Contents

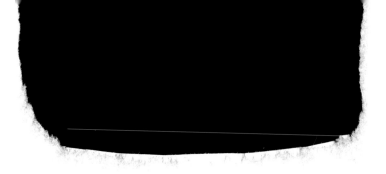

OXFORD READINGS IN FEMINISM

Feminism and Politics

Edited by
Anne Phillips

Oxford · New York

OXFORD UNIVERSITY PRESS

1998

Oxford University Press, Great Clarendon Street, Oxford OX2 6DP

Oxford New York
Athens Auckland Bangkok Bogota Bombay
Buenos Aires Calcutta Cape Town Dar es Salaam
Delhi Florence Hong Kong Istanbul Karachi
Kuala Lumpur Madras Madrid Melbourne
Mexico City Nairobi Paris Singapore
Taipei Tokyo Toronto Warsaw
and associated companies in
Berlin Ibadan

Oxford is a trade mark of Oxford University Press

Published in the United States
by Oxford University Press Inc., New York

Introduction and Selection © Oxford University Press 1998

British Library Cataloguing in Publication Data
Data available

Library of Congress Cataloging in Publication Data
Feminism and politics / edited by Anne Phillips.
(Oxford readings in feminism)
Includes bibliographical references and index.
1. Feminism—Political aspects. 2. Women in politics. 3. Women's rights.
I. Phillips, Anne. II. Series.
HQ1236.F446 1998 305.42—dc21 97–31035
ISBN 0–19–878206–3
ISBN 0–19–878205–5 (Pbk)

Typeset by Hope Services (Abingdon) Ltd.
Printed in Great Britain
on acid-free paper by
Biddles Ltd.,
Guildford and King's Lynn

Notes on Contributors

SUSAN C. BOURQUE is the E. B. Wiley Professor of Government and Dean for Academic Development at Smith College. Until 1994 she was chair of the Government department and Director of the Smith Project on Women and Social Change. Her most recent book is *The Politics of Women's Education*, co-edited with Jill K. Conway (Ann Arbor: University of Michigan Press, 1993). Dr Bourque received her Ph.D. from Cornell University.

TERESA BRENNAN is Professor of Philosophy at the New School for Social Research, New York; she was previously Professor of Women's Studies at the University of Amsterdam. She is the author of *The Interpretation of the Mind* (Routledge) and *History after Lacan* (Routledge 1994), and the editor of *Between Psychoanalysis and Feminism* (Routledge).

JUDITH BUTLER is Chancellor's Professor in the Department of Rhetoric at UCLA. Her books include *Gender Trouble* (Routledge, 1990), *Bodies That Matter* (Routledge, 1993), and *The Psychic Life of Power* (Stanford University Press, 1997).

KIMBERLE CRENSHAW is Professor of Law at the Los Angeles Law School, University of California.

IRENE DIAMOND is Professor of Political Science at the University of Oregon. She is the author of many books and articles, including *Fertile Ground: Women, Earth and the Limits of Control* (Beacon Press, 1994) and *Feminism and Foucault: Reflection on Resistance* (Northeastern University Press, 1988).

MARY G. DIETZ is a Professor in the Department of Political Science, University of Minnesota. She is the author of *Between the Human and the Divine: The Political Thought of Simone Weil* and editor of *Thomas Hobbes and Political Theory* and has written essays on Machiavelli, Arendt, Habermas, patriotism, feminist politics, and the meaning of political action.

JEAN BETHKE ELSHTAIN is the Laura Spelman Rockefeller Professor of Social and Political Ethics at the University of Chicago. She is the author of many books, including *Public Man, Private Woman: Women in Social and Political Thought*. Books she has edited include *The Family in Political Thought*; *Politics and the Human Body*; and *Just War Theory*. Elshtain is also the author of over two hundred articles and essays in scholarly journals and journals of civic opinion. In 1996 she was elected a Fellow of the American Academy of Arts and Sciences. She also writes a regular column for *The New Republic*.

NANCY FRASER is Professor of Political Science at the Graduate Faculty of the New School for Social Research. She is the author of *Unruly Practices*:

Minnesota Press, 1989), the co-author of *Feminist Contentions: A Philosophical Exchange* (Routledge, 1994) and the co-editor of *Revaluing French Feminism: Critical Essays on Difference, Agency and Culture* (Indiana University Press, 1992). Her new book, *Justice Interruptus*, was published by Routledge in 1996.

JEAN GROSSHOLTZ is a political activist and Professor of Politics and Women's Studies at Mount Holyoke College. She has written books on Philippine and Sri Lankan politics and articles on Southeast Asian politics, violence against women, the peace movement and global feminism.

NANCY HARTSOCK is Professor of Political Science at the University of Washington. She is author of *Money, Sex, and Power: Toward a Feminist Historical Materialism* (New York: Longman, 1983; Boston, Northeastern University Press, 1984) and many other essays in feminist theory. She is interested in the relationships between politics and epistemologies, and a collection of her essays on these issues, *The Feminist Standpoint Revisited*, will be published by Westview Press in 1998.

BERNICE JOHNSON REAGON, Distinguished Professor of History at American University and Curator Emeritus at the Smithsonian Institution, she is also a composer and recording producer. She resides in Washington, DC and continues to perform with Sweet Honey In The Rock, the African American female acapella ensemble she founded in 1973.

CATHARINE A. MACKINNON is a lawyer, teacher, writer, activist, and expert on sex equality. She has been Professor of Law at the University of Michigan Law School since 1990, and is Visiting Professor of Law at the University of Chicago Law School. She is currently representing *pro bono* Croatian and Muslim women and children victims of Serbian genocidal atrocities seeking remedies under international law.

Her recent publications include *Toward a Feminist Theory of the State* (Harvard, 1989) and *Only Words* (Harvard, 1993). Forthcoming works include *In Harm's Way: The Pornography Civil Rights Hearings* (with Andrea Dworkin, Harvard, 1998) and *Sex Equality* (Foundation, 1998), a legal casebook.

JANE MANSBRIDGE is Professor of Public Policy at the John F. Kennedy School of Government at Harvard University. She is the author of *Beyond Adversary Democracy* and *Why We Lost the ERA*, editor of *Beyond Self Interest*, and co-editor, with Susan Moller Okin, of *Feminism*, a two-volume collection.

SUSAN MOLLER OKIN teaches in Political Science and in the Ethics in Society Program at Stanford University. She is the author of *Women in Western Political Thought* (1979, 1992), *Justice, Gender and the Family* (1979) and articles on topics ranging from feminist theory to the ethics of nuclear deterrence policy.

CAROLE PATEMAN is Professor of Political Science, UCLA and Adjunct Professor in the Research School of Social Sciences, Australian National

University. Her books include *Participation and Democratic Theory* and *The Sexual Contract*.

ANNE PHILLIPS is Professor of Politics at London Guildhall University. Her publications include *The Politics of Presence* (1995), *Democracy and Difference* (1993), *Destabilizing Theory*: *Contemporary Feminist Debates* (co-edited with Michèle Barrett, 1992) and *Engendering Democracy* (1991).

ROSEMARY PRINGLE is Professor of Women's Studies at Griffith University. Her publications include *Transitions: New Australian Feminisms*, which she co-edited with Barbara Caine (Allen and Unwin, 1995) and *Sex and Medicine* (forthcoming Allen and Unwin, 1998).

DEBORAH L. RHODE is Professor of Law and Director of the Keck Centre on the Legal Profession at Stanford University. She is the author of *Justice, Gender and Speaking of Sex* and was a former Director of Stanford's Institute for Research on Women and Gender. She is currently President Elect of the Association of American Law Schools.

VIRGINIA SAPIRO is the Sophonisba P. Breckinridge Professor of Political Science and Women's Studies at the University of Wisconsin-Madison and directs the American National Election Studies. Her books include *The Political Integration of Women* (1983), *Women in American Society* (1998) and *A Vindication of Political Virtue: The Political Theory of Mary Wollstonecraft* (1992).

CHRISTINE SYLVESTER's recent work on feminist international relations appears in US, Australian, Finnish, Swedish and German journals. She has also completed a study of 'women', 'production' and 'progress' in Mashonaland, Zimbabwe, and has several projects underway on art, gender, development and international relations. She is at the National Centre for Development Studies, Research School of Pacific and Asian Studies, Australian National University.

CHANDRA TALPADE MOHANTY teaches feminist and anti-racist studies at Hamilton College, Clinton. She has co-edited *Third World Women* and *The Politics of Feminism* (Indiana University Press, 1991) and *Feminist Genealogies, Colonial Legacies, Democratic Futures* (Routledge, 1997).

SOPHIE WATSON is a Professor in the Centre for Urban Studies in the School for Policy Studies at the University of Bristol. Her recent publications include (with P. Murphy) *Surface City*: *Sydney at the Millennium* (Pluto Press) and *Postmodern Cities and Spaces* (edited collection with K. Gibson, Basil Blackwell).

IRIS MARION YOUNG teaches ethics and political theory in the Graduate School of Public and International Affairs at the University of Pittsburgh. Her most recent book is entitled *Intersecting Voices: Dilemmas of Gender, Political Philosophy, and Policy* (Princeton University Press, 1997).

Introduction

Anne Phillips

Feminism is politics. Yet, judging from its impact on either theory or practice, feminism has been less successful in challenging 'malestream' politics than in the near-revolution it has achieved elsewhere. We are living through a time of major transformation in sexual relations: transformations that can be measured in the global feminization of the workforce, the rapid equalization between the sexes (at least in the richer countries) in educational participation and qualifications, and a marked increase in women's self-confidence and self-esteem that is probably the most lasting legacy of the contemporary women's movement. The changes cannot be attributed to feminism alone, and are often ambiguous in their effects; but even if the reshaping of gender relations is partial and deeply problematic, it would be hard not to notice this as a period of significant change. In politics, by contrast, it still seems like business as usual. Certainly, the politics portrayed to us via the daily newspapers and television accounts remains overwhelmingly masculine in personnel and style; while in some parts of the world, women face direct attacks on recently achieved civil rights by parties and governments resisting the implications of sexual equality.

Politics as pursued in academic departments is also surprisingly untouched, for while the literature on gender and politics or feminist political theory has grown from a few seminal articles into a rich diversity of work, 'feminism and politics' is still treated as a discrete object of study, of interest only to those inside it. Sociologists have always included the family among their objects of study. Literary critics have never been able to avoid women writers. Students of politics, by contrast, have taken this as referring to a domain of public power from which women are largely absent. In one of the early discussions of feminism and politics, Joni Lovenduski noted that 'there was never any way that the modern study of politics could fail to be sexist' for 'women usually do not dispose of public power,

1

belong to political elites, or hold influential positions in government institutions'.[1] The very definition of the subject matter has made politics peculiarly intransigent to feminist transformations.

This relative intransigence has had one—rather unexpected—result: that the feminists who once sighted politics everywhere are not particularly enthused by the study of politics, and are far more readily engaged by work in cultural studies or philosophy or film. Michèle Barrett has written of a 'turn to culture' in recent feminism that has shifted the words/things balance away from the more materialist preoccupations of the social sciences (their preoccupation, as she puts it, with 'things') and towards the cultural salience of words. 'Feminism sells best as fiction', and even in the more academic literature, 'the rising star lies with the arts, humanities and philosophy'.[2] This turn to culture need not be construed as an anti-politics; indeed, Barrett suggests that the later preoccupations could help us towards a better account of subjective political motivation and open up space for a more explicitly ethical politics. But the effects can be somewhat perplexing for feminists studying on politics courses or researching in areas normally associated with political science or political theory. I remember rushing out to buy a new collection of essays published under the title *Feminists Theorize the Political*,[3] a collection packed with fascinating essays, but organized, as it turned out, around confirming or contesting the value of poststructuralist theories. It can be hard to know what to do with this in a world where 'the political' still conjures up images of governments and elections and parties: should feminists simply refuse to engage with this dreary universe, or do we have to engage in order to transform?

In the stories we tell ourselves of the development of feminist thinking, we often construct histories that demonstrate a movement from naïvety to sophistication, a progression from simpler to more complex beliefs. It is sometimes suggested, for example, that feminists began their explorations with a relatively uncomplicated notion of 'filling the gaps', and only later moved on to more conceptually challenging questions. Joan Scott describes feminist historians in the first years of the contemporary women's movement as setting out to establish women's presence and participation through history—as making visible what was previously ignored.[4] Such work perhaps began as a relatively simple process of historical recovery, but when 'the questions of why these facts had been ignored and how they were now to be understood were raised, history became more than a search for facts'.[5] Accounts of feminism and politics often make similar points. Virginia Sapiro writes in

Chapter 3 of an initial period when 'most work was of the "add women and stir" or compensatory variety', while a recent collection on feminism and politics suggests that '(e)arly efforts to explore women's participation in the traditional political arenas were basically descriptive or mapping exercises',[6] and that it was only as the limitations of this became apparent that feminists embarked on a paradigm shift that more fundamentally questioned the categories of analysis.

These histories do convey something of the growing sophistication of feminist thought, but there is a troubling neatness to their pattern, and as applied to feminist thinking about politics they underestimate one crucial feature. Contemporary feminism developed out of a period of radical disillusionment with the post-war political settlement in North America and Europe, and both its language and forms of organization were significantly influenced by the radical sub-cultures from which it emerged. Earlier generations of feminists had often employed a vocabulary of women's equality or women's emancipation. The activists of the contemporary women's movement typically talked of 'women's liberation', and David Bouchier has suggested that this phrase originated in sardonic reference to the way women were treated in liberation movements for black or Third World peoples.[7] Many of those who read the new feminist literature or marched in the women's-movement demonstrations were experiencing their first involvement in politics, but a significant minority came from a prior engagement with new-left or civil-rights politics. They came, that is, with a conception of politics that was already at odds with the dull routines of political parties, or the backstage manœuvrings through which public policy is made. In the formative years of the contemporary women's movement, the 'politics' that feminists were contesting was already a deviation from conventional norms.

'The personal is political' is probably the best-known slogan of those early years, but the key point about this is that it was directed primarily at socialist or radical men. It signalled a move away from the contestations between capital and labour that had preoccupied generations of Marxist activists, and questioned the radicalism of those new social movements that were themselves extending the meaning of politics, but rarely to the point of including who did the housework or who typed the leaflets or who had the power in bed. It also, of course, queried that more academic literature on politics which looked to states or interest groups or rational individuals and failed to spot women in any of these places. But 'the personal is political' derived most of its force from arguments within radical politics, for it was in this context that the preoccupations with sexual equality were most consistently sneered at as a trivial diversion. The feminism of the 1960s or 70s issued a potentially devastating challenge to both conventional and radical understandings of politics. There was no naïve early moment before anyone paused to ask what was wrong with the way politics was conceived.

The problem, if any, was that 'politics' was subjected to such devastating criticism that it threatened to dissolve as a distinct category of analysis. The notion of power as ubiquitous is often attributed to Michel Foucault (and feminists have indeed made much use of Foucault in analysing the power of discursive practices or challenging what Rosemary Pringle and Sophie Watson in Chapter 9 term 'essentialist' notions of the state), but feminists were already acting on a more relational understanding of power long before any of them cited Foucault's work. Representations of masculinity and femininity were seen as forms of control over women just as effective as the nineteenth-century legislation that had denied them the vote; and the regulation of sexuality—including what many have described as 'compulsory heterosexuality'—was seen as a central mechanism in sustaining sexual inequality. Politics was power, power was everywhere, and politics was no longer much different from anything else.

Against this background, feminist thinking on politics has often been characterized by a double movement towards both critique *and* recuperation. In her influential analysis of *Public Man, Private Woman*, Jean Bethke Elshtain traced the different ways that distinctions between public and private have operated in the traditions of Western political thought: sometimes as a sharp demarcation that allocated certain kinds of people to the realm of politics and others to the realm of the household; sometimes as a differentiation within each individual between the public language of reason and the private language of sentiment; always as a thoroughly gendered analysis that sought to protect politics from contamination by the private sphere. In one particularly evocative sentence, Elshtain suggests that 'politics is in part an elaborate defence against the tug of the private, against the lure of the familial, against evocations of female power'.[8] The implication, it might seem, is that the barriers should be finally torn down—but Elshtain is equally critical of what she views as a total collapse of public and private in radical feminist thought. Against the starker interpretations of 'the personal is political', Elshtain wants to recapture both the centrality of the family and the importance of politics *per se*. She objects, that is, to the over-politicization of childrearing that understates the importance of a permanent relationship between child and caring adult; she also objects to the *de*politicization of 'politics' that discourages feminists from addressing issues of citizenship or political authority. If we are to reconstruct the public/private divide so that it no longer silences or marginalizes women, we must first comprehend its recurring power.

Elshtain's own reconstruction has proved particularly contentious within feminism—she is associated with what Mary Dietz describes as a 'maternal feminism' that looks to the values and practices of mothering as the basis for a more ethical polity—but that double imperative towards critique and recuperation has remained a defining characteristic. Feminists have developed and deepened their critical assessment of the various ways in which politics is conceived. They have increasingly combined this, however, with a calling back to politics, stressing the insights feminism can bring to the theorization of public power. Some of this recuperates the more self-evidently 'political' preoccupation with women's under-representation in decision-making assemblies; some of it focuses on the complex dilemmas that arise in developing legislation for sexual equality; much of it involves a retheorization of citizenship that takes feminist issues right to the heart of the public domain.

In many ways, the theoretical debates then replicate the tension between 'reformism' and 'utopianism' that has been played out on more practical terrain. Should women be trying to get into politics? Or setting their sights on much higher goals? Many have warned against uncritical assimilation of traditional social-science methodology: the dangers, for example, in presenting women as just another interest group, or the impoverishment of understanding that comes with the preference for quantitative over qualitative analysis in contemporary political science.[9] Others, meanwhile, have warned against wholesale repudiation of traditional research methods, arguing that feminism has a distinctive approach to politics but not a unique methodology, and that feminists should avoid attacks on 'male' rationality or science *per se*.[10] Feminism is necessarily subversive, but there is no unified position on the kind of subversion required.

FEMINIST CRITIQUES OF POLITICS

So what, if anything, characterizes feminist critiques of politics? Most of the arguments share three common starting-points: that existing definitions are saturated with gender; that this saturation has worked in such a way as to legitimate women's lack of political power; and that much of the process depends on a particular way of conceiving of the public–private divide. We might think that women are less visible in politics simply because they do less politics than men. The complacent version of this (described by Susan Bourque and Jean Grossholtz in Chapter 1 as 'the assumption of male dominance') raises no awkward questions about women's lesser visibility, and simply takes it for granted that men will do politics while women tend the children and home. The more critical version views this state of affairs as a consequence of the sexual division of labour in employment and carework, and focuses its energies on combating the structures of sexual inequality that make it so hard for women to enter the political domain. The literature on feminism and politics often includes this last point—the idea, that is, that society is structured in such a way as to keep women politically marginal—but it always looks to the additional power of the categories in making women less politically visible. Notions of political rationality, for example, often derive from a 'masculine' paradigm that disdains what it perceives as the more gossipy preoccupations of women. This can have very direct political effects, in making it harder for women to win recognition as serious candidates for political office, or harder for groups campaigning around what are seen as women's issues to win recognition as serious actors on the political stage. It also has more indirect consequences in turning the public domain into what Elshtain in Chapter 17 describes as 'amoral statecraft'—emptying out of politics what are regarded as more feminine (read 'soppy') concerns.

Distinctions between public and private play a central role in this critique. Most feminists now query the tendency to dissolve *all* distinction between public and private—'women, just as much as men, need privacy for the development of intimate relations with others, for the space to shed their roles temporarily, and for the time by themselves that contributes to the development of the mind and of creativity' (Okin, Chapter 5)—but all argue that the boundaries should become more permeable, and that changing the way we view them gives us new insight into the processes of political exclusion. The point here is not that the literature on politics has ignored the public–private divide. In many formulations of liberalism, this demarcation appears as the first line of defence against tyranny, reminding expansionist governments of the dangers of establishing state control over the 'private' workings of the economy, and securing to individual citizens their rights to decide for themselves what religion, if any, to practise, or what books, if any, to read. In socialist arguments, by contrast, the demarcation is often seen as reinforcing tyranny, encouraging us to believe that political equality is secured despite all the gross inequalities in social and economic life, discouraging the notion that democracy is as relevant in the workplace as in the regulation of political life. Political theorists have talked often enough about the public–private divide, but one of the key points made by feminists (most notably in an article by Carole Pateman)[11] is that their arguments proceed as if the distinction refers only to that between state and economy, or state and civil society. They fail to register that 'public–private' refers to not one but two distinctions; they gloss over that further distinction that differentiates both state and civil society from the deeper privacy of the domestic sphere.

This suppression has had serious consequences for political thought. When political theorists cast the veil of deep privacy over relations in the domestic sphere, this makes it much easier for them to perform the sleight of hand that turns the innocent-sounding 'individual' into a synonym for 'male head of household'. It also enables them to presume that arguments about equality or justice do not apply to the relationship between wife and husband or between parent and child. Feminist scholarship has established the complex and often quirky consequences of this in the writings of classical political theorists, and re-examination of the history of political thought has proved one of the most exciting developments of the 1980s.[12] That the 'great thinkers' suffered from various degrees of misogyny or sexual evasion is not, perhaps, so suprising. More unexpectedly, feminists have been able to demonstrate a continuing slippage between 'the individual' and 'the male head of household' even in contemporary writers like John Rawls.[13]

The implications for normative political theory are profound. At their most obvious, they require us to extend into the domestic sphere questions previously considered relevant only to the public arrangements between citizens: to ask why those who regard freedom as the capacity to give or withdraw consent still hear rape victims saying 'yes' when they so clearly mean 'no'; or why those who write so eloquently on justice within and between states seem so untroubled by injustice between husbands and wives. This line of argument takes notions of equality or freedom or justice from the public sphere and looks at what happens when we apply them to the private. An alternative line of argument starts from the other direction, begins, that is, from notions of care or responsibility for others that have been more closely associated with practices in the private sphere and asks what happens when we apply such notions to public life. These represent very different starting-points; but in either case, the process throws up questions that redefine what we understand by equality or freedom or justice. It has been argued, for example, that justice should be retheorized so that ideals of strict impartiality no longer rule out the compassion associated with care;[14] or citizenship reformulated, in Carole Pateman's words, 'to open up space for two figures: one masculine, one feminine'.[15] Once we break the silence over our private existence, we are enabled to see the problems of politics in a new light.

As the above examples indicate, feminism has often seen itself as restoring the more grainy reality of everyday life—including the bodies through which we live our existence—to a discourse that has viewed us as rational calculators or abstract individuals. Critiques of false abstraction figure prominently in the literature. In their discussion of classical liberalism in Chapter 4, Teresa Brennan and Carole Pateman expose the ambiguities of liberal contract theory by focusing on the status of married women: arguments that looked wonderfully egalitarian when they were delivered in terms of 'free individuals' turn out to be acutely problematic once these individuals are translated into women and men. Looking at later literature on citizenship, Iris Marion Young in Chapter 19 discerns a tendency to equate good citizenship with the capacity to set aside one's own perspectives or experiences—with the capacity, that is, to turn oneself into a desexed, declassed, deracialized abstraction—and she argues that this suppression of particular affiliations or experiences ends up reinforcing the privileges of already dominant groups. Feminists have been quick to spot the pretended universality that appears in references to 'citizens', 'people', 'mankind'. They have also been quick to spot the unthinking association between masculinity and normality that presents anything different in women's lives as a deviation from a supposedly gender-neutral norm. This last has developed as a major theme in the literature on equality, where feminists have challenged the assumption that equality means levelling up (perhaps we should say down) to some male-defined norm, or that treating people equally means treating them as if they were already the same. One of the standard assumptions in legislation for equality or against discrimination is that laws and institutions should be gender-neutral: that people should be treated as people, not treated differently because they are women or men. This denial of difference, however, can make it difficult to argue for special treatment for groups who are unequally positioned in the social hierarchy, leading to contentious conclusions, such as that pregnancy leave is unfair because only women will ever take it, or quotas for women illegitimate because they attach undue weight to sexual difference.

When these two elements are put together—the critique of false abstraction and the reformulation of relationships between public and private spheres—they lead to a much greater emphasis on historically situated differences. There is an element in this of bringing the politics back home: putting the real human beings, some male, some female, back into analyses distorted by the formality of their conventions. Where standard studies of political behaviour have relied on mass surveys of anonymous respondents, and barely registered whether these were male or female, feminists have often preferred in-depth interviews with a smaller number of people, and have been fascinated by the differences between women and men. Feminists have scrutinized local politics with as much interest as national politics; have studied social movements or *ad hoc* pressure groups in preference to political élites; and have frequently focused on people who describe themselves as unpolitical rather than self-appointed leaders of political fashion. Some of this might appear as a relatively straightforward process of 'filling the gaps', but it always raises questions about the meaning of politics, and often involves a self-consciously irreverent disruption of the norms. In Chapter 2, for example, Christine Sylvester moves from the canonical writings of international relations theory to a pregnant woman at the Greenham Common peace camp, warming her stomach in the sun: exposing pregnancy, as she puts it, 'as a political act at a military base'.

The further element to this—already signalled in some of Jean Bethke Elshtain's comments—is that feminists have often stressed the nurturant qualities of women's experiences and drawn on notions of care or intimacy to transform the vocabulary of politics. When we look at politics through the prism of either self- or group interest, we take our models of political interaction from the way people relate in the market-place or in the corridors of power. What happens if we turn this around, to develop models of political inter-action from the way mothers relate to their children, or the more trusting co-operation that characterizes a group of friends? In their critique of 'interests' as the central category for political analysis, Irene Diamond and Nancy Hartsock suggest in Chapter 8 that '(t)he reduction of all human emotions to interests and interests to the rational search for gain reduces the human community to an instru-mental, arbitrary, and deeply unstable alliance, one which rests on the private desires of isolated individuals.' Such an account fails to capture a mother's characteristically nurturant relationship to her child; in imposing a 'masculine' model of instrumental interests and individual gain, it also fails to account for political motivation. This weakens our understanding of politics as it currently exists. Even more importantly, it weakens our capacity for constructing a better world. Closer attention to the practices or values associated with women's experiences promises a more transformative politics that will deal with us in the fullness of our humanity and help us combat the bureaucratic regulation that distorts our lives.

This third element is more controversial (within feminism) than the first two, but it overlaps closely with commonsense notions about the difference women could make to politics. It is frequently suggested, for example, that women are less aggressive than men, that they are more likely to value listening to others over the capac-ity for humiliating one's opponents, or that they are more con-cerned with longer-term issues, like the future of the environment, than short-term material gain. The experiences women have as the carers in society are often seen as providing a model for a more gen-erous and less conflictual democracy. In this more visionary recon-struction, it is not a matter of getting women 'into' politics, a formulation that too readily accepts conventional notions of what politics is about, but of enabling women's experiences and values to transform the political realm.

THEORIZING DIFFERENCE

At the risk of too hasty a generalization, I would say that all feminist writing about politics involves some reinsertion—and revalua-tion—of the scorned female, the not-to-be-mentioned body, the politics of everyday life. But there is also an uneasiness about this that surfaces in some of the readings in this collection. In Chapter 18 Mary Dietz, for example, criticizes the atomistic rationalism of liberal political theory, and suggests that feminism provides an 'alternative conception of politics that is historically concrete and very much a part of women's lives': all this fits neatly enough within what I am presenting as a near-consensus. She fears, however, that feminists have too readily domesticated their own contribution, and that, focusing too exclusively on 'questions of social and economic concern—questions about children, family, schools, work, wages, pornography, abortion, abuse—they will not articulate a truly political vision, nor will they address the problem of citizenship'. Dietz writes from within a broadly Arendtian tradition that is particularly insistent on the distinctiveness of politics from other practices in our social life, but her argument echoes worries frequently expressed by women in politics. We often talk as if we want to make politics less distant and more grounded, but in doing so we gamble with our own marginality: think of the many female politicians through this century who have resisted the identification with 'women's issues' and thought it better to be the spokesperson on economic policy than the Minister for Women's Affairs. Focusing on the differences between women and men can lend itself to a sentimentalized vision of women's place or role—and, in the sentimental vision, women are usually subordinate.

Susan Moller Okin notes various examples of 'false gender-neutrality' that have emerged out of the confrontation between feminism and orthodox political theory: a balanced alternation of 'he' and 'she' that simply ignores the current positioning of the sexes in the distribution of political power; an extraordinary denial of women's unique relationship to pregnancy that turns arguments over abortion into a discussion of the relationship between parents and foetuses, and hardly seems to register that women have a different relationship to the foetus than men. Pretending the differences away produces very peculiar results. Women *are* different from men, and if these differences are not explicitly acknowledged, political analysis will continue as an analysis of men. But feminists writing about politics have also wanted to contest the misogynist assumptions that present women as so *very* different from men: as apolitical, sentimental, incapable of rising from the particularities of their family and neighbourhood to the generalities of the public sphere. The emphasis on sexual difference threatens to legitimate precisely those notions of the 'eternal feminine' that have so often served to close down questions about the inequity of political arrangements;

ANNE PHILLIPS

and even when the analysis is explicitly linked to a revaluation of
women's experiences and priorities, it can still end up with what
Kathleen Jones describes as an 'idealized image of an all-nurturing,
all loving woman'[16] that is dangerously indebted to the patriarchal
system that first bestowed on us this image. Where, then, should
feminists position themselves? Should they be querying the supposed, but perhaps much exaggerated, differences between the
sexes? Or should they be building sexual difference more explicitly
into political theory and practice?

Discussions of this reflect and inform wider debates in feminist
theory. 'Difference' has emerged as one of the central motifs in feminist analysis, referring both to the weight to be attached to sexual
difference, and to the many differences between women themselves.[17] The readings in this collection illustrate the variety of positions adopted on the first issue. All involve some claim about the
difference gender makes—it is hard to see what constitutes a feminist analysis of politics, if not some idea that the sexes are different
and some notion that focusing on this difference changes the way we
understand political life. But most distance themselves from what
might be deemed an 'essentialist' reading of the difference, and
many register concern about defining women by their practices of
nurturance or care. Jane Mansbridge notes in Chapter 6 that a 'fairly
small difference in experience can become a large difference in self-
image and social perception', and that while psychological research
in empathy shows up relatively minor variations between the sexes
when they are measured on 'objective' physiological scales, the same
research throws up enormous differences when the respondents
know they are being tested on their capacity for emotional identification.[18] This suggests that the gender coding of difference is more
powerful than the actual difference between the sexes: women know
they are supposed to be more empathetic than men; men know that
emotionality conflicts with a reputation for masculine behaviour;
both sexes deliver what they perceive as expected and reinforce the
conventional assumptions. Difference matters, but we may not differ as much as we have been encouraged to believe.

Uncertainty about how much weight to attach to sexual difference is reinforced by the second issue that goes under the heading of
'difference': how much weight to attach to differences between
women. When we draw on notions of 'women' or 'women's experience' or 'women's interests' to fuel the assault on existing analysis,
we risk generating yet another abstraction: we may find ourselves
deconstructing one set of fictions only to put another set in their

place. Women are indeed women (no-one is seriously questioning this), and women are indeed different from men. As Catharine MacKinnon in Chapter 14 puts it, in a nicely pointed question: 'I mean, can you imagine elevating one half of a population and denigrating the other half and producing a population in which everyone is the same?' But our identities as women invariably intersect with racial identities, class identities, regional or national identities—and these do more than complicate the picture, they introduce very real conflicts and divides. When black feminists accused the women's movement of racism, they were not just drawing attention to an over-generalized image of womanhood that had obliterated differences between white women and black; that had failed to notice, to take an example from the British context, that the much-discussed problems of part-time employment were primarily problems for white women, and that Afro-Caribbean women were more typically working full-time; or that had failed to register that the problems of the nuclear family were being read off one of a variety of family forms. Serious as they were, these 'oversights' could always be corrected, leading to a more nuanced picture of women's experiences and a less parochial understanding of women's interests and concerns. But the accusations of racism were not only about the failure to notice; they were about a reluctance on the part of white women to concede their racially achieved power. In this context, 'women' looks as dangerous an abstraction as the gender-neutral categories of orthodox political thought.

I noted earlier that there is a significant 'calling back to politics' in contemporary feminist writing; this is particularly marked in the current theorization of difference. As feminists feel their way towards a more satisfactory understanding of racial or class differences, they have turned to notions of coalition-building—the construction of explicitly *political* alliances—as the best way of approaching the possibilities of women's solidarity. Discussions of women's experience or women's interests sometimes give the impression of a unity founded on the shared experience of oppression; once we acknowledge that the experience of oppression varies according to one's location in class and racial hierarchies, this reveals itself as rather a fantastic dream. One—rather despairing—response continues to treat identities as given by experience, but sees 'women' as fragmenting into the multiple identities associated with gender, class, race, sexuality, nationality, and their almost infinite combinations. (This is not just a theoretical response, but a reasonably accurate description of what happened in the contemporary women's movement in the later 1970s.) The alternative developed by Bernice Reagon in Chapter 11 and Chandra Talpade Mohanty in Chapter 12 stresses politics as action and engagement: a complex, dangerous, but always necessary process of building coalitions.

In the presentation she made to a Women's Music Festival in 1981, Bernice Reagon talked of the 'barred rooms' that constitute our homes: the spaces we retreat to—maybe women-only spaces, maybe for lesbians only, maybe for black women only—where we mix with those most like us, those we want to have in our homes. We need these spaces, she suggests, but we cannot survive in these safe enclaves alone: they become less safe and homelike when people we never thought of including turn up thinking they fall into our category (the black women, for example, who thought they belonged in the women-only home); and even if they could sustain their pristine purity, they are far too vulnerable against the onslaughts of the outside world. Getting beyond what Reagon calls the 'womb' stage means going into coalition, venturing out into connections with people who are not only different but dangerous, and always disturbing to one's sense of oneself. As picked up by Chandra Talpade Mohanty in Chapter 12, this imagery of home and coalition splinters the presumed unities of experience and pushes feminism towards 'a politics of engagement rather than a politics of transcendence'. We have to engage with others, but this should be construed as a political process rather than a reflection of deep similarity.

Like all political processes, it may well fail. In her own highly critical analysis of what is meant by identity in Chapter 13, Judith Butler warns that we should not presume that people entering coalitions will be guaranteed some ultimate unity. We cannot, she argues, figure the forms of coalition in advance, and if we must (as it seems) abandon the notion of 'women' as some slumbering entity waiting to be raised for battle, we should be equally sceptical of 'women' achieving existence at the end of the coalitional process. The point is not that there are no women, but that as a subject of politics, or a subject of feminist politics, 'women' does not—and may never— exist. 'It would be wrong to assume in advance that there is a category of "women" that simply needs to be filled in with various components of race, class, age, ethnicity, and sexuality in order to become complete.' The very notion of identity has become deeply problematic for feminism, and we should no longer expect to fix it in some final, unambiguous way.

Difference figures in these discussions, not as a descriptive category (women are more different from one another than they may have wanted to believe), but as a new way of thinking about political processes and political tasks. It might be said, I suppose, that this just brings feminism back to a more standard way of thinking, for the idea of politics as alliances and compromises and fragile coalitions is hardly foreign to orthodox political analysis. What is striking, however, is the way feminism has moved from an identity politics associated with women to issues raised by identity politics in general, and then almost beyond a politics of identity to what is increasingly termed a politics of difference. The critique of false abstraction focused initially on the abstraction from sexual difference that had presented us with a homogenized world of individuals or citizens: those men in gender-neutral guise. The subsequent focus on differences between women has combined with a post-structuralist deconstruction of fixed, unambiguous identities to generate a more searching emphasis on difference and diversity *per se*. Contemporary work then becomes less defined by any particular object of study (looking at women, looking at gender, looking at what goes on in the private rather than the public sphere), and more by its scepticism towards universalizing theory, or its perception of difference as positive rather than always and inevitably a problem. Iris Young talks of an 'emancipatory politics that affirms group difference';[19] Susan Mendus of the search 'for an understanding of democracy as something to be aimed at *through* difference, not something to be attained via the *removal* of difference'.[20] Much recent writing draws explicit parallels between sexual and other kinds of difference. This moves feminism beyond the question of women's exclusion/inclusion to a less gender-specific set of issues associated with homogeneity/heterogeneity, sameness/diversity, and universality/difference.

The association between feminism and a politics of difference is particularly marked in the last two readings in the collection: Iris Young's discussion of a 'differentiated citizenship' that would explicitly recognize differences of sex, race, class, sexuality, or language in order to guarantee that all groups are fully included; and Nancy Fraser's exploration of tensions between those struggles for recognition that are most closely associated with identity politics and those struggles for redistribution that arise in the context of traditional socialist politics. In both cases, feminism provides the tools with which to deconstruct exclusionary notions of the common good or the class-defined preoccupations of earlier struggles for social

ANNE PHILLIPS

equality. Feminism also generates the insights that clarify the importance of particular identities (female, black, lesbian, gay) while questioning the solidity of these identities. But the issues addressed hardly fit within a notion of 'women's politics' or 'women's issues'. They confirm, rather, the promise of feminism in transforming how we think about any kind of politics at all.

Despite the wealth of this literature, Virginia Sapiro in Chapter 3 suggests that feminism and politics still faces a double marginality: marginality in relation to political studies, where research labelled 'feminist' is still widely ignored or rejected 'because the label taints it with political values'; but also marginality in relation to women's studies, where there is a widespread view 'that feminist theory and research in the social sciences is much less developed and sophisticated and even less "feminist" than work in the humanities.' The political studies community continues to define politics in ways that make feminist concerns seem either inappropriate or irrelevant. It over-emphasizes the importance of elections and electoral behaviour; is far more interested in party politics than the politics of social movements or non-governmental organizations; and is inclined to distrust research that is overtly influenced by a prior commitment to sexual equality. But the womens' studies community sometimes seems to have travelled to the opposite extreme, preferring the study of cultural representation to the drearier realms of political representation, or writing off things governmental as irrelevant to any feminist project.

I think Sapiro is right about this: there *is* a marginality about feminist work on politics, a continuing failure to incorporate feminist insights into the standard analyses of politics, juxtaposed with a lack of enthusiasm among feminists that may reflect deeper disillusionments with the political world. But marginality has its own strengths, and a number of readings in this collection turn marginality on its head to make a virtue out of failing to fit. Christine Sylvester in Chapter 2 indicates a variety of positions now being staked out in the feminist literature in international relations; of these, she identifies most closely with a postmodern turn that does not 'insert women into international relations or international relations into some notion of real women', but focuses on 'the homeless places' or 'no-man's borderlands' that unsettle territorial assumptions. Women are (what so many misogynists have claimed them to be) a disruptive force. They do not fit the neat patterns that supposedly bind individuals to a state, and then set states in conflict with one another. Building on arguments represented elsewhere in this volume, Sylvester notes that women's citizenship is always more ambiguous than men's, and that while their place in the nation is in one sense particularly homebound, they are in another sense homeless in the world of what she calls 'citizensandstates'. This opens up, however, new possibilities for thinking about the norms of international justice and new ways of imagining the communities to which we belong. Though often experienced as a weakness, not fitting can be a great source of strength.

Kimberle Crenshaw also makes an explicit case for the margins in her analysis of anti-discrimination law. Black women frequently fall out of existing categories of analysis: they do not fit the categories of sex discrimination because they cannot establish that they were discriminated against solely by sex; they do not fit the categories of race discrimination because they cannot establish that they were discriminated against solely by race. In a move that is controversial but not untypical of feminist approaches to politics, Crenshaw argues in Chapter 15 for a shift of perspective that places those most marginalized at the centre of analysis. Instead of a top-down compartmentalization that requires people to choose one issue over another, what about beginning from the needs and problems of those who experience compound disadvantage? 'When they enter, we all enter' (p. 167). When analyses address the most marginal, they can more reliably hope to address us all.

All the essays in this collection raise critical questions about the way politics has been conceived, but those in Parts I and II are most explicit in challenging the mainstream politics literature. Part I includes essays that take issue with what its practitioners like to consider the more 'scientific' side of political analysis; Part II addresses canonical work in both classical and contemporary political theory. The essays in Part III move on to a discourse about interests and representation that has always played a major part in orthodox political analysis, and looks at what happens when we put sexual difference more firmly into the picture. Part IV explores further the resulting ambiguities around 'women': who or what do we mean by this? and what are the limits to identity politics? Essays in Part V take up the tensions between equality and difference in formulating policies for equality and against discrimination, while those in Part VI explore new ways of thinking about citizenship when we problematize the relationship between public and private or give greater weight to sexual—and other—differences.

Running through all sections are those questions that recurrently arise in thinking about feminism and politics. Does a feminist approach to politics lead to the conclusion that there has been too much gender in previous analyses, too much stereotyping of male and female? Does it lead, on the contrary, to the conclusion that there has not been enough gender, not enough attention to differences between women and men? Is the implication that public notions of equality and justice should be applied equally to relations in the private sphere? Or that private notions of care and intimacy should be applied more imaginatively in the public? Should feminists see themselves as challenging male dominance by opening up politics more fully to women? Or should they consider 'women' a fictitious entity that pretends to a spurious coherence but fails to address differences by class or race? Does feminism see politics as the expression of diverse and heterogeneous identities, identities previously swept under the carpet by grand notions about the citizen or the common good? Or does it see identity as too inherently ambiguous to form the basis for any politics at all? Do we think, in the now-classic terms of the 'equality versus difference' debate, that equality is best served by denying differences between the sexes? Or do we believe that equality can only be promoted by stressing the special needs of women?

The readings reflect diverse responses, but even where there is clear disagreement, the arguments are more nuanced than these formulations might suggest. The articles that address the political representation of women, for example, conjure up a notion of 'women' or 'women's interests' that would seem indefensible from Judith Butler's critique of the category of women or Rosemary Pringle and Sophie Watson's analysis of interests as discursively constructed through past and present interactions. But the difficulties in defining a set of women's interests form a central plank in all the arguments about women's political representation; and Butler herself notes that 'the political task is not to refuse representational politics—as if we could' (p. 5). None of the essays grouped together in the discussion of equality and anti-discrimination can be placed on one side or other of an equality/difference dichotomy. Catharine MacKinnon employs the notion of domination to cut through what she sees as the utterly ineffective alternation between sameness *or* difference; Deborah Rhode draws on the notion of disadvantage to similar effect; while Kimberle Crenshaw exposes the single-axis framework that forces Black women to represent themselves as facing either sex *or* race discrimination, and makes it impossible to address the intersection between these two. The readings on citizenship do indeed represent contrasting perspectives—particularly in the very different conceptions of citizenship developed by Mary Dietz and Jean Bethke Elshtain—but here, too, it would be misleading to locate these on one side or other of a public/private divide. It would also be misleading to try to locate the readings on one side or other of a 'politics of difference' or a 'politics of common concerns'. Iris Young makes a trenchant attack on the false impartiality that appeals to us to disregard our differences, but she sees specifically group representation as something that will promote better public discussion on matters of social justice: this is no narrow assertion of each group's specific and competing concerns. In related vein, Nancy Fraser in Chapter 20 stresses the importance of struggles for recognition by groups defined by their gender or race, but argues for a 'deconstructive cultural politics' (rather close to some of the arguments developed by Judith Butler) as the best way to finesse the redistribution–recognition dilemma. In all these arguments, there is an element of both critique and recuperation: politics matters, but what we understand by politics must first be transformed.

Journalistic accounts of contemporary politics often suggest that political disillusionment has reached an all-time high. This is not, I think, because political institutions are more corrupt or less inspiring than usual, but because the apparent inclusiveness of contemporary politics deprives us of the usual scapegoats and makes it harder to envisage the forces for change. There are more democracies in the world than ever before: more countries where the rights to citizenship have been detached from either sexual or racial qualifications; more countries where citizens ostensibly control their governments. In this context, we can no longer pin our hopes on widening the franchise, returning the army to its barracks, or overthrowing one-party rule—and if the politics continues to disappoint us, we are inclined to think that it is politics that carries the blame. Feminism provides a much needed counterweight to the resulting cynicism or apathy. It enables us to think more critically about the exclusions still practised under apparent inclusiveness. It also enables us to think more imaginatively about the many ways in which politics can still be transformed.

Notes

1. Joni Lovenduski, 'Toward the Emasculation of Political Science', in Dale Spender (ed.), *Men's Studies Modified* (Oxford: Pergamon, 1981), 89.
2. Michèle Barrett, 'Words and Things: Materialism and Method in

Contemporary Feminist Analysis', in M. Barrett and A. Phillips (eds.), *Destabilizing Theory: Contemporary Feminist Debates* (Oxford: Polity Press, 1992), 204.

3. Judith Butler and Joan W. Scott (eds.), *Feminists Theorize the Political* (New York and London: Routledge, 1992).

4. Joan Wallach Scott, 'Introduction', in Scott (ed.), *Feminism and History* (Oxford: Oxford University Press, 1996).

5. Ibid. 3.

6. M. Githens, P. Norris, and J. Lovenduski, 'Introduction', in Githens *et al.* (eds.), *Different Roles, Different Voices: Women and Politics in the United States and Europe* (New York: Harper Collins, 1994), p. ix.

7. David Bouchier, *The Feminist Challenge* (London: Macmillan, 1983), 52.

8. Jean Bethke Elshtain, *Public Man Private Woman: Women in Social and Political Thought* (Princeton: Princeton University Press, 1981), 15-16.

9. This last is one of the points argued in Joni Lovenduski's 'Toward the Emasculation of Political Science'.

10. Vicky Randall, 'Feminism and Political Analysis', *Political Studies*, 39 (1991), 513–32.

11. Carole Pateman, 'Feminist Critiques of the Public/Private Dichotomy', in S. I. Benn and G. F. Gaus (eds.), *Public and Private in Social Life* (London: Croom Helm, 1985).

12. See e.g. the essays collected together in Mary Lyndon Shanley and Carole Pateman (eds.), *Feminist Interpretations and Political Theory* (Oxford: Polity Press, 1991).

13. Susan Moller Okin, *Justice, Gender and the Family* (New York: Basic Books, 1989).

14. This is most associated with Carol Gilligan's *In a Different Voice* (Cambridge, Mass.: Harvard University Press, 1982). For an overview of some of the subsequent debates, see Diemut Bubeck, 'A Feminist Approach to Citizenship', in O. Hufton and Y. Kravaritou (eds.), *Gender and the Use of Time* (The Hague: Kluwer Law International, forthcoming).

15. Carole Pateman, *The Sexual Contract* (Oxford: Polity Press, 1988), 224.

16. Kathleen B. Jones, 'Citizenship in a Woman-Friendly Polity', *Signs*, 15 (1990), 794.

17. Two very useful essays exploring the different meanings now attached to 'difference' are Michèle Barrett, 'The Concept of "Difference" ' *Feminist Review*, 26 (1987), 29–41; and Linda Gordon, 'On "Difference" ' *Genders*, 10 (1991), 91–111.

18. For a fuller discussion of this literature, see Jane Mansbridge, 'Feminism and Democratic Community', in *Democratic Community: NOMOS XXXV*, eds. John Chapman and Ian Shapiro (New York: New York University Press, 1993), 339–95.

19. Iris Marion Young, *Justice and the Politics of Difference*, (Princeton: Princeton University Press, 1990), 157.

20. Susan Mendus, 'Losing the Faith: Feminism and Democracy', in John Dunn (ed.), *Democracy: The Unfinished Journey 508BC to AD1993* (Oxford: Oxford University Press, 1992), 218.

Part I. Feminism and Political Studies

Politics an Unnatural Practice: Political Science Looks at Female Participation

Susan Bourque and Jean Grossholtz

That politics is a man's world is a familiar adage; that political science as a discipline tends to keep it that way is less well accepted, but perhaps closer to the truth. This paper addresses itself to both concerns: the sexual definition accorded to politics and the manner in which the discipline of political science perpetuates this definition. We argue that in the choice of data to be analysed and in the interpretation of that data, the discipline insists upon a narrow and exclusive definition of politics which limits political activity to a set of roles which are in this society, and many others, stereotyped as male. Since society assigns roles by sex, this differentiation is carried over into political roles.

The tendency for political scientists to explain disparities in the political participation of certain groups (women, blacks, minorities, those of low income and status) as a reflection of their social position and purported innate proclivities, has provided a justification for those disparities and relieved the discipline from the need to seek alternate explanations which would question the distribution of roles, status, and power, as well as the very definition of politics. The conclusion reached by this sort of orientation is that the fault lies with the excluded group who simply will not get organized and participate in the ways open to them. We agree with Bella Abzug on this point:

I suggest what is really ludicrous is a political structure that denies representation to a majority of its population and then winds up fingering the victims of this situation as somehow responsible for it because of their personal inadequacies.[1]

By accepting the behaviour of those who presently exercise power as *the* standard of political behaviour, political science explains the

From J. Siltanen and M. Stanworth (eds.), *Women and the Public Sphere* (Hutchinson, 1984), 103–21. The full text of this chapter with more extensive examples, can be found in *Politics and Society*, 4/2 (Winter 1974), 225–66. Reprinted by permission of Routledge (Unwin Hyman) and Sage Publications, Inc.

failure of others to participate by their inability to approximate that behaviour. Unfortunately, political scientists do not go on to ask why or if this *should* be so, or how to overcome the impediments to 'proper' behaviour. Nor does the discipline ever deal adequately with the ramifications of this standard for the political system itself and for such other values as equal participation and government by consent.[2]

We argue in this paper that we have misconceived politics (pun not intended) and political life, and that the exclusion of women and numerous others may be a product of that misconception. Consequently, we should set ourselves the task of redefining the study of politics to adhere to the unqualified and uncorrupted demand and expectation of equal participation. We maintain that women, as women, can never be full participants in politics as presently defined by political scientists, given the assumptions made about the nature of politics and the necessity for sex role differentiation in society.

This paper illuminates the content and pervasiveness of these assumptions. We have not developed, in this analysis, specific alternatives. Rather, we define the problem. We look first at the way women are treated in some classic studies, and then at the basis of the statements which are made about the participation of women in politics.

We found that we could sort our findings into four categories of distortion of the participation of women in politics. Some studies fell into only one category, others fit into all four.

Our first category, 'fudging the footnotes', comprises those statements of female political characteristics, attitudes, or behaviour which are not substantiated in the material cited as the source. Misuse of the data of earlier studies usually involves removing all the qualifications and careful language of the original study, thus misrepresenting and in some cases falsifying the data.

Our second category is 'the assumption of male dominance'. This comprises the most pervasive expectation about sex differences in politics: that men will occupy dominant political roles and control political decisions. There is no doubt that males hold the vast majority of public offices at every level and control influence at every level as well. That political scientists report this cannot be faulted. What we find unacceptable is the failure to question this occurrence, to ask why this happens and to worry about the implications.

The reason for this is simply that it has been asserted and accepted, without proper evidence, that men dominate and women are dependent at the primary level of community life—the family. This asserted dominance of the male is then extended to a wider realm. For example, women's political attitudes are assumed to be reflections of those of the father or husband. This unwarranted assumption about family life and its relationship to the broader community is doubly damning because it suggests that it is women's preferences which give men control of politics. Moreover, whereas it is quite clear that males are dominant in politics, it is often asserted on the prior basis of assumed family relationships, not on the basis of evidence.

The third category of distinction is the acceptance of 'masculinity as ideal political behaviour'. This refers to the unexplained and unexamined assumption that those stereotyped characteristics held up as the masculine ideal (for example, aggressiveness, competitiveness, pragmatism, etc.) are the norms of political behaviour as well.[3] The distortion is most frequent when discussing explicit political behaviour (candidate preferences, issue preference, and saliency). Rational political behaviour is defined by the male pattern: it is by definition the expression of male values, and irrationality is by definition the expression of female values.

The fourth category of distortion we have called 'commitment to the eternal feminine'. In this sense feminine political behaviour is explained as a direct product of a woman's social role as wife and mother and her mythical status as purity personified. This distortion involves an assumption that women's present weak political position is necessary and functional. Society relies upon the services provided by women in the social realm, therefore there must be no corruption of that role and no change in it. We must tolerate limited participation by women in order to assure that we have wives to nurture our leaders and mothers to preserve the race.

STUDIES OF POLITICAL PARTICIPATION

We examined in detail three of the frequently quoted studies of political participation which summarize the question of sex differences: Angus Campbell *et al.*, *The American Voter*; Gabriel Almond and Sidney Verba, *The Civic Culture*; and Robert Lane, *Political Life*. These studies are, in turn, cited by the students of childhood and adult political socialization as the source of their knowledge of sex differences in participation. Here is the picture of female participation that we found in each.

Campbell *et al.*'s *The American Voter*, written in 1960, is a study of voting: the influences on turnout and partisan choice.[4] It concluded that there is an average difference of about 10 per cent in the turnout rates of men and women. The authors' examination of sex differences in turnout revealed that at succeeding levels of education the similarity of rates increases. At the upper end of the scale, male and female rates approach one another. Among the young, the single, and the married without children, they found 'no average difference in turnout between men and women across categories of education and age, outside the South'.[5]

What then, apart from age, accounts for the difference in turnout rate? According to Campbell *et al.*:

Mothers of young children, however, are consistently less likely to vote than are fathers of young children across all levels of education. . . . Furthermore, this dip in participation among mothers of small children does not appear to be matched by a slackened political involvement within this grouping. . . . The presence of young children requiring constant attention serves as a barrier to the voting act.[6]

Here we find direct evidence of the relationship between female social roles and limited political participation. But rather than suggesting that this impediment to female voting might change through some new division of childcare responsibilities, the authors conclude that the situation is hopeless:

Our analysis may be brought to bear on our expectations for future female participation. If primary responsibility for young children leads to some reduction in turnout potential, this effect is likely to leave a permanent discrepancy in participation between the sexes.[7]

This is the eternal feminine in action.

Campbell *et al.* also report a difference in the degree of political efficacy sensed by men and women. The data on differences in political efficacy supposedly demonstrate:

Men are more likely than women to feel that they can cope with the complexities of politics and to believe that their participation carries some weight in the political process. We conclude, then, . . . what has been less adequately transmitted to the woman is a sense of some personal competence *vis à vis* the political world.[8]

The authors of *The American Voter* found an explanation for this lower sense of political efficacy among women in the sex roles that prevail in this society:

The man is expected to be dominant in action directed toward the world outside the family; the woman is to accept his leadership passively. She is not expected, therefore, to see herself as an effective agent in politics.[9]

The authors are building an explanation on an assertion that males are expected to be dominant. This is a case of *assuming* male dominance.

The authors imply that men's and women's expressions of political efficacy are rational for both, given the societal sex roles. By the same reasoning it is irrational for a woman to express a sense of political efficacy comparable to a man's. But the fact is, under these criteria there are a large number of irrational women in this sample. Among the women polled, 68 per cent of the college educated, 40 per cent of the high school, and 14 per cent of the grade school expressed high efficacy, in contrast to 83 per cent, 47 per cent cent, and 32 per cent of the men respectively.[10] Obviously, there are differences between men and women, but an explanation based on societal sex roles is inadequate.

One might offer the alternative hypothesis, that given the very limited number of issues that citizens can affect, the lower sense of political efficacy expressed by women is a perceptive assessment of the political process. Men, on the other hand, express irrationally high rates of efficacy because of the limitations of their sex role which teaches them that they are masterful and capable of affecting the political process. In fact, few of us have any political influence in any case.

This second interpretation of the data will not be taken seriously as long as male political behaviour is considered the standard by which all other responses should be measured. Furthermore, the second hypothesis rests on granting women a degree of political cynicism, realism, sophistication, and understanding greater than that of men. This is something that these authors are unwilling to do.

In choosing to use Robert Lane's *Political Life* we wondered if it would be fair to criticize a book published in 1959 before some of the more comprehensive studies of voters had appeared. However, when we consulted the 1964 paperback edition of *Political Life* we found in the preface the author's assurance that the book had 'weathered well' and that he had 'modified the relevant comments on changing patterns of electoral participation'.[11]

Lane reports that there is a high degree of political agreement among members of the same family. But there are disagreements, and what happens then?

27

What evidence we have shows that conflict between husband and wife, when it occurs, produces a greater degree of discussion than political conflict in other groups [here he cites Maccoby 1954] followed usually by the wife's being 'persuaded' on the point. The wife is 'persuaded' rather than the husband partly, at least, because her role is culturally prescribed as less political; she loses less by yielding.[12]

Here Lane finds his pattern of male dominance. He argues that wives are 'persuaded' to adopt their husband's position, or when failing to do so, decide not to vote.

Lane's comments on the effect of political conflict among married people were probably triggered by a section in the Maccoby article in which the amount of political discussion in various groups is compared. Here is what the original study found:

we find that people who prefer the same party as their fellow workers tend to talk politics with them quite a bit while those who have a different political position than their fellow workers less often engage in political discussion at work. The opposite situation tends to hold true in the home of the young married couples: when they disagree on politics they discuss them extensively, while with agreement, politics become a less central subject of discussion.[13]

There is no indication here, or anywhere in the article, that wives are 'persuaded' because it is somehow less costly for them to do so. On the contrary, the authors conclude quite the opposite:

our data suggest that the husband–wife team is a cohesive group and that political agreement is important to the smooth functioning of the group, so that disagreement produces discussion and *mutual influence*.[14] (Our emphasis)

The data presented by Maccoby and her colleagues cannot be said to substantiate the conclusions drawn by Lane. However, a more recent study by Kent Jennings and Richard Niemi supports the Maccoby findings.[15] The authors describe two different models of husband-and-wife political behaviour:

In the measure that participation in matters political represents an instrumental action *vis a vis* the outside world, then clearly the role differentiation model points towards fathers rather than mothers as the chief actors. . . . Conversely the role sharing model suggests that fathers have no necessary monopoly on instrumental and adaptive behavior, that sharing may occur within a family or that patterns vary from family to family.[16]

As Jennings and Niemi point out, the predominance of one of these models over the other has deep ramifications for the position accorded women in politics.[17] The authors studied 430 conjugal pairs who were parents of high school age children. Their conclusion was that 'the evidence for the role sharing view of political participation is rather marked'.[18] And they argue that forces are at work pushing in the direction of even greater overlapping.[19]

Lane's treatment of this data suggests a case of fudging the footnotes to fit his assumption of male dominance.

A more subtle effect of these images, however, in Lane's terms, is that they perpetuate a moralistic or reform orientation towards politics among women. He notes that this moralistic orientation has its roots in the female responsibility to engender morality in the young. There are, in addition, other factors which lead to this orientation, and these, in Lane's view, have some rather important consequences for female political behaviour:

the more limited orbits of women, their more restricted contacts in society and narrower range of experience may tend to reinforce the view that the values they are familiar with are the only values—a lack of cultural relativism.[20] The evidence of the somewhat greater intolerance of women seems to support this view.[21]

The net effect of this moralistic orientation has been not only to provide an ineffective and relatively 'ego-distant' tie with political matters but also, as Riesman has remarked, to limit attention to the superficial and irrelevant aspects of politics.[22] Furthermore, such an orientation gives an illusion of comprehension because it is relatively easy to compare political acts and statements with moral symbols to assay moral worth, while it is difficult, indeed, to ascertain causes and estimate results. Finally such moralism may account for the relatively greater candidate orientation of women,[23] since persons—as contrasted to issues—are even more clearly perceived as 'good' or 'bad'. Hence, women, more than others contribute to the personification of politics both in the United States and abroad.[24]

What Lane appears to be saying is that the limited roles open to women lead directly to their greater intolerance, an ineffective tie to political matters, and an interest in the superficial, irrelevant aspects of politics. Women may appear to understand politics because of their manipulation of moral symbols, but they have actually missed the deeper currents, and more critical concerns.

Lane concluded that the moralistic orientation of women towards politics had led them to limit their attention to 'the superficial and irrelevant aspects of politics'. Here he cites page 58 of an article by David Riesman. On this page Riesman cites three incidents in which women or women's groups have been aroused about corruption in the political process. This he takes as an indication of their greater political conservatism and lesser sophistication. One example from Riesman will suffice:

I recall the grimness of my own reception when I spoke several years ago to a politically active women's organization and criticized Kefauver and his TV hearings as a lure for the unpolitical, a mobilization of the indignants, and a distraction from more important issues . . . a men's group of like education, perhaps worldly wise and cynical, would have gotten the point more easily—perhaps too easily.

It is clear that Lane believes that masculine behaviour is ideal political behaviour. But he does not pause to speculate on the consequences of this view of politics for the participatory political life he sets up as ideal. However, when he turns to his suggestions for improving participation he does consider the implications of change. One of the suggestions is to politicize the female role. Here is his assessment of that remedy:

Politicize the female role. Since the rate of political interest, knowledge and activity of women is generally lower than that of men, it is appropriate to consider how to relieve this depressed area of politics. Broadly speaking, political affairs are considered by the culture to be somewhat peripheral to the female sphere of competence and proper concern. Would it be wise to reinforce the feminist movement, emphasizing politics on the women's page along with the garden club and bridge club news, and making ward politics something like volunteer work for the Red Cross or the hospital auxiliary? No doubt something along this line could be done, *but it is too seldom remembered in the American society that working girls and career women who insistently serve the community in volunteer capacities, and women with extra-curricular interests of an absorbing kind are often borrowing their time and attention and capacity for relaxed play and love from their children to whom it rightfully belongs. As Kardiner points out, the rise in juvenile delinquency (and he says, homosexuality) is partly to be attributed to the feminist movement and what it did to the American mother.*[25] (Our emphasis)

Better to have 50 per cent of society operating in their political behaviour with only an 'illusion of comprehension' than to risk more juvenile delinquency and homosexuality.

Even Lane, after all his dire descriptions of female political participation (or perhaps he meant images), is reluctant to make any changes in the social roles of women that might change their assignments in the sexual division of labour. This is the eternal feminine response. In it women are caught in a 'damned if you do and damned if you don't' situation: they do not behave politically like men because of their social roles—and as a result they do not behave very well; but you cannot change their social roles because, if you did, the fabric of society would be torn asunder.

The Civic Culture, a comparative study of political attitudes in the USA, Britain, Germany, Italy, and Mexico, makes several important departures in its analysis of the political behaviour of women. At times the authors do not seem to be aware of the dramatic departures they have taken from the standard interpretations of the political behaviour of American women. Their opening statements match the interpretations we have previously discussed:

> Wherever the consequences of women's suffrage have been studied, it would appear that women differ from men in their political behavior only in being somewhat more frequently apathetic, parochial, conservative, and sensitive to the personality, emotional and aesthetic aspects of political life in electoral campaigns.[26]

The authors claim that their data are consistent with previous findings in the literature,[27] and their figures support this except in the American case. In the US data the differences between men and women, it is claimed, are not impressive and suggest a remarkable degree of similarity between the sexes, given the rather different political roles that are open to them.[28]

Almond and Verba point out the comparatively high rate of female participation in the United States and devote some attention to the importance of the role of women in determining the shape and direction of a society's political culture. Since political culture consists of an orientation to action, women are important in shaping political behaviour. The authors note that other studies of the role of women in politics have erred in treating sex as simply another demographic category.

> What they have overlooked is the fact that the great majority of adults are married; that they create families, raise children and help to 'socialize' these children into their adult roles and attitudes. Thus the political characteristics of women affect the family as a unit in the political system and affect the way in which the family performs the socialization function.
>
> It makes a great deal of difference whether women tend to live outside the political system in an intra-mural family existence, . . . or within the political system . . . which tends to be the case in the United States and Britain.[29]

In a refreshing admission of the limitations of their data, and the frequent propensity to make assertion without evidence, the authors go on to say:

8339

While our data do not permit us to demonstrate it directly and explicitly, we are suggesting that in the United States and Britain the family tends to be a part of the political system, that events and issues in the polity tend to be transmitted into the family via both marriage partners, and that political discussion tends to be frequent and reciprocal, rather than male dominated.[30]

While this flies in the face of the assertions of both Lane and Campbell and his colleagues, Almond and Verba give it scant attention. It may be an indication that their assessment of the literature on this question indicated it did not merit refutation.

Almond and Verba conclude that as a result of the family unit 'being in' the political system, which is a direct result of women 'living-in' the political system:

that the problems of family life, the needs of women and children are more directly and effectively transmitted into the polity through this kind of politically open family. The aesthetic quality and emotional tone of political life are probably also affected by the political competence and activity of women in the United States and Britain.[31]

As they see it, women in the US, and to a lesser extent in Britain, make their greatest political contributions in their roles as wives and mothers. It is in the home, through the political attitudes they instil in their children and the atmosphere of political discussion in which they participate, that the civic culture is passed on from one generation to the next.

Thus, Almond and Verba present a new view of American women, one that accepts the notion of comparable levels of political interest, involvement and competence between men and women. But, at the same time, this view underscores and praises the traditional sexual division of labour and uses that division to justify the exclusion of women from the leadership levels of political life. This is a case of commitment to the eternal feminine combined with an assertion of male dominance.

STUDIES OF POLITICAL SOCIALIZATION

The study of sex differences in political socialization is confined almost exclusively to childhood. The studies of childhood socialization show very few significant differences between the sexes although there is wide disagreement in the profession about the evidence.

The classic modern study of childhood learning about politics is that of Fred Greenstein, *Children and Politics*,[32] which includes an entire chapter on sex differences.

Greenstein collected information by questionnaire for children in grades four to eight and found differences between boys and girls in his sample on the following items:[33]

1. amount of political information;
2. ability to name an interesting news story;
3. naming a news story that was political in nature;
4. interest in national news.

Amount of political information was measured by the number of 'reasonably accurate answers' to questions asking the names of the incumbent mayor, governor, and president, and the duties of such officials and of legislative bodies. Although, as Greenstein reports, the amount of such information held by the children in the sample was 'infinitesimal', boys were significantly better informed. When asked to name an interesting news story boys were more likely than girls to be able to do so, and furthermore were significantly more likely to name a story that Greenstein classified as 'political'.

The sex differences reported in Greenstein all hang on what is meant by political. When asked, for example, 'if you could change the world what would you do?' girls are likely either not to respond at all or to give 'a distinctly non-political response' such as 'get rid of all the criminals and bad people'. We have no examples of what the 'political' responses of boys were.

Another sex difference used by Greenstein in his study to show the natural enthusiasm of boys for politics involves children's attitudes towards the Second World War. This difference is based on a study of twenty-one children between the ages of 6 and 7, which was conducted during the war. Although the sample was small, only twelve boys and nine girls, the differences were strikingly clear cut, Greenstein reports. 'When asked which of a series of pictures they preferred nine of the boys and none of the girls picked war pictures.' A look at this study shows that on other measures as well, the sex difference exists. In general, the attitude of the boys was classified as enthusiastic or excited about the war in eleven out of twelve cases, while only two girls were so classified.[34] Seven girls but only one boy were indifferent to the war. The exception among the boys was described by the authors as:

almost a genius in mathematics and music, reads at the fifth grade level and has unusual ability in spelling. He is the most immature member of the class socially and engages little in group activities.[35]

It is worth noting as well that part of the measure of interest was taken to be the report of three boys that they actually read the newspaper to get their news of the war, while girls relied on conversations with their parents or the radio.

A major part of Greenstein's orientation, if not explanation, relies upon Lewis M. Terman and Leona E. Tyler, 'Psychological Sex Differences', a review of the literature on sex differences among children published in the *Manual of Child Psychology* in 1954.[36]

They find sufficient evidence of aggressive behaviour on the part of boys, although some part of that difference they assign to teacher bias in reporting.[37] On emotional differences they report a study which shows girls rating their own response in thirty-four situations more emotional than boys, but they caution that girls and boys are not equally willing to confess emotion. They also note that girls get credit for more moral superiority than they possess.

From the basis of this data Greenstein argues that the demonstrated differences in aggressive and dominant behaviour means that more men are willing to express hostility and engage in controversy. He also relates this finding to the fact that 'women are more pacifist in their issue positions'. These relationships must remain speculative as must the following:

In a field as controversial as politics, it also seems possible that differential aggressiveness would affect the degree of participation.[38]

The tendency of women to have 'an absorbing interest in persons and personal relations' that Terman and Taylor report, is related by Greenstein to the fact that 'adult women are more likely than men to be candidate oriented'.

In conclusion, Greenstein argues that some factors inhibiting the participation of women in political life (such as having small children at home to care for, low levels of education, etc.) can be changed, but there are other 'less malleable psychological causes of political differences such as "deeply engrained sex roles" and the female dependence on males'. Greenstein quotes, with obvious pleasure, what he calls Duverger's charmingly Gallic remarks:

While women have legally ceased to be minors, they still have the mentality of minors in many fields and particularly in politics, they usually accept paternalism on the part of men. The man—husband, fiancé, lover, or myth—is the mediator between them and the political world.[39]

Greenstein says that his data give him no basis for final conclusions as to the explanation of adult sex differences. None the less, the data 'cast doubt on theories which suggest that such sex differences will disappear in the near future', that is, changes in educational level, work experience, and so on that adults experience will not have any significant effect, because differences in political involvement and orientation by sex emerge early in life.

An adequate theory must account for the psychological underpinnings of political sex differences, understood in terms of sex roles in society, how they develop, and what maintains them.

Further research is needed to discover what these underpinnings are. In part they may be curiosity, interest, and other related positive drives, channeled from tender age in one direction for girls and in another for boys. Politics, although not of deep interest to children of either sex, is resonant with the 'natural' enthusiasms of boys.[40]

Like the designation 'political', 'natural' is also in quotes, and never defined, so we do not know why politics is natural for boys. Greenstein has accepted without question masculinity as ideal political behaviour.

THE NOT SO HIDDEN BASIS FOR SEX DIFFERENCES IN POLITICS

The first conclusion we can draw from this research is that there is a high level of distortion in this literature. Much of the conventional wisdom on sex differences in politics is based on what we have called 'fudging the footnotes'. Consider the notion that women are more intolerant than men. This is consistently repeated and assigned to evidence presented by Samuel Stouffer.[41] On the question solely of the right of communists or communist doctrine to a public forum, Stouffer found 'women tend to be somewhat less tolerant'.[42] However, he goes on to point out that despite this attitude women are far more likely than men to be tolerant of deviance in their children. There is no evidence in the Stouffer study for the statement in Lane referring to 'the somewhat greater intolerance of women' about politics generally.[43] In the same pages Lane cites another source which, upon investigation, also notes that women are more likely to defend their children from 'patriarchal legalisms' and insist on the right of their children to be idiosyncratic.[44]

A second set of distortions result from the political scientists' acceptance of a sexual division of labour and function in the society, and their transference of that division of labour to politics. We disagree with this both on the basis of the assumed immutability of the sexual division of labour and on the basis of the validity of its transference to political behaviour. Despite the fact that differences between males and females, as shown by the research cited in this paper, are modest, i.e., that many women act just like men, these political scientists have assumed a fundamental difference between masculine and feminine political behaviour. The sexual stereotype of females as more emotional and sensitive is used to describe the contribution of women to political life. The forum for female participation is still the family and the primary function of the politically competent woman is to socialize children and to filter the needs of home and family into the political system.

The hidden message that femininity precludes politics becomes, in the hands of political scientists, a curious weapon. They seem unduly concerned that the attitude be assigned to women's self-evaluation, to her free choice. A widely used text published in 1967 put it all together:

The political inactivity of women evidently results mainly from the view widely held in our society that a woman's proper business is caring for her home, her husband, and her children, and she should leave the rough and dirty world of business and politics to her menfolk. As one woman respondent put it, 'Woman is a flower for men to look after', and another, 'I have never voted, I never will . . . a woman's place is in the home . . . leave politics to men.'[45]

Significantly the source of these quotes came from women respondents in the Merriam and Gosnell study, 43 years earlier.

Nowhere in the literature is there any attempt to treat seriously and systematically the exclusion of women from political leadership roles. Almond and Verba, conscious of the importance of women to the creation of civic sentiments, make it clear:

The significance of the political emancipation of women is not in the suffragette's dream of women in cabinets, parliaments, at the upper levels of the civil service, and the like. . . . [Greenstein] points out, correctly, that there are inherent limitations in the adult female role, which set an outer boundary to political participation for the great majority of women.[46]

Campbell *et al.*, Lane, and Greenstein all explicitly adhere to the assumption of male dominance. All the élite studies implicitly support this assumption. Many of the supplementary sources we have used in this paper also accept this assumption. Let the reader be clear, we firmly believe that political life in the United States is dominated by males. But we also believe that the character and explanation of the dominance has never been explored or tested by political scientists. On the contrary, the distortion arises from the political scientists' acceptance of male dominance without questioning why that should be a social fact, or if it is a valid explanation.

The clearest expression of commitment to this belief involves the explanations for the fact that conjugal pairs usually vote alike and hold similar political opinions. From this it is concluded that women vote according to their husbands' dictates.

A variation of this distortion is the notion that male dominance exists because women lack interest. This notion is buttressed by some unexplained and undocumented assertions, such as Greenstein's 'deeply engrained sex roles', or female dependence on men, or the assertion of 'a set of norms that women hold that they should not be as participatory as men'. We have not found in any of the literature cited in these studies, or anywhere else for that matter, a study of female socialization and political attitudes that supports this assertion.[47] Rather, it appears that political scientists have very clear and decisive beliefs about adult women's attitudes and roles which they are using in lieu of evidence.

The second and most basic conclusion we can draw from this research is that politics is defined as a masculine activity. The basis for assertions of male political dominance and the unwillingness to take female participation seriously, derives from this definition of politics. Those characteristics and enthusiasms which supposedly sway men (war, controversy, electoral manipulation) are defined as specifically political, while those characteristics and enthusiasms which supposedly sway women (human needs for food, clothing and shelter, adherence to consistent moral principles, the pre-emption of national by human concerns, a rejection of war as rational) are simply not considered political.

A 'political' response becomes by definition a male response. Note the ease with which Lane and Riesman are willing to relegate some political concerns, such as morality in public life, to the irrelevant category. In the same way élite studies, such as Presthus,[48] find that women in the élite are concerned with 'community improvement of a welfare kind' which really carries no weight in 'politics'. This is an arbitrary judgement which is used to support the image of women in political life that the author has in mind. We do not argue that in the reality which Presthus describes his assessment of the importance given to 'community improvement of a welfare kind' is incorrect, only that to deem this less political is to adopt a limited and strange notion of that classification.

One of the sources often cited as evidence of sex difference in political attitudes is the catalogue of public opinion polls compiled by Hadley Cantril and Mildred Strunk for the period 1935–46.[49] The belief that women have fewer opinions than men is based on the fact that women are said to give 'don't know' responses more often than men. Greenstein, for example, cites the following questions in Cantril and Strunk on all of which women gave more 'don't know' responses than men:

Would you approve or disapprove of a speed limit on open roads? Do you think the Russians are planning a world revolution or do you think they have given it up? If there had been a Liberal candidate (in the British election of July 1945) would you have voted for him? Are you in favor of a union of Western nations? Do you know what workers councils are and what their task is? (asked of a Czech sample in 1946). It has been said that quarreling among political parties has interfered with Canada's war effort. Do you agree or disagree? (asked of Canadians in 1942).

On the basis of the percentage of 'don't know' responses women are assumed to be less willing to take a controversial stand and also, it is presumed, to have less information.

However, in the same volume we find that women, more often than men, said they thought the people should be consulted before any declaration of war (in both 1935 and 1939); women, more often than men, opposed capital punishment; women, more often than men, were willing to continue food rationing in order to feed hungry Europeans and even the defeated Germans. Women also expressed strong opinions about draft laws, divorce law reform, and women in high office. On all these issues there were no significant differences by sex on the 'don't know' responses. These opinions we submit are 'political'.

In short, it is not a question of women not having opinions on controversial matters, it is a question of which matters one takes as being most important to politics. It is clear that the assumptions being made here exclude those interests about which women are most concerned.

Fundamentally those things which society defines as stereotypically masculine (aggressiveness, pragmatism, etc.) are considered to be the norms of politics. One must have these characteristics to be a 'real' man and to be a 'real' *politico* one must have these same characteristics. Our response to that message is that we must redefine politics and political life in terms that will allow political science to treat human persons as necessarily participatory in the collective decisions that shape their lives. Furthermore, the definition of human persons must not be restricted by stereotypical images of what human beings are all about, whether they are male or female.

THE IMPLICATIONS FOR POLITICAL SCIENCE

There is in our view a distressing compatibility between the stereotypical model of politics that political science has accepted and the denial of moral values and acceptance of pragmatic political expediency that the Watergate scandal represents. There is as well, a frightening similarity between assumptions that war is exciting and glorious, that aggressiveness and controversy are politically mature, and the long and bitter bloodletting in Indo-China. We would not argue that women would bring anything different to politics in the present circumstances. Rather, women who enter this polity carry the same ideals, norms and orientations as men. As the material in this paper makes specifically clear—there are relatively few differences between men and women in politics. This is a tragedy in our eyes, for it means that women have accepted the masculine ethos in politics.

But there *are some differences* in the political behaviour of men and women. Paradoxically, it is the discipline's treatment of these differences which demonstrates the problem. What we see in the treatment of women is a symptom of a larger problem in the discipline—a willingness to either avoid questions of power and justice by blaming the victims, or to substitute explanations based on societal norms while at the same time ignoring the political system's role in the maintenance of those norms.

Perhaps if political scientists had subjected the data they found on these differences to more searching analysis, and avoided the assumptions that they have used as explanations, they might have found some interesting hypotheses about our political life and even some suggestions as to where it goes awry. Let us illustrate with some examples.

Women were found to have a moralistic orientation towards politics. We think the evidence cited is not striking, although there are significant but small differences between men and women on those things which political scientists label moral positions. This classification is never truly explained but at times seems to consist of

SUSAN BOURQUE AND JEAN GROSSHOLTZ

women's application of individual moral principles to political life, at other times it seems to deal with women's assessment of government officials as doing their job, or with the need to obey the law, or with pacifist notions. But the most difficult problem and the most revealing factor in this entire category of difference is the fact that political scientists who assume the category is real and who believe it is a view held by women more often than men, deem this a concern with the irrelevant, and a lack of sophistication. Clearly politics in the United States has been conducted as if moral concerns were irrelevant, but should political scientists accept this as mature political style? Are we satisfied with an assessment of political life which calls a concern for consistent principles, obedience to the law, and concern for human life irrelevant?

Another example is women's attitude towards elections. Women do not see much difference between the parties, preferring instead to search out candidates they can believe in. Might this not be interpreted as a realistic appraisal of conventional political life? Women, like Lipsitz's poor, may well have grievances, and when allowed or encouraged to voice them come forth loud and clear.[50] But those who determine which issues will be discussed and which emerge in party platforms are not women.

Initially, in our own research, we thought the treatment of women in political science could be explained by the assumption of social roles as determinant and the acceptance of this assumption as legitimate justification for low levels of participation on the part of women. This view holds that both men and women have come to accept certain divisions within the society (of labour, status, behaviour) along sex lines and those have been translated into politics. But as we read the literature, looking critically at both the data and the interpretations which were offered, we came to a rather different conclusion. If politics was to be the man's realm, then at the levels that political scientists measured political involvement, women were not getting the message. Women turned out to vote at about the same rate as men, except when the care of small children kept them at home. Moreover, they had about the same level of interest and involvement in politics as most men. Many of the differences in the political orientations of men and women were created by the political scientists out of their own notions of what should be the case.

What happens to our understanding of political life and our very definition of 'politics' if we assume that women are as interested in and competent to exercise political power as men?

Notes

1. B. Abzug in *Women's Role in Contemporary Society: The Report of the New York City Commission of Human Rights* (New York: Avon Books, 1972), 639.
2. The discipline's justification of existing power holders has been challenged in the case of class and occupation, and that challenge is now taken seriously. There is a growing body of literature criticizing political science on this source. See e.g. C. Pateman, *Participation and Democratic Theory* (Cambridge: Cambridge University Press, 1970); L. Lipsitz, 'The Grievances of the Poor', in P. Green and S. Levinson (eds.), *Power and Community: Dissenting Essays in Political Science* (New York: Vintage, 1969); A. Wolfe, *The Seamy Side of Democracy: Repression in America* (New York: McKay, 1973); etc. However, political scientists still dismiss as polemics the same criticism when it is made on the basis of sex or race. Why this should be the case is one of our major concerns.
3. This is similar to the findings in recent psychological studies that ideal, or healthy, personalities are made up of what are regarded as masculine characteristics. I. K. Broverman, D. M. Broverman, F. E. Carlson, P. S. Rosenkrantz, and S. R. Vogel, 'Sex-Role Stereotypes and Clinical Judgements of Mental Health', in J. M. Bardwick (ed.), *Readings on the Psychology of Women* (New York: Harper and Row, 1972), 320–4.
4. A. Campbell *et al.*, *The American Voter* (New York: Wiley, 1960).
5. Ibid. 487.
6. Ibid. 488.
7. Ibid.
8. Ibid. 490.
9. Ibid.
10. Ibid., Table 15.4, 260. These are figures for the non-South only. The differences in the South were of the same order.
11. R. E. Lane, *Political Life* (New York: Free Press, 1965), paperback edition, preface.
12. Ibid. 208.
13. E. E. Maccoby, R. Mathews, and A. S. Morton, 'Youth and Political Change', *Public Opinion Quarterly*, **18** (1954), 23–9.
14. Ibid. 33.
15. M. Kent Jennings and R. G. Niemi, 'The Division of Political Labor Between Mothers and Fathers', *American Political Science Review*, **65** (March 1971), 69–82.
16. Ibid. 69.
17. Ibid. 70.
18. Ibid. 73.
19. The study also found that variation in this model was related to whether the wife worked and the level of education. Although they concede that there is still a built-in edge for males: 'Even in those cases where the male ego is clearly dominant, there are abundant instances where the distaff side of the family is paramount or the male advantage seriously impaired.' Ibid. 82.
20. D. Riseman, 'Orbits of Tolerance, Interviews, and Élites', *Public Opinion Quarterly*, **20** (1956), 49–73, 57. Cited in Lane, *Political Life*, 213.
21. S. Stouffer, *Communism, Conformity and Civil Liberties: A Cross Section of the Nation Speaks Its Mind* (New York: Doubleday, 1955), 131–55.

22. Riesman, 'Orbits of Tolerance, Interviews, and Élites', 58.
23. A. Campbell, G. Gurin, and W. Miller, *The Voter Decides* (Evanston, Ill.: Row Peterson, 1954), 152–6.
24. Lane, *Political Life*, 213.
25. Ibid. 354, 355.
26. The sources cited on this statement are: Lane's *Political Life*; M. Duverger, *The Political Role of Women* (Paris: UNESCO, 1955); F. Greenstein, 'Sex-Related Political Differences in Childhood', *Journal of Politics*, 23 (1961), 353–71; M. Dogan and J. Narbonne, 'Les Françaises Facent à la Politique', and G. Bremme, 'Die Politische Rolle der Frau in Deutschland'; all in G. Almond and S. Verba, *The Civic Culture* (Princeton: Princeton University Press 1963), 388.
27. Ibid.
28. For this data consult the tables on 390–5 in Almond and Verba, *The Civic Culture*.
29. Ibid. 398.
30. Ibid.
31. Ibid., pp. 398–9.
32. F. Greenstein, *Children and Politics* (New Haven: Yale University Press, 1965).
33. This information is displayed in Table 6.1 in Greenstein, *Children and Politics*, 117. The table is somewhat hard to read and the actual questions are not given. The table is divided into 'specifically political responses', which includes the political information score which shows significant differences, although all other measures show no significant differences; and 'politically relevant responses'.
34. Ibid. 97.
35. Ibid. 96.
36. L. M. Terman and L. E. Tyler, 'Psychological Sex Differences', in L. Carmichael (ed.), *Manual of Child Psychology* (New York: Wiley, 1954).
37. Ibid. 1097–8.
38. Greenstein, *Children and Politics*, 121.
39. Ibid. 126, n. 51.
40. Ibid. 127.
41. Stouffer, *Communism, Conformity and Civil Liberties*.
42. Ibid. 131.
43. Lane, *Political Life*, 213.
44. Lane cites David Reisman, 'Orbits of Tolerance, Interviews and Élites'.
45. H. A. Bone and A. Ranney, *Politics and Voters* (New York: McGraw-Hill, 1967).
46. Ibid. 399.
47. The documented source for the low rates of turnout for women in Greenstein was based on women's belief that voting is for men, as reported by R. Lane, C. E. Merriam, and H. F. Gosnell, *Non-Voting: Causes and Methods of Control* (Chicago: University of Chicago Press, 1924), which is in turn the source of the Lane statement. It is worth looking at Merriam and Gosnell since this study has become the basis for so much assertion. These authors, studying Chicago voters in April 1923, found that over half the adult citizens not voting were women (p. 27). One-third of these women were foreign-born women who had acquired citizenship by marriage. Of the women in the sample some 11.4 per cent said they did not vote out of disbelief. This number included 414 who disbelieved *and 54 more* who did not vote because their husbands objected. The authors conclude that the disbelief in women's voting was 'an important but

vanishing factor in the civic life of the community' (115–16). It is worth noting that this study, completed only three years after the women's suffrage amendment was passed, was the source of statements regarding women's low rates of turnout and male dominance in voting choices. The authors made no such claims, even in 1923.

48. R. Presthus, *Men at the Top* (Oxford: Oxford University Press, 1964).
49. H. Cantril, and M. Strunk, *Public Opinion 1935–1946* (Princeton: Princeton University Press, 1951).
50. Lipsitz, 'The Grievances of the Poor'.

Homeless in International Relations? 'Women's' Place in Canonical Texts and Feminist Reimaginings

Christine Sylvester

William Connolly's essay, 'Democracy and Territoriality', tells us of a nostalgia in late modernity 'for a time when a coherent politics of "place" could be imagined as a real possibility for the future'.[1] For feminists, that 'nostalgia' reads as 'backlash'; as a dream of certain people to return in the future to a golden age where women knew their place, to a Wo(e)begon(e) where all the women are good looking and all the men are strong, to an imagined community of naturalized gender.[2]

Where is women's place? For nostalgia buffs, it lies in two linked realms: the liberal nation and its sub-unit of mythical proportions, the household and the family. And what are women doing in these places? Far more, say feminist historians, than the gender nostalgias suggest, yet much less than nostalgias for liberal democracy can provide for all citizens.[3] Women are the food preparers and the main caretakers of adult men and children. In many locations today, they are still the food growers who are excluded from the gross national product and, when GNP calls for it, they are the Rosie Riveters. Women are also the protected ones: the Beautiful Souls, and delicate beings who are too disorderly and irrational to be of the disorder we know as international relations.[4]

Lately, some feminists have recovered a third 'home' for women, unacknowledged in mainstream texts of international relations, at the interstices of national and international spaces: as home-bound workers for Benetton International; as models evoking 'exotic nations' and exotic sexuality for the logo of Chiquita bananas; as First-World nation-based tourists adding the refuse of our middle-class need for respite to the dirty laundry that women in 'other' national locations must wash; and as nation-based soldiers in the Persian Gulf War.[5] We are now, in the eyes of some feminist writers,

Chapter 4 in M. Ringrose and A. J. Lerner (eds.), *Reimagining the Nation* (Open University Press, 1993), 76–97. Reprinted by permission.

international actors. However, it does not require enormous imagination to see, in the newly viewed homeland of international relations for 'women', the markings of a zone of domestic politics of
nation and household that keeps us locked out of the 'truly important' realms of canonical international relations.

In this essay, I pursue the traces of gender in the sections of
Connolly's essay that discuss the intersection of nostalgic idealism
of territorial democracy and the nostalgic realism of international
relations. I argue that an unacknowledged principle of co-operative
autonomy from 'women' is discernible in the mainstream texts of
international relations. This principle rehearses a gender nostalgia
in which a particular sex–gender absence is required and must be
invented in order to enable the encoding of international relations
as masculine territory. Through autonomy from 'women', both as
embodied people and as an ensemble of ascriptive traits, it becomes
axiomatic that 'women' may merely visit international relations for
brief periods of time in roles that are assigned to us. Since our
homes are presumed to be elsewhere, 'women' cannot be permanently in international relations. Only 'men' have a 'coherent politics of place' in that sphere. Cooperative autonomy can be sighted
whenever the Janus-faced territorial markers of anarchy and reciprocity are raised in international relations theory and practice. It
has an antidote in a variety of feminist strategies of homesteading.

WOMEN AT HOME IN REALIST IMAGINARIES?

Two theorists on a critical edge inside the canonical community of
international relations, Frederick Kratochwil and John Ruggie, tell
us that:

it has been widely assumed throughout the history of modern international relations theory that there exists one realm of international life
which is intrinsically conflictual and another which is intrinsically more
cooperative.[6]

The realm of intrinsic conflict is cloaked in the dark anarchies of an
international realm which has no governance. This conflictual
realm, a place apart from the co-operative sphere of legitimately
governed nations, is inhabited by states, statesmen, soldiers, and a
few 'particles of government' found in international law and organization.[7] Without external authority, states rely on 'the means they

can generate and the arrangements they can make for themselves'.[8] Often, states 'fail to co-operate even when they have common interests'[9] because they primarily compete for power, security, survival, and dominance. A ghostly transmogrified Adam Smith stalks this realm holding in his second hand a market-like thing which brings about the reciprocity of oligopolistic relations rather than the total decentralization of anarchy. This market-like thing is the balance of power. Great states are rational to create it and others are rational to accept it: 'as in any self-help system, the units of greatest capability set the scene of action for others as well as for themselves'.[10] In this intrinsic realm of conflict where 'interdependence is always a marginal affair',[11] the other intrinsic of co-operation is actually disallowed. It is treated as a totally separate and snug home port outside international relations where 'pretty girls' kiss the boys and wave the flags of domestic democracy.

In some manner or form, a realist imaginary of international relations, as a place with a politics apart, has held sway for 300 years.[12] It was conjured up in the writings of Thucydides, toyed with by Hobbes, and defended with gusto in the twentieth century when actions by fascist Germany threatened the balance of power and precipitated a chain of events that created a bipolar world. Realism came to the aid of war in Korea and in Vietnam and it assisted the build-up of nuclear and conventional weapons. It underlaid 'constructive engagement' with racist South Africa in the 1980s and was sighted during the British invasion of the Malvinas. It warred, it walled, kept the peace (so some claim), and it produced a bigger-than-life security dilemma. It made the Carter administration's hopes on behalf of human rights sound radical. It made Noriega, Batista, Marcos, Chiang Kai-Shek, Samosa, Smith, and Mobutu look good. It made outpost Berlin and the diplomatic isolation of Cuba necessary. It was spouted by theorists and bosses, experts and presidents. It was everything: the hipboots for all bogs. The S and M of realism wounded many people in these Third World proxy wars and kept all of us in the First World tied up and beaten by a trumped-up sense of our security needs.

Jean Bethke Elshtain argues that realism in international relations 'is one of the most dubious of many dubious sciences that present truth claims that mask the power plays embedded in the discourse and in the practices it legitimates'.[13] Realism's long reign as the king of international relations means that it sets powerful dynamics of 'social relations in which all parties are forced to participate— women as well as men, unmasculine as well as masculine men'.[14]

One might add that colonizing countries and victims of sovereign property rights have also been subsumed by realist understandings of the international. Yet, like the Schumpeterian realism of democratic theory, realist international relations denies a common sociality that binds domestic democracies to the nation-state acting in international relations.[15] It also denies the possibility that the household is bound to the nation-state that acts in the international system. These linkages place 'women' in the sociality of realism. Nevertheless, 'women', like other groups which are seemingly dispensable to realist international relations (e.g. working-class men, and people of colour when they are not soldiers), are under-theorized and even unseen as the visitors in canonical texts who support the coherent politics of 'men's' place when they are statesmens' wives, companions to men at military bases, designated weepers over anarchy's debris of lost lives, and patriots. Masculine international relations protects others by doing violence to their presence in international relations: indeed, it renders them homeless in the canon.

Carole Pateman provides the basis for a genealogy of the gender-coded territory of international relations. This genealogy centres on Hobbes, the social contractarian whom theorists of international relations love to remember.[16] Pateman suggests that Hobbes's route of escape from a mythical state of nature, which was anarchical and warlike, in part required the subordination of women in collective units, captained by men, that occasionally warred against other similar units. 'Women' in the state of nature were as strong and cunning as men, but the mother-rights to children that Hobbes granted to women weighed them down during periods of war.[17] Having to defend children and themselves, women tended to be conquered by men who had already shown, through tacit acceptance of mother-right, that they were not similarly inclined to assume involuntary obligations to weaker parties. The conquering men often had 'weaker' men to assist them. These were confederates who had been overcome by the conqueror or who had voluntarily capitulated to his power. The conquering man, his confederates and conquered women made a family which consisted of 'a man, and his children, and servants together; wherein the father or master is the sovereign'.[18]

Families did not negotiate the mythical social contract. Only free-standing (unconquered) men did that for other free-standing men. Because they did not stand free, women were partly left behind in the state of nature. They were also partly brought under men's formal control by the civic contract of marriage, which was made possible by the contracting logic of the social contract. Faced with an ambiguous status in the social contract, women 'consented' to become wives under the domain of their husbands. This sexual contract, which had roots in male–female relations in the state of nature and which was the only logical option for non-free-standing women, made for a troubled relationship of 'women' to 'citizenship'. One might say that it made for a tenuous home in the intrinsic of co-operation in the nation-state because some of us were only partly accommodated in rights-bearing categories.[19]

Of course, we must not fail to see that the (male) citizen can lose as well as gain in his national territory despite his privileged location in a nostalgia of place. At once, the (male citizen) exchanges identities for identity and ends up 'as subject diminished, as Sovereign empowered and increased. . . . Reconstituted by this Constitution, the citizen's regard for himself follows from his participation in sovereignty'.[20] Whether he wants it or not, the identity of 'men' becomes fused with the identity of the conquering, or naturally entitled, authority of the state. That is, a variety of (male) citizens of the state become fused into an imaginary of (and here even the words must be fused) citizensandstates. This fusion has an analogue in Hobbes' implicit imaginary of womenandchildren.[21] The citizenandstate is 'free that can defend itself and gain the recognition of others, and shore up an acknowledged identity' as the sovereign state.[22] *L'état c'est moi* becomes *l'état c'est les citoyens*, and the *citoyen(ne)s* with the fullest rights are men.

This conflation of citizen and state catapults the local nation-state into another zone of liberal gender relations. It is in realist international relations that the imaginary state of nature is wild and is left behind by the social contract to be reimagined beyond territorial boundaries. International relations is a disorderly place where citizensandstates gaze out on other citizensandstates competing for power, security, dominance, and survival. Despite balances of power 'out there', the local authority of the conqueror sovereign is threatened by the unconquered, unterritorialized intrinsic of anarchy. If another citizenandstate trumpets war, 'To preserve the larger civic body, which must be "as one", particular bodies must be sacrificed'.[21] Citizensandstates must, at that moment, disaggregate into sacrificing citizen men who enter the second (international) imaginary of nature and mark its zones through war. These men prove thereby that they are what they were meant to be: 'war and the state'.[24] This identity is often unleashed against the gendered representatives of hearth and home; warring citizens often rape the 'enemy's women' as part of war. People called women are thereby thrust into realist international relations. But they are not admitted into most realist studies of war.

Jean-Jacques Rousseau gives us a different, though complementary, genealogy of gender place, that focuses on women's second home—the household. With a powerful nostalgia that romanticizes and does violence to the Hobbesian notion of a sexual contract, Rousseau nativizes (or assigns a natural place) for women in marriage and family. To Rousseau, the family is 'the oldest of all societies and the only natural one'.[25] The family is based on a social constitution of gender—a primary difference 'in the ways of life of the two sexes'. This difference marks a passage from a presocial situation in which the two sexes are not differentiated into a social situation in which 'Women became more sedentary, and grew accustomed to looking after the Hut and Children, while the man went in quest of the common subsistence'.[26]

Rousseau subsequently countervenes the *social* constitution of gender by saying, in *Emile*, that '[t]he physical [difference] leads us unawares to the moral'.[27] The morality of women is grounded in the irrational uterus and its unlimited sexual needs that refuse sublimation. Men's morality, on the other hand, is grounded in the mind, in reason, things that civilization helps develop in him to augment his physical strength.[28] Because 'women' is on the fringe of socially contracted civilization, and because her sex difference drives her to disorderly behaviour, Rousseau says that women must 'be subjected either to a man or to the judgments of men'.[29] Women must strive to 'please men, to be useful to them, to be loved and honoured by them'[30] and to pass on to sons the virtues of citizenship and to daughters the virtues of subordination. We are homebound to the family where the violence of its scripted founding, as described by Hobbes, is simultaneously abusively rehearsed and cancelled out by implying that it is natural.[31]

Although 'women' continue to be protected, debated, denied, denounced, or rejected, there is a considerable history of resistance to marginalization.[32] It includes feminist struggles of the 1970s, when women declared that the personal was political and thereby exposed the family as a site of politics without the type of recompense available in the public sphere. It also includes Aida Hurtado's reminder that women of colour in the United States cannot even take solace in some of the genuinely warm spaces of the private household because their 'private' child-bearing decisions are publicly scrutinized and their marketing lists checked for signs of squandered public assistance money. The public in their lives 'is *personally* political'.[33] Historical epilogues show people called women struggling in liberal societies to attain even the most rudimentary of Schumpeter's democratic imperative—access to periodic elections.

'Women's places' are required to maintain equivalences of men, heads-of-households, citizens, states, and war. These categories mark the territory of domestic realism and realist international relations. Citizens fight for their mother country rather than admit that all wars are civil wars over masculinized spaces. Mother's milk is made into the 'foundation for civic-spiritedness and willingness to die'.[34] Therefore, as Connolly says of Schumpeterian democratic realism, realist international relations can be seen as 'instantiating masculine rationality through feminine strategems while simultaneously denying the indispensability of these tactics through masculinist imperatives'.[35]

There is in all of this a grand conflation *cum* subversion of citizenship. Citizens draw identity from a relationship among themselves, which culminates in the state. Simultaneously, when states face threats from other states, they sacrifice their citizens. Citizens are secure in their rights as conquerors–creators–rulers of private and public places in liberal societies, but that security is disturbed by the displacing activities of other conquerors–creators–rulers 'out there'. At home, fighting citizens can wait and wait for the state-self they have protected to reconnect with its heroes of war. American veterans of the Vietnam War waited until 1991 to receive state compensation for Agent Orange related illnesses. Their monument was late in coming and their activities on behalf of mother country were labelled as baby-killing by the womenandchildren and citizen-soldiers they ostensibly protected.[36]

At moments of such waiting and sacrifice, being a citizen on the 'inside' of the sovereign state's borders can be as taxing as being on the 'outside'. But Rousseau at least leaves spaces in liberal societies for men who, 'by constitution rather than by distance from the society of men',[37] are self-sufficient and can therefore stay aloof from citizenandstate in order to gain (or retain) more comprehensive identities, wisdoms, and virtues. These 'solitaries' do not need others to raise them since they 'raise themselves in spite of what one does'.[38] They are well placed, accordingly, to assist others in exploring broader identities that lie submerged in the identity 'citizen'. Women are not allotted an equivalent social task and opportunity for rebellion. We are too busy raising ordinary men, the ones who 'need to be raised',[19] in places that are sequestered from the realist imaginary. Solitaries can be autonomous within the privileges of citizenandstate, but women cannot be autonomous from mothersandchildren. When we attempt to take some autonomy, the nostalgia for gender place reminds us of our transgression.

The interrelated genealogical stories of Hobbes and Rousseau have a gender intrinsic, within the realist intrinsic, that brings even the action of warring citizensandstates into some harmony. The gender intrinsic is co-operative autonomy from 'women'. It stipulates that the place of 'women' is somewhere other than where the citizenandstate rules. In the genealogical texts of Western liberal democracy, readers are told why 'women' occupies a separate place. In the zone of realism known as international relations, the gender intrinsic, though implied, is a notable textual absence that belies the claim that co-operation and interdependence are marginal aspects of international relations. It also belies the claim that co-operation is located in an intrinsic marked by domestic politics in nation-states. In other words, co-operative autonomy counters the realist notion that the international realm is one of intrinsic conflict between citizensandstates and exposes it as a realm of partial coop-eration that serves to distract us from the 'real' conflict over sex-gender territories.

Co-operative autonomy is not the product of any direct agreement to exclude 'women' from international relations, just as the social contract was, in fact, not a negotiated agreement. It is a myth that is honoured as though it was scripture. It is common sense. It is acceptable to flaunt co-operative autonomy in order to bring women into status as a public resource in building up the nation (the Rosie Riveter syndrome) or in conducting international relations (for which diplomats' wives are used), but it seems unacceptable to study women in realist international relations. Irrespective of the level of analysis, sightings of 'women' 'out there' (including traits such as caretaking, co-operation, and modesty that are assigned to us) are not chronicled.[40] When 'women' cross the boundaries and step into masculine international territory (for example, by volunteering for duty in the Persian Gulf), public debate springs up about the propriety of pairing menandchildren at home.

Cooperative autonomy fits Michel Foucault's poststructuralist characterization of places apart from the state where particular notions of truth, knowledge, and beliefs are produced and veiled by the concept of 'legitimacy'. Co-operative autonomy's 'politics of discursive regime'[41] involves multiple forms of constraint over:

the types of discourse to accept and make function as true; the mechanisms and instances which enable one to distinguish true and false statements; the means by which each is sanctioned; the techniques and procedures accorded value in the acquisition of truth; [and] the status of those who are charged with saying what counts as true.[42]

The discourse of cooperative autonomy is realist: the authorities are masculinist; and the mechanisms, techniques and procedures revolve around forms of 'agreement' that are silent about 'women's' third home in the international spaces that feminists find and record.

REGINAS AT HOME IN NEO-LIBERAL INSTITUTIONS?

Neo-liberal institutionalism in international relations theory, which is closely associated with the work of Robert Keohane, claims to be different from realism on two points. First, it advances the argument that the international system is indeed anarchic, but that it nevertheless has conventions, treaties, and regimes that save us from a Hobbesian drama of war of all against all. There is a co-operative realm of international relations. Second, the 'neo-liberal' in neo-liberal institutionalism signifies that 'co-operation and liberalism are conceptually distinct'.[43] While liberalism in its realist guise grants a superior regulatory position to market-like mechanisms (i.e. balance of power), neo-liberalism emphasizes 'the importance of international institutions, constructed by states, in facilitating mutually beneficial policy coordination among governments'.[44]

There can be co-operation under anarchy, under the security dilemma, among egoists, and after hegemony[45] because:

As everyone understands by now, rational egoists making choices in the absence of effective rules or social conventions can easily fail to realize feasible joint gains, ending up with outcomes that are suboptimal (sometimes drastically suboptimal) for all parties concerned.[46]

Thus, under certain situations, citizensandstates will co-operate and not wage war or perniciously compete. The acceptance of anarchy as a first principle of international relations, however, structures the neo-liberal understanding of co-operation such that the difference it presents is derivative of, rather than alternative to, realist system structure. Keohane tries to script a possible way out of the realist intrinsic through the gradual formation of an international social democracy with Walzerian idealist components of 'plurality, diversity, spheres, complex equality [and complex interdependence], membership, belonging, shared understandings'.[47]

Keohane claims that states are woven together around 'conventions'—implicit rules and shared understandings that hold anarchy in check in the absence of more formal cooperation. Reciprocity is one such convention; indeed, it is the key convention which activates pluralist pulling and hauling in a way that can enable a healthy communitarian system to emerge in the zone of war. It provides a basis for states to accept obligations that preclude:

making calculations about advantage in particular situations, if they believe that doing so will have better consequences in the long run than failure to accept any rules or acceptance of any other politically feasible set of rules.[48]

These rules, called regimes or institutions, 'prescribe behavioral roles, constrain activity, and shape expectations'[49] as a Foucaultian 'politics of discursive regime' anticipates. The General Agreement on Tariffs and Trade (GATT) is one such regime. I argue that an unnamed and less formal international regime reproduces and maintains the gender intrinsic of co-operative autonomy from 'women'.

Keohane argues that, once established, regimes can broaden the options for co-operation by offering states high-quality information in environments where norms of honesty and straightforwardness may emerge to counter realist values. Acceptance of initial obligations may begin a complex train of events in which states accept more obligations, moving from specific reciprocity ('I trade if you trade') to more generalized commitments to regime-negotiated outcomes (e.g. lower tariffs), and to the welfare of other states with whom they interact via regimes (by, for example, avoiding trade wars). In a formal sense, diffuse reciprocity occurs where states gradually 'contribute one's share, or behave well toward others, not because of ensuing rewards from specific actors, but in the interests of continuing satisfactory overall results for the group of which one is part, as a whole'.[50]

The gender regime encourages diffuse reciprocity for masculine international relations: 'I recognize men in international relations if you do' gradually becomes 'I will take on obligations to safeguard the rights of men to that territory for the good of the group.' The realist intrinsic of co-operative autonomy from 'women' thereby slips unproblematized into neo-liberal institutionalism—that which is meant to be distinct from realism.

There are at least two consequences of this slippage. First, neo-liberal institutionalist texts rarely point out that co-operation is a usual sign of 'women' in Western societies—a sign of handmaidens of men, eternal volunteers in communities and homes and carriers of obligations to children that fathers often ignore.[51] Rather, neo-liberal institutionalism assigns co-operating states a rationality that is usually associated with men. This move maintains gender nostalgia and the sense that international relations, whether conflictual or cooperative, is a coherent politics of place where 'men' rule. Second, in this literature there is no mention that international reciprocity is restricted to men and citizensandstates because 'women' are not officially in international relations. At the level of daily experience, people called women who work in the administration of formal neo-liberal regimes are trapped in a regime of gender that exists within the international regime, such that most can only be civil caretakers of international civil servants and of member citizensandstates. This is evidenced by the fact that 'women occupy less than 3 per cent of [United Nations] "senior level" positions . . . and only 22.3 per cent of the professional international civil-service posts, as compared with 83 per cent of its clerical and secretarial jobs'.[52] This is so despite the efforts of a Co-ordinator for the Improvement of the Status of Women in the Secretariat of the United Nations. The message is that women can visit the citadels of co-operative international relations in support roles for men. At the end of the work day, the women go home and the men go to receptions and dinners where the business of international relations continues.

In a related sense, women can be covered by international human rights conventions of the United Nations,[53] but 'a male-as-norm orientation persists in treating women's rights as secondary'.[54] In an essay entitled 'Crime of Gender', Heise writes:

International human rights conventions specifically reject the principle of nonintervention when violations of rights occur. Yet systematic violence against women is treated as 'customary' or a 'private matter', and thus immune to international condemnation. 'If a person is murdered because of his or her politics, the world justifiably responds with outrage. But if a person is beaten or allowed to die because she is female, the world dismisses it as "cultural tradition".'[55]

When gender is undertheorized, it is easy for us to overlook, as does neo-liberal institutionalism, the possibility that reciprocity is only a partial, gender-specific convention in international relations. It is also easy to misinterpret the neo-liberal institutionalist disclaimer that it does not make the idealist mistake of 'incorporating . . . excessively optimistic assumptions about the role of ideals in world politics or about the ability of statesmen to learn what the theorist considers "right lessons" '.[56] Neo-liberalism may not put forth the agreements of men as the answer to war. Nevertheless, the dream of sandblasting anarchic structure with man-to-man obligations resonated during the 1991 Gulf War. One way of interpreting the international citizenandstate turn to the United Nations as an agent of war would be to think of a fit of nostalgia for (masculine) collective security (if all good men man the torpedoes, the result of war is justice). This action recalls the faith before the Second World War in a benevolent modernity of idealism captained reasonably by rational statesmen.

Oran Young, who is associated with institutionalism, reports that 'The most striking features of international society . . . are its relatively small number of formal members and its high level of decentralization of authority'.[57] Responsibility in this system, he says, is dispersed to such a degree that its institutions are primitive and underdeveloped. Viewed through feminist lenses, the international society does indeed have relatively few formal members, but it is remarkably centralized around intrinsics, nostalgias, and regimes of ascriptive gender. Realism offers us anarchy as a community of men, and neo-liberal institutionalism tells us that citizensandstates are forced into moments of co-operative community that retain realist limits against gender reciprocities. If realism is the S and the M of international relations, neo-liberal institutionalism is the set of street gangs that enforce the rule of honour among scoundrels and thieves. It is the gender subterfuge, the furtive (as opposed to joyful, hopeful, and gender-thwarting) den of drag.

FEMINIST HOMESTEADINGS

The gender-joining of realism and neoliberal institutionalism to 'an' international relations of strikingly masculinist proportions 'elide[s] the fragmentation, diversity, and pluralism of social identity that we find in global political space'[58] and renders 'the skills and orientations of individuals somehow . . . fixed and peripheral'.[59] It creates a discursive politics within which the raising of gender issues sounds dissident and out of place.

CHRISTINE SYLVESTER

Women are 'special' solitaries in international relations theory and in the worlds theorists describe; we are awkwardly situated at the intersection of barbarism, primitivism, and heresy (to borrow Rostow's categories).[60] Women carry the sign of inferiority and disorder. Indeed, according to Rousseau, we have a barbaric lack of restraint that precludes our absorption into the realist citizenand-state. Instead, women are accommodated as providers of the mother's milk of citizenship and as interlopers who are needed to define rationality as masculine. We are also innocent primitives. Our natures not having evolved very far, we are meant to stay in home places in the nation and the family, and not aspire to join citizensandstates or go beyond civilized governance into international relations. This is the case even though (and this is the rub) our 'barbarism' makes us 'naturals' for 'anarchy'. Finally, some of us commit heresy by suggesting that 'shared meanings' of realism are marked 'with specific cognitive and perceptual tendencies which reflect and reproduce the special interests of men as men'.[61] We blaspheme by saying that 'women's capacity to challenge the men in their families, their communities, and their political movements, will be a key to remaking the world'.[62]

At this intersection of barbarism, primitivism, and heresy, women are beyond studied dissidence in the system, and enjoy instead earnest, but none the less passing, nods in the alternative international-relations literature. This attitude is especially evident in the special issue of *International Studies Quarterly* (34/3, 1990) entitled 'Speaking the Language of Exile: Dissidence in International Studies', where women are mentioned, but our dilemmas of gender are not considered important enough to warrant article-length treatment. With shared understandings biased to one side, even dissidence is more credible when it is represented to us mostly by men.

Feminists are only beginning to deconstruct the exile of 'women' from international relations. We are only beginning to recognize the devices that keep some people and their experiences officially out of the 'out there' and to recover the places where 'women' transgress the rules. Feminist positions, however, are forming, and strange homesteads are being staked out that unsettle inherited knowledge and displace turf. These homesteads are something other than parcels of space *for* and *as* 'women's' proper homes in a hostile wilderness.

One form of homesteading counters liberal realism with a feminist liberalism that reveals the inequalities of 'our' field. Many feminists who study and rewrite international relations incorporate some liberal observations into their work, which means that they point out the biases and distortions that are hidden by the implicit gendering of international relations as the citizenandstate 'out there'.[61] At the same time, most feminists are critical of liberalism and the gender-hiding ideology which suggests that law is 'potentially principled, meaning predisposed to no substantive outcome, or manipulable to any ends, thus available as a tool that is not fatally twisted'.[64]

Mona Harrington, an exception, defends liberalism and distinguishes between support for the liberal state and support for liberal international institutions. The liberal state, she argues, 'is a suitable, even elegant, agent to advance a feminist agenda in both domestic and international relations'.[65] That state has enabled political power to be centralized in ways that bring strength to bear against traditional patriarchy, class, and race hierarchies. She reminds us that the liberal state moved against industrial giants in the late nineteenth century and towards a welfare ethos in the middle of the twentieth century. Feminists should not be taken in, she warns, by institutionalist currents in international relations that remove the exercise of power from public scrutiny. International institutions simply 'shift policymaking . . . from potentially democratic and constituent-based to definitively bureaucratic and élite-based authority'.[66]

Harrington encourages feminists to invest greater support in the type of democracy that Connolly associates with Walzer, where the state is treated as a democratic preserve of many spheres, including the sphere of relatively powerless people. These are the people for whom social liberalism makes more sense than a contractarian understanding of the liberal state because plural society has 'internal understandings of justice . . . that can be brought to bear whenever: (a) an injustice is discovered within it; or (b) its internal principles illicitly leak into other spheres'.[67] Powerless people are the ones who stand to gain from liberal stands against oppressive tyrannies because, in these cases, the individual receives social support 'for self-definition, a resistance against socially imposed identities, stereotypes, limitations to the range of mind, imagination, movement, work or role'.[68]

It is noteworthy that Harrington does not address the historical trends that conflate citizensandstates with people called 'men'. She therefore underestimates the extent to which canonical liberal realism weaves domesticities associated with the family and nation into international zones of gender politics. It is a circular endeavour for women to use liberalism for a sustained assault on recalcitrant liberalism. As Spike Peterson contends, 'good intentions and liberal commitments are not in themselves sufficient'.[69] What is needed is a reconstitution of international norms from women's perspectives or from a combination of perspectives.

Standpoint feminism attempts such a reconstitution. It homesteads the field with knowledges that people called women develop as a consequence of being socially subordinate and excluded from centres of power. Nancy Hirschmann writes:

> If the entrenchment in liberal theory of the public/private dichotomy guarantees the obliteration of women's experience from our ordinary-language understanding of political obligation, and if gender bias relates to the very epistemological framework that defines the conceptual terminology in which theories operate, then any analysis of 'the problem of women' within the boundaries of existing theories of obligation will only be able to go so far.[70]

Other feminist standpoint insights are specifically pertinent to the international relations canon. Christine Di Stefano argues that, from the perspective of women who mother, the Hobbesian imaginary assumes the existence of 'orphans who have reared themselves, whose desires are situated within and reflect nothing but independently generated movement'.[71] Hirschmann's work helps us think of a genealogy of co-operative autonomy from 'women' as nesting in early gendering experiences in liberal societies. In those societies, boy babies struggle to individuate against a mother whose body is different from theirs and whose position in liberal society is lowly. The genealogy of co-operative autonomy is finalized in contractarian liberalism, which records the experiences of wary adult 'individuals' with government instead of recording their relations of gender heteronomy that begin at birth.[72] Ann Tickner offers the insight that realist international relations enshrines masculine principles and diminishes the capacity 'to tolerate cultural differences and to seek potential for building community in spite of these differences'.[71]

The challenge of the feminist standpoint is to explore and valorize these and other insights from the 'other side' and bring them to bear on fields that base their knowledge on the experience of people called men. One increasingly important facet of the feminist standpoint project is to bring 'women' who are tucked inside realism's geo-political sociality, yet who reside far from the oligopolistic centres of power, into this homesteading project.[74] If one becomes situated in a local arena, either through area studies or by 'reinventing oneself as other',[75] it is possible to see how repetitions of realist refrains make their way through the world system.

My work regularly takes me to Zimbabwe. Zimbabwe is a postindependence state that pulls a gender nostalgia over its own effort to proclaim the dawn of women's rights. It has a small, but none the less impressive, body of legislation that redresses colonial injustices against women by outlawing inheritances of Rhodesian law which, for example, stipulated that women were legal minors for life. Simultaneously, people called women are severely constrained from speaking too loudly and moving too quickly into places that are marked out by gender nostalgias. For example, a Ministry of Women's Affairs, still an unusual devotion in liberal states, was created at the time of independence as part of a Ministry of Community Development and Women's Affairs. Within six years, Women's Affairs was joined to the Ministry of Cooperatives to form the unwieldy Ministry of Community and Cooperative Development and Women's Affairs. The merger was dissolved a year later when Women's Affairs landed on its own feet only to be cradled a short time later by a (male) Senior Minister of Political Affairs who was given the orphan women to oversee.[76] These forced migrations of 'women's' identity and political salience are set in motion when masculinist standpoints guide reformist political efforts. Standpoint feminism can help to bring the forced migrations to light and expose the local resentments, compliances and resistances that combine to form cross-cutting, nostalgia-crashing, nostalgia-reinforcing homesteading efforts. These identity shores seem far from the centre of international relations, but it remains to be seen through additional research whether 'distant' political territories are any less a part of international gender relations than are the domestic relations of Western nations.[77]

Feminisms associated with the postmodern turn in philosophy and epistemology offer another type of challenge to realist liberalism. These feminisms do not insert women into international relations or international relations into some notion of real women. Rather, they explore the homeless places, which are often found in over-defined subject statuses, that defy the seeming totality of our nostalgic gender intrinsics. It is thought that a 'quick find our homes or we are lost' approach merely fences in certain places before other possibilities of location, identity and work are fully explored. The no-man's borderlands are more interesting. There one finds the good soldier and the good mother, both immersed in, among other things, 'worlds revolving around stomachs, bodily harm or well-being, and the search for protection'.[78] One also finds Greenham Common protesters fixing Rousseau's wagon by putting implements of domesticity (potatoes) up the exhaust pipes of trucks carrying self-sacrificing men and their nuclear armour around Britain.[79]

The idea is to bring to the fore the homesteadings on 'men's' and 'women's' assigned places which take place without any reach for gender control, for co-operative autonomy from difference, or for the triumph of 'a' standpoint. One begins to see these home-steadings when considering the experiences of variously located 'women' in international relations. This is not to assert that real women exist or that certain bodies fit pre-given rules of standpoint. Rather, it is radically decentring to begin in an official void and find 'women' in unlikely places and in unexpected comminglings of identities.

Consider a commingling at Greenham Common:

I remember sitting in a blockade and a woman, just a few yards away from me, was lying down, and she was pregnant—about six months pregnant. She was quite thin, and so her pregnancy really showed, because it was just a small, nice hump. And she took her dungarees off, and let her stomach just—like show to the sun. And that was when I really decided that I had come to Greenham again, and that women's actions were the way forward for me. Dunno; just sitting watching that stomach; I just made so many connections . . . about patriarchy and male violence and nuclear weapons being male violence. I just thought, 'It's so right. There's no way I'm ever going to doubt it ever again.'[80]

To expose pregnancy as a political act at a military base is at once to confirm the Rousseauian conviction that women are fuelled by the passions of their uteruses, and to reverse the related and lingering notion that women should properly display 'the modesty and shame with which Nature armed the weak in order to subjugate the strong'.[81] This act homesteads the nation-securing meanings of pregnancy with something that is not fully articulated, but that rings with a very different sense of mother's milk from that which we find in national homes for 'women'. The commingling expressed here evokes a homestead of creative homelessness.

One also creatively builds homeless identities by unravelling real-ist defences. This causes the unravellers to homestead from posi-tions of gender homelessness that they themselves help to create through their unravellings:

We'd practised getting up on each other's shoulders. And we unravelled lots [of fence after] our bolt-cutters had been taken. And cut a massive section down, because we went to quite a deserted place. . . . So we cut about 200 yards down. . . . All it is is just snipping at the side of the posts, and then these big sections just fall down. . . . It was just an amazing sense of relief and freedom . . . to be able to see . . . a space where it was, and to know that you personally were responsible for taking it down.[82]

The politics 'on each other's shoulders' and the 'amazing sense of relief and freedom' as the unravelled fence 'just falls down' decentres and subverts the realist nostalgia of women properly in their national-household places at home. Thus, 'women who come today no longer have to spend their time justifying themselves or fighting for political space. They can get on with what they came to do, confronting the base and the issues it raises.'[83]

Similarly, when military wives strike up friendships with women military officers—neither really belonging in the realist scenario of international security—there is a startling subversion of the hierarchies that maintain realism. When diplomats' wives struggle to be declared 'private' persons in order that they be less obligated to serve the national interest by feeding the world of diplomats, their struggle subverts dependence on a mother's milk and announces a refusal to be a visiting resource for the citizenandstate. Ironically, it also asserts a privacy that is, after all, supposed to be a hallmark of 'women' in liberal democracy.[84] Homesteading can occur in 'innocuous' ways that fool the eye but pulverize the basis of gender nostalgias.

DISTURBING

These feminist approaches constitute, in Connolly's term, a 'politics of disturbance'[85] that unsettles realist-insinuating knowledges and ploughs up inherited turfs without planting the same old seeds in the field. We must beware of colonial possibilities lurking in any recreated metaphor of 'Westward Ho!' and homestead differently. We must reappropriate and rework 'homestead' so that it is less emblematic of heartless barbarism and nationalist primitivism and more a heretical shifting that unravels some walls and makes others translucent and light and movable and disposable. This feminist homesteading must be available for all to see, help and critique because any sense of 'Woman (with a capital W) may . . . kill women if She loses the contact and speaks of Herself only according to what She wants to hear about Herself'.[86]

I have in mind homesteading places that have been homesteaded to death by the conquering cavalry of realist democracy. This should not be done in emulation of those acts and not in a frenzy of Western feminist narcissism, but rather in practices of profound deterritorialization that leave all of us appropriately homeless and ready to negotiate identity fields rather than derive them from nostalgias.[87] Other feminisms may homestead a bit differently, preferring a more liberal or feminist standpointed point of entry. We certainly need not agree on what constitutes waywarding agendas.

In the interstices of feminist projects lies a knowing alertness to co-op(t)erative nostalgias of place—seductive appeals to build anew on the pylons of realist, colonial, and masculine homes—and a shared sense that it is none the less around homefronts that imagined communities and nostalgias roost and take flight.

Notes

1. William Connolly, 'Democracy and Territoriality', in M. Ringrose and A. J. Lerner (eds.), *Reimagining the Nation* (Open University Press, 1993), 49.
2. For writing on backlash, see Susan Faludi, *Backlash: The Undeclared War Against American Women* (New York: Crown Publishers, 1991). The Wo(e)begon(e) reference recalls the imagined small town of Lake Wobegon, Minnesota, where Garrison Keillor, its creator-narrator and spinner of ironic tales, suggests that all the *women* are strong and all the *men* are good-looking and everyone is, in the long run, basically happy. This is from the live radio show, *A Prairie Home Companion*, and found in its written follow-up tales, the latest being *Leaving Home* (New York: Viking, 1987).
3. See e.g. Bonnie Anderson and Judith Zinsser, *A History of Their Own: Women in Europe from Prehistory to the Present* (New York: Harper and Row, 1988); and Marilyn Boxer and Jean Quataert, *Connecting Spheres: Women in the Western World, 1500 to the Present* (Oxford: Oxford University Press, 1987).
4. See Jean Elshtain's discussion of Beautiful Souls in *Women and War* (New York: Basic Books, 1987). Also see Judith Stiehm, 'The Protected, the Protector, the Defender', in Judith Stiehm (ed.), *Women and Men's Wars* (Oxford: Pergamon Press, 1983); and Maria Mies, *Patriarchy and Accumulation on a World Scale: Women and the International Division of Labour* (London: Zed Books, 1986).
5. Cynthia Enloe, *Bananas, Beaches, and Bases: Making Feminist Sense of International Politics* (London: Pandora, 1989); and Cynthia Enloe, 'Womenandchildren: Making Feminist Sense of the Persian Gulf Crisis', *Village Voice*, 25 (September 1990), 29–32.
6. Frederick Kratochwil and John Ruggie, 'International Organization: A State of the Art on an Art of the State', *International Organization*, 40/4 (1986), 762.
7. Kenneth Waltz is the great champion of this view. See Kenneth Waltz, *Theory of International Politics* (Reading, Mass.: Addison-Wesley, 1979), 114.
8. Ibid. 111.

9. Joseph Grieco, *Cooperation among Nations: Europe, America, and Non-Tariff Barriers to Trade* (Ithaca, NY: Cornell University Press, 1990), 4. Grieco is a present-generation defender of Waltz's story of international relations.

10. Waltz, *Theory of International Politics*, 72.

11. Kenneth Waltz, 'The Myth of National Interdependence', in Charles Kindleberger (ed.), *The International Corporation* (Cambridge, Mass.: MIT Press, 1970), 206.

12. K. J. Holsti, *The Dividing Discipline: Hegemony and Diversity in International Theory* (Boston: Unwin Hyman, 1985), p. vii.

13. Elshtain, *Women and War*, 91.

14. Nancy Hartsock, *Money, Sex, and Power: Toward Feminist Historical Materialism* (Boston: Northeastern University Press, 1983), 178.

15. Connolly, 'Democracy and Territoriality', 60–1.

16. Carole Pateman, *The Sexual Contract* (Stanford, Calif.: Stanford University Press, 1988). See a discussion of her work in Christine Sylvester, 'Feminists and Realists View Autonomy and Obligation in International Relations', in V. Spike Peterson (ed.), *Gendered States: Feminist (Re)Visions of International Relations Theory* (Boulder, Colo.: Lynne Reinner, 1992), 155–77.

17. Hobbes says that 'every woman that bears children becomes both a mother and a lord [over the child]'. Thomas Hobbes, *Philosophical Rudiments Concerning Government and Society*, in *The English Works of Thomas Hobbes of Malmesbury* (Germany: Scientia Verlag Aalen, 1966), ii. 116, quoted in Pateman, *Sexual Contract*, 44. In return for her nurturing of a child, the mother presumably wins an ally in the war of all against all and reduces her chances of being conquered. Yet she rarely makes it to that point without falling under a master, because the child is helpless for years.

18. Thomas Hobbes, *Leviathan*, in *The English Works of Thomas Hobbes of Malmesbury* (Germany: Scientia Verlage Aalen, 1966), ii. 191. A family could also consist of a man and his children who are contracted to him by their mother or, one supposes, abandoned by the mother or conquered father. Mother-rights and father-conquerings exist in a tension with Hobbes's admonition, in *The Citizen*, 'to consider men as if but even now sprung out of the earth, and suddenly, like mushrooms, come to full maturity, without all kind of engagement with one another'. See Christine Di Stefano, 'Masculinity as Ideology in Political Theory: Hobbesian Man Considered', *Women's Studies International Forum*, 6/6 (1983), 637.

19. Men conquered by other men are later released from servitude to become citizens. Women remained bound to the sexual contract and to subservience until the latter part of the twentieth century.

20. Anne Norton, *Reflections on Political Identity* (Baltimore: Johns Hopkins University Press, 1988), 32.

21. Cynthia Enloe, 'Womenandchildren', 29, coined the word 'womenandchildren' in the context of the Persian Gulf. 'In the torrents of media coverage that accompany an international crisis women typically appear as symbols, victims, or dependents. "Womenandchildren" rolls so easily off network tongues because in network minds women are family members rather than independent actors, presumed to be almost childlike in their innocence about the realpolitik of international affairs.'

22. Jean Bethke Elshtain, 'Sovereignty, Identity, Sacrifice', in M. Ringrose and A. J. Lerner (eds.), *Reimagining the Nation* (Open University Press, 1993), 162.

23. Ibid.
24. Ibid.
25. Jean-Jacques Rousseau, *Social Contract* (Harmondsworth: Penguin Books, 1968), 50.
26. Jean-Jacques Rousseau, *First and Second Discourses*, ed. V. Gourevitch (New York: Harper and Row, 1986), 173–4.
27. Jean-Jacques Rousseau, *Emile or On Education*, trans. and ed. A. Bloom (New York: Basic Books, 1979), 360.
28. Anne Norton, *Reflections on Political Identity*, 40–1, writes about the change in consciousness of man that accompanies the social contract.
29. Rousseau, *Emile*, 370.
30. Translated from *Emile* by Sarah Kofman, 'Rousseau's Phallocratic Ends', in Nancy Fraser and Sandra Bartky (eds.), *Revaluing French Feminism: Critical Essays on Difference, Agency, and Culture* (Bloomington, Ind.: Indiana University Press, 1992), 58.
31. Ibid. Kofman argues that the nature to which Rousseau appealed reflected his own erotic obsession with dominant but maternal women as well as his phallocratic defence of male domination. Contextualizing Rousseau in this way lays bare his claims to be noting an objective empirical reality.
32. In the United States, the portrayal of Anita Hill as a cunning and deceptive woman trying to prevent a good man (Clarence Thomas) from sitting on the US Supreme Court is a case of 'women' being denied, denounced, and rejected. The spectacle of the US Democratic Party asserting the importance of women candidates in the 1992 election, while attempting to hold off a backlash of white men who, according to television newscasters, feel they have been abandoned by the party, is a case of debating the fitness and fairness of heretofore protected 'women' as agents of national politics. This debate does not have an analogue for 'men'.
33. Aido Hurtado, 'Relations to Privilege: Seduction and Rejection in the Subordination of White Women and Women of Color', *Signs* 14/4 (1989), 849. Also see 833–55.
34. Elshtain, 'Sovereignty, Identity, Sacrifice', 161.
35. Connolly, 'Democracy and Territoriality', 55.
36. I am grateful to Adam Lerner for helping me expand this example.
37. Norton, *Reflections on Political Identity*, 33.
38. Rousseau, *Emile*, 52.
39. Ibid.
40. Cooperative autonomy runs through Zeev Maoz's realist discussion of what happens when a strong state enhances its power by acquiring extra resources. Nowhere does Maoz suggest that women are resources of states or question whether resource-inferior states will respond to others augmenting this particular resource in the same way that they would respond to other augmentations of power. Zeev Maoz, 'Power, Capabilities, and Paradoxical Conflict Outcomes', *World Politics*, 41/1 (1989), 239–66. I discuss this case in 'Feminists and Realists View Autonomy and Obligation', in Peterson, *Gendered States*, 169–71.
41. Michel Foucault, 'Truth and Power', in *Power/Knowledge: Selected Interviews and Other Writings 1972–1977*, ed. and trans. Colin Gordon (New York: Pantheon Books, 1980), 118.
42. Michel Foucault, 'Truth and Power', in *The Foucault Reader*, ed. Paul Rabinow (New York: Penguin Press, 1984), 60.

43. Robert Keohane, *After Hegemony: Cooperation and Discord in the World Political Economy* (Princeton: Princeton University Press, 1984), 34.
44. Robert Keohane, *International Institutions and State Power: Essays in International Relations Theory* (Boulder, Westview Press, 1989), 10.
45. See Robert Axelrod and Robert Keohane, 'Achieving Cooperation Under Anarchy', *World Politics*, 38/1 (1985), 226–54; Robert Jervis, 'Cooperation Under the Security Dilemma', *World Politics*, 30/2 (1978), 167–86; Robert Axelrod, 'The Emergence of Cooperation Among Egoists', *American Political Science Review*, 75/2 (1981), 306–18; and Keohane, *After Hegemony*.
46. Oran Young, *International Cooperation: Building Regimes for Natural Resources and the Environment* (Ithaca, NY: Cornell University Press, 1989), 1.
47. Connolly, 'Democracy and Territoriality', 55. On complex interdependence, see Robert Keohane and Joseph Nye, *Power and Interdependence: World Politics in Transition* (Boston: Little, Brown, 1977).
48. Keohane, *International Institutions and State Power*, 13.
49. Ibid. 3.
50. Ibid. 146.
51. Keohane is on record as saying that one of the benefits of integrating feminism into international relations is that it will help the field reformulate basic concepts to reflect the connectedness that informs women's experiences. Indeed, he has called for an alliance between feminism and neo-liberal institutionalism based on overlaps that he thinks exist in our two projects. See Robert Keohane, 'International Relations Theory: Contributions of a Feminist Standpoint', *Millennium: Journal of International Studies*, 18/2 (1989), 245–55.
52. Enloe, *Bananas, Beaches, Bases*, 121.
53. Many states do not cooperate with human rights regimes: 134 heads of state have yet to sign the related United Nations Convention on the Rights of the Child.
54. V. Spike Peterson, 'Whose Rights? A Critique of the "Givens" in Human Rights Discourse', *Alternatives*, 15/3 (1990), 305.
55. L. Heise, 'Crime of Gender', *Worldwatch* (March–April 1989), quoted in Peterson, 'Whose Rights?'
56. Keohane, *After Hegemony*, 8.
57. Young, *International Cooperation*, 19.
58. Stephen Rosow, 'The Forms of Internationalization: Representation of Western Culture on a Global Scale', *Alternatives*, 15/3 (1990), 288.
59. James N. Rosenau, *Turbulence in World Politics: A Theory of Change and Continuity* (Princeton: Princeton University Press, 1990), 25.
60. These categories are taken from Rosow, 'Forms of Internationalization'.
61. Di Stefano, 'Masculinity as Ideology in Political Theory', 634.
62. Enloe, *Bananas, Beaches, Bases*, 17.
63. See e.g. ibid.: Judith Stiehm, *Arms and the Enlisted Woman* (Philadelphia: Temple University Press, 1989); and Mies, *Patriarchy and Accumulation*.
64. Catharine MacKinnon, *Toward a Feminist Theory of the State* (Cambridge, Mass.: Harvard University Press, 1989), 160.
65. Mona Harrington, 'What Exactly is Wrong with the Liberal State as an Agent of Change?', in Peterson, *Gendered States*, 65.
66. Ibid. 67.
67. Connolly, 'Democracy and Territoriality', 56.
68. Harrington, 'What Exactly is Wrong', 74.

69. Peterson, 'Whose Rights?', 305.
70. Nancy Hirschmann, *Rethinking Obligation* (Ithaca, NY: Cornell University Press, 1992), 186.
71. Di Stefano, 'Masculinity as Ideology', 639.
72. Hirschmann summarizes this argument in 'Freedom, Recognition, and Obligation: A Feminist Approach to Political Theory', *American Political Science Review*, 83/4 (1989), 1227–44.
73. J. Ann Tickner, 'Hans Morgenthau's Principles of Political Realism: A Feminist Reformulation', *Millennium: Journal of International Studies*, 17/3 (1988), 433.
74. See 'Feminists Write International Relations', a special issue I edited of the journal *Alternatives: Social Transformations and Human Governance*, 18/1 (1993). The issue challenges the heretofore geospatially limited discussion of feminist international relations.
75. Sandra Harding, *Whose Science? Whose Knowledge? Thinking From Women's Lives* (Ithaca, NY: Cornell University Press, 1991), writes about the necessity of reinventing ourselves as other.
76. See the discussion in Christine Sylvester, ' "Urban Women Cooperators", "Progress", and "African Feminism" in Zimbabwe', *Differences*, 3/1, (1991), pp. 31–62. For an overview of 'women' in Zimbabwe, see Chapter 5 in Christine Sylvester, *Zimbabwe: The Terrain of Contradictory Development* (Boulder, Colo.: Westview Press, 1991).
77. Maria Mies, *Patriarchy and Accumulation on a World Scale: Women in the International Division of Labour* (London: Zed Books, 1986), suggests that such shores are not distant from Western international relations.
78. Elshtain, *Women and War*, 223.
79. Gwyn Kirk, 'Our Greenham Common: Feminism and Nonviolence', in Adrienne Harris and Ynestra King (eds.), *Rocking the Ship of State* (Boulder, Colo.: Westview Press, 1989), 115–32.
80. Nina Hall, quoted in Jill Liddington, *The Road to Greenham Common: Feminism and Anti-Militarism in Britain Since 1820* (Syracuse, NY: Syracuse University Press, 1990), 265–6.
81. Rousseau, *Emile*, 50.
82. Nina Hall in Liddington, *The Road to Greenham Common*, 270.
83. *New Statesman* (5 September 1986). Quoted ibid. 279.
84. These examples are mentioned in Enloe, *Bananas, Beaches, Bases*, and discussed in Christine Sylvester, 'Feminists and Realists View Autonomy and Obligation', 155–78.
85. Connolly, 'Democracy and Territoriality', 61.
86. Trinh T. Minh-ha, *Woman, Native, Other: Writing Postcoloniality and Feminism* (Bloomington, Ind.: Indiana University Press, 1989), 28.
87. Wendy Brown, 'Feminist Hesitations, Postmodern Exposures', *Differences*, 3/1 (1991), 63–84, advocates politically deciding rather than deriving ourselves from known authority sources.

Feminist Studies and Political Science— and Vice Versa

Virginia Sapiro

Women's studies in political science is now more than a generation old. When the Women's Caucus in Political Science was founded in 1969, women who openly considered focusing any of their research or teaching on women were discouraged and dissuaded by teachers and colleagues convinced that such work had to be 'political' rather than 'scholarly'; in any case, it was deemed of little interest to the wider concerns of political science. In the early 1990s the Women's Caucus remained large and active. At the same time, and following the institution of 'Organized Sections' within the American Political Science Association, membership in the Organized Section on Women and Politics Research grew to 450 out of the nearly 12,000 political scientists. A special journal devoted to this area, *Women and Politics*, has been in publication since 1980, and its contents represent only a fraction of the periodical literature published by political scientists each year.

But how much has really changed for political scientists pursuing women's or feminist studies? The discipline is slightly less gender segregated than it was. In 1972–3 11 per cent of faculty were women. In 1990 19 per cent of faculty were women, including 16 per cent of full-time faculty and 10 per cent of those with tenured positions. Clearly, the amount of research and teaching has grown substantially. Feminist work has matured considerably in many areas of the discipline. In the early days most work was of the 'add women and stir' or compensatory variety, taking conventional questions in different fields, but especially political behaviour and political theory, and asking, 'What about the women?'[1] In political behaviour this meant trying to find out whether women and men differed in political action or public opinion, and searching for the mechanisms of the exclusion of women from political leadership. In political theory

From Domna Stanton and Abigail Stewart (eds.) *Feminisms in the Academy* (University of Michigan Press, 1995), 291–310. Copyright © The University of Michigan (1995). Reprinted by permission of the University of Michigan Press.

this meant asking what the canonical political philosophers such as Aristotle and Plato, Hobbes, Locke, and Rousseau, or Mill and Marx said—or didn't say—about women. This work was and is important, but it was not sufficient.

In the early days defining this field as *women and politics* seemed unproblematic because we were primarily interested in how women fitted into politics and what their impact was.[2] Some of us now prefer *gender politics*, explicitly reconceptualizing the field as exploring the relationships between gender and politics more broadly defined. Adequate feminist analysis of government and politics cannot conceivably be limited to focusing on *women* and politics.

Now there is feminist scholarship in almost every branch of political science, and in many areas scholars are formulating their own questions and concepts, often in conjunction with feminist studies colleagues in other disciplines.[3] But, for those of us who define ourselves simultaneously in political science and women's studies, two problems remain troubling. First, despite the size of the gender-politics community, and despite the fact that most political science departments now offer at least one course in the area, gender politics has not been fully integrated into political science; its theories, questions, and conclusions have not been 'mainstreamed' to any significant degree. Both graduate and undergraduate students still often find that, when they try to pursue gender questions in their courses, they meet with resistance or a considerable amount of simple ignorance. After a twenty-year history of gender-politics research in political science, students must often take the lead in introducing this area into their studies, as though it were a new field. Of course, many professors have integrated some of this work into their courses. But some resent even the suggestion to do so, as if it were an affront to their expertise or professional judgement.[4] In general, although there has been improvement over the years, political scientists in most fields show little interest in or even awareness of feminist work, even in their own general areas of teaching and research.

The other problem facing the same feminist scholars in political science is that our work has not been fully integrated into women's studies. The representation of political scientists' work in interdisciplinary women's studies journals is low, although for a variety of reasons political scientists may be less likely than scholars in some other fields to submit their work on these journals. But an interdisciplinary field is not interdisciplinary just because publishing outlets are shared by people in different disciplines; it is also interdisciplinary because participants seek out relevant work where it can be found, and borrow and reintegrate concepts, theories, and conclusions for their own purposes. With the exception of a very few areas in the social sciences and history, women's studies shows little interest in or awareness of the work of feminist political scientists.

The remainder of this essay will revolve around these two problems, briefly seeking to explain them and suggest remedies. I will begin with the relation of gender politics to political science, focusing especially on the special issues arising from the nature of the subfield in professional political science. I will then turn to the relation of feminist studies in political science to women's studies, focusing especially on the relative standing of the humanities and social sciences, especially with regard to the 'science question', but also consider the politics of politics in women's studies and the implications for political science. Since the birth of women's studies, feminist scholars have repeatedly turned a critical eye toward their disciplines in search of the reasons for their marginality. The same must be done within women's studies.

GENDER POLITICS IN POLITICAL SCIENCE

The past two decades of gender politics work in political science has witnessed the production of many—perhaps too many—critical reviews of the inattention of professional political science to women and gender issues.[5] As elsewhere, the underlying problem can be defined in two different ways. The first is primarily sociological or sociopolitical, emphasizing the low number of women and their subordination within the profession. Women's structural position can be understood as causing both suppression of attention to women as subjects and a relatively unchallenged androcentric scholarly conception of women, gender, and sexuality.

The other type of critique focuses primarily on epistemological and conceptual questions, including professional constructions of the nature of knowing and analysis and the impact of these constructions on understanding gender and sexuality in both feminist and non-feminist theory and research.[6] As in other disciplines, epistemological and logic of inquiry debate in political science surrounding the 'feminism question' is informed by many different approaches, including 'standpoint' and materialist theories, postmodern and poststructuralist theories, and different varieties of empiricism.[7]

Although the small number of women in political science surely has an impact on the reception of feminist research and teaching, problems having to do with the theoretical and methodological underpinnings of political science are important to understand. I will outline some of these, emphasizing their impact on the integration of gender politics into political science. Specifically, I will focus on definitions of public, private, and politics; the legacy of positivism in empirical methodology; the legacy of the canon in defining theoretical importance; and the political and gender-based construction of professional norms. These constructions are not 'caused' by gender, but they do have a bearing on how the gender basis of political science is changed or maintained.

The Public, Private, and Politics

Ever since the early feminist anthropological work of the 1970s, especially essays appearing in Rosaldo and Lamphere's collection, *Women, Culture, and Society* (1974), feminist scholars across the humanities and social scientists have taken the 'public/private split', especially the common if not ubiquitous relegation of women and low status to the 'private' sphere and men and high status to the 'public' sphere, as a central problem of inquiry. Certainly, the public/private split has played a key role in theory and research in anthropology and history as well as philosophy. But it takes on special importance in political science, the one field whose disciplinary boundaries are conventionally defined by the public/private split.

Political science is 'about' politics and government; it is 'about' public life. A standard opening in introduction to politics courses is to reach back to classical notions of the polis, or community, for a means to define the turf of politics. Certainly, even the most mainstream political scientists know that one might talk about the politics of personal life and that personal life may 'have an impact on' politics, but the divide for purposes of defining academic boundaries is not widely questioned, and students are often counselled to leave analysis of the politics of private life to the sociologists and psychologists.

Not surprisingly, among the earliest important works of feminist scholarship in political science are those examining the meaning of the public/private divide within historical political thinking (e.g. Elshtain 1974, 1981).[8] Soon feminist scholars began not just to engage in critical discussion of the political significance of the public/private split, but also to criticize conventional definitions of politics or political activity, and to incorporate into their research human activities and problems usually left to the side by their colleagues. By its subject matter alone, then, feminist research in political science can appear to the mainstream to be outside the boundaries of the discipline or, at least, at its margins.

The Legacy of Positivism

Political science is one of the social sciences in which the bulk of research is empirical in character; indeed, 'scientific method' is widely viewed as the ideal approach to research, and quantitative research is accorded high status in at least some of the major sub-fields of political science. In the large and dominant area of *behavioural* political science (i.e. research focusing primarily on human behaviour and thinking rather than e.g. institutional structures or law themselves), some of the original practitioners were also advocates of *behaviourism*, a theoretical stance derived from a branch of psychology that allows investigation only of phenomena widely believed to be directly visible. This position has largely been abandoned, although it may be reviving to some degree among those working with the increasingly popular rational choice models.[9]

As feminist theorists of inquiry have often noted, many aspects of positivist stances toward research have been employed to suppress feminist research, but chief among these is the dominant construction of *objectivity* and the value placed on it within the positivist tradition.[10] Briefly stated, 'good' social science is supposed to be 'value free'. Objectivity and freedom from values is accomplished by following agreed-upon procedures that can be replicated by any other scientist. Any scientist following the procedures properly will discover the same accurate or true picture of what is 'out there'. Without repeating the criticisms and issues raised so often and comprehensively by other feminist theorists, even feminist scholars who follow most of the practices of conventional social science methods tend to accept the central point of the diverse criticisms: no research and no set of research procedures can be value-free.[11] Indeed, regardless of feminism, a large proportion of empirical political scientists generally hold considerably altered conceptions of the relationship between values and research.

Research labelled 'feminist' is widely ignored or rejected within the discipline because the label taints it with political values, because to do research on women appears especially motivated by political or social values, and because the results often do not fit with the personal and professional experience of more conventional researchers, and therefore *seem* tainted with 'perspective'. For all the professional arguments about objectivity and logic, it sometimes seems that it is only the feeling of familiarity and comfort that proves objectivity.

It is crucial to recognize that the conventions of science have had a double-edged effect on feminist research in political science. Whatever may be said about the antagonism between positivist norms and feminism, the sub-field of the discipline in which science is most valued as a model of research is also the sub-field in which there has been the greatest amount of feminist research and one that has probably received the most widespread reading by scholars who do not themselves do research on women or gender. A very large proportion of feminist research in political science focuses on mass and élite political behaviour and orientations, exploring such problems as gender differences in public opinion, perception, and political participation and action; gender-based political socialization; and the gender basis of recruitment to political office and the behaviour of women and men once they hold leadership positions.

Arguing that the legacy of positivism both inhibits and promotes the study of women, including feminist research, is not as self-contradictory as it might at first seem. Women could 'break into' the field by applying many of its own conventions. If an important test of research is whether it follows conventional procedures, the new research on women could often pass the test.[12] Many of us in that field in its early days made what was *in context* a powerful claim: the statements usually made by political scientists about women's political behaviour and orientations were generally based on stereotypes, and had not been subjected to empirical tests. At the most basic level statements about dramatic differences in women's and men's attitudes toward politics and political issues—some of which persist in the public mind and, indeed, in feminist theory—were, for the most part, unfounded or starkly non-dramatic (Shapiro and Mahajan 1986). The relationships between gender-based familial roles and political attitudes and behaviour are both more complicated and less clear than conventional wisdom indicates (Darcy, Welch, and Clark 1987; Sapiro 1983). In the legacy of positivism, no empirical statement may rest immune to testing. 'Everyone knows that' is no defence; neither is 'self-evidence'.[13]

The Legacy of the Canon

The dominance of the legacy of positivism offers a part of the explanation for the difficulty of integrating feminist research into political science, but it cannot be anything like the whole explanation. Indeed, although many of the critiques of the dominance of positivism and behaviouralism are penned by political theorists, the sub-field of theory has been as bad or worse in integrating feminist work. In the non-'science' sub-fields and communities of the discipline there are values beside 'scientific objectivity' that render feminist research suspect. In theory (as in other fields), for example, the measure of scholarly worth is the probing of 'universal' or 'perennial' problems. Here women lose not on the measure of objectivity versus subjectivity and 'bias' but, rather, on the measure of universalism versus parochialism, or centrality versus marginality.

This problem will be especially familiar to those in the humanities who have been party to the debate over the canon. Political theory and philosophy, like the literary disciplines, is commonly a text-and/or author-based field of inquiry; it is largely structured around a historical parade, or canon, of great authors, great works ranging from Plato and Aristotle through Machiavelli to the central figures of modern political thought such as Hobbes, Locke, and Rousseau and Mill and Marx, with many others in between. The contemporary works are probably more variable, but include debates over democratic theory and justice, or liberalism, republicanism, and communitarianism, and revolve around such theorists as John Rawls, J. G. A. Pocock, Michael Walzer, and Michael Sandel.[14]

In political theory, as in other fields, canonical works are said to be self-evidently ('objectively'?) laden with the universal and important human political problems. Although, ironically, a large proportion of the pre-twentieth-century canonical works and authors dwelt very explicitly on questions about women and gender, in this century the explicit attention to women and gender was likely to be ignored as unimportant or inessential to the work.[15] Issues about women have been relegated to the parochial (rather than universal) except, perhaps, as objects of 'our' desire (as texts say, not incidentally, in a male voice). For women to write about women and gender, especially in a manner critical of canon and canonical interpretation, is to degrade political theory by making it parochial and particularistic rather than perennial and universal.

FIRST CONCLUSION

There has been considerable research on women and gender in political science over the last two decades, but, judging by the syllabi and footnotes of non-specialists, it has been integrated into the discipline in only minor ways and sporadically. There are some obvious reasons why this has been the case. Politics remains a distinctly 'male' cultural domain, and political science remains a male-dominated field. Just as race is not 'a problem' for members of a dominant race in a racially structured society, so gender is not a problem for men in a male-dominated arena. As in many other areas, feminists and others differ over where we see gender in the first place; traditional political scientists can see a legislative body overwhelmingly dominated by people of one sex and not see gender as relevant to the picture. Clearly, feminist scholars cannot.

It is not enough to attribute the difficulty merely to the proportion of women in the discipline or even, in any simple way, to the fact that the subject of this discipline—politics—remains culturally identified as masculine. Rather, as I have tried to indicate, there are also professional norms, values, and practices that become part of the process of obstruction. Further, in order to understand a discipline as intellectually diverse as political science, it is necessary to recognize that it consists of overlapping scholarly communities with different values and practices. Somewhat different problems face feminist scholars in different subfields, an issue rarely noted in critical reviews of the discipline.

SCIENCE AND POLITICS IN WOMEN'S STUDIES

Critiques of intellectual inclusion and exclusion of women's studies typically focus on its marginalization within the traditional disciplines. But many within the community of those who live our scholarly lives in both political science and women's studies also sense a lack of integration of our (collective) work into women's studies. Indeed, feminist social scientists in different disciplines often discuss among themselves a shared perception that the social sciences generally are marginalized within women's studies. This is especially strongly felt where empirical research is concerned, but also with regard to feminist theory in the social sciences. As in the case of the exclusion of gender issues from political science, this state of affairs must be regarded as a historical phenomenon shaped by continuing shifts in social relations and larger sets of intellectual issues involved in scholarly work. But, as in the case of understanding the integration—or lack of it—of feminism within the disciplines, it is important to analyse the structure lent to inclusion and exclusion by the currently dominant theories, methods, and assumptions.

The forms, objects, and practices of theory and theorizing are somewhat different in the social sciences and humanities, largely because of the different treatment of empirical statements within theory and the different relationship between theory and empirical research. In some areas of social science the term *theory* implies a hypothetical statement that must be examined against evidence, and in which the theorist must make clear the ways the theory could be shown to be wrong. Clearly, such a definition would be foreign to most scholars in the humanities, especially in the more antiempirical areas. Indeed, what social scientists and humanities scholars[16] identify as theory is probably an overlapping but not identical set; standards of what constitutes good theory certainly differ in some respects. Given that the majority of scholars are probably not aware of the differences in the very definition of *theory* between the humanities and social sciences, it is no wonder that some conflicts and misunderstanding have emerged.[17] In any case, in recent years humanities-based theorizing has held a privileged position in the eyes of both humanities and social-science scholars within the community of feminist scholars.

A widespread view held among feminists in the humanities states that feminist theory and research in the social sciences is much less developed and sophisticated, and even less 'feminist', than work in the humanities. Just as we see few references to our work among non-feminists in our own discipline, we note relatively sparse treatment of social-science theory and research in interdisciplinary feminist studies; certainly, the attention of humanities feminists to social-science feminists is not equivalent to the attention social-science feminists pay to the humanities.[18]

There is a difference between claiming women's studies is a 'multidisciplinary' or an 'interdisciplinary' effort. It is certainly the former; there are parallel research communities and bodies of literature across all of the humanities and social sciences and some of the natural sciences as well. But many of us also claim it is interdisciplinary, meaning that the community of scholars that thinks, theorizes, and seeks answers together crosses disciplinary boundaries.[19]

Thus, just as it is possible and important to explore the barriers between feminist research and the larger disciplinary communities, so it is possible and important to explore the barriers between discipline-based feminist research and the larger women's studies community. Here I will suggest four aspects of the logic and practice of inquiry that inhibit more reciprocal interdisciplinarity especially with regard to political science, both as a social science and as a distinct discipline. These are: (1) the 'science' question in feminist studies; (2) the discovery of politics; (3) the political climate and relation to the concerns of political science; and (4) the contrast between text- and non-text-centred disciplines in the light of post-structuralism. As before, I will outline each briefly and not attempt complete elaboration.

The 'Science Question'

Feminist studies has played a leading role in contemporary criticism of the dominant theoretical underpinnings and practices of science. This attention to theory, method, and philosophies of knowing has helped to maintain a vitality and critical edge in feminist studies that is remarkable. But there is an unfortunate side to such widespread raising of epistemological banners. This literature in its (academically) popularized version tends to caricature and homogenize the sciences and social sciences, rendering research that displays signs of accepting any set of scientific norms in making empirical claims suspicious and possibly non-feminist.[20] These views gain added resonance from both popular stereotype and the 'different voices' literature supporting the notion that women are more intuitive, holistic, and connected, in contrast to scientific and mathematical thinking, which is also defined as 'masculine' in character.

Logics and practices of inquiry are undeniably related to gender culture and the gender basis of the social structure of related professions. But there is not 'science', there are 'sciences' (in the same sense as 'feminisms'); there is not computer usage, there are different means and styles of using computers (Perry and Greber 1990; Turkle and Papert 1990). Feminist scholars should not buttress traditional dichotomies by making assumptions about what can and cannot be said or accomplished using scientific and empirical modes of analysis. Feminist social scientists who use quantitative analytical methods are not just 'squashing people into little numbers'. To suggest they do because of an assumed logic of inquiry without considering their work more carefully is simply to fall prey to a revised but nevertheless dangerous form of math anxiety. Feminist scholars in the social sciences are, in fact, exploring the implications of feminist theory for the practices of empirical social science. This requires studying and understanding research practices as well as probing the theory-based logic of inquiry.

The Discovery of Politics

In the era in which women's studies was founded, politics was 'everywhere'. Whereas explicit attention to politics and government had earlier been relatively restricted in the liberal arts outside a few fields—for example, political science, history, sociology, and philosophy—scholars influenced by the cultural politics of the student and counterculture movement, feminists influenced by the declaration that 'the personal is political', as well as others similarly grounded in the politics of the 1960s, increasingly pressed their examination of politics in their substantive studies and in the practices of academia.

For those of us in political science, similarly influenced, but also having chosen a field of study explicitly and consciously about politics, the overwhelming academic attention to politics was exciting and encouraging, but in the long run it has also contributed to a certain degree of isolation of political scientists. The excitement of the discovery of politics led to a proliferation of political theorizing often based loosely on current trends and fashions but ungrounded in the long tradition of political debate, discussion, and research; naïve with regard to the complexities of politics and political discourse; and resistant to the idea that empirical research about politics has told us much worth knowing. Political-science-based feminist theorists often voice frustration with feminist theory that ignores the knowledge gained from the long-standing debates in political theory, even within the 'male-stream'.[21]

Even recognizing the fact that political science has been undeniably androcentric, and despite the fact that politically involved people who pay close attention to the news know a lot about politics, systematic and scholarly study adds considerably to political understanding, political deliberation, and political action. Of course, any simple statement of what has been achieved and what could be offered by one of the liberal arts disciplines is bound to sound silly. But one of the central missions of political science, for example, is engaging in critical reading of major theoretical debates in politics over the last two thousand years. One could not begin in such a short space to outline the knotty problems that are standard fare for consideration by historical political theorists—the questions about the relationships between human character and political organization, the nature and dynamics of power and authority, the problems of human political action and inaction, resistance, and acquiescence, and considerations of democracy, authoritarianism, justice, community, and how these and the range of other political norms relate to political process and structure. In the more empirical vein, the mission of political science includes understanding the dynamics of politics at all levels of analysis, from the individual to the international, including political thinking and activity, organization, and processes, and all of these both in their abstract and generalizable aspects and in their particular, national, cultural, or locally bound contexts. Certainly, the recent emphasis on 'globalism' is nothing new to a discipline in which two of the major divisions of the discipline are comparative politics (including area studies) and international politics.

Political Climate

In theory (as it were) one might expect a field as devoted to politics as women's studies to seek scholarly counsel from the discipline most self-consciously devoted to the study of politics, much as scholars might turn to historians to help them learn history, to psychologists to learn psychology, or to literary critics to learn how to read. But feminist studies has not tended to look to political science for political theory or analysis very often, partly because of the political climate in which feminist studies developed and the political ideology dominant within feminist studies.

Most feminist political scientists have criticized their own discipline for focusing too much on conventional and formal definitions of politics and political action (e.g. concentrating so heavily on elections and electoral behaviour as compared with other forms) and certainly for ignoring the politics of non-governmental organizations. But the dominant political ideologies of feminist studies have tended to rest at the other extreme of the political continuum, regarding things governmental and electoral as male-dominated, irrelevant, and, almost worst of all, 'liberal' and 'reformist'.[22]

Here there are two related problems. First, while the demand to expand the definition of the political is absolutely correct, the tendency in the process to downplay the theoretical importance of the state and government to the point at which they appear only where unavoidable (as in analysis of reproductive 'rights') is a mistake. Government and politics play a crucial role in structuring sex/gender systems; it simply will not do to ignore scholarly study of how this works. The current worldwide changes in governance and politics should make it overwhelmingly clear this is the case. The fears on the part of Russian feminists, for example, that even if a new democracy is constructed it will be 'minus women', and therefore no democracy at all, bears witness to the primary importance of politics and government (Ashwin 1991). In the short history of contemporary feminist studies the crucial influence of two theoretical traditions has contributed to this problem. In the founding days of women's studies one of the most fruitful sources of theory was theoretical Marxism, which defined government as epiphenomenal with respect to economic organization. From a very different direction cultural theories tend to downplay the importance of the institutional and material arrangements such as government. This is not to say that either theoretical Marxism or cultural theory necessitates stripping the governmental out of feminist political analysis, as the work of Petchesky (1984) and Eisenstein (1988), among others shows. But these two theoretical forces together combined, in their actual usage as opposed to theoretical possibilities, to leave government to the side.

A second issue is of concern as well. For a scholarly field that devotes so much energy to theory, including theories of politics, feminist studies tends to be remarkably inattentive to taking care with political theory. Often, to the eye of theorists trained in political theory, terms such as *liberalism* and *reform* seem to serve as much as symbolic flags as they do analytic concepts. Certainly, it is wrong to say that 'a concern' with particular problems, such as representation or specific policy changes, is in itself 'merely' reformist or even indicative of liberalism. Likewise, merely incorporating class into theoretical analysis does not make it Marxist. A topic is not liberal—or Marxist, or sufficient to identify any given theory or ideology—an argument is.

My point is not, as it will be taken by some, to argue that liberalism or reformism are adequate bases for feminist theory or politics. Rather, it is that a substantial portion of feminist discussion of what constitutes liberalism, reformism, democratic theory, and their relation to feminism has been distinctly inadequate, at least until the recent analyses by scholars such as Carole Pateman (1988, 1989) and Anne Phillips (1991). More often comparisons of liberalism in feminist theory with other forms such as socialist or radical feminism are vague, underspecified, and make less clear and useful distinctions among these different types of theory than is often thought. As many political theorists have pointed out, even if the dominant traditions of political theory and political theory debate are affected with profound androcentrism and patriarchalism, intensive study of these traditions nevertheless has a considerable amount to offer feminist theory that is, in any case, affected by these traditions. The same is true of the body of work devoted to empirical study of power, governance, collective decision-making, and conflict and conflict resolution on the local, national, and global scale. These, after all, are the central subjects of political science.

In fact, attention in women's studies to these problems is already changing as, perhaps, world events make it impossible to be casual about government. There has been a tremendous growth in feminist political history in the last decade, accompanied by a burgeoning of the feminist law literature and some key contributions by political philosophers such as Nancy Fraser (1989). Interdisciplinary efforts to understand gender and the welfare state (e.g. Gordon 1990) bear impressive witness to the change. My argument is not simply that feminist political scientists have been undervalued in the feminist studies community but, rather, that feminist scholars, who, like political scientists, have been developing theoretical, methodological, and substantive expertise with respect to political institutions and processes, have more to contribute to feminist studies than has been recognized in recent years.

The Impact of Poststructuralism and Postmodernism

Poststructuralism and its relatives have had profound effects on scholarship in the last decade, not just within the humanities but also in the social sciences.[23] Certainly, it is possible to see its effects even beyond the community of scholars who accept the name. But, even so, important differences among disciplines mean the influence, reaction, and use, for the most part, will be different. Here I will briefly suggest two differences. First is the distinction between text- and non-text-centred disciplines, together with the standing of empirical statements, and second is the question of intentionality.

Important disciplinary differences must affect the reception of poststructuralist and postmodernist messages. (Such a modern construction!) The disciplines of literature are text-centred; the social sciences (and some humanities disciplines, such as history) are not. The point holds even granting that each of these disciplines relies heavily on written texts and even accepting the view that language is not a medium to separate and distinct 'reality'. To be pedestrian about it, even among those of us especially interested in gender politics, some of us went into our particular disciplines because we wanted to study written texts and some because we wanted to study those things the texts are talking about. Regardless of theoretical background, literature specialists want to produce or read literature as their main task. For others of us the written text is only a medium for holding a conversation about how to solve problems that must be understood in their material dimensions: war, poverty, apartheid, education, natural resources, violence, and so forth. Despite the problem of values and objectivity within social science discussed earlier, for social scientists, including political scientists, that conversation is supposed to include the public as citizens and policymakers.

Part of the goal of a considerable portion of political science is at least the development of citizenship, if not the shaping of policy and government. Certainly, US social science from the beginning has pressed towards acting in the world (Ross 1991). If one's scholarly passion is devoted especially to the literary texts themselves, the products of the creative imaginations of authors—even without Author(ity)—the idea that there is nothing but language (at least for scholarly purposes) does not pose as fundamental a problem as it must to the others of us whose primary scholarly passion is devoted to trying to understand and perhaps affect social conditions and problems. Even in the more theoretical and philosophical communities of this social science, and among those whose method is primarily interpretive rather than empirical, scholars are likely to be more sensitive to the empirical and hypothetical aspects and implications of theory and theorizing than may be true in literary fields.

Even in the most text-centred of the fields of political science, historical political philosophy, the conception of the task nevertheless makes the project more one of holding a conversation about things outside the written text. Although historical political philosophers study written texts of political philosophy, training in political philosophy often emphasizes that these texts are media through which political philosophers hold conversations about politics across time and space.

The problem of communication among writers and readers raises a second fundamental difficulty posed by important premises of poststructuralism: the deconstruction of the authorial voice. Certainly, one of the common foci of dispute with regard to poststructuralism and postmodernism is the 'empowering of the reader', as it is sometimes put, or the denial of the author and of intention. The importance of this debate for understanding the position of social science is not as simple as whether there is simple meaning or whether meaning can be transferred from person to person or anything of the sort. It should not be forgotten that some of these points, which form empirical assumptions on the part of some poststructuralists, have long been subjects of empirical questions and investigation on the part of many social scientists, especially in social psychology and the fields influenced by social psychology.[24]

The power issue raised by poststructuralists is an important one. Even were it possible to recover pristine authorial meaning or intention, to require that the only way readers may approach a text is to search for and lock themselves into that pristine text is to require a form of slavery on the part of readers. That slavery is even more dehumanizing when placed in the context of the sociopolitical relations within which texts are produced and read. This is, in part, what arguments about 'the canon' are about.[25] Feminist scholars and other marginalized groups have fought to release themselves from that slavery.

But for political scientists the political questions, not just of power but also of responsibility, are likely to be even more compelling. In political science the study of the day-to-day life of politics and government reminds us that denial of voice or intention, and certainly the denial of responsibility to seek to understand others' voices and intentions is a fundamental part of some of the most dangerous and terrifying politics the world has seen. Among the common objects of our study are Berlin, Chernobyl, Soweto, Tiananmen Square, and the Plaza de Mayo. The political theorist who has spent a career focusing on the nature of the political, the governmental, in all its tangible aspects must have trouble forgetting how the denial of voice and intention can become part of the 'banality of evil', as Arendt (1964) described the character of the Holocaust.[26] Thus, if the empirical urges of political and other social scientists appear banal to those more enveloped in poststructuralism, it is preferable to the more deadly and profoundly painful banalities of life.

SECOND CONCLUSION

These arguments will no doubt seem cranky to some. But the relations within the community of scholars known as women's studies can be subjected to the same kind of analysis feminists have for so long aimed at the communities of scholars within disciplines. Once upon a time (as they say in fairy tales) women's studies scholars tended to claim to be developing a field, a scholarly community. The intellectual differences between feminist scholars and their home fields seemed more pressing than the intellectual differences among feminist scholars across fields.

This is no longer the case. The bodies of literature and theory among feminist scholars within many fields have grown immensely. Those of us who are old enough can remember when it seemed possible to keep up with scholarly activity in the far corners of the academic world. Many of us are now overwhelmed by our own academic neighbourhoods.

What is the nature of the relationship among different feminist communities of scholars? What is their future? The answer cannot be found in the sociological aspects of the problem alone—that is, where feminists are housed and whether they talk to one another. Rather, intellectual and methodological questions are crucial as well.

If, as many of us are inclined to believe, feminist studies is more than the sum of its parts, but not a completely separate discipline undefined by the existent disciplinary boundaries and differences, the interdisciplinary feminist community has considerable work left to do drawing connections and developing methods for this joint project.

Notes

1. It is not entirely correct to call the early 1970s the 'early days' of research on women and politics among political scientists; there was sporadic work reaching back to the first decades of the existence of professional political science, founded in 1909 by discontented members of the American Economics Association. Most notably, excellent research was carried out by women such as Sophinisba Breckinridge, the first woman to earn a Ph.D. degree in political science. She, like most other women in the field, was unable to find an academic job within political science and carried her work out within an applied research setting and, ultimately, an academic social welfare programme.
2. Throughout this essay *we* refers to the community of scholars doing women-and-politics or gender-politics research within political science.

3. I discuss the current state of the field in Sapiro (1991).
4. The reaction is most evident in the organization of the National Association of Scholars, which sees changes such as the growing influence of women's studies as an assault on the integrity of scholarship and higher education.
5. See Bourque and Grossholtz (1974); Elshtain (1979); Flax (1983); Goot and Reid (1975); Kelley, Ronan, and Cawley (1987); Keohane (1981); Lovenduski (1981); Morgan (1974); Nelson (1989); and Sapiro (1979, 1987*a*, 1987*b*, 1991).
6. These different constructions are, of course, related to one another, and a substantial body of work ties them together, largely now through the train of work spun from Carol Gilligan's very influential thesis *In a Different Voice* (1982), as well as Belenky *et al.*, *Women's Ways of Knowing* (1986); and in the sciences, such as Evelyn Fox Keller's writing (e.g. 1985). My point here, however, is to distinguish an argument that focuses primarily on who does the thinking (which itself can be explained) to what is thought. For some lively and contentious treatments of the place of the 'different voices' discussion in political science, see Tronto (1987); Steuernagel (1987); and Sapiro (1987).
7. These different viewpoints are well summarized and discussed (outside of political science) in Harding (1991). For one of the few theorists of feminist empiricism, see Nelson (1990).
8. For one of the more recent and best essays on the public and private in political theory, see Okin (1990).
9. Many of these terms—*empirical, quantitative, scientific, behavioural, behaviourist*—are widely confused and are often caricatured by critics of the related practices who are not themselves involved in the relevant types of research. For present purposes, at least, let it be noted that these are not synonymous terms. Rational-choice theories are derived from economic models, in which people are posited as individuals with consistent, stable, and conscious goals based in their self-interest and whose choices are based in rational goal-seeking behaviour. Research employing rational-actor models is a matter of defining optimal solutions for self-interested goal-seekers and determining the situations under which optimality is not reached. Many (if not most) rational-choice theorists see no reason to study preferences themselves, or the sources of preferences, and argue that one can only study manifest behaviour in any case and infer preferences from that. For a brief and relatively jargon-free introduction, see Monroe (1991).
10. I use the term *legacy of positivism* rather than *positivism* itself to recognize that critics of social science, especially those based outside social science, often overestimate the degree to which those who practise empirical social science actually adhere to positivism in any classic sense.
11. For more complete discussion of these issues, see Harding (1987, 1991) and Nielson (1989). Sandra Harding's work is probably the most well-known among feminist scholars.
12. On the other hand, when, as a very young scholar, I had presented in a convention paper a cross-national comparison of public opinion on the status of women, a very senior and eminent political scientist serving as discussant dismissed my paper on the grounds that one cannot look at public opinion on the status of women the way one could examine other public issues because, after all, 'our views of women have to do with emotions, and libidos, and that part of life. It's just not rational in the way other issues are.'
13. Having been one of the people who made this claim in print (Sapiro 1979), I

am also painfully aware that these claims in turn became subject to intense criticism by other feminist writers, who interpreted the argument to say that androcentric research was a simple matter of 'bad science'. I suspect that most people who argue that androcentric and misogynist research is bad science would not also argue that it is only that.

14. There are women among the list of contemporary political theorists who must be read by any serious student of political theory according to almost anyone's criteria; among these are Hanna Arendt, Hanna Pitkin, and Judith Shklar.

15. For more discussion, see Sapiro (1992: ch. 9).

16. Although it is common for humanities scholars to be referred to as 'humanists', nothing essential about the nature of humanities disciplines makes their practitioners any more humanist than are practitioners of social science, especially given the variety within both.

17. The definition and evaluation of feminist theory would be a good topic for a feminist studies conference or other serious interdisciplinary efforts. Indeed, at this point it is difficult to define precisely what the differences are. I have experienced a number of situations in which feminist social-science scholars could not see what was 'theoretical' about a theoretical discussion offered by a humanities scholar. I would not be surprised if the reverse were also true.

18. The primary exception is the widespread attention in the humanities to Carol Gilligan's book *In a Different Voice*, although its findings and theories are often misinterpreted and certainly exaggerated, and the bulk of the empirical research responding to that work (other than Belenky, Clinchy, Goldberger, and Tarule, 1986) has been ignored.

   One of my favourite examples of the contrast concerns an interdisciplinary graduate research seminar in women's studies at my university, in which professors based in social science and in humanities alternate teaching. The seminar is intended and advertised as broadly interdisciplinary, attempting to foster the development of skills to work in an interdisciplinary field. One year, when it was taught by a social scientist, students in a literature department reported that students there discussed the course and argued with one another that they should wait until a humanities professor taught the course; only one humanities-based student took the course with the social scientist. The following year I witnessed many social-science students discussing how valuable it would be to take the course that year *because* it would be taught by a humanities professor and therefore would give them important exposure to a different and highly valuable area.

19. I am impressed with Lynn Hankinson Nelson's argument (1990: 314) that 'individuals are knowers only in a derivative sense', meaning that 'epistemological communities' and not just individuals need to be self-reflective in their science, which I would extend to scholarly inquiry more generally. I further accept the view that much of the vitality of women's studies comes from grounding in traditional disciplines and its continual traffic with the questions, issues, and methods of those disciplines.

20. Many of us have been charged with not being able to do truly feminist work *because* of using empirical tools of social science such as statistics or surveys, even by members of our own disciplines. See, in my case, Steuernagel (1987). It is interesting to note that in their discussion of a conference on women and computers many women—many feminists—felt similarly excluded by virtue of their participating in this 'masculine' field. See Perry and Greber (1990: 90).

21. For a few recent examples admittedly chosen haphazardly, see Elshtain (1987); Tronto (1987); di Stefano (1988); Phelan (1990); and Sapiro (1992). This list should also bear witness to the fact that political-science-based feminist theorists have considerable disagreements among themselves as well.

22. I remember all too clearly the number of feminist-studies activists who declared before the 1980 US presidential election that politics, and especially elections, make no difference, or at least none that goes beyond minor reformist changes. I later saw some of them at demonstrations protesting the effects of the Supreme Court appointments made in the following decade.

23. Although some use the terms identically, when I use *poststructuralist* I am referring to one distinct characteristic that distinguishes it from the broader movement of postmodernism, as suggested in Pauline Marie Rosenau's (1992) work on postmodernism and the social sciences: the former is more 'uncompromisingly' anti-empirical, which is one of the important tendencies at issue here.

24. It is important to be mindful that this anti-empirical approach to knowledge is based in part on empirical statements about the state of the world and mind, just as the arguments against theory within postmodernism themselves constitute a theory, as Rosenau (1992) has pointed out. Of course, that doesn't make these arguments wrong, simply more complicated and interesting.

25. I suspect that, in any case, students of political theory have not been asked to lock themselves into specific texts as much as may be true in some areas of literature. While there are certainly many political theorists whose work is devoted to understanding what Rousseau or Plato or especially Marx 'really meant', probably more political theorists are devoted, for example, to trying to figure out the potential for political community by reading smart and thoughtful writers like Rousseau, Plato, or Marx. One would read the same texts, but the task is quite different. If my point is correct, this difference in task would also constitute one of the points of misunderstanding between scholars in different fields.

26. Lest anyone believe I am claiming a superiority of social science as compared with literature—which I am not—I also recommend David Hughes's 1984 novel, *The Pork Butcher*, for its comprehension of the banality of the evil of the Holocaust.

References

Arendt, Hannah (1964), *Eichmann in Jerusalem: A Report on the Banality of Evil* (New York: Viking Press).

Ashwin, Sarah (1991), 'Development of Feminism in the *Perestroika* Era', *Report on the USSR* (30 August): n.p.

Belenky, Mary Field, Blythe McVicker Clinchy, Nancy Rule Goldberger, and Jill Mattuck Tarule (1986), *Women's Ways of Knowing: The Development of Self, Voice, and Mind* (New York: Basic Books).

Bourque, Susan C., and Jean Grossholtz (1974), 'Politics as an Unnatural Practice: Political Science Looks at Female Participation', *Politics and Society*, 4, 255–66.

Brown, Wendy (1988), *Manhood and Politics: A Feminist Reading in Political Theory* (Totowa, NJ: Rowman and Littlefield).

Darcy, R., Susan Welch, and Janet Clark (1987), *Women, Elections, and Representation* (New York: Longman).

Di Stephano, Christine (1988), 'Dilemmas of Difference: Feminism, Modernity, and Postmodernism', *Women and Politics*, 8, 1–24.

Eisenstein, Zillah R. (1988), *The Female Body and the Law* (Berkeley: University of California Press).

Elshtain, Jean Bethke (1974), 'Moral Woman and Immoral Man: A Consideration of the Public-Private Split and Its Political Ramifications', *Politics and Society*, 4, 453–74.

—— (1979), 'Methodological Sophistication and Conceptual Confusion: A Critique of Mainstream Political Science', in *The Prism of Sex: Essays in the Sociology of Knowledge*, ed. Julia Sherman and Evelyn Beck (Madison, Wis.: University of Wisconsin Press), 229–52.

—— (1981), *Public Man, Private Woman: Women in Social and Political Thought* (Princeton: Princeton University Press).

—— (1987), *Women and War* (New York: Basic).

Flax, Jane (1983), 'Political Philosophy and the Patriarchal Unconscious: A Psychoanalytic Perspective on Epistemology and Metaphysics', in *Discovering Reality*, ed. Sandra Harding and Merrill Hintikka (Dordrecht: D. Reidel), 245–82.

Fraser, Nancy (1989), *Unruly Practices: Power, Discourse, and Gender in Contemporary Social Theory* (Minneapolis: University of Minnesota Press).

Gilligan, Carol (1987), *In a Different Voice: Psychological Theory and Women's Development* (Cambridge, Mass.: Harvard University Press).

Gordon, Linda (ed.) (1990), *Women, the State, and Welfare* (Madison, Wis.: University of Wisconsin Press).

Harding, Sandra (1991), *Whose Science? Whose Knowledge? Thinking from Women's Lives* (Ithaca: Cornell University Press).

—— (ed.) (1987), *Feminism and Methodology: Social Science Issues* (Bloomington, Ind.: Indiana University Press).

Hughes, David (1984), *The Pork Butcher* (Harmondsworth: Penguin).

Keller, Evelyn Fox (1985), *Reflections on Gender and Science* (New Haven: Yale University Press).

Kelley, Rita Mae, Bernard Ronan, and Margaret E. Cawley (1987), 'Liberal Positivistic Epistemology and Research on Women and Politics', *Women and Politics*, 7, 11–28.

Keohane, Nannerl O. (1981), 'Speaking from Silence: Women and the Silence of Politics', in *A Feminist Perspective in the Academy: The Difference It Makes*, ed. Elizabeth Langland and Walter Gove (Chicago: University of Chicago Press), 86–100.

Lovenduski, Joni (1981), 'Toward the Emasculation of Political Science: The Impact of Feminism', in *Men's Studies Modified: The Impact of Feminism on the Disciplines*, ed. Dale Spender (New York: Pergamon), 83–92.

Monroe, Kirsten Renwick (1991), 'The Theory of Rational Action: What Is It? How Useful Is It for Political Science?' in *Political Science: Looking to the Future*, i. *The Theory and Practice of Political Science*, ed. William Crotty (Evanston, Ill.: Northwestern University Press), 77–98.

Morgan, Jan (1974), 'Women and Political Socialization: Fact and Fantasy in Easton and Dennis and in Lane', *Politics*, 9, 50–5.

Nelson, Barbara J. (1989), 'Women and Knowledge in Political Science: Texts, Histories, and Epistemologies', *Women and Politics*, 9, 1–26.

Nelson, Lynn Hankinson (1990), *Who Knows? From Quine to a Feminist Empiricism* (Philadelphia: Temple University Press).

Nielsen, Joyce McCarl (ed.) (1989), *Feminist Research Methods: Readings from the Social Sciences* (Boulder, Colo.: Westview Press).

Okin, Susan Moller (1990), 'Gender, the Public, and the Private', in *Modern Political Theory*, ed. David Held (London: Polity Press), 67–90.

Pateman, Carole (1988), *The Sexual Contract* (Stanford, Calif.: Stanford University Press).

—— (1989), *The Disorder of Women*. Stanford, Calif.: Stanford University Press.

Perry, Ruth, and Lisa Greber (1990), 'Women and Computers: An Introduction', *Signs*, 16, 74–101.

Petchesky, Rosalind Pollack (1984), *Abortion and Woman's Choice: The State, Sexuality, and Reproductive Freedom* (New York: Longman).

Phelan, Shane (1990), 'Feminism and Individualism', *Women and Politics*, 10, 1–18.

Phillips, Anne (1991), *Engendering Democracy* (University Park, Pa.: Pennsylvania State University Press).

Rosaldo, Michelle, and Louise Lamphere (eds.) (1974), *Women, Culture, and Society* (Stanford, Calif.: Stanford University Press).

Rosenau, Pauline Marie (1992), *Post-Modernism and the Social Sciences: Insights, Inroads, and Intrusions* (Princeton: Princeton University Press).

Ross, Dorothy (1991), *The Origins of American Social Science* (Cambridge: Cambridge University Press).

Sapiro, Virginia (1979), 'Women's Studies and Political Conflict', in *The Prism of Sex: Essays in the Sociology of Knowledge*, ed. Julia Sherman and Evelyn Beck (Madison, Wis.: University of Wisconsin Press), 318–24.

—— (1983), *The Political Integration of Women: Roles, Socialization, and Politics* (Urban, Ill.: University of Illinois Press).

—— (1987*a*), 'Reflections on Reflections: Personal Ruminations', *Women and Politics*, 7, 21–29.

—— (1987*b*), 'What the Political Socialization of Women Can Tell Us about the Political Socialization of People', in *The Impact of Feminist Research in the Academy*, ed. Christie Farnham (Bloomington, Ind.: Indiana University Press), 148–73.

—— (1991), 'Gender Politics, Gendered Politics: The State of the Field', in *Political Science: Looking to the Future*, i. *The Theory and Practice of Political Science*, ed. William Crotty (Evanston, Ill.: Northwestern University Press), 165–88.

—— (1992), *A Vindication of Political Virtue: The Political Theory of Mary Wollstonecraft* (Chicago: University of Chicago Press).

Shapiro, Robert Y., and Harpeet Mahajan (1986), 'Gender Differences in Policy Preferences: A Summary of Trends from the 1960s to the 1980s', *Public Opinion Quarterly*, 50, 42–61.

Steuernagel, Gertrude A. (1987), 'Reflections on Women and Political Participation', *Women and Politics*, 7, 3–14.

Tronto, Joan C. (1987), 'Political Science and Caring: Or, the Perils of Balkanized Social Science', *Women and Politics*, 7, 85–98.

Turkle, Sherry, and Seymour Papert (1990), 'Epistemological Pluralism: Styles and Voices within the Computer Culture', *Signs*, 16, 128–57.

Part II. Feminism and Political Theory

'Mere Auxiliaries to the Commonwealth': Women and the Origins of Liberalism

Teresa Brennan and Carole Pateman

> The peculiar character of man's domination over woman in the modern family, and the necessity, as well as the manner, of establishing real social equality between the two, will be brought out into full relief only when both are completely equal before the law.
>
> F. Engels, *The Origin of the Family, Private Property and the State*

Women, more specifically married women, constitute a permanent embarrassment and problem for liberal political theory. If this is not usually acknowledged, it is only because theorists rarely bother to consider whether their arguments have any relevance to women as well as men. Both the character and magnitude of the problem posed by married women, and the form of certain popular contemporary feminist arguments, can only be properly appreciated through an examination of the origins of liberal theory in the social contract theory of the seventeenth century. The arguments of Hobbes and Locke, which we shall discuss here, were developed as part of a conflict with patriarchal theorists. Yet, today, if women are taken into account in liberal theory, most writers retreat to patriarchal assumptions and assertions. The conflict between liberal and patriarchal theory is far from concluded: liberal theorists still have to confront, and answer, a very embarrassing question, namely, why it is that a free and equal female individual should always be assumed to place herself under the authority of a free and equal male individual.

The idea of individual freedom and equality, or the view that individuals are all 'by nature' free and equal to each other, and its corollary that authority relationships are grounded in convention, have been bequeathed to liberal theory by the social contract theorists. The emergence of these ideas in the seventeenth century marked a decisive break with the traditional view that people were

First published in *Philosophical Quarterly* 27/2 (1979), 183–200. Copyright © The Management Committee of the Philosophical Quarterly (1979).

'naturally' bound together in an hierarchy of inequality and subordination. Traditionally, the family had also been seen as a model of, and symbol for, authority relationships throughout society. The belief that the family is the source of all authority relationships is basic to patriarchal theory, but the latter, as Schochet points out, emerged as a developed political theory at the same time as social contract theory.[1] Commentators on the political theory of the seventeenth century have recently begun to emphasize the importance of patriarchal ideas to all writers of the period, obscure as well as famous. For some, this provides another key to the reading of the classic texts; for Hinton, for example, 'the least assailable side of [Hobbes's] argument' is his patriarchalism.[2] But such a claim can be made only by ignoring the fact that the contract theorists, and Hobbes in particular, denied the central tenets of patriarchal theory. Moreover, to emphasize patriarchal arguments does nothing to explain why it is that social contract theory and patriarchal theory emerged together and engaged in mutual criticism.

To find an explanation it is necessary to consider the integral relationship between political theories and specific forms of social life, a relationship that is also crucial to an understanding of the difficulties that married women pose for liberal theorists. Once the idea had gained ground that individuals were 'naturally' free and equal, or were born free and equal to each other, the patriarchalists were forced to clarify and systematize their arguments in order to combat the spread of such a subversive conception. But why should the contract theorists have argued that individuals were born free and equal; why, in their theories, do such creatures inhabit the state of nature? Social contract theory was part and parcel of the emergence of the capitalist, market economy, and the liberal, constitutional state—of the emergence of liberal society. Individuals cannot be seen as freely entering contracts and making exchanges with each other in the market, and as able freely to pursue their interests, unless they have come to be conceived as free and equal to each other. Furthermore, unless they are seen in this fashion, they have no need voluntarily to agree to, or consent to, government or the exercise of authority. To show that individuals were justified in consenting to government the contract theorists used the device of the state of nature. However, for individuals to be seen as free and equal 'by nature', they must to some degree be seen in isolation from (or as separate from) other individuals, and in abstraction from their social relationships. Now, if individuals are conceived of in this abstract manner, their sex is irrelevant. Each abstract entity, taken singularly, is an 'individual' with specified 'natural' characteristics. But this means that the conception of 'natural' individual freedom and equality is incompatible with patriarchal authority, whether that authority is exercised in the state or the family.

Or, at least, the two are incompatible all the time that females as well as males are seen as 'individuals'. *Logically*, there is no good reason why a liberal theorist should exclude females from this category; *in practice*, and in most liberal political theory, for three centuries the 'free and equal individual' has been a male. Discussions of patriarchal arguments unfailingly concentrate on the relationship between the father and the male children. The mother remains a shadowy figure indeed, and her status is obscure. Of course, the relationship between father and son is central to the conflict between the contract theorists and their opponents; how can it realistically be said that sons are not born in subjection to their fathers? Furthermore, in the strict sense, 'patriarchy' refers to rule by fathers. Sir Robert Filmer's *Patriarcha* is the best known statement of the patriarchal case. He argues that God gave Adam, the first father, absolute monarchical power by virtue of his procreative powers, and this power passed to his male heirs. All political authority is absolute and monarchical, and the power of kings is identical to that of fathers, and vice versa. However, fathers are, at one and the same time, husbands. Filmer also argued that God gave kingly power to Adam over Eve. Eve was made naturally fit for subordination, to be ruled by her husband.[3] This aspect of patriarchalism is generally ignored, although the status of wives and mothers within the family remains as an unsolved problem at the heart of liberal theory. Contemporary theorists conspicuously fail to address themselves to the question of how a husband's authority over a wife is to be justified without giving up some basic principles of liberal theory.

Discussions of social contract theory tend to gloss over the question of who exactly enters the contract and so consents to government. This is not surprising, for once the question is asked it exposes a profound ambiguity in the contract theorists' conception of the state of nature. If the state of nature is purely a logical fiction (useful in aiding us to understand the proper basis of obligation to government) then it is peopled by abstractly conceived, 'naturally' free and equal individuals, all of whom can participate in the social contract. On the other hand, if the state of nature is conceived as a sociologically and anthropologically realistic condition, or as an historical reality, it will be seen as composed of families, and an explicit attack must then be maintained on all aspects of patriarchalism if fathers *and* mothers of families are to enter the social contract. Neither the social contract theorists—with the notable, if partial, exception of Hobbes—nor their successors, have been willing to take their criticism of patriarchal ideas to its logical conclusion. Explicitly or implicitly the 'individuals' who enter the social contract are assumed to be fathers of families,[4] with all that this implies for the place of the sexes in civil society.

It might be objected that, in the seventeenth century, if not today, such an assumption was hardly unexpected. The authority of the father as head of the household was taken for granted by everyone, and the contract theorists were merely reflecting the convictions of their time when they supposed that fathers entered the social contract on behalf of their families. However, the conjugal and productive relationships of the seventeenth century also suggest that the contract theorists could have extended the logic of their individualism to women without stepping completely outside their own world. We have emphasized the interrelationship of contract theory and the emerging capitalist, market economy, but the contract theorists and patriarchalists fought their battle in a period that lies at the beginning of the long process of social change that brought liberal society into being. In the seventeenth century world we have lost, the family was still the main unit of economic production. Although fathers exercised authority within the family, the relationship of husband and wife within this productive unit presents a striking contrast to the conjugal relationship which we assume is proper and 'natural' today.

Historians, like political theorists, have concentrated almost exclusively on men in their analyses, and, with the important exception of Clark's *Working Life of Women in the Seventeenth Century*, there is little material available about the position of women in this period. Nevertheless, the broad picture is clear enough. Three centuries ago there was 'strong prejudice against bachelors and masterless men'.[5] Marriage 'was the entry to full membership' in society, and it constituted 'the creation of a new economic unit as well as a lifelong association of persons previously separate and caught-up in existing families'.[6] Within marriage, however, 'the idea is seldom encountered that a man supports his wife'.[7] In all classes of society women were engaged in productive work and were economically independent of their husbands: 'The wife was subject to her husband, . . . but she was by no means regarded as his servant.'[8] Even humble households had servants (of both sexes) so that wives were not exclusively occupied with domestic tasks as we think of these today. In the seventeenth century 'able business women' were common, and the wives of tradesmen and farmers were their husband's economic associates and partners.[9] On the death of a husband, 'surprisingly often, the widow, if she could, would herself carry on the trade'.[10] Women could also engage in trade on their own account; the 'early Customs of the Boroughs', and the by-laws of some corporations, allowed married women to trade as *femme sole*, with 'certain proprietary and legal rights independent of their husbands'.[11] Moreover, some trades and professions, notably brewing and midwifery, were the exclusive preserve of women. Even if the husband was a wage labourer, his wife fed and clothed the family; women 'can hardly have been regarded as mere dependants on their husbands when the clothing for the whole family was spun by their hands'.[12]

In the seventeenth century both women and men could 'shift for themselves', and thus there was a sound socio-economic basis for both sexes being regarded as, or abstracted into the state of nature as, 'free and equal individuals'. The contract theorists were well aware that their starting point of 'natural' individual freedom and equality had implications for the family as well as for political authority. If (like Hobbes) they contrived to remain silent about the status of wives in the family in civil society, or (like Locke) they capitulated to the patriarchalists, they nevertheless knew that there was a *problem* about the position of married women. Today, political theorists no longer acknowledge that such a problem exists; the authority of husbands over wives is excluded from theoretical scrutiny. To understand why this is the case it is necessary to examine the impact of the consolidation of capitalism in the eighteenth and nineteenth centuries on the socio-economic position of married women. We shall discuss this in more detail in the final section of this paper. At this point, it should be noted that as the development of capitalism separated economic production from the household, the relationship of husband and wife was transformed. They were no longer economic associates and partners, but either competed with each other in the market for individual wages, or the wife became her husband's economic dependent. This was an ironic, and tragic, development for women since at one and the same time, and as part of the same social process, liberal individualist ideas emerged that held out a promise of freedom and equality for women, yet socio-economic changes denied that promise and reinforced patriarchy.

HOBBES AND THE ONE-PARENT FAMILY

In order to treat Hobbes as a patriarchal thinker it is necessary to see his state of nature as inhabited by families, with fathers at their head. At times Hobbes' statements provide support for this view, but to interpret his state of nature in this fashion is inconsistent with his radical individualism which, in turn, is a logical consequence of his scientific method. Furthermore, to present Hobbes as a patriarchalist is to ignore his repeated denial that generation entails authority, and his insistence that all authority relationships are based on consent. It is also to ignore his scathing rejection of the argument from testimony and example on which the patriarchalists rested their case.[13]

In *Leviathan*, Hobbes begins his argument from an imaginative 'resolution' of a commonwealth into the physiological entities, or machines in perpetual motion, that are its component parts. He then builds these entities into recognizable human individuals by attributing various 'natural' characteristics to them. Hobbes' method thus leads him to a radical, abstractly individualist conception of the state of nature and its inhabitants. It is not a historically realistic condition, but a logical fiction in the most complete sense. In the state of nature each individual has an equal right of freedom to secure everything that is judged necessary for self-preservation. All are naturally equal because each one is strong enough, and has sufficient prudence, to kill another if required for survival. Hobbes' natural condition is asocial; it lacks a common moral language that provides a stable meaning for 'good' or 'bad' or 'justice'; it is without property, law, or 'Dominion'—and it has 'No Matrimoniall lawes'.[14] Hobbes' atomized individuals have no 'natural' connections with each other, and, in their mutual competition and war for survival in the state of nature, settled and ordered relationships, such as those in the patriarchal family, are extremely unlikely to exist. It is precisely because of Hobbes' singular picture of the natural condition that his 'view of the family subverts patriarchal attitudes'.[15]

When each 'individual' is considered completely abstractly, in separation from others, its sex is irrelevant. In Hobbes' state of nature, female individuals are as capable of protecting themselves as male individuals: he writes that 'the inequality of their natural forces is not so great, that the man could get . . . domination over the woman without war'.[16] There is, therefore, no reason why a free and equal female individual should always place herself under the protection, or authority, of a male. In the Hobbesian natural state there are no 'natural' relationships of authority. When all individuals are free and equal to each other, relationships of authority must be based on convention or consent. Hobbes pushes this argument to its limit and challenges every aspect of the patriarchal thesis. According to Hobbes, even an infant consents to the rule of a parent. In this particular argument, as in the rest of his political theory, Hobbes is helped by his conception of 'consent'. He identifies 'consent' with submission, or the 'voluntary' acceptance of protection in return for life, whether the submission is given by the subject in the face of the conqueror's sword, by a victim to a robber with a gun, or by a child to a parent who has the power to expose or abandon it.[17] In the latter case the 'parent' who has this power is the mother who gives birth to the child, and it is to her authority and protection that the child gives its 'consent'. In Hobbes' state of nature, 'every woman that bears children, becomes both a *mother* and a *lord*.[18] The procreative powers of the father are irrelevant to authority over children:

it cannot be known who is the Father, unless it be declared by the Mother: and therefore the right of Dominion over the Child dependeth on her will, and is consequently hers. Again, seeing the Infant is first in the power of the Mother, . . . is therefore obliged to obey her, rather than any other; and by consequence the Dominion over it is hers.[19]

A mother can lose the right to authority over her children if she is taken prisoner, when they too come under the rule of her captor. She may also consent to a man exercising authority over her children, although a covenant between a man and a woman does not always have this consequence. If the mother enters a contract 'for society of bed only' she retains dominion over her children; if it is a contract 'for society of all things' then 'sometimes the government may belong to the wife', notably if she is a queen.[20]

Like the patriarchalists, Hobbes sees authority as all of a piece throughout society, but as grounded in convention, not nature. The 'Rights and Consequences' of parental domination and sovereignty by institution (contract) and acquisition (conquest, which is to say, submission or 'consent') are all the same.[21] Hobbes is theoretically consistent enough to present the family as an 'artificial' or entirely conventional institution. He sees it 'strictly in rational terms': 'It is a "civil person" by virtue of jurisdiction, not by virtue of marriage or biological parenthood'.[22] The family, Hobbes argues, rests not on the natural ties of generation or sentiment, but is, like the state, grounded in the consent of its individual members and is 'united in one Person Representative'.[23] But which parent exercises jurisdiction in the family in civil society; which parent is the 'Person Representative'? The doctrine of indivisible sovereignty is a cornerstone of Hobbes' political theory, but in the state, although he prefers a monarch, he allows that sovereignty could be exercised by an assembly. Given the equality between the sexes, it would seem logical that the mother and father should rule jointly, as an 'assembly', in the family in civil society. However, as shown in his discussion of covenants between men and women, Hobbes insists that only *one* of the parents can govern. Within the 'matrimonial laws' of civil society he also assumes, although both mothers and fathers have the right of dominion, that it is the father who will exercise jurisdiction within the household. Most of Hobbes' commentators see nothing surprising in this: indeed it is offered as an example of his patriarchalism. Even Chapman, who emphasizes that the mother has an equal right to govern in the family, fails to discuss the status of the husband or wife who is ruled. Yet the precise status of this parent is extremely obscure, the more so if it is the status of the father that must be explained.

The problem is revealed in Hobbes' definition of a 'family'. The striking feature of his definition is that the mother silently fades from sight. In *Leviathan*, Hobbes refers to the 'family' as 'a man and his children; or . . . a man and his servants; or . . . a man, and his children, and servants together'.[24] At first sight, in *The Elements of Law*, his definition is conventional; Hobbes writes of the family as 'the father or mother, or both', together with the children and servants.[25] However, he concludes the sentence by stating that 'the father or master . . . is sovereign of the same; and the rest (both children and servants equally) subjects'. But what has happened to the mother? Similarly, he argues in *De Cive* that a '*father* with his *sons* and *servants*, grown into a civil person by virtue of his paternal jurisdiction, is called a *family*'.[26] Again, this leaves a large question to be answered about the status of the 'disappearing' free and equal individual who is the mother. One possibility is that the wife has the same status as a servant. This is unlikely, however, for the master-servant relationship, like slavery, originates in force.[27] The master makes a contractual grant of 'corporall liberty' to a servant, whereas marriage is a contract between two individuals of equal status, both of whom, in principle, have the right of dominion in the household. In addition, as we have shown, wives were economic associates of their husbands, not their servants, in this period. Chapman argues that Hobbes took his model of the 'artificial' family from ancient Rome.[28] This suggests that the wife's status might be that of a child. Either she would remain under the jurisdiction of her father, or, if the marriage was with *manus*, she would become part of her husband's household but have the position of a daughter in regard to property rights.[29] But this is hardly a plausible solution to the problem; everyone knew in the seventeenth century that wives and husbands were part of one family. Moreover, Hobbes' conception of the family follows logically from his theoretical individualism, so it is unnecessary to look to ancient Rome.

In fact, there is no solution to the problem of the 'disappearing parent' within Hobbes' political theory. He must remain silent about the status of wives and mothers in civil society if the inconsistency of his capitulation to the patriarchalists is not to be brought to the surface. The only 'argument' that he offers to justify the rule of fathers within the family is that 'for the most part Commonwealths have been erected by the Fathers, not by the Mothers of families'.[30] When discussing the problem of succession to the sovereign in the state, he says that it will usually pass to a male child, because 'generally men are endued with greater parts of wisdom and courage',[31] and they are 'naturally fitter than women, for actions of labour and danger'.[32] He also argues that children should be taught, as part of a process of political socialization designed to secure the absolute rule of the sovereign, that it is fathers who have instituted commonwealths.[33] All this is not only in blatant contradiction to his attack on patriarchal claims, but ignores his own strictures against arguments that rely on history and the 'Practise of men' rather than reason.[34]

The problem of the status of the 'missing parent' arises from Hobbes' refusal to allow that married individuals might rule jointly within their families. Because he falls back on patriarchal assertions about the 'natural' fitness of males to govern, the problem has gone unnoticed. The 'disappearance' of the mother in his definition of the family, and its implication that women always have good reason to submit to (consent to) the authority of men, seems unremarkable today after three centuries of liberal accommodation to patriarchy. Hinton has argued that there is an 'inherent dilemma' in patriarchalism:

for if kings are fathers, fathers cannot be patriarchs. If fathers are patriarchs at home, kings cannot be patriarchs on their thrones. Patriarchal kings and patriarchal fathers are a contradiction in terms. The patriarchalist therefore walks a tightrope. On the one hand he wants to emphasize sovereignty in kings and obedience in subjects, but on the other hand he has to preserve the father's property and freedom.[35]

This dilemma arises because the patriarchalists argue that authority structures are homologous throughout society. Hobbes agrees with them on this point, although he insists that all authority relationships are based on convention, not nature. But Hobbes avoids the dilemma; his radical individualism leads him to argue that just as family cohesion depends on the jurisdiction of a single 'person representative', so socio-political cohesion depends on the sword of an absolute monarch. If the security provided by the sword is to be maintained, then no father can have '*an absolute Propriety in his Goods; such, as excludeth the Right of the Sovereign*'.[36] Hobbes' theory, like patriarchalism, is thus ideologically inadequate for a developing liberal, market society. It was Locke who led the way forward, who argued against an homologous structure of authority, distinguishing between paternal and political rule, and who also showed how patriarchal claims about women could be neatly fitted into a liberal theoretical framework.

'HE FOR THE MARKET ONLY, SHE FOR THE MARKET THROUGH HIM'[37]

If, in Hobbes' theory, the lady vanishes, women have their place in Locke's argument from the beginning of the *First Treatise*, where he accuses Filmer of ignoring God's command that both mothers and fathers should be honoured. In part, Locke escapes Hobbes' peculiar difficulties over the position of wives in the family in civil society because his individualism is more moderate and so more anthropologically and sociologically adequate. But he also avoids the problem of the 'disappearing parent' because he has no quarrel with the patriarchalists about the status of wives and husbands. Locke retains all the patriarchal claims about the 'natural' authority of fathers, but hidden beneath a gloss of 'consent'. In this respect, as in others, his theory is 'fully as much a defense against radical democracy as an attack on traditionalism'.[38] However, just as some theorists wish to see Hobbes as a patriarchalist, so Locke is presented as an anti-patriarchalist. Schochet, for example, argues that Locke 'more fully than anyone else, analyzed the patriarchal political theory and tried to put something in its place', and 'by asking all the right questions' he rejected 'the presumptions on which patriarchalism rested'.[39] Hinton makes the extraordinary comment that 'Locke countered the patriarchalist case almost too effectively'.[40] Such arguments are plausible only if attention is exclusively concentrated on Locke's attack on absolute monarchy, his distinction between 'paternal' and 'political' power, and his insistence that mature male children are as free as their fathers. They are most implausible if Locke's arguments about wives and mothers are also considered.

At first sight women appear to fare well in Locke's *Two Treatises*. He argues against Filmer that God gave Adam no political power over Eve; the curse on Eve 'only foretels what should be the Womans Lot'. Locke argues that a woman might be free from subjection to her husband 'if the Circumstances either of her Condition or Contract with her Husband should exempt her from it' (i. 47).[41] The crux of his attack on Filmer is contained in the distinction between political and other forms of authority: 'the Power of a *Magistrate* over a Subject may be distinguished from that of a *Father* over his Children, a *Master* over his Servant, a *Husband* over his Wife, and a *Lord* over his Slave' (ii. 2). Political rule is distinguished by the right to impose the death penalty. Neither parents nor husbands have the right to exercise this ultimate power over children or wives. Under certain circumstances a wife may even be at liberty to leave her husband (ii. 82, 86). Parents have a natural authority over their children, but this does not, Locke argues against the patriarchalists, derive from procreation. Rather, it is a consequence of the parents' duty to care for and educate children while they are in their nonage and incapable of shifting for themselves (i. 52–3: ii. 58, 65). Locke repeatedly states that the mother 'hath an equal Title' with the father to authority over children, and this form of authority should therefore be called 'parental' not 'paternal' (e.g. ii. 52). In his discussion of conquest he even suggests that a wife might own property by virtue of her own labour (ii. 183).

All this appears to imply that Locke regarded women as well as men as free and equal individuals, and that his picture of the state of nature reflected women's productive role in the seventeenth century. However, this is only one side of Locke's argument and the least important. He sweeps away all that his individualism appears to promise women. It is no accident that Locke persistently forgets his own distinction between 'parental' and 'paternal' authority, and usually refers to the father and paternal rule in the *Second Treatise*.

An examination of Locke's discussion of the natural right to appropriate private property, and his account of the origins of government, reveal that patriarchal assertions about the 'natural' authority of fathers are basic to his political theory.

In his discussion of Adam and Eve, Locke takes the sting out of his attack on Filmer by adding that a wife's subjection to her husband has 'a Foundation in Nature' (i. 47). A husband's authority rests on contract, not nature, but Locke assumes that a free and equal female individual will always enter a marriage contract that places her in subjection to her husband. The extent of a wife's subjection may appear to be strictly limited, for Locke states that she has her own 'peculiar Right'. However, this refers to the right she has to her life, and her right to share in the exercise of authority over children. Her 'peculiar Right' excludes her from the crucial area of decision-making about family property. Notwithstanding his discussion of conquest, it is clear that Locke regards the labour of a wife, like that of a servant, as contributing to the property appropriated by her husband, or a master (ii. 28). The authority of a husband, father, and master does not extend to the property that members of the household have in their lives, but paternal and political authority have one important feature in common; in both forms the locus of authority must be placed somewhere determinate. Locke argues that the rule of one man is no longer justified in political life but, within the family, it is precisely this form of authority which must prevail. The power of decision-making in the family, or 'the last Determination, *i.e.* the Rule', will 'naturally' belong to the father because he is 'the abler and the stronger'. His right, unlike that of his wife, reaches 'to the things of their common Interest and Property' (ii. 82). The father is the 'Proprietor of the Goods and Land', and 'his Will take(s) place before that of his wife in all things of their common Concernment' (i. 48).

Locke's picture of the state of nature offers an excellent illustration of the integral connection between political concepts and theories and specific forms of social life. It reflects the social relationships of an emerging capitalist, market economy and, in his conjectural history of the state of nature, Locke provides a moral justification for these relationships.[42] In addition, he provides an account of the origins of government. His commentators have often overlooked the fact that Locke's state of nature contains government—the government of fathers. Once this is taken into account the distinction between 'political' and 'paternal' authority becomes exceedingly fine. Schochet makes the important point that discussions of social contract theory usually fail to differentiate between the contract and consent.[43] Locke is able to meet the patriarchalist objection to his principle of individual freedom and equality, that an original contract cannot bind future generations of sons. He argues that they consent to the political arrangements made, through the contract, by their fathers. A sharp contrast thus seems to exist between Locke and Filmer; a Lockean father will rule by consent, not by virtue of his generative powers. But how far does Locke's argument about consent actually undermine patriarchal assertions? Pitkin has argued convincingly that Locke's conception of 'consent' is of hypothetical consent; he argues that if a government is legitimate then consent ought to be given.[44] Indeed, Locke goes much further and argues that, given a legitimate government (such as that instituted through the social contract), then consent is given, or, at least, that it can always reasonably be inferred or hypothesized that it is given.

In the Lockean state of nature, male children who are out of their nonage remain under the authority of their father. God has 'appointed' government to enable humans to live peacefully together (i. 105, 13). The 'first' fathers in the state of nature become rulers through an 'insensible change', a change in which the 'first' mature male children give a 'tacit and scarce avoidable consent' to them becoming monarchs (ii. 76, 75). Locke says nothing about wives and mothers in this context, but he obviously takes it for granted that the marriage contract involves the wife's 'consent' to her husband's transmogrification. Such a reconciliation of liberal contract theory and patriarchal theory was made all the easier because patriarchalists, too, had recourse to ideas of contracts and consent.[45] For example, Dudley Digges in the 1640s claimed that the 'King hath paternall powers from the consent of the people'. If this is a 'curious union of consent with patriarchalism',[46] it is no more curious than Locke's 'consent' which gives kingly power to fathers in the face of his own argument that paternal and political power must be distinguished.

It might be objected that, even if there is little difference between a Lockean and a patriarchal account of the origins of government, Locke's argument in the *Second Treatise* for limited, representative government marks a complete break with patriarchal theory. It is true that Locke argues that, at a certain stage of the historical development of the state of nature, a single father-monarch is no longer able to provide adequate security for property, and that government must be reconstituted. He also adds that 'at best an Argument from what has been, to what should of right be, has no great force' (ii. 903); but there is an important continuity between what 'has been' in Locke's conjectural history and what 'should be'. Locke's history shows why it is rational for individuals to enter the social contract through which the new, liberal government of representatives is instituted.[47] Given this justification for the liberal state, it can then be inferred that succeeding generations 'consent' to this political act of their fathers. There is no separation of Locke's conjectural history from his theory of government; he does not turn the history 'into a descriptive and politically neutral anthropology and then [insert] his own theory of consent . . . in place of the moral patriarchalism Filmer had improperly derived from history'.[48] Locke's conjectural history is neither merely descriptive nor politically neutral. It provides the necessary basis for his brilliant justification of the liberal, constitutional state as the only form of government appropriate to a developing capitalist society. Furthermore, it provides a new contractual dress for the patriarchal assertion that wives are 'naturally' subordinate to their husbands, and legitimizes the exclusion of women from political life.

The 'individuals' who enter Locke's social contract and establish the liberal state are the fathers of families. They act to secure their property, whether this consists of estates or merely the 'property' that members of the family have in their lives, liberty and labour. In so acting, they also secure the 'property' that they have in their own position of authority within the family. Locke states that 'no rational Creature can be supposed to change his condition with an intention to be worse (ii. 131). During the change from the state of nature to civil society, inequalities of property and all the social relationships of the natural condition are preserved (indeed consolidated), including the authority relationships within the family. The *Second Treatise* offers no reason to suppose that Locke would have disagreed with James Tyrrell, his friend and fellow critic of Filmer, who argued that consent to government 'needed no Compact of all the People of the world, since every Father of a Family . . . had a power to confer his Authority of governing himself and his Family upon whom he pleased'; and who added that women were 'concluded by their Husbands'.[49]

The emergence of patriarchal theory in the seventeenth century was, Schochet argues, a 'direct result' of the differentiation of political from other forms of authority.[50] But this distinction is also crucial to the accommodation of social contract with patriarchal theory. It enables Locke to assume that women are 'naturally' fit only for a restricted role within the family. Men alone can make the transition to political life; it is they who are the 'individuals' who have the capacity to enter the social contract and to be authors of their own subjection in political life. A striking and sad corollary of this assumption is that women are seen as lacking in the rationality required to take these steps. The 'moderate and sensible'[51] character of Locke's theory has been challenged by Macpherson who argues that Locke regards propertyless males as less than fully rational. He concludes his discussion of Locke's theory with these words:

the greatness of seventeenth-century liberalism was its assertion of the free rational individual as the criterion of the good society; its tragedy was that this very assertion was necessarily a denial of individualism to half the nation.[52]

But Macpherson has completely overlooked *literally* 'half the nation' for whom the development of liberal, capitalist society, which compounded and reinforced (while transforming) patriarchy, was an even greater tragedy. We would argue that for Locke every male, whether owning material property or not, is rational and an 'individual'. Every male is assumed to be sufficiently rational, or 'naturally' to have the capacity, to govern a family. Rationality, it can be said, comes not just with age, but with the tying of the conjugal knot, and with fatherhood. In Locke's theory, it is women who are seen as 'naturally' lacking in rationality and as 'naturally' excluded from the status of 'free and equal individual', and so unfit to participate in political life.

LIBERALISM AND FEMINISM

The claim that women are lacking in rationality and unfitted for political life is still widely accepted; indeed, in 1978, this is frequently presented as one of the 'natural' differences of character and attributes between the sexes. That it can seem unremarkable for women to be so regarded when today, as *citizens*, they are formally equal to men and have the same opportunities for political participation open to them, can be explained only by taking account of *both* the reconciliation of liberal and patriarchal theory and the economic changes that forced married women into dependence on their husbands. The failure of more recent liberal theorists, with the honourable exception of J. S. Mill, to extend their principles to one half of humankind remains unchallenged because it is now seen as 'natural' for married women to be economic dependants, and so 'naturally' unfree and unequal.

In the eighteenth century, economic independence (especially as exemplified in property ownership) became the major criterion for citizenship. Kant, listing all those unfit to vote because of their dependence and subordination, remarked that they had 'no civil personality and their existence is, so to speak, purely inherent'. He included in this group 'women in general'.[53] Women could be lumped into one undifferentiated group, forever dependent, whereas males might be able to transcend their position as 'mere auxiliaries to the commonwealth'. During the nineteenth century they began to do so. The fight for manhood suffrage had the advantage that all men, even the propertyless, were seen as able to govern within their families. Consequently, it was not implausible to claim that they had the capacities required for citizenship in the liberal state.

Richards has pointed out that the impact on women of the development of capitalist industry in England, from the seventeenth into the twentieth century, provides an extremely interesting comparison with the current effects of industrialization and the expansion of wage-labour in the developing countries. In both cases the participation rates of women decline as development proceeds.[54] From the end of the seventeenth century in England women's economic independence and legal status began to be undermined. Businesswomen were less prominent by the end of the century and, although married women continued to participate in trades and crafts well into the eighteenth century, more and more avenues of employment became closed to them. Men began to organize themselves into professional and trade associations from which women were excluded, even from brewing, which was once a female trade. Women also lost control of dairying, midwifery, and medicine.[55] Summing up the effects of capitalist development upon the wives of tradesmen and craftsmen, Clark writes:

it seems probable that the wife of the prosperous capitalist tended to become idle, the wife of the skilled journeyman lost her economic independence and became his unpaid domestic servant, while the wives of other wage earners were driven into the sweated industries.[56]

We have earlier drawn attention to the importance for married women of the gradual divorce of home and work and the expansion of wage-labour. On the land and in the new workplaces, men and women had to compete for an individual wage, and wages for women were rarely sufficient for them to feed and clothe themselves and their children.[57] Moreover, the employment of women (and children) in the textile factories was an atypical development. From the beginning of the nineteenth century in existing and newly developing industries, opportunities for employment of women declined: 'the loss of employment in the traditional lines was probably greater than the creation of new opportunities'.[58]

These economic changes were also accompanied by a deterioration in the legal status of women. Legal customs which had favoured women were abrogated in favour of common law focused on the individual male. By the mid-nineteenth century when 'the range of [economic] opportunities for . . . women was tragically restricted',[59] the formal status of married women had also reached its lowest point; their position reflected Blackstone's Common Law doctrine of 'unity of person'. He wrote, 'a man cannot grant any thing to his wife, or enter into covenant with her, for the grant would suppose her separate existence'.[60] Women were deemed incapable of acting for themselves or assuming responsibility for so doing; that was a burden that husbands carried. Mothers had lost the authority over their children of which Locke had made so much, and a husband could legally imprison his wife in the matrimonial home to prevent her from leaving him.[61] It is not surprising that so many of the early champions of women's rights were abolitionists, or that married women were frequently compared to slaves, for legally and civilly they did not exist. Their social, political, and economic dependence upon, and subordination to, their husbands was virtually complete.

Neither liberal theorists' acceptance of the dependence and subordination of wives to husbands as 'natural', and so theoretically irrelevant, nor feminists' response to this view, can be fully understood in the absence of an appreciation of this historical background and of the integral connection between political and social concepts, theories, and ideas, and specific forms of social life. Ideas are not merely automatic reflections of socio-economic developments, but nor do they exist in an independent timeless world of their own. The nineteenth- and early-twentieth-century feminist movement was a response to the social, legal, and economic position of women, and to the failure of theorists and men of affairs to grant that women were 'individuals' capable of exercising civil rights. It was a largely middle-class movement, a class which included large numbers of women who could not be 'concluded by their husbands' for they had no husbands, and few means of supporting themselves.[62] The consolidation of capitalist production had fostered a sharp class division between women. Many working-class women continued to work from necessity, especially, of course, in domestic service (although the ideal of the non-working wife had spread to 'respectable' households of all classes by the middle of the nineteenth century).[63]

The narrow limits of acceptable and accessible female employment in the mid-century provoked from some women—almost entirely middle-class in origin—a response which generated fuel for the feminist developments of the age. . . . The real origins of the 'emancipation of women' (in the modern sense of economic opportunity and independence) must be sought in the shifting balance of the occupational framework which began to emerge in the last quarter of the 19th century.[64]

The assertion that they too were rational was central to the earlier feminists' fight for women's emancipation. It is central to women's formal recognition as free and equal individuals capable of enjoying legal and civil rights; the vote, the right to enter economic contracts and control property, the right to education, and to work in the professions, and the right to dispose of the property they have in their persons. In a *formal* sense the battle is more or less over. In the last quarter of the twentieth century, the principle of individual equality and freedom, which the social-contract theorists used to attack patriarchalism, is now being institutionalized in the liberal democracies—for both males and females. This could be seen as the last stage of the bourgeois revolution; yet, far from fulfilling the promise of liberalism, this formal recognition of women as individual human persons has served to highlight the contradiction between women seen formally as free and equal individuals, and women as wives and mothers within the family. The theoretical embarrassment that women posed to seventeenth-century theorists, reluctant or unwilling to question the authority of husbands and fathers within the family, has now returned as a practical contradiction between institutionalized liberal individualism and the authority structure of the twentieth-century family.

The new feminist movement of the last decade has been particularly concerned with the private world of the family, rather than the public world that preoccupied their predecessors. This concern, too, can be related to economic developments. Since the Second World War there has been a dramatic increase in the participation rate of married women in the paid workforce. This increase is a result of new employment created by the rapid growth of the tertiary sector of the economy.[65] Married women now have the opportunity for economic independence and all that it implies for social and political life. Or, at least, this is true for educated middle-class women with special skills, who can compete for work that pays enough for them to be self-supporting.[66] The jobs open to most working-class women are very poorly paid, and many women are once more, perhaps have always been, in a position of interdependence in the family. In many cases their families can survive only through the combined incomes of husband and wife.[67]

However, many current feminist arguments and slogans fail to take account of the different positions of wives in the middle and working classes. Unlike liberal theorists, they are concerned with women; but like those theorists they implicitly appeal to an abstractly individualist liberalism that ignores socioeconomic and historical realities and developments, and their importance for the married woman question. Some feminist aims and demands constitute a mirror-image of the abstractly individualist conception of social life, or resemble the liberal picture of the atomistic classless state of nature. Such a response leads to a politics of negation that is encapsulated in the popular slogans 'the personal is the political' and 'smash the family', and in the claim that 'nature' is the oppressor and must be abolished.[68] Firestone, for instance, argues that women will only be free through artificial means of human reproduction.[69] Because so many women are now constrained by the burden of two jobs (paid and unpaid), it can easily appear as if the family must be 'smashed' if women are to be independent, and the three-centuries-old promise of liberalism is to be achieved. Feminists have implicitly attacked Locke's always fragile separation of paternal and political authority and argue that males rule in an identical fashion in the family and in the state; 'the personal is the political'. Like Hobbes and the patriarchalists, they see authority relationships as all of a piece, and, ideally, as conventional. Once the family is 'smashed' there will be no 'natural' restrictions of the ability of equal individuals freely to interact; even 'all adult–child relationships will [be] mutually chosen'.[70] With these feminist arguments the wheel has turned full circle, back to Hobbes' radical abstractly individualist, and conventionalist, attack on patriarchy.

But if the liberal accommodation to patriarchy is to be broken, we must move forward, not backward, in both theory and practice. It is necessary to look beyond the abstract categories of liberal theory that have assisted the consolidation and transformation of patriarchy, to a theoretical perspective explicitly grounded in the present socioeconomic realities. As we have shown, the social place of married women is not 'natural' and unchanging, but forms part of specific socioeconomic and political relationships. Nor is the family an unchanging social entity or an eternal, timeless enemy of women. The relationship between the class structure of advanced liberal-capitalist societies and the status of married women within the family is only just beginning to be investigated, and much work remains to be done. In this paper our aim has been to perform some of the groundwork necessary for this wider task: to show how and why married women pose an acute problem for liberal political theory and practice, and how popular beliefs about women's place, and the feminist attack on these, are bound up with the historical development of the capitalist economy and the liberal state.

Notes

1. G. J. Schochet, *Patriarchalism in Political Thought* (Oxford, Blackwell, 1975), 19 and 55–6.
2. R. W. K. Hinton, 'Husbands, Fathers and Conquerors: II', *Political Studies*, 16 (1968), 58.
3. We have no space here to explore the opportunities opened up for women by the religious dimension of individualism. See e.g. K. V. Thomas, 'Women and the Civil War Sects', *Past and Present*, 13 (1958); and C. Hill, *The World Turned Upside Down* (London: Temple Smith, 1972), ch. 15. The Reformation also reinforced patriarchy as fathers took on priestly tasks; see Schochet, *Patriarchalism in Political Thought*, 57.
4. In Rawls' revival of contract theory it is significant that he says of his original position that 'we may think of the parties as heads of families'. J. Rawls, *A Theory of Justice* (Oxford: Oxford University Press, 1972), 128. The veil of ignorance may be intended to hide the parties' knowledge of their sex, but it is unlikely that Rawls could make so many appeals to 'our' intuitions and considered judgements if, for example, the heads of families are not seen in conventional terms as fathers.
5. Thomas, 'Women and the Civil War Sects', 42.
6. P. Laslett, *The World We Have Lost* (London: Methuen, 1965), 11–12 and 90.
7. A. Clark, *Working Life of Women in the Seventeenth Century* (London: Frank Cass, 1968), 12. First published in 1919.
8. Ibid. 41.
9. Ibid. 35.
10. Laslett, *The World We Have Lost*, 8.
11. Clark, *Working Life of Women in the Seventeenth Century*, 151; R. Thompson, *Women in Stuart England and America: A Comparative Study* (London: Routledge and Kegan Paul, 1974), 163.
12. Clark, *Working Life of Women in the Seventeenth Century*, 145.
13. Hobbes argues that the authority of the Bible rests only on the authority of the church, which, in turn, derives from the Commonwealth and its head; and 'hath the head of the Commonwealth any other authority than that which hath

been given him by the members?' Cited (from *Liberty, Necessity and Chance*), in P. Riley, 'Will and Legitimacy in the Philosophy of Hobbes: Is He a Consent Theorist?', *Political Studies*, 21 (1973), 504.

14. T. Hobbes, *Leviathan*, ed. C. B. Macpherson (Harmondsworth: Penguin Books, 1968), xiii. 188; xx. 254.
15. R. A. Chapman, '*Leviathan* Writ Small: Thomas Hobbes on the Family', *American Political Science Review*, 69 (1975), 77.
16. T. Hobbes, *De Cive*, ed. B. Gert (New York: Anchor Books, 1972), ix. 3, 213. And see *Leviathan*, xx. 253.
17. P. King, *The Ideology of Order* (London: Allen and Unwin, 1974), ch. 15, over-looks Hobbes's general conception of 'consent' when he argues how implausi-ble it is to speak of an infant's 'consent'. Hobbes's notion of 'consent' is discussed in detail in C. Pateman, *The Problem of Political Obligation* (Chichester: Wiley, 1979).
18. Hobbes, *De Cive*, ix. 3, 213.
19. Hobbes, *Leviathan*, xx. 254; compare his views in T. Hobbes, *The Elements of Law*, ed. F. Tönnies (2nd edn., London: Frank Cass, 1969), pt. 2, iv. 3, 132.
20. Ibid. 5–6, 133; and see *De Cive*, ix. 5–7. The reference to 'queens' suggests a social state of nature—or is Hobbes referring to civil society here?
21. Hobbes, *Leviathan*, xx. 256.
22. Chapman, '*Leviathan* Writ Small', 78, 80.
23. Hobbes, *Leviathan*, xxii. 285.
24. Ibid. 257; see Chapman, '*Leviathan* Writ Small', 80.
25. Hobbes, *The Elements of Law*, Pt. II, iv. 10, 135.
26. Hobbes, *De Cive*, ix. 10, 217.
27. Hobbes, *Leviathan*, xx. 255–6; *The Elements of Law*, Pt. II, ch. III: *De Cive*, ch. VIII.
28. Chapman, '*Leviathan* Writ Small', 82–4.
29. S. B. Pomeroy, *Goddesses, Whores, Wives and Slaves: Women in Classical Antiquity* (New York: Schocken Books, 1975), esp. 152, 162. In ch. VIII, Pomeroy shows that male relatives, especially fathers, retained considerable power over married women, even if married with *manus*.
30. Hobbes, *Leviathan*, xx. 253.
31. Hobbes, *The Elements of Law*, Pt. II, IV. 14, 136.
32. Hobbes, *Leviathan*, xix. 250; and see *De Cive*, ix. 16, 219, where Hobbes states this is 'for the most part' and that it has 'grown a custom'.
33. Hobbes, *Leviathan*, xxx. 382.
34. Ibid. xx. 261.
35. R. W. K. Hinton, 'Husbands, Fathers and Conquerors: I', *Political Studies*, 15 (1967), 294.
36. Hobbes, *Leviathan*, xxix. 367.
37. C. Hill's felicitous phrase.
38. S. Wolin, *Politics and Vision* (London: Allen and Unwin, 1961), 294.
39. Schochet, *Patriarchalism in Political Thought*, 245, 268.
40. Hinton, 'Husbands, Fathers and Conquerors: II', 66.
41. References in brackets in the text refer to paragraphs of the 'First Treatise' and the 'Second Treatise' in J. Locke, *Two Treatises of Government*, ed. P. Laslett (2nd edn.; Cambridge: Cambridge University Press, 1967).
42. The conjectural history is discussed in more detail in C. Pateman, 'Sublimation

and Reification: Locke, Wolin and the Liberal Democratic Conception of the Political', *Politics and Society*, 5 (1975).

43. Schochet, *Patriarchalism in Political Thought*, 9, 262.
44. H. Pitkin, 'Obligation and Consent', in P. Laslett, W. G. Runciman, and Q. Skinner (eds.), *Philosophy, Politics and Society* (4th ser., Oxford: Blackwell, 1972).
45. Hinton, 'Husbands, Fathers and Conquerors: II', 62, comments that 'Hobbes's patriarchalism was for Locke the strongest patriarchalism because it was based on consent'. For a detailed discussion of the use of the marriage contract as an analogue of the social contract by both royalists and republicans in the seventeenth century, see M. L. Shanley, 'Marriage Contract in Seventeenth-Century Political Thought', paper presented to the Annual Meeting of the American Political Science Association (1976).
46. Cited by Schochet, *Patriarchalism in Political Thought*, 104.
47. This argument is developed further in Pateman, 'Sublimation and Reification'.
48. Schochet, *Patriarchalism in Political Thought*, 259.
49. Cited by Schochet, *Patriarchalism in Political Thought*, 202. It should be noted that although all fathers take part in the contract, only a few propertied fathers become politically relevant members of civil society, who can act as, and choose, representatives.
50. Ibid. 55.
51. J. Plamenatz, *Man and Society* (London: Longmans, 1963), i. 241.
52. C. B. Macpherson, *The Political Theory of Possessive Individualism* (Oxford: Oxford University Press, 1962), 262.
53. I. Kant, *Kant's Political Writings*, ed. H. Reiss (Cambridge: Cambridge University Press, 1971), 139.
54. E. Richards, 'Women in the British Economy Since About 1700: An Interpretation', *History*, 59 (1974), 337–57.
55. Clark, *Working Life of Women in the Seventeenth Century*, especially ch. VI. On male trade and professional organizations and their effect on women's employment, see also H. Hartmann, 'Capitalism, Patriarchy and Job Segregation by Sex', *Signs*, 1 (1976), 3, Pt. 2. On women's economic role, see also I. Pinchbeck, *Women Workers and the Industrial Revolution, 1750–1850* (London: Routledge, 1930).
56. Clark, *Working Life of Women in the Seventeenth Century*, 235.
57. Ibid. 92, 145, 304; also Thompson, *Women in Stuart England and America*, 241.
58. Richards, 'Women in the British Economy Since About 1700', 345–6.
59. Ibid. 347.
60. Sir W. Blackstone, *Commentaries on the Laws of England* (London: Sweet, Maxwell, Stevens and Norton, 1844) 21st edn. i. Book I, ch. 15, 442. The *Commentaries* were first published in 1765–9. Blackstone (444) adds, 'even the disabilities the wife lies under, are for the most part intended for her protection and benefit. So great a favourite is the female sex of the laws of England!'
61. See the examples in J. O'Faolain and L. Martines (ed.), *Not in God's Image* (New York: Harper, 1973), 318–28.
62. See R. McWilliams-Tullberg, *Women at Cambridge* (London: Gollancz, 1975), 21. In 1861 46 per cent of women aged 20–34 were unmarried.
63. See e.g. the comments in G. Stedman-Jones, *Outcast London* (Harmondsworth: Penguin, 1976), 83–4; and D. Thompson, 'Women and Nineteenth-Century Radical Politics: A Lost Dimension', in J. Mitchell and A. Oakley

(eds.), *The Rights and Wrongs of Women* (Harmondsworth: Penguin, 1976), 136–7.

64. Richards, 'Women in the British Economy Since About 1700', 350–1.

65. Ibid. 348, 354–7.

66. There is considerable (if sometimes unconscious) resentment of this potential independence, revealed in the current attacks on married women for depriving male school-leavers and other males of jobs in a period of high unemployment. Such attacks also reveal a considerable ignorance of the sexual structuring of the labour market. In fact women are usually channelled into sectors of the economy in which men (including male school-leavers) are unwilling to compete. On the structure of the labour-market see M. Reich, D. M. Gordon, and R. C. Edwards, 'A Theory of Labor Market Segmentation', *American Economic Review*, Papers and Proceedings, 63 (1973).

67. The economic interdependence of working-class women and men, as opposed to the potential economic independence of middle-class women, is discussed in T. Brennan, 'Women and Work', *The Journal of Australian Political Economy*, 1 (1977).

68. It is also reflected in the proposals for 'contract' marriages. See e.g. L. J. Weitzman, 'Legal Regulation of Marriage: Tradition and Change', *California Law Review*, 62 (1974), 1169–288.

69. S. Firestone, *The Dialectic of Sex* (London: Paladin, 1972), 187 ff.

70. Ibid. 222.

5 Gender, the Public, and the Private

Susan Moller Okin

The concepts of public and private spheres of life have been central to Western political thought at least since the seventeenth century. In some respects, they have origins in classical Greek thought.[1] In much of mainstream (as contrasted with feminist) political theory today, these concepts continue to be used as if relatively unproblematical. Important arguments in contemporary debates depend upon the assumption that public concerns can with relative ease be distinguished from private ones, that we have a solid basis for separating out the personal from the political. Sometimes explicitly, but more often implicitly, the idea is perpetuated that these spheres are sufficiently separate, and sufficiently different, that the public or political can be discussed in isolation from the private or personal. As I shall argue in this chapter, such assumptions can be sustained only if very persuasive arguments of feminist scholars are ignored.

Feminist scholarship in various disciplines has placed on the agenda a new category of analysis, gender, which raises many new questions about previous distinctions between public and private spheres. 'Gender' refers to the social institutionalization of sexual difference; it is a concept used by those who understand not only sexual inequality but also much of sexual differentiation to be socially constructed. So far, feminist scholarship in political theory tends to be marginalized, as it still is to some extent in history, but in contrast with its now central place in literary theory. As I shall attempt to explain here, however, such marginalization will continue only at the expense of the continued coherence, comprehensiveness, and persuasiveness of political theory.

There is a certain irony to be noted here. The 'rebirth' of normative political theory has occurred contemporaneously with the rebirth of feminism and, not coincidentally, at a time of major changes in the family and its relations to the rest of society. But the new political theory has paid almost no attention to the family, and

Chapter 3 in David Held (ed.), *Political Theory Today* (Polity Press, 1991), 67–90. Reprinted by permission of Blackwell Publishers Ltd. and Stanford University Press. Copyright © Susan Moller Okin (1991).

continues its central debates with little regard for the challenges of recent feminism.

DEFINITIONS AND AMBIGUITIES

Distinctions between public and private have played a crucial role, especially in liberal theory, 'the private' being used to refer to a sphere or spheres of social life in which intrusion or interference with freedom requires special justification, and 'the public' to refer to a sphere or spheres regarded as more generally or more justifiably accessible. Sometimes it is the control of information about what goes on in the private sphere that is stressed, sometimes freedom from being observed, sometimes freedom from actual interference with or intrusion upon one's activities, solitude, or decisions.[2] All too frequently in political theory, the terms 'public' and 'private' are used with little regard for clarity and without precise definition, as if we all knew what they meant in whatever context the theorist uses them. There are, however, as feminist scholarship has made increasingly clear, two major ambiguities involved in most discussions of the public and the private.

The first ambiguity results from the use of the terminology to indicate at least two major conceptual distinctions, with variations within each. 'Public/private' is used to refer both to the distinction between state and society (as in public and private ownership), and to the distinction between non-domestic and domestic life. In both dichotomies, the state is (paradigmatically) public, and the family, domestic, and intimate life are (again paradigmatically) private. The crucial difference between the two is that the intermediate socio-economic realm (what Hegel called 'civil society') is in the first dichotomy included in the category of 'private', but is in the second dichotomy 'public'. There has been little discussion of this major ambiguity by mainstream political theorists. Even anthologies devoted to the subject of public and private pay little attention to analysing it, in spite of the fact that they may include some articles about one distinction and some about the other. In Benn and Gaus's recent anthology,[3] for example, the only paper in the volume that pays serious and sustained attention to the ambiguity is Pateman's highly lucid feminist critique.[4] In other anthologies one or other definition seems simply to be assumed, and only that version of the dichotomy is addressed. In the collection edited by Hampshire, for example, there is virtually no mention in any of the essays of the domestic sphere or the dichotomy that specifies it as distinct from the rest of social life.[5]

A rare exception to the general glossing over of the fact that 'public/private' has more than one meaning is to be found in a discussion by Weinstein.[6] He draws a useful analogy between publicness and privateness and the layers of an onion; just as a layer that is outside one layer will be inside another, so something that is public with regard to one sphere of life may be private in relation to another. While Weinstein is correct in pointing out that the distinction therefore has a multiplicity of meanings, rather than simply a dual meaning, the state/society and the non-domestic/domestic meanings are those most frequently used in political theory, where both play major roles. I shall focus on the second in this chapter, because it is the continuation of this dichotomy that enables theorists to ignore the political nature of the family, the relevance of justice in personal life, and, as a consequence, a major part of the inequalities of gender. I shall refer to the dichotomy as 'public/ domestic'.

Second, even *within* the public/domestic dichotomy, there remains an ambiguity, resulting directly from the patriarchal practices and theories of our past, that has serious practical consequences—especially for women. Fundamental to this dichotomy from its theoretical beginnings has been the division of labour between the sexes. Men are assumed to be chiefly preoccupied with and responsible for the occupations of the sphere of economic and political life, and women with those of the private sphere of domesticity and reproduction. Women have been regarded as 'by nature' both unsuited to the public realm and rightly dependent on men and subordinated within the family. These assumptions, not surprisingly, have pervasive effects on the structuring of the dichotomy and of both its component spheres. As feminist scholarship has revealed, from the seventeenth-century beginnings of liberalism both political rights and the rights pertaining to the modern liberal conception of privacy and the private have been claimed as rights of individuals; but these individuals were assumed, and often explicitly stated, to be adult, male heads of households.[7] Thus, the rights of these individuals to be free from intrusion by the state, or by the church, or from the prying of neighbours, were also these individuals' rights *not* to be interfered with as they controlled the other members of their private sphere—those who, whether by reason of age, or sex, or condition of servitude, were regarded as rightfully controlled by them and existing within *their* sphere of privacy. There is no notion that these subordinate members of households might have privacy rights of their own. Some of the contemporary consequences of this theoretical and legal legacy will be discussed below.

THE NEGLECT OF GENDER AND THE PERPETUATION OF AN UNREFLECTIVE PUBLIC/DOMESTIC DICHOTOMY

Many political theorists in the past used to discuss both public and domestic spheres, and to be explicit in their claims that they were separate and operated in accordance with different principles. Locke, for example, *defines* political power by distinguishing it from the power relations operating within the household.[8] Rousseau and Hegel clearly contrast the particularistic altruism of the family with the need for impartial reason in the state, and cite this contrast in legitimating male rule in the domestic sphere.[9] These theorists make explicit arguments about the family, and closely related ones about the nature of women. By contrast, most contemporary political theorists continue the same 'separate spheres' tradition by *ignoring* the family, and in particular its division of labour, related economic dependencies, and power structure. The judgement that the family is 'non-political' is implicit in the very fact that it is *not* discussed in most works of political theory today.[10] The family is clearly *assumed*, for example in that political theorists take as the subjects of their theories mature, independent human beings, without explaining how they came to be that way; but it is not much talked about. Rawls, in constructing his theory of justice, does not discuss the internal justice of the family, although he both includes the family in his initial components of the basic structure (to which the principles of justice are to apply) and requires a just family for his conception of moral development.[11] Even in a recent book entitled *Justice, Equal Opportunity and the Family* we find no discussion of the division of labour between the sexes or the internal justice of families.[12]

Among the few exceptions to this rule are theoretical discussions explicitly focused on the public/private distinction, which occasionally point to the sphere of family life as the paradigm case of 'the private'. Apart from these, the widely disparate arguments about the family of Walzer and Green, who *are* concerned with its internal justice, Bloom, who claims (following Rousseau) that it is naturally and inevitably *un*just, and Sandel, whose argument against the primacy of justice depends upon an idealized vision of families operating in accordance with virtues nobler than justice, are rare exceptions in recent works of political theory.[13]

Along with the typical assumptions about and neglect of family life goes a phenomenon that I shall call 'false gender neutrality'. In the past, political theorists used explicitly male terms of reference, such as 'he' and 'man'. Usually it was clear that their major arguments were, indeed, about male heads of families. These arguments have often been read as if they pertain to all of us, but feminist interpretations of the last fifteen years or so have revealed the falsity of this 'add women and stir' assumption.[14] Since about the mid-1970s most theorists have tried to avoid, in one way or another, the allegedly generic use of male terms of reference. Instead, they tend to use terms such as 'one', 'he or she', 'men and women', 'persons', or 'selves', or to use masculine and feminine terms of reference alternately in a random manner. The problem with these merely terminological responses to feminist challenges is that they often strain credulity and sometimes result in nonsense. Gender-neutral terms, if used without real awareness of gender, frequently obscure the fact that so much of the real experience of 'persons', so long as they live in gender-structured societies, does in fact depend on what sex they are. Two particularly striking examples should elucidate this point.

First, in *Social Justice in the Liberal State*, Bruce Ackerman in general employs scrupulously gender-neutral language.[15] He breaks with this neutrality only, it seems, to defy existing sex roles; he refers to 'the Commander', who plays the lead role in his theory, as 'she'. However, the argument of the book does not address the existing inequality or role differentiation between the sexes. The full impact of the use of neutral language without gender awareness is revealed in Ackerman's discussion of abortion. A two-page discussion of the topic, with the exception of a single 'she', is written in completely gender-neutral language, in terms of 'parents' and 'foetuses'.[16] The impression given is that there is no relevant respect in which the relationship of a mother to a foetus is different from that of a father. Now it is of course possible to imagine (and in the view of many feminists, it would be desirable to achieve) a society in which differences in the respective relationships of women and men to foetuses would be so slight as reasonably to play only a minor role in a discussion of abortion. Such would be the case in a society without gender—where sex difference carried no social significance, the sexes were equal in power and interdependence, and parenting and earning responsibilities were completely shared. But this is certainly not now the case. Moreover, there is no discussion of this possibility in Ackerman's book. Family life, as so often, seems to be assumed rather than discussed, and the division of labour between the sexes is not considered to be a matter of social justice. In this context, especially on a topic such as abortion, gender-neutral language is very misleading.[17]

Striking examples of false gender neutrality also occur in the works of Alasdair MacIntyre. He is careful in recent works to avoid the old 'generic' male terms of reference, yet his rejection of both liberalism and Marxism has led him into a return to 'our traditions', especially the Aristotelian–Christian tradition, that is fraught with problems from a feminist perspective. When he gives examples of the characters in the stories 'we' need to imbibe, in order for 'our' lives to have coherence as narratives, we find them filled with both assumptions about gender and explicitly negative images of women.[18] Moreover, when MacIntyre confronts feminist criticism of Aristotle as a theorist whose social vision depends centrally on the subordination of women, his response is briefly to refer us to the solution envisaged by Plato.[19] But he makes no mention of the fact that Plato's integration of the guardian women into society rests on his abolition of the family, which seems hardly to be a tenable solution for an Augustinian Christian, as MacIntyre now defines himself. Thus his gender-neutral language remains false, since he has offered no evidence that the traditions he draws on to provide us with moral and political guidance can be adapted so as fully to include women.

Failure on the part of recent political thought to consider the family, and the use of falsely gender-neutral language, have together resulted in the continuing neglect by mainstream theorists of the highly political issue of gender. The language they employ makes little difference to what they actually do, which is to write about men, and about only those women who manage, in spite of the gendered structure of the society in which they live, to adopt patterns of life that have developed to suit men. The fact that human beings are born helpless infants, not the supposedly autonomous actors who populate political theories, is obscured by the implicit assumption of gendered families, operating outside the scope of political theories. To a very large extent, contemporary theory, like that of the past (though less obviously), is about men with wives at home.

FEMINISM AND THE POLITICIZATION OF THE PERSONAL

The neglect of gender in mainstream political theory has persisted despite the persuasive arguments of a generation of feminist scholars, many of whom emerged (whether as radicals, liberals or socialists) from the New Left of the 1960s.[20] As Joan Scott has explained in an influential recent article, 'gender' is a term used by those who claimed that women's scholarship would 'fundamentally transform disciplinary paradigms', that the study of women would 'not only add new subject matter but would also force a critical reexamination of the premises and standards of existing scholarly work'.[21] As I shall explain here, feminist analyses of and discoveries about gender are of crucial significance for political theory, and affect in particular its continuing reliance on the public/domestic dichotomy. I shall show how, by demonstrating the legitimacy of gender as an important category of political and social analysis, and particularly by focusing on gender as itself a social construction needing to *be explained*, feminist scholars have pointed out numerous flaws in the dichotomy and the ways it continues to be used in mainstream political theory. As Pateman has said, 'the separation and opposition between the public and private spheres in liberal theory and practice . . . is, ultimately, what the feminist movement is about'.[22]

A parallel can be drawn here between the critiques of liberalism offered by Marxists and some other socialists, and those offered by feminists. Since Marx wrote *On the Jewish Question* and the *Critique of Hegel's Philosophy of Right*, those on the left, by focusing on class and arguing the close interrelation of political and economic power and practices, have exposed the extent to which the dichotomy between state and society, reified and exaggerated by liberal theory, serves ideological functions. 'The economic is political' is a claim central to the left's challenge to liberalism.[23] In a parallel way, feminist theorists, focusing on gender and arguing that both political and economic power and practices are closely interrelated with the structure and practices of the domestic sphere, have exposed the extent to which the dichotomy between public and domestic, also reified and exaggerated by liberal theory, serves equally ideological functions.[24] The corresponding feminist slogan, of course, is 'the personal is political.'

'The personal is political' is at the root of feminist critiques of the conventional liberal public/domestic dichotomy. This being the case, it is important to start by explaining its origins and its mean-ing. Most nineteenth- and early twentieth-century feminists did not question or challenge women's special role within the family. Indeed, they often argued for women's rights and opportunities, such as education or the suffrage, on the grounds that these would either make them better wives and mothers or enable them to bring their special moral sensibilities, developed in the domestic sphere, to bear on the world of politics.[25] Thus, though they struggled to overturn the legal subordination of wives and claimed equal rights for women in the public sphere, they accepted the prevailing assumption that women's close association with and responsibility for the domestic sphere were natural and inevitable. Even at the beginning of the 'second wave' of feminism in the 1960s, some tried to argue for dismantling all barriers against women in the world of work and politics while at the same time endorsing women's special responsibilities in the family. The contradictions in this acceptance of the 'dual role' of women are clearly evident, for example, in the 1963 report of the Kennedy Commission on the Status of Women.[26] At the opposite end of the spectrum of feminist views, early radical feminists argued that since the family was at the root of women's oppression it must be 'smashed'.[27] It was not long, however, before most feminists developed positions between these two extremes, refusing to accept the division of labour between the sexes as natural and unchangeable, but refusing also to give up on the family. We recognized that the family was not inevitably tied to its gender structure, but that until that structure was successfully challenged there could be no hope of equality for women in either the domes-tic or the public sphere.

In time, then, it was not only radical feminists who turned their attention to the politics of what had previously been regarded as paradigmatically non-political—the personal sphere of sexuality, of housework, of the family. Though not always explicitly stated, 'the personal is political' in fact became the claim that underlay what most feminist thinkers were saying. Feminists of different political leanings and in a variety of disciplines have revealed and analysed the multiple interconnections between women's domestic roles and their inequality and segregation in the workplace, and between their socialization in gendered families and the psychological aspects of their subordination. Thus the family became, and has since remained, central to the politics of feminism and a major focus of feminist theory. Contemporary feminism thus poses a significant challenge to the long-standing underlying assumption of political

SUSAN MOLLER OKIN

theories that the sphere of family and personal life is so separate and distinct from the rest of social life that such theories can legitimately ignore it.

By way of a proviso, I must point out what many feminists who critique the traditional dichotomy of public and domestic do *not* claim, especially because it is a claim rightly associated with some. Jaggar says that both radical and socialist feminists argue for total abolition of the distinction between public and private,[28] while liberal feminists argue for a narrower definition of the private sphere. I do not think this correlation can be drawn so clearly. Many feminists of various political persuasions deny neither the usefulness of a concept of privacy nor the value of privacy in human life. Nor do we deny that there are *some* reasonable distinctions to be made between the public and domestic spheres. Both Pateman and Nicholson, for example, distance themselves from the literal interpretation of 'the personal is political' made by some radical feminists,[29] and I agree with them in not interpreting it as a statement of simple and total identification of the two. Allen argues that many claims important to feminists—from reproductive rights to protection against sexual harassment—are most effectively grounded on women's rights to various types of privacy.[30] And I have argued elsewhere that only in so far as a high degree of equality is maintained within the domestic sphere of family life is its being regarded as a private sphere consistent with the privacy and the physical and socio-economic security of women and children.[31] As Nicholson points out, the question 'How political *is* the personal?' is an important source of tension within both liberal and socialist feminism.[32]

What, then, do other feminists, as well as the most radical, mean by 'the personal is political'? We mean, for one thing, that what happens in personal life, particularly in relations between the sexes, is not immune from the dynamic of *power*, which has typically been seen as a distinguishing feature of the political. And we also mean that neither the realm of domestic, personal life, nor that of non-domestic, economic, and political life, can be understood or interpreted in isolation from the other. Olsen has argued lucidly and most persuasively that the whole notion that the state can choose whether or not to intervene in family life makes no sense at all; the only intelligible question is *how* the state both defines and influences family life.[33] Others have shown that, once the significance of gender is understood, neither the public nor the domestic realm, in terms of its structures and practices, assumptions and expectations, division of labour and distribution of power, can intelligibly be discussed without constant reference to the other. We have demonstrated how the inequalities of men and women in the worlds of work and politics are inextricably related, in a two-way causal cycle, with their inequalities within the family.[34] While very much aware that the actual organization of contemporary society is deeply affected by the prevailing perception of social life as divided into separate and distinct spheres, feminists have argued persuasively that much of this thinking is misleading—and that it operates so as to reify and thus legitimize the gendered structure of society, and to immunize a significant sphere of human life (and especially of women's lives) from the scrutiny to which the political is subjected.

Thus feminists claim that the existing liberal distinction between public and domestic is ideological in the sense that it presents society from a traditional male perspective, that it is based on assumptions about the different natures and natural roles of men and women and that, as presently conceived, it cannot serve as a central concept in a political theory that will, for the first time, include all of us. Challenging the approach of those theorists who still seem silently to assume that female child-rearing and domesticity are 'natural' and therefore fall outside the scope of political inquiry, feminist scholars have argued that the domestic division of labour, and especially the prevalence of female child-rearing, are socially constructed, and therefore matters of political concern. Not only are these major causal factors in the gender structure of society at large, but their continuance cannot itself be explained without reference to elements of the non-domestic sphere, such as the current sex segregation and sex discrimination in the labour force, the scarcity of women in high-level politics, and the structural assumption that workers and holders of political office are not responsible for the care of small children.

FEMINIST SCHOLARSHIP ON GENDER: FROM EXPLANATION TO DECONSTRUCTION

Current theories about gender have resulted from two decades of intensive thought, research, analysis, criticism and argument, rethinking, more research, and reanalysis. Feminist scholars in many disciplines and with some radically different points of view have contributed to the enterprise. Most radical feminist explanations

125

of sexual asymmetry have focused primarily on bodily sexual and reproductive differences.[35] Emphasizing the biological basis of both the social differentiation of the sexes and the domination of women by men, their solutions range from the technological to the separatist. Marxists have tended to see the roots of sex inequality in the realm of production, stressing the connections between patriarchy and capitalism.[36] Socialist feminists have built on the insights of both radical feminism and Marxism, while criticizing the former for ahistoricism and biological determinism, and the latter for insufficient attention to the reproductive dimension of human life.[37] The critical combination of various feminist emphases has led to attempts to understand gender as a social and political construct, *related to but not determined by* biological sex difference. As Scott points out: 'In its most recent usage, "gender" seems to have first appeared among American feminists who wanted to insist upon the fundamentally social quality of distinctions based on sex. The word denoted a rejection of the biological determinism implicit in the use of such terms as "sex" or "sexual difference".'[38] Two major foci of the theories of gender developed by feminists are psychology and history. I shall explain each briefly, for I consider them to be potentially the most significant elements of the new feminist scholarship for political theory.

Psychologically focused complex theories of gender

Psychoanalytic and other psychologically based theories of gender have filled out Simone de Beauvoir's insight, fundamental to the feminist concept of gender, that 'one is not born, but rather becomes, a woman'.[39] They have provided perceptive and complex theories in answer to a crucial question that had not previously been asked, since the answer was assumed self-evident: 'Why do women mother?' One of the earliest, but still most influential, of such explanations is to be found in the psychoanalytically based work of Nancy Chodorow.[40] Chodorow has paid special attention to the effects on the psychological development of both sexes of the fact that, in a gender-structured society such as ours, children of both sexes are raised primarily by women. She has argued, on the basis of object-relations theory, that the experience of individuation—of separating oneself from the caregiver with whom one is at first psychologically fused—is a very different experience for those of the same sex as the nurturer than for those of the opposite sex. In addition, the developmental task of identification with the same-sex parent is very different for girls, for whom this parent is usually present, and for boys, for whom the parent to identify with is often absent for long periods in the day. Thus, she argues, the personality characteristics in women that lead them to be more psychologically connected with others, to be more likely to choose nurturing and to be regarded as especially suited for it, and those in men that lead them to a greater need and capacity for individuation and orientation towards achieving 'public' status, can be explained as originating in the assignation of primary parenting within the existing gender structure itself.

Moreover, as Chodorow makes clear, the complete answer to the question of why women *are* primary parents cannot be arrived at by looking only at the domestic sphere or at the psychology of the sexes.[41] Part of the answer is to be found in the sex segregation of the workplace, where women, despite some recent and much publicized changes among élites, are still concentrated in the lower-paid and more dead-ended occupations. This fact makes it economically 'rational' in most families for women to be the primary childrearers, which keeps the whole cycle of gender going.

It has also been argued that the experiences of *being* a primary nurturer and of growing up with the anticipation of this role are likely to affect women's psychology.[42] In addition, feminist psychologists have indicated the significance for women of the overall experience of growing up in a society in which members of one's sex are in many ways less valued than and subordinated to the other.[43] Once we admit the idea that significant differences between women and men are *created by* the existing division of labour within the family, we begin to see the depth and the extent of the social construction of gender. Such explanations of differences between the sexes in terms of central aspects of the social structure itself reveal the impossibility of developing a human, as opposed to a patriarchal or masculinist, political theory without including discussion of gender, and its linchpin, the family.

Historically and Anthropologically Focused Explanations of Gender

Recently, a number of feminist theorists, while acknowledging that gender seems to have been a feature of all known cultures and historical periods, have stressed the need for resisting unicausal, universalist, and ahistorical explanations of it.[44] These theorists analyse gender as a social construction that has been universally present in human societies but subject to change over time, because it results from a number of complex factors.

Some of the earlier attempts to explain differences between the sexes in terms of social practices placed particular emphasis on the public/domestic dichotomy itself. Anthropologist Rosaldo, for example, argued on the basis of cross-cultural research that the *degree* to which women are subjected to the authority (culturally legitimized power) of men in a given society is correlated with the degree to which the public/domestic dichotomy is stressed.[45] And Ortner argued that there was a more or less universal association in human societies among the dichotomies male/female, culture/nature, and public/private.[46]

As Rosaldo pointed out a few years later, however, these explanations themselves tend towards universalistic and ahistorical accounts of gender. They also tend to reify the public/domestic dichotomy, instead of understanding that it, as well as gender, has differed from one time and place to another. She wrote: 'a model based upon the opposition of two spheres assumes—where it should rather help illuminate and explain—too much about how gender really works,' and saw gender as instead 'the complex product of a variety of social forces.'[47] Rosaldo and, more recently, historian of ideas Linda Nicholson and historian Joan Scott have been major influences in the historicization of the public/domestic opposition and in providing complex, multifaceted accounts of gender. As Nicholson has said, in considering categories of analysis such as public, domestic, and the family, 'we need to ferret out that which is specific to our culture from that which might be truly cross-cultural.'[48]

Such feminists reject the search for *origins* or unicausal explanations of the inequality of the sexes. They see it as a universal phenomenon in one sense, in that it appears to have been present in all known societies and historical periods, but they emphasize that it has taken diverse forms and been affected by various causal factors at different times and in different social contexts. Nicholson stresses the importance of history in comprehending both the public/domestic distinction and gender. She argues against the powerful tendency, particularly present in political theory, to reify the distinction, to perceive it as rigid and timeless.[49] We must recognize, instead, that concepts of public and domestic have not only been used to divide up social life very differently in different periods (for example, production has moved almost entirely from the domestic to the public sphere in the past 300 years), but have also had very different connotations (intimacy, for example, not being seen as characteristically domestic before the late seventeenth century). Nicholson argues persuasively that the gender structure of a particular time and place is causally affected not only by other contemporary structures (economic, political, and so on) but also by the *previous* history of gender, and consequently, that without a historical approach to gender, we can never hope fully to comprehend it.

Scott elaborates a position that similarly stresses the centrality of history. She analyses historical, political, socio-economic, and psychological aspects of the perpetuation of gender, which she too sees as a universal phenomenon taking diverse forms. She looks at, first, cultural myths and symbols (often contradictory) of woman, such as Eve and Mary in the Western Christian tradition; second, normative interpretations of these symbols, expressed in religious, educational, scientific, legal, and political doctrines that categorically fix the 'binary opposition' of male and female, masculine and feminine; third, social institutions—not only family and household, but also sex-segregated labour markets, various educational institutions, and a male-dominated polity—which are all parts of the construction of gender; and fourth, the psychological reproduction of gender in the subjective identity formation of individuals.[50] All of these aspects, Scott emphasizes, must be understood as interrelated and, of course, subject to change over time. The task at hand is to expose the social construction of gender by deconstructing it. This involves 'a refusal of the fixed and permanent quality of the binary opposition, a genuine historicization and deconstruction of the terms of sexual difference . . . [We must] revers[e] and displac[e] its hierarchical construction, rather than accepting it as real or self-evident or in the nature of things.' She adds: 'In a sense, of course, feminists have been doing this for years.'[51]

To the extent to which all this is persuasive—and I think that a great deal of feminist scholarship bears out what Chorodow, Rosaldo, Nicholson, and Scott argue—its impact on political theory could be profound. For in the feminist attempt to comprehend gender we find the personal and the political mixed in a way that confounds the separate categories of public and domestic, and points out the necessary incompleteness of theories of politics that persist in confining themselves to the study of what has been defined in a pre-feminist era as legitimately political. We cannot hope to understand the 'public' spheres—the state of the world of work or the market—without taking account of their genderedness, of the fact that they have been constructed under the assumption of male superiority and dominance, and that they presuppose female responsibility for the domestic sphere. We must ask: would the structure or practices of the workplace, the market, or the legislature be the same if they had developed with the assumption that their participants had to accommodate to the needs of child-bearing, child-rearing, and the responsibilities of domestic life? Would policy-making or its outcomes be the same if those who engaged in them were persons who also had significant day-to-day responsibilities for caring for others, rather than being some of those least likely in the entire society to have such experience? Despite the compelling nature of such questions, and many others like them, most political theory today, remaining unreflective about the old public/domestic dichotomy, fails to consider them.

PRIVACY—FOR WHOM? FROM WHOM?

One reason why the exclusion of women from the scope of ostensibly universal arguments goes unnoticed is that 'the separation of the private and public is presented in liberal theory as if it applied to all individuals in the same way'.[52] Clearly, this is still to a very large extent true of contemporary theory. The liberal idea of the non-intervention of the state into the domestic realm, rather than maintaining neutrality, in fact reinforces existing inequalities within that realm. It is an insight not unique to feminism that the privacy of groups and the privacy of their individual members can conflict, that 'where the privacy of the individual may mean the maximum of freedom for him, the privacy of the group may imply precisely the opposite for the individual'.[53] But it has been primarily feminists and advocates of children's rights who have pointed out in recent years the extent to which the nature of the right to privacy in the domestic sphere has been heavily influenced by the patriarchal nature of liberalism. I shall explore this question here by first looking at some classic liberal defences of domestic privacy, and then pointing out some new problems that have been posed for this conception by recent developments towards the legal equality of women and the advocacy of rights for children.

While Locke's most famous distinctions between political and other forms of power are made in the *Second Treatise of Government*, his strongest arguments for the protection of a private sphere from governmental intrusion or regulation are found in the *Letter on*

Toleration. Here, in this classic argument for *laissez-faire* liberalism, Locke's defence of religious toleration rests in part on an appeal to what he clearly considers to be an already widely recognized right of privacy. In appealing to a realm of 'private domestic affairs' in which no one would consider interfering, he specifies as one of those obviously private things a man's marrying off his daughter.[54] That the daughter herself might have an interest in the choice, and might therefore have a privacy right to choose her own husband, does not seem to have crossed his mind. Nor does the fact that men had, at the time and long after, the legal right to beat their wives and children, and to force sexual intercourse on their wives, cause him any hesitation in specifying that 'all force . . . belongs only to the magistrate', so that private associations may not use force against their members.[55] There is no doubt at all that Locke's privacy rights adhere to male heads of households in their relations with each other, and *not* to their subordinate members in relation to them. This fact, however, is frequently ignored by contemporary liberals who appeal to these rights.[56]

The same assumption is immediately apparent in another, more recent, classic argument for the liberal right to privacy, Warren and Brandeis's 'The Right to Privacy'.[57] The argument starts with the assertion: 'That the individual shall have full protection in person and in property is a principle as old as the common law.' In the very next paragraph, however, the limited meaning of 'individual' is revealed, as we are told that 'man's family relations became a part of the legal conception of his life, and the alienation of a wife's affections was held to be remediable.' Clearly, underlying the law that allowed husbands but not wives to sue third parties for 'alienation of affections' was the notion that a wife fell within the aegis of a man's privacy, much as his property did.

It is all the more remarkable that contemporary discussions of privacy, in referring to such classic sources, do not mention this aspect of them, once we realize that some of these aspects of patriarchy lasted until very recently, and some of them are still with us. While most aspects of *coverture* were abolished in the nineteenth century, forced sexual relations within marriage have only been recognized as rape in English law since the 1990s; they have become so recognized in fewer than half of the states of the USA, and there only since the late 1970s. Moreover, recent studies have shown that from 10 to 14 per cent of married women in the USA have suffered sexual assaults by their husbands that would qualify under the legal definitions of rape or attempted rape had they been committed by someone else.[58] Wife-beating was clearly illegalized in Britain only in 1962, and though now illegal, the prevalence of the practice, long denied and hidden, was 'rediscovered' both in Britain and in the USA in the 1970s. A recent US government study of marital violence in Kentucky found that 9 per cent of women had been kicked or bitten, struck with a fist or object, beaten up, or either threatened or attacked with a knife or gun by the male partner they lived with, and some estimates of actual incidence are far higher.[59] The 'full protection [of the individual] of person and in property' is still not provided by the law for many women, for whom their home, in all its privacy, may be the most dangerous of all places.

The patriarchal nature of liberal notions of domestic privacy is being significantly challenged by the increasing demand from feminists and children's rights advocates that individuals within families have privacy rights that sometimes need protection against the family unit. In a number of important recent decisions about privacy, the US Supreme Court has been grappling with this issue. Until the last two decades, decisions of the Court that rested on a presumed constitutional right of family privacy roughly followed the old model, and some still do; they confirmed the rights of *families* (in practice, therefore, those of their more powerful members) to make decisions regulating their members.

The attitude of the Court's majority about traditional sex roles changed distinctly during the 1970s. So also, for the most part, did its decisions regarding privacy issues. Most earlier rulings that had upheld the rights of families—for example, to educate their children in the school of their choice, to have their children educated bilingually, or even to be exempted on religious grounds from a state compulsory education statute—had generally followed the notion that domestic privacy entailed the protection of the family's freedom to make decisions regarding its individual members.[60] In practice, this notion of the family as a single entity having rights against the state in regulating its members reinforced the authority of husbands over wives and parents over children.[61] More recently, in some (though not all) decisions, the Court has moved in the direction of viewing privacy rights as rights of individuals rather than of families. This notion of what might more appropriately be called privacy within the family than family privacy gives constitutional protection to the rights of individual family members even against the preferences of more powerful family members, or the collective decision of the family as a whole. Thus, for example, rights to make decisions about contraception and abortion, while first upheld by the Court under the rubric of family or marital privacy, soon evolved into rights of individuals, whether married or not, and sometimes constitute rights against families, viewed as collective entities.

The speed of this development can be seen by comparing a series of cases concerning contraception and abortion. In 1965 the Court held that the right of married couples to use contraceptives was part of 'a right of privacy older than the Bill of Rights' that 'protected the sacred precincts of marital bedrooms'. By 1972, while citing this precedent, the Court declared: 'If the right to privacy means any-thing, it is the right of the *individual*, married or single, to be free from unwarranted governmental intrusion into matters so funda-mentally affecting a person as the decision whether to bear or beget a child.' The following year, the individual woman's right of privacy was the basis on which state laws prohibiting abortion were declared unconstitutional, and this was confirmed by subsequent decisions that struck down laws requiring spousal or parental consent for abortion.[62] What had quickly developed from a notion of marital privacy consistent with the patriarchal conceptions of Locke or Warren and Brandeis were individual rights of women and minors that these earlier liberals would have found incomprehensible. As Minow concludes: 'Legal protections for families have often rein-forced patriarchal family relations, yet the rhetoric of legal rights has also provided a basis for protecting individuals against the patriar-chal family.'[63] These cases, many of them involving difficult and highly controversial issues, have finally brought into the light of day a fundamental problem long obscured by the public/domestic rhetoric that enabled a highly patriarchal liberalism to appear indi-vidualistic from its beginnings.

CONCLUSIONS: GENDER AND THE VALUE OF PRIVACY

While feminists challenge much in political theory that has depended upon the traditional public/domestic dichotomy, few of us would deny the value of personal privacy. When we look at the arguments of mainstream liberal theorists about some of the rea-sons for and the value of having a private sphere, however, it seems that, unaware of the significance of gender, they unselfconsciously assume the perspective of a person who is not primarily responsible for the work and the organization of domestic life. Since it seems likely that women need privacy for much the same reasons as men do, the final question I wish to address here is whether and to what extent they are likely to *find* it in the domestic sphere, in a gender-structured society. Three reasons that are often given for the value of privacy are that it is necessary for the development of intimate personal relations, that it is an essential sphere in which we can temporarily shed our public 'roles', and that it gives us the freedom to develop our mental and creative capacities. Let us look at each of these in turn, with gender in mind.

A number of theorists argue that private space is needed as a prerequisite for intimacy.[64] The family, with its private domestic household, is often specified as the space in which this personal intimacy is to be found. Clearly there is no reason to doubt that women *need* privacy for this reason, just as much as men do; the question that is raised by awareness of gender is how likely they are to *find* it, in the domestic sphere. Some feminists have argued that real intimacy or love between the sexes is incompatible with the condition of sexual inequality.[65] Moreover this claim is reinforced by one of the points made by those who argue that privacy is essential for intimacy. Pennock, for example, specifies that the kind of small groups necessary for intimacy must be ones in which 'ultimate reliance upon force (the distinctive element of the political) is entirely absent'.[66] But this condition, of course, is not met for all in the domestic sphere, and especially not for the many women and children who live with the daily experience of physical abuse and the many more who live under the constant threat of it. For them, the domestic sphere does not provide the kind of privacy in which intimacy is likely to flourish.

Another recurrent argument for the importance of a private sphere is that it is needed as an escape from the tension of maintaining the various public roles in which most of 'one's' life is presumably occupied. Since, it is claimed, there exists a gap between a natural person and the roles he (*sic*) bears, only in a private realm in which he can get out of these roles will there be room for the development of personality.[67] Privacy is a kind of 'backstage' where the social actor can put on and take off his masks. That this claim involves problems for those who find the domestic sphere paradigmatic of privacy is immediately apparent once gender is considered.[68] If there *is* a need for this kind of privacy, if we need, for the development of personality, a backstage where we can temporarily shed our social roles, then most women are unlikely to find it in the domestic sphere. Whether or not they also have non-domestic roles, far more is generally expected of them in their roles as mothers and family caretakers than is expected of men in their family roles. This is evidenced by the fact that publicly successful men, but not women, are still often excused for neglecting their families. Indeed, a whole different standard of what constitutes 'neglect of one's family' is generally applied to women, just as 'mothering' a child means something entirely different from 'fathering' one.

It is interesting that some of those who have written recently about privacy as a sphere for unmasking have questioned whether it is in fact to be found in the private home, or whether it may be better found somewhere else.[69] Perhaps the raising of this question is due to the fact that, with the entry of more mothers into the workforce, some men are not so well 'buffered' from the needs of their children as they once were. Thus the demands of the role of father are intruding more into their previously private realms at home. Ryan seems to suggest this, when in the course of an argument for private home ownership, he suddenly concedes that a private home is in certain respects *not* the most private of places. He says, 'Many men at least feel that their privacy is a great deal more secure in an office whose door will not be opened by every Tom, Dick and Harry than it is in their own homes, where young Samantha may come bursting through the bedroom or bathroom door at any moment.'[70] It is worth asking why Ryan attributes this feeling that their privacy is more likely to be violated at home than in the office to 'many men at least' when, given the current division of labour in most households, it is much likelier to be her mother's than her father's privacy that young Samantha will invade. Perhaps, realistically, he means to allude to the fact that a man is far more likely than a woman to *have* an office from which he can shut out Tom, Dick, and Harry (as well as Samantha, of course). All of which goes to show that arguments about privacy frequently do not have the same ring when we think about them with any consciousness of gender. 'Many men' and 'many women' are not likely, in current social conditions, to find the same extent of privacy for unmasking, or to find it in the same places.

Closely related to this argument for privacy as backstage is the argument for privacy as space for mental self-development. Solitude and the opportunity to concentrate are central to this defence of a private sphere. But as feminists have long been aware, this aspect of privacy too is far less available to women than to men so long as the present gender structure lasts.[71] Even assuming the presence of domestic servants, J. S. Mill cited women's being 'expected to have

135

[their] time and faculties always at the disposal of everybody' as part of the explanation for their lesser achievements in the arts and sciences.[72] Similar reasoning led Virginia Woolf to her conclusion that in order to be a writer a woman must start out with an independent living and 'a room of her own'. It is still very much the case that, for men, having a family is far less in tension with artistic or other creative achievement than it is for women, and many women feel that they must choose between the two. As those who have refused to make this choice testify, it is exceedingly difficult under current conditions for a woman to have her work, her children, and her relationship with a male partner all flourishing at the same time.

The assumption that a clear and simple distinction can be drawn between the political and the personal, the public and the domestic, has been basic to liberal theory at least since Locke, and remains as a foundation of much political theory today. As feminist theorists have demonstrated, this fundamental division was based in the culture and social practices of patriarchy, and it cannot last unchanged if the long era of patriarchy is to end. While some feminists have argued that there is no need to maintain a private sphere, many, including myself, would agree with mainstream liberal theorists about the need for a sphere of privacy and, on the whole, with the reasons for that need.[73] I have suggested here that women, just as much as men, need privacy for the development of intimate relations with others, for the space to shed their roles temporarily, and for the time by themselves that contributes to the development of the mind and of creativity. And I conclude that the institutions and practices of gender will have to be greatly altered if women are to have equal opportunities with men either for participating in the non-domestic spheres such as work, the market, and politics, or for benefiting from the advantages that privacy has to offer.[74] We must aim at a society in which men and women will share as equals the nurturing and other domestic tasks that mainstream political thought has explicitly assumed, and continues by its silence about gender and the family implicitly to assume, are 'naturally' women's. As has already happened to some extent with food production, child care, and health care, activities that have previously taken place in the domestic sphere will move outside it. The boundary between the two, never as distinct in fact as in theory, will continue to fluctuate. While we need to maintain some protection of personal and private life from intrusion and control, the dichotomy between public and domestic is not likely, in the theory or the practices of a gender-free world, to be anything like as distinct as that which has prevailed in mainstream political theory from the seventeenth century to the present.

Notes

1. I shall confine my discussion here to Western theories and the cultures from which they emanate. For an interesting cross-cultural study of privacy and the public/private dichotomy (including discussion of the theories and practices of the classical Greeks, Hebrews, ancient Chinese and contemporary Eskimos), see Barrington Moore, Jr., *Privacy: Studies in Social and Cultural History* (Armonk, NY: Sharpe, 1984). Moore concludes that although what is private and the extent to which privacy is valued differ considerably from one society to another, 'it seems highly likely that all civilized societies display some awareness of the conflict between public and private interests', and he finds no culture which does not value privacy of some sort.

2. See Hyman Gross, 'Privacy and Autonomy', Ernest van den Haag, 'On Privacy', and W. L. Weinstein, 'The Private and the Free: A Conceptual Inquiry', in J. Roland Pennock and John W. Chapman (eds.), *Privacy* (*Nomos* XIII) (New York: Atherton, 1971); Anita L. Allen, *Uneasy Access: Privacy for Women in a Free Society* (Totowa, NJ: Rowman and Littlefeld, 1988), esp. chs. 1 and 2.

3. S. I. Benn and G. F. Gaus (eds.), *Public and Private in Social Life* (London: Croom Helm, 1983).

4. Carole Pateman, 'Feminist Critiques of the Public/Private Dichotomy', in Benn and Gaus (eds.), *Public and Private in Social Life*; see also Frances E. Olsen, 'The Family and the Market: A Study of Ideology and Legal Reform', *Harvard Law Review*, 96 (1983), 7, 1497–1578.

5. Stuart Hampshire (ed.), *Public and Private Morality* (Cambridge: Cambridge University Press, 1978).

6. W. L. Weinstein, 'The Private and the Free: A Conceptual Inquiry', in Pennock and Chapman (eds.), *Privacy*, 32–5.

7. Much of feminist political theory to date has been concerned with formulating critiques of these arguments and analysing the impact of such critiques on the theories. See e.g. Lorenne Clark and Lynda Lange, *The Sexism of Social and Political Thought* (Toronto: University of Toronto Press, 1979); Jean Bethke Elshtain, *Public Man, Private Woman: Women in Social and Political Thought* (Princeton: Princeton University Press, 1981); Susan Moller Okin, *Women in Western Political Thought* (Princeton: Princeton University Press, 1979); Carole Pateman and Elizabeth Gross (eds.), *Feminist Challenges: Social and Political Theory* (Boston: Northeastern University Press, 1987); Carole Pateman and Mary L. Shanley, *Feminist Critiques of Political Theory* (Cambridge: Policy, 1990).

8. John Locke, *Two Treatises of Government*, ed. Peter Laslett (Cambridge: Cambridge University Press, 1960), 308.

9. Susan Moller Okin, 'Women and the Making of the Sentimental Family', *Philosophy and Public Affairs*, 11 (1982), 1, 65–8; Carole Pateman, ' "The Disorder of Women": Women, Love, and the Sense of Justice', *Ethics*, 91 (1980), 1, 20–34.

10. See e.g. Bruce A. Ackerman, *Social Justice in the Liberal State* (New Haven: Yale

University Press, 1980); Ronald Dworkin, *Taking Rights Seriously* (Cambridge, Mass.: Harvard University Press, 1977); William A. Galston, *Justice and the Human Good* (Chicago: University of Chicago Press, 1980); Robert Nozick, *Anarchy, State and Utopia* (New York: Basic Books, 1974).

11. John Rawls, *A Theory of Justice* (Cambridge, Mass.: Harvard University Press, 1971); see Deborah Kearns, 'A Theory of Justice—and Love: Rawls on the Family', *Politics* (Journal of the Australasian Political Studies Association), 18 (1983), 2, 36–42; Susan Moller Okin, 'Justice and Gender', *Philosophy and Public Affairs*, 16 (1987), 1, 42–72, and 'Reason and Feeling in Thinking about Justice', *Ethics*, 99 (1989), 2, 229–49.

12. James S. Fishkin, *Justice, Equal Opportunity, and the Family* (New Haven: Yale University Press, 1983).

13. Michael L. Walzer, *Spheres of Justice* (New York: Basic Books, 1983); Philip Green, *Retrieving Democracy: In Search of Civic Equality* (Totowa, NJ: Rowman and Allanheld, 1985); Allan Bloom, *The Closing of the American Mind* (New York: Simon and Schuster, 1987); Michael J. Sandel, *Liberalism and the Limits of Justice* (Cambridge: Cambridge University Press, 1982).

14. See n. 7 above.

15. Ackerman, *Social Justice in the Liberal State*.

16. Ibid. 127–8.

17. Consider, for example, Ackerman's hypothesis: 'Suppose a couple simply *enjoy* abortions so much that they conceive embryos simply to kill them a few months later?' (ibid. 128).

18. Alasdair MacIntyre, *After Virtue* (Notre Dame: University of Notre Dame Press, 1st edition, 1981), 201.

19. Alasdair MacIntyre, *Whose Justice? Which Rationality?* (Notre Dame: University of Notre Dame Press, 1988), 105.

20. The most comprehensive analyses of the variety of theories and practices of recent feminism are Alison M. Jaggar, *Feminist Politics and Human Nature* (Totowa, NJ: Rowman and Allanheld, 1983), and Rosemarie Tong, *Feminist Thought: A Comprehensive Introduction* (Boulder, Colo.: Westview, 1989). For a very good, briefer analysis, see Linda J. Nicholson, *Gender and History* (New York: Columbia University Press, 1986), parts 1 and 2.

21. Joan W. Scott, 'Gender: A Useful Category of Historical Analysis', *American Historical Review*, 91 (1986), 5, 1054.

22. Carole Pateman, 'Feminist Critiques of the Public/Private Dichotomy', in Benn and Gaus (eds.), *Public and Private in Social Life*, 281.

23. See G. F. Gaus, 'Public and Private Interests in Liberal Political Economy, Old and New', in Benn and Gaus (eds.), *Public and Private in Social Life*, citing Galbraith and Lindblom; Pateman, 'Feminist Critiques of the Public/Private Dichotomy', on Wolin and Habermas; and Walzer, *Spheres of Justice*, esp. ch. 12.

24. Olsen, 'The Family and the Market', 1560–78.

25. Jean Bethke Elshtain, 'Moral Woman/Immoral Man: The Public/Private Distinction and its Political Ramifications', *Politics and Society*, 4 (1974), 4, 453–73.

26. See Nicholson, *Gender and History*, 20, 58.

27. Firestone's argument, unique but for a time influential within the movement, went further: locating women's oppression in their reproductive biology, she argued that equality between the sexes could occur only with the attainment

and use of techniques of artificial reproduction. Shulamith Firestone, *The Dialectic of Sex* (New York: William Morrow, 1971).

28. Jaggar, *Feminist Politics and Human Nature*, 145, 254.

29. Pateman, 'Feminist Critiques of the Public/Private Dichotomy'; Nicholson, *Gender and History*.

30. Allen, *Uneasy Access*.

31. Susan Moller Okin, *Justice, Gender, and the Family* (New York: Basic Books, 1989).

32. Nicholson, *Gender and History*, 19.

33. Frances E. Olsen, 'The Myth of State Intervention in the Family', *University of Michigan Journal of Law Reform*, 18 (1985), 1, 835–64.

34. Barbara R. Bergmann, *The Economic Emergence of Women* (New York: Basic Books, 1986); Kathleen Gerson, *Hard Choices: How Women Decide about Work, Career, and Motherhood* (Berkeley: University of California Press, 1985); Okin, *Justice, Gender, and the Family*.

35. Firestone, *The Dialectic of Sex*; Susan Brownmiller, *Against Our Will: Men, Women and Rape* (New York: Bantam, 1975); Catharine A. MacKinnon, 'Feminism, Marxism, Method, and the State: An Agenda for Theory', *Signs*, 7 (1982), 3; Mary Daly, *Gyn/Ecology: The Metaethics of Radical Feminism* (Boston: Beacon Press, 1978), and some French and English Lacanian feminists; however, compare MacKinnon, *Feminism Unmodified* (Cambridge, Mass.; Harvard University Press, 1987) and Adrienne Rich, 'Compulsory Heterosexuality and Lesbian Existence', *Signs*, 5 (1980), 4.

36. Frederick Engels, 'The Origin of the Family, Private Property and the State', in *Karl Marx and Frederick Engels: Selected Works*, ii. (Moscow: Foreign Language Publishing House, 1955); Heidi Hartmann, 'Capitalism, Patriarchy and Job Segregation by Sex', in Z. Eisenstein (ed.), *Capitalist Patriarchy and the Case for Socialist Feminism* (New York: Monthly Review Press, 1979).

37. Jaggar, *Feminist Politics and Human Nature*.

38. Scott, 'Gender', 1054.

39. Simone de Beauvoir, *The Second Sex*, trans. H. M. Parshley (New York: Vintage Books, 1974), 301.

40. Nancy Chodorow, 'Family Structure and Feminine Personality', in M. Z. Rosaldo and L. Lamphere (eds.), *Woman, Culture, and Society* (Stanford, Calif.: Stanford University Press, 1974), 43–66, and *The Reproduction of Mothering* (Berkeley, University of California Press, 1978).

41. Here my reading of Chodorow differs from that of Scott, who says that her interpretation 'limits the concept of gender to family and household experience and, for the historian, leaves no way to connect the concept (or the individual) to other social systems of economy, politics or power'. Scott, 'Gender', 1063. Cf. Chodorow, *The Reproduction of Mothering*, 214–15; also Nicholson, *Gender and History*, 84–8.

42. Sara Ruddick, 'Maternal Thinking', *Feminist Studies*, 6 (1980), 2; Jane Flax, 'The Conflict Between Nurturance and Autonomy in Mother–Daughter Relationships and Within Feminism', *Feminist Studies*, 4 (1978), 2.

43. Jean Baker Miller, *Toward a New Psychology of Women* (Boston: Beacon Press, 1976); Jaggar, *Feminist Politics and Human Nature*.

44. See especially Michelle Z. Rosaldo, 'The Use and Abuse of Anthropology', *Signs*, 5 (1980), 3, 389–417; Nicholson, *Gender and History*; and Scott, 'Gender'.

45. Rosaldo, 'Women, Culture and Society: A Theoretical Overview' in Rosaldo

and Lamphere (eds.), *Women, Culture and Society* (Stanford University Press, 1974).

46. Sherry B. Ortner, 'Is Female to Male as Nature is to Culture?', in Rosaldo and Lamphere (eds.), *Woman, Culture, and Society*, 67–87.

47. Rosaldo, 'The Use and Abuse of Anthropology', 399, 401.

48. Nicholson, *Gender and History*, 83.

49. Ibid.; also Olsen, 'The Family and the Market', esp. 1566.

50. Scott, 'Gender', 1067–9.

51. Ibid. 1065–6.

52. Pateman, 'Feminist Critiques of the Public/Private Dichotomy', 283.

53. Arnold Simmel, 'Privacy is Not an Isolated Freedom', in Pennock and Chapman (eds.), *Privacy*, 86.

54. John Locke, *A Letter Concerning Toleration* (Indianapolis: Bobbs-Merrill, 1950), 28–9.

55. Ibid. 23–4.

56. Pateman and Nicholson both provide excellent commentaries on this contradiction of liberal individualism, its basis in individual rights and its denial of such rights to women (Pateman, 'Feminist Critiques of the Public/Private Dichotomy'; Nicholson, *Gender and History*, esp. chs. 5 and 7). Both the fact and the feminist challenge to it are noted briefly by Benn and Gaus (*Public and Private in Social Life*, 38), but this has little effect on their subsequent discussion, in which they proceed as if liberal rights or privacy adhered to everyone in the same way.

57. Samuel D. Warren and Louis D. Brandeis, 'The Right to Privacy', *Harvard Law Review*, 4 (1890), 5, 193–220.

58. David Finkelhor and Kersti Yllo, *License to Rape: Sexual Abuse of Wives* (New York: Free Press, 1985), ch. 1.

59. *A Survey of Spousal Violence Against Women in Kentucky* (Washington, DC: Law Enforcement Assistance Administration, 1979); see also R. Emerson Dobash and Russell Dobash, *Violence against Wives* (New York: Free Press, 1979), on marital violence in Scotland.

60. *Pierce* v. *Society of Sisters*, 268 US (1925); *Meyers* v. *Nebraska*, 262 US (1923); *Wisconsin* v. *Yoder*, 406 US (1972). One exception to this was *Prince* v. *Massachusetts*, 321 US (1944), in which a Child Labor Law was upheld against the claim of the plaintiff that its prohibition on her allowing her nine-year-old niece to distribute religious literature was in violation of both her niece's freedom of religion and parental rights to control the child's religious upbringing.

61. Olsen, 'The Family and the Market', 1504–13, 1521–2; Nikolas Rose, 'Beyond the Public/Private Division: Law, Power and the Family', *Journal of Law and Society*, 14 (1987), 1, 61–76.

62. The cases referred to are: *Griswold* v. *Connecticut*, 381 US (1965); *Eisenstadt* v. *Baird*, 405 US (1972); *Roe* v. *Wade*, 410 US (1973); *Planned Parenthood* v. *Danforth*, 428 US (1976); *Carey* v. *Population Services International*, 431 US (1976); and *Bellotti* v. *Baird*, 443 US (1976).

63. Martha Minow, 'We, the Family: Constitutional Right and American Families', *The American Journal of History*, 74, 3, 978. As Minow notes, *Parham* v. *J.R.*, 442 US (1979), while recent, is an example of the former; in this case, the Court upheld the right of parents to commit children to mental hospitals without such legal safeguards as apply in the case of adults.

64. Charles Fried, 'Privacy', in Graham Hughes (ed.), *Law, Reason, and Justice*

(New York: New York University Press, 1969), 145–69; Stanley I. Benn, 'Privacy, Freedom, and Respect for Persons', in Pennock and Chapman (eds.), *Privacy*; Ruth Gavison, 'Information Control: Availability and Exclusion', and Alan Ryan, 'Public and Private Property', in Benn and Gaus (eds.), *Public and Private in Social Life*.

65. Firestone, *The Dialectic of Sex*; Elizabeth Rapaport, 'On the Future of Love: Rousseau and the Radical Feminists', in C. Gould and M. Wartofsky (eds.), *Women and Philosophy* (New York: Putnam, 1980).

66. J. Roland Pennock, 'Introduction', in Pennock and Chapman (eds.), *Privacy*, p. xv.

67. Benn, 'Privacy, Freedom, and Respect for Persons'; Gavison, 'Information Control'; and Ryan, 'Public and Private Property'.

68. Olsen, 'The Family and the Market', 1565.

69. Ryan, 'Public and Private Property'; S. I. Benn and G. F. Gaus, 'The Public and the Private: Concepts and Action', in Benn and Gaus (eds.), *Public and Private in Social Life*.

70. Ryan, 'Public and Private Property', in Benn and Gaus (eds.), *Public and Private in Social Life*, 241.

71. See Allen, *Uneasy Access*, chs. 2 and 3 for comprehensive and careful argument of this point. Class, as well as gender, is likely to affect considerably one's chances of enjoying the privacy that is needed for intimacy, unmasking, and mental development. Thus élite women may enjoy more of these aspects of privacy than working-class men, and working- or underclass women are least likely to enjoy them.

72. J. S. Mill, *The Subjection of Women* (Indianapolis: Hackett, 1988), 80.

73. See also Allen, *Uneasy Access*.

74. See also Okin, *Justice, Gender, and the Family*, esp. chs. 6–8.

6 Feminism and Democracy

Jane Mansbridge

For centuries, while men ran governments and wrote political philosophy, the experience of women had little influence on democratic practice or thought. Recently, however, feminist ideas have been at the centre of an emerging debate about the nature of democratic politics.

The dominant tradition in political science sees democracy primarily as a method of summing up individual desires rooted in self-interest. The tradition's critics emphasize that any workable democracy requires that its citizens and representatives think not only as 'I', but also as 'we'. Democracy involves public discussion of common problems, not just a silent counting of individual hands. And when people talk together, the discussion can sometimes lead the participants to see their own stake in the broader interests of the community. Indeed, at its best, the democratic process resolves conflict not only by majority will, but by discovering answers that integrate the interests of minorities. Thus a 'deliberative democracy' does not simply register preferences that individuals already have; it encourages citizens to think about their interests differently.

Two strands of feminist writing illuminate the debate on deliberative democracy. One strand, which celebrates women's greater nurturance, modifies and enriches the deliberative framework by providing images and models of practice from women's experience. In this view, women's socialization and role in child-rearing, among other causes, makes them especially concerned to transform 'I' into 'we' and to seek solutions to conflict that accommodate diverse and often suppressed desires. In our society women are usually brought up to identify their own good with that of others, especially their children and husbands. More than men, women build their identities through relationships with friends. As Jennifer Nedelsky puts it, the female self has more 'permeable' boundaries. Feminist writers

Reprinted by permission from *The American Prospect*, 1/1 (Spring 1991), 126–39. Copyright © *The American Prospect*, P.O. Box 383080, Cambridge, MA 02138 (1991). For an expanded version of this article, see Jane Mansbridge, 'Feminism and Democratic Community', in John W. Chapman and Ian Shapiro (eds.), *Democratic Community*: NOMOS XXXV (New York University Press, 1993).

propose this capacity for broader self-definition as a model for democratic politics.

Yet, as feminists are also well aware, the very capacity to identify with others can easily be manipulated to the disadvantage of women. A second strand of feminist thought, which focuses on male oppression, warns against deliberation serving as a mask for domination. Permeability, Andrea Dworkin demonstrates, is the avenue for invasion as well as intimacy. The transformation of 'I' into 'we' brought about through political deliberation can easily mask subtle forms of control. Even the language people use as they reason together usually favours one way of seeing things and discourages others. Subordinate groups sometimes cannot find the right voice or words to express their thoughts, and when they do, they discover that they are not heard. Feminists who focus on the inequality of power between men and women point to the ways women are silenced, encouraged to keep their wants inchoate, and heard to say 'yes' when they mean 'no'. These same insights help us to grasp other forms of domination, such as those based on wealth, that can also infect the deliberative process.

So, as political theorists turn to thinking about democracy as deliberation, feminist thought lends both encouragement and caution. Feminists bring to the new stress on deliberation experiences of a self accustomed to encompassing others' welfare in its own and achieving that common welfare more by persuasion than by power. Yet feminists also bring a vivid recognition of the capacity of a dominant group to silence or ignore voices it does not wish to hear.

DEMOCRACY AS DELIBERATION

Democracy originally meant deliberative democracy. Aristotle, while not a democrat, still concluded that the people in their deliberative capacity could come to better decisions on many matters than could an expert—'just as a feast to which many contribute is better than one provided by a single person'. The great writers on democracy in the eighteenth and nineteenth centuries saw democracy as primarily a way of reasoning together to promote the common good. James Madison thought that factions pitted against one another could cancel each other out, allowing men of public virtue the space to deliberate and make wise decisions. John Stuart Mill argued that the most important business of a representative assembly was 'talk', bringing to bear different perspectives on the public's interests. Before the Second World War, Ernest Barker, the great translator of Aristotle's *Politics*, defined democracy not, in its essence, as a matter of voting, but rather as 'a method of government by laying heads together, in a common debate in which all share, to attain a result which as many as possible are agreed in accepting'.

The political thought that emerged from World War II reversed this emphasis on deliberation and the common good, demanding the recognition of power and conflict. Schools of thought as disparate and mutually contradictory as those of Marx, Freud, Arthur Bentley (founder of the group conflict view of politics), and neoclassical economics all assumed a political world based on self-interest, power, and competing interests.

In 1942 the economist Joseph Schumpeter formalized a deeply influential theory that recast democracy as a marketplace. In democracy, as Schumpeter understood it, there is no common good or public interest. Voters pursue their individual interests by making demands on the political system in proportion to the intensity of their feelings. Politicians, also pursuing their own interests, adopt policies that buy them votes, thus ensuring accountability. To stay in office, politicians act like entrepreneurs and brokers, looking for formulas that satisfy as many interests as possible. The decisions that emerge from the interchange between self-interested voters and self-interested brokers come as close as possible to a balanced sum of individual interests. In politics as marketplace, candidates are commodities, selling themselves or being sold.

For a generation, in American political science, Schumpeter's formulation underlay the dominant understanding of democratic practice. It also seemed to many to represent a democratic ideal. The study of pluralism, interest groups and who gets what, where, when, and how, typically assumed that citizens (and their representatives) were self-interested and that interests would conflict. Most of those who criticized the American polity, whether from the right, the mainstream, or the left, also agreed with these underlying assumptions about politics as power.

Ten years ago, the tide began to turn again. A few political scientists began to point out that some legislative actions were inexplicable unless representatives cared about good public policy as well as re-election. Legislators in the House and Senate, for example, voted in the late 1970s and early 1980s to deregulate the airline and trucking industries, a move they thought would benefit the public. They did so against strong lobbying by both the unions and the industries, which had close relations with the regulatory commissions. Political scientists now also noticed that citizens took stands on issues like Vietnam and bussing less because the policy they favoured would benefit them than because they thought that policy was right.

In small towns the concern of citizens for the common good was, if anything, even stronger. My own study of a small New England town and a collectively run workplace convinced me that the implicit theory of democracy in these small polities differed sharply from Schumpeter's marketplace model. Schumpeter handled conflict, in theory, by counting and weighing preferences. The members of the communities I came to know assumed that on many issues there was a common good and that reasoning together—deliberation—could let them discover or create that good.[1]

When recent democratic theorists reject the conception of democracy as only a mechanism for aggregating conflicting and self-interested preferences, they draw on several independent philosophical traditions. J. G. A. Pocock and Garry Wills have demonstrated that the framers of the American Constitution, far from reflecting only Lockean individualism, wanted to promote both public spirit and benevolence. Pocock traces the concern for public spirit to Machiavelli's writing on the corruption of republican virtue in Florence; Wills traces the concern for benevolence to the Scottish Enlightenment. Cass Sunstein argues that the United States Supreme Court has never countenanced a theory of democracy based purely on aggregating preferences. Although the Court will generally not look beneath the rationale that legislators present, it has always insisted in principle that legislation be guided by a public interest. Jürgen Habermas, writing on public spaces and the characteristics of an ideal 'speech situation', has inspired many to ask what institutions and structures of power are most hospitable to public deliberation.

The new deliberative theorists have suggested various institutional changes to renew the democratic process.

- *Infusions of direct democracy.* Decentralizing some decisions to neighbourhood assemblies and relying more on city, state, and national referenda might help promote deliberation. Benjamin Barber suggests that the first stage of a referendum be multiple choice, phrased to allow voters to express their intensity of support and to endorse a principle but not the specific proposal. That stage might be tied to attendance at a deliberative neighbourhood assembly. The second stage, after a deliberative period of several months, would be the more traditional yes/no ballot.

- *Election reforms.* The framework of campaign debates is a proper subject for legislation. The League of Women Voters' format for debates should be reinstated and expanded to cover candidates on the state and city levels. Public funds should finance large blocks of television time for discussing the issues. And by closing schools and stores and prohibiting sports events on election day as well as the last day of campaigns, the nation could explicitly set aside time for discussion and voter registration. The purpose would be symbolic as well as practical: to signal the value and importance of public discussion.
- *Policy juries.* Governments could empanel a representative sample of an affected population to review evidence, deliberate on specific policy issues, and advise the appropriate legislature. Minnesota's experiments with policy juries give legislators a better grasp of considered public opinion than do surveys; and the juries' deliberations give participants and their friends a chance to exert creative influence over policy.

The quality of deliberation makes or breaks a democracy. Good deliberation produces, along with good solutions, the emotional and intellectual resources to accept hard decisions. Active participation in decisions makes it easier to bear—and understand the reasons for—the losses some decisions entail. The manipulation of participation generates cynicism both in the factory and the polity. Deliberation that accords respect to all participants and rests outcomes on reasons and points of view that stand up under questioning generates outcomes that even opponents can respect.

Theorists who promote deliberation, however, sometimes conflate deliberation and the common good. The language not only of Mill and Barker but also of more recent theorists like Benjamin Barber and Joshua Cohen suggests that deliberation must be deliberation on the common good. Deliberation, in this view, must be framed in terms of 'we'; claims of self-interest are invalid. Yet ruling self-interest out of order makes it harder for any participant to sort out what is going on. In particular, the less powerful may not find ways to discover that the prevailing sense of 'we' does not adequately include them. Deliberation, and the political process more broadly speaking, ought to make participants more aware of their real interests, even when those interests turn out to conflict.

Deliberative theorists also sometimes forget power. When, as often happens, no policy will benefit everyone, democracies require some way of legitimating a process by which one group of people makes another do something that it does not want to do. To avoid giving too much weight to the status quo, democracies must facilitate some exercise of power. They can legitimate the coercion by, in theory, giving each citizen equal power in the process. The system succeeds where each loses on some issues but wins on others. Feminism, in both its nurturant and anti-oppression strands, can correct the vision of both the unrealistically 'hard-nosed' political scientists who insist that politics is nothing but power and the deliberative theorists who either reject power altogether or overlook the ways the powerful often use to their advantage the openness of deliberation, its procedures, and the orientation of many participants toward the common good.

NURTURANCE: A POLITICS WITHOUT POWER?

Politics without domination is an ideal with a long ancestry on both its paternal and maternal sides. Claude Henri de Saint-Simon, an early prophet of socialism, and Edward Bellamy, the nineteenth-century American utopian, both wanted to replace the government of men by the administration of things. Karl Marx envisioned the withering away of 'political power properly so called', that is, class domination. John Stuart Mill and Ernest Barker replaced crude power not with administration but with deliberation. Yet when women arrived at their own understanding of politics without domination, their language often carried overtones of their experiences as mothers. The outcome was not quite the same. Nurturance—a particular form of making the other's good your own—invaded the political sphere.

In 1818, Hannah Mather Crocker, an early feminist, argued in almost the same breath that God had 'endowed the female mind with equal powers and faculties' to those of men and that 'it must be the appropriate duty and privilege of females, to convince by reason and persuasion'. One hundred years later the suffragists used the same formula of equality with difference. Strategically, the suffragists relied on persuasion because they had little political power. Yet many also believed that women would bring virtue into politics by extending the stance of motherhood to the public sphere, substituting persuasion for power, and replacing party politics with Progressive good government.

In *Herland*, a feminist utopian novel published six years before women won the suffrage, Charlotte Perkins Gilman painted a society peopled only by women, where domination had no place. Of the three men who stumble on this utopia, the most aggressive aches to fight, tries to 'master' the women, and glorifies competition. The women return patient understanding, meting out no punishments, and experiencing no competitive feeling stronger than 'a mild triumph as of winning some simple game'.

Without Gilman's explicit concern for nurturance, Mary Parker Follett, an organizational theorist writing a generation later, also argued against 'domination' ('a victory of one side over the other'). She even opposed 'compromise' ('each side gives up a little in order to have peace'), in favour of 'integration', which allows neither side 'to sacrifice anything'. Follett often gave as an example of integration how one day sitting in a library she had wanted a window shut, while another reader had wanted it open. Instead, they opened the window in an unoccupied adjacent room. 'There was no compromise', she wrote, 'because we both got all we really wanted.'

What we would now call 'win/win' solutions, like those Follett proposed, pose a necessary corrective to politics as a battle of wills. Yet it is easy in some feminist visions to mistake the corrective for the whole story, or to mistake the stress on nurturance or empathy for the conclusion that all of human relations can be encompassed in nurturance.

It is also easy to confuse the normative claim that nurturant or attentive approaches to relationships are good in themselves (or promote other values good in themselves) with the empirical claim that women are more likely than men to adopt these approaches. Whether or not women differ from men in nurturance or attentiveness, the moral claims should stand on their own. We should be able to find the language to make a persuasive case for any claim without appeal to gender. Yet because persuasion rests on experience and some experiences are more socially salient to women (whether or not they have actually had the experience of, say, motherhood itself), the persuasive images that come most easily to women will not always strike a responsive chord in men. Some claims will have to take shape within a community that shares the relevant experiences and later be 'translated' for other audiences.

As early as 1968 and 1969, for example, in almost the same moment as discovering themselves as a 'class', with separate and sometimes conflicting interests to those of men, women discovered they had a distinct and in some ways superior 'culture'. For non-separatist strands in feminist thought, the problem became how to integrate the nurturance, listening, and emotional sensitivity of this culture into the politics that women had inherited from men. This project now finds allies among political theorists promoting deliberative democracy.

FEMINIST THEORIES OF POWER

Consider the 'femaleness' of nurturance. Some feminists have reacted to the prevailing definition of politics as only power, and power as only domination, by elaborating what Nancy Hartsock calls 'the feminist theory of power'. Adopting Mary Parker Follett's distinction between 'power over' and 'power with', they have portrayed power not only as dominance but also as 'energy, capacity, and effectiveness'. In 1980 Sara Ruddick became the first academic theorist to bring maternal ideals into politics. Arguing against the conjunction of power and powerlessness in the received understanding of motherhood, Ruddick stated as her project 'the construction of an image of maternal power which is benign, accurate, sturdy and sane', suggesting that women bring to the public world a culture and tradition embodied in the ideal of 'maternal thinking', with its characteristics of 'humility', resilient good humour, realism, respect for persons, and responsiveness to growth'. Kathy Ferguson soon urged that in creating new forms of organization, women draw upon values 'structured into women's experience—caretaking, nurturance, empathy, connectedness'. Virginia Held pointed out that the relation between 'mothering parent' and child provides an understanding of power that does not involve bending another to one's will: 'The mothering person seeks to empower the child to act responsibly. She wants neither to wield power nor to defend herself against the power wielded by the child.' When they are physically weakest, as in infancy and illness, children can 'command' the greatest amount of attention and care—because then their needs are so serious.

Neither Ruddick, nor Ferguson, nor Held, nor any of the many theorists now writing in this vein are trying to replace a political vocabulary based on power with one based on care or intimacy. Their aim is to integrate into political thought a right but neglected vocabulary and set of experiences—neglected because usually allocated to the domestic realm and defined as private, non-political, or even anti-political. This project of integration requires some subtlety. It requires maintaining useful distinctions between the

149

governmental and non-governmental, and between the particular-
ism of one-to-one empathy and the universalism of solidarity with
all humankind. The project does not require merging the public with
the private. But it does require seeing relations formed in the private,
domestic, and particular realm as reasonable models for, or the first
steps toward, some forms of public spirit. The step the ancient
Greeks took in using 'philia', or friendship, as 'civic friendship', the
basis of the state, does not differ in form from the suffragists' step, in
'social motherhood', of applying the maternal relation to the larger
polity.

Taking motherhood seriously, for example, reveals the radical
limitations of political theories based on a misplaced analogy to the
marketplace. When Robert Nozick suggests that individuals have a
primordial right to own and sell what they produce, Susan Okin
replies that in that case mothers own and have a right to sell their
children. Mothers' relations with their children usefully undermine
neo-classical models of independent individuals, rights, contracts,
or owning and selling.

LISTENING AND DEMOCRATIC DELIBERATION

Attentiveness to relationships is not the same as 'nurturance'. Nancy
Chodorow has proposed that boy children may be required, in a
society where women give the most care in early childhood, to separate themselves more firmly and oppositionally than girls from
their mothers. Thus in later relationships men may feel less intrinsically connected with others. Whether for this reason or for reasons
derived from a history of subordination, girls and women in the
United States do seem to value relationships more than do boys and
men. Girls' games, at least in white middle-class communities, take
place in small, relatively homogeneous groups, and de-emphasize
the rules and competition that characterize boys' games. Girls and
women are better than men at interpreting facial expressions and
other interpersonal cues. Women speak less in public than men do,
and listen more. As Marlene Dixon put it in 1970, 'Women are
trained to nuances, to listening for the subtle cues which carry the
message hidden under the words. It is part of that special skill called
"intuition" or "empathy" which all female children must learn if
they are to be successful in manipulating others to get what they
want and to be successful in providing sympathy and understanding

to their husbands and lovers.' While the 'all' in her sentence undoubtedly exaggerates, it is true that generations upon generations of women have been taught to be good listeners. As early as the fifth century BC, Sophocles said, 'Silence is a woman's crown.'

The skills of listening—though not of silence—do seem to produce better decisions. The laboratory experiments of social psychologists suggest that the best group decisions (those most likely to produce a 'correct' answer or a creative solution) come when members solicit the opinions of individuals who are initially in a minority. When an experimenter instructs a group to consult every member, the group makes more correct decisions than without these instructions. When leaders facilitate the emergence of minority opinion, their groups perform better than leaderless groups. Organizational consultants have learned from the psychologists the useful though rather jarring phrase, 'I hear you saying . . .' To say those words, you need to have listened, and others have a chance to correct what you think you've heard. Without this jargon, feminists teach the same lesson—listening.

Along with promoting an ethic of care and skill in listening, feminist thinkers have also suggested a critical role for the emotions in deliberation. Emotions help tell us who we want to be. Good deliberation is not fostered by 'keeping emotion out of it'. Rather, 'integrative' or 'win/win' solutions often require the emotional capacity to guess what others want, or at least to ask in a genuinely curious and unthreatening way. It takes emotional ability to elicit from people in conflict the sometimes subconscious sentiments and unobserved facts that can help create an integrative solution.

Union members sometimes strike in support of another union's demands; some childless property-owners vote for higher taxes to improve the schools. Such actions are based not only on a rational commitment to maxims that one would will to be universal or on a belief in achieving the greatest good for the greatest number, but also on a process that has evoked empathy, solidarity, or the commitment of one's identity and actions to a principle. The presence of others with interests different from one's own makes it hard, rightly or wrongly, to insist on claims based on pure self-interest. When people with competing claims come face to face, the conflict not only creates selfish competitiveness; it also often becomes emotionally clearer how self-interested behaviour can harm others. When individuals are capable of principled commitment or solidarity, engaging the emotions helps create the self-transformations necessary to think 'we' instead of 'I'.

OVERCOMING THE SUBTLE FORMS OF POWER

But who is the 'we' in a deliberation? 'We' can easily represent a false universality, as 'mankind' used to do. Even if spoken and believed by the subordinate, 'we' may mask a relationship that works against the subordinate's interests. Women's experience of silence, of unexplored wants, of words that do not mean (and are not heard to mean) what they say, and of subtle forms of domination generalize beyond gender to alert both theorists and practitioners to the pitfalls of unequal power in deliberation.

Silence, on its positive side, permits listening. On the negative side, a history of relative silence makes women political actors more likely to understand that when deliberation turns into theatre, it leaves out many who are not, by nature or training, actors. When deliberation turns into a demonstration of logic, it leaves out many who cannot work their emotionally felt needs into a neat equation. When many voices compete for the deliberative floor, the sample that gets heard is not representative.

Many shy men are quiet, but the equivalent percentage of shy women is increased by learning silence as appropriate to their gender. So, too, it is the human condition, not just a gendered condition, not to know what one wants. But over and above the human condition, many women like myself—white middle class citizens of the United States, born in the 1930s and 1940s—were taught not to have too strongly defined wants. Boys wondered, as early as 'soldier, sailor, Indian chief', which kinds of work they were suited for. Middle-class boys wondered what careers they would choose. Girls like myself wondered, instead, what kind of man they would marry. My mother, always practical, increased my range of options in the best way she knew how. She brought me up with an array of skills, she told me more than once, so that I might marry either 'a prince or a pauper'.

Training to be chosen rather than to choose includes not allowing one's wants to become too definite. Keeping one's wants indefinite makes it even harder than usual for one's intellect to learn the signs the self emits of wanting one thing rather than another. Knowing how easy it is to keep one's wants indefinite makes women realize that deliberative assemblies must work actively at helping participants discover and create what they truly want. Preferences themselves, let alone interests, are not given. They must be tentatively voiced, tested, examined against the causes that produced them, explored, and finally made one's own. Good deliberation must rest on institutions that foster dissent and on images of appropriate behaviour that allow for fumbling and changing one's mind, that respect the tentativeness of this process. Only such safeguards can help participants find where they themselves want to go.

Words are the very stuff of deliberation. But women traditionally have been trained not to say what they mean. Carole Pateman directs us to the last chapter of Rousseau's *Emile*, the first handbook of progressive education, designed to produce a virtuous and naturally healthy man and woman. After all the brave first chapters, where Emile is raised to emotional honesty and to despise the hypocrisy of the city and the court, it comes as a shock, when Rousseau turns to Sophie, to have him teach her to say 'no' when she means 'yes', and teach Emile, in response, to act as if she had said 'yes', not 'no'. In the very paragraph where Rousseau puts forth the radical doctrine that all sexual intercourse, even in marriage, must be based on mutual desire, he states that men must disregard verbal signs of non-consent to read consent in women's looks.

As rapes increase across the United States, but it becomes gradually illegal, state by state, to have intercourse with one's wife against her will, women have particular reason to want their 'nos' taken to mean 'no' and not 'yes', and to want women taught, like men, to say 'no' when they mean 'no'.

It is not hard to see how deliberation is distorted when subordinates say 'yes' ('Yes, boss') when they mean 'no'. The convolutions of mismeaning embedded in men's and women's dance of domination and subordination reveal other layers, and other types of distortion, of which both parties may be unaware, and in which the larger culture is complicit.

It has been the decade of deconstruction, semiotics, and Foucault. As deconstruction picks apart a piece of literature to see what lies behind, as semiotics sees every pause, word, or non-word as a signifier, as Foucault uncovers power in the interstices of every social act, these currents have served as allies, often consciously unwanted, in the feminist enterprise of unmasking, and guarding against, subtle forms of domination.

An important example of this enterprise, on the theoretical plane, is Andrea Dworkin and Catharine MacKinnon's analysis of the domination implicit in the act of intercourse. Dworkin and MacKinnon suggest that in the average act of sexual intercourse the fact that one person penetrates and the other is penetrated, one thrusts and the other receives, encodes a pattern of domination and

subordination, reinforced in some cases by top versus bottom position, initiator versus initiate, and other reflections or coy reversals of
external structures of power. Feminists have brought out the power
imbalances inherent in many subtle acts—the clothing the two genders use, hairstyle, makeup, laughter, and attitudes toward food or
one's own body.

Women, more than most oppressed groups, have come to learn the
covert as well as the overt faces of power. Many women, no matter
how active as feminists, have loved their fathers, sons, sometimes
their male lovers or husbands. And many men have loved women,
sometimes (at least in the modern era) with a strong conscious commitment to creating in the social world, or at least their intimate relations, the equality they perceive 'underneath'. Because this love and
commitment to equality are also bound up tightly with conscious and
unconscious forms of domination, women have had to begin learning to parse out the confused grammars of love and power.

Sensitivity to subtle forms of power pervaded the egalitarianism
and commitment to consensus of the early radical women's movement. It continues today to inspire the National Women's Studies
Association's experiments with equalizing power, like its caucuses
for constituencies who feel they have a less than equal voice.
Mainstream women's organizations share the same concerns. The
League of Women Voters from its beginning has made decisions by
what the organization calls 'consensus', namely 'agreement among a
substantial number of members, representative of the membership
as a whole, reached after sustained study and group discussion'. The
aim is deliberation, and decision through persuasion. Throughout
the 1970s and 1980s state and local branches of the National
Organization for Women fought inequalities in power among their
members, suggesting in Massachusetts in 1972, for example, a rotat-
ing president because 'they didn't want to have a star system'.

Used indiscriminately, practices aimed at ensuring equality and
consensus can undermine deliberation, not advance it. We need laboratories, which feminist practice abundantly provides, to assess
which forms work and which do not.

'DIFFERENCE' AS A POLITICAL STRATEGY

To say that feminists can add something new to political theory
through their understanding of women's experience does not

require believing that women and men are 'essentially' different. It requires only that certain experiences be distributed unequally between men and women. A fairly small difference in experience can become a large difference in self-image and social perception. If one group is dominant, as men are, they typically take pains to avoid the language and images attributed to the subordinates. The subordinate group, on the other hand, is torn between pride in its own language and images and a desire to emulate the dominant group.

Empathy—the quality of being able to put oneself emotionally in another's place—may serve as an example. Women are typically seen, and see themselves, as more empathetic than men. Research on empathy, however, shows gender difference to vary dramatically depending on how empathy is measured. In experimental studies simulating emotional situations, few differences between men and women show up in physiological reactions or reports of feelings of sympathy or concern. But when asked on questionnaires to respond to items such as 'I tend to get emotionally involved with a friend's problems', girls and women score much higher on empathy than do boys and men. The social reputation for difference is as important as any difference in behaviour. For it suggests an alternative model—an ideal type of behaviour valued by the subordinate group.

In some parts of their lives, women and men do have dramatically different experiences. Women give birth, nurse, and are socialized for childrearing. They are far more likely to be raped, battered, and the victims of incest, or to have to plan their lives around the fear of rape. They are more likely to become secretaries, nurses, or elementary school teachers, to have interrupted careers, and to experience poverty. But not every woman has given birth or been raped. Some manage to avoid the pervasive fear of rape. A few arrange job trajectories much like those of men.

In many other respects, men's and women's experiences overlap greatly. Since on many psychological, social, and political measures the means between the two sexes are so close, almost half the men in any group have had a certain 'female' experience or trait more often than half the women. The same is true of women in regard to 'masculine' traits and experiences.

Because socialization to gender is not merely a passive response to punishment and reward but rather the result of an active, engaged building of the personality, and because healthy people tend to like and want to be who they are, children probably value being a boy or a girl long before they know what that means. As children create themselves, they learn that gender is a salient identifying characteristic and adopt the traits their social milieux associate with women or men. Even in the future, when I expect the significance of gender to diminish greatly, biological sex will continue to be sexy.

Whenever we learn, as adults or children, that certain features of human personality or action are socially salient, we become more conscious of those features, perhaps even exaggerating them in our minds, as we absorb them into our self-image. Social images grow in much the same way. When a distinction makes a difference in a culture, we build those distinctions into schemas, or stories, that explain the world. The mirror of society magnifies emotions and behaviour already enlarged in the mirror of the self.

These magnified distinctions influence our ways of knowing. Ways of knowing associated with women can be scorned as 'soft', ways of knowing associated with men praised as 'hard'. The nature of inquiry itself can become part of an overall pattern of domination. When the subordinate classes fight back, they can expose the power relations inherent in the dominant paradigm. Fighting as women for women's ways of knowing binds women closer in sisterhood, reinforcing common experience. It also shoots adrenaline into the collective intellectual system, helping to see the world differently, and sometimes more clearly.

Out of this process can come critical intellectual tools. Take Carol Gilligan's distinction between the 'male' emphasis on rights versus the 'female' emphasis on relationships. Differences between men and women do appear both at the 'higher' level of Kohlberg's scales of moral development (among the professional classes, women are more likely to appear at a 'lower' stage of development) and on Carol Gilligan's and her colleagues' more recent measures of orientation to rights and relationships among upper middle-class men and women. In mixed-class populations, these differences do not usually reach statistical significance. But even if there were no differences at all between men and women on these dimensions in actual behaviour, if the differences persisted in social image they would help us understand how one way of looking at moral questions—a 'different voice' that stresses relationships rather than rights—could have been passed over in the development of moral theory.

That different voice is by no means unanimously female. Gilligan herself points out that many men also speak with a different voice. But by signalling that the previously overlooked and discredited perspective has been stereotyped as a woman's perspective and thus can easily be perceived, through the lens of self- and social image, as a woman's perspective, she not only explains its previous subordination. She also mobilizes to fight for it as a legitimate perspective in its own right. Reading Gilligan's *A Different Voice* angers women. It helps explain why whole disciplines have devalued what 'women' do, and it gives women the energy to fight back, with their sisters, the next time it happens. As they fight back, the men who also adopt a 'different voice' benefit, too. And so, with luck, does the larger human analytic enterprise.

A focus on women's differences from men goes a long way toward building feminist solidarity. However, for the purpose of changing mainstream—that is, male—practices and ideas, the strategy is double-edged. Any idea should be persuasive in its own right. Harnessing that idea to women's differences from men assures it the automatic attention given anything related to sex. At the same time, yoking the idea to the age-old 'war between the sexes' will work for or against it, depending on the audience. There are costs to such a strategy—in possibly neglecting non-gendered arguments for the idea, in seeming to diminish its scope, in seeming to suggest that the differences between men and women are large, innate, or ineradicable, in eliminating potential audiences, in discounting the experiences of the many, both men and women, whose feelings are not congruent with gendered social expectations, and in tapping emotional sources of intellectual activity that can blind as well as clarify. There are also benefits—in generating the idea in the first place, getting people to think about it, explaining previous denigration, and providing through the connection with gender the language and additional perspectives that help the idea make sense.

In the next decades feminism is bound to be a fertile source of insight not only into its main subject of gender relations, but also into most other human relations that involve inequalities of power or making another's good one's own. Regardless of the strategy chosen, feminists need allies when their goal is improving mainstream political practice and thought. In the near future feminists can find allies in the political theorists and empirical political scientists who are newly concerned with the quality of deliberation. And when democratic theorists are in search of provocative and useful new ideas, they can find them in the constantly growing corpus of feminist theory.

Notes

1. Jane Mansbridge, *Beyond Adversary Democracy* (Chicago: University of Chicago Press, 1980/1983).

157

References

On Feminist Political Thought

Andrea Dworkin, *Intercourse* (Free Press, 1987).

Catharine A. MacKinnon, *Feminism Unmodified* (Harvard University Press, 1987).

Jennifer Nedelsky, 'Reconceiving Autonomy', *Yale Journal of Law and Feminism* 1 (1989): 7–36.

Susan Okin, *Justice, Gender and the Family* (Basic Books, 1989).

Carole Pateman, *The Sexual Contract* (Polity Press, 1988).

On Deliberative Democracy

Benjamin Barber, *Strong Democracy* (University of Chicago Press, 1984).

Ernest Barker, *The Citizen's Choice* (Cambridge University Press, 1938).

Joshua Cohen, 'Deliberation and democratic legitimacy', in Alan Hamlin and Phillip Pettit, eds. *The Good Polity* (Blackwell, 1989).

Jürgen Habermas, *The Structural Transformation of the Public Sphere*, trans. Thomas Burger and Frederick Lawrence (MIT Press, 1989).

J.G.A. Pocock, *The Machiavellian Moment* (Princeton University Press, 1975).

Cass Sunstein, 'Political self-interest in constitutional law' in Jane Mansbridge, ed. *Beyond Self-Interest* (University of Chicago Press, 1990).

Garry Wills, *Inventing America* (Doubleday, 1978).

On Gender Differences

Nancy Chodorow, *The Reproduction of Mothering: Psychoanalysis and the Sociology of Gender* (University of California Press, 1978).

Hannah Mather Crocker, 'Observations on the real Rights of Women' (1818).

Marlene Dixon, in *It Ain't Me Babe* 1. (1970).

Kathy E. Ferguson, *The Feminist Case Against Bureaucracy* (Temple University Press, 1984).

Mary Parker Follet, *Dynamic Administration* (Harper & Brothers, 1940).

Carol Gilligan, *In a Different Voice: Psychological Theory and Women's Development* (Harvard Univesity Press, 1982).

Carol Gilligan, Jance Victoria Ward, and Jill MacLean Taylor, eds. *Mapping the Moral Domain* (Harvard University Press, 1988).

Charlotte Perkins Gilman, *Herland* [1915] (Pantheon, 1979).

Nancy Hartsock, *Money, Sex and Power* (Longman, 1983).

Virginia Held, 'Mothering versus contract' in Jane Mansbridge, ed. *Beyond Self-Interest* (University of Chicago Press, 1990).

Lawrence Kohlberg, 'A Cognitive-Developmental Analysis of Children's Sex Role Concepts and Attitudes', in Eleanor E. Maccoby, ed. *The Development of Sex Differences* (Stanford University Press, 1966).

Sara Ruddick, 'Maternal Thinking'. *Feminist Studies* 6 (Summer, 1980).

Part III. Interests and Representation

When are Interests Interesting? The Problem of Political Representation of Women

Virginia Sapiro

In the beginning there was no problem of political representation of women. The reason was not that everyone agreed that women should not be represented; rather, the argument was that women *were* represented. The justification for this argument is best exemplified by the often-quoted common law view found in Blackstone's *Commentaries*:

By marriage, the husband and wife are one person in law: that is, the very being or legal existence of the women is suspended during the marriage, or at least is incorporated and consolidated into that of the husband: under whose wing, protection, and cover, she performs everything (Okin 1979: 249).

The most serious legal objections to women's participation in electoral politics, both at citizen and élite levels, was that the male is the head of the family (the 'head of household', as he is still known), and in him was invested the authority to rule his family and to represent his family's interests in the 'outside' world. The question many opponents of women's suffrage asked was how it could be possible for a woman to have interests separate and distinct from those of her husband; that is, how could a woman be considered an individual citizen with the rights of a distinct individual?

The most widely discussed political reform movements of the nineteenth century might be said to have rested on the principle that 'all individuals who enter the social contract are members of the political community, but only the males who own substantial amounts of material property are politically relevant members of society' (Pateman 1979: 71). The reform movements of that time considered the most 'important' are those that sought to make males who did *not* own substantial amounts of property 'politically

Reprinted by permission from *The American Political Science Review*, 75/3 (1981), 701–16.

relevant members of society', that is, to confer upon them political rights, including representation. For women, perhaps the greatest reform issue of the time was not whether political rights could be conferred upon individuals who did not now own property, but whether women were indeed individuals who could own property. It was not until the 1840s in the United States, 1882 in England, and even later throughout most of Europe that married women could own and manage their own property or make contracts. It was only when these reforms were achieved that it became clear that attaining 'personhood', even if accompanied by substantial amounts of property, did not confer *political* personhood on women equivalent to that possessed by men of their own class. Liberal democratic theory and reforms did little to weaken the patriarchal concept of social organization where women were concerned.

The contradictions of a political tradition that combines the individualism of liberal theory with patriarchalism has been dealt with extensively elsewhere (Schochet 1975; Brennan and Pateman 1979; Okin 1979). The basic problems have not yet been solved; nowhere are they more evident than in public policies on the family. One might argue, however, that for all practical purposes the problem of women and representation has been solved. Despite the remaining contradictions in democratic theory and practice, women have gained full rights of political participation in most Western nations, and they serve in political offices at all levels of government, although in small numbers. It would seem that women, as individual members of the political community, now have the right of representation.

New demands by feminist movements have opened a different question. Women (as well as many others) ask not for representation as individual citizens, but as members of a group. They ask not only that citizens who happen to be women be represented, but also that women be represented *because* they are women. What does this demand mean? On what grounds can we argue that women are entitled to representation as members of a group, rather than simply as individuals? Is the demand for representation of women simply or necessarily a demand for more women in political office? These questions point to vast gaps in political research, gaps that exist for two reasons. One is that barely a decade has passed since the development of interest in the study of women and politics; one could hardly expect scholars in a new field to ask and answer all of its research questions in that amount of time, particularly given the lack of training in women's studies available in universities.[1] The second problem is that most political scientists who study core political questions such as representation have tended to ignore issues concerning women, or have regarded such issues as 'special topics' worthy of only limited interest. Political scientists have shown little inclination to pursue questions concerning women. This 'guide to the frontiers', then, will focus on the problem of research on women and politics as it concerns questions of representation. It is designed for two overlapping audiences: those with a specific substantive interest in women and politics, and those who study representation, interest groups, and policy-making.[2]

We turn, then, to the fundamental question of group interests and representation. This discussion is framed by two straightforward questions: (1) What is political representation of women? and (2) To what degree and under what circumstances are political institutions and decision-makers responsive to female citizens? The discussion focuses primarily on contemporary empirical research— although the themes are, or should be, puzzles of long-standing interest to political theory. As the responses to these questions are presented, more complex and less straightforward questions will emerge. Evidence and examples will be drawn from a variety of cultural contexts. As anthropologists have shown, people in any given culture tend to think that the roles of women and men, the sexual division of status and labour, are natural and universal (Ardener 1975, 1978). One way forcefully to bring to light the patterns and meaning of gender stratification is to demonstrate how variable the contours of the 'natural and universal' really are. The examples offered here might appear to be drawn rather promiscuously from a range of cultures and times; sometimes the way to spur thought and research is to make statements demanding rebuttal or elaboration. Evidence and arguments are also drawn from a range of disciplines. The problem of representation of women raises economic, psychological, sociological, and biological questions. Moreover, much of the most suggestive work has been done in the allied social sciences, partly because of the distribution of women's researchers in the social sciences and partly because of the greater attention other disciplines have paid to the relevant issues.

WHAT IS TO BE REPRESENTED?

One of the few truly obvious facts of political life is that the proportion of women among those designated as representatives is considerably smaller than the proportion of women found among the represented. This is the fact to which many people turn when they argue that women are under-represented. This rationale frays under close scrutiny. Let us say, for example, that I am a redheaded woman. Why should I wish to be represented by a woman, indeed, a redheaded woman? I could say, as many people would, that such a person, resembling me, would represent my interests.

— 'And how do you know that?' (the attentive reader asks).
— 'Because she is in the same position I am in and could act for me. She would understand and feel the same way' (I answer).
— 'When you say, "the same position", do you mean as a woman or as a redhead?'
— 'As a woman, of course.'
— 'Why as a woman and not as a redhead?'
— 'Because being a redhead is not politically relevant and being a woman is.'

It is clear that the real question is not whether my representative looks like me—it is whether my interests are being represented. What matters is whether my representative is 'acting in the interest of the represented, in a manner responsive' to me (Pitkin 1967: 209).[3]

In order to discuss representation of women we must consider whether women as a group have unique politically relevant characteristics, whether they have special interests to which a representative could or should respond. Can we argue that women as a group share particular social, economic, or political problems that do not closely match those of other groups, or that they share a particular viewpoint on the solutions to political problems? If so, we can also argue that women share interests that may be represented. Framing the working definition of 'representable interests' in this fashion does not mean that the problems or issues are exclusively those of the specified interest group any more than we can make the same argument about other types of groups more widely accepted as interest groups. The fact that there is a labour interest group, for example, reflects the existence of other groups such as the business establishment, consumers, and government, which in a larger sense share labour's concern, but often have viewpoints on the nature of, or solutions to, the problems which conflict with those of labour. That in the abstract 'good wages', 'fair prices', or 'efficiency' sound good for everyone does not eliminate the differences of interest among the groups pursuing these goals. We would not suggest that business people or consumers can adequately represent the interests of labour simply because they too are somehow involved in the industrial enterprise. Nor does our working definition of an interest group mean that all of the potential members of that group are consciously allied, or that there is a clear and obvious answer to any given problem articulated by the entire group that differs substantially from answers articulated by others. In fact, I am not using 'interest group' in the narrow sense generally found in political science, which seems to require an organized group of people interacting through conventional political channels in opposition to other organized interest groups. As we shall see, studies of women (and other oppressed groups) demonstrate that part of the political relevance of some groups is that they have been systematically denied the means with which to form themselves into an interest organization: self-consciousness and identification (Sapiro 1979a). The terms 'interest group' and 'interest organization' are therefore not interchangeable here, although the latter is formed primarily out of the former.[4]

The term 'women's issues' usually refers to public concerns that impinge primarily on the private (especially domestic) sphere of social life, and particularly those values associated with children and nurturance. But even within this domain 'women's issues' can be interpreted in three distinct, although related ways. One interpretation is simply that women are more interested in these issues than in others as a result of their 'parochial' domestic concerns (suggested by Lane 1959). Another is that they are more interested in these issues than are men—that there is, in a sense, a division of labour in political attention. Finally, one could say that regardless of their relative level of concern with these issues, women have a 'special' interest, or a particular (potential) viewpoint from which their positions or preferences might be derived. In discussing representation, we are more concerned with the latter two, and especially the final interpretation. In order to analyse women's interests, we will follow two lines of inquiry. The first is the problem of women's 'objective situation' and its relevance to political interests; the other is the hardly less difficult question of women's consciousness of their own interests and the 'subjective' condition of women.

Research in various fields of social science provides evidence that women do have a distinct position and a shared set of problems that characterize a special interest. Many of these distinctions are located in the institution in which women and men are probably most often assumed to have common interests, the family. Much has been made of the 'sharing' or 'democratic' model of the modern family, but whatever democratization has taken place it has not come close to erasing the division of labour and, indeed, stratification, by sex.[5] A case in point, time-use studies show that housework and child care are the responsibilities of the woman, regardless of her employment status, and that she spends about the same amount of time on and does the same proportion of housework and childcare now as women did at the turn of the century (Robinson 1980; Vanet 1980). We are accustomed to the idea that divisions of labour and stratification in public life define group interests in politics; can the same case be made for divisions of labour in private life? (See the editors of *Questions Feministes*, 1980; Delphy, 1980). One can make such a case if these 'private arrangements' are either determined at least in part by public policy or governmental organization, or if they affect objects of public policy and policy debate. Gender divisions of labour and stratification within the family meet these tests. Law and policy serve as direct and indirect buttresses of such differentiation and stratification. In addition, gender differentiation and stratification in private life buttresses the political economy, affecting, at minimum, child care and welfare, education, consumption, employment and labour supply, and property and wealth arrangements.

Law and public policy continue to create and reinforce differences between women and men in property and contract matters (especially regarding marriage, divorce, and widowhood), economic opportunity (including employment, credit, and social security), protection from violence (rape and wife battery), control over fertility and child care, educational opportunities, and civic rights and obligations.[6] Women and men have different relationships to pregnancy, childbirth, and lactation. These biological differences are exaggerated by women's having been given nearly total responsibility for reproduction, child care, and even child support. Marxist and non-Marxist scholars alike understand a group's relation to the mode of production, their relative control over both processes and products, as at least part of the basis for defining political interests. Children are perhaps the most important 'products' of a society. Reproduction must be considered in a serious way as a factor in the political economy of governance (as in Eisenstein 1979; Delphy 1980).

The indicators generally used to describe differences in socioeconomic position also show that the politically relevant situations of women and men are different. Social and individual goods are very unevenly divided between the sexes. Women in almost all countries have less education than men, and where they achieve equivalent levels of education, segregation by field and therefore skills and market value remains. Women are less likely to be in the labour market. Men and women remain segregated in different sectors of the labour market and in jobs of different status within the same sectors. Wealth and credit are unevenly distributed. Men and women do not have the same access to physical and mental health, in large part because of socio-political factors. When we consider the half of the female population in paid employment, we find that they do not have equal access to leisure. Few groups in any society have a lower proportion of its members in positions accorded high status, value, or power. Only in life expectancy do women 'outdo' men, a bonus that has little compensatory value in some countries, given the poverty of the aged and the inadequate support services available to them.

To say that women are in a different social position from that of men and therefore have interests to be represented is not the same as saying that women are conscious of these differences, that they define themselves as having special interests requiring representation, or that men and women as groups now disagree on policy issues on which women might have a special interest.[7] Studies of public opinion on the status and roles of women show relatively few significant differences between the sexes, and do not reveal women to be consistently more feminist than men (e.g. Sapiro 1980; Inglehart and Inglehart 1975). Some of the problems in such research cannot be resolved until more validation studies have been done. Why do American men receive high scores on vague, abstract questions on sex equality when they continue to leave childcare and housework to their wives? What is the relationship between conscious replies to questions and non-conscious prejudice and stereotyping? (On non-conscious prejudice, see Deaux 1976; Sapiro 1979a).

Political systems are not likely to represent previously unrepresented groups until those groups develop a sense of their own interests and place demands upon the system. This requires the development of political consciousness and political activism based on this new group consciousness. Social movements and protest activity, especially in their early stages, are intended to develop such group consciousness as much as to place demands on other groups. It is no coincidence that the women's movement has emphasized 'consciousness raising' so heavily, using phrases such as, 'the personal is the political'. These efforts are meant to increase awareness

167

among women that what they might perceive as personal and iso-lated problems (such as underdeveloped skills, poor pay, or even feelings of 'middle-aged depression') are widely shared problems that are due in large part to widespread social, economic, and polit-ical factors. Research on women and politics has begun to make contributions to our knowledge of how political interests develop, and especially how development of subjective group interests is repressed or inhibited in the cases of non-dominant and minority groups. However, much more work needs to be done (Freeman 1975; Hole and Levine 1971; Rowbotham 1973; Sapiro 1980; DuBois 1978; Evans 1980). It should be fascinating to a political sci-entist to ponder how a group could so long accept as in its interest the denial of education, income, economic and physical security, and political power to its own members. Women's studies scholars have taken a strong hand in demonstrating how a sub-group learns to adopt the viewpoint of opposing groups, leading them to act against their own interests (Hacker 1951; Thorne and Henley 1975; Deaux 1976; Daly 1979; and Sapiro 1979a).

What are the limits of the issues on which one might find a woman's interest? This would be difficult to answer, especially before a wider range of policies are investigated for their differential impact on women and men. Such laws and policies need not have 'women' in the title or text. When a local council grants or does not grant zoning approval for a new shopping centre or parking facility, women's time and work are affected. When the government restricts the money supply, women's work is increased; it is women's domes-tic labour that compensates for relative unavailability of money to provide food, clothing, childcare, or household equipment.[8] One problem worth investigating is how interest groups come to define their issues; an early bone of contention between the American Federation of Labour and the Congress of Industrial Organization, for example, was how widely the term 'labour issues' should be con-strued. Similar arguments may be heard in the women's movement. It would be wrong, however, to ignore the division of interest among women. Although women share many common problems, they are also divided, for example, by class, race, age, and marital status. It sometimes appears that while mainstream social scientists overplay these 'cross-cutting cleavages', feminist scholars often underplay them.

WHEN DOES REPRESENTATION OCCUR?

We have argued that there is a woman's interest to be represented. Let us, for now, limit the conception of this interest to the expansion of rights, liberties, and opportunities for women where these have been denied or inhibited in comparison with those of men. We now turn to a new set of questions: Under what circumstances are political systems representative of women? Under what circumstances do they act in the interests of the represented—in this case, women? In order to answer these questions we must look at the sources and effects of public policies that concern the quality of women's lives and women's ability to control the quality of their lives. This discussion will offer four possible explanations for change in public policy on women. They are (1) problems of the general political economy, including the structure of government and secular political needs, (2) ideology, (3) interest organization, including especially feminist movements, and (4) the effects of women as members of the political élite. Not all of these sources directly concern the relationship between the representative and the represented. Rather, they focus on the relationship between the actions of government and the interests of citizens.

Political Economy

A careful examination of women's political history suggests that women's own actions have sometimes played only minor roles in some of the most profound legal or policy changes in comparison with other current problems and features of the political system. The 1940s Married Women's Property Acts in the United States provide a case in point; the women's rights movement of the time was led by a relatively tiny group of women with virtually no influence on public officials, and certainly no mass following. Even in the instances in which women's movements were active, influential, and successful, as in the case of a number of suffrage movements, it would be a mistake to analyse the movement activities without paying careful attention to the more general political context. Social movements and interests succeed and fail only partly because of their own goals and strategies. In New Zealand and Australia (the first two nations to grant women the vote) and in Britain and the United States, for example, the political questions of women's suffrage must be understood in the context of current waxing, waning, and jockeying of contemporary political parties, and in the pitting of women's suffrage against other issues such as progressivism, governmental reform, the immigrant question, and the Irish question (Morgan 1972, 1974). In Germany and Russia the women's movements appear to have played very little part indeed; rather, one must look to the general wash of the Weimar Republic or the Communist revolution (Stites 1978; Thönnessen 1969; Evans 1976). In many cases policies that affect and even expand the status and opportunities of women appear to be propelled by sources other than women's interest organizations.

One rather commonplace assumption, based in the functionalist school of political development, is that modernization breeds secularization, mass communication, merit rather than parochially based social systems, and ultimately egalitarianism, including equality for women and men. As pleasant as such a parsimonious, comprehensive theory might be, it is wrong in many respects and in many cases. It is also misleading or silent on the evolution of specific policies. Numerous anthropologists have pointed not to a linear but to a curvilinear relationship between economic development and egalitarianism (especially Sanday 1974). Some African countries offer stark examples of the effects of modernization and especially the 'reforms' of Western nations which destroyed many of the rights and opportunities of women and increased the gap between the power and status of women and men (Hafkin and Bay 1976). Although the sweeping view of development theory *per se* is of little help, comparative studies uncover certain aspects of the needs and structures of the political economy that appear to support or inhibit change in the status of women. What follows is merely a laundry list; the work that remains is to develop these into more coherent theory and, especially, to model their interaction.

1. *Economic Needs.* Women constitute a marginal labour force whose status and specific activities fluctuate according to systemic needs for production, reproduction, and consumption. Changes in policies concerning women appear especially linked to the rise and fall of population needs. Among the policies most linked to population needs are those concerning birth control, childcare, marriage and sexuality, and employment. Birth-control policies offer an interesting example of this link. Many of the laws barring contraception and abortion (and, for that matter, homosexuality) were instituted in the nineteenth century and at times in the twentieth century when expansion of the population was needed (Gordon

1976; Kennedy 1970; Weeks 1977). The legalization of contraception and abortion in many nations at about the same time as the boom of postwar babies reached adulthood, and the remarkable fluctuations in population policy in Nazi Germany and in the Soviet Union from the 1920s on, testify to how the supply of labour (including military labour) influences policies that directly affect women.

Fertility and employment of women are directly related; employment policies appear to have histories similar to that of birth control. Women were, in effect, drafted into traditionally male employment during the Second World War. When new sectors of the economy expand and, especially when auxiliary or lower-status workers are demanded for this expansion, women have often provided the new source of labour. The massive expansion of the female labour force as a result of the need for communication facilitators (clerical workers, including those associated with computer technology) was accompanied by the first major governmental encouragements for female employment (in the US, the 1963 Equal Pay Act and the 1964 Civil Rights Act). Similarly, provision of services that affect childcare and household management seem to depend on national needs (Steinfels 1973). The United States offered limited day-care facilities during the Second World War; nursery schools and kindergartens were expanded in the same postwar period that saw the rise of female employment. Particularly interesting are the cases in which national needs require both female *productive* and *reproductive* labour. The result has been the creation of a 'double burden', by which is meant the longer hours of labour faced by women as compared with men. Rarely has there been any attempt by government to shift part of the burden of domestic labour onto men.[9]

2. *War*. Although war is supposed to be the domain of men, not to mention a major force shaping male life, war has often had profound effects on the status and roles of women. As a marginal labour force, women have been used as substitutes for men in the domestic labour force, which has meant both the expansion of female employment and, to some degree, expansion of the types of jobs in which women are employed. During and especially after wars, policies are also designed to restock the population, which means pushing women out of productive and into reproductive work. In some cases, as we have suggested, contradictory needs lead to contradictory, or at least fluctuating, policies, as in the cases of Germany and

the USSR just prior to and during the Second World War. Just as war encourages female entry into the labour force, war can develop new political roles for women, which are often institutionalized by law and policy after the war is over. In some cases governments have used women's part in the war as part of the justification for extending women's rights, as in the case of suffrage in Britain following the First World War. Sometimes governmental attention to women's roles and rights seems to flow from their participation in revolutions, as in the cases of the USSR, India, Cuba, and Mozambique. Changes that accompany war must be treated with care; one would want to distinguish between changes that are part of temporary dislocations and compromises of a period of national crisis and those which are more directly due to these crises but more lasting. (On women, war, and the military, see Enloe 1980; *Armed Forces and Society*, 1978).

3. *International Politics.* With the exception of some of the studies of Third World women, most research on policy and law on women (and, for that matter, domestic law and policy in general) is confined to domestic sources. Scattered throughout studies of women and policy are suggestions that international politics play an important role as well. We have already suggested the roles of war. Colonialism and neo-colonialism, as was mentioned earlier, have worked against the interests of women, but the direction of effects has by no means been uniform. These forces have also supported increased education for women, reform of marriage laws, attacks on the initiation rites of female genital mutilation, and, despite recent events, have helped to chip away at the walls of *purdah*.

It should not be assumed that the effects of international politics are limited to the Third World. Both the nineteenth- and twentieth-century women's movements were international ones. Just as ideas and policies associated with the Enlightenment, property reform, and Marxism spread from one country to the next, so too do ideas and policies associated with the emancipation of women. One of the unstudied aspects of policy on women is the process by which international politics affects domestic policy. In some cases it appears that feminists of one nation use the example of policies discussed or employed in another, as in the case of the growing interest in American affirmative-action policies in Europe. In others, the role of women may be used as a national sign of status or a symbol to other nations; in an odd sense, in this case the women represent the government rather than the reverse. One of the clearest examples is found in Germany at the turn of the century, when women were allowed into universities in part because German leaders felt they could not convincingly lead the world as a rational, scientific nation as long as they were among the few 'advanced' nations to bar women from higher education (Evans 1976: 19). The sex equality clause of the Japanese constitution, like the rest of the original postwar document, was imposed by Americans, but of course not by Americans using their own Constitution as an example. Many communist nations have used the image of women working as an important symbol to the non-communist world. Although such examples abound, it is not yet clear under what circumstances international politics enters the picture, and how this happens.

4. *Federalism and International Organization.* One common observation in American politics in the 1960s, and one of the assumptions of many political reform groups, is that alteration of civil liberties and rights is most easily accomplished at the federal rather than at the state level, that a federal structure is particularly conducive to change. American history offers numerous examples of this principle with regard to women. Land-grant colleges were among the leaders in extending higher education to women. The Nineteenth Amendment to the Constitution accomplished what could have taken years longer in the South and much of the East. In the post-Second World War era, the Supreme Court in particular, but also Congress and the executive branch, have pushed change far beyond what most states would initiate on their own. Examples are not limited to the American case. International organizations such as the United Nations (Galey 1979; Hevener 1978) and the organizations associated with European integration have been far ahead of most of their member nations and have, in some cases, stimulated changes in domestic policies. Federalism is becoming a more important feature of politics worldwide; its effects on women must be more clearly understood.

5. *Intergroup Tensions.* One of the points suggested earlier is that policy on women must be considered in the context of conflicting political demands and problems. Progress on the status of women appears to occur at times when the status of other social groups is under question as well, but it seems just as apparent that women's demands are often blocked by policy considerations involving those other groups, and often other minority groups. From the time of consideration of the Civil War amendments to recent debates over

policies of preferential treatment, women's fate has been tied in part to racial problems and policies (Chafe 1977; DuBois 1980). Women were introduced into Title VII of the 1964 Civil Rights Act in an effort to block the bill, which resulted in a curious temporary coalition of opponents of black civil rights and supporters of extensions of civil rights. Recent immigration policies in Britain, which discriminate between the rights of entry for males and females, are based on the desire to restrict entry of nonwhites into the country. Soviet population policies and thinking are based in part on fears that the eastern Muslim populations will out-reproduce the more 'desirable' Western groups. Revitalization of *purdah* in the Mideast and continued support of the practice of clitoridectomy in some parts of Africa are due in large part to the desire of male leaders and governments to combat foreign, especially Western, influence. Under what circumstances are policies on women linked to the fortunes of other social groups rather than to the women's interests? Do these linkages serve the function of blocking the development of effective coalitions?

Ideology

The previous section presents what might be considered rather mechanistic forces shaping policy on women. It points to sociopolitical forces beyond ideology or specific attitudes toward women's roles and status. There should be little doubt that ideology is an important factor as well, but its exact role is unclear. Parties of the left are not always remarkably different from parties on the right in their policy efforts toward women. Until 1980 Republican and Democratic parties alike gave the nod to the Equal Rights Amendment, and, despite his general recalcitrance on matters of civil rights, it was Richard Nixon who extended the executive order of affirmative action.

If left–right ideology is truly the linchpin of women's rights policy, differences between communist and non-communist parties and systems should constitute an important test. Every communist nation made conscious efforts to improve the relative status of the sexes at a very early stage, and the communist parties of the predominantly Catholic nations of France and Italy have, in general, been forces for improvement. But, as numerous analysts have pointed out, the matter is not a simple one. Both liberal and social democratic systems and Marxist systems have within their ideologies fundaments on which to base emancipatory policies. Policy history shows great fluctuation in all these types of systems. When we compare *overall* degrees of stratification and segregation in economy and politics across these different systems, we find little difference. The question, 'Does socialism liberate women?' still ends with a question mark (Atkinson, Dallin, and Lapidus 1977; Scott 1974; Eisenstein 1979; Wolchik 1979).

Religiosity versus secularism is another important dimension of ideology that serves as a basis from which to understand governmental actions on women's interests. The Catholic nations of the West (and Canada's Quebec province) lagged far behind the Protestant nations in granting women basic civil rights, such as the vote or property rights, and the Catholic nations have also been slower to change marriage and reproduction policies. (On women and politics in Catholic European nations, see Caldwell 1978; Cantarow 1976; Makward 1975; Porter and Venning 1974.) Islamic nations have tended to lag even more (Mernissi 1975; Nelson 1974). Religion and secularism have played very important roles within nations, often in interaction with left–right politics that is well worth untangling and examining. In France and more so in Italy the communist parties have led in battles for reform of women's status not simply as the parties of the left but as the anti-clerical or, at least, secular parties. In Israel feminists clash with religious authorities as well. In the United States degrees of religions fundamentalism or orthodoxy may be more important than religious denomination *per se*, but 'separation of church and state' has by no means eliminated the role of religion in political debates on the status of women as the 'moral majority' shows. Indeed, some of the major rifts within religious organizations, regardless of the specific religion or country, are based on attitudes toward women's role and status.

Feminist Movements and Interest Organizations

Thus far we have said little about feminism *per se* as an influence in policies on women. Although there are numerous worthwhile studies of women's movements, there are vast gaps in analysis of the role of women's movements and organizations in the policy-making process (but see Boles 1979; Freeman 1974; Morgan 1972, 1974; O'Connor 1980).

The very nature of patriarchalism makes the development of a woman's interest group and strategies for successful influence a complex and interesting problem. Conflict that may be understood as a battle between the sexes tears at the most basic structures of

VIRGINIA SAPIRO

society as well as personal life. Pressures against such an interpretation make it difficult for women's interest organizations to define
the grounds of political conflict over the status of women (Sapiro
1980). Whereas most interest organizations would be loath to blame
their socio-political problems on themselves (especially when members of their own group are notably absent from positions of
power), women are under pressure to underscore their own participation in their oppression in order not to appear to be staging the
battle for greater equality as a battle between women and men.
Thus, women's organizations are caught in a dilemma regarding
which strategies will suit the needs of *intra*group mobilization and
*inter*group influence. If women's groups feel pressed to criticize
themselves in the early stages of the development of a movement,
they are unlikely to mobilize vast numbers of other women, particularly because a principal problem among women is low self-esteem
and a relatively low sense of personal and political efficacy (Deaux
1976). On the other hand, if women's movements blame those in
power, who tend to be men, they are often labelled as cranks and
'man-haters', and on those grounds may again be easily dismissed by
those—male and female—they attempt to influence. This is a common tactic used to undermine the legitimacy of interest groups:
blacks who point to the injustices against them perpetrated by white
society have often been labelled racists; early labour organizers who
pointed to the ills of industrial organization were attacked as anti-
American. Women's movements, then, provide a case study of conflicts among strategies of mobilization and influence in women's
efforts to press their interests.

Women's movements and organizations include a wide variety of
strategies and ideologies. One cannot analyse the impact of women's
interest organization without at least outlining these differences.
Taking the problem of strategies first, we can identify at least eight
different types used by women's organizations. One is *conventional
pressure techniques*, including legal action, lobbying, electoral participation, and contact with public officials and the press. These
strategies have been the basis of action for perhaps the best-known
women's organizations, such as the National American Women's
Suffrage Association (NAWSA) of the nineteenth century, and the
National Organization of Women (NOW) and the National
Women's Political Caucus (NWPC) of today. A second form is the
use of *nonconventional pressure techniques*, including symbolic
political action, protest, and demonstrations, and, from time to
time, violence. When American and British suffragists chained

themselves to the gates of important governmental buildings, when the British suffragists smashed windows of MPs' houses, when American feminists crowned a pig Miss America, and when French feminists put a wreath on the tomb of the unknown soldier for that man's wife, they were adopting serious political strategies designed to force the unaware to see that there was a problem to which the political system had to respond.

A third strategy which identifies particular types of feminist organization is *consciousness-raising*, or activities oriented directly toward intragroup mobilization. Included here would be not only groups specifically devoted to 'consciousness-raising', but also other means designed to develop knowledge about women and gender stratification. Fourth, women have established *alternative institutions*, providing services to women as diverse as health, transportation, banking, protection, legal aid, publishing, and education. These institutions have been established with the goal of satisfying the needs of women that are not covered by existing, especially male-dominated, organizations. In some cases they have not remained self-contained; rather, they have created demands for more comprehensive and public coverage and investment. Many of the rape crisis centres, womens' transit systems, and shelters for battered wives that now have some public funding were begun as organizations operated solely by volunteer work and private funds. As the use of these services increased and stretched beyond the limits of volunteer organizations, more widespread and forceful demands began to be placed on public authorities. In the United States these services were often given partial federal funding to serve as experimental social services, to be picked up later by local and state authorities. A fifth strategy, related to the former, is *separatism*, or the establishment of groups, institutions, and networks whose goal is to provide self-contained services and communities. One of the principles underlying separatist strategies is the desire to avoid having the goals, styles, and motivations of women's organizations reshaped or diverted by male institutions or nonfeminist ideology.

A sixth strategy might be called *caucus* organization. A vast number, and indeed many of the oldest women's groups, are formed as a subset of women within occupational, educational, or political organizations and institutions. These, of course, tend to restrict themselves to the specific concerns of women within these organizations. Sometimes, rather than working within other organizations, women's groups attempt to form *coalitions* with others, which requires emphasizing shared concerns and, often, submerging what can be profound differences. This is a seventh variety. Finally, as mentioned above, women have engaged in *international organization*. International congresses of women's groups extend back to the nineteenth century and women's history books are filled with references to women in one country importing the people, ideas, and strategies of women in other countries. Although these efforts often take place within larger organizations, such as the United Nations, international socialist organizations, or international congresses of other sorts, many and various international organizations have been established by women specifically for the purpose of discussing and solving problems of women's political status and social roles.

Women's groups also differ widely in their ideologies, or their understanding of the nature and sources of women's problems, as well as their solutions. The various types of feminism share three components: (1) a belief that women's opportunities and the quality of their lives are limited in part simply because they are women, (2) a desire to release the constraints imposed by patriarchy and sexism, and (3) a belief not simply in individual action, but also in group action to improve the conditions of women. Beyond these points, varieties of feminism differ widely. Some are derived primarily from traditions of liberal individualistic thought, others from socialist thought. In France, and to a lesser extent in England and the United States, psychoanalytic theory is serving as an important underpinning of feminism. Increasing numbers of feminists are attempting to wrench themselves from the context of theories and ideologies developed within and reflective of gender-stratified societies, in an effort to find new ways of understanding and responding to women's interests (Rich 1979; Daly 1978; editors of *Questions Feministes*, 1980). Of course here we are discussing more sophisticated ideologies than would commonly be found across the wide span of mass-level politics, but the various types of feminism among leaders and activists in women's organizations reflect these different strains.

The point of presenting this catalogue is not merely to describe, but also to provide means for comparison and analysis. Women's political organization and activities differ in strategy and ideology, in the breadth of their issue concerns, in their degree of self-containment, in the directness with which they approach women's problems as political problems, and political problems as government problems, in the size and type of their constituencies, and in the degree to which they, individually or together, are likely to be effective instruments of change. If feminism and feminist organizations stand as 'independent variables' in analyses of governmental action regarding women's interests, the complexity of those variables must be understood.

Analysis of women's interest organizations cannot be restricted to examination of the groups themselves, but rather must focus on the response of governmental and quasi-governmental groups as well. A variety of studies discuss the content of law and policy on women, but in general these provide only indirect information about the process of governmental response to interest-based demands, and the conditions under which demands are successfully placed (Brown, Freedman, Katz, and Price 1977; Goldstein 1979; Sachs and Wilson 1979). Taking a cue from William Gamson's study of responses to social movements (1975), we observe that the range of responses is more complex than a simple dichotomy of rejection and acceptance. It has been argued, for example, that while governments and political parties may display 'interest' in women's status, at the same time there is a constant attempt to depoliticize and diffuse the issues (Dahlerup 1980). One reason this is possible is that women's issues, perhaps more than any others, tend to fall somewhere between what are considered 'public' and 'private' interests and welfare. Every time someone questions the impact of a new policy affecting women's status on 'the basic unit of society, the family', that public–private distinction is being questioned.

At times governmental response is predominantly one of co-optation, diffusion, or symbolic manipulation. A most interesting example in the United States is provided by the executive actions of President Kennedy and the ensuing 1963 Equal Pay Act. Although Kennedy's Presidential Commission on the Status of Women and the resulting state commissions of similar title can be seen as important steps in both politicizing women's problems and in seeking solutions (Freeman 1975), it has also been argued that Kennedy's efforts were designed in part to forestall serious interest in the Equal Rights Amendment, for which he, along with previous presidents, had voiced support. More broadly, the history of governmental response to women provides an excellent case study of the function of study commissions and conferences in policy making. Non-decision-making does not necessarily mean that issues are not raised. If issues can be discussed long enough and in a manner confusing enough to allow time, energy, interest, or money to run out, the effect can be the same.

Women as Representatives

Certainly one of the most often-voiced desires of the women's movement is placing women in positions of influence. The very term 'representation of women' is usually taken very specifically to mean increasing the number of women in political office because of the assumption that women in power would be more responsive to women's interests than men would be. Questions about the validity of this assumption have led to a wealth of research on women in élite positions, much of which provides some clues, and much of which raises further questions.

The major questions posed in the literature on women as public officeholders are (1) are women different from men; and (2) if so (or not), why (or why not)? Research on these questions reveals considerably more similarity between the sexes than difference, although some of the differences are of great importance to the problem of representation.

Very few women seek political offices with the intention of representing women's interests *per se* (Kirkpatrick 1974; Carroll 1979; Mezey 1978*b*, 1977; Vallance 1979). Female candidates tend not to initiate discussion of women's issues, in part because 'too much emphasis upon women's issues in a campaign might generate speculation that the candidate is too narrow in her concerns and will not adequately represent all the people' (Carroll 1979: 27). Emily Stoper shows that women candidates place less emphasis on their home lives in their campaigning than do men, presumably because it is suspected that a woman is easily distracted from her public work by her private concerns, while for a man reference to family shows the solidity of character of a good 'family man' (Stoper 1977).

There is evidence that a woman's desire to represent women, if voiced, would be a drawback in campaign politics. In a recent experimental study, a pro-equal rights male defeats an anti-equal rights male by 28 percentage points, but a man who says nothing on the subject defeats a woman who runs as a representative of women by 32 percentage points (Perkins and Fowlkes 1980). In a study of candidates for state legislative seats in 1976 Susan Carroll finds that women who did not discuss women's issues at all during their campaigns fared somewhat better than did those who discussed the issues (Carroll 1979).

Although women might fare better, in terms of campaign strategy, not to discuss women's interests or, especially, not to claim to represent them, female candidates and officeholders are forced into a 'woman's role', or at least they are forced to be defined as 'woman' candidates or politicians rather than, simply as candidates or politicians. They are more often asked about their families than are men (Mezey 1978*a*). Once women are in office, their committee assignments, initiation of legislation, and the topics on which they speak tend to reflect traditional women's concerns (Vallance 1979; Diamond 1977; Hough 1977). What we do not know, however, is the degree to which these differences are attributable to self-initiation or to the constraints of organizations and other élites. Research does show that perceptions of women among the politically élite are shaped in part by stereotypes, and that sexism plays a role in élite recruitment and promotion (Dubeck 1976; Hedlund, Freeman, Hamm, and Stein 1979; Welch 1978; Sapiro 1981; Carroll 1979). Do women, then constitute a group that must stay 'in the closet' (Carroll 1979) or sneak into office?

Do women make a difference in office? There is little evidence of differences when general policy questions are asked (Mezey 1978*b*; Francovic 1977), although this result is not universal (Cook 1978). Beverly Cook's study of judges shows women, who are more feminist on some issues than are men, are more likely to 'transfer symbolic resources to women' than are men (Cook 1979: 27). Although women may not run 'as women', they tend to be sympathetic toward feminism, and may become partially concerned with women's issues once in office (Carroll 1979; Mezey 1978*a*, 1978*b*). Even when it appears that male and female officeholders share preferences on women's issues, it is often up to the women to do the real legislative work (Vallance 1979). Although sympathetic attitudes are important, legislative work is crucial.

With more research on élite behaviour it may become possible to determine the effects of organizational roles and structures on the ability of members of the élite to respond to women's interests. Although legislators may become most effective when they become specialists, or take a leading role on specialized committees, is the same true when the speciality is women's issues? Or, as suggested above, is this type of speciality interpreted as a narrow interest compared with, for example, the fortunes of the aeroplane industry in Washington? What policy implications can be drawn from studies that show that women are less likely to be promoted or placed in important positions within governmental bodies, or that they may be less well integrated informally and socially into the 'men's club' called government (Vallance 1979; Mezey 1978*b*; Diamond 1977)?

Research in social psychology shows that men and women use

different communication styles and strategies, and studies of group interaction show that men can effectively—even if unintentionally—freeze women out of conversations and debates, or simply render their communication ineffective (Deaux 1976; Frieze *et al.* 1978). Most of these studies focus on informal groups; are these forces at work in legislative halls, executive offices, and judicial chambers as well? Reports from the earliest studies (Breckinridge 1933) to the most recent (Vallance 1979) suggest that they are; more rigorous communication studies will determine the degree. Social psychology research also suggests that women's leadership in primarily male domains such as politics may be curbed by the difficulties which all people, and especially men, have in being supervised or led by a woman (Deaux 1976; Frieze *et al.* 1978). How does this problem affect, for example, personnel relations and effectiveness in organizations such as Congress, where large staff are critical to legislative work? Studies in social psychology and organizational behaviour are filled with suggestions for forces that may affect policy making and implementation as they concern women's issues.

In recent years governments increasingly include special offices, commissions, committees, or people whose job it is to concern themselves with the problems of women (Stewart 1980). Political parties of all types have generally contained women's sections. These offices do not always appear designed to promote change; in some cases it appears more that these groups are designed very much for appeasement or cooptive purposes (Mossink 1980). Although special women's offices may be important symbols, indicating that women's status is a topic of concern, their mere presence does not necessarily indicate that governments are responding to women's interests. All states in the United States formed special commissions in the early 1960s in response to President Kennedy's call, and a vast number of countries have done the same, particularly as part of the United Nations' declaration of an International Women's Decade. Masses of policy agendas were drawn up by the appointed commissions. What were the results?

We may also look at formalization of the women's interest in terms of strategies of segregation and integration. Special offices within parties or governments have important symbolic meaning and they are generally, although not always, staffed by activists and specialists in women's problems. At the same time, however, segregation can 'ghettoize' the problems; it can segregate the issues both from other related problems and from experts and leaders in other fields. How do these forces balance in the policy process?

These observations about the problems of women as representatives of women returns us to a question posed at the beginning: is an increase in the number of women in positions of power the key to representing women? We can now argue that it is a necessary condition, but it is not sufficient. We have seen that the presence of female officeholders is only one element among the factors determining the degree to which government responds to the interests of women. Moreover, the role of women in government is shaped by the effects of recruitment procedures and organizational constraints in a political system dominated by patriarchal norms. Not the least of the problems is the presence of many female leaders who, to varying degrees, accept and make decisions according to these patriarchal norms. (For a radical example, see Koonz 1977.)

Can we argue that the presence of more women among public officeholders will mean women will be more represented than they were? Increasing the number of women in government is not sufficient, but it is necessary. First, we have seen that women in office do make some difference in government responsiveness to women's interests. Second, the mere presence of women in positions of power readjusts what is now a thoroughly inequitable distribution of political values in society: power, participation, and decision-making. If we accept the democratic ideal that participation in governance is valuable, can we argue that systematic exclusion of a particular social group is acceptable? Finally, increased representation of people who 'look like' women will effect powerful symbolic changes in politics. Women and men continue to think of politics as a male domain because the empirical truth at this moment is that politics *is* a male domain. People of both sexes find governance by women odd, remarkable, extraordinary, and even inappropriate. Can we consider a governing system to be representative of women if women are not considered 'representative' of governance? More women in office will increase the acceptability of women in government (MacManus 1981).

CONCLUSION: WHEN WOMEN'S INTERESTS ARE INTERESTING

The question of what is to be represented and under what circumstances are women represented has left us with a vast web that needs untangling. Research on these questions will serve two functions.

First, it will develop knowledge about a large portion of humanity that has received little serious attention in the past. But just as knowledge developed about specific institutions, leaders, policies, or nations is useful to those who spend most of their time focusing on these specific areas, research on women and politics or, more properly, gender and politics, will fill gaps in our understanding of politics more generally. What does 'representation of women' mean? What is to be represented? Under what circumstances are women's interests represented? The answers require new investigations of fundamental questions of politics, informed by a recognition that gender differentiation and stratification profoundly structure human life. The relation between women and politics is no mere 'special topic'. It is a field of study from which political scientists have much to learn. Some suggestions of what these things are follow.

Analysis of women's political interests and how governments represent and respond to them require renewed attention to the thorny problem of the limits of politics and government, the boundaries of and relationship between the private and public domains. Women are largely defined as belonging to the private rather than the political world; often the objections raised against the demands of feminist movements are framed as rejection of government incursions into private life. Protection against violence is a good example. Many of the legislators who most strongly advocate 'law and order' are bitter opponents of domestic-violence legislation which is designed to protect women from one of the most common forms of violence, wife battery, on the grounds that what happens within the family is beyond the proper reach of government. Conservatives label shelters for battered women 'houses for runaway wives', thus defining these women not as people escaping from crime, but wives abandoning their proper domain.

As we asked earlier, why is an individual's relationship to the production of children not commonly accepted as a matter of political interest while one's relationship to other forms of production is? The answer cannot be dismissed simply by arguing that reproduction is a private matter with no political or social interest; myriad laws on birth control, legitimacy, and sex education show that our political system does regard reproduction as a state matter. Indeed, many of the justifications for restricting women's educational, employment, and civic opportunities have been phrased in terms of the overriding state interest in the quality of motherhood and in assuring 'necessary' production levels. The Supreme Court has stated repeatedly that reproduction and children are fundamental concerns of the state. Women's interests have played key roles in the historical fluidity of our definitions of 'public' and 'private'. It is no coincidence that the development of women as political persons and of their status and roles as policy questions coincides with twentieth-century expansion of government in social welfare and socialist states. The Supreme Court first explicitly delineated a constitutional right to privacy in a 1965 case involving contraception (*Griswold* v. *Ct.* 381 US 479) and expanded upon it in later cases on abortion. Scholarship profits most from attention to the most difficult questions; in debates over what is private and what is public, what is personal and what is political, many of the most difficult questions have unique relevance to women's lives and interests.

Taking a serious interest in women and politics will also change some of the ways in which political scientists approach and discuss politics. Women's studies research has already pointed out flaws and gaps in accepted political theories and models. It has also revealed many pieces of conventional wisdom to be false, usually by transforming common and sometimes unstated assumptions into questions and hypotheses (e.g. Shabad and Andersen 1979). Research on women uncovers critical problems in democratic theory and research which are of direct relevance to the problem of representation (Brennan and Pateman 1979; Okin 1979; Sapiro 1979a, 1979b).

Women's studies research also criticizes and refines the basic tool of any type of research: language. We have already suggested that analysis of women and representation offers an opportunity to scrutinize the 'political', the core concept in our vocabulary. We have made many of our words more blunt tools than they need be. 'What is the nature of man, what are his needs and wants? How do these relate to political interests, goals, strategies, and structures?' If we ask these questions of our political philosophers and psychologists, the answers depend in large part upon whether we understand 'man' to be a generic term or one that refers to a specific gender. Most of our great philosophers held that the nature of males and females is very different. What do we mean, then, when we ask about the political implications of the 'nature of man'? (On the 'generic man', see Moulton 1977; Silveira 1980; Martyna 1978; Schneider and Hacker 1980.) Political scientists have difficulty incorporating women into the political world because they lack or reject the appropriate language. 'Patriarchy', 'sexism', 'feminist' and 'male-dominated' appear to be emotionally charged words, the tools of the polemicist rather than the scholar. But are these words necessarily more charged than 'monarchy', 'democratic', 'Democratic', or 'authoritarian'?

For now, the root of the study of politics is, as an eminent political scientist has argued, 'man' (Eulau 1963). In politics the sum of the parts is not equal to the whole. The argument of women's studies is that by focusing our attention primarily on half of humanity, assuming that that half speaks for—represents—all, we have done worse than understanding half of politics. Political science can only benefit by expanding its view. As one of the first sociologists wrote in 1837, 'If a test of civilization be sought, none can be so sure as the condition of that half of society over which the other half has power—from the exercise of the right of the strongest' (Martineau 1974: 125).

Afterword

This article was originally written in 1980 in response to a request to summarize what we then knew about the representation of women and what research was still needed. Of course, it reflects the scholarly literature of the time, but perhaps more significantly, it reflects the state of the world at that time. Two important events would have to be central to any consideration of this topic now. Both the fall of the communist regimes in the Soviet Union and surrounding countries and the move towards retrenchment of the welfare states of the advanced industrial nations in the face of the economic crises of the 1980s and 1990s reinforce a central point in this essay: namely, that the analysis of the representation of women requires contextualization in an understanding of larger problems of the political economy *in interaction with* the gender ideology of popular cultures. A large literature, beginning with Barbara Einhorn's *Cinderella Goes to Market* (London: Verso, 1993), demonstrates the point well, as does a growing literature on women and the welfare state in both historical and contemporary perspective. For an updated bibliographic essay on the problems raised in this discussion, see Virginia Sapiro, *Transforming the Curriculum in Political Science* (Towson State College: National Centre for Curriculum Transformation Resources on Women, 1997).

Notes

1. Moreover, it is important to note that the question of representation *per se* has been subjected to reconsideration and revitalization in recent years. See, for example, Eulau and Wahlke (1978) and Lawson (1980).

2. One of the recurrent problems that women's studies scholars (and probably those of any interdisciplinary field) face is the lack of familiarity people in the 'home field' have with the literature of the interdisciplinary field, resulting in questions about lack of evidence. The purpose of this discussion is not to review the literature for those unfamiliar with it, although the major relevant work and especially review works and anthologies are cited in references.

3. I will return to this question later, suggesting that having a representative who looks like me may well serve my interests.

4. If we were to argue that an 'interest group' must be entirely self-conscious and organized, we must then argue that an entirely oppressed group has no special interest and is, in fact, theoretically irrelevant to the political system. For a defence of the more orthodox definition of 'interest group' see Wilson (1981).

5. Evidence suggests that familial modernization and democratization have altered relations between the sexes very little. Indeed, the burden of socio-historical research points to these as forces that have decreased women's value within the family and, in many cases, increased the gap between the sexes. See especially Rosaldo and Lamphere (1974), Rowbotham (1974), and Boserup (1970).

6. A catalogue of specific policies would be too long to mention here because of the vast number of restrictive policies. For international comparison see Adams and Winston (1980) and the 'World Plan of Action' in Tinker and Bramsen (1976). For an introduction to American law and policy, see the Sage Yearbooks in Women's Policy Studies (Chapman, 1976; Chapman and Gates, 1977; Chapman and Gates, 1978; Feinstein, 1979; and Berk, 1980) as well as Goldstein (1979) and Brown, Freedman, Katz, and Price (1977).

7. For further discussion see Jennings and Farah (MS., n.d.).

8. When money becomes tight, except in the case of poverty, a family will not do without food; rather, it will avoid paying for the labour costs of prepared foods. Similarly, it will not purchase as many new items of clothing. In the former case women do more cooking, in the latter they do more sewing and mending.

9. For an exception, see King (1977). In addition there have been policy suggestions that would create government-sponsored incentives for some women to remain full-time homemakers. For analysis of some of the possible implications of these policies, see the excellent novel by Fairbairns (1979).

References

Adams, Carolyn Teich, and Kathryn Teich Winston (1980), *Mothers at Work: Public Policies in the United States, Sweden, and China* (New York: Longman).

Ardener, Shirley (ed.) (1975), *Perceiving Women* (London: Malaby).

—— (ed.) (1978), *Defining Females: The Nature of Women in Society* (New York: John Wiley).

Armed Forces and Society (1978), Special issue, Summer, entire issue.

Atkinson, Dorothy, Alexander Dallin, and Gail Warshovsky Lapidus (eds.) (1977), *Women in Russia* (Stanford, Calif.: Stanford University Press).

Berk, Sara Fenstermaker (ed.) (1980), *Women and Household Labor* (Beverly Hills, Calif.: Sage).

Boles, Janet K. (1979), *The Politics of the Equal Rights Amendment: Conflict and the Decision Process* (New York: Longman).

Boserup, Ester (1970), *Women's Role in Economic Development* (London: Allen and Unwin).

Breckinridge, Sophinisba (1933), *Women in the Twentieth Century: A Study of their Political, Social, and Economic Activities* (New York: McGraw-Hill).

Brennan, Teresa, and Carole Pateman (1979), ' "Mere Auxiliaries to the Commonwealth": Women and the Origins of Liberalism', *Political Studies*, 27, 183–200.

Brown, Barbara, Ann Freedman, Harriet Katz, and Alice Price (1977), *Women's Rights and the Law: The Impact of the ERA on State Laws* (New York: Praeger).

Cantarow, Ellen (1976), 'Abortion and Feminism in Italy: Women against Church and State', *Radical America*, 10, 8–28.

Carroll, Susan (1979), 'Women Candidates and Support for Women's Issues: Closet Feminists', Presented at the annual meeting of the Midwest Political Science Association, Chicago.

Chapman, Jane Roberts (ed.) (1976), *Economic Independence for Women: The Foundation for Equal Rights* (Beverly Hills, Calif.: Sage).

—— and Margaret Gates (eds.) (1977), *Women into Wives: The Legal and Economic Impact of Marriage* (Beverly Hills, Calif.: Sage).

—— (eds.) (1978), *The Victimization of Women* (Beverly Hills, Calif.: Sage).

Caldwell, Lesley (1978), 'Church, State, and Family: The Women's Movement in Italy', in A. Kuhn and A. M. Wolpe (eds.), *Feminism and Materialism* (Boston: Routledge and Kegan Paul), 68–95.

Cook, Beverly Blair (1979), 'Judicial Attitudes on Women's Rights: Do Women Judges Make a Difference?' Presented at the IPSA Roundtable on Women, Essex.

Dahlerup, Drude (1980), 'Approaches to the Study of Public Policy Towards Women', presented at the joint sessions of the European Consortium for Political Research, Florence.

Daly, Mary (1978), *Gyn/Ecology: The Metaethics of Radical Feminism* (Boston: Beacon).

Deaux, Kay (1976), *The Behavior of Women and Men* (Monterey, Calif.: Wadsworth).

Delphy, Christine (1980), 'The Main Enemy', *Feminist Issues*, 1, 23–40.

Diamond, Irene (1977), *Sex Roles in the State House* (New Haven, Conn.: Yale University Press).

Dubeck, Paula J. (1976), 'Women and Access to Political Office: A Comparison of Female and Male State Legislators', *Sociological Quarterly*, 17, 42–52.

DuBois, Ellen Carol (1980), *Feminism and Suffrage: The Emergence of an Independent Women's Movement in America, 1848–1869* (Ithaca, NY: Cornell University Press).

Editors of *Questions Feministes* (1980), 'Variations on Some Common Themes', *Feminist Issues*, 1, 3–22.

Eisenstein, Zillah R. (ed.) (1979), *Capitalist Patriarchy and the Case for Socialist Feminism* (New York: Monthly Review Press).

Enloe, Cynthia (1980), 'Women—The Reserve Army of *Army* Labor', *Review of Radical Political Economy*, 12, 42–52.

Eulau, Heinz (1963), *The Behavioural Persuasion in Politics* (New York: Random House).

—— and John C. Wahlke (eds.) (1978), *The Politics of Representation* (Beverly Hills, Calif.: Sage).

Evans, Richard J. (1976), *The Feminist Movement in Germany, 1894–1933* (Beverly Hills, Calif.: Sage).

Evans, Sara (1980), *Personal Politics: The Roots of Women's Liberation in the Civil Rights Movement and the New Left* (New York: Random House).

Fairbairns, Zoe (1979), *Benefits* (London: Virago).

Flexner, Eleanor (1973), *A Century of Struggle: The Women's Rights Movement in the USA* (New York: Atheneum).

Feinstein, Karen Wolk (ed.) (1979), *Working Women and Families* (Beverly Hills, Calif.: Sage).

Francovic, Kathleen A. (1977), 'Sex and Voting in the United States House of Representatives, 1961–1975', *American Politics Quarterly*, 5, 315–30.

Freeman, Jo (1975), *The Politics of Women's Liberation* (New York: David McKay).

Frieze, Irene, *et al.* (eds.) (1978), *Women and Sex Roles: A Social Psychological Perspective* (New York: Norton).

Galey, Margaret E. (1979), 'Promoting Nondiscrimination against Women: The United nations Commission on the Status of Women', *International Studies Quarterly*, 23, 273–302.

Gamson, William A. (1975), *The Strategy of Social Protest* (Homewood, Ill.: Dorsey).

Goldstein, Leslie Friedman (1979), *The Constitutional Rights of Women: Cases in Law and Social Change* (New York: Longman).

Gordon, Linda (1976), *Woman's Body, Woman's Right: A Social History of Birth Control in America* (New York: Viking).

Grimes, Alan (1967), *The Puritan Ethic and Woman Suffrage* (New York: Oxford University Press).

Hedlund, Ronald D., Patricia K. Freeman, Keith Hamm, and Robert Stein (1979), 'The Electability of Women Candidates: The Effects of Sex Role Stereotypes', *Journal of Politics*, 41, 513–25.

Hevener, Natalie Kaufman (1978), 'International Law and the Status of Women: An Analysis of International Legal Instruments Related to the Treatment of Women', *Harvard Women's Law Journal*, 1, 131–56.

Hole, Judith, and Ellen Levine (1971), *The Rebirth of Feminism* (New York: Quadrangle).

Hough, Jerry F. (1977), 'Women and Women's Issues in Soviet Policy Debates', in D. Atkinson *et al.* (eds.), *Women in Russia* (Stanford, Calif.: Stanford University Press), 355–74.

Inglehart, Ronald, and Margaret Inglehart (1975), *European Men and Women* (Brussels: European Economic Community).

Jennings, M. Kent, and Barbara G. Farah (1981), 'Gender and Politics: When Is a Cleavage Not a Cleavage?' in H. Kerr, H. D. Klingermann, and P. Personen (eds.), *People and Their Polities*, forthcoming.

Kennedy, David M. (1970), *Birth Control in America: The Career of Margaret Sanger* (New Haven: Yale University Press).

King, Marjorie (1977), 'Cuba's Attack on Women's Second Shift, 1974–1976', *Latin American Perspectives*, 4, 106–19.

Kirkpatrick, Jeane (1974), *Political Woman* (New York: Basic).

Koonz, Claudia (1977), 'Mothers in the Fatherland: Women in Nazi Germany', in R. Bridenthal and C. Koonz (eds.), *Becoming Visible: Women in European History* (Boston: Houghton Mifflin), 445–73.

Kraditor, Aileen (1965), *The Ideas of the Women's Suffrage Movement: 1890–1920* (New York: Columbia University Press).

Kreps, Juanita M. (ed.) (1976), *Women and the American Economy: A Look to the 1980's* (Englewood Cliffs, NJ: Prentice-Hall).

Lane, Robert (1959), *Political Life* (Glencoe: Free Press).

Lapidus, Gail Warshovsky (1977), *Women in Soviet Society* (Berkeley: University of California Press).

Lawson, Kay (ed.) (1980), *Political Parties and Linkage: A Comparative Perspective* (New Haven, Conn.: Yale University).

Lewis, Gwendolyn L. (1978), 'Changes in Women's Role Participation', in I. Frieze *et al.* (eds.), *Women and Sex Roles* (New York: Norton), 137–56.

Makward, Christiane (1975), 'French Women in Politics, 1975', *Michigan Papers in Women's Studies*, 1, 123–38.

Martineau, Harriet (1974), 'Society in America', in A. Rossi (ed.), *The Feminism Papers* (New York: Bantam), 125–43.

Martyna, Wendy (1978), 'What Does *He* Mean—The Use of the Generic Masculine', *Journal of Communication*, 28, 131–38.

Mernissi, Fatima (1975), *Beyond the Veil: Male–Female Dynamics in a Modern Muslim Society* (New York: Wiley).

Mezey, Susan Gluck (1978*a*), 'Does Sex Make a Difference? A Case Study of Women in Politics', *Western Political Quarterly*, 31, 492–501.

—— (1978*b*), 'Support for Women's Rights Policy: An Analysis of Local Politicians', *American Politics Quarterly*, 6, 485–97.

Morgan, David (1972), *Suffragists and Democrats: The Politics of Woman Suffrage in America* (Ann Arbor: University of Michigan Press).

—— (1974), *Suffragists and Liberals: The Politics of Women's Suffrage in England* (Totowa, NJ: Rowman and Littlefield).

Mossink, Maryke (1980), 'Emancipation or Liberation? Government Emancipation Policies and the Feminist Movement', presented at the joint sessions of the European Consortium for Political Research, Florence.

Moulton, Janice (1977), 'The Myth of the Neutral "Man"', in M.

Vetterling-Braggin, F. Ellison, and J. English (eds.), *Feminism and Philosophy* (Totowa, NJ: Littlefield, Adams), 124–37.

Nelson, Cynthia (1974), 'Public and Private Politics: Women in the Middle Eastern World', *American Ethnology*, 1, 551–63.

O'Connor, Karen (1980), *Women's Groups' Use of the Courts* (Lexington, Mass.: Lexington Books).

Okin, Susan Moller (1979), *Women in Western Political Thought* (Princeton, NJ: Princeton University Press).

Pateman, Carole (1979), *The Problem of Political Obligation: A Critical Analysis of Liberal Theory* (New York: John WIley).

Perkins, Jerry, and Diane L. Fowlkes (1980), 'Opinion Representation versus Social Representation: Or, Why Women Can't Run as Women and Win', *American Political Science Review*, 75, 92–103.

Pitkin, Hannah (1967), *The Concept of Representation* (Berkeley: University of California Press).

Porter, Mary Cornelia, and Corey Venning (1974), 'Church, Law, and Society: The Status of Women in Italy and the Republic of Ireland', *Michigan Papers in Women's Studies*, 1, 125–41.

Rich, Adrienne (1979), *On Lies, Secrets, and Silence* (New York: Norton).

Robinson, John P. (1980), 'Housework Technology and Household Work', in S. F. Berk (ed.) *Women and Household Labor* (Beverly Hills, Calif.: Sage), 53–68.

Rosaldo, Michelle, and Louise Lamphere (eds.) (1974), *Women, Culture, and Society* (Stanford, Calif.: Stanford University Press).

Rowbotham, Sheila (1973), *Woman's Consciousness, Man's World* (Baltimore: Penguin).

—— (1974), *Hidden from History: Rediscovering Women in History from the Seventeenth Century to the Present* (New York: Random House).

Sachs, Albie, and Joan Hoff Wilson (1979), *Sexism and the Law: Male Beliefs and Legal Bias in Britain and the U.S.* (New York: Free Press).

Sandy, Peggy (1974), 'Female Status in the Public Domain', in M. Rosaldo and L. Lamphere (eds.), *Women, Culture, and Society* (Stanford, Calif.: Stanford University Press), 189–209.

Sapiro, Virginia (1979*a*), 'Sex and Games: On Oppression and Rationality', *British Journal of Political Science*, 9, 385–408.

—— (1979*b*), 'Women's Studies and Political Conflict', in J. Sherman and E. Beck (eds.), *The Prism of Sex: Essays in the Sociology of Knowledge* (Madison, Wis.: University of Wisconsin Press), 253–66.

—— (1980), 'News from the Front: Inter-Sex and Intergenerational Conflict over the Status of Women', *Western Political Quarterly*, 2, 260–77.

—— (1981), 'If Senator Baker Were a Woman: An Experimental Study of Candidate Images', *Political Psychology*, 3 (Spring/Summer 1981–2), 61–83.

Schneider, Joseph W., and Sally Hacker (1980), 'Sex Role Imagery and the

Use of Generic *Man* in Introductory Texts', *American Sociologist*, 8, 12–18.

Schochet, Gordon J. (1975), *Patriarchalism in Political Thought* (New York: Basic Books).

Scott, Hilda (1974), *Women and Socialism: Experiences from Eastern Europe* (Boston: Beacon).

Shabad, Goldie, and Kristi Andersen (1979), 'Candidate Evaluations by Men and Women', *Public Opinion Quarterly*, 43, 18–35.

Silveira, Jeanette (1980), 'Generic Masculine Words and Thinking', *Women's Studies International Quarterly*, 3, 165–78.

Steinfels, Margaret O'Brien (1973), *Who's Minding the Children? The History and Politics of Day Care in America* (New York: Simon and Schuster).

Stewart, Debra W. (1980), 'Institutionalization of Female Participation at the Local Level: Commissions on the Status of Women and Agenda Building', *Women and Politics*, 1, 37–63.

Stites, Richard (1978), *The Women's Liberation Movement in Russia: Feminism, Nihilism, and Bolshevism, 1860–1930* (Princeton, NJ: Princeton University Press).

Stoper, Emily (1977), 'Wife and Politician: Role Strain among Women in Public Office', in M. Githens and J. Prestage (eds.), *A Portrait of Marginality* (New York: Longman), 320–38.

Thorne, Barrie, and Nancy Henley (eds.) (1975), *Language and Sex: Differences and Dominance* (Rowley, Mass.: Newbury House).

Tinker, Irene, and Michele Bo Bramsen (eds.) (1976), *Women and World Development* (Washington, DC: overseas Development Council).

Vallance, Elizabeth (1979), *Women in the House: A Study of Women Members of Parliament* (London: Athlone Press).

Vanek, Joann (1980), 'Household Work, Wage Work, and Sexual Equality', in S. F. Berk (ed.), *Women and Household Labor* (Beverly Hills, Calif.: Sage), 275–92.

Weeks, Jeffrey (1977), *Coming Out: Homosexual Politics in Britain, from the Nineteenth Century to the Present* (London: Quartet).

Welch, Susan (1978), 'Recruitment of Women to Public Office: A Discriminant Analysis', *Western Political Quarterly*, 31, 372–80.

Wilson, Graham, K. (1981), *Interest Groups in the United States* (New York: Oxford University Press).

Wolchik, Sharon L. (1979), 'The Status of Women in a Socialist Order: Czechoslovakia, 1948–78', *Slavic Review*, 38, 583–602.

8

Beyond Interests in Politics: A Comment on Virginia Sapiro's 'When Are Interests Interesting? The Problem of Political Representation of Women'

Irene Diamond and Nancy Hartsock

In 'When Are Interests Interesting?' Virginia Sapiro makes a number of stimulating and important arguments. Her article is particularly useful because it both suggests new research directions and serves as an example of the difficulties of approaching the study of women and politics within the conventional categories of political analysis. We disagree with Sapiro on a number of points, but rather than addressing these here, we hope to expand the discussion by focusing on the ways in which Sapiro's arguments illuminate the problems created by attempting to make do with the conventional categories.[1] Recent developments in feminist theory have begun to uncover fundamental weaknesses in the categories of political analysis themselves, thus forcing researchers to move beyond the positions Sapiro has taken.[2]

Sapiro's treatment of women's representation underscores the major problem her article presents: on the one hand, she holds that women are an interest group, but on the other, she states that conflict over the issues raised by including women in politics 'tears at the most basic structures and conceptions of society'. If women are simply another interest group, however seriously one may take their interests, they remain a special interest group not fundamentally different from others, and in discussing their concerns one need raise no important new political or methodological questions. But if the inclusion of women in politics threatens the most basic structures of society, one cannot fit their concerns into the framework of interests. These inconsistent positions are an inevitable consequence of trying to work within the conventional categories of political analysis. Here we will point to the new directions which research

Reprinted by permission from *The American Political Science Review*, 75/3 (1981), 717–21.

can take if one follows the implications raised by the question of women's political representation.

If women have common interests, as both we and Sapiro believe they do, any attempt to ascertain these interests involves one in the difficult problem of understanding objective social situations and their relevance to political interests. In addition, one must recognize that the different objective situations of the sexes may not necessarily be clearly reflected in women's consciousness of these differences. While Sapiro understands these things, she is vague about which characteristics are most salient and how they relate to women's objective interests.[3]

Instead of a consideration of these issues—all of them presenting complicated problems for research—Sapiro's essay offers a mixed list of factors and social indicators which may be politically relevant, and some references to the few significant differences between women's and men's attitudes as these emerge from public opinion data. The attribution of common concerns to women needs a firmer institutional foundation than this.

If women's issues have been defined by the division of labour in private life, as Sapiro and others have suggested, why not base an account of women's common concerns on a more thoroughgoing analysis of this division of labour? We hold that despite the real differences among women, there are commonalities which grow from women's life activity of producing and sustaining human beings. At the level of grand theory, it may be fruitful to proceed on the basis of the radical-feminist hypothesis that all forms of oppression and domination are modelled on male/female oppression. However, the power relations of race and class which mediate this common female experience remain important for middle-level theory and empirical accounts; failure to take account of them will lead to errors and may even undermine the legitimacy of feminist scholarship.

In schematic and simplified terms, 'women's work' occurs in a context characterized by concrete involvement with the necessities of life rather than abstraction from them, a context in which the specific qualities of individuals and objects are central, and in which the unification of mind and body, of mental and manual labour, is inherent in the activities performed. In this context, relations with others take a variety of forms which transcend instrumental cooperation for the attainment of joint ends. Feminist theorists have pointed out that the depth and variety of a woman's relations with others grows both from her socialization as a female human being and from the biological fact of living in a female body (e.g. Rich 1976: 63; Chodorow 1978: 59). In the face of menstruation, coitus, pregnancy, childbirth, lactation—all challenges to bodily bounds— a female cannot maintain in any simple way the distinction Freud saw as central to human existence, the clear disjunction between me and not-me (1961: 12–13). And the social circumstance that typically women, but not men, nurture the young has meant that the child's task of differentiating from the mother follows different patterns in each sex; this differentiation reinforces boundary confusion in female egos and boundary-strengthening in males.[4] Psychoanalytic evidence suggests that, as a result of these early experiences, women tend to define and experience themselves relationally, while men are more likely to form a sense of self as separate and disconnected from the world (Chodorow (1978: 198).

We hypothesize that these different psychic experiences both grow out of and in turn reinforce the sexual division of labour. And different male and female life-activity leads toward profoundly different social understandings. For men, 'masculinity' can only be attained by means of opposition to the concrete world of daily life, by escaping from contact with the 'female' world of the household into the 'masculine' world of public life, and at least in the *polis*, politics. This experience of two worlds—one considered valuable, if largely attainable, the other considered useless and demeaning, if concrete and necessary—organizes what might be termed *phallocentric* social existence. In contrast, women's relationally defined existence, as constructed through the sexual division of labour, results in a social understanding in which dichotomies are less foreign, everyday life is more valued, and a sense of connectedness and continuity with other persons and the natural world is central.

Our argument is that female experience not only inverts that of the male but also forms a basis on which to expose the traditional conceptions of masculine existence and the political community men have constructed as both partial and fundamentally flawed (Hartsock 1981: ch. 10, discusses this in more depth). Throughout Western history the life-activities most important to survival— motherwork, housework, and, until the rise of capitalism, any work necessary to basic subsistence or survival—have been held to be unworthy of those who are fully human.

One result of these 'reversals' of the proper order of things, perhaps the most devastating of all, is illustrated by the Western cultural preoccupation with violence and death. In both philosophy and practice one finds the pervasive belief that it is the ability deliberately to risk one's life, to seek with Achilles a short life but a glorious one, which sets human beings above animals. From Homeric times to our own, this belief has carried such power that even a feminist theorist such as Simone de Beauvoir held that combat, whether against nature in the form of hunting or fishing, or against men in the form of war, is essential to the affirmation of 'spirit' as against mere life. Thus she argued that 'the worst cause that was laid upon woman was that she should be excluded from these warlike forays. For it is not in giving life but in risking life that man is raised above the animal; that is why superiority has been accorded in humanity not to the sex that brings forth but to that which kills' (1961: 58).

A systematic examination of the psychic and institutional consequences of the sexual division of labour could provide the necessary base for the attribution of common interests to women. The processes which both create and reinforce the sexual division of labour and translate its psychic and institutional consequences into hierarchical relations of power would need to be specified. Clearly this is no small task. Yet pursuing this line of inquiry becomes even more compelling when one recognizes that while the meanings of 'public' and 'private' have changed over time, women as a group have remained excluded from public authority. What feminist theorist Mary Daly (1979: 14, 233) has labeled 'gynephobia' may be inherent in the very construction of state societies in the West.

Attention to the sexual division of labour also calls into question the appropriateness of the language of interests for understanding political life. As Christian Bay has remarked, this language fails to assign priorities to human wants, needs, objectives, and purposes, and in so doing implicitly supports the 'right of the strong to prevail in every contest' (Bay 1980: 332). We should remember that the language of interests emerged along with the changes in the division of labour in production and reflected society's understanding of itself as dominated by rational economic men seeking to maximize their satisfactions. But human beings are moved by more than interests. The reduction of all human emotions to interests and interests to the rational search for gain reduces the human community to an instrumental, arbitrary, and deeply unstable alliance, one which rests on the private desires of isolated individuals. An account of social life such as this is clearly partial: certainly a mother's characteristically nurturing relationship to her child is difficult to describe in terms of instrumental interests in individual gain. Close attention to women's activity rather than men's, and the consequent thoroughgoing focus on whole human beings, necessitates the development of *more* encompassing categories of analysis for political life.

A focus on the expansion of rights for women leads to similar questions. But here, too, Sapiro's discussion of the circumstances where political systems have responded to the expansion of the rights previously denied women in comparison with men does not go far enough. By focusing the discussion as she does, Sapiro perpetuates the belief that women are primarily seeking to catch up with men; instead she should address the fact that much of what women want and need is not the same as what men want and need. Reproductive freedom and access to abortion are perhaps the most prominent examples. Perhaps the best way to determine whether a public issue is concerned with advancing the representation of women is to establish whether it merely advocates extending to women rights established for men, or whether the discussion moves into new territory. Our outline of the sexual division of labour points to why issues centring on the reproduction of life cannot be covered by agendas which take account only of the demands appropriate to male individuals.

The problems feminism poses for the conventional understanding of individual rights can, ironically, be found in their shared intellectual roots in the seventeenth and eighteenth centuries: not only has feminism used the theory as far back as the eighteenth century, where feminism was based on the conception of the independent and autonomous self, but also at the same time it has argued for a recognition of women as a sexual class. (Eisenstein 1981: 3–173, traces this history.) More recently feminist theory has challenged the use of the rights framework on the issue of abortion and forced sterilization. For example, while liberal, pro-choice activists in the US articulated the need for abortion in terms of rights, recent work argues that the achievements of this struggle have had contradictory impacts, and that failures are partly attributable to the inappropriateness of the language of rights and the problematic nature of communities constructed around rights (see Petchesky 1980).

Sapiro's implicit adherence to the language of interests and rights and the assumptions of individualism which this language carries makes her discussion of the conditions that permit women to control the quality of their lives less useful than it might be. Her discussion is both too comprehensive and too narrow, since we are offered a bibliography of explanations at a variety of levels of analysis with no suggestion about their relative importance or interrelationships.

Sapiro's unwillingness to focus on the importance of any group, female or otherwise, leads her to ignore the influence of three of the most significant factors that structure social relations—sex, race, and class. This blank in the midst of comprehensiveness grows from her failure to make a clean break with the assumptions of the interest group framework. Though Sapiro clearly holds that the state is not neutral *vis-à-vis* women, her conceptual tools do not permit her to develop this insight. Where can she put her own recognition of the important ways in which gender differentiation and stratification structure human life? Indeed, her very use of the term 'responsiveness' carries with it the hidden and untested assumption that women's demands can be integrated into political systems. Before one accepts this assumption, or the counter-claim of the inherent impenetrability of political life, one must have more precise empirical specification of the dynamics of representation, the tensions which emerge in response to demands, and the contradictions which accompany policy success.

Marxists have long argued that state policy is intimately linked to the social divisions deriving from productive activity. We are suggesting, with Sapiro, that this concept should be expanded to recognize the profound implications of the social divisions deriving from *reproductive* activity. The task at hand is to begin to take seriously the full complexity of state power and state policies. Within ongoing states, the entire policy process—from identifying legitimate needs to implementing specific policies that affect the lives of women—is shaped by a social fabric in which hierarchies based on gender, class, and race are heavily intertwined. Empirical work needs to dissect the changing character of these interconnections, and thus we propose more systematic investigations both of the different phases of the policy process and the survival strategies of women of different classes and races. Once issues have been defined and political coalitions have been mobilized, the votes of female and male legislators do not differ substantially. Men seem to be able in these circumstances to represent and 'act for' women. Our hypothesis, however, is that the ability of men to act for women varies considerably through the different phases of the policy process: only women can 'act for' women in identifying 'invisible' problems affecting the lives of large numbers of women. At the same time, women's ability to 'act for' women must be understood in the context of the survival strategies women have created in response to their powerlessness. Thus, in dealing with policy changes made without the agitation of women, such as the Married Women's Property Acts, one must recognize that this advance was of little material consequence for the survival of the vast majority of women in nineteenth-century America. In contrast, the current attention public officials are giving to the abuse of women in the family is a direct outcome of women's collective action on 'invisible' problems. A focus on women's survival strategies which takes account of women's lack of access to resources and information would also be useful for understanding how differences in consciousness among women develop during periods of change, and why women's own actions sometimes conflict with their own welfare and survival. For instance, early pregnancy among black teenage girls lacking job opportunities might be examined as their way of achieving adult status and a sense of self-worth. In a somewhat different vein, women's participation in right-wing political activities concerning the family and sexual issues might be better viewed as efforts to achieve human dignity in the face of change: these women's opposition to the routine assaults on female sexuality in the contemporary news and entertainment media has taken the form of banning sex education in public schools, and their response to the socioeconomic changes undermining survival strategies appropriate to family-based patriarchy has been to attack feminism.

The most fundamental question to be addressed, one which has been only hinted at in our discussion thus far, is the extent to which inclusion of questions regarding reproduction and sexuality may change the political process itself. We believe that taking women's lives seriously would have far-reaching and profound consequences, and that the very concepts of what is political and what is public may be threatened by the inclusion of women's concerns in political life.

From women's perspective, one sees the intimate interconnections between the purportedly separate private and public realms. Yet the origins of Western politics in the Greek city-states provides a forceful reminder of the extent to which politics has been structured by the exclusion of women's concerns. In ancient Greece the public, political world was constructed as an arena in which participants were freed of the constraints of necessary labour, and political power rested on courage in war and courage in speech. Women, slaves, and all the concerns associated with the household and the world of necessity were excluded from the public world. This public world, of course, depended in reality on and could not have existed without the private world of household production. Yet this dependence was rarely recognized by political thinkers. While the content of the public world has changed, and the formal barriers between the spheres have been removed, the refracted impact of the ancient dualities still structures much of our thinking about politics. That the ancient understanding of the citizen as warrior is still with us is illustrated by the depth of opposition in the United States to authorizing women to serve in combat. Civic personality is not yet separate from military capacity, but the need to rethink the relationship between war and politics is made more urgent by the present technological possibilities for total destruction.

In sum, we are not saying, as Sapiro does, that recent scholarship in women's studies can show that political science has been studying the actions of only half of humanity, and that the subject matter of political science should be expanded. Instead, we are suggesting that the focus on the activity of only half of humanity is fundamental to what has been understood as political life for the last 2,500 years. To include women's concerns, to represent women in the public life of our society might well lead to a profound redefinition of the nature of public life itself.

Notes

1. Among our specific points of disagreement with Sapiro are her claim that women have accepted a denial of equality as in their interest, that separatism is best understood as related to self-help and involving self-contained services to other women, that the major goal of the women's movement has more than anything else been to put women in positions of influence, and that women developed as political persons and women's roles became policy questions in the context of the twentieth-century expansion of social welfare. We hold instead that there is a centuries-old tradition of female resistance to inequality, that separatism must be understood as more strategy and philosophy than as delivery of services to other women, that important parts of the women's movement have as their goal the creation of a just society for all human beings rather than the installation of women in powerful positions, and finally, that women's roles have been policy questions in political theorizing at least as far back as Plato's Republic.

2. A representative selection of the work most central to the study of politics would include Bunch *et al.*, Chodorow, Daly, Dinnerstein, Eisenstein, Elshtain, Ferguson, Griffin, Harding and Hintikka, Hartsock, Okin, Sargent, and Young. For a more comprehensive discussion, see the two review essays by Berenice Carroll (1979, 1980).

3. There are two important difficulties with Sapiro's description of what it means to share common interests. First, her definition of what it means (objectively) to share an interest is so vague that it cannot even differentiate the interests of labour from capital. Second, she fails to address the several important methodological problems presented by the concept of objective interests. An adequate ground for attributing common interests to a group must address issues such as (1) control over the political agenda, (2) latent possibilities for conflict as well as

observable conflict, (3) the relation of 'real' to subjectively held interests, and (4) the relation of interests and desires to human needs. The attribution of common interests requires an understanding of human nature and social structure which can satisfactorily account for the systematic failure of large groups to perceive and act on politics from which, arguably, they would benefit. Whether or not one finds the Marxian account of political and economic domination persuasive, it does at least meet these formal requirements for an attribution of objective interests.

4. We have not failed to notice that recently some fathers have begun to participate more fully in child-rearing. The small scale on which this has so far occurred, however, does not vitiate our general point.

References

Bay, Christian (1980), 'Peace and Critical Political Knowledge as Human Rights', *Political Theory*, 8, 293–318, 331–34.

Bunch, Charlotte, *et al.* (1981), *Building Feminist Theory: Essays from Quest* (New York: Longman).

Carroll, Berenice (1979), 'Part I: American Politics and Political Behavior', *Signs: Journal of Women in Culture and Society*, 5, 289–306.

—— (1980), 'Part II: International Politics, Comparative Politics, and Feminist Radicals', *Signs: Journal of Women in Culture and Society*, 5, 449–58.

Chodorow, Nancy (1978), *The Reproduction of Mothering* (Berkeley: University of California Press).

Daly, Mary (1978), *Gyn/Ecology* (Boston: Beacon).

de Beauvoir, Simone (1961), *The Second Sex*, translated by H. M. Parshley (New York: Bantam).

Dinnerstein, Dorothy (1976), *The Mermaid and the Minotaur* (New York: Harper and Row).

Elshtain, Jean (1981), *The Public and the Private: A Critical Inquiry* (Princeton: Princeton University Press).

Eisenstein, Zillah (ed.) (1979), *Capitalist Patriarchy and the Case for Socialist Feminism* (New York: Monthly Review Press).

—— (1981), *The Radical Future of Liberal Feminism* (New York: Longman).

Ferguson, Ann (1979), 'Women as a New Revolutionary Class in the U.S.', in Pat Walker (ed.), *Between Labor and Capital* (Boston: South End Press), 279–304.

Freud, Sigmund (1961), *Civilization and Its Discontents* (New York: Norton).

Griffin, Susan (1978), *Woman and Nature* (New York: Harper and Row).

Harding, Sandra, and Merrill Hintikka (eds.) (1981), *Dis-Covering Reality: Feminist Perspectives on Epistemology, Metaphysics, Methodology, and Philosophy of Science* (Dordrecht: Reidel).

Hartsock, Nancy (1981), *Money, Sex, and Power: An Essay on Domination and Community* (New York: Longman).

Lukács, Georg (1968), *History and Class Consciousness* (Cambridge, Mass.: MIT Press).

Okin, Susan (1979), *Women in Western Political Thought* (Princeton: Princeton University Press).

Petchesky, Rosalind (1980), 'Reproductive Freedom: Beyond "A Woman's Right to Choose"', *Signs: Journal of Women, Culture, and Society*, 5, 661–85.

Rich, Adrienne (1976), *Of Woman Born* (New York: Norton).

Sargent, Lydia (ed.) (1981), *Women and Revolution* (Boston: South End Press).

Young, Iris (1980), 'Socialist Feminism and the Limits of Dual Systems Theory', *Socialist Review*, 10, 169–88.

9 'Women's Interests' and the Poststructuralist State

Rosemary Pringle and Sophie Watson

We killed the Queen. We picked our way through a series of state-rooms and stabbed Her. It was all very abstract: no blood or noise. We left, taking any papers that might incriminate us. Apparently we had Her cremated—there was no sign of a body—but we had trouble getting rid of the ashes. We gave them to a priest-like figure to dispose of but he couldn't do so without giving us another set in its place. So we had this urn, which we had exchanged several times for different sets of ashes. Though we'd freed ourselves of the original we were still carrying around an urn full of ashes.

Then we found ourselves in court amongst a large group of women who were dressed in sackcloth and demonstrating with placards. All were chanting, 'I killed the Queen', which created a great deal of confusion.

These are fragments of a dream produced by one of us as we started thinking about this paper. It encapsulates our key themes and dilemmas. Sovereignty, as theorized by the classical political theorists, was assassinated a long time ago and the sovereign was displaced by a bureaucratic/legal/coercive order. The state became complex and differentiated; no longer embodying the will of the sovereign, it was rather the arena, or set of arenas, in which the action takes place. While this is a familiar enough story to mainstream social scientists, many socialists and feminists invoke the older model: they are still carrying the sovereign's ashes around. The question we take up here is why those ashes are so difficult to bury, and why we cling to them. Given that the dream represents both the sovereign and her assassins as *female*, it is clear that feminism is heavily implicated. Why then are we in 'sackcloth and ashes' when we should be celebrating?

The reasons have to do with the threats and confusions posed by postmodern and poststructuralist thought. While their relation to feminism has been widely discussed in the area of cultural politics,

Chapter 4 in M. Barrett and A. Phillips (eds.), *Destabilizing Theory: Contemporary Feminist Debates* (Polity Press, 1992), 57–73. Copyright © Rosemary Pringle and Sophie Watson (1992). Reprinted by permission.

less has so far been said about the state. Yet essentialist notions of women's political 'interests' and of 'the state' are under challenge just at the point when feminist political scientists are gaining a hearing in their discipline, on the importance of gender as a central analytic category.[1] We argue here that while the ashes of sovereignty do need to be buried, the state itself remains an important focus. But the state, the interests articulated around it, and feminist political strategies need to be reconsidered in the light of poststructuralist theory.

For feminists there are both risks and gains in these new emphases. In treating gender as discursively constructed rather than objectively or structurally given, there is a danger of its being decentred or trivialized, with the fundamental quality of gender domination being lost. Wendy Hollway has expanded on discourse theory to show how gender-differentiated meanings and positions are made available to men and women.[2] All discourse is gendered, but this point is systematically ignored outside of feminism. In the work of Foucault,[3] and of Laclau and Mouffe,[4] gender identity is no more than a subject position within a discourse. The latter pay lip-service to feminism, but treat the women's movement merely as one against many new social movements which can be recruited to the project of 'radical democracy'. Women might well complain that just at the moment when they are achieving 'identity' and articulating 'interests', these fundamental categories are being rejected by a group of predominantly male theorists. While these are real problems, we none the less argue that they are outweighed by the benefits of engaging with poststructuralist approaches to the state. These include an ability to respond more contextually and strategically to shifting frameworks of power and resistance; and a fuller recognition of multiplicity and difference amongst women. A consideration of the ways the state has been discursively constructed creates the possibility of deconstructing existing discourses, including feminist ones, as well as assessment of the strategic possibilities open to feminists in different frameworks.

'The state' has been one of the major casualties of recent social theory. While behaviourists have always seen it as too broad a conceptual category to be subjected to empirical analysis, it was the focus of considerable intellectual activity within both Marxism and feminism in the 1970s. Since then it has been so reduced in status in these same circles that not only its relevance and centrality but its very existence have been questioned. Where the concept remains in everyday use, it is used descriptively, most by the 'practitioners' of social policy and social welfare.

Marxists and many feminists had assumed that the state has an objective existence as a set of institutions or structures; that it plays a key role in organizing relations of power in any given society; that it operates as a unity, albeit a contradictory and complex one; and that there is a set of coherent interests, based on underlying economic or, in the case of some feminisms, sexual relations, which exist outside the state and are directly represented by or embodied in it. As key concepts like the mode of production and the labour theory of value came under challenge, along with the objective reality of the 'economic' and the 'social', it was inevitable that 'the state' would have to be either reformulated or rejected.

Feminists unmoved by the Marxist and post-Marxist projects have in any case ignored the state as an object of theoretical concern.[5] In stressing that 'the personal is political' they had already emphasized the omnipresence of power and the continuities between men's power in the state and in other domains. The collapse of Marxist certainties and the emergence of discourse analysis has provided a certain intellectual vindication for this position. In a recent paper, Judith Allen argues not only that feminists don't need a theory of the state but that the retention of the concept actually obscures many of the connections which they want to make.[6] Reflecting on the history of prostitution and abortion, she claims that the state is 'a category of abstraction that is too aggregative, too unitary and too unspecific to be of much use in addressing the disaggregated, diverse and specific (or local) sites that must be of most pressing concern to feminists'. Since 'the state' is not an 'indigenous' category of feminist thought, it should, she believes, be abandoned. Leaving aside for a moment the question of the 'indigenous', we can see that Allen's concern echoes that of many thinkers on the left for whom Marxist accounts of capitalism and the capitalist state appeared too general, too rigid and too functionalist to explain the nature of power relations in the late twentieth century.

Foucault's much-quoted writings on power have been of obvious importance in this transition. He argues that power is not imposed from the top of a social hierarchy nor derived from a fundamental opposition between rulers and ruled.[7] It is relational rather than owned or seized, and it operates in a capillary fashion from below. Power finds a shifting and unstable expression in networks and alliances that permeate every aspect of life. 'The state' is an overall effect of all these relations and cannot be assumed to act coherently as the agent of particular groups.

Foucault shifts the emphasis away from the intentionality of the state to pose questions about its techniques and apparatuses of regulation. Though he starts with the localized and specific mechanisms and technologies of power he is no pluralist. He aims to show how these mechanisms and technologies get annexed and appropriated to more global forms of domination. But these interconnections are not to be read off from a general theory; in each case they have to be established through analysis. To place the state 'above' or outside society is to miss its main significance and to insist on a homogeneity in the operations of power which simply is not there. He warns that we should not assume that 'the sovereignty of the state, the form of the law or the overall unity of a domination are given at the outset; rather, these are only the terminal forms power takes'. Power does not reside in institutions or structures, and rather than there being a 'unity of state power' there is a 'complex strategical situation in a particular society'.[8]

Foucault deliberately makes few direct references to 'the state' because he wants to confront the view of it as Leviathan, a sovereign being from which power emanates. Yet as a historian of power Foucault remains much more interested in discourses and practices concerning the state than other poststructuralists who have concentrated more exclusively on language and culture. In particular he is concerned with the discourses on 'governmentality',[9] including social science and statistics, and the diplomatic-military techniques of policing and surveillance of populations that characterize the modern state. Though he does not say so, these domains are clearly masculine. 'Governmentality' was originally conceived on the model of (a father's) management of a family, and family remains an important instrument of government.

It is possible to distinguish between the discourses that in some sense found the modern state and those that produce 'the state' as it appears in feminist discourses. The former assume a masculine subject rather than self-consciously defending or creating 'men's interests'. Here we can include not only 'governmentality' but 'fraternity' as evoked by the social-contract theorists. Pateman argues that the original social contract was in reality a sexual-social contract, in which men overthrew the rule of fathers but only to institute a fraternal agreement which guaranteed men access to women's bodies.[10] She argues that while fraternity has evoked less attention than liberty and equality, its specific gender connotations largely explained away, it 'does not appear by accident as one of the basic liberal and contractarian principles, and it means exactly what it says—brotherhood'.[11] This cannot be dismissed as a fairy story, for 'fraternity' underpins liberalism, and the 'social contract' forms a powerful mythical basis of the contemporary state.

The discourse of 'fraternity', we suggest, presumes and evokes the notion that men alone are the political actors, that state and civil society have been established by men, who act on behalf of the population as a whole. Political differences tend to be constituted as differences between men, reinforcing at a more fundamental level the notion of the public, political domain as a masculine one. In modern 'fraternal' discourse, like the specifically patriarchal ones that preceded them, women are treated as the objects or recipients of policy decisions rather than full participants in them. What feminists are confronted with is not a state that represents 'men's interests' as against women's, but government conducted as if men's interests are the only ones that exist. Claims to be representing 'women's interests', however disunified they may be, may actually be tossed around among groups of men and used as a strategy for achieving their own goals. In the 1990 Australian election campaign, for example, the major parties competed for 'the women's vote' with substantial childcare packages, particularly after the polls showed that more women than men were undecided about which way to vote. Even the reactionary National Party, after being attacked by Prime Minister Hawke for being 'sexist', entered the fray, offering increased funding for breast-cancer testing.

Before taking up the question of interests we must go back to consider more concretely some key feminist discourses around the state and the contexts in which they operate. Our concern is not with how 'accurately' they describe or theorize the state, but with the political implications of particular theories. We draw in particular on Britain, Australia, and Scandinavia.

FEMINISMS AND THE STATE

The state only became an object of feminist theoretical concern in the late 1970s when Marxist feminists attempted to adapt current Marxist theories of the state to women. Within this paradigm, a feminist analysis of social reproduction, the family and gender was grafted on to an analysis of the capitalist state, which was still seen as acting predominantly in the interests of preserving the dominant class relations and assisting the accumulation of capital. At the level of the state, the emphasis was on how the capitalist state created and reproduced patriarchal relations. Elizabeth Wilson[12] and Mary McIntosh[13] analysed the ways in which the welfare state reproduces the capitalist modes of production and women's dependence upon men within the family. In this account gender domination is seen as functional to capitalism:

Capitalist society is one in which men as men dominate women, yet it is not this, but class domination that is fundamental to the society. It is a society in which the dominant class is composed mainly of men; yet it is not as men but as capitalists that they are dominant . . . the state must be seen as a capitalist one.[14]

Such accounts over-emphasized the effectiveness with which the welfare state reproduces the capitalist mode of production through women's dependence upon men within the family. And they were unable to explain convincingly just why the state should need to reinforce masculine dominance and privilege. Zillah Eisenstein attempted to solve the problem by treating the state as the mediator between the dual systems of patriarchy and capitalism.[15] This raised another set of difficulties in establishing where these systems began and ended, and produced an analysis that was overly functionalist. Most tended to focus on the oppressive aspects of the state.[16]

The 'capitalist state' view was particularly dominant in British feminism, reflecting the importance of class divisions in British political life and the tendency of radicals to interpret inequality and oppression in terms of class. Attempts to work within the state arenas were viewed with suspicion and likely to be dismissed as co-option. The influential text *In and Against the State*[17] treats the state as a form of social relations which acts in the interests of capital. Though it discusses working within the institutions, it exhorts people to build a culture of opposition. As a result of adopting such a position feminists were ambivalent about working within state institutions, which retained their masculinist and exclusionary culture of white male and class privilege.

It was only after the Thatcher government came to power that the picture began to change. Provoked by the increase of central government control over local government expenditure and the privatization of public services, many became involved in local government as a significant site of resistance and reaction. Women began to enter these local political and bureaucratic arenas. The Greater London Council set up the first women's committee in 1981 and other local authorities followed. 'Local' came to symbolize 'humanitarian', in opposition to the privatization policies of the

Thatcher government. Even at this level, working with the state was regarded as 'tainting'. Feminist interventions retained a marginal character and focused on the 'interests' of particular disadvantaged groups rather than the more general policy issues. There was suspicion of local government workers and concern about accountability. As open meetings were held and working parties set up, particular efforts were made to secure the representation of black, disabled, older, and lesbian women. Yet open or co-ordinating meetings were always susceptible to domination by well-organized groups (such as the 'Wages for Housework' group) and by those women who were articulate and had the time and resources to attend.[18] Women who were co-opted on to committees as lesbian or black women found themselves having to represent the interests of women from their respective constituency or local area. Membership of a particular group thus allowed a speaking position as, say, lesbian, which had direct impact on the way certain policies were formulated. In some instances this meant that one woman could define the issues for the group in question with little or no accountability to her own constituency. While such problems may be seen as endemic to participatory democracy, the 'against the state' discourse gave them a sharp edge. This discourse is still alive and well. A recent review dismissed feminist bureaucrats in Australia as a group whose lives are lived out 'on the borderland between radicalism and conservatism', as they uncritically embraced a pragmatic form of social democracy.[19]

The problems in Australia and Scandinavia have been of a rather different order. The Australian working class has had a long pragmatic tradition of expecting the state to be concerned with the welfare of its citizens and to act as an arbitrator of conflict. This is reflected particularly in the wage-fixing of the arbitration and industrial relations commissions. The bureaucracy has been perceived as more open and less under the control of the establishment. Despite a relatively small welfare state, a positive value has been placed on state intervention. The more diverse bases of feminism in Australia combined with the political culture to create a space where feminist interventions were possible and not immediately subject to widespread criticism.

In the early 1970s, the liberal feminist Women's Electoral Lobby (WEL) grew up alongside Women's Liberation. By the time the Whitlam Labour government was elected in 1972, WEL was well placed to lobby for women's advisers, anti-discrimination legislation, equal opportunity programmes, an integrated childcare policy and so on. The Whitlam government was committed to opening up the public service and creating bureaucratic structures which reflected changing community needs, and feminist interventions were constituted by and through such discourse. Throughout the seventies a number of feminists entered key positions within the bureaucratic and ministerial staff. Many of the personal links made in the seventies have been maintained and developed. The channels of intervention, the interests represented, and the policies initiated reflect the players, their histories, and their connections. This is not to deny the importance of feminist pressure groups and networks outside. But the particular flavour of Australian feminism, its strengths and its limitations, lie in this relation to the bureaucracy.

Two problematic areas can be identified. One concerns the positioning of the 'femocrats' as mediators of the 'interests' of all Australian women. There is an issue here not only about how representative they are, but of the discursive practices within which 'interests' are constructed. Where British feminists might be suspicious of the procedure, there is in Australia a recognition that femocrats are actually articulating interests that are by no means pre-given, and which have to be constructed in the context of the machinery of government. Whatever the debates and conflicts, they have played an important part in securing funding for a range of women's services, even if this has involved tensions for the feminist groups involved, trying to maintain feminist principles as well as being accountable to the funding authority.[20]

A second question concerns the relationship between the feminist bureaucrats and the Australian Labor Party (ALP). The Hawke Labour government, which was in power from 1983, was committed not to radical reform but to change through the mechanisms of tripartism and consensus. One of the main mechanisms was a prices-and-incomes accord with the unions, which did rather reinstate the primacy of the older political contestants. Feminists drew attention to the marginality of women in the accord, and debated whether it was inevitable or inherent. Given that it was an attempt by Labour to persuade the unions to exercise wage restraint, women's near-exclusion is no surprise. The accord was seen as a pact between men. There is a strong resonance here with social-contract mythology, and particularly its fraternal dimension, as identified by Carole Pateman.[21] As the main strategy for maintaining living standards in Australia since the early part of the century has been through the protection of jobs through tariff barriers, the arbitration system, and the family wage, we could argue a long history of a fraternal contract in welfare creating women's 'dependence'. Fraternalism has a particular meaning in Australia, where male 'mateship' amounts almost to a religious cult. The emotionalism concerning the return of the surviving diggers to Anzac Cove on the seventy-fifth anniversary of Gallipoli reminds us that the national identity, and the myths that legitimate the Australian state, celebrate masculine separatism and treat women as 'other'.

Femocrats have debated whether women would be better off with or without the accord. They have also had to adapt themselves to the discourses of corporatism and managerial efficiency, which have become smoothly conjoined with the philosophy of 'mateship'. While gains have been made through partnership with the ALP, the price has at times been high. Anna Yeatman argues that femocrats have colluded in the rolling-back of the welfare state, and been rather too ready to endorse the official discourse of 'Labourism'.[22] This locates 'people' as workers, and 'workers' as 'men'. Instead of citizens with 'rights' there are 'disadvantaged groups', mostly women, who fall outside of the contract. For them a 'social justice strategy' is offered, which effectively entrenches them in a position of disadvantage.

Yeatman also criticizes the women's movement for failing to challenge the government's use of feminist rhetoric to enforce child maintenance payments from non-custodial parents, mostly fathers, thus reprivatizing parenting arrangements. Others might see this as constructing competing masculine interests: those of individual fathers in dodging liability versus the collective interests of the fraternity. Given the history of child desertion in Australia, it is not immediately obvious that feminists should oppose the legislation. Many argued that, in the context of budget constraints, it was a positive move that will significantly improve the situation of single mothers. Others have suggested that it reinforces traditional heterosexual dependent relations and scares off men from donating sperm to single women who want children.

Yeatman stresses that politics is pre-eminently a set of debates and struggles over meaning. And she finds femocrats, whether they work in the bureaucracy, in academia or in women's services, rather wanting in their capacity to engage at this level. Certainly it is true that little informed social policy debate takes place in Australia. While sophisticated critiques of degendering have been applied to the public sphere,[23] the implications for policy development are rarely spelt out. Because of the pragmatism towards the state it has not been the subject of intellectual debate in the way it has in

Britain, and many feminists would endorse Allen's view that it is not a priority.[24]

In Scandinavia the state is seen as 'an instrument of popular will', which is used to control the private forces of market and family.[25] Norwegians and Swedes use the words 'society' and 'state' interchangeably, and notions of community, rights and entitlements, and distributive justice have been important in women's claims for equality. In feminist engagements with the state in Scandinavia the emphasis has been less on 'class' or 'bureaucracy' than on 'power', and particularly on sexual power hierarchy. This perhaps reflects the relatively high level of representation of women within the elective bodies on the one hand, and an extensive welfare state on the other. Such gains, it has become clear, do not necessarily imply a major shift in gender relations. As Hernes points out,[26] women's increased political power in Sweden has to be balanced against shifts in the centre of the power to the administrative arena. This relates to the significance of corporate structures, where decision-making takes place with little input from women. In some accounts power is represented as a possession, while in others there is a sense of power as shifting. There is also some doubt about the extent of women's integration into Scandinavian labour markets. The development of the welfare state has seen a partnership between state and family which compromises women's labour-force participation. Women's 'interests' have been centrally constructed in relation to welfare rather than to jobs (which have been the emphasis in Australia). Ongoing gender inequalities can thus be linked to differences in labour-market participation, which in turn affects representation in the corporate system.

The Marxist, liberal, and social democratic perspectives within which feminists have operated in these countries have not come to grips with the gendered nature of the state. The state is described as masculine or patriarchal, but these words have only an adjectival force. Birte Siim comments, typically, that 'state policies can be said to reflect male dominance to the extent they have incorporated the dominant male assumptions and have been governed mainly by male interests and, therefore, have not permitted any real threat to male supremacy'.[27] The American radical feminist Catharine MacKinnon has attempted to theorize the fundamentally patriarchal nature of the state, emphasizing the ways in which the law incorporates a male standpoint and institutionalizes masculine interests.[28] Here too, the 'maleness' of the state is simply a reflection of the maleness of everything else in patriarchal society. She does not add much to our conceptualizations of either 'maleness' or 'the state'. More than this, she backs into a political corner, since it is not at all clear how the patriarchal state might be effectively challenged, or from what quarters. She paints women as both total victims of this all-encompassing system and yet able to use the state in a variety of ways for their own ends.[29] 'Men' and 'women' are taken for granted here as unified categories.

Feminist theories of the state have frequently assumed unitary interests between men, between sections of capital, and between women. Debates among feminist political scientists focus on the questions of subjective versus objective interests, and interests versus needs.[30] Some writers, like Halsaa,[31] argue that there is an objective basis to women's interests in the reproductive work that only women are able to do. Others raise questions about who is to define women's needs and act on behalf of them; while those concerned with subjective needs have stressed the necessity for participation of 'being among' those creating the alternatives. We believe that the notion of objective versus subjective interests fails to capture the diverse, shifting, and conflicting nature of the experiences and representations which form the human subject. While complexity is acknowledged, the framework here is still that of representation rather than articulation. The issue needs to be shifted from how women's interests can be most accurately represented to the processes whereby they are constituted.

The state should be seen as erratic and disconnected rather than contradictory. It is not an object or an actor so much as a series of arenas or, in Yeatman's words, a 'plurality of discursive forums'.[32] The current collection of practices and discourses which construct 'the state' are a historical product, not structurally 'given'. What intentionality there is comes from the success with which various groupings are able to articulate their interests and hegemonize their claims: it is always likely to be partial and temporary. If we take this view we do not have to puzzle about why the state acts so contradictorily or, on occasion, fails to act at all. We do not have to conclude in advance that it will act uniformly to maintain capitalist or patriarchal relations, or that this is its 'purpose'. The outcomes of particular policies will depend not purely on the limits placed by 'structures', but on the range of discursive struggles which define and constitute the state and specific interests from one moment to the next.

More recent socialist and feminist work has recognized that there are many varieties of state, spatially and historically. The state is now regarded as too diverse, divided, and contradictory to evoke as an entity. Each has its own combination of institutions, apparatuses, and arenas, which have their own histories, contradictions, relations, and connections, internally and externally. Work on the welfare state has recognized the need to shift our analyses to particular institutions and their specific histories, rather than assuming any unity or integration of its parts.[33] Local, regional, and national as well as historical and cultural specificities have to be acknowledged. To argue that the welfare state supports the traditional patriarchal family is no longer useful, if it ever was. As Alison Smith suggests in her discussion of women's refuges,[34] the legal agencies cannot be perceived as simply shoring up some 'archetypal conception of family relations but instead should be seen as contribution to their changing forms'.

Work is being done on the ways in which gender inequalities are embedded in the state and vice versa. Nancy Fraser,[35] for example, has pointed to the divisions in the US welfare system between work-oriented social-insurance programmes (masculine) and the 'unearned' public-assistance schemes which cater predominantly for women. Franzway, Court, and Connell emphasize the practices that construct the state rather than taking its structures as given.[36] Unlike MacKinnon, they establish a dynamic relationship between gender and the state. The state does not simply reflect gender inequalities but, through its practices, plays an important role in constituting them; simultaneously, gender practices become institutionalized in historically specific state forms. It is a two-way street.

This emphasis on practice and discourse is characteristic of newly emerging feminist and post-Marxist accounts of the state. There is a move away from abstract theorizing, and from any belief in the fixed or coherent character of state structures. At first sight this might look like a retreat to pluralism. But poststructuralist theorists share the view that analyses of power should proceed from a micro-level. Much traditional social science tends towards the empirical and the behaviourist, while poststructuralist thinking is concerned with fragmentation and multiplicity of meaning. It emphasizes the importance of language and discourse, not just in describing the world, but in constituting social reality. Neither social reality nor the natural world has fixed, intrinsic meanings which language reflects or expresses; instead, there has been an emphasis on the relational, historical, and precarious character of 'reality'. Language is also the place where our 'identities' are constructed. Subjectivity is produced in a whole range of discursive practices, the meanings of which are a constant site of struggle over power. It is neither unified nor fixed, but a site of disunity and conflict. Poststructuralists regard the 'real world' and the notion of 'interests' as anything but clear-cut; their concern is therefore with the discursive fields in which social reality and individual and group identities and interests are constituted. Power is regarded as immanent in all social relationships, rather than based on deeper economic or sexual divisions. Meaning arises out of the play of differences in language rather than being already given in reality; and meanings are not fixed or static but dynamic and contextual. In poststructuralist accounts of the state, 'discourse' and 'subjectivity' rather than structures and interests become the key terms.

DISCOURSE AND SUBJECTIVITY

In Foucault's work, discourses are much more than ways of constituting knowledge. They include the social practices, and the forms of subjectivity and power relations that inhere in such knowledges. The most powerful discourses have firm institutional locations—in law, medicine, social welfare, and so on—though these too must be seen as sites of contest. Laclau and Mouffe suggest that the distinction between the discursive and the non-discursive is unnecessary:[37] that if we look closely at the 'non-discursive' complexes, such as institutions, productive organizations, or techniques, we will always find that they are given meaning through discursive structures.

Laclau and Mouffe's analysis draws together in a systematic way many of the themes that we have already posed. It also raises some major questions for feminist strategy. We shall therefore discuss their position in some detail before concluding with a discussion of the implications for feminism.

First, their work marks a complete break with any essentialist conceptions of social structure or relations. While not denying that the 'real' world has an objective existence, Laclau and Mouffe insist that it can only be known through discourse.[38] They reject totalizing theories of society, stressing that the social constitutes itself as a *symbolic* order. 'Symbolic' is used here in place of ideology to mark the intended break with the base–superstructure model, and it is meant to include material practices. The social formation is not a totality governed by an organizing principle, the determination of the economic in the last instance. The mode of production itself is a conceptual and social construct dependent, for example, on legal discourse. Relations of production therefore do not have any explanatory priority. Society is not a closed system.

The 'relative autonomy' of the state from the economy is thus rendered meaningless, while 'its' relation to civil society becomes more complex. As Laclau and Mouffe put it, the state 'is not a homogeneous medium, separated from civil society by a ditch, but an uneven set of branches and functions, only relatively integrated by the hegemonic practices which take place within it'.[39]

The emphasis on the symbolic order implies that the social can never be permanently fixed and will always be subject to contested meanings: 'Society never manages fully to be society, because everything in it is penetrated by its limits which prevent it from constituting itself as an objective reality'.[40] Given the impossibility of permanently 'fixing' meaning, one might ask how meaning is possible at all. Laclau and Mouffe stress the 'articulatory practices' which temporarily arrest the flow of differences to construct privileged sites or nodal points which partially fix meaning. 'Man' is one such nodal point which underlies the 'humanization' of a number of social practices since the eighteenth century. In the case of 'woman', they add slightly patronizingly, there is an ensemble of practices and discourses that mutually reinforce and act on each other, making it possible to speak of a sex/gender system. 'Men' and 'women' and their 'interests' rest not on biological difference, reproductive relations, or the sexual division of labour, but on the discursive practices that produce them.

Classes do not arise automatically out of the mode of production and are given no presumed primacy in political struggles. Members of classes (and by implication, genders and other interest groups) do not simply know their material interests, but have to form conceptions of them. Any connections among groups have to be constructed, articulated, and maintained; they are not pre-given. Groups make these connections using the discursive frameworks available to the time and culture.

'Interests', then, are precarious historical products which are always subjected to processes of dissolution and redefinition. They are not self-constituted identities, but rather 'differences' in the Saussurian sense, whose only identity is established relationally. Subjects cannot be the origin of social relations, but rather, are subject positions in discursive structures. And *every* social practice is articulatory: it cannot simply be the expression of something already acquired but involves a continuous process of constructing new differences.

Laclau and Mouffe are concerned to establish links between struggles. They are aware that such struggles all have a partial character and, left to themselves, can be articulated to a variety of discourses, including those of the right. Here the establishment of nodal points is very important. These may be compared with Lacan's '*points de capiton*', or with the points at which a loose cover is held on to an armchair.[41] They are the privileged points or signifiers which, at least partially, fix meaning. Without such reference points communication would be impossible, for meaning would be constantly sliding away. The sense of permanence and fixity that they evoke is, however, an illusion. While nodal points are always necessary, they do in fact shift. Laclau and Mouffe castigate the British left for treating one set of nodal points as if it were absolute, and thus limiting their capacity for action and analysis, handing over to the right the capacity to fix meanings.

What, then, are the discursive conditions under which collective action against *all* forms of inequality and subordination might emerge? Their own nodal points would be established in a programme for radical democracy. This recognizes a plurality of antagonisms, based not on 'objective' interests but on a plurality of subject positions. While each should be given maximum autonomy, it should be in an overall context of a 'democratic equivalence' between group demands: that is, not only a respect for the rights of others but a willingness to modify their subjectivities in the process. For example, the class subjectivity of white male workers is overdetermined by both racial and sexual attitudes which must be contested; and workers' control could be established so as to ignore ecology or the demands of other groups affected by production decisions. It is precisely because the identity of each social movement can never be acquired once and for all that we can expect modifications. Given that so much depends on the extension of democracy, the 'against the state' discourse, which has informed radical political practice in Britain, is rejected here, and we believe rightly so, in favour of the consolidation and democratic reform of the constitutive principles of the liberal state.

FEMINIST STRATEGIES

We are not arguing that 'the state' as a category ought to be abandoned, but for a recognition that, far from being a unified structure, it is a by-product of political struggles. If we accept that power resides in all social relations this opens up the possibility of a multiplicity of forms of resistance. Interests are also constructed discursively and constituted in their intersection with the state arenas. Notions of women's interests have been crucial in the different discourses around state activity. A focus on interests provides a way of avoiding some of the traps of analysing the state as a given entity. The critique of a category of unified subject opens the way to recognition of a plurality of antagonisms constituted on the basis of different subject positions.

From the discussion so far, we may draw out three key issues for feminist strategies in the 1990s: our relation to the categories of man/woman, our relation to differences among women, and our relation to a wider democratic politics. It seems clear that feminism can no longer ground itself in an essentialist conception of 'woman' or on an understanding of a 'gender identity' or 'interest' shared by all women. The tendency of white, middle-class women to treat their own experience as normative has already been widely criticized.[42] Yet many feminists would still be reluctant to let go of some core of common identity which unites women across class, ethnic and racial boundaries. While we reject such notions of 'identity' we do believe that, along with continuing inequalities at every level, women have in common a discursive marginality. 'Woman' is only knowable in so far as she is similar to, different from or complementary to 'man': phallocentric discourse makes women and their interests virtually unrepresentable except in relation to a masculine norm.[43] In the fact of this, the assertion of the feminine may be an important political tactic. This is not a return to essentialism so much as a technique of empowerment: in Braidotti's words, 'essentialism with a difference'.[44] This is an act of self-legitimation which, she suggests, 'opens up the field of possible "becoming", providing the foundation for a new alliance among women, a symbolic bond among woman *qua* female sexed beings'.[45]

If 'women's interests' are constructed rather than pre-given, so are men's. If we have to let go of the authentic female subject, then we can let go too of the male subject. Patriarchal discourse need not be seen as homogeneous and uniformly repressive, and women do not need to be portrayed as victims. This opens up possibilities of exposing differences between men and, where appropriate, creating alliances. The interests of men as 'fathers', for example, do not always coincide with their interests as 'brothers' or 'mates', and each in turn will shift and change each time they are articulated.[46] We might note in passing that men as men are now beginning to associate formally against what they see as the unfair advantages of women. The association for 'weekend fathers' in Sweden is just one of many organizations that aim to influence judicial procedures surrounding custody and divorce. 'Fathers' rights' have even extended to rights over the unborn foetus. As Carol Smart warns,[47] in the face of these developments, feminists need to rethink their relation to the whole discourse of 'rights' and remember that discourses should be evaluated not in the abstract but always in a social context.

The political demands of 'women' on the state presuppose a coherent set of interests outside the political and bureaucratic arenas which can be met, rather than recognizing that these interests are actively constructed in the process of responding to some demands and not others. It is in the process of engagement with the arenas of the state that interests are constructed. Through creating a framework of meanings, through the use of particular languages or discourses, certain possibilities for change emerge. Interests are produced by conscious and unwitting practices by the actors themselves in the processes of engagement. Feminists who engage with the state do so within a set of parameters that are discursively constituted and will formulate their interests accordingly. Interests are constituted and constrained by the discursively available possibilities for representation and action in any particular situation. These will also be a result of 'past struggles in which the "interests" of certain forms of interest representation have been constituted in the constraints and pressures on discursive availability'.[48]

If we include a perspective of heterogeneity of women and of feminist response, no one policy will be a gain for all women. Take the example of pornography. There is no one feminist position, but a variety of demands for government regulation or latitude. The absence of a coherent feminist position mirrors the lack of coherence, interest, or clarity within the state arenas. Each and every instance of policymaking reflects a different configuration of power relations and networks. Policy and its implementation will depend not only on how strongly these different interests are articulated, but on how they mesh with the demands of other groups. 'Women's interests' will here be articulated in a variety of competing ways. In Britain a new group, Women Against Pornography and Censorship, has cleverly sought to occupy the discursive field, by arguing that the sexual exploitation of women is a civil-liberties issue, and that pornography itself is a form of censorship in so far as it establishes a particular representation of women as normative. Drawing on community support for legislation against sex and race discrimination, the group locates pornography both as a form of sex discrimination and as an incitement to sexual hatred and violence in analogous terms to racial hatred and violence.[49] This is calculated to draw support from across the discursive board, including the right. It is also intended to pull the rug from under their feminist opponents, who situate pornography in more complex terms in relation to representation and fantasy.

A feminist orientation to the politics of difference means that we each recognize that any standpoint we take is necessarily partial, and based on the way in which we are positioned in relation to class, race, educational background, and any number of other factors. Our subjectivity will have been formed within a multiplicity of discourses, many of them conflicting and contradictory.[50] While this may be threatening, it also allows change and flexibility. Rather than seeking a politics based on 'unity', we can move towards one based on respect for the differences of others, and on alliances with them.

This brings us back to the 'radical democracy' project, which we endorse with some reservations. Precisely because subjectivity can never be acquired once and for all, and is constructed as part of a chain of differences, it should be possible for all who are committed to the project to construct their identities and interests in ways that are respectful of others. It makes obvious sense for feminists to ally themselves with those committed to working collectively to end all forms of inequality and subordination. Nevertheless, we consider that this seriously underplays gender inequality. While acknowledging surface sexism, it takes no account of the problem of phallocentrism in discourse, and neither does it take any serious account of sexual difference. It assumes one sex only, and that sex is male. The class subjectivity of white male workers remains a reference point, even as it is acknowledged that this group must reconsider its standpoint. Laclau and Mouffe are very low-key about 'socialism', but they obviously regard the socialization of production as a necessary (if not sufficient) condition of radical democracy.[51] Given that no other 'necessary' conditions are laid down, it is not clear why this one is privileged. Feminists could justifiably see this as (male) socialist hegemony back in a more sophisticated form. This being said, such a project offers interesting possibilities for feminism in the nineties.

Rethinking the state, we conclude, requires a shift away from seeing the state as a coherent, if contradictory, unity. Instead we see it as a diverse set of discursive arenas which play a crucial role in organizing relations of power. Rather than abandoning the state as an analytic or political category, it is important to analyse the strategic possibilities available at any one time. Women's interests and thereby feminist politics are constructed in the process of interaction with specific institutions and sites. The policies that ensue depend not just on the constraints of structures but on the discursive struggles which define and constitute particular interests and the state at any one time.

Notes

1. K. Jones and A. Jonasdottir, *The Political Interests of Gender* (London: Sage, 1988).
2. W. Hollway, 'Gender Difference and the Production of Subjectivity', in J. Henriques, W. Hollway, C. Urwin, C. Venn, and V. Walkerdine, *Changing the Subject* (London: Methuen, 1984).
3. Especially his *History of Sexuality*, i (New York: Vintage Books, 1981); 'On Governmentality', *Ideology and Consciousness*, 6 (1979); 'Truth and Power', in C. Gordon (ed.), *Power/Knowledge: Selected Interviews and Other Writings 1972–1977: Michel Foucault* (Brighton: Harvester Press, 1980); and see M. Morris and P. Patton (eds.), *Michel Foucault: Power, Truth, Strategy* (Sydney: Feral Publications, 1979).
4. E. Laclau and C. Mouffe, *Hegemony and Socialist Strategy* (London: Verso, 1985).
5. M. Frye, *The Politics of Reality* (Trumansberg, NY: The Crossing Press, 1983).
6. J. Allen, 'Does Feminism Need a Theory of the State?', in S. Watson (ed.), *Playing the State* (London: Verso, 1990).
7. Foucault, *History of Sexuality*, i.
8. Foucault, 'On Governmentality', 20.
9. Ibid.
10. C. Pateman, *The Sexual Contract* (London: Polity Press, 1988).
11. Ibid. 74.
12. E. Wilson, *Women and the Welfare State* (London: Tavistock, 1977).
13. M. McIntosh, 'The State and the Oppression of Women', in A. Kuhn and A. Wolpe (eds.), *Feminism and Materialism* (London: Routledge, 1978). Other accounts tended to be more descriptive, e.g. H. Land, 'Who Still Cares for the Family?', *Journal of Social Policy*, 7 (1978).
14. McIntosh, 'The State and the Oppression of Women', 259.
15. Z. Eisenstein, *Capitalist Patriarchy and the Case for Socialist Feminism* (New York: Monthly Review Press, 1978).
16. B. Siim, 'Towards a Feminist Rethinking of the Welfare State', in Jones and Jonasdottir, *Political Interests of Gender*, 171.
17. London/Edinburgh Return Group, *In and Against the State* (London: Pluto Press, 1979).
18. S. Goss, 'Women's Initiatives in Local Government', in M. Boddy and C. Fudge (eds.), *Local Socialism* (London: Macmillan, 1984).
19. L. Loach, 'Feminists Abroad', *New Statesman and Society*, 2 March 1990.

20. L. McFerren, 'Interpretations of a Frontline State: Australian Women's Refuges and the State', in Watson, *Playing the State*.
21. Pateman, *The Sexual Contract*.
22. A. Yeatman, *Bureaucrats, Technocrats, Femocrats: Essays on the Contemporary Australian State* (Sydney: Allen and Unwin, 1990).
23. C. Pateman and E. Gross (eds.), *Feminist Challenges* (Sydney: Allen and Unwin, 1987); B. Sullivan, 'Sex Equality and The Australian Body Politic', in Watson, *Playing the State*.
24. Allen, 'Does Feminism Need a Theory of the State?'
25. H. Hernes, 'Women and the Welfare State: The Transition from Private to Public Dependence', in A. Showstack Sasson (ed.), *Women and the State* (London: Hutchinson, 1987), 156.
26. H. Hernes, *Welfare State and Woman Power: Essays in State Feminism* (Oslo: Norwegian University Press, 1987), 151.
27. Siim, 'Towards a Feminist Rethinking of the Welfare State', 178.
28. C. A. MacKinnon, 'Feminism, Marxism, Method and the State: Toward a Feminist Jurisprudence', *Signs*, 8 (1983).
29. See C. Smart, *Feminism and the Power of Law* (London: Routledge, 1989).
30. A. Jonasdottir, 'On the Concept of Interest, Women's Interests, and the Limitations of Interest Theory', in Jones and Jonasdottir, *Political Interests of Gender*; D. Dahlerup, 'Overcoming the Barriers: An Approach to the Study of how Women's Issues are Kept from the Political Agenda', in J. H. Stiehm (ed.), *Women's Views of the Political World of Men* (New York: Transitional Publishers, 1984).
31. B. Halsaa, 'Har kuïnnor gemensamma intressen?', discussed in H. Skjeie, *The Feminisation of Power: Norway's Political Experiment (1986–)* (Oslo: Institute for Social Research, 1988), 48.
32. Yeatman, *Bureaucrats, Technocrats, Femocrats*, 170.
33. S. Shaver, 'Gender, Class and the Welfare State: The Case of Income Security', *Feminist Review*, 32 (1989).
34. A. Smith, 'Women's Refuges: The Only Resort? Feminism, Domestic Violence and the State', in D. Barry and P. Botsman (eds.), 'Public/Private', *Local Consumption*, ser. 6, Sydney (1985).
35. N. Fraser, 'Women, Welfare and the Politics of Need Interpretation', *Thesis Eleven*, 17 (1987).
36. S. Franzway, D. Court, and R. W. Connell, *Staking a Claim: Feminism, Bureaucracy and the State* (London: Paladin, 1989).
37. Laclau and Mouffe, *Hegemony and Socialist Strategy*, 107.
38. Ibid.
39. Ibid. 180.
40. Ibid. 127.
41. Ibid. 112–14.
42. For example, M. Barrett and M. McIntosh, 'Ethnocentrism and Socialist Feminism', *Feminist Review*, 20 (1985).
43. See especially L. Irigaray, *This Sex Which Is Not One* (Ithaca, NY: Cornell University Press, 1985); E. Grosz, *Sexual Subversions* (Sydney: Allen and Unwin, 1989).
44. R. Braidotti, 'The Politics of Ontological Difference', in T. Brennan (ed.), *Between Feminism and Psychoanalysis* (London: Routledge, 1989).
45. Ibid. 102.

46. R. Pringle and S. Watson, 'Fathers, Brothers, Mates: The Fraternal State in Australia', in Watson, *Playing the State*, 229–43.
47. Smart, *Feminism and the Power of Law*.
48. S. Clegg, *Frameworks of Power* (London: Sage, 1988), 181.
49. Women Against Pornography and Censorship, 'Questions and Answers' (Women Against Pornography and Censorship, London, April 1989); C. Itzin, 'Pornography: Is the New Campaign Against Pornography and Censorship a Contradiction?', *Observer* (16 April 1989).
50. R. Pringle, *Secretaries Talk: Sexuality, Power and Work* (London: Verso, 1989).
51. Laclau and Mouffe, *Hegemony and Socialist Strategy*.

10 Democracy and Representation: Or, Why Should it Matter Who our Representatives Are?

Anne Phillips

Though the overall statistics on women in politics continue to tell their dreary tale of under-representation, this under-representation is now widely regarded as a problem, and a significant number of political parties have adopted measures to raise the proportion of women elected. That the issue is even discussed marks a significant change. Even more remarkable is that growing support for a variety of *enabling* devices (day-schools, for example, to encourage potential women candidates) now combines with some minority backing for measures that *guarantee* parity between women and men. Parties in the Nordic countries took the lead in this, introducing gender quotas for the selection of parliamentary candidates from the mid-1970s onwards, but a quick survey across Europe throws up a number of parallel developments. Positive action to increase the proportion of women elected is now on the political agenda. It has become one of the issues on which politicians disagree.

In some ways, indeed, this is an area where those engaged in the practice of politics have edged ahead of those engaged in its theory. Gatherings of party politicians are significantly more likely to admit the problem of women's under-representation than gatherings of political scientists, for while the former remain deeply divided over the particular measures they will support, most can manage at least a lukewarm expression of 'regret' that so few women are elected. The pressures of party competition weigh heavily on their shoulders. In an era of increased voter volatility, they cannot afford to disparage issues that competitors might turn to electoral advantage. Hence the cumulative effect noted in Norwegian politics, where the Socialist Left Party first adopted gender quotas in the 1970s; this was followed in the 1980s by similar initiatives from the Labour and Centre

First published in *Schweizerisches Jahrbuch für Politische Wissenschaften* (1994), 63–76. Reprinted by permission of Editions Paul Haupt Berne. An expanded version of this argument is in *The Politics of Presence* (Oxford University Press, 1995).

Parties; and was accompanied by substantial increases in the number of women selected by the Conservative Party as well (Skjeie 1991). Hence the impact of the German Green Party, which decided to alternate women and men on its list for the 1986 election; the threat of this small—but at the time, rapidly growing—party contributed to the Christian Democrats' adoption of a voluntary quota, and the Social Democrat's conversion to a formal one (Chapman 1993: ch. 9). Hence the otherwise surprising consensus that has emerged among Britain's major political parties—at central office level if not yet in local constituencies—in favour of selecting a higher proportion of women candidates (Lovenduski and Norris 1989). None of this would have happened without vigorous campaigning inside the political parties, but the campaigns have proved particularly effective where parties were already worried about their electoral appeal.

This pragmatically driven conversion contrasts with a more tough-minded resistance inside the political science community, where arguments range from a supposed lack of evidence that sex affects policy decisions, to a distaste with what is implied in saying that it should. Women's under-representation in politics is in one sense just empirical fact: they are not present in elected assemblies in the same proportions as they are present in the electorate. But the characteristics of those elected may diverge in any number of ways from the characteristics of those who elect them, and this is not always seen as a matter of democratic consequence. In a much cited article on representation, A. Phillips Griffiths (1960: 190) argued that some divergences are regarded as positively beneficial. We do not normally consider the interests of lunatics as best represented by people who are mad, and 'while we might well wish to complain that there are not enough representative members of the working class among Parliamentary representatives, we would not want to complain that the large class of stupid or maleficent people have too few representatives in Parliament: quite the contrary'. Feminists may find the implied parallels unconvincing, especially when we recall the many decades in which women were classified with children and the insane as ineligible for the right to a vote; but the general point remains. Establishing an empirical under-representation of certain categories of people does not in itself add up to a normative case for their equal or proportionate presence. It may alert us to overt forms of discrimination that are keeping certain people out, but does not yet provide the basis for radical change.

The contemporary version of Phillips Griffiths' argument takes the form of the notorious 'slippery slope': if measures are proposed for achieving a fair 'representation' of the proportion of women in the electorate, why not also of homosexuals, of pensioners, of the unemployed, of people with blue eyes and red hair? Though usually raised with deliberately facetious intent, such questions combine with more serious work on representation which has tended to dismiss ideals of 'descriptive' or 'mirror' representation as a nostalgic yearning for direct democracy. In her influential work on *The Concept of Representation*, Hanna Pitkin (1967: 86) suggests that the metaphors of descriptive representation are most commonly found among those who regard representative democracy as a poor second-best, and who therefore look to more 'accurate' or pictorial representation of the electorate as a way of approximating the old citizen assemblies. Yet representatives, she argues, are supposed to act—what would be the point of a system of representation that involved no responsibility for delivering policy results?—and too much emphasis on who is present may divert us from the more urgent questions of what the representatives actually do. 'Think of the legislature as a pictorial representation or a representative sample of the nation, and you will almost certainly concentrate on its composition rather than its activities' (1967: 226). In Pitkin's preferred version, it is the activities rather than the characteristics that matter, and what happens after the action rather than before it that counts. Representing 'means acting in the interests of the represented, in a manner responsive to them' (1967: 209). Fair representation cannot be guaranteed in advance; it is achieved in more continuous process, which depends on a (somewhat unspecified) level of responsiveness to the electorate. The representatives may and almost certainly will differ from those they act for, not only in their social and sexual characteristics, but also in their understanding of where the 'true' interests of their constituents lie. What renders this representative is the requirement for responsiveness. 'There need not be a constant activity of responding, but there must be a constant condition of responsive*ness*, of potential readiness to respond' (1967: 233).

Radicals may challenge this resolution as allowing too much independence of judgement and action to the representatives, but the direction their criticisms take also lends little support to arguments for gender parity. The most radical among them will scorn what they see as a reformist preoccupation with the composition of political élites—and they may express some dismay that a once obsessively democratic women's movement could retreat to such limited ambitions. Others will give more serious consideration to reforms that increase the representative nature of existing national assemblies, but they will prefer mechanisms of accountability that minimize the significance of the individuals elected. The shift from direct to representative democracy has shifted the emphasis from *who* the politicians are to *what* (policies, preferences, ideas) they represent, and in doing so, has made accountability to the electorate the pre-eminent concern. We may no longer have much hope of sharing in the activities of government, but we can at least demand that our politicians do what they promised to do. The quality of representation is then thought to depend on tighter mechanisms of accountability that bind politicians more closely to the opinions they profess to represent. Where such processes are successful, they reduce the discretion and autonomy of individual representatives; in the process, they seem to minimize the importance of whether these individuals are women or men.

Consider, in this context, the guidelines that were introduced by the US Democrats in the early 1970s, to make their National Convention (which carries the crucial responsibility of deciding on the presidential candidate) more representative of the party rank and file. Dismay at the seemingly undemocratic nature of the 1968 Convention prompted the formation of a Commission on Party Structure and Delegate Selection, which recommended more extensive participation by party members in the selection of delegates, as well as quota guidelines to increase the proportion of delegates who were female, black, and young. As a result of this, the composition of the 1972 Convention was markedly more 'descriptive' of Party members than previous ones had been: 40 per cent of the delegates were women, 15 per cent were black, and 21 per cent were aged between 18 and 30. But the reforms pointed in potentially contradictory directions, for they simultaneously sought to increase rank and file participation in the selection of delegates, to bind delegates more tightly to the preferences of this rank and file, and to ensure a more descriptive representation according to age, gender, and race. As Austin Ranney (1982: 196)—one of the members of the Commission—later noted, the success of the first two initiatives undermined the importance of the third. By 1980, the overwhelming majority of delegates were being chosen in party primaries which bound them to cast their votes for one particular candidate; they became in consequence mere ciphers, who were there to register preferences already expressed. 'If that is the case,' Ranney argues, 'then it really doesn't matter very much who the delegates are.' The more radical the emphasis on accountability, the less significance attaches to who does the work of representation.

Those engaged in campaigns for gender quotas have worked with some success on the electoral sensitivities of party politicians, but have made less headway among the tough-minded theorists of representation. My concern here is to address the latter, and to create maximum difficulties for myself I will focus on the stronger claim of gender parity, rather than the more modest claim for some more women elected.[1] This reflects what may be a naïve confidence on my part: that no one who seriously considers the matter could regard the current balance between the sexes as a fair process of representation. At the lowest points of women's under-representation (it was only in 1987 for example, that the British House of Commons lifted itself above the 5 per cent mark), one need only reverse the position of the sexes to demonstrate the democratic deficit. What would men think of a system of political representation in which they were outnumbered nineteen to one? At such gross levels of gender imbalance, rhetorical devices are all that we need—one would have to be a pretty determined patriarch to defend this as an appropriate state of affairs. But recent initiatives have raised the stakes considerably higher, insisting on positive action as a condition for effective change, and aiming at fifty/fifty parity, or a 40 per cent minimum for either sex. What are the arguments for this more radical position, and how do they engage with current conventions of accountability and representation?

Arguments for raising the proportion of women elected fall broadly into four groups. There are those that dwell on the role model successful women politicians offer; those that appeal to principles of justice between the sexes; those that identify particular interests of women that would be otherwise overlooked; and those that point towards a revitalized democracy that bridges the gap between representation and participation. The least interesting of these, from my point of view, is the role model. When more women candidates are elected, their example is said to raise women's self-esteem, encourage others to follow in their footsteps, and dislodge deep-rooted assumptions on what is appropriate to women and men. I leave this to one side, for I see it as an argument that has no particular purchase on politics *per se*. Positive role models are certainly beneficial, but I want to address arguments that engage more directly with issues of democracy and representation.

One final preamble. Though I deal here only with general issues of justification, there is a second order question, which is how legitimate objectives can be best achieved. The emphasis on quota mechanisms and other such guarantees has aroused strong resistance even among those who claim to share the ultimate goal of women's equality in politics, and while some of this can be discounted as intellectual or political dishonesty, much of it relates to pragmatic judgements of what is possible in any particular context. The potential backlash against women is one consideration here, as are the difficulties some political parties claim to experience in finding enough women candidates. Some of the resistance depends on more general arguments against positive action; some of it reflects still unresolved tensions between gender and class; some relates to a familiar problem in political argument, which is that mechanisms proposed for achieving one desired goal can conflict with other desirable ends. Considerations of space prevent me dealing with this second order question, and I will merely note that there *are* pragmatic judgements to be made, which do not flow simply from the conclusions on general objectives. But if gender parity can be shown to matter, and existing structures can be shown to discourage it, this constitutes a case for positive action.

I. THE CASE FOR GENDER PARITY:
THE JUSTICE ARGUMENT

One of the most powerful arguments for gender parity is simply in terms of justice: that it is patently and grotesquely unfair for men to monopolize representation. If there were no obstacles operating to keep certain groups of people out of political life, then we would expect positions of political influence to be randomly distributed between both sexes and across all the ethnic groups that make up the society. There might be some minor and innocent deviations, but any more distorted distribution of political office is evidence of intentional or structural discrimination (Phillips 1991). In such contexts (that is, most contexts!) women are being denied rights and opportunities that are currently available to men. There is a *prima facie* case for action.

There are three things to be said about this argument. One is that it relies on a strong position on the current sexual division of labour as inequitable and 'unnatural'. Consider the parallel under-representation of the very young and very old in politics. Most people will accept this as part of a normal and natural life-cycle, in which the young have no time for conventional politics, and the old have already contributed their share; and since each in principle has a chance in the middle years of life, this under-representation does not strike us as particularly unfair. The consequent 'exclusion' of certain views or experiences may be said to pose a problem. But however much people worry about this, they rarely argue for proportionate representation for the over-70s and the under-25s.[2] The situation of women looks more obviously unfair, in that women will be under-represented throughout their entire lives, but anyone wedded to the current division of labour can treat it as a parallel case. A woman's life-cycle typically includes a lengthy period of caring for children, and another lengthy period of caring for parents as they grow old. It is hardly surprising, then, that fewer women come forward as candidates, or that so few women are elected. Here, too, there may be an under-representation of particular experiences and concerns, but since this arises quite 'naturally' from particular life-cycles it is not at odds with equality or justice.

I do not find the parallel convincing, but my reasons lie in a feminist analysis of the sexual division of labour as 'unnatural' and unjust. The general argument from equal rights or opportunities only translates into a specific case for gender parity in politics when it is combined with some such analysis; failing this, it engages merely with the more overt forms of discrimination that exclude women from political office, and cannot deliver any stronger conclusion. Justice requires us to eliminate discrimination (this is already implied in the notion of justice), but the argument for women's *equal* representation in politics depends on that further ingredient which establishes structural discrimination. Feminists will have no difficulty adding this. This first point then helps clarify what is involved in moving from a description of women's under-representation to an analysis of its injustice.

The second and third points are more intrinsically problematic, and relate to the status of representation as a political act. If we treat the under-representation of women in politics as akin to their under-representation in management or the professions, we seem to treat being a politician as on a continuum with all those other careers that should be opened up equally to women. In each case, there is disturbing evidence of sexual inequality; in each case, there should be positive action for change. The argument appeals to our sense of justice, but it does so at the expense of an equally strong feeling that being a politician is not just another kind of job. 'Career politician' is still—and rightly—a term of abuse; however accurately it may describe people's activities in politics, it does not capture our political ideals. If political office *has* been reduced to yet another favourable and privileged position, then there is a clear argument from justice for making such office equally available to women. Most democrats, however, will want to resist pressures to regard political office in this way. So while men have no 'right' to monopolize political office, there is something rather unsatisfying in basing women's claim to political equality on an equal right to an interesting job.

An alternative and more promising formulation considers the under-representation of women in elected assemblies as analogous to their under-representation in the membership of political parties or the attendance at political meetings, and thus treats the equal right to be an elected representative as part of an equal right to political participation. This provides a more theoretically satisfying foundation, for equality in participation is one of the criteria by which democracies are judged, and the systematic under-participation of particular social groups is normally regarded as a political problem (Verba, Nie, and Kim 1978; Parry, Moyser, and Day 1992). This is not to say that everyone must be equally enthralled by the political process: the interest in politics is unevenly distributed, as is the interest in sport or in jazz. But when the distribution coincides too neatly with divisions by class or gender or ethnicity, political participation is by definition unequal and political influence as a consequence skewed. The principle of a rough equality between various social groups is already implicit in our idea of participation, and too marked a deviation from this is already regarded as a political failing. Once gender is admitted as an additional and relevant imbalance, it is easy enough to argue for equal participation between women and men.

As applied to representation, however, the argument seems to assert what has still to be established: that representation is just another aspect of participation, to be judged by the same criteria. Yet many theorists of democracy proceed from just the opposite direction, and they have based much of their critique of direct or participatory democracy on precisely what differentiates representation from participation. Participation implies activity, and yet activity is always a minority affair. By setting the requirements for participation impossibly high, theorists of participatory democracy are said to promote a politics that becomes 'unrepresentative' and unequal, for while most citizens can manage an occasional foray into the polling booth, few are willing or able to take on more continuous engagement, and the power then slips into the hands of those who most love politics. Representative democracy claims to solve this conundrum by removing the requirement for physical presence. As long as there is a minimal level of equality in the act of voting, then the representation can be said to be equal; we do not have to commit ourselves additionally to the hard labour of the political life.

Equality of presence—a rough approximation to the social groups that make up the society—is already implicit in the notion of participation. But it is not so obviously implicit in the notion of representation, which was, if anything, dreamt up to get round this bothersome condition. The two are, of course, related, for a society that provided genuinely equal access to participation in meetings and pressure groups and parties would almost certainly produce the same kind of equality among the people elected. In principle, however, they are separate, for in distancing itself from participating democracy, representative democracy has distanced itself from physical presence as the measure of political equality. Representative democracy claims, for example, to represent the competing interests of capital and labour by giving each of us an equal right to vote, and this is said to encourage a variety of parties to emerge that will speak to our different concerns. But representative democracy makes no claims about achieving a proportionate representation of working class people inside the legislative assemblies: workers, should be equally represented, but not necessarily by workers themselves. So while we can readily appeal to existing understandings of democracy as the basis for women's equal *participation*, the case for gender parity among elected representatives moves onto more unchartered ground.

What we can perhaps do is turn the argument around, and ask by what 'natural' superiority of talent or experience men could claim a right to dominate assemblies? The burden of proof then shifts to the men, who would have to establish either some genetic distinction which makes them better at understanding problems and taking decisions, or some more socially derived advantage which enhances their political skills. Neither of these looks particularly persuasive: the first has never been successfully established; and the second is no justification if it depends on structures of discrimination. There is no argument from justice that can defend the current state of affairs; and in this more negative sense, there *is* an argument from justice for parity between women and men. But there is still a troubling sense in which the argument overlooks what is peculiar to representation as a political act. When democracy has become largely a matter of representing particular policies or programmes or ideas, this leaves a question-mark over why the sex of the representatives should matter.

II. THE CASE FOR GENDER PARITY: WOMEN'S INTERESTS

The second way of arguing for gender parity is in terms of the interests that would be otherwise discounted: this is an argument from political realism. In the heterogeneous societies contained by the modern nation state, there is no transparently obvious 'public interest', but rather a multiplicity of different and potentially conflicting interests which must be acknowledged and held in check. Our political representatives are only human, and as such they cannot pretend to any greater generosity of spirit than those who elected them to office. There may be altruists among them, but it would be unwise to rely on this in framing our constitutional arrangements. Failing Plato's solution to the intrusion of private interest (a class of Guardians with no property or family of their own) we must look to other ways of limiting tyrannical tendencies, and most of these will involve giving all interests their legitimate voice.

This, in essence, was James Mill's case for representative government and an extended franchise, though he notoriously combined this with the argument that women could 'be struck off without inconvenience' from the list of potential claimants, because they had no interests not already included in those of their fathers or husbands. (He also thought we could strike off 'young' men under forty years of age.) Part of the argument for increasing women's political representation looks like a feminist rewrite and extension of this. Women occupy a distinct position within society: they are typically concentrated, for example, in lower-paid jobs; and they carry the primary responsibility for the unpaid work of caring for others. There are particular needs, interests, and concerns that arise from women's experience, and these will be inadequately addressed in a politics that is dominated by men. Equal rights to a vote have not proved strong enough to deal with this problem; there must also be equality among those elected to office.

At an intuitive level, this is hard to fault. It takes what is a widely accepted element in our understanding of democracy and applies it to women's situation. Looked at more closely, however, the argument from women's interests or women's concerns seems to rest on three conditions: that women have a distinct and separate interest as women; that this interest cannot be adequately represented by men; and that the election of women ensures its representation. As critics of gender quotas will be quick to point out, each condition is vulnerable to attack. The notion that women have at least some interests distinct from and even in conflict with men's is relatively straightforward (we can all think of appropriate examples), but this falls a long way short of establishing a set of interests shared by all women. If interests are understood in terms of what women express as their priorities and goals, there is considerable disagreement among women, and while attitude surveys frequently expose a 'gender gap' between women and men, the more striking development over recent decades has been the convergence in the voting behaviour of women and men. There may be more mileage in notions of a distinct woman's interest if this is understood in terms of some underlying but as yet unnoticed 'reality', but this edges uncomfortably close to notions of 'false consciousness', which most feminists would prefer to avoid. Indeed the presumption of a clearly demarcated 'woman's interest' which holds true for all women in all classes and all countries has been one of the casualties of recent feminist critique, and the exposure of multiple differences between women has undermined more global understandings of women's interests and concerns (see, for example, Mohanty 1992). If there is no clearly agreed and recognized 'women's interest', does it really matter if the representatives are predominantly men?

Definitive as this might seem, it does not seriously undermine the claim to gender parity; if anything, it can be said to strengthen it. Consider, in this context, Edmund Burke's rather odd understanding of interests as reflecting 'an objective, impersonal, unattached reality', which can then be represented by any sufficiently competent and honest individual (Pitkin 1967: 168). Odd as this is, it conveys a partial truth. The more fixed the interests, or the more definite and easily defined, the less significance attaches to who does the work of representation. So if women's interests were transparently obvious to any intelligent observer, there might be no particular case—beyond the perennial one of trust—for insisting on representatives who also happen to be women. We might feel that men will be less diligent in pressing women's interests or concerns, but if we all know what these are, it will be correspondingly easy to tell whether they are being adequately pursued. If, however, the interests are varied, unstable, perhaps still in the process of formation, it will be far more difficult to separate out what is to be represented from who is to do the representation. The greater problems arise, that is, where interests are not so precisely delineated, where the political agenda has been constructed without reference to certain areas of concern, or where much fresh thinking is necessary to work out the appropriate policies. To this extent, the very difficulties in defining what are in women's interests strengthen the case for more women as representatives.

The more decisive problem lies in the third condition. Does the election of more women then ensure their representation? Again, at an intuitive level, an increase in the number of women elected seems likely to change both the practices and the priorities of politics, increasing the attention given to matters of childcare, for example, or ensuring that women's poor position in the labour market is more vigorously addressed. This intuition is already partially confirmed by the experience of those countries which have changed the gender composition of their elected assemblies. But what does this mean in terms of political representation? Elections are typically organized by geographical constituencies, which sometimes coincide with concentrations of particular ethnic or religious groups, or concentrations of certain social classes, but which never coincide with concentrations of women or men. Elections typically take place through the medium of political parties, each of which produces candidates who are said to represent that party's policies and programmes and goals. In what sense can we say that the women elected through this process carry an additional responsibility to represent women? In the absence of mechanisms to establish accountability, the equation of more women with more adequate representation of women's interests looks suspiciously undemocratic. How do the women elected know what the women who elected them want? By what right do they claim responsibility to represent women's concerns?

Though this is rarely stated in the literature, the argument from women's interests implies that representatives will have considerable autonomy: that they do have currently, and by implication, that this ought to continue. Women's exclusion from politics is said to matter precisely because politicians do not abide by pre-agreed policies and goals. As any observer of the political process knows, policy decisions are *not* settled in advance by party programmes, for new problems and issues emerge alongside unanticipated constraints, and in the subsequent weighing of interpretations and priorities, it matters immensely who the representatives are. Feminists have much experience of this, gained through painful years of watching hard won commitments to sexual equality drop off the final agenda. When there is a significant under-representation of women at the point of final decision, this can and does have serious consequences, and it is partly in reflection of this that feminists have shifted their attention from the details of policy commitments to the composition of the decision-making group. Political experience tells us that all male or mostly male assemblies will be poor judges of women's interests and priorities and concerns, and that trying to shore up this judgement by pre-agreed programmes has only limited effect. There is a strong dose of political realism here. Representatives *do* have considerable autonomy, which is why it matters who those representatives are.

It is worth dwelling on this point, for it highlights a divergence between current feminist preoccupations and what has long been the main thrust in radical democracy. Radical democrats distrust the wayward autonomy of politicians and the way they concentrate power around them, and they typically work to combat these tendencies by measures that will bind politicians more tightly to their promises, and disperse over-centralized power. Feminists have usually joined forces in support of the second objective: feminism is widely associated with bringing politics closer to home; and women are often intensely involved in local and community affairs. But when feminists insist that the sex of the representatives matters, they are expressing a deeper ambivalence towards the first objective. The politics of binding mandates, for example, turns the representatives into glorified messengers: it puts all the emphasis onto the content of the messages, and makes it irrelevant who the messengers are. In contesting the sex of the representatives, feminists are querying this version of democratic accountability.

The final point about the argument from interests is that it may not of itself justify equal or proportionate presence. In a recent discussion of demands for group representation in Canada, Will Kymlicka (1993) makes a useful distinction between arguments for equal or proportionate presence (where the number of women or aboriginal Indians or francophone Canadians in any legislative assembly would correspond to their proportion in the citizenry as a whole), and the case for a threshold presence (where the numbers would reach the requisite level that ensured each group's concerns were adequately addressed). When the group in question is a numerically small minority, the threshold might prove larger than their proportion in the population as a whole; when the group composes half the population, the threshold might be considerably lower. On this basis, there might be an argument for greater than proportionate representation of Indians, for example, but less than proportionate representation of women: not that women would be formally restricted to 25 or 30 per cent of the seats, but that they might not require any more than this in order to change the political agenda. It is the argument from justice that most readily translates into strict notions of equality; the argument from women's interests need not deliver such strong results.

III. THE CASE FOR GENDER PARITY: TOWARDS A REVITALISED DEMOCRACY

The third argument is less developed, and I offer it here as a way of dealing with some of the problems I identify above. The argument from justice works well enough on the limited ground that treats being a politician like any other kind of job, or on the negative ground that denies any just basis for a male monopoly. The argument from women's interests works well enough as a case for a threshold, but not necessarily equal, presence, but is best understood in terms of a realistic assessment of how rarely politicians abide by their pre-agreed programmes. These are powerful arguments, but they are not, on the whole, the kinds of arguments that feminists most admire: they are too much grounded in an impoverished experience of democracy to bear the full weight of feminist ambition. And they leave unresolved that recurrent radical concern about controlling wayward politicians. Apart from the argument that women should get an equal chance at a political career (which is a fair enough argument, but not intrinsically about democracy), we can only believe that the sex of the representatives matters if we think it will change what the representatives do. In saying this, we seem to be undermining accountability through party programmes. We are saying we expect our representatives to do more—or other—than they promised in the election campaign.

There is often an expectation, for example, that women politicians will operate on a cross-party basis, forging alliances to press for improvements in childcare provision or changes in the abortion laws. In her study of Norwegian representatives, Hege Skjeie (1991) records a number of such initiatives, but she notes that it is the priorities of their party that finally dictate the way women politicians vote. If we are either surprised or disappointed by this, it must be because we see an increase in the number of women politicians as challenging the dominance of the party system or the tradition of voting along party lines. Those who feel that the tighter controls of party discipline have discouraged serious discussion and debate may be happy enough with this conclusion. But in the absence of alternative mechanisms of consultation or accountability, it does read like a recipe for letting representatives do what *they* choose to do.

What makes sense of this, I believe, is an additional presumption that is implicit in most feminist arguments, a conviction that changing the composition of existing elected assemblies is only part of a wider project of increasing and enhancing democracy. When the argument for gender parity is taken out of this context, it has to rely more heavily on arguments from political realism, and while these are powerful enough arguments in themselves, they fall short on some key concerns. Put back into its context, the argument often reveals a more ambitious programme of dispersing power through a wider range of decision-making assemblies, and changing the balance between participation and representation.

We might think here of the further initiatives that are so typical of women in politics: the use of the open forum, for example, as a way of consulting women in a local community; the report back to women's sections or women's conferences; or just the extraordinary energy so many women politicians devote to what they see as their responsibilities for representing women. Even among those most committed to party politics (and many women deliberately stay outside, in the more amorphous politics of women's movement groups and campaigns), the political party is frequently viewed as an inadequate vehicle for representation. In 1980s Britain, for example, there was a flowering of women's committees within the framework of local government (usually associated with more left-wing Labour councils), and these made extensive use of co-option or the open forum as a way of consulting women outside the political parties. Now you could think of this as a short term compensation for women's current under-representation among elected councillors, but there is little to support this view. More commonly, those associated with the development of women's committees saw the additional mechanisms of consultation and participation as always and everywhere desirable—even under some future scenario where women might hold 50 per cent of council seats. The women involved were querying the exclusive emphasis on the party as the vehicle for representation; they were pursuing complementary (sometimes conflicting) ways of empowering women to make their needs better known.

The case for gender parity in politics should, I believe, be understood within this broader context, and to this extent, it confirms Hanna Pitkin's intuition. The argument for more 'descriptive' or 'mirror' representation does move in close parallel with arguments for a more participatory form of democracy; and those concerned with the under-representation of women in politics do look to additional mechanisms of consultation and accountability and participation that would complement our occasional vote. We do not need this additional ammunition to argue for more women in politics; there are arguments enough from justice or interests that provide a basis for substantial change. But as a more profound set of issues about democracy and representation, the case for gender parity is at its strongest when it is associated with the larger dream.

Notes

1. I use the term parity to indicate a rough equality between the proportion of women and men elected. My use of this term should not be confused with the arguments that have recently surfaced within the Council of Europe for so-called parity democracy. See Outshoorn (1993) for a critical review of this literature.
2. There *are* parties which operate quotas for youth—as with my own example of the 1972 Democratic National Convention—but when it comes to parliamentary candidatures, few people worry about the paucity of those under 25.

References

Chapman, Jenny (1993), *Politics, Feminism, and the Reformation of Gender* (London: Routledge).

Grofman, B., Lijphart, A., McKay, R.B., Scarrow, H.A. (eds.) (1982), *Representation and Redistricting Issues* (Lexington, Mass.: D. C. Heath and Co.).

Kymlicka, Will (1993), 'Group Representation in Canadian Politics'. Paper prepared for IRPP project on 'Communities, the Charter and Interest Advocacy'.

Lovenduski, Joni and Norris, Pippa (1989), 'Selecting Women Candidates: Obstacles to the Feminisation of the House of Commons', *European Journal of Political Research*, 17, 533–63.

Mohanty, Chandra (1993), 'Feminist Encounters: Locating the Politics of Experience', in Michèle Barrett and Anne Phillips (eds.), *Destabilizing Theory: Contemporary Feminist Debates* (Cambridge: Polity Press), 74–92.

Outshoorn, Joyce (1993), 'Parity Democracy: A Critical Look at a "New" Strategy', paper prepared for workshop on 'Citizenship and Plurality', European Consortium for Political Research, Leiden.

Parry, Geraint, Moyser, George, and Day, Neil (1992), *Political Participation and Democracy in Britain* (Cambridge: Cambridge University Press).

Phillips, Anne (1991) *Engendering Democracy* (Cambridge: Polity Press).

Phillips Griffiths, A. (1960), 'How Can One Person Represent Another?' *Aristotelian Society*, Supplementary vol. xxxiv, 187–208.

Pitkin, Hanna F. (1967), *The Concept of Representation* (Berkeley: University of California Press).

Ranney, Austin (1982), 'Comments on Representation Within the Political Party System', in Grofman *et al.* (1982), 193–7.

Skjeie, Hege (1991), 'The Rhetoric of Difference: On Women's Inclusion into Political Elites', *Politics and Society*, 19/2, 233–63.

Verba, Sidney, Nie, Norman H., and Kim, Jae-on (1978), *Participation and Political Equality: A Seven National Comparison* (Cambridge: Cambridge University Press).

Part IV. Identities and Coalitions

Coalition Politics: Turning the Century

Bernice Johnson Reagon

I've never been this high before. I'm talking about the altitude. There is a lesson in bringing people together where they can't get enough oxygen, then having them try to figure out what they're going to do when they can't think properly. I'm serious about that. There probably are some people here who can breathe, because you were born in high altitudes and you have big lung cavities. But when you bring people in who have not had the environmental conditioning, you got one group of people who are in a strain— and the group of people who are feeling fine are trying to figure out why you're staggering around, and that's what this workshop is about this morning.

I wish there had been another way to graphically make me feel it because I belong to the group of people who are having a very difficult time being here. I feel as if I'm gonna keel over any minute and die. That is often what it feels like if you're *really* doing coalition work. Most of the time you feel threatened to the core and if you don't, you're not really doing no coalescing.

I'm Bernice Reagon. I was born in Georgia, and I'd like to talk about the fact that in about twenty years we'll turn up another century. I believe that we are positioned to have the opportunity to have something to do with what makes it into the next century. And the principles of coalition are directly related to that. You don't go into coalition because you just *like* it. The only reason you would consider trying to team up with somebody who could possibly kill you, is because that's the only way you can figure you can stay alive.

A hundred years ago in this country we were just beginning to heat up for the century we're in. And the name of the game in terms of the dominant energy was technology. We have lived through a period where there have been things like railroads and telephones, and radios, TVs and airplanes, and cars, and transistors, and com-

Author, Bernice Johnson Reagon © Songtalk Publishing Company. Originally published in *Home Girls: A Black Feminist Anthology,* Kitchen Table Press, 1983. This chapter is based upon a presentation at the West Coast Women's Music Festival 1981, Yosemite National Forest, California.

puters. And what this has done to the concept of human society and human life is, to a large extent, what we in the latter part of this century have been trying to grapple with. With the coming of all that technology, there was finally the possibility of making sure no human being in the world would be unreached. You couldn't find a place where you could hide if somebody who had access to that technology wanted to get to you. Before the dawning of that age you had all these little cute villages and the wonderful homogenous societies where everybody looked the same, did things the same, and believed the same things, and if they didn't, you could just kill them and nobody would even ask you about it.

We've pretty much come to the end of a time when you can have a space that is 'yours only'—just for the people you want to be there. Even when we have our 'women-only' festivals, there is no such thing. The fault is not necessarily with the organizers of the gathering. To a large extent it's because we have just finished with that kind of isolating. There is no hiding-place. There is nowhere you can go and only be with people who are like you. It's over. Give it up.

Now every once in awhile there is a need for people to try to clean out corners and bar the doors and check everybody who comes in the door, and check what they carry in and say, 'Humph, inside this place the only thing we are going to deal with is X or Y or Z.' And so only the Xs or Ys or Zs get to come in. That place can then become a nurturing place or a very destructive place. Most of the time when people do that, they do it because of the heat of trying to live in this society where being an X or Y or Z is very difficult, to say the least. The people running the society call the shots as if they're still living in one of those little villages, where they kill the ones they don't like or put them in the forest to die. (There are some societies where babies are born and if they are not wanted for some reason they are put over in a corner. They do that here too, you know, put them in garbage cans.) When somebody else is running a society like that, and you are the one who would be put out to die, it gets too hard to stay out in that society all the time. And that's when you find a place, and you try to bar the door and check all the people who come in. You come together to see what you can do about shouldering up all of your energies so that you and your kind can survive.

There is no chance that you can survive by staying *inside* the barred room. That will not be tolerated. The door of the room will just be painted red and then when those who call the shots get ready to clean house, they have easy access to you.

But that space while it lasts should be a nurturing space where you sift out what people are saying about you and decide who you really are. And you take the time to try to construct within yourself and within your community who you would be if you were running society. In fact, in that little barred room where you check everybody at the door, you act out community. You pretend that your room is a world. It's almost like a play, and in some cases you actually grow food, you learn to have clean water, and all of that stuff, you just try to do it all. It's like 'If *I* was really running it, this is the way it would be.'

Of course the problem with the experiment is that there ain't nobody in there but folk like you, which by implication means you wouldn't know what to do if you were running it with all of the other people who are out there in the world. Now that's nationalism. I mean it's nurturing, but it is also nationalism. At a certain stage nationalism is crucial to a people if you are going to ever impact as a group in your own interest. Nationalism at another point becomes reactionary because it is totally inadequate for surviving in the world with many peoples.

Sometimes you get comfortable in your little barred room, and you decide you in fact are going to live there and carry out all of your stuff in there. And you gonna take care of everything that needs to be taken care of in the barred room. If you're white and in the barred room and if everybody's white, one of the first things you try to take care of is making sure that people don't think that the barred room is a racist barred room. So you begin to talk about racism and the first thing you do is say, 'Well, maybe we better open the door and let some Black folks in the barred room.' Then you think, 'Well, how we gonna figure out whether they're Xs or not?' Because there's nothing in the room but Xs. You go down the checklist. You been working a while to sort out who you are, right? So you go down the checklist and say, 'If we can find Black folk like that we'll let them in the room.' You don't really want Black folks, you are just looking for yourself with a little colour to it.

And there are those of us Black Folk who are like that. So if you're lucky you can open the door and get one or two. Right? And everything's wonderful. But no matter what, there will be one or two of us who have not bothered to be like you and you know it. We come knocking on your door and say, 'Well, you let them in, you let me in too.' And we will break your door down trying to get in. As far as we can see we are also Xs. Cause you didn't say, 'THIS BARRED ROOM IS FOR WHITE XS ONLY.' You just said it was for Xs. So everybody who thinks they're an X comes running to get into the room. And because you trying to take care of everything in this room, and you know you're not racist, you get pressed to let us all in.

The first thing that happens is that the room don't feel like the room anymore. And it ain't home no more. It is not a womb no more. And you can't feel comfortable no more. And what happens at that point has to do with trying to do too much in it. You don't do no coalition building in a womb. It's just like trying to get a baby used to taking a drink when they're in your womb. It just don't work too well. Inside the womb you generally are very soft and unshelled. You have no covering. And you have no ability to handle what happens if you start to let folks in who are not like you.

Coalition work is not work done in your home. Coalition work has to be done in the streets. And it is some of the most dangerous work you can do. And you shouldn't look for comfort. Some people will come to a coalition and they rate the success of the coalition on whether or not they feel good when they get there. They're not looking for a coalition; they're looking for a home! They're looking for a bottle with some milk in it and a nipple, which does not happen in a coalition. You don't get a lot of food in a coalition. You don't get fed a lot in a coalition. In a coalition you have to give, and it is different from your home. You can't stay there all the time. You go to the coalition for a few hours and then you go back and take your bottle wherever it is, and then you go back and coalesce some more.

It is very important not to confuse them—home and coalition. Now when it comes to women—the organized women's movement—this recent thrust—we all have had the opportunity to have some kind of relationship with it. The women's movement has perpetuated a myth that there is some common experience that comes just cause you're women. And they're throwing all these festivals and this music and these concerts happen. If you're the same kind of women like the folk in that little barred room, it works. But as soon as some other folk check the definition of 'women' that's in the dictionary (which you didn't write, right?) they decide that they can come because they are women, but when they do, they don't see or hear nothing that is like them. Then they charge, 'This ain't no women's thing!' Then if you try to address that and bring them in, they start to play music that ain't even women's music! And you try to figure out what happened to your wonderful barred room. It comes from taking a word like 'women' and using it as a code. There is an in-house definition so that when you say 'women only' most of the time that means you had better be able—if you come to this place—to handle lesbianism and a lot of folks running around with

245

no clothes on. And I'm being too harsh this morning as I talk to you, but I don't want you to miss what I'm trying to say. Now if you come and you can't handle that, there's another term that's called 'woman-identified'. They say you might be a woman but you're not woman-identified, and we only want women who are 'woman-identified'. That's a good way to leave a lot of women out of your room.

So here you are and you grew up and you speak English and you know about this word 'woman' and you know you one, and you walk into this 'woman-only' space and you ain't there. Because 'woman' in that space does not mean 'woman' from your world. It's a code word and it traps, and the people that use the word are not prepared to deal with the act that if you put it out, everybody that thinks they're a woman may one day want to seek refuge. And it ain't no refuge place! And it's not safe! It should be a coalition! It may have been that in its first year the Michigan National 'Women-Only' festival was a refuge place. By the fourth year it was a place of coalition, and it's not safe anymore. It ain't safe for nobody who comes. When you walk in there you in trouble—and everybody who comes is trying to get to their home there. At this festival they said: whatever you drink, bring it with you—tea, honey, you know, whatever it is—and we will provide hot water. Now I understand that you got here and there was no hot water. Can't get nothing! That is the nature of coalition. You have to give it all. It is not to feed you; you have to feed it. And it's a monster. It never gets enough. It always wants more. So you better be sure you got your home someplace for you to go to so that you will not become a martyr to the coalition. Coalition *can* kill people; however, it is not by nature fatal. You do not have to die because you are committed to coalition. I'm not so old, and I don't know nothing else. But you do have to know how to pull back, and you do have to have an old-age perspective. You have to be beyond the womb stage.

None of this matters at all very much if you die tomorrow—that won't even be cute. It only matters if you make a commitment to be around for another fifty more years. There are some grey-haired women I see running around occasionally, and we have to talk to those folks about how come they didn't commit suicide forty years ago. Don't take everything they say because some of the stuff they gave up to stay around ain't worth considering. But be sure you get on your agenda some old people and try to figure out what it will be like if you are a raging radical fifty years from today.

Think about yourself that way. What would you be like if you had white hair and had not given up your principles? It might be wise as you deal with coalition efforts to think about the possibilities of going for fifty years. It calls for some care. I'm not gonna be suicidal, if I can help it. Sometimes you don't even know you just took a step that could take your head off cause you can't know everything when you start to coalesce with these people who sorta look like you in just one aspect but really they belong to another group. That is really the nature of women. It does not matter at all that biologically we have being women in common. We have been organized to have our primary cultural signals come from some other factors than that we are women. We are not from our base acculturated to be women people, capable of crossing our first people boundaries—Black, White, Indian, etc.

Now if we are the same women from the same people in this barred room, we never notice it. That stuff stays wherever it is. It does not show up until somebody walks into the room who happens to be a woman but really is also somebody else. And then out comes who we really are. And at that point you are not a woman. You are Black or you are Chicana or you are Disabled or you are Racist or you are White. The fact that you are a woman is not important at all and it is not the governing factor to your existence at that moment. I am now talking about bigotry and everybody's got it. I am talking about turning the century with some principles intact. Today wherever women gather together it is not necessarily nurturing. It is coalition building. And if you feel the strain, you may be doing some good work. So don't come to no women's festival looking for comfort unless you brought it in your little tent. And then if you bring it in your tent don't be inviting everybody in because everybody ain't your company, and then you won't be able to stand the festival. Am I confusing you? Yes, I am. If coalition is so bad, and so terrible, and so uncomfortable, why is it necessary? That's what you're asking. Because the barred rooms will not be allowed to exist. They will all be wiped out. That is the plan that we now have in front of us.

Now these little rooms were created by some of the most powerful movements we have seen in this country. I'm going to start with the Civil Rights movement because of course I think that that was the first one in the era we're in. Black folks started it, Black folks did it, so everything you've done politically rests on the efforts of my people—that's my arrogance! Yes, and it's the truth; it's my truth. You can take it or leave it, but that's the way I see it. So once we did what we did, then you've got women, you've got Chicanos, you've got the Native Americans, and you've got homosexuals, and you got all of these people who also got sick of somebody being on their neck. And maybe if they come together, they can do something about it. And I claim all of you as coming from something that made me who I am. You can't tell me that you ain't in the Civil Rights movement. You are in the Civil Rights movement that we created that just rolled up to your door. But it could not stay the same, because if it was gonna stay the same it wouldn't have done you no good. Some of you would not have caught yourself dead near no Black folks walking around talking about freeing themselves from racism and lynching. So by the time our movement got to you it had to sound like something you knew about. Like if I find out you're gay, you gonna lose your job.

There were people who came South to work in the movement who were not Black. Most of them were white when they came. Before it was over, that category broke up—you know, some of them were Jewish, not simply white, and some others even changed their names. Say if it was Mary when they came South, by the time they were finished it was Maria, right? It's called finding yourself. At some point, you cannot be fighting oppression and be oppressed yourself and not feel it. Within the Black movement there was also all of the evils of the society, so that anything that was happening to you in New York or the West Coast probably also happened to you in another way, within the movement. And as you became aware of that you tried to talk to these movement people about how you felt. And they say, 'Well let's take that up next week. Because the most important thing now is that Black people are being oppressed and we must work with that.' Watch these mono-issue people. They ain't gonna do you no good. I don't care who they are. And there are people who prioritize the cutting line of the struggle. And they say the cutting line is this issue, and more than anything we must move on this issue and that's automatically saying that whatever's bothering you will be put down if you bring it up. You have to watch these folks. Watch these groups that can only deal with one thing at a time. On the other hand, learn about space within coalition. You can't have everybody sitting up there talking about everything that concerns you at the same time or you won't get no place.

There is not going to be the space to continue as we are or as we were. There was a time when folks saw the major movement force coming out of the Black community. Then, the hottest thing became the Native Americans and the next, students' rights and the next, the anti-war movement or whatever. The movement force just rolled around hitting various issues. Now, there were a few people who kept up with many of those issues. *They are very rare.* Anytime you find a person showing up at all of those struggles, and they have some sense of sanity by your definition, not theirs (cause almost everybody thinks they're sane), one, study with them, and two, protect them. They're gonna be in trouble shortly because they are the most visible ones. They hold the key to turning the century with our principles and ideals intact. They can teach you how to cross cultures and not kill yourself. And you need to begin to make a checklist—it's not long, you can probably count on your two hands. When it comes to political organizing, and when it comes to your basic survival, there are a few people who took the sweep from the 60s to the 80s and they didn't miss a step. They could stand it all. If they're painters, there's a picture about everything as best they can do it. And if they're singers, there's a song showing that they were awake through all the struggles. Now the songs and the pictures and poems ain't all right, cause you ain't dealing with people who are free from bigotry. I remember a song I wrote about Vietnam. It wasn't about Vietnam, it was about the whole world. And it started, of course, with Black people—I don't start nothing except with Black people:

> Black people taken from an ancient land
> Suffered trials by cruel white hands
> In the circle there's gotta be room for them
> Move on over. Make a little room for them
> We're in trouble cause there's no room for them . . .

By that time I'd been listening to the Vietnam war, right? And we called them the Viet Cong. I started to pull for the Viet Cong to win. I didn't know at that time that they were all the same people, but just before I wrote the song, somebody hit on me that Viet Cong are Vietnamese. So I say, 'Oh,' cause I wanna be correct whenever I write a song, so my next verse was:

> The Vietnamese with slanted eyes
> Fighting for their land, not standing by
> They can't make it cause there's no room . . .

Okay, did you see what I did? Reduced these people to the slant of their eyes. If I ran into a Vietnamese who didn't have slanted eyes, I'd be in trouble. They may not have even had slanted eyes, but you know when people talked about them, they had slanted eyes. The next verse was:

> Little brown boy with straight black hair
> Fighting in India land, there's no food there . . .

Reduced all of the people in India to straight hair! Do you understand? Brown skin. Then I ran into some of them who were so black and some of them got kinky hair. Do you understand what I'm talking about? So all of these people who hit every issue did not get it right, but if they took a stand, at least you know where their shit is.

It must become necessary for all of us to feel that this is our world. And that we are here to stay and that anything that is here is ours to take and to use in our image. And watch that 'our'—make it as big as you can—it ain't got nothing to do with that barred room. The 'our' must include everybody you have to include in order for you to survive. You must be sure you understand that you ain't gonna be able to have an 'our' that don't include Bernice Johnson Reagon, cause I don't plan to go nowhere! That's why we have to have coalitions. Cause I ain't gonna let you live unless you let me live. Now there's danger in that, but there's also the possibility that we can both live—if you can stand it.

I want to talk a little about turning the century and the principles. Some of us will be dead. We won't be here. And many of us take ourselves too seriously. We think that what we think is really the cutting line. Most people who are up on the stage take themselves too seriously—it's true. You think that what you've got to say is special and that somebody needs to hear it. That is arrogance. That is egotism, and the only checking line is when you have somebody to pull your coattails. Most of us think that the space we live in is the most important space there is, and that the condition that we find ourselves in is the condition that must be changed or else. That is only partially the case. If you analyse the situation properly, you will know that there might be a few things you can do in your personal, individual interest so that you can experience and enjoy the change. But most of the things that you do, if you do them right, are for people who live long after you are long forgotten. That will only happen if you give it away. Whatever it is that you know, give it away, and don't give it away only on the horizontal. Don't give it away like that, because they're gonna die when you die, give or take a few days. Give it away *that* way (up and down). And what I'm talking about is being very concerned with the world you live in, the condition you find yourself in, and be able to do the kind of analysis that says that what you believe in is worthwhile for human beings in general, and in the future, and do everything you can to throw yourself into the next century. And make people contend with your baggage, whatever it is. The only way you can take yourself seriously is if you can throw yourself into the next period beyond your little meager human-body-mouth-talking all the time.

I am concerned that we are very short-sighted, and we think that the issue we have at this moment has to be addressed at this moment or we will die. It is not true. It is only a minor skirmish. It must be waged guerrilla-warfare style. You shoot it out, get behind the tree so you don't get killed, because they ain't gonna give you what you asked for. You must be ready to go out again tomorrow and while you're behind the tree you must be training the people who will be carrying the message forward into the next period, when they do kill you from behind the tree.

You must believe that believing in human beings in balance with the environment and the universe is a good thing. You must believe—and I'm being biased and bigoted here again—that having a society that doesn't solve everything with guns is a good thing. You must believe that when they sell bread to Russia and then go to El Salvador and say that the biggest problem in El Salvador is Russia, that they're pulling your leg. And you must not let them pull your leg. There are some people who have a problem with people killing people, and people robbing people, and people raping people, and people exploiting people, and people not giving people jobs because of the way they look and because of the way they're born. Some of you are in here trying to change all of that right now. The thing that must survive you is not just the record of your practice, but the principles that are the basis of your practice. If in the future, somebody is gonna use that song I sang, they're gonna have to strip it or at least shift it. I'm glad the principle is there for others to build on.

I had never left Georgia until after the Civil Rights movement, so I didn't know nothing about all of these people in the world. I knew two people. White people and Black people. When I went to New York, the white people were not the same white people. I was being very sensible at this time. They were too dark. I tried to make them become Black. They didn't like that at all. I would try to ask them: Who are you and where are you from? They say: Well, what do you mean? And I say: Well, you don't look white. And they say: Well, we're white. And I say: But you don't look white-white. If you all had let me run it, we would all be coloured. Because I grew up in Albany, Georgia, and I knew what white people looked like, and they looked like none of them dark-skinned white folks I saw up in New York who got mad at me when I tried to bring them over. Respect means when somebody joins you and they need to be white, you give it to them. You turn it over and you say: Okay you got it—you are white. I could save your life, but okay you got it—you are white. That's called allowing people to name themselves. And dealing with them from that perspective. Shaking your head in your little barred room about it, or if somebody's crazy enough to let you sit on the stage for a little while will not help the situation. It won't stretch your perimeter.

I didn't have anything to do with being alive at this time, but if I had been running it I couldn't have picked a better time. I have lived through the brilliant heat of the Civil Rights struggle. I have lived through a war that was stopped. I mean they talked about these women who tell these men that if you go to war we won't sleep with you, right? That is not how Vietnam got stopped. Not that they have told us. I've lived at a time when people stopped a country from beating another country. Of course they don't tell you *you* did that and so you are still trying to figure out where you went wrong! I hear it on TV all the time. Jane Pauley was talking to this man who wrote this book about what was wrong with the 60s—he had been in Washington when they closed down Washington that May—(they closed the city down!) and she leaned over to him, and she said, 'Where did we go wrong?' And I say, You fool. You wouldn't be on the Today show to even ask the question, if we had gone wrong! We have not gone wrong! The period I have lived through saw a president of a country come down and he was not assassinated. That is the way we like to do things. And if you want to know the other side of it, take a look at Iran, or take a look at the way they took care of all of those leaders years back. When you don't like who's in power, you kill 'em. That is not what happened with Nixon. And we did it. We did that. Any of you who have jobs that your mama didn't have, we did that. Nobody else did that!! It is a very good time to be alive—to be in this place, complete with its racism, and its classism, and its garbage trucks running through.

People who think that the only 'women-only' there are are lesbian women give me a big problem, cause I would have to leave too many of my folk out cause they ain't gonna take that for one second. *And if they came in they would be homophobic.* And you'll have to challenge them about it. Can you handle it? This ain't no nurturing place no more. Cause we're taking over. Anything that says 'Women', we're gonna come. You can forget it. Now if you clean it up and name what it is you want, then you might be able to have it—but we might storm *that* if we don't think it should exist. Cause like it is, it is our world, and we are here to stay. And we are not on the defensive. We are not on the defensive.

There is an offensive movement that started in this country in the

60s that is continuing. The reason we are stumbling is that we are at the point where in order to take the next step we've go to do it with some folk we don't care too much about. And we got to vomit over that for a little while. We must just keep going. The media says that the Civil Rights movement was a dream. The media says that nothing happened in the 70s, and most of us get up on stage and we talk as if that in fact is the case, and it's a lie. The only way it will be true is if you believe them and do not take the next step. Everybody who is in this space at this time belongs here. And it's a good thing if you came. I don't care what you went through or what somebody did to you. Go for yourself. *You* give this weekend everything you can. Because no matter how much of a coalition space this is, it ain't nothing like the coalescing you've got to do tomorrow, and Tuesday and Wednesday, when you really get out there, back into the world: that is ours too.

12 Feminist Encounters: Locating the Politics of Experience

Chandra Talpade Mohanty

Feminist and anti-racist struggles in the 1990s face some of the same urgent questions encountered in the 1970s. After two decades of engagement in feminist political activism and scholarship in a variety of sociopolitical and geographical locations, questions of difference (sex, race, class, nation), experience and history remain at the centre of feminist analysis. Only, at least in the US academy, feminists no longer have to contend as they did in the 1970s with phallocentric denials of the legitimacy of gender as a category of analysis. Instead, the crucial questions in the 1990s concern the construction, examination and, most significantly, the institutionalization of difference *within* feminist discourses. It is this institutionalization of difference that concerns me here. Specifically, I ask the following question: how does the politics of location in the contemporary USA determine and produce experience and difference as analytical and political categories in feminist 'cross-cultural' work? By the term 'politics of location' I refer to the historical, geographical, cultural, psychic, and imaginative boundaries which provide the ground for political definition and self-definition for contemporary US feminists.[1]

Since the 1970s there have been key paradigm shifts in Western feminist theory. These shifts can be traced to political, historical, methodological, and philosophical developments in our understanding of questions of power, struggle, and social transformation. Feminists have drawn on decolonization movements around the world, on movements for racial equality, on peasant struggles, and gay and lesbian movements, as well as on the methodologies of Marxism, psychoanalysis, deconstruction, and poststructuralism to situate our thinking in the 1990s. While these developments have often led to progressive, indeed radical analyses of sexual difference,

Reprinted from *Destabilizing Theory: Contemporary Feminist Debates*, edited by Michèle Barrett and Anne Phillips, with the permission of the publishers, Stanford Univesity Press. Collection and Introduction © 1992 Michèle Barrett and Anne Phillips. The individual chapters © the several contributors.

the focus on questions of subjectivity and identity which is a hall-mark of contemporary feminist theory has also had some problem-atic effects in the area of race and Third World/post-colonial studies. One problematic effect of the postmodern critique of essen-tialist notions of identity has been the dissolution of the category of race—however, this is often accomplished at the expense of a recog-nition of racism. Another effect has been the generation of dis-courses of diversity and pluralism which are grounded in an apolitical, often individualized identity politics.[2] Here, questions of *historical interconnection* are transformed into questions of discrete and separate histories (or even herstories) and into questions of identity politics.[3] While I cannot deal with such effects in detail here, I work through them in a limited way by suggesting the impor-tance of analysing and theorizing difference in the context of femi-nist cross-cultural work. Through this theorization of experience, I suggest that historicizing and locating political agency is a necessary alternative to formulations of the 'universality' of gendered oppres-sion and struggles. This universality of gender oppression is prob-lematic, based as it is on the assumption that the categories of race and class have to be invisible for gender to be visible. In the 1990s the challenges posed by black and Third World feminists can point the way towards a more precise, transformative feminist politics. Thus, the juncture of feminist and anti-racist/Third World/post-colonial studies is of great significance, materially as well as methodologically.[4]

Feminist analyses which attempt to cross national, racial, and ethnic boundaries produce and reproduce difference in particular ways. This codification of difference occurs through the naturaliza-tion of analytic categories which are supposed to have cross-cultural validity. I attempt an analysis of two recent feminist texts which address the turn of the century directly. Both texts also foreground analytic categories which address questions of cross-cultural, cross-national differences among women. Robin Morgan's 'Planetary Feminism: The Politics of the 21st Century' and Bernice Johnson Reagon's 'Coalition Politics: Turning the Century' are both *move-ment* texts and are written for diverse mass audiences. Morgan's essay forms the introduction to her 1984 book, *Sisterhood is Global: The International Women's Movement Anthology*, while Reagon's piece was first given as a talk at the West Coast Women's Music Festival in 1981, and has since been published in Barbara Smith's 1983 anthology, *Home Girls: A Black Feminist Anthology*.[5] Both essays construct contesting notions of experience, difference, and struggle within and across cultural boundaries. I stage an encounter between these texts because they represent for me, despite their differences from each other, an alternative presence—a thought, an idea, a record of activism and struggle—which can help me both locate and position myself in relation to 'history'. Through this presence, and with these texts, I can hope to approach the end of the century and not be overwhelmed.

The status of 'female' or 'woman/women's' experience has always been a central concern in feminist discourse. After all, it is on the basis of shared experience that feminists of different political persuasions have argued for unity or identity among women. Teresa de Lauretis, in fact, gives this question a sort of foundational status: 'The relation of experience to discourse, finally, is what is at issue in the definition of feminism.'[6] Feminist discourses, critical and liberatory in intent, are not thereby exempt from inscription in their internal power relations. Thus, the recent definition, classification, and assimilation of categories, of experientially based notions of 'woman' (or analogously, in some analyses, 'lesbian') to forge political unity require our attention and careful analysis. Gender is *produced* as well as uncovered in feminist discourse, and definitions of experience, with attendant notions of unity and difference, form the very basis of this production. For instance, gender inscribed within a purely male/female framework reinforces what Monique Wittig has called the heterosexual contract.[7] Here difference is constructed along male/female lines, and it is being female (as opposed to male) which is at the centre of the analysis. Identity is seen as either male or female. A similar definition of experience can also be used to craft lesbian identity. Katie King's analysis indicates this:

The construction of political identity in terms of lesbianism as a magical sign forms the pattern into which the feminist taxonomic identities of recent years attempt to assimilate themselves . . . Identifying with lesbianism falsely implies that one knows all abut heterosexism and homophobia magically through identity or association. The 'experience' of lesbianism is offered as salvation from the individual practice of heterosexism and homophobia and the source of intuitive institutional and structural understanding of them. The power of lesbianism as a privileged signifier makes analysis of heterosexism and homophobia difficult since it obscures the need for counter-intuitive challenges to ideology.[8]

King's analysis calls into question the authority and presence of 'experience' in constructing lesbian identity. She criticizes feminist analyses in which difference is inscribed simply within a lesbian/

heterosexual framework, with 'experience' functioning as an unexamined, catch-all category. This is similar to the female/male framework Wittig calls attention to, for although the terms of the equation are different, the status and definition of 'experience' are the same. The politics of being 'woman' or 'lesbian' are deduced from the *experience* of being woman or lesbian. Being female is thus seen as *naturally* related to being feminist, where the experience of being female transforms us into feminists through osmosis. Feminism is not defined as a highly contested political terrain; it is the mere effect of being female.[9] This is what one might call the feminist osmosis thesis: females are feminists by association and identification with the experiences which constitute us as female.

The problem is, however, we cannot avoid the challenge of *theorizing* experience. For most of us would not want to ignore the range and scope of the feminist political arena, one characterized quite succinctly by de Lauretis: 'feminism defines itself as a political instance, not merely a sexual politics but a politics of everyday life, which later . . . enters the public sphere of expression and creative practice, displacing aesthetic hierarchies and generic categories, and . . . thus establishes the semiotic ground for a different production of reference and meaning'.[10] It is this recognition that leads me to an analysis of the status of experience and difference, and the relation of this to political praxis in Robin Morgan's and Bernice Reagon's texts.

'A PLACE ON THE MAP IS ALSO A PLACE IN HISTORY'[11]

The last decade has witnessed the publication of numerous feminist writings on what is generally referred to as an international women's movement, and we have its concrete embodiment in *Sisterhood is Global*, a text which in fact describes itself as '*The* International Women's Movement Anthology'. There is considerable difference between international feminist networks organized around specific issues like sex-tourism and multinational exploitation of women's work, and the notion of *an* international women's movement which, as I attempt to demonstrate, implicitly *assumes* global or universal sisterhood. But it is best to begin by recognizing the significance and value of the publication of an anthology such as this. The value of documenting the indigenous histories of women's struggles is unquestionable. Morgan states that the book took twelve years in conception and development, five years in actual work, and innumerable hours in networking and fundraising. It is obvious that without Morgan's vision and perseverance this anthology would not have been published. The range of writing represented is truly impressive. At a time when most of the globe seems to be taken over by religious fundamentalism and big business, and the colonization of space takes precedence over survival concerns, an anthology that documents women's organized resistances has significant value in helping us envision a better future. In fact, it is because I recognize the value and importance of this anthology that I am concerned about the political implications of Morgan's framework for cross-cultural comparison. Thus my comments and criticisms are intended to encourage a greater internal self-consciousness within feminist politics and writing, not to lay blame or induce guilt.

Universal sisterhood is produced in Morgan's text through specific assumptions about women as a cross-culturally singular, homogeneous group with the same interests, perspectives, and goals and similar experiences. Morgan's definitions of 'women's experience' and history lead to a particular self-presentation of Western women, a specific codification of differences among women, and eventually to what I consider to be problematic suggestions for political strategy.[12] Since feminist discourse is productive of analytic categories and strategic decisions which have material effects, the construction of the category of universal sisterhood in a text which is widely read deserves attention. In addition, *Sisterhood is Global* is still the only text which proclaims itself as the anthology of *the* international women's movement. It has had world-wide distribution, and Robin Morgan herself has earned the respect of feminists everywhere. And since authority is always charged with responsibility, the discursive production and dissemination of notions of universal sisterhood is a significant political event which perhaps solicits its own analysis.

Morgan's explicit intent is 'to further the dialogue between and solidarity of women everywhere' (8). This is a valid and admirable project to the extent that one is willing to assume, if not the reality, then at least the possibility, of universal sisterhood on the basis of shared goodwill. But the moment we attempt to articulate the operation of contemporary imperialism with the notion of an international women's movement based on global sisterhood, the awkward political implications of Morgan's task become clear. Her particular notion of universal sisterhood seems predicated on the erasure of the history and effects of contemporary imperialism.

Robin Morgan seems to situate *all* women (including herself) outside contemporary world history, leading to what I see as her ultimate suggestion that transcendence rather than engagement is the model for future social change. And this, I think, is a model which can have dangerous implications for women who do not and cannot speak from a location of white, Western, middle-class privilege. A place on the map (New York City) is, after all, also a locatable place in history.

What is the relation between experience and politics in Robin Morgan's text? In 'Planetary Feminism' the category of 'women's experience' is constructed within two parameters: woman as victim, and woman as truth-teller. Morgan suggests that it is not mystical or biological commonalities which characterize women across cultures and histories, but rather a common condition and world-view:

The quality of feminist political philosophy (in all its myriad forms) makes possible a totally new way of viewing international affairs, one less concerned with diplomatic postures and abstractions, but focused instead on concrete, *unifying* realities of priority importance to the survival and betterment of living beings. For example, the historical, cross-cultural opposition women express to war and our healthy skepticism of certain technological advances (by which most men seem overly impressed at first and disillusioned at last) are only two instances of shared attitudes among women which seem basic to a common world view. Nor is there anything mystical or biologically deterministic about this commonality. It is the result of a *common condition* which, despite variations in degree, is experienced by all human beings who are born female. (4)

This may be convincing up to a point, but the political analysis that underlies this characterization of the commonality among women is shaky at best. At various points in the essay, this 'common condition' that women share is referred to as the suffering inflicted by a universal 'patriarchal mentality' (1), women's opposition to male power and androcentrism, and the experience of rape, battery, labour, and childbirth. For Morgan, the magnitude of suffering experienced by most of the women in the world leads to their potential power as a world political force, a force constituted in opposition to Big Brother in the US, Western and Eastern Europe, Moscow, China, Africa, the Middle East, and Latin America. The assertion that women constitute a potential world political force is suggestive; however, Big Brother is *not exactly the same* even in, say, the US and Latin America. Despite the similarity of power interests and location, the two contexts present significant differences in the manifestations of power and hence of the possibility of struggles against it.

I part company with Morgan when she seems to believe that Big Brother is the same the world over because 'he' simply represents male interests, notwithstanding particular imperial histories or the role of monopoly capital in different countries.

In Morgan's analysis, women are unified by their shared perspective (for example, opposition to war), shared goals (betterment of human beings), and shared experience of oppression. Here the homogeneity of women as a group is produced not on the basis of biological essentials (Morgan offers a rich, layered critique of biological materialism), but rather through the psychologization of complex and contradictory historical and cultural realities. This leads in turn to the assumption of women as a unified group on the basis of secondary sociological universals. What binds women together is an ahistorical notion of the sameness of their oppression and, consequently, the sameness of their struggles. Therefore in Morgan's text cross-cultural comparisons are based on the assumption of the singularity and homogeneity of women as a *group*. This homogeneity of women as a group, is, in turn, predicated on a definition of the *experience of oppression*, where difference can only be understood as male/female. Morgan assumes universal sisterhood on the basis of women's shared opposition to androcentrism, an opposition which, according to her, grows directly out of women's shared status as its victims. The analytic elision between the *experience* of oppression and the *opposition* to it illustrates an aspect of what I referred to earlier as the feminist osmosis thesis: being female and being feminist are one and the same, we are *all* oppressed and hence we *all* resist. Politics and ideology as self-conscious struggles and choices necessarily get written out of such an analysis.

Assumptions pertaining to the relation of experience to history are evident in Morgan's discussion of another aspect of women's experience: woman as truth-teller. According to her, women speak of the 'real' unsullied by 'rhetoric' or 'diplomatic abstractions'. They, as opposed to men (also a coherent singular group in this analytic economy), are authentic human beings whose 'freedom of choice' has been taken away from them: 'Our emphasis is on the individual voice of a woman speaking not as an official representative of her country, but rather as a truth-teller, with an emphasis on reality as opposed to rhetoric' (p. xvi). In addition, Morgan asserts that women social scientists are 'freer of androcentric bias' and 'more likely to elicit more trust and . . . more honest responses from female respondents of their studies' (p. xvii). There is an argument to be made for women interviewing women, but I do not think this is it.

The assumptions underlying these statements indicate to me that Morgan thinks women have some kind of privileged access to the 'real', the 'truth', and can elicit 'trust' from other women purely on the basis of their being not-male. There is a problematic conflation here of the biological and the psychological with the discursive and the ideological. 'Women' are collapsed into the 'suppressed feminine' and men into the dominant ideology.

These oppositions are possible only because Morgan implicitly erases from her account the possibility that women might have *acted*, that they were anything but pure victims. For Morgan, history is a male construction; what women need is herstory, separate and outside of his-story. The writing of history (the discursive and the representational) is confused with women as historical actors. The fact that women are representationally absent from his-story does not mean that they are/were not significant social actors in history. However, Morgan's focus on herstory as separate and outside history not only hands over all of world history to the boys, but potentially suggests that women have been universally duped, not allowed to 'tell the truth', and robbed of all *agency*. The implication of this is that women as a group seem to have forfeited any kind of material referentiality.

What, then, does this analysis suggest about the status of experience in this text? In Morgan's account, women have a sort of cross-cultural coherence as distinct from men. The status or position of women is assumed to be self-evident. However, this focus on the position of women whereby women are seen as a coherent group in *all* contexts, regardless of class or ethnicity, structures the world in ultimately Manichaean terms, where women are always seen in opposition to men, patriarchy is always essentially the invariable phenomenon of male domination, and the religious, legal, economic and familial systems are implicitly assumed to be constructed by men. Here, men and women are seen as whole groups with *already constituted* experiences as groups, and questions of history, conflict, and difference are formulated from what can only be this privileged location of knowledge.

I am bothered, then, by the fact that Morgan can see contemporary imperialism only in terms of a 'patriarchal mentality' which is enforced by men as a *group*. Women across class, race and national boundaries are participants to the extent that we are 'caught up in political webs not of our making which we are powerless to unravel' (25). Since women as a unified group are seen as unimplicated in the process of history and contemporary imperialism, the logical strategic response for Morgan appears to be political transcendence: 'To fight back in solidarity, however, as a real political force requires that women transcend the patriarchal barriers of class and race, and furthermore, transcend even the solutions the Big Brothers propose to the problems they themselves created' (18). Morgan's emphasis on women's transcendence is evident in her discussions of (1) women's deep opposition to nationalism as practised in patriarchal society, and (2) women's involvement in peace and disarmament movements across the world, because, in her opinion, they desire peace (as opposed to men who cause war). Thus, the concrete reality of women's involvement in peace movements is substituted by an abstract 'desire' for peace which is supposed to transcend race, class and national conflicts among women. Tangible responsibility and credit for organizing peace movements is replaced by an essentialist and psychological unifying desire. The problem is that in this case women are not seen as political agents; they are merely allowed to be well intentioned. Although Morgan does offer some specific suggestions for political strategy which require resisting 'the system', her fundamental suggestion is that women transcend the left, the right, and the centre, the law of the father, God, and the system. Since women have been analytically constituted outside real politics or history, progress for them can only be seen in terms of transcendence.

The *experience* of struggle is thus defined as both personal and ahistorical. In other words, the political is *limited to* the personal and all conflicts among and within women are flattened. If sisterhood itself is defined on the basis of personal intentions, attitudes, or desires, conflict is also automatically constructed on only the psychological level. Experience is thus written in as simultaneously individual (that is, located in the individual body/psyche of woman) and general (located in women as a preconstituted collective). There seem to be two problems with this definition. First, experience is seen as being immediately accessible, understood, and named. The complex relationships between behaviour and its representation are either ignored or made irrelevant; experience is collapsed into discourse and vice versa. Second, since experience has a fundamentally psychological status, questions of history and collectivity are formulated on the level of attitude and intention. In effect, the sociality of collective struggles is understood in terms of something like individual–group relations, relations which are commonsensically seen as detached from history. If the assumption of the *sameness* of experience is what ties woman (individual) to women (group),

regardless of class, race, nation, and sexualities, the notion of experience is anchored firmly in the notion of the individual self, a determined and specifiable constituent of European modernity.
However, this notion of the individual needs to be self-consciously
historicized if as feminists we wish to go beyond the limited bourgeois ideology of individualism, especially as we attempt to understand what cross-cultural sisterhood might be made to mean.

Towards the end of 'Planetary Feminism' Morgan talks about
feminist diplomacy.

> What if feminist diplomacy turned out to be simply another form of the
> feminist aphorism 'the personal is political'? Danda writes here of her own
> feminist epiphany, Amanda of her moments of despair, La Silenciada of
> personally bearing witness to the death of a revolution's ideals. Tinne con-
> fides her fears, Nawal addresses us in a voice direct from prison, Hilkla tells
> us about her family and childhood; Ama Ata confesses the anguish of the
> woman artist, Stella shares her mourning with us, Mahnaz communicates
> her grief and her hope, Nell her daring balance of irony and lyricism, Paola
> the story of her origins and girlhood. Manjula isn't afraid to speak of pain,
> Corrine traces her own political evolution alongside that of her movement.
> Maria de Lourdes declares the personal and the political inseparable.
> Motlalepula still remembers the burning of a particular maroon dress,
> Ingrid and Renate invite us into their private correspondence, Marielouise
> opens herself in a poem, Elena appeals personally to us for help,
> Gwendoline testifies about her private life as a public figure . . .
> And do we not, after all, recognize one another? (35–6)

It is this passage more than any other that encapsulates Morgan's
individualized and essentially equalizing notion of universal sisterhood, and its corresponding political implications. The lyricism, the
use of first names (the one and only time this is done), and the insistence that we must easily 'recognize one another' indicate what is
left unsaid: we must identify with *all* women. But it is difficult to
imagine such a generalized identification predicated on the commonality of women's interests and goals across very real divisive
class and ethnic lines—especially, for example, in the context of the
mass proletarianization of Third World women by corporate capital
based in the US, Europe, and Japan.

Universal sisterhood, defined as the transcendence of the 'male'
world, thus ends up being a middle-class, psychologized notion
which effectively erases material and ideological power differences
within and among groups of women, especially between First and
Third World women (and, paradoxically, removes us all as actors
from history and politics). It is in this erasure of difference as

inequality and dependence that the privilege of Morgan's political 'location' might be visible. Ultimately in this reductive utopian vision, men *participate* in politics while women can only hope to *transcend* them. Morgan's notion of universal sisterhood *does* construct a unity. However, for me, the real challenge arises in being able to craft a notion of political unity without relying on the logic of appropriation and incorporation and, just as significantly, a denial of *agency*. For me the unity of women is best understood not as *given*, on the basis of a natural/psychological commonality; it is something that has to be worked for, struggled towards—*in history*. What we need to do is articulate ways in which the historical forms of oppression relate to the category 'women', and not to try to deduce one from the other. In other words, it is Morgan's formulation of the relation of synchronous, alternative histories (herstories) to a diachronic, dominant historical narrative (History) that is problematic. One of the tasks of feminist analysis is uncovering alternative, non-identical histories which challenge and disrupt the spatial and temporal location of a hegemonic history. However, sometimes attempts to uncover and locate alternative histories code these very histories as either totally dependent on and determined by a dominant narrative, or as isolated and autonomous narratives, untouched in their essence by the dominant figurations. In these rewritings, what is lost is the recognition that it is the very co-implication of histories with History which helps us situate and understand oppositional agency. In Morgan's text, it is the move to characterize alternative herstories as separate and different from history that results in a denial of feminist agency. And it is this potential repositioning of the relation of oppositional histories/spaces to a dominant historical narrative that I find valuable in Bernice Reagon's discussion of coalition politics.

'IT AIN'T HOME NO MORE': RETHINKING UNITY

While Morgan uses the notion of sisterhood to construct a cross-cultural unity of women and speaks of 'planetary feminism as the politics of the 21st century', Bernice Johnson Reagon in Chapter 11 uses *coalition* as the basis to talk about the cross-cultural commonality of struggles, identifying *survival*, rather than *shared oppression*, as the ground for coalition. She begins with this valuable political reminder: 'You don't go into coalition because you *like* it. The only reason you would consider trying to team up with somebody who could possibly kill you, is because that's the only way you can figure you can stay alive'.

The governing metaphor Reagon uses to speak of coalition, difference, and struggle is that of a 'barred room'. However, whereas Morgan's barred room might be owned and controlled by the Big Brothers in different countries, Reagon's internal critique of the contemporary left focuses on the barred rooms constructed by oppositional political movements such as feminist, civil rights, gay and lesbian, and chicano political organizations. She maintains that these barred rooms may provide a 'nurturing space' for a little while, but they ultimately provide an illusion of community based on isolation and the freezing of difference. Thus, while sameness of experience, oppression, culture, etc. may be adequate to construct this space, the moment we 'get ready to clean house' this very sameness in community is exposed as having been built on a debilitating ossification of difference.

Reagon is concerned with differences *within* political struggles, and the negative effects, in the long run, of a nurturing, 'nationalist' perspective: 'At a certain stage nationalism is crucial to a people if you are going to ever impact as a group in your own interest. Nationalism at another point becomes reactionary because it is totally inadequate for surviving in the world with many peoples' (p. 245). This is similar to Gramsci's analysis of oppositional political strategy in terms of the difference between wars of manœuvre (separation and consolidation) and wars of position (re-entry into the mainstream in order to challenge it on its own terms). Reagon's insistence on breaking out of barred rooms and struggling for coalition is a recognition of the importance—indeed the inevitable necessity—of wars of position. It is based, I think, on a recognition of the need to resist the imperatives of an expansionist US state, and of imperial History. It is also, however, a recognition of the limits of identity politics. For once you open the door and let others in, 'the room don't feel like the room anymore. And it ain't home no more' (p. 245).

The relation of coalition to home is a central metaphor for Reagon. She speaks of coalition as opposed, by definition, to home.[13] In fact, the confusion of home with coalition is what concerns her as an urgent problem, and it is here that the status of experience in her text becomes clear. She criticizes the idea of enforcing 'women-only' or 'woman-identified' space by using an 'in-house' definition of woman. What concerns her is not a sameness which allows us to identify with each other as women, but the exclusions particular normative definitions of 'woman' enforce. It is the exercise of violence in creating a legitimate *inside* and an illegitimate *outside* in the name of identity that is significant to her—or, in other words, the exercise of violence when unity or coalition is confused with home and used to enforce a premature sisterhood or solidarity. According to her this 'comes from taking a word like "women" and using it as a code' (p. 246). The experience of being woman can create an illusory unity, for it is not the experience of being woman, but the meanings attached to gender, race, class, and age at various historical moments that is of strategic significance.

Thus, by calling into question the term 'woman' as the automatic basis of unity, Bernice Reagon would want to splinter the notion of experience suggested by Robin Morgan. Her critique of nationalist and culturalist positions, which after an initial necessary period of consolidation work in harmful and exclusionary ways, provides us with a fundamentally political analytic space for an understanding of experience. By always insisting on an analysis of the operations and effects of power in our attempts to create alternative communities, Reagon foregrounds our *strategic* locations and positionings. Instead of separating experience and politics and basing the latter on the former, she emphasizes the politics that always define and inform experience (in particular, in left, anti-racist, and feminist communities). By examining the differences and potential divisions *within* political subjects as well as collectives, Reagon offers an implicit critique of totalizing theories of history and social change. She underscores the significance of the traditions of political struggle, what she calls an 'old-age perspective'—and this is, I would add, a global perspective. What is significant, however, is that the global is forged on the basis of memories and counter-narratives, not on an ahistorical universalism. For Reagon, global, old-age perspectives are founded on humility, the gradual chipping away of our assumed, often ethnocentric centres of self/other definitions.

Thus, her particular location and political priorities lead her to emphasize a politics of engagement (a war of position), and to interrogate totalizing notions of difference and the identification of exclusive spaces as 'homes'. Perhaps it is partly also her insistence on the urgency and difficult nature of political struggle that leads Reagon to talk about difference in terms of racism, while Morgan often formulates difference in terms of cultural pluralism. This is Bernice Reagon's way of 'throwing yourself into the next century':

Most of us think that the space we live in is the most important space there is, and that the condition we find ourselves in is the condition that must be changed or else. That is only partially the case. If you analyse the situation properly, you will know that there might be a few things you can do in your personal, individual interest so that you can experience and enjoy change. But most of the things that you do, if you do them right, are for people who live long after you are forgotten. That will happen if you give it away . . . The only way you can take yourself seriously is if you can throw yourself into the next period beyond your little meager human-body-mouth-talking all the time. (p. 251)

We take ourselves seriously only when we go 'beyond' ourselves, valuing not just the plurality of the differences among us but also the massive presence of the Differences that our recent planetary history has installed. This 'Difference' is what we see only through the lenses of our present moment, our present struggles.

I have looked at two recent feminist texts and argued that feminist discourse must be self-conscious in its production of notions of experience and difference. The rationale for staging an encounter between the two texts, written by a white and black activist respec- tively, was not to identify 'good' and 'bad' feminist texts. Instead, I was interested in foregrounding questions of cross-cultural analysis which permeate 'movement' or popular (not just academic) femi- nist texts, and in indicating the significance of a politics of location in the US of the 1980s and the 1990s. Instead of privileging a certain limited version of identity politics, it is the current *intersection* of anti-racist, anti-imperialist, and gay and lesbian struggles which we need to understand to map the ground for feminist political strat- egy and critical analysis.[14] A reading of these texts also opens up for me a temporality of *struggle*, which disrupts and challenges the logic of linearity, development, and progress which are the hallmarks of European modernity.

But why focus on a temporality of struggle? And how do I define *my* place on the map? For me, the notion of a temporality of strug- gle defies and subverts the logic of European modernity and the 'law of identical temporality'. It suggests an insistent, simultaneous, non- synchronous process characterized by multiple locations, rather than a search for origins and endings which, as Adrienne Rich says, 'seems a way of stopping time in its tracks'.[15] The year 2000 is the end of the Christian millennium, and Christianity is certainly an indelible part of post-colonial history. But we cannot afford to forget those alternative, resistant spaces occupied by oppositional histories and memories. By not insisting on *a* history or *a* geography, but focusing on a temporality of struggle, I create the historical ground from which I can define myself in the USA of the 1990s, a place from which I can speak to the future—not the end of an era, but the promise of many.

The USA of the 1990s: a geopolitical power seemingly unbounded in its effects, peopled with 'natives' struggling for land and legal rights, and 'immigrants' with their own histories and memories. Alicia Dujovne Ortiz writes about Buenos Aires as 'the very image of expansiveness'.[16] This is also how I visualize the USA of the 1990s. Ortiz writes of Buenos Aires:

A city without doors. Or rather, a port city, a gateway which never closes. I have always been astonished by those great cities of the world which have such precise boundaries that one can say exactly where they end. Buenos Aires has no end. One wants to ring it with a beltway, as if to point an index finger, trembling with uncertainty, and say: 'You end there. Up to this point you are you. Beyond that, God alone knows!' . . . a city that is impossible to limit with the eye or the mind. So, what does it mean to say that one is a native of Buenos Aires? To belong to Buenos Aires, to be *Porteno*—to come from this Port? What does this mean? What or who can we hang onto? Usually we cling to history or geography. In this case, what are we to do? Here geography is merely an abstract line that marks the separation of the earth and sky.[17]

If the logic of imperialism and the logic of modernity share a notion of time, they also share a notion of space as territory. In the North America of the 1990s geography seems more and more like 'an abstract line that marks the separation of the earth and sky'. Witness the contemporary struggle for control over oil in the name of 'democracy and freedom' in Saudi Arabia. Even the boundaries between space and outer space are not binding any more. In this expansive and expanding continent, how does one locate oneself? And what does location as I have inherited it have to do with self-conscious, strategic location as I choose it now?

A National Public Radio news broadcast announces that all immigrants to the United States now have to undergo mandatory AIDS testing. I am reminded very sharply of my immigrant status in this country, of my plastic identification card which is proof of my legitimate location in the US. But location, for feminists, necessarily implies self- as well as collective definition, since meanings of the self are inextricably bound up with our understanding of collectives as social agents. For me, a comparative reading of Morgan's and Reagon's documents of activism precipitates the recognition that experience of the self, which is often discontinuous and fragmented, must be historicized before it can be generalized into a collective vision. In other words, experience must be historically interpreted and theorized if it is to become the basis of feminist solidarity and struggle, and it is at this moment that an understanding of the politics of location proves crucial.

In this country I am, for instance, subject to a number of legal/political definitions: 'post-colonial', 'immigrant', 'Third World'. These definitions, while in no way comprehensive, do trace an analytic and political space from which I can insist on a temporality of struggle. Movement *between* cultures, languages, and complex configurations of meaning and power have always been the territory of the colonized. It is this *process*, what Caren Kaplan in her discussion of the reading and writing of home/exile has called 'a continual reterritorialization, with the proviso that one moves on',[18] that I am calling a temporality of struggle. It is this process, this reterritorialization through struggle, that allows me a paradoxical continuity of self, mapping and transforming my political location. It suggests a particular notion of political agency, since my location forces and enables specific modes of reading and knowing the dominant. The struggles I choose to engage in are, then, an intensification of these modes of knowing—an engagement on a different level of knowledge. There is, quite simply, no transcendental location possible in the USA of the 1990s.

I have argued for a politics of engagement rather than a politics of transcendence, for the present and the future. I *know*—in my own non-synchronous temporality—that by the year 2000 apartheid will be discussed as a nightmarish chapter in black South Africa's history, the resistance to and victory over the efforts of the US government and multinational mining conglomerates to relocate the Navajo and Hopi reservations from Big Mountain, Arizona, will be written into elementary-school textbooks, and the Palestinian homeland will no longer be referred to as the 'Middle East question'—it will be a reality. But that is my preferred history: what I hope and struggle for, I garner as *my* knowledge, create it as the place from where I seek to know. After all, it is the way in which I understand, define, and engage in feminist, anti-imperialist, and anti-racist collectives and movements that anchors my belief in the future and in the efficacy of struggles for social change.

Notes

1. I am indebted to Adrienne Rich's essay, 'Notes Toward a Politics of Location' (1984), for the notion of the 'politics of location', in her *Blood, Bread, and Poetry: Selected Prose 1979–1985* (New York: W. W. Norton and Company, 1986), 210–31. In a number of essays in this collection Rich writes eloquently and provocatively about the politics of her own location as a white, Jewish, lesbian feminist in North America. See especially 'North American Tunnel Vision' (1983), and 'Blood, Bread and Poetry: The Location of the Poet' (1984).

   While I attempt to modify and extend Rich's notion, I share her sense of urgency as she asks feminists to re-examine the politics of our location in North America:

   > A natural extension of all this seemed to me the need to examine not only racial and ethnic identity, but location in the United States of North America. As a feminist in the United States it seemed necessary to examine how we participate in mainstream North American cultural chauvinism, the sometimes unconscious belief that white North Americans possess a superior right to judge, select, and ransack other cultures, that we are more 'advanced' than other peoples of this hemisphere . . . It was not enough to say 'As a woman I have no country; as a woman my country is the whole world.' Magnificent as that vision may be, we can't explode into breadth without a conscious grasp on the particular and concrete meaning of our location here and now, in the United States of America. ('North American Tunnel Vision', 162.)

2. I address one version of this, the management of race and cultural pluralism in the US academy, in some depth in my essay 'On Race and Voice: Challenges for Liberal Education in the 1990s', *Cultural Critique*, 14 (1989–90), 179–208.

3. Two recent essays develop the point I am trying to suggest here. Jenny Bourne identifies the problems with most forms of contemporary identity politics which equalize notions of oppression, thereby writing out of the picture any analysis of structural exploitation or domination. See her 'Jewish Feminism and Identity Politics', *Race and Class*, 29 (1987), 1–24.

   In a similar vein, S. P. Mohanty uses the opposition between 'History' and 'histories' to criticize an implicit assumption in contemporary cultural theory that pluralism is an adequate substitute for political analyses of dependent relationships and larger historical configurations. For Mohanty, the ultimate target is the cultural and historical *relativism* which he identifies as the unexamined philosophical 'dogma' underlying political celebrations of pure difference. This is how he characterizes the initial issues involved:

   > Plurality [is] thus a political ideal as much as it [is] a methodological slogan. But . . . a nagging question [remains]: How do we negotiate between my history and yours? How would it be possible for us to recover our commonality, not the humanist myth of our shared human attributes which are meant to distinguish us all from animals, but, more significantly, the imbrication of our various pasts and presents, the ineluctable relationships of shared and contested meanings, values, material resources? It is necessary to assert our dense particularities, our lived and imagined differences. But could we afford to leave unexamined the question of how our differences are intertwined and indeed hierarchically organized? Could we, in other words, really afford to have *entirely* different histories, to see ourselves as living—and having lived`—in entirely heterogeneous and discrete spaces?

   See his 'Us and Them: On the Philosophical Bases of Political Criticism', *The Yale Journal Of Criticism*, 2 (1989), 1–31; 13.

4. For instance, some of the questions which arise in feminist analyses and politics which are situated at the juncture of studies of race, colonialism, and Third World political economy pertain to the systemic production, constitution, operation, and reproduction of the institutional manifestations of power. How does power operate in the constitution of gendered and racial subjects? How do we talk about contemporary political praxis, collective consciousness, and collective struggle in the context of an analysis of power? Other questions concern the discursive codification of sexual politics and the corresponding feminist political strategies these codifications engender. Why is sexual politics defined around particular issues? One might examine the cultural and historical processes and conditions under which sexuality is constructed during conditions of war. One might also ask under what historical conditions sexuality is defined as sexual violence, and investigate the emergence of gay and lesbian sexual identities. The discursive organization of these questions is significant because they help to chart and shape collective resistance. Some of these questions are addressed by contributors in a collection of essays I have co-edited with Ann Russo and Lourdes Torres, entitled *Third World Women and the Politics of Feminism* (Bloomington, Ind., and Indianapolis: Indiana University Press, 1991).

5. Robin Morgan, 'Planetary Feminism: The Politics of the 21st Century', in her *Sisterhood is Global: The International Women's Movement Anthology* (New York: Anchor Press/Doubleday, 1984), 1–37; I also refer to the 'Prefatory Note and Methodology' section (pp. xiii–xxiii) of *Sisterhood is Global* in this essay. Bernice Johnson Reagon, 'Coalition Politics: Turning the Century', in Barbara Smith (ed.), *Home Girls: A Black Feminist Anthology* (New York: Kitchen Table, Women of Color Press, 1983), 356–68.

6. Teresa de Lauretis, 'Feminist Studies/Critical Studies: Issues, Terms and Contexts', in de Lauretis (ed.), *Feminist Studies/Critical Studies* (Bloomington, Ind.: Indiana University Press, 1986), 1–19; 5.

7. Monique Wittig develops this idea in 'The Straight Mind', *Feminist Issues*, 1 (1980), 103–10; 103.

8. Katie King, 'The Situation of Lesbianism as Feminism's Magical Sign: Contests for Meaning and the US Women's Movement, 1968–1972', *Communication*, 9 (1986), 65–91; 85.

9. Linda Gordon discusses this relation of female to feminist in her 'What's New in Women's History', in de Lauretis, *Feminist Studies/Critical Studies*, 20–31.

10. de Lauretis, 'Feminist Studies/Critical Studies: Issues, Terms and Contexts', 10.

11. Rich, 'Notes Toward a Politics of Location', 212.

12. Elsewhere I have attempted a detailed analysis of some recent western feminist social-science texts about the Third World. Focusing on works which have appeared in an influential series published by Zed Press of London, I examine this discursive construction of women in the Third World and the resultant Western feminist self-representations. See 'Under Western Eyes: Feminist Scholarship and Colonial Discourses', *Feminist Review*, 30 (1988), 61–88.

13. For an extensive discussion of the appeal and contradictions of notions of home and identity in contemporary feminist politics, see Biddy Martin and Chandra Talpade Mohanty, 'Feminist Politics: What's Home Got to Do With It?', in de Lauretis, *Feminist Studies/Critical Studies*, 191–212.

14. For a rich and informative account of contemporary racial politics in the US, see Michael Omi and Howard Winant, *Racial Formation in the United States*:

From the 1960s to the 1980s (New York and London: Routledge and Kegan Paul, 1986). Surprisingly, this text erases gender and gay politics altogether, leading me to wonder how we can talk about the 'racial state' without addressing questions of gender and sexual politics. A good companion text which in fact emphasizes such questions is G. Anzaldua and C. Moraga (eds.), *This Bridge Called My Back*: *Writings By Radical Women of Color* (New York: Kitchen Table, Women of Color Press, 1983). Another, more contemporary text which continues some of the discussions in *This Bridge*, also edited by Gloria Anzaldua, is entitled *Making Face, Making Soul, Haciendo Caras, Creative and Critical Perspectives by Women of Color* (San Francisco: Aunt Lute, 1990).

15. Rich, 'Notes Toward a Politics of Location', 227.
16. Alicia Dujovne Ortiz, '*Buenos Aires* (an excerpt)', *Discourse*, 8 (1986–7), 73–83; 76.
17. Ibid. 76.
18. Caren Kaplan, 'The Poetics of Displacement in *Buenos Aires*', *Discourse*, 8 (1986–7), 94–102; 98.

13   Subjects of Sex/Gender/Desire

Judith Butler

> One is not born a woman, but rather becomes one.
> —Simone de Beauvoir
>
> Strictly speaking, 'women' cannot be said to exist.
> —Julia Kristeva
>
> Woman does not have a sex.
> —Luce Irigaray
>
> The deployment of sexuality . . . established this notion of sex.
> —Michel Foucault
>
> The category of sex is the political category that founds society as heterosexual.
> —Monique Wittig

'WOMEN' AS THE SUBJECT OF FEMINISM

For the most part, feminist theory has assumed that there is some existing identity, understood through the category of women, who not only initiates feminist interests and goals within discourse, but constitutes the subject for whom political representation is pursued. But *politics* and *representation* are controversial terms. On the one hand, *representation* serves as the operative term within a political process that seeks to extend visibility and legitimacy to women as political subjects; on the other hand, representation is the normative function of a language which is said either to reveal or to distort what is assumed to be true about the category of women. For feminist theory, the development of a language that fully or adequately represents women has seemed necessary to foster the political visibility of women. This has seemed obviously important considering the pervasive cultural condition in which women's lives were either misrepresented or not represented at all.

Extracted from chapter 1 in J. Butler, *Gender Trouble: Feminism and the Subversion of Identity* (Routledge, 1990), 1–16. Reprinted by permission.

Recently, this prevailing conception of the relation between feminist theory and politics has come under challenge from within feminist discourse. The very subject of women is no longer understood in stable or abiding terms. There is a great deal of material that not only questions the viability of 'the subject' as the ultimate candidate for representation or, indeed, liberation, but there is very little agreement after all on what it is that constitutes, or ought to constitute, the category of women. The domains of political and linguistic 'representation' set out in advance the criterion by which subjects themselves are formed, with the result that representation is extended only to what can be acknowledged as a subject. In other words, the qualifications for being a subject must first be met before representation can be extended.

Foucault points out that juridical systems of power *produce* the subjects they subsequently come to represent.[1] Juridical notions of power appear to regulate political life in purely negative terms— that is, through the limitation, prohibition, regulation, control, and even 'protection' of individuals related to that political structure through the contingent and retractable operation of choice. But the subjects regulated by such structures are, by virtue of being subjected to them, formed, defined, and reproduced in accordance with the requirements of those structures. If this analysis is right, then the juridical formation of language and politics that represents women as 'the subject' of feminism is itself a discursive formation and effect of a given version of representational politics. And the feminist subject turns out to be discursively constituted by the very political system that is supposed to facilitate its emancipation. This becomes politically problematic if that system can be shown to produce gendered subjects along a differential axis of domination or to produce subjects who are presumed to be masculine. In such cases, an uncritical appeal to such a system for the emancipation of 'women' will be clearly self-defeating.

The question of 'the subject' is crucial for politics, and for feminist politics in particular, because juridical subjects are invariably produced through certain exclusionary practices that do not 'show' once the juridical structure of politics has been established. In other words, the political construction of the subject proceeds with certain legitimating and exclusionary aims, and these political operations are effectively concealed and naturalized by a political analysis that takes juridical structures as their foundation. Juridical power inevitably 'produces' what it claims merely to represent; hence, politics must be concerned with this dual function of power:

the juridical and the productive. In effect, the law produces and then conceals the notion of 'a subject before the law'[2] in order to invoke that discursive formation as a naturalized foundational premise that subsequently legitimates that law's own regulatory hegemony. It is not enough to inquire into how women might become more fully represented in language and politics. Feminist critique ought also to understand how the category of 'women', the subject of feminism, is produced and restrained by the very structures of power through which emancipation is sought.

Indeed, the question of women as the subject of feminism raises the possibility that there may not be a subject who stands 'before' the law, awaiting representation in or by the law. Perhaps the subject, as well as the invocation of a temporal 'before', is constituted by the law as the fictive foundation of its own claim to legitimacy. The prevailing assumption of the ontological integrity of the subject before the law might be understood as the contemporary trace of the state of nature hypothesis, that foundationalist fable constitutive of the juridical structures of classical liberalism. The performative invocation of a non-historical 'before' becomes the foundational premise that guarantees a presocial ontology of persons who freely consent to be governed and, thereby, constitute the legitimacy of the social contract.

Apart from the foundationalist fictions that support the notion of the subject, however, there is the political problem that feminism encounters in the assumption that the term *women* denotes a common identity. Rather than a stable signifier that commands the assent of those whom it purports to describe and represent, *women*, even in the plural, has become a troublesome term, a site of contest, a cause for anxiety. As Denise Riley's title suggests, *Am I That Name?* is a question produced by the very possibility of the name's multiple significations.[3] If one 'is' a woman, that is surely not all one is; the term fails to be exhaustive, not because a pregendered 'person' transcends the specific paraphernalia of its gender, but because gender is not always constituted coherently or consistently in different historical contexts, and because gender intersects with racial, class, ethnic, sexual, and regional modalities of discursively constituted identities. As a result, it becomes impossible to separate out 'gender' from the political and cultural intersections in which it is invariably produced and maintained.

The political assumption that there must be a universal basis for feminism, one which must be found in an identity assumed to exist cross-culturally, often accompanies the notion that the oppression of women has some singular form discernible in the universal or hegemonic structure of patriarchy or masculine domination. The notion of a universal patriarchy has been widely criticized in recent years for its failure to account for the workings of gender oppression in the concrete cultural contexts in which it exists. Where those various contexts have been consulted within such theories, it has been to find 'examples' or 'illustrations' of a universal principle that is assumed from the start. That form of feminist theorizing has come under criticism for its efforts to colonize and appropriate non-Western cultures to support highly Western notions of oppression, but because they tend as well to construct a 'Third World' or even an 'Orient' in which gender oppression is subtly explained as symptomatic of an essential, non-Western barbarism. The urgency of feminism to establish a universal status for patriarchy in order to strengthen the appearance of feminism's own claims to be representative has occasionally motivated the shortcut to a categorial or fictive universality of the structure of domination, held to produce women's common subjugated experience.

Although the claim of universal patriarchy no longer enjoys the kind of credibility it once did, the notion of a generally shared conception of 'women', the corollary to that framework, has been much more difficult to displace. Certainly, there have been plenty of debates: Is there some commonality among 'women' that pre-exists their oppression, or do 'women' have a bond by virtue of their oppression alone? Is there a specificity to women's cultures that is independent of their subordination by hegemonic, masculinist cultures? Are the specificity and integrity of women's cultural or linguistic practices always specified against and, hence, within the terms of some more dominant cultural formation? If there is a region of the 'specifically feminine', one that is both differentiated from the masculine as such and recognizable in its difference by an unmarked and, hence, presumed universality of 'women'? The masculine/feminine binary constitutes not only the exclusive framework in which that specificity can be recognized, but in every other way the 'specificity' of the feminine is once again fully decontextualized and separated off analytically and politically from the constitution of class, race, ethnicity, and other axes of power relations that both constitute 'identity' and make the singular notion of identity a misnomer.[4]

My suggestion is that the presumed universality and unity of the subject of feminism is effectively undermined by the constraints of the representational discourse in which it functions. Indeed, the premature insistence on a stable subject of feminism, understood as a seamless category of women, inevitably generates multiple refusals to accept the category. These domains of exclusion reveal the coercive and regulatory consequences of that construction, even when the construction has been elaborated for emancipatory purposes. Indeed, the fragmentation within feminism and the paradoxical opposition to feminism from 'women' whom feminism claims to represent suggest the necessary limits of identity politics. The suggestion that feminism can seek wider representation for a subject that it itself constructs has the ironic consequence that feminist goals risk failure by refusing to take account of the constitutive powers of their own representational claims. This problem is not ameliorated through an appeal to the category of women for merely 'strategic' purposes, for strategies always have meanings that exceed the purposes for which they are intended. In this case, exclusion itself might qualify as such an unintended yet consequential meaning. By conforming to a requirement of representational politics that feminism articulate a stable subject, feminism thus opens itself to charges of gross misrepresentation.

Obviously, the political task is not to refuse representational politics—as if we could. The juridical structures of language and politics constitute the contemporary field of power; hence, there is no position outside this field, but only a critical genealogy of its own legitimating practices. As such, the critical point of departure is *the historical present*, as Marx put it. And the task is to formulate within this constituted frame a critique of the categories of identity that contemporary juridical structures engender, naturalize, and immobilize.

Perhaps there is an opportunity at this juncture of cultural politics, a period that some would call 'postfeminist', to reflect from within a feminist perspective on the injunction to construct a subject of feminism. Within feminist political practice, a radical rethinking of the ontological constructions of identity appears to be necessary in order to formulate a representational politics that might revive feminism on other grounds. On the other hand, it may be time to entertain a radical critique that seeks to free feminist theory from the necessity of having to construct a single or abiding ground which is invariably contested by those identity positions or anti-identity positions that it invariably excludes. Do the exclusionary practices that ground feminist theory in a notion of 'women' as subject paradoxically undercut feminist goals to extend its claims to 'representation'?[5]

Perhaps the problem is even more serious. Is the construction of the category of women as a coherent and stable subject an unwitting regulation and reification of gender relations? And is not such a reification precisely contrary to feminist aims?

To what extent does the category of women achieve stability and coherence only in the context of the heterosexual matrix?[6] If a stable notion of gender no longer proves to be the foundational premise of feminist politics, perhaps a new sort of feminist politics is now desirable to contest the very reifications of gender and identity, one that will take the variable construction of identity as both a methodological and normative prerequisite, if not a political goal.

To trace the political operations that produce and conceal what qualifies as the juridical subject of feminism is precisely the task of *a feminist genealogy* of the category of women. In the course of this effort to question 'women' as the subject of feminism, the unproblematic invocation of that category may prove to *preclude* the possibility of feminism as a representational politics. What sense does it make to extend representation to subjects who are constructed through the exclusion of those who fail to conform to unspoken normative requirements of the subject? What relations of domination and exclusion are inadvertently sustained when representation becomes the sole focus of politics? The identity of the feminist subject ought not to be the foundation of feminist politics, if the formation of the subject takes place within a field of power regularly buried through the assertion of that foundation. Perhaps, paradoxically, 'representation' will be shown to make sense for feminism only when the subject of 'women' is nowhere presumed.

THE COMPULSORY ORDER OF SEX/GENDER/DESIRE

Although the unproblematic unity of 'women' is often invoked to construct a solidarity of identity, a split is introduced in the feminist subject by the distinction between sex and gender. Originally intended to dispute the biology-is-destiny formulation, the distinction between sex and gender serves the argument that whatever biological intractability sex appears to have, gender is culturally constructed: hence, gender is neither the causal result of sex nor as seemingly fixed as sex. The unity of the subject is thus already potentially contested by the distinction that permits of gender as a multiple interpretation of sex.[7]

If gender is the cultural meanings that the sexed body assumes, then a gender cannot be said to follow from a sex in any one way. Taken to its logical limit, the sex/gender distinction suggests a radical discontinuity between sexed bodies and culturally constructed genders. Assuming for the moment the stability of binary sex, it does not follow that the construction of 'men' will accrue exclusively to the bodies of males or that 'women' will interpret only female bodies. Further, even if the sexes appear to be unproblematically binary in their morphology and constitution (which will become a question), there is no reason to assume that genders ought also to remain as two.[8] The presumption of a binary gender system implicitly retains the belief in a mimetic relation of gender to sex whereby gender mirrors sex or is otherwise restricted by it. When the constructed status of gender is theorized as radically independent of sex, gender itself becomes a free-floating artifice, with the consequence that *man* and *masculine* might just as easily signify a female body as a male one, and *woman* and *feminine* a male body as easily as a female one.

This radical splitting of the gendered subject poses yet another set of problems. Can we refer to a 'given' sex or a 'given' gender without first inquiring into how sex and/or gender is given, through what means? And what is 'sex' anyway? Is it natural, anatomical, chromosomal, or hormonal, and how is a feminist critic to assess the scientific discourses which purport to establish such 'facts' for us?[9] Does sex have a history?[10] Does each sex have a different history, or histories? Is there a history of how the duality of sex was established, a genealogy that might expose the binary options as a variable construction? Are the ostensibly natural facts of sex discursively produced by various scientific discourses in the service of other political and social interests? If the immutable character of sex is contested, perhaps this construct called 'sex' is as culturally constructed as gender; indeed, perhaps it was always already gender, with the consequence that the distinction between sex and gender turns out to be no distinction at all.[11]

It would make no sense, then, to define gender as the cultural interpretation of sex, if sex itself is a gendered category. Gender ought not to be conceived merely as the cultural inscription of meaning on a pre-given sex (a juridical conception); gender must also designate the very apparatus of production whereby the sexes themselves are established. As a result, gender is not to culture as sex is to nature; gender is also the discursive/cultural means by which 'sexed nature' or 'a natural sex' is produced and established as 'prediscursive', prior to culture, a politically neutral surface *on which* culture acts. It is already clear that one way the internal stability and binary frame for sex is effectively secured is by casting the duality of sex in a prediscursive domain. This production of sex *as* the prediscursive ought to be understood, however, as the effect of the apparatus of cultural construction designed by *gender*. How, then, does gender need to be reformulated to encompass the power relations that produce the effect of a prediscursive sex and so conceal that very operation of discursive production?

GENDER: THE CIRCULAR RUINS OF CONTEMPORARY DEBATE

Is there 'a' gender which persons are said *to have*, or is it an essential attribute that a person is said *to be*, as implied in the question 'What gender are you?'? When feminist theorists claim that gender is the cultural interpretation of sex or that gender is culturally constructed, what is the manner or mechanism of this construction? If gender is constructed, could it be constructed differently, or does its constructedness imply some form of social determinism, foreclosing the possibility of agency and transformation? Does 'construction' suggest that certain laws generate gender differences along universal axes of sexual difference? How and where does the construction of gender take place? What sense can we make of a construction that cannot assume a human constructor prior to that construction? On some accounts, the notion that gender is constructed suggests a certain determinism of gender meanings inscribed on anatomically differentiated bodies, where those bodies are understood as passive recipients of an inexorable cultural law. When the relevant 'culture' that 'constructs' gender is understood in terms of such a law or set of laws, then it seems that gender is as determined and fixed as it was under the biology-is-destiny formulation. In such a case, not biology, but culture, becomes destiny.

On the other hand, Simone de Beauvoir suggests in *The Second Sex* that 'one is not born a woman, but, rather, becomes one'.[12] For de Beauvoir, gender is 'constructed', but implied in her formulation is an agent, a *cogito*, who somehow takes on or appropriates that gender and could, in principle, take on some other gender. Is gender as variable and volitional as de Beauvoir's account seems to suggest? Can 'construction' in such a case be reduced to a form of choice? De

Beauvoir is clear that one 'becomes' a woman, but always under a cultural compulsion to become one. And clearly, the compulsion does not come from 'sex'. There is nothing in her account that guarantees that the 'one' who becomes a woman is necessarily female. If 'the body is a situation',[13] as she claims, there is no recourse to a body that has not always already been interpreted by cultural meanings; hence, sex could not qualify as a prediscursive anatomical facticity. Indeed, sex, by definition, will be shown to have been gender all along.[14]

The controversy over the meaning of *construction* appears to founder on the conventional philosophical polarity between free will and determinism. As a consequence, one might reasonably suspect that some common linguistic restriction on thought both forms and limits the terms of the debate. Within those terms, 'the body' appears as a passive medium on which cultural meanings are inscribed or as the instrument through which an appropriative and interpretive will determines a cultural meaning for itself. In either case, the body figures as a mere *instrument* or *medium* for which a set of cultural meanings are only externally related. But 'the body' is itself a construction, as are the myriad 'bodies' that constitute the domain of gendered subjects. Bodies cannot be said to have a signifiable existence prior to the mark of their gender; the question then emerges: To what extent does the body *come into being* in and through the mark(s) of gender? How do we reconceive the body no longer as a passive medium or instrument awaiting the enlivening capacity of a distinctly immaterial will?[15]

Whether gender or sex is fixed or free is a function of a discourse which, it will be suggested, seeks to set certain limits to analysis or to safeguard certain nets of humanism as presuppositional to any analysis of gender. The locus of intractability, whether in 'sex' or 'gender' or in the very meaning of 'construction', provides a clue to what cultural possibilities can and cannot become mobilized through any further analysis. The limits of the discursive analysis of gender presuppose and preempt the possibilities of imaginable and realizable gender configurations within culture. This is not to say that any and all gendered possibilities are open, but that the boundaries of analysis suggest the limits of a discursively conditioned experience. These limits are always set within the terms of a hegemonic cultural discourse predicated on binary structures that appear as the language of universal rationality. Constraint is thus built into what that language constitutes as the imaginable domain of gender.

JUDITH BUTLER

Although social scientists refer to gender as a 'factor' or a 'dimension' of an analysis, it is also applied to embodied persons as 'a mark' of biological, linguistic, and/or cultural difference. In these latter cases, gender can be understood as a signification that an (already) sexually differentiated body assumes, but even then that signification exists only *in relation* to another, opposing signification. Some feminist theorists claim that gender is 'a relation', indeed, a set of relations, and not an individual attribute. Others, following de Beauvoir, would argue that only the feminine gender is marked, that the universal person and the masculine gender are conflated, thereby defining women in terms of their sex and extolling men as the bearers of a body-transcendent universal personhood.

In a move that complicates the discussion further, Luce Irigaray argues that women constitute a paradox, if not a contradiction, within the discourse of identity itself. Women are the 'sex' which is not 'one'. Within a language pervasively masculinist, a phallogocentric language, women constitute the *unrepresentable*. In other words, women represent the sex that cannot be thought, a linguistic absence and opacity. Within a language that rests on univocal signification, the female sex constitutes the unconstrainable and undesignatable. In this sense, women are the sex which is not 'one', but multiple.[16] In opposition to de Beauvoir, for whom women are designated as the Other, Irigaray argues that both the subject and the Other are masculine mainstays of a closed phallogocentric signifying economy that achieves its totalizing goal through the exclusion of the feminine altogether. For de Beauvoir, women are the negative of men, the lack against which masculine identity differentiates itself; for Irigaray, that particular dialectic constitutes a system that excludes an entirely different economy of signification. Women are not only represented falsely within the Sartrian frame of signifying-subject and signified-Other, but the falsity of the signification points out the entire structure of representation as inadequate. The sex which is not one, then, provides a point of departure for a criticism of hegemonic Western representation and of the metaphysics of substance that structures the very notion of the subject.

What is the metaphysics of substance, and how does it inform thinking about the categories of sex? In the first instance, humanist conceptions of the subject tend to assume a substantive person who is the bearer of various essential and nonessential attributes. A humanist feminist position might understand gender as an *attribute* of a person who is characterized essentially as a pregendered substance or 'core', called the person, denoting a universal capacity for

282

reason, moral deliberation, or language. The universal conception of the person, however, is displaced as a point of departure for a social theory of gender by those historical and anthropological positions that understand gender as a *relation* among socially constituted subjects in specifiable contexts. This relational or contextual point of view suggests that what the person 'is', and, indeed, what gender 'is', is always relative to the constructed relations in which it is determined.[17] As a shifting and contextual phenomenon, gender does not denote a substantive being, but a relative point of convergence among culturally and historically specific sets of relations.

Irigaray would maintain, however, that the feminine 'sex' is a point of linguistic *absence*, the impossibility of a grammatically denoted substance, and, hence, the point of view that exposes that substance as an abiding and foundational illusion of a masculinist discourse. This absence is not marked as such within the masculine signifying economy—a contention that reverses de Beauvoir's argument (and Wittig's) that the female sex *is* marked, while the male sex is not. For Irigaray, the female sex is not a 'lack' or an 'Other' that immanently and negatively defines the subject in its masculinity. On the contrary, the female sex eludes the very requirements of representation, for she is neither 'Other' nor the 'lack', those categories remaining relative to the Sartrian subject, immanent to that phallogocentric scheme. Hence, for Irigaray, the feminine could never be the *mark of a subject*, as de Beauvoir would suggest. Further, the feminine could not be theorized in terms of a determinate *relation* between the masculine and the feminine within any given discourse, for discourse is not a relevant notion here. Even in their variety, discourses constitute so many modalities of phallogocentric language. The female sex is thus also *the subject* that is not one. The relation between masculine and feminine cannot be represented in a signifying economy in which the masculine constitutes the closed circle of signifier and signified. Paradoxically enough, de Beauvoir prefigured this impossibility in *The Second Sex* when she argued that men could not settle the question of women because they would then be acting as both judge and party to the case.[18]

The distinctions among the above positions are far from discrete; each of them can be understood to problematize the locality and meaning of both the 'subject' and 'gender' within the context of socially instituted gender asymmetry. The interpretive possibilities of gender are in no sense exhausted by the alternatives suggested above. The problematic circularity of a feminist inquiry into gender is underscored by the presence of positions which, on the one hand,

presume that gender is a secondary characteristic of persons and
those which, on the other hand, argue that the very notion of the
person, positioned within language as a 'subject', is a masculinist
construction and prerogative which effectively excludes the structural and semantic possibility of a feminine gender. The consequence of such sharp disagreements about the meaning of gender
(indeed, whether *gender* is the term to be argued about at all, or
whether the discursive construction of *sex* is, indeed, more fundamental, or perhaps *women* or *woman* and/or *men* and *man*) establishes the need for a radical rethinking of the categories of identity
within the context of relations of radical gender asymmetry.

For de Beauvoir, the 'subject' within the existential analytic of
misogyny is always already masculine, conflated with the universal,
differentiating itself from a feminine 'Other' outside the universalizing norms of personhood, hopelessly 'particular', embodied, con-
demned to immanence. Although de Beauvoir is often understood
to be calling for the right of women, in effect, to become existential
subjects, and hence for inclusion within the terms of an abstract
universality, her position also implies a fundamental critique of the
very disembodiment of the abstract masculine epistemological subject.[19] That subject is abstract to the extent that it disavows its
socially marked embodiment and, further, projects that disavowed
and disparaged embodiment on to the feminine sphere, effectively
renaming the body as female. This association of the body with the
female works along magical relations of reciprocity whereby the
female sex becomes restricted to its body, and the male body, fully
disavowed, becomes, paradoxically, the incorporeal instrument of
an ostensibly radical freedom. De Beauvoir's analysis implicitly
poses the question: Through what act of negation and disavowal
does the masculine pose as a disembodied universality and the feminine get constructed as a disavowed corporeality? The dialectic of
master–slave, here fully reformulated within the nonreciprocal
terms of gender asymmetry, prefigures what Irigaray will later
describe as the masculine signifying economy that includes both the
existential subject and its Other.

De Beauvoir proposes that the female body ought to be the situation and instrumentality of women's freedom, not a defining and
limiting essence.[20] The theory of embodiment informing de
Beauvoir's analysis is clearly limited by the uncritical reproduction
of the Cartesian distinction between freedom and the body. Despite
my own previous efforts to argue the contrary, it appears that de
Beauvoir maintains the mind/body dualism, even as she proposes a

synthesis of those terms.[21] The preservation of that very distinction can be read as symptomatic of the very phallogocentrism that de Beauvoir underestimates. In the philosophical tradition that begins with Plato and continues through Descartes, Husserl, and Sartre, the ontological distinction between soul (consciousness, mind) and body invariably supports relations of political and psychic subordination and hierarchy. The mind not only subjugates the body, but occasionally entertains the fantasy of fleeing its embodiment altogether. The cultural associations of mind with masculinity and body with femininity are well documented within the field of philosophy and feminism.[22] As a result, any uncritical reproduction of the mind/body distinction ought to be rethought for the implicit gender hierarchy that the distinction has conventionally produced, maintained, and rationalized.

The discursive construction of 'the body' and its separation from 'freedom' in de Beauvoir fails to mark along the axis of gender the very mind–body distinction that is supposed to illuminate the persistence of gender asymmetry. Officially, de Beauvoir contends that the female body is marked within masculinist discourse, whereby the masculine body, in its conflation with the universal, remains unmarked. Irigaray clearly suggests that both marker and marked are maintained within a masculinist mode of signification in which the female body is 'marked off', as it were, from the domain of the signifiable. In post-Hegelian terms, she is 'cancelled', but not preserved. On Irigaray's reading, de Beauvoir's claim that woman 'is sex' is reversed to mean that she is not the sex she is designated to be, but, rather, the masculine sex *encore* (and *en corps*) parading in the mode of otherness. For Irigaray, that phallogocentric mode of signifying the female sex perpetually reproduces phantasms of its own self-amplifying desire. Instead of a self-limiting linguistic gesture that grants alterity or difference to women, phallogocentrism offers a name to eclipse the feminine and take its place.

THEORIZING THE BINARY, THE UNITARY, AND BEYOND

De Beauvoir and Irigaray clearly differ over the fundamental structures by which gender asymmetry is reproduced; de Beauvoir turns to the failed reciprocity of an asymmetrical dialectic, while Irigaray suggests that the dialectic itself is the monologic elaboration of a masculinist signifying economy. Although Irigaray clearly broadens the scope of feminist critique by exposing the epistemological, onto-logical, and logical structures of a masculinist signifying economy, the power of her analysis is undercut precisely by its globalizing reach. Is it possible to identify a monolithic as well as a monologic masculinist economy that traverses the array of cultural and histor-ical contexts in which sexual difference takes place? Is the failure to acknowledge the specific cultural operations of gender oppression itself a kind of epistemological imperialism, one which is not ame-liorated by the simple elaboration of cultural differences as 'exam-ples' of the selfsame phallogocentrism? The effort to *include* 'Other' cultures as variegated amplifications of a global phallogocentrism constitutes an appropriative act that risks a repetition of the self-aggrandizing gesture of phallogocentrism, colonizing under the sign of the same those differences that might otherwise call that totalizing concept into question.[23]

Feminist critique ought to explore the totalizing claims of a mas-culinist signifying economy, but also remain self-critical with respect to the totalizing gestures of feminism. The effort to identify the enemy as singular in form is a reverse-discourse that uncritically mimics the strategy of the oppressor instead of offering a different set of terms. That the tactic can operate in feminist and antifeminist contexts alike suggests that the colonizing gesture is not primarily or irreducibly masculinist. It can operate to effect other relations of racial, class, and heterosexist subordination, to name but a few. And clearly, listing the varieties of oppression, as I began to do, assumes their discrete, sequential coexistence along a horizontal axis that does not describe their convergences within the social field. A verti-cal model is similarly insufficient; oppressions cannot be summar-ily ranked, causally related, distributed among planes of 'originality' and 'derivativeness'.[24] Indeed, the field of power structured in part by the imperializing gesture of dialectical appropriation exceeds and encompasses the axis of sexual difference, offering a mapping of intersecting differentials which cannot be summarily hierarchized either within the terms of phallogocentrism or any other candidate for the position of 'primary condition of oppression'. Rather than an exclusive tactic of masculinist signifying economies, dialectical appropriation and suppression of the Other is one tactic among many, deployed centrally but not exclusively in the service of expanding and rationalizing the masculinist domain.

The contemporary feminist debates over essentialism raise the question of the universality of female identity and masculinist oppression in other ways. Universalistic claims are based on a common or shared epistemological standpoint, understood as the articulated consciousness or shared structures of oppression or in the ostensibly transcultural structures of femininity, maternity, sexuality, and/or *écriture feminine*. The opening discussion in this chapter argued that this globalizing gesture has spawned a number of criticisms from women who claim that the category of 'women' is normative and exclusionary and is invoked with the unmarked dimensions of class and racial privilege intact. In other words, the insistence upon the coherence and unity of the category of women has effectively refused the multiplicity of cultural, social, and political intersections in which the concrete array of 'women' are constructed.

Some efforts have been made to formulate coalitional politics which do not assume in advance what the content of 'women' will be. They propose instead a set of dialogic encounters by which variously positioned women articulate separate identities within the framework of an emergent coalition. Clearly, the value of coalitional politics is not to be under-estimated, but the very form of coalition, of an emerging and unpredictable assemblage of positions, cannot be figured in advance. Despite the clearly democratizing impulse that motivates coalition building, the coalitional theorist can inadvertently reinsert herself as sovereign of the process by trying to assert an ideal form for coalitional structures *in advance*, one that will effectively guarantee unity as the outcome. Related efforts to determine what is and is not the true shape of a dialogue, what constitutes a subject-position, and, most importantly, when 'unity' has been reached, can impede the self-shaping and self-limiting dynamics of coalition.

The insistence in advance on coalitional 'unity' as a goal assumes that solidarity, whatever its price, is a prerequisite for political action. But what sort of politics demands that kind of advance purchase on unity? Perhaps a coalition needs to acknowledge its contradictions and take action with those contradictions intact. Perhaps also part of what dialogic understanding entails is the acceptance of divergence, breakage, splinter, and fragmentation as part of the often tortuous process of democratization. The very notion of 'dialogue' is culturally specific and historically bound, and while one speaker may feel secure that a conversation is happening, another may be sure it is not. The power relations that condition and limit dialogic possibilities need first to be interrogated. Otherwise, the model of dialogue risks relapsing into a liberal model that assumes that speaking agents occupy equal positions of power and speak with the same presuppositions about what constitutes 'agreement' and 'unity' and, indeed, that those are the goals to be sought. It would be wrong to assume in advance that there is a category of 'women' that simply needs to be filled in with various components of race, class, age, ethnicity, and sexuality in order to become complete. The assumption of its essential incompleteness permits that category to serve as a permanently available site of contested meanings. The definitional incompleteness of the category might then serve as a normative ideal relieved of coercive force.

Is 'unity' necessary for effective political action? Is the premature insistence on the goal of unity precisely the cause of an ever more bitter fragmentation among the ranks? Certain forms of acknowledged fragmentation might facilitate coalitional action precisely because the 'unity' of the category of women is neither presupposed nor desired. Does 'unity' set up an exclusionary norm of solidarity at the level of identity that rules out the possibility of a set of actions which disrupt the very borders of identity concepts, or which seek to accomplish precisely that disruption as an explicit political aim? Without the presupposition or goal of 'unity', which is, in either case, always instituted at a conceptual level, provisional unities might emerge in the context of concrete actions that have purposes other than the articulation of identity. Without the compulsory expectation that feminist actions must be instituted from some stable, unified, and agreed-upon identity, those actions might well get a quicker start and seem more congenial to a number of 'women' for whom the meaning of the category is permanently moot.

This anti-foundationalist approach to coalitional politics assumes neither that 'identity' is a premise nor that the shape or meaning of a coalitional assemblage can be known prior to its achievement. Because the articulation of an identity within available cultural terms instates a definition that forecloses in advance the emergence of new identity concepts in and through politically engaged actions, the foundationalist tactic cannot take the transformation or expansion of existing identity concepts as a normative goal. Moreover, when agreed-upon identities or agreed-upon dialogic structures, through which already established identities are communicated, no longer constitute the theme or subject of politics, then identities can come into being and dissolve depending on the concrete practices that constitute them. Certain political practices institute identities on a contingent basis in order to accomplish whatever aims are in view. Coalitional politics requires neither an expanded category of 'women' nor an internally multiplicitous self that offers its complexity at once.

Gender is a complexity whose totality is permanently deferred, never fully what it is at any given juncture in time. An open coalition, then, will affirm identities that are alternately instituted and relinquished according to the purposes at hand; it will be an open assemblage that permits of multiple convergences and divergences without obedience to a normative telos of definitional closure.

Notes

1. See Michel Foucault, 'Right of Death and Power over Life', in *The History of Sexuality, Volume I, An Introduction*, trans. Robert Hurley (New York: Vintage, 1980), originally published as *Histoire de la sexualité 1: La volonté de savoir* (Paris: Gallimard, 1978). In that final chapter, Foucault discusses the relation between the juridical and productive law. His notion of the productivity of the law is clearly derived from Nietzsche, although not identical with Nietzsche's will-to-power. The use of Foucault's notion of productive power is not meant as a simple-minded 'application' of Foucault to gender issues. The consideration of sexual difference within the terms of Foucault's own work reveals central contradictions in his theory.

2. References throughout this work to a subject before the law are extrapolations of Derrida's reading of Kafka's parable 'Before the Law', in *Kafka and the Contemporary Critical Performance: Centenary Readings*, ed. Alan Udoff (Bloomington: Indiana University Press, 1987).

3. See Denise Riley, *Am I That Name?: Feminism and the Category of 'Women' in History* (New York: Macmillan, 1988).

4. See Sandra Harding, 'The Instability of the Analytical Categories of Feminist Theory', in *Sex and Scientific Inquiry*, eds. Sandra Harding and Jean F. O'Barr (Chicago: University of Chicago Press, 1987), 283–302.

5. I am reminded of the ambiguity inherent in Nancy Cott's title, *The Grounding of Modern Feminism* (New Haven: Yale University Press, 1987). She argues that the early-twentieth-century US feminist movement sought to 'ground' itself in a programme that eventually 'grounded' that movement. Her historical thesis implicitly raises the question of whether uncritically accepted foundations operate like the 'return of the repressed'; based on exclusionary practices, the stable political identities that found political movements may invariably become threatened by the very instability that the foundationalist move creates.

6. I use the term *heterosexual matrix* throughout the text to designate that grid of cultural intelligibility through which bodies, genders, and desires are naturalized. I am drawing from Monique Wittig's notion of the 'heterosexual contract' and, to a lesser extent, on Adrienne Rich's notion of 'compulsory heterosexuality' to characterize a hegemonic discursive/epistemic model of gender intelligibility that assumes that for bodies to cohere and make sense there must be a stable sex expressed through a stable gender (masculine expresses male, feminine expresses female) that is oppositionally and hierarchically defined through the compulsory practice of heterosexuality.

7. For a discussion of the sex/gender distinction in structuralist anthropology and feminist appropriations and criticisms of that formulation, see chapter 2,

JUDITH BUTLER

section i, 'Structuralism's Critical Exchange', in my *Gender Trouble: Feminism and the Subversion of Identity* (Routledge, 1990).

8. For an interesting study of the *berdache* and multiple-gender arrangements in Native American cultures, see Walter L. Williams, *The Spirit and the Flesh: Sexual Diversity in American Indian Culture* (Boston: Beacon Press, 1988). See also Sherry B. Ortner and Harriet Whitehead (eds.), *Sexual Meanings: The Cultural Construction of Sexuality* (New York: Cambridge University Press, 1981). For a politically sensitive and provocative analysis of the *berdache*, transsexuals, and the contingency of gender dichotomies, see Suzanne J. Kessler and Wendy McKenna, *Gender: An Ethnomethodological Approach* (Chicago: University of Chicago Press, 1978).

9. A great deal of feminist research has been conducted within the fields of biology and the history of science that assess the political interests inherent in the various discriminatory procedures that establish the scientific basis for sex. See Ruth Hubbard and Marian Lowe (eds.), *Genes and Gender*, 1 and 2 (New York: Gordian Press, 1978, 1979); the two issues on feminism and science of *Hypatia: A Journal of Feminist Philosophy*, 2/3 (Fall 1987), and 3/1 (Spring 1988), and especially The Biology and Gender Study Group, 'The Importance of Feminist Critique for Contemporary Cell Biology', in this last issue (Spring 1988); Sandra Harding, *The Science Question in Feminism* (Ithaca: Cornell University Press, 1986); Evelyn Fox-Keller, *Reflections on Gender and Science* (New Haven: Yale University Press, 1984); Donna Haraway, 'In the Beginning was the Word: The Genesis of Biological Theory', *Signs: Journal of Women in Culture and Society*, 6/3 (1981); Donna Haraway, *Primate Visions* (New York: Routledge, 1989); Sandra Harding and Jean F. O'Barr, *Sex and Scientific Inquiry* (Chicago: University of Chicago Press, 1987); Anne Fausto-Sterling, *Myths of Gender: Biological Theories About Women and Men* (New York: Norton, 1979).

10. Clearly Foucault's *History of Sexuality* offers one way to rethink the history of 'sex' within a given modern Eurocentric context. For a more detailed consideration see Thomas Lacquer and Catherine Gallagher (eds.), *The Making of the Modern Body: Sexuality and Society in the 19th Century* (Berkeley: University of California Press, 1987), originally published as an issue of *Representations*, 14 (Spring 1986).

11. See my 'Variations on Sex and Gender: Beauvoir, Wittig, Foucault', in *Feminism as Critique*, eds. Seyla Benhabib and Drucilla Cornell (Basil Blackwell, dist. by University of Minnesota Press, 1987).

12. Simone de Beauvoir, *The Second Sex*, trans. E. M. Parshley (New York: Vintage, 1973), 301.

13. Ibid. 38.

14. See my 'Sex and Gender in de Beauvoir's *Second Sex*', *Yale French Studies, Simone de Beauvoir: Witness to a Century*, 72 (Winter 1986).

15. Note the extent to which phenomenological theories such as Sartre's, Merleau Ponty's, and de Beauvoir's tend to use the term *embodiment*. Drawn as it is from theological contexts, the term tends to figure 'the' body as a mode of incarnation, and hence to preserve the external and dualistic relationship between a signifying immateriality and the materiality of the body itself.

16. See Luce Irigaray, *The Sex Which Is Not One*, trans. Catherine Porter with Carolyn Burke (Ithaca: Cornell University Press, 1985), originally published as *Ce sexe qui n'en est pas un* (Paris: Éditions de Minuit, 1977).

17. See Joan Scott, 'Gender as a Useful Category of Historical Analysis', in *Gender*

and the Politics of History (New York: Columbia University Press, 1988), 28–52, repr. from *American Historical Review*, 91/5 (1986).

18. De Beauvoir, *The Second Sex*, p. xxvi.

19. See my 'Sex and Gender in de Beauvoir's *Second Sex*'.

20. The normative ideal of the body as both a 'situation' and an 'instrumentality' is embraced by both de Beauvoir with respect to gender and Frantz Fanon with respect to race. Fanon concludes his analysis of colonization through recourse to the body as an instrument of freedom, where freedom is, in Cartesian fashion, equated with a consciousness capable of doubt: 'O my body, make of me always a man who questions!' Frantz Fanon, *Black Skin, White Masks* (New York: Grove Press, 1967), 323; orig. published as *Peau noire, masques blancs* (Paris: Éditions de Seuil, 1952).

21. The radical ontological disjunction in Sartre between consciousness and the body is part of the Cartesian inheritance of his philosophy. Significantly, it is Descartes' distinction that Hegel implicitly interrogates at the outset of the 'Master-Slave' section of *The Phenomenology of Spirit*. De Beauvoir's analysis of the masculine Subject and the feminine Other is clearly situated in Hegel's dialectic and in the Sartrian reformulation of that dialectic in the section on sadism and masochism in *Being and Nothingness*. Critical of the very possibility of a 'synthesis' of consciousness and the body, Sartre effectively returns to the Cartesian problematic that Hegel sought to overcome. De Beauvoir insists that the body can be the instrument and situation of freedom and that sex can be the occasion for a gender that is not a reification, but a modality of freedom. At first this appears to be a synthesis of body and consciousness, where consciousness is understood as the condition of freedom. The question that remains, however, is whether this synthesis requires and maintains the ontological distinction between body and mind of which it is composed and, by association, the hierarchy of mind over body and of masculine over feminine.

22. See Elizabeth V. Spelman, 'Woman as Body: Ancient and Contemporary Views', *Feminist Studies*, 8/1 (Spring 1982).

23. Gayatri Spivak most pointedly elaborates this particular kind of binary explanation as a colonizing act of marginalization. In a critique of the 'self-presence of the cognizing supra-historical self', which is characteristic of the epistemic imperialism of the philosophical cogito, she locates politics in the production of knowledge that creates and censors the margins that constitute, through exclusion, the contingent intelligibility of that subject's given knowledge-regime: 'I call "politics as such" the prohibition of marginality that is implicit in the production of any explanation. From that point of view, the choice of particular binary oppositions . . . is no mere intellectual strategy. It is, in each case, the condition of the possibility for centralization (with appropriate apologies) and, correspondingly, marginalization.' Gayatri Chakravorty Spivak, 'Explanation and Culture: Marginalia', in *In Other Worlds: Essays in Cultural Politics* (New York: Routledge, 1987), 113.

24. See the argument against 'ranking oppressions' in Cherríe Moraga, 'La Güera', in *This Bridge Called My Back: Writings of Radical Women of Color*, eds. Gloria Anzaldua and Cherríe Moraga (New York: Kitchen Table, Women of Color Press, 1982).

Part V. Equality and Anti-Discrimination

14 Difference and Dominance: On Sex Discrimination

Catharine MacKinnon

What is a gender question a question of? What is an inequality question a question of? These two questions underlie applications of the equality principle to issues of gender, but they are seldom explicitly asked. I think it speaks to the way gender has structured thought and perception that mainstream legal and moral theory tacitly gives the same answer to them both: these are questions of sameness and difference. The mainstream doctrine of the law of sex discrimination that results is, in my view, largely responsible for the fact that sex equality law has been so utterly ineffective at getting women what we need and are socially prevented from having on the basis of a condition of birth: a chance at productive lives of reasonable physical security, self-expression, individuation, and minimal respect and dignity. Here I expose the sameness/different theory of sex equality, briefly show how it dominates sex discrimination law and policy and underlies its discontents, and propose an alternative that might do something.

According to the approach to sex equality that has dominated politics, law, and social perception, equality is an equivalence, not a distinction, and sex is a distinction. The legal mandate of equal treatment—which is both a systemic norm and a specific legal doctrine—becomes a matter of treating likes alike and unlikes unlike; and the sexes are defined as such by their mutual unlikeness. Put another way, gender is socially constructed as difference epistemologically; sex discrimination law bounds gender equality by difference doctrinally. A built-in tension exists between this concept of equality, which presupposes sameness, and this concept of sex, which presupposes difference. Sex equality thus becomes a contradiction in terms, something of an oxymoron, which may suggest why we are having such a difficult time getting it.

First published in C. MacKinnon, *Feminism Unmodified* (Harvard Univ 1987). Reprinted by permission.

Upon further scrutiny, two alternate paths to equality for women emerge within this dominant approach, paths that roughly follow the lines of this tension. The leading one is: be the same as men. This path is termed gender neutrality doctrinally and the single standard philosophically. It is testimony to how substance gets itself up as form in law that this rule is considered formal equality. Because this approach mirrors the ideology of the social world, it is considered abstract, meaning transparent of substance; also for this reason it is considered not only to be *the* standard, but *a* standard at all. It is so far the leading rule that the words 'equal to' are code for, equivalent to, the words 'the same as'—referent for both unspecified.

To women who want equality yet find that you are different, the doctrine provides an alternate route: be different from men. This equal recognition of difference is termed the special benefit rule or special protection rule legally, the double standard philosophically. It is in rather bad odour. Like pregnancy, which always calls it up, it is something of a doctrinal embarrassment. Considered an exception to true equality and not really a rule of law at all, this is the one place where the law of sex discrimination admits it is recognizing something substantive. Together with the Bona Fide Occupational Qualification (BFOQ), the unique physical characteristic exception under ERA policy, compensatory legislation, and sex-conscious relief in particular litigation, affirmative action is thought to live here.[1]

The philosophy underlying the difference approach is that sex *is* a difference, a division, a distinction, beneath which lies a stratum of human commonality, sameness. The moral thrust of the sameness branch of the doctrine is to make normative rules conform to this empirical reality by granting women access to what men have access to: to the extent that women are no different from men, we deserve what they have. The differences branch, which is generally seen as patronizing but necessary to avoid absurdity, exists to value or compensate women for what we are or have become distinctively as women (by which is meant, unlike men) under existing conditions.

My concern is not with which of these paths to sex equality is preferable in the long run or more appropriate to any particular issue, although most discourse on sex discrimination revolves about these questions as if that were all there is. My point is logically prior: to treat issues of sex equality as issues of sameness and difference *is to take a particular approach*. I call this the difference approach because it is obsessed with the sex difference. The main theme in the fugue is 'we're the same, we're the same, we're the same'. The counterpoint theme (in a higher register) is 'but we're different, but we're different, but we're different'. Its underlying story is: on the first day, difference was; on the second day, a division was created upon it; on the third day, irrational instances of dominance arose. Division may be rational or irrational. Dominance either seems or is justified. Difference *is*.

There is a politics to this. Concealed is the substantive way in which man has become the measure of all things. Under the sameness standard, women are measured according to our correspondence with man, our equality judged by our proximity to his measure. Under the difference standard, we are measured according to our lack of correspondence with him, our womanhood judged by our distance from his measure. Gender neutrality is thus simply the male standard, and the special protection rule is simply the female standard, but do not be deceived: masculinity, or maleness, is the referent for both. Think about it like those anatomy models in medical school. A male body is the human body; all those extra things women have are studied in ob/gyn. It truly is a situation in which more is less. Approaching sex discrimination in this way—as if sex questions are difference questions and equality questions are sameness questions—provides two ways for the law to hold women to a male standard and call that sex equality.

Having been very hard on the difference answer to sex equality questions, I should say that it takes up a very important problem: how to get women access to everything we have been excluded from, while also valuing everything that women are or have been allowed to become or have developed as a consequence of our struggle either not to be excluded from most of life's pursuits or to be taken seriously under the terms that have been permitted to be our terms. It negotiates what we have managed in relation to men. Legally articulated as the need to conform normative standards to existing reality the strongest doctrinal expression of its sameness idea would prohibit taking gender into account in any way.

Its guiding impulse is: we're as good as you. Anything you can do, we can do. Just get out of the way. I have to confess a sincere affection for this approach. It has gotten women some access to employment[2] and education,[3] the public pursuits, including academic,[4] professional,[5] and blue-collar work;[6] the military;[7] and more than nominal access to athletics.[8] It has moved to change the dead ends that were all we were seen as good for and has altered what passed for women's lack of physical training, which was really serious training in passivity and enforced weakness. It makes you want to cry sometimes to know that it has had to be a mission for many women just to be permitted to do the work of this society, to have the dignity of doing jobs a lot of other people don't even want to do.

The issue of including women in the military draft[9] has presented the sameness answer to the sex equality question in all its simple dignity and complex equivocality. As a citizen, I should have to risk being killed just like you. The consequences of my resistance to this risk should count like yours. The undercurrent is: what's the matter, don't you want me to learn to kill . . .just like you? Sometimes I see this as a dialogue between women in the afterlife. The feminist says to the soldier, 'we fought for your equality.' The soldier says to the feminist, 'Oh, no, *we* fought for *your* equality.'

Feminists have this nasty habit of counting bodies and refusing not to notice their gender. As applied, the sameness standard has mostly gotten men the benefit of those few things women have historically had—for all the good they did us. Almost every sex discrimination case that has been won at the Supreme Court level has been brought by a man.[10] Under the rule of gender neutrality, the law of custody and divorce has been transformed, giving men an equal chance at custody of children and at alimony.[11] Men often look like better 'parents' under gender-neutral rules like level of income and presence of nuclear family, because men make more money and (as they say) initiate the building of family units.[12] In effect, they get preferred because society advantages them before they get into court, and law is prohibited from taking that preference into account because that would mean taking gender into account. The group realities that make women more in need of alimony are not permitted to matter, because only individual factors, gender-neutrally considered, may matter. So the fact that women will live their lives, as individuals, as members of the group women, with women's chances in a sex-discriminatory society, may not count, or else it is sex discrimination. The equality principle in this guise mobilizes the idea that the way to get things for women is to get them for men. Men have gotten them. Have women? We still have not got equal pay,[13] or equal work,[14] far less equal pay for equal work,[15] and we are close to losing separate enclaves like women's schools through this approach.[16]

Here is why. In reality, which this approach is not long on because it is liberal idealism talking to itself, virtually every quality that distinguishes men from women is already affirmatively compensated in this society. Men's physiology defines most sports,[17] their needs define auto and health insurance coverage, their socially designed biographies define workplace expectations and successful career patterns, their perspectives and concerns define quality in scholarship, their experiences and obsessions define merit, their objectification of life defines art, their military service defines citizenship, their presence defines family, their inability to get along with each other—their wars and rulerships—defines history, their image defines god, and their genitals define sex. For each of their differences from women, what amounts to an affirmative action plan is in effect, otherwise known as the structure and values of American society. But whenever women are, by this standard, 'different' from men and insist on not having it held against us, whenever a difference is used to keep us second-class and we refuse to smile about it, equality law has a paradigm trauma and it's crisis time for the doctrine.

What this doctrine has apparently meant by sex inequality is not what happens to us. The law of sex discrimination that has resulted seems to be looking only for those ways women are kept down that have *not* wrapped themselves up as a difference—whether original, imposed, or imagined. Start with original: what to do about the fact that women actually have an ability men still lack, gestating children in utero. Pregnancy therefore is a difference. Difference doctrine says it is sex discrimination to give women what we need, because only women need it. It is not sex discrimination not to give women what we need because then only women will not get what we need.[18] Move into imposed: what to do about the fact that most women are segregated into low-paying jobs where there are no men. Suspecting that the structure of the marketplace will be entirely subverted if comparable worth is put into effect, difference doctrine says that because there is no man to set a standard from which women's treatment is a deviation, there is no sex discrimination here, only sex difference. Never mind that there is no man to compare with because no man would do that job if he had a choice, and of course he has because he is a man, so he won't.[19]

Now move into the so-called subtle reaches of the imposed category, the *de facto* area. Most jobs in fact require that the person, gender neutral, who is qualified for them will be someone who is not the primary caretaker of a preschool child.[20] Pointing out that this raises a concern of sex in a society in which women are expected to care for the children is taken as day one of taking gender into account in the structuring of jobs. To do that would violate the rule

299

against not noticing situated differences based on gender, so it never emerges that day one of taking gender into account was the day the job was structured with the expectation that its occupant would have no childcare responsibilities. Imaginary sex differences—such as between male and female applicants to administer estates, or between males ageing and dying and females ageing and dying[21]—I will concede, the doctrine can handle.

I will also concede that there are many differences between women and men. I mean, can you imagine elevating one half of a population and denigrating the other half and producing a population in which everyone is the same? What the sameness standard fails to notice is that men's differences from women are equal to women's differences from men. There is an *equality* there. Yet the sexes are not socially equal. The difference approach misses the fact that hierarchy of power produces real as well as fantasied differences, differences that are also inequalities. What is missing in the difference approach is what Aristotle missed in his empiricist notion that equality means treating likes alike and unlikes unlike, and nobody has questioned it since. Why should you have to be the same as a man to get what a man gets simply because he is one? Why does maleness provide an original entitlement, not questioned on the basis of *its* gender, so that it is women—women who want to make a case of unequal treatment in a world men have made in their image (this is really the part Aristotle missed)—who have to show in effect that they are men in every relevant respect, unfortunately mistaken for women on the basis of an accident of birth?

The women that gender-neutrality benefits, and there are some, show the suppositions of this approach in highest relief. They are mostly women who have been able to construct a biography that somewhat approximates the male norm, at least on paper. They are the qualified, the least of sex discrimination's victims. When they are denied a man's chance, it looks the most like sex bias. The more unequal society gets, the fewer such women are permitted to exist. Therefore, the more unequal society gets, the *less* likely the difference doctrine is to be able to do anything about it, because unequal power creates both the appearance and the reality of sex differences along the same lines as it creates its sex inequalities.

The special benefits side of the difference approach has not compensated for the differential of being second-class. The special benefits rule is the only place in mainstream equality doctrine where you get to identify as a woman and not have that mean giving up all claim to equal treatment—but it comes close. Under its double standard, women who stand to inherit something when their husbands die have gotten the exclusion of a small percentage of the inheritance tax, to the tune of Justice Douglas waxing eloquent about the difficulties of all women's economic situation.[22] If we're going to be stigmatized as different, it would be nice if the compensation would fit the disparity. Women have also gotten three more years than men get before we have to be advanced or kicked out of the military hierarchy, as compensation for being precluded from combat, the usual way to advance.[23] Women have also gotten excluded from contact jobs in male-only prisons because we might get raped, the Court taking the viewpoint of the reasonable rapist on women's employment opportunities.[24] We also get protected out of jobs because of our fertility. The reason is that the job has health hazards, and somebody who might be a real person some day and therefore could sue—that is, a foetus—might be hurt if women, who apparently are not real persons and therefore can't sue either for the hazard to our health or for the lost employment opportunity, are given jobs that subject our bodies to possible harm.[25] Excluding women is always an option if equality feels in tension with the pursuit itself. They never seem to think of excluding men. Take combat.[26] Somehow it takes the glory out of the foxhole, the buddiness out of the trenches, to imagine us out there. You get the feeling they might rather end the draft, they might even rather not fight wars at all than have to do it with us.

The double standard of these rules doesn't give women the dignity of the single standard; it also does not (as the differences standard does) suppress the gender of its referent, which is, of course, the female gender. I must also confess some affection for this standard. The work of Carol Gilligan on gender differences in moral reasoning[27] gives it a lot of dignity, more than it has ever had, more, frankly, than I thought it ever could have. But she achieves for moral reasoning what the special protection rule achieves in law: the affirmative rather than the negative valuation of that which has accurately distinguished women from men, by making it seem as though those attributes, with their consequences, really are somehow ours, rather than what male supremacy has attributed to us for its own use. For women to affirm difference, when difference means dominance, as it does with gender, means to affirm the qualities and characteristics of powerlessness.

Women have done good things, and it is a good thing to affirm them. I think quilts are art. I think women have a history. I think we create culture. I also know that we have not only been excluded from

301

making what has been considered art; our artifacts have been excluded from setting the standards by which art is art. Women have a history all right, but it is a history both of what was and of what was not allowed to be. So I am critical of affirming what we have been, which necessarily is what we have been permitted, as if it is women's, ours, possessive. As if equality, in spite of everything, already ineluctably exists.

I am getting hard on this and am about to get harder on it. I do not think that the way women reason morally is morality 'in a different voice'.[28] I think it is morality in a higher register, in the feminine voice. Women value care because men have valued us according to the care we give them, and we could probably use some. Women think in relational terms because our existence is defined in relation to men. Further, when you are powerless, you don't just speak differently. A lot, you don't speak. Your speech is not just differently articulated, it is silenced. Eliminated, gone. You aren't just deprived of a language with which to articulate your distinctiveness, although you are; you are deprived of a life out of which articulation might come. Not being heard is not just a function of lack of recognition, not just that no-one knows how to listen to you, although it is that; it is also silence of the deep kind, the silence of being prevented from having anything to say. Sometimes it is permanent. All I am saying is that the damage of sexism is real, and reifying that into differences is an insult to our possibilities.

So long as these issues are framed this way, demands for equality will always appear to be asking to have it both ways: the same when we are the same, different when we are different. But this is the way men have it: equal and different too. They have it the same as women when they are the same and want it, and different from women when they are different and want to be, which usually they do. Equal and different too would only be parity.[29] But under male supremacy, while being told we get it both ways, both the specialness of the pedestal and an even chance at the race, the ability to be a woman and person, too, few women get much benefit of either.

There is an alternative approach, one that threads its way through existing law and expresses, I think, the reason equality law exists in the first place. It provides a second answer, a dissident answer in law and philosophy, to both the equality question and the gender question. In this approach, an equality question is a question of the distribution of power. Gender is also a question of power, specifically of male supremacy and female subordination. The question of equality, from the standpoint of what it is going to take to get it, is at root a question of hierarchy, which—as power succeeds in constructing social perception and social reality—derivatively becomes a categorical distinction, a difference. Here, on the first day that matters, dominance was achieved, probably by force. By the second day, division along the same lines had to be relatively firmly in place. On the third day, if not sooner, differences were demarcated, together with social systems to exaggerate them in perception and in fact, *because* the systematically differential delivery of benefits and deprivations required making no mistake about who was who. Comparatively speaking, man has been resting ever since. Gender might not even code as difference, might not mean distinction epistemologically, were it not for its consequences for social power.

I call this the dominance approach, and it is the ground I have been standing on in criticizing mainstream law. The goal of this dissident approach is not to make legal categories trace and trap the way things are. It is not to make rules that fit reality. It is critical of reality. Its task is not to formulate abstract standards that will produce determinate outcomes in particular cases. Its project is more substantive, more jurisprudential than formulaic, which is why it is difficult for the mainstream discourse to dignify it as an approach to doctrine or to imagine it as a rule of law at all. It proposes to expose that which women have had little choice but to be confined to, in order to change it.

The dominance approach centres on the most sex-differential abuses of women as a gender, abuses that sex equality law in its difference garb could not confront. It is based on a reality about which little of a systematic nature was known before 1970, a reality that calls for a new conception of the problem of sex inequality. This new information includes not only the extent and intractability of sex segregation into poverty, which has been known before, but the range of issues termed violence against women, which has not been. It combines women's material desperation, through being relegated to categories of jobs that pay nil, with the massive amount of rape and attempted rape—44 per cent of all women—about which virtually nothing is done;[30] the sexual assault of children—38 per cent of girls and 10 per cent of boys—which is apparently endemic to the patriarchal family;[31] the battery of women that is systematic in one-quarter to one-third of our homes;[32] prostitution, women's fundamental economic condition, what we do when all else fails, and for many women in this country, all else fails often;[33] and pornography, an industry that traffics in female flesh, making sex inequality into sex to the tune of eight billion dollars a year in profits largely to organized crime.[34]

These experiences have been silenced out of the difference definition of sex equality largely because they happen almost exclusively to women. Understand: for this reason, they are considered *not* to raise sex-equality issues. Because this treatment is done almost uniquely to women, it is implicitly treated as a difference, the sex difference, when in fact it is the socially situated subjection of women. The whole point of women's social relegation to inferiority as a gender is that for the most part these things aren't done to men. Men are not paid half of what women are paid for doing the same work on the basis of their equal difference. Everything they touch does not turn valueless because they touched it. When they are hit, a person has been assaulted. When they are sexually violated, it is not simply tolerated, or found entertaining, or defended as the necessary structure of the family, the price of civilization, or a constitutional right.

Does this differential describe the sex difference? Maybe so. It does describe the systematic relegation of an entire group of people to a condition of inferiority and attribute it to their nature. If this differential were biological, maybe biological intervention would have to be considered. If it were evolutionary, perhaps men would have to evolve differently. Because I think it is political, I think its politics construct the deep structure of society. Men who do not rape women have nothing wrong with their hormones. Men who are made sick by pornography and do not eroticize their revulsion are not under-evolved. This social status in which we can be used and abused and trivialized and humiliated and bought and sold and passed around and patted on the head and put in place and told to smile so that we look as though we're enjoying it all is not what some of us have in mind as sex equality.

This second approach—which is not abstract, which is at odds with socially imposed reality and therefore does not look like a standard according to the standard for standards—became the implicit model for racial justice applied by the courts during the sixties. It has since eroded with the erosion of judicial commitment to racial equality. It was based on the realization that the condition of Blacks in particular was not fundamentally a matter of rational or irrational differentiation on the basis of race, but was fundamentally a matter of white supremacy, under which racial differences became invidious as a consequence.[35] To consider gender in this way, observe again that men are as different from women as women are from men, but socially the sexes are not equally powerful. To be on the top of a hierarchy is certainly different from being on the bottom, but that is an obfuscatingly neutralized way of putting it, as a hierarchy is a great deal more than that. If gender were merely a question of difference, sex inequality would be a problem of mere sexism, of mistaken differentiation, of inaccurate categorization of individuals. This is what the difference approach thinks it is and is therefore sensitive to. But if gender is an inequality first, constructed as a socially relevant differentiation in order to keep that inequality in place, then sex inequality questions are questions of systematic dominance, of male supremacy, which is not at all abstract and is anything but a mistake.

If differentiation into classifications, in itself, is discrimination, as it is in difference doctrine, the use of law to change group-based social inequalities becomes problematic, even contradictory. This is because the group whose situation is to be changed must necessarily be legally identified and delineated, yet to do so is considered in fundamental tension with the guarantee against legally sanctioned inequality. If differentiation is discrimination, affirmative action, and any legal change in social inequality, is discrimination—but the existing social differentiations which constitute the inequality are not? This is only to say that, in the view that equates differentiation with discrimination, changing an unequal status quo is discrimination, but allowing it to exist is not.

Looking at the difference approach and the dominance approach from each other's point of view clarifies some otherwise confusing tensions in sex equality debates. From the point of view of the dominance approach, it becomes clear that the difference approach adopts the point of view of male supremacy on the status of the sexes. Simply by treating the status quo as 'the standard', it invisibly and uncritically accepts the arrangements under male supremacy. In this sense, the difference approach is masculinist, although it can be expressed in a female voice. The dominance approach, in that it sees the inequalities of the social world from the standpoint of the subordination of women to men, is feminist.

If you look through the lens of the difference approach at the world as the dominance approach imagines it—that is, if you try to see real inequality through a lens that has difficulty seeing an inequality as an inequality if it also appears as a difference—you see demands for change in the distribution of power as demands for special protection. This is because the only tools that the difference paradigm offers with which to comprehend disparity equate the recognition of a gender line with an admission of lack of entitlement to equality under law. Since equality questions are primarily confronted in this approach as matters of empirical fit[36]—that is, as matters of accurately shaping legal rules (implicitly modelled on the standard men set) to the way the world is (also implicitly modelled on the standard men set)—any existing differences must be negated to merit equal treatment. For ethnicity as well as for gender, it is basic to mainstream discrimination doctrine to preclude any true diversity among equals or true equality within diversity.

To the difference approach, it further follows that any attempt to change the way the world actually is looks like a moral question requiring a separate judgment of how things ought to be. This approach imagines asking the following disinterested question that can be answered neutrally as to groups: against the weight of empirical difference, should we treat some as the equals of others, even when they may not be entitled to it because they are not up to standard? Because this construction of the problem is part of what the dominance approach unmasks, it does not arise with the dominance approach, which therefore does not see its own foundations as moral. If sex inequalities are approached as matters of imposed status, which are in need of change if a legal mandate of equality means anything at all, the question of whether women should be treated unequally means simply whether women should be treated as less. When it is exposed as a naked power question, there is no separable question of what ought to be. The only real question is what is and is not a gender question. Once no amount of difference justifies treating women as sub-human, eliminating that is what equality law is for. In this shift of paradigms, equality propositions become no longer propositions of good and evil, but of power and powerlessness, no more disinterested in their origins or neutral in their arrival at conclusions than are the problems they address.

There came a time in Black people's movement for equality in this country when slavery stopped being a question of how it could be justified and became a question of how it could be ended. Racial disparities surely existed, or racism would have been harmless, but at that point—a point not yet reached for issues of sex—no amount of group difference mattered any more. This is the same point at which a group's characteristics, including empirical attributes, become constitutive of the fully human, rather than being defined as exceptions to or as distinct from the fully human. To one-sidedly measure one group's differences against a standard set by the other incarnates partial standards. The moment when one's particular qualities become part of the standard by which humanity is measured is a millenial moment.

To summarize the argument: seeing sex equality questions as matters of reasonable or unreasonable classification is part of the way male dominance is expressed in law. If you follow my shift in perspective from gender as difference to gender as dominance, gender changes from a distinction that is presumptively valid to a detriment that is presumptively suspect. The difference approach tries to map reality; the dominance approach tries to challenge and change it. In the dominance approach, sex discrimination stops being a question of morality and starts being a question of politics.

You can tell if sameness is your standard for equality if my critique of hierarchy looks like a request for special protection in disguise. It's not. It envisions a change that would make possible a simple equal chance for the first time. To define the reality of sex as difference and the warrant of equality as sameness is wrong on both counts. Sex, in nature, is not a bipolarity; it is a continuum. In society it is made into a bipolarity. Once this is done, to require that one be the same as those whose who set the standard—those which one is already socially defined as different from—simply means that sex equality is conceptually designed never to be achieved. Those who most need equal treatment will be the least similar, socially, to those whose situation sets the standard as against which one's entitlement to be equally treated is measured. Doctrinally speaking, the deepest problems of sex inequality will not find women 'similarly situated'[37] to men. Far less will practices of sex inequality require that acts be intentionally discriminatory.[38] All that is required is that the status quo be maintained. As a strategy for maintaining social power, first structure reality unequally, then require that entitlement to alter it be grounded on a lack of distinction in situation; first structure perception so that different equals inferior, then require that discrimination be activated by evil minds who *know* they are treating equals as less.

I say, give women equal power in social life. Let what we say matter, then we will discourse on questions of morality. Take your foot off our necks, then we will hear in what tongue women speak. So long as sex equality is limited by sex difference, whether you like it or don't like it, whether you value it or seek to negate it, whether you stake it out as a grounds for feminism or occupy it as the terrain of misogyny, women will be born, degraded, and die. We would settle for that equal protection of the laws under which one would be born, live, and die, in a country where protection is not a dirty word and equality is not a special privilege.

Notes

1. The Bona Fide Occupational Qualification (BFOQ) exception to Title VII of the Civil Rights Act of 1964, 42 USC § 2000 e–(2)(e), permits sex to be a job qualification when it is a valid one. The leading interpretation of the proposed federal Equal Rights Amendment would, pursuing a similar analytic structure, permit a 'unique physical characteristic' exception to its otherwise absolute embargo on taking sex into account. Barbara Brown, Thomas I. Emerson, Gail Falk, and Ann E. Freedman, 'The Equal Rights Amendment: A Constitutional Basis for Equal Rights for Women,' *Yale Law Journal*, 80 (1971), 893.

2. Title VII of the Civil Rights Act of 1964, 42 USC § 2000 e; Phillips v. Martin-Marietta, 400 US 542 (1971) Frontiero v. Richardson, 411 US 484 (1974) is the high-water mark of this approach. See also City of Los Angeles v. Manhart, 435 US 702 (1978); and Newport News Shipbuilding and Dry Dock Co. v. EEOC, 462 US 669 (1983).

3. Title IX of the Education Amendments of 1972, 20 USC § 1681; Cannon v. University of Chicago, 411 US 677 (1981); Mississippi University of Women v. Hogan, 458 US 718 (1982); see also De La Cruz v. Tormey, 582 F.2d 45 (9th Cir. 1978).

4. My impression is that women appear to lose most academic sex discrimination cases that go to trial, although I know of no systematic or statistical study on the subject. One case that won eventually, elevating the standard of proof in the process, is Sweeney v. Board of Trustees of Keene State College, 439 US 29 (1979). The ruling for the plaintiff was affirmed on remand, 604 F.2d 106 (1st Cir. 1979).

5. Hishon v. King and Spalding, 467 US 69 (1984).

6. See e.g. Vanguard Justice v. Hughes, 471 F. Supp. 670 (D. Md. 1979); Moyer v. Missouri State Highway Commission, 567 F.2d 804, 891 (8th Cir. 1977); Payne v. Travenol Laboratories Inc., 416 F. Supp. 248 (N.D. Mass. 1976). See also Dothard v. Rawlinson, 433 US 321 (1977) (height and weight requirements invalidated for prison guard contact positions because of disparate impact on sex).

7. Frontiero v. Richardson, 411 US 484 (1974); Schlesinger v. Ballard, 419 US 498 (1975).

8. This situation is relatively complex. See Gomes v. R. I. Interscholastic League, 469 F. Supp. 659 (D. R.I. 1979); Brenden v. Independent School District, 477 F.2d 1292 (8th Cir. 1973); O'Connor v. Board of Education of School District No. 23, 645 F.2d 578 (7th Cir. 1981); Cape v. Tennessee Secondary School Athletic Association, 424 F. Supp. 732 (E.D. Tenn. 1976), rev's, 563 F.2d 793 (6th Cir. 1977); Yellow Springs Exempted Village School District Board of Education v. Ohio High School Athletic Association, 443 F. Supp. 753 (S.D. Ohio 1978); Aiken v. Lieuallen, 593 P.2d 1243 (Or. App. 1979).

9. Rostker v. Goldberg, 453 US 57 (1981). See also Lori S. Kornblum, 'Women Warriors in a Men's World: The Combat Exclusion', *Law and Inequality: A Journal of Theory and Practice*, 2 (1984), 353.

10. David Cole, 'Strategies of Difference: Litigating for Women's Rights in a Man's World', *Law and Inequality: A Journal of Theory and Practice*, 2 (1984) 34, n. 4 (collecting cases).

11. Devine v. Devine, 398 So. 2d 686 (Ala. Sup. Ct. 1981); Danielson v. Board of Higher Education, 358 F. Supp. 22 (S.D.N.Y. 1972); Weinberger v. Wiesenfeld,

420 US 636 (1975); Stanley v. Illinois, 405 US 645 (1971); Caban v. Mohammed, 441 US 380 (1979); Orr v. Orr, 440 US 268 (1979).

12. Lenore Weitzman, 'The Economics of Divorce: Social and Economic Consequences of Property, Alimony and Child Support Awards', *U.C.L.A. Law Review*, 28 (1982) 1118, 1251, documents a decline in women's standard of living of 73 per cent and an increase in men's of 42 per cent within a year after divorce.

13. Equal Pay Act, 29 USC § 206(d)(1) (1976) guarantees pay equality, as does case law, but cf. data on pay gaps.

14. Examples include Christenson v. State of Iowa, 563 F.2d 353 (8th Cir. 1977); Gerlach v. Michigan Bell Tel. Co., 501 F. Supp. 1300 (E.D. Mich. 1980); Odomes v. Nucare, Inc., 653 F.2d 246 (6th Cir. 1981) (female nurse's aide denied Title VII remedy because her job duties were not substantially similar to those of better-paid male orderly); Power v. Barry County, Michigan, 539 F. Supp. 721 (W.D. Mich. 1982); Spaulding v. University of Washington, 740 F.2d 686 (9th Cir. 1984).

15. County of Washington v. Gunther, 452 US 161 (1981) permits a comparable-worth-type challenge where pay inequality can be proved to be a correlate of intentional job segregation. See also Lemons v. City and County of Denver, 17 FEP Cases 910 (D. Colo. 1978), aff'd 620 F.2d 228 (10th Cir. 1977), cert. denied, 449 US 888 (1980); AFSCME v. State of Washington, 770 F.2d 1401 (9th Cir. 1985). See generally Carol Jean Pint, 'Value, Work and Women', *Law and Inequality: A Journal of Theory and Practice* (1983) 159.

16. Combine the result in Bob Jones University v. United States, 461 US 547 (1983) with Mississippi University for Women v. Hogan, 458 U.S. 718 (1982), and the tax-exempt status of women-only schools is clearly threatened.

17. A particularly pungent example comes from a case in which the plaintiff sought to compete in boxing matches with men, since there were no matches sponsored by the defendant among women. A major reason that preventing the woman from competing was found not to violate her equality rights was that the 'safety rules and precautions [were] developed, designed, and tested in the context of all-male competition'. Lafler v. Athletic Board of Control, 536 F. Supp. 104, 107 (W.D. Mich. 1982). As the court put it: 'In this case, the real differences between the male and female anatomy are relevant in considering whether men and women may be treated differently with regard to their participating in boxing. The plaintiff *admits* that she wears a protective covering for her breasts while boxing. Such a protective covering . . . would violate Rule Six, Article 9 of the Amateur Boxing Federation rules currently in effect. The same rule *requires* contestants to wear a protective cup, a rule obviously designed for the unique anatomical characteristics of men.' Id. at 106 (emphasis added). The rule is based on the male anatomy, therefore not a justification for the discrimination but an example of it. This is not considered in the opinion, nor does the judge discuss whether women might benefit from genital protection, and men from chest guards, as in some other sports.

18. This is a reference to the issues raised by several recent cases which consider whether states' attempts to compensate pregnancy leaves and to secure jobs on return constitute sex discrimination. California Federal Savings and Loan Assn. v. Guerra, 758 F.2d 390 (9th Cir. 1985), cert. granted 54 USLW 3460 (US Jan. 13, 1986); see also Miller-Wohl v. Commissioner of Labor, 515 F. Supp. 1264 (D. Montana 1981), vacated and dismissed, 685 F.2d 1088 (9th Cir. 1982).

The position argued in 'Difference and Dominance' here suggests that if these benefits are prohibited under Title VII, Title VII is unconstitutional under the equal protection clause.

This argument was not made directly in either case. The American Civil Liberties Union argued that the provisions requiring pregnancy to be compensated in employment, without comparable coverage for men, violated Title VII's prohibition on pregnancy-based classifications and on sex. Montana had made it illegal for an employer to 'terminate a woman's employment because of her pregnancy' or to 'refuse to grant to the employee a reasonable leave of absence for such pregnancy'. Montana Maternity Leave ACt § 49–2–310(1) and (2). According to the ACLU, this provision 'grants pregnant workers certain employment rights not enjoyed by other workers . . . Legislation designed to benefit women has . . . perpetuated destructive stereotypes about their proper roles and operated to deny them rights and benefits enjoyed by men. The [Montana provision] deters employers from hiring women who are or may become pregnant, causes resentment and hostility in the workplace, and penalizes men.' Brief of American Civil Liberties Union, *et al. amicus curiae*, Montana Supreme Court No. 84–172, at 7. The National Organization for Women argued that the California provision, which requires employers to give pregnant workers unpaid disability leave with job security for up to four months, would violate Title VII should Title VII be interpreted to permit it. Brief of National Organization for Women, *et al.*, United States Court of Appeals for the Ninth Circuit, 685 F.2d 1088 (9th Cir. 1982).

When Congress passed the Pregnancy Discrimination Act, amending Title VII, 42 USC § 2000 e(k), it defined 'because of sex' or 'on the basis of sex' to include 'because of or on the basis of pregnancy, childbirth, or related medical conditions; and women affected by pregnancy, childbirth, or related medical conditions shall be treated the same for all employment-related purposes'. In so doing, Congress arguably decided that one did not have to be the same as a man to be treated without discrimination, since it guaranteed freedom from discriminatory treatment on the basis of a condition that is not the same for men as it is for women. It even used the word 'women' in the statute.

Further, Congress made this decision expressly to overrule the Supreme Court decision in General Electric v. Gilbert, 429 US 125 (1976), which had held that failure to cover pregnancy as a disability was not sex discrimination because the line between pregnant and non-pregnant was not the line between women and men. In rejecting this logic, as the Court found it did expressly in Newport News Shipbuilding and Dry Dock Co. v. EEOC, 462 US 669, 678 (1983), Congress rejected the implicit measuring of women's entitlement to equality by a male standard. Nor need all women be the same, that is, pregnant or potentially so, to have pregnancy-based discrimination be sex-based discrimination.

Upholding the California pregnancy leave and job security law, the Ninth Circuit opinion did not require sameness for equality to be delivered: 'The PDA does not require states to ignore pregnancy. It requires that women be treated equally . . . [E]qually under the PDA must be measured in employment opportunity, not necessarily in amounts of money expended—or in amounts of days of disability leave expended. Equality . . . compares coverage to actual need, not coverage to hypothetical identical needs.' California Federal v. Guerra, 758 F.2d 390 (9th Cir. 1985) (Ferguson, J.). "We are not the first court to announce the goal of Title VII is equality of employment opportunity, not necessarily same-ness of treatment.' Id. at 396 n. 7.

19. Most women work at jobs mostly women do, and most of those jobs are paid less than jobs that mostly men do. See e.g. Pint, n. 15 above, at 162–63 nn. 19, 20 (collecting studies). To the point that men may not meet the male standard themselves, one court found that a union did not fairly represent its women in the following terms: 'As to the yard and driver jobs, defendants suggest not only enormous intellectual requirements, but that the physical demands of those jobs are so great as to be beyond the capacity of any female. Again, it is noted that plaintiffs' capacity to perform those jobs was never tested, despite innu-merable requests therefore. It is also noted that defendants have never sug-gested *which* of the innumerable qualifications they list for these jobs (for the first time) the plaintiffs might fail to meet. The court, however, will accept without listing here the extraordinary catalogue of feats which defendants argue must be performed in the yard, and as a driver. That well may be. However, one learns from this record that one cannot be too weak, too sick, too old and infirm, or too ignorant to perform these jobs, *so long as one is a man.* The plaintiffs appear to the layperson's eye to be far more physically fit than many of the drivers who moved into the yard, over the years, according to the testimony of defense witnesses . . . In short, they were all at least as fit as the men with serious physical deficits and disabilities who held yard jobs.' Jones v. Cassens Transport, 617 F. Supp. 869, 892 (1985) (emphasis in original).

20. Phillips v. Martin-Marietta, 400 US 542 (1971).

21. Reed v. Reed, 404 US 71 (1971) held that a statute barring women from admin-stering estates is sex discrimination. If few women were taught to read and write, as used to be the case, the gender difference would not be imaginary in this case, yet the social situation would be even more sex discriminatory than it is now. Compare City of Los Angeles v. Manhart, 434 US 815 (1978), which held that requiring women to make larger contributions to their retirement plan was sex discrimination, in spite of the allegedly proven sex difference that women on the average outlive men.

22. Kahn v. Shevin, 416 US 351, 353 (1974).

23. Schlesinger v. Ballard, 419 US 498 (1975).

24. Dothard v. Rawlinson, 433 US 321 (1977); see also Michael M. v. Sonoma County Superior Court, 450 US 464 (1981).

25. Doerr v. B. F. Goodrich, 484 F. Supp. 320 (N.D. Ohio 1979). Wendy Webster Williams, 'Firing the Woman to Protect the Fetus: The Reconciliation of Fetal Protection with Employment Opportunity Goals Under Title VII', *Georgetown Law Journal*, 69 (1981), 641. See also Hayes v. Shelby Memorial Hospital, 546 F. upp. 259 (N.D. Ala. 1982); Wright v. Olin Corp., 697 F.2d 1172 (4th Cir. 1982).

26. Congress requires the Air Force (10 USC § 8549 [1983]) and the Navy (10 USC § 6015 [1983]) to exclude women from combat, with some exceptions. Owens v. Brown, 455 F. Supp. 291 (D.D.C. 1978), had previously invalidated the prior Navy combat exclusion because it prohibited women from filling jobs they could perform and inhibited Navy's discretion to assign women on combat ships. The Army excludes women from combat based upon its own policies under congressional authorization to determine assignment: 10 USC § 3012(e) (1983).

27. Carol Gilligan, *In a Different Voice* (1982).

28. Ibid.
29. I argued this in Appendix A of my *Sexual Harassment of Working Women: A Case of Sex Discrimination* (1979). That book ends with 'Women want to be equal and different, too.' I could have added 'Men are.' As a standard, this would have reduced women's aspirations for equality to some corresponding version of men's actualities. But as an observation, it would have been true.
30. Diana Russell and Nancy Howell, 'The Prevalence of Rape in the United States Revisited', *Signs: Journal of Women in Culture and Society*, 8 (1983), 689 (44 per cent of women in 930 households were victims of rape or attempted rape at some time in their lives).
31. Diana Russell, 'The Incidence and Prevalence of Intrafamilial and Extrafamilial Sexual Abuse of Female Children', *Child Abuse and Neglect: The International Journal*, 7 (1983), 133.
32. R. Emerson Dobash and Russell Dobash, *Violence against Wives: A Case against the Patriarchy* (1979); Bruno v. Codd, 90 Misc. 2d 1047, 396 N.Y.S. 2d 974 (Sup. Ct. 1977), *rev'd*, 64 A.D. 2d 582, 407 N.Y.S. 2d 165 (1st Dep't 1978), *aff'd* 47 N.Y. 2d 582, 393 N.E. 2d 976, 419 N.Y.S. 2d 901 (1979).
33. Kathleen Barry, *Female Sexual Slavery* (1979); Moira K. Griffin, 'Wives, Hookers and the Law: The Case for Decriminalizing Prostitution', *Student Lawyer*, 10 (1982) 18; Report of Jean Fernand-Laurent, Special Rapporteur on the Suppression of the Traffic in Persons and the Exploitation of the Prostitution of Others (a United Nations report), in *International Feminism: Networking against Female Sexual Slavery*, ed. Kathleen Barry, Charlotte Bunch, and Shirley Castley (Report of the Global Feminist Workshop to Organize against Traffic in Women, Rotterdam, Netherlands, Apr. 6–15, 1983 [1984]), 130.
34. Galloway and Thornton, 'Crackdown on Pornography—A no-Win Battle', *US News and World Report* (June 4, 1984), 84. See also 'The Place of Pornography', *Harper's* (November 1984), 31 (citing $7 billion per year).
35. Loving v. Virginia, 388 US 1 (1967), first used the term 'white supremacy' in invalidating an antimiscegenation law as a violation of equal protection. The law equally forbade whites and Blacks to intermarry. Although going nowhere near as far, courts in the athletics area have sometimes seen that 'same' does not necessarily mean 'equal', nor does 'equal' require 'same'. In a context of sex inequality like that which has prevailed in athletic opportunity, allowing boys to compete on girls' teams may diminish overall sex equality. 'Each position occupied by a male reduces the female participation and increases the overall disparity of athletic opportunity which generally exists.' Petrie v. Illinois High School Association, 394 N.E. 2d 855, 865 (Ill. 1979). 'We conclude that to furnish exactly the same athletic opportunities to boys as to girls would be most difficult and would be detrimental to the compelling governmental interest of equalizing general athletic opportunities between the sexes.' Id.
36. The scholars Tussman and ten Broek first used the term 'fit' to characterize the necessary relation between a valid equality rule and the world to which it refers. J. Tussman and J. ten Broek, 'The Equal Protection of the Laws', *California Law Review*, 37 (1949), 341.
37. Royster Guano C. v. Virginia, 253 US 412, 415 (1920): '[A classification] must be reasonable, not arbitrary, and must rest upon some ground of difference having a fair and substantial relation to the object of the legislation, so that all persons similarly circumstanced shall be treated alike.' Reed v. Reed, 404 US 71,

76 (1971): 'Regardless of their sex, persons within any one of the enumerated classes . . . are similarly situated . . . By providing dissimilar treatment for men and women who are thus similarly situated, the challenged section violates the Equal Protection Clause.'

38. Washington v. Davis, 426 US 229 (1976) and Personnel Administrator of Massachusetts v. Feeney, 442 US 256 (1979) require that intentional discrimination be shown for discrimination be said to have occurred.

Demarginalizing the Intersection of Race and Sex: A Black Feminist Critique of Antidiscrimination Doctrine, Feminist Theory, and Antiracist Politics

Kimberle Crenshaw

One of the very few Black women's studies books is entitled *All the Women Are White, All the Blacks Are Men, But Some of Us are Brave.*[1] I have chosen this title as a point of departure in my efforts to develop a Black feminist criticism[2] because it sets forth a problematic consequence of the tendency to treat race and gender as mutually exclusive categories of experience and analysis.[3] In this talk, I want to examine how this tendency is perpetuated by a single-axis framework that is dominant in antidiscrimination law and that is also reflected in feminist theory and antiracist politics.

I will centre Black women in this analysis in order to contrast the multidimensionality of Black women's experience with the single-axis analysis that distorts these experiences. Not only will this juxtaposition reveal how Black women are theoretically erased, it will also illustrate how this framework imports its own theoretical limitations that undermine efforts to broaden feminist and antiracist analyses. With Black women as the starting point, it becomes more apparent how dominant conceptions of discrimination condition us to think about subordination as disadvantage occurring along a single categorical axis. I want to suggest further that this single-axis framework erases Black women in the conceptualization, identification and remediation of race and sex discrimination by limiting inquiry to the experiences of otherwise-privileged members of the group. In other words, in race discrimination cases, discrimination tends to be viewed in terms of sex- or class-privileged Blacks; in sex discrimination cases, the focus is on race- and class-privileged women.

Reprinted by permission from *The University of Chicago Legal Forum*, 139 (1989), 139–67.

This focus on the most privileged group members marginalizes those who are multiply-burdened and obscures claims that cannot be understood as resulting from discrete sources of discrimination. I suggest further that this focus on otherwise-privileged group members creates a distorted analysis of racism and sexism because the operative conceptions of race and sex become grounded in experiences that actually represent only a subset of a much more complex phenomenon.

After examining the doctrinal manifestations of this single-axis framework, I will discuss how it contributes to the marginalization of Black women in feminist theory and in antiracist politics. I argue that Black women are sometimes excluded from feminist theory and anti-racist policy discourse because both are predicated on a discrete set of experiences that often does not accurately reflect the interaction of race and gender. These problems of exclusion cannot be solved simply by including Black women within an already established analytical structure. Because the intersectional experience is greater than the sum of racism and sexism, any analysis that does not take intersectionality into account cannot sufficiently address the particular manner in which Black women are subordinated. Thus, for feminist theory and anti-racist policy discourse to embrace the experiences and concerns of Black women, the entire framework that has been used as a basis for translating 'women's experience' or 'the Black experience' into concrete policy demands must be rethought and recast.

As examples of theoretical and political developments that miss the mark with respect to Black women because of their failure to consider intersectionality, I will briefly discuss the feminist critique of rape and separate spheres ideology, and the public policy debates concerning female-headed households within the Black community.

I. THE ANTIDISCRIMINATION FRAMEWORK

A. The Experience of Intersectionality and the Doctrinal Response

One way to approach the problem of intersectionality is to examine how courts frame and interpret the stories of Black women plaintiffs. While I cannot claim to know the circumstances underlying the cases that I will discuss, I nevertheless believe that the way courts interpret claims made by Black women is itself part of Black women's experience and, consequently, a cursory review of cases involving Black female plaintiffs is quite revealing. To illustrate the difficulties inherent in judicial treatment of intersectionality, I will consider three Title VII[4] cases: *DeGraffenreid* v. *General Motors*,[5] *Moore* v. *Hughes Helicopter*[6] and *Payne* v. *Travenol*.[7]

1. *DeGraffenreid* vs. *General Motors.* In *DeGraffenreid*, five Black women brought suit against General Motors, alleging that the employer's seniority system perpetuated the effects of past discrimination against Black women. Evidence adduced at trial revealed that General Motors simply did not hire Black women prior to 1964 and that all of the Black women hired after 1970 lost their jobs in a seniority-based layoff during a subsequent recession. The district court granted summary judgment for the defendant, rejecting the plaintiffs' attempt to bring a suit not on behalf of Blacks or women, but specifically on behalf of Black women. The court stated:

[P]laintiffs have failed to cite any decisions which have stated that Black women are a special class to be protected from discrimination. The Court's own research has failed to disclose such a decision. The plaintiffs are clearly entitled to a remedy if they have been discriminated against. However, they should not be allowed to combine statutory remedies to create a new 'super-remedy' which would give them relief beyond what the drafters of the relevant statutes intended. Thus, this lawsuit must be examined to see if it states a cause of action for race discrimination, sex discrimination, or alternatively either, but not a combination of both.[8]

Although General Motors did not hire Black women prior to 1964, the court noted that 'General Motors has hired . . . female employees for a number of years prior to the enactment of the Civil Rights Act of 1964'.[9] Because General Motors did hire women—albeit *white women*—during the period that no Black women were hired, there was, in the court's view, no sex discrimination that the seniority system could conceivably have perpetuated.

After refusing to consider the plaintiffs' sex discrimination claim, the court dismissed the race discrimination complaint and recommended its consolidation with another case alleging race discrimination against the same employer.[10] The plaintiffs responded that such consolidation would defeat the purpose of their suit since theirs was not purely a race claim, but an action brought specifically on behalf of Black women alleging race *and* sex discrimination. The court, however, reasoned:

The legislative history surrounding Title VII does not indicate that the goal of the statute was to create a new classification of 'black women' who would have greater standing than, for example, a black male. The prospect of the creation of new classes of protected minorities, governed only by the mathematical principles of permutation and combination, clearly raises the prospect of opening the hackneyed Pandora's box.[11]

Thus, the court apparently concluded that Congress either did not contemplate that Black women could be discriminated against as 'Black women' or did not intend to protect them when such discrimination occurred.[12] The court's refusal in *DeGraffenreid* to acknowledge that Black women encounter combined race and sex discrimination implies that the boundaries of sex and race discrimination doctrine are defined respectively by white women's and Black men's experiences. Under this view, Black women are protected only to the extent that their experiences coincide with those of either of the two groups.[13] Where their experiences are distinct, Black women can expect little protection as long as approaches, such as that in *DeGraffenreid*, which completely obscure problems of intersectionality prevail.

2. *Moore* vs. *Hughes Helicopter, Inc.* *Moore* v. *Hughes Helicopter, Inc.*[14] presents a different way in which courts fail to understand or recognize Black women's claims. *Moore* is typical of a number of cases in which courts refused to certify Black females as class representatives in race *and* sex discrimination actions.[15] In *Moore*, the plaintiff alleged that the employer, Hughes Helicopter, practised race and sex discrimination in promotions to upper-level craft positions and to supervisory jobs. Moore introduced statistical evidence establishing a significant disparity between men and women, and somewhat less of a disparity between Black and white men in supervisory jobs.[16]

Affirming the district court's refusal to certify Moore as the class representative in the sex discrimination complaint on behalf of all women at Hughes, the Ninth Circuit noted approvingly:

Moore had never claimed before the EEOC that she was discriminated against as a female, *but only* as a Black female. . . . [T]his raised serious doubts as to Moore's ability to adequately represent white female employees.[17]

The curious logic in *Moore* reveals not only the narrow scope of antidiscrimination doctrine and its failure to embrace intersectionality, but also the centrality of white female experiences in the conceptualization of gender discrimination. One inference that could be drawn from the court's statement that Moore's complaint did not entail a claim of discrimination 'against females' is that discrimination against Black females is something less than discrimination against females. More than likely, however, the court meant to imply that Moore did not claim that *all* females were discriminated against *but only* Black females. But even thus recast, the court's rationale is problematic for Black women. The court rejected Moore's bid to represent all females apparently because her attempt to specify her race was seen as being at odds with the standard allegation that the employer simply discriminated 'against females'.

The court failed to see that the absence of a racial referent does not necessarily mean that the claim being made is a more inclusive one. A white woman claiming discrimination against females may be in no better position to represent all women than a Black woman who claims discrimination as a Black female and wants to represent all females. The court's preferred articulation of 'against females' is not necessarily more inclusive—it just appears to be so because the racial contours of the claim are not specified.

The court's preference for 'against females' rather than 'against Black females' reveals the implicit grounding of white female experiences in the doctrinal conceptualization of sex discrimination. For white women, claiming sex discrimination is simply a statement that but for gender, they would not have been disadvantaged. For them there is no need to specify discrimination as *white* females because their race does not contribute to the disadvantage for which they seek redress. The view of discrimination that is derived from this grounding takes race privilege as a given.

Discrimination against a white female is thus the standard sex discrimination claim; claims that diverge from this standard appear to present some sort of hybrid claim. More significantly, because Black females' claims are seen as hybrid, they sometimes cannot represent those who may have 'pure' claims of sex discrimination. The effect of this approach is that even though a challenged policy or practice may clearly discriminate against all females, the fact that it has particularly harsh consequences for Black females places Black female plaintiffs at odds with white females.

Moore illustrates one of the limitations of anti-discrimination law's remedial scope and normative vision. The refusal to allow a multiply disadvantaged class to represent others who may be singularly disadvantaged defeats efforts to restructure the distribution of opportunity and limits remedial relief to minor adjustments within an established hierarchy. Consequently, 'bottom-up' approaches, those which combine all discriminatees in order to challenge an entire employment system, are foreclosed by the limited view of the wrong and the narrow scope of the available remedy. If such 'bottom-up' intersectional representation were routinely permitted, employees might accept the possibility that there is more to gain by collectively challenging the hierarchy rather than by each discriminatee individually seeking to protect her source of privilege within the hierarchy. But as long as anti-discrimination doctrine proceeds from the premise that employment systems need only minor adjustments, opportunities for advancement by disadvantaged employees will be limited. Relatively privileged employees probably are better off guarding their advantage while jockeying against others to gain more. As a result, Black women—the class of employees which, because of its intersectionality, is best able to challenge all forms of discrimination—are essentially isolated and often required to fend for themselves.

In *Moore*, the court's denial of the plaintiff's bid to represent all Blacks and females left Moore with the task of supporting her race and sex discrimination claims with statistical evidence of discrimination against Black females alone.[18] Because she was unable to represent white women or Black men, she could not use overall statistics on sex disparity at Hughes, nor could she use statistics on race. Proving her claim using statistics on Black women alone was no small task, due to the fact that she was bringing the suit under a disparate impact theory of discrimination.[19]

The court further limited the relevant statistical pool to include only Black women who it determined were qualified to fill the openings in upper-level labour jobs and in supervisory positions.[20] According to the court, Moore had not demonstrated that there were any qualified Black women within her bargaining unit or the general labour pool for either category of jobs.[21] Finally, the court stated that even if it accepted Moore's contention that the percentage of Black females in supervisory positions should equal the percentage of Black females in the employee pool, it still would not find discriminatory impact.[22] Because the promotion of only two Black women into supervisory positions would have achieved the expected mean distribution of Black women within that job category, the court was 'unwilling to agree that a prima facie case of disparate impact ha[d] been proven'.[23]

The court's rulings on Moore's sex and race claim left her with such a small statistical sample that even if she had proved that there were qualified Black women, she could not have shown discrimination under a disparate impact theory. *Moore* illustrates yet another way that anti-discrimination doctrine essentially erases Black women's distinct experiences and, as a result, deems their discrimination complaints groundless.

3. *Payne* vs. *Travenol.* Black female plaints have also encountered difficulty in their efforts to win certification as class representatives in some race discrimination actions. This problem typically arises in cases where statistics suggest significant disparities between Black and white workers and further disparities between Black men and Black women. Courts in some cases[24] have denied certification based on logic that mirrors the rationale in *Moore*: The sex disparities between Black men and Black women created such conflicting interests that Black women could not possibly represent Black men adequately. In one such case, *Payne* v. *Travenol*,[25] two Black female plaintiffs alleging race discrimination brought a class action suit on behalf of all Black employees at a pharmaceutical plant.[26] The court refused, however, to allow the plaintiffs to represent Black males and granted the defendant's request to narrow the class to Black women only. Ultimately, the district court found that there had been extensive racial discrimination at the plant and awarded back pay and constructive seniority to the class of Black female employees. But, despite its finding of general race discrimination, the court refused to extend the remedy to Black men for fear that their conflicting interests would not be adequately addressed;[27] the Fifth Circuit affirmed.[28]

Notably, the plaintiffs in *Travenol* fared better than the similarly situated plaintiff in *Moore*: They were not denied use of meaningful statistics showing an overall pattern of race discrimination simply because there were no men in their class. The plaintiffs' bid to represent all Black employees, however, like Moore's attempt to represent all women employees, failed as a consequence of the court's narrow view of class interest.

Even though *Travenol* was a partial victory for Black women, the case specifically illustrates how anti-discrimination doctrine generally creates a dilemma for Black women. It forces them to choose between specifically articulating the intersectional aspects of their subordination, thereby risking their ability to represent Black men, or ignoring intersectionality in order to state a claim that would not lead to the exclusion of Black men. When one considers the political consequences of this dilemma, there is little wonder that many people within the Black community view the specific articulation of Black women's interests as dangerously divisive.

In sum, several courts have proved unable to deal with intersectionality, although for contrasting reasons. In *DeGraffenreid*, the court refused to recognize the possibility of compound discrimination against Black women and analysed their claim using the employment of white women as the historical base. As a consequence, the employment experiences of white women obscured the distinct discrimination that Black women experienced.

Conversely, in *Moore*, the court held that a Black woman could not use statistics reflecting the overall sex disparity in supervisory and upper-level labour jobs because she had not claimed discrimination as a woman, but 'only' as a Black woman. The court would not entertain the notion that discrimination experienced by Black women is indeed sex discrimination—provable through disparate impact statistics on women.

Finally, courts, such as the one in *Travenol*, have held that Black women cannot represent an entire class of Blacks due to presumed class conflicts in cases where sex additionally disadvantaged Black women. As a result, in the few cases where Black women are allowed to use overall statistics indicating racially disparate treatment Black men may not be able to share in the remedy.

Perhaps it appears to some that I have offered inconsistent criticisms of how Black women are treated in anti-discrimination law: I seem to be saying that in one case, Black women's claims were rejected and their experiences obscured because the court refused to acknowledge that the employment experience of Black women can be distinct from that of white women, while in other cases the interests of Black women were harmed because Black women's claims were viewed as so distinct from the claims of either white women or Black men that the court denied to Black females representation of the larger class. It seems that I have to say that Black women are the same and harmed by being treated differently, or that they are different and harmed by being treated the same. But I cannot say both.

This apparent contradiction is but another manifestation of the conceptual limitations of the single-issue analyses that intersectionality challenges. The point is that Black women can experience discrimination in any number of ways and that the contradiction arises from our assumptions that their claims of exclusion must be unidirectional. Consider an analogy to traffic in an intersection, coming and going in all four directions. Discrimination, like traffic through an intersection, may flow in one direction, and it may flow in another. If an accident happens in an intersection, it can be caused by cars travelling from any number of directions and, sometimes, from all of them. Similarly, if a Black woman is harmed because she is in the intersection, her injury could result from sex discrimination or race discrimination.

Judicial decisions which premise intersectional relief on a showing that Black women are specifically recognized as a class are analogous to a doctor's decision at the scene of an accident to treat an accident victim only if the injury is recognized by medical insurance. Similarly, providing legal relief only when Black women show that their claims are based on race or on sex is analogous to calling an ambulance for the victim only after the driver responsible for the injuries is identified. But it is not always easy to reconstruct an accident. Sometimes the skid marks and the injuries simply indicate that they occurred simultaneously, frustrating efforts to determine which driver caused the harm. In these cases the tendency seems to be that no driver is held responsible, no treatment is administered, and the involved parties simply get back in their cars and zoom away.

To bring this back to a non-metaphorical level, I am suggesting that Black women can experience discrimination in ways that are both similar to and different from those experienced by white women and Black men. Black women sometimes experience discrimination in ways similar to white women's experiences; sometimes they share very similar experiences with Black men. Yet often they experience double-discrimination—the combined effects of practices which discriminate on the basis of race, and on the basis of sex. And sometimes, they experience discrimination as Black women—not the sum of race and sex discrimination, but as Black women.

Black women's experiences are much broader than the general categories that discrimination discourse provides. Yet the continued insistence that Black women's demands and needs be filtered through categorical analyses that completely obscure their experiences guarantees that their needs will seldom be addressed.

B. The Significance of Doctrinal Treatment of Intersectionality

DeGraffenreid, Moore and *Travenol* are doctrinal manifestations of a common political and theoretical approach to discrimination which operates to marginalize Black women. Unable to grasp the importance of Black women's intersectional experiences, not only courts, but feminist and civil rights thinkers as well have treated Black women in ways that deny both the unique compoundedness of their situation and the centrality of their experiences to the larger classes of women and Blacks. Black women are regarded either as too much like women or Blacks and the compounded nature of their experience is absorbed into the collective experiences of either group or as too different, in which case Black women's Blackness or femaleness sometimes has placed their needs and perspectives at the margin of the feminist and Black liberationist agendas.

While it could be argued that this failure represents an absence of political will to include Black women, I believe that it reflects an uncritical and disturbing acceptance of dominant ways of thinking about discrimination. Consider first the definition of discrimination that seems to be operative in anti-discrimination law. Discrimination which is wrongful proceeds from the identification of a specific class or category; either a discriminator intentionally identifies this category, or a process is adopted which somehow disadvantages all members of this category.[29] According to the dominant view, a discriminator treats all people within a race or sex category similarly. Any significant experiential or statistical variation within this group suggests either that the group is not being discriminated against or that conflicting interests exist which defeat any attempts to bring a common claim.[30] Consequently, one generally cannot combine these categories. Race and sex, moreover, become significant only when they operate to explicitly *disadvantage* the victims; because the *privileging* of whiteness or maleness is implicit, it is generally not perceived at all.

Underlying this conception of discrimination is a view that the wrong which anti-discrimination law addresses is the use of race or gender factors to interfere with decisions that would otherwise be fair or neutral. This process-based definition is not grounded in a bottom-up commitment to improve the substantive conditions for those who are victimized by the interplay of numerous factors. Instead, the dominant message of anti-discrimination law is that it will regulate only the limited extent to which race or sex interferes with the process of determining outcomes. This narrow objective is facilitated by the top-down strategy of using a singular 'but for' analysis to ascertain the effects of race or sex. Because the scope of anti-discrimination law is so limited, sex and race discrimination have come to be defined in terms of the experiences of those who are privileged *but for* their racial or sexual characteristics. Put differently, the paradigm of sex discrimination tends to be based on the experiences of white women; the model of race discrimination tends to be based on the experiences of the most privileged Blacks. Notions of what constitutes race and sex discrimination are, as a result, narrowly tailored to embrace only a small set of circumstances, none of which include discrimination against Black women.

To the extent that this general description is accurate, the following analogy can be useful in describing how Black women are marginalized in the interface between anti-discrimination law and race and gender hierarchies: Imagine a basement which contains all people who are disadvantaged on the basis of race, sex, class, sexual preference, age and/or physical ability. These people are stacked—feet standing on shoulders—with those on the bottom being disadvantaged by the full array of factors, up to the very top, where the heads of all those disadvantaged by a singular factor brush up against the ceiling. Their ceiling is actually the floor above which only those who are *not* disadvantaged in any way reside. In efforts to correct some aspects of domination, those above the ceiling admit from the basement only those who can say that 'but for' the ceiling, they too would be in the upper room. A hatch is developed through which those placed immediately below can crawl. Yet this hatch is generally available only to those who—due to the singularity of their burden and their otherwise privileged position relative to those below—are in the position to crawl through. Those who are multiply burdened are generally left below unless they can somehow pull themselves into the groups that are permitted to squeeze through the hatch.

As this analogy translates for Black women, the problem is that they can receive protection only to the extent that their experiences are recognizably similar to those whose experiences tend to be reflected in anti-discrimination doctrine. If Black women cannot conclusively say that 'but for' their race or 'but for' their gender they would be treated differently, they are not invited to climb through the hatch but told to wait in the unprotected margin until they can be absorbed into the broader, protected categories of race and sex.

Despite the narrow scope of this dominant conception of discrimination and its tendency to marginalize those whose experiences cannot be described within its tightly-drawn parameters, this approach has been regarded as the appropriate framework for addressing a range of problems. In much of feminist theory and, to some extent, in anti-racist politics, this framework is reflected in the belief that sexism or racism can be meaningfully discussed without paying attention to the lives of those other than the race-, gender- or class-privileged. As as result, both feminist theory and anti-racist politics have been organized, in part, around the equation of racism with what happens to the Black middle-class or to Black men, and the equation of sexism with what happens to white women.

Looking at historical and contemporary issues in both the feminist and the civil rights communities, one can find ample evidence of how both communities' acceptance of the dominant framework of discrimination has hindered the development of an adequate theory and praxis to address problems of intersectionality. This adoption of a single-issue framework for discrimination not only marginalizes Black women within the very movements that claim them as part of their constituency, but it also makes the illusive goal of ending racism and patriarchy even more difficult to attain.

II. FEMINISM AND BLACK WOMEN: 'AIN'T WE WOMEN?'

Oddly, despite the relative inability of feminist politics and theory to address Black women substantively, feminist theory and tradition borrow considerably from Black women's history. For example, 'Ain't I a Woman' has come to represent a standard refrain in feminist discourse.[31] Yet the lesson of this powerful oratory is not fully appreciated because the context of the delivery is seldom examined. I would like to tell part of the story because it establishes some themes that have characterized feminist treatment of race and illustrates the importance of including Black women's experiences as a rich source for the critique of patriarchy.

In 1851, Sojourner Truth declared 'Ain't I a Woman?' and challenged the sexist imagery used by male critics to justify the disenfranchisement of women.[32] The scene was a Women's Rights Conference in Akron, Ohio; white male hecklers, invoking stereotypical images of 'womenhood', argued that women were too frail and delicate to take on the responsibilities of political activity. When Sojourner Truth rose to speak, many white women urged that she be silenced, fearing that she would divert attention from women's suffrage to emancipation. Truth, once permitted to speak, recounted the horrors of slavery, and its particular impact on Black women:

Look at my arm! I have ploughed and planted and gathered into barns, and no man could head me—and ain't I a woman? I could work as much and eat as much as a man—when I could get it—and bear the lash as well! And ain't I a woman? I have borne thirteen children, and seen most of 'em sold into slavery, and when I cried out with my mother's grief, none but Jesus heard me—and ain't I a woman?[33]

By using her own life to reveal the contradiction between the ideological myths of womanhood and the reality of Black women's experience, Truth's oratory provided a powerful rebuttal to the claim that women were categorically weaker than men. Yet Truth's personal challenge to the coherence of the cult of true womanhood was useful only to the extent that white women were willing to reject the racist attempts to rationalize the contradiction—that because Black women were something less than real women, their experiences had no bearing on true womanhood. Thus, this 19th-century Black feminist challenged not only patriarchy, but she also challenged white feminists wishing to embrace Black women's history to relinquish their vestedness in whiteness.

Contemporary white feminists inherit not the legacy of Truth's challenge to patriarchy but, instead, Truth's challenge to their forbears. Even today, the difficulty that white women have traditionally experienced in sacrificing racial privilege to strengthen feminism renders them susceptible to Truth's critical question. When feminist theory and politics that claim to reflect *women's* experience and *women's* aspirations do not include or speak to Black women, Black women must ask: 'Ain't *We* Women?' If this is so, how can the claims that 'women are', 'women believe' and 'women need' be made when such claims are inapplicable or unresponsive to the needs, interests and experiences of Black women?

The value of feminist theory to Black women is diminished because it evolves from a white racial context that is seldom acknowledged. Not only are women of colour in fact overlooked, but their exclusion is reinforced when *white* women speak for and as *women*. The authoritative universal voice—usually white male subjectivity masquerading as non-racial, non-gendered objectivity[34]— is merely transferred to those who, but for gender, share many of the same cultural, economic, and social characteristics. When feminist theory attempts to describe women's experiences through analyzing patriarchy, sexuality, or separate-spheres ideology, it often overlooks the role of race. Feminists thus ignore how their own race functions to mitigate some aspects of sexism and, moreover, how it often privileges them over and contributes to the domination of other women.[35] Consequently, feminist theory remains *white*, and its potential to broaden and deepen its analysis by addressing non-privileged women remains unrealized.

An example of how some feminist theories are narrowly constructed around white women's experiences is found in the separate-spheres literature. The critique of how separate-spheres ideology shapes and limits women's roles in the home and in public life is a central theme in feminist legal thought.[36] Feminists have attempted to expose and dismantle separate-spheres ideology by identifying and criticizing the stereotypes that traditionally have justified the disparate societal roles assigned to men and women.[37] Yet this attempt to debunk ideological justifications for *women's* subordination offers little insight into the domination of *Black* women. Because the experiential base upon which many feminist insights are grounded is white, theoretical statements drawn from them are over-generalized at best, and often wrong.[38] Statements such as 'men and women are taught to see men as independent, capable, powerful; men and women are taught to see women as dependent, limited in abilities, and passive',[39] are common within this literature. But this 'observation' overlooks the anomalies created by cross-currents of racism and sexism. Black men and women live in a society that creates sex-based norms and expectations which racism operates simultaneously to deny; Black men are not viewed as powerful, nor are Black women seen as passive. An effort to develop an ideological explanation of gender domination in the Black community should proceed from an understanding of how cross-cutting forces establish gender norms and how the conditions of Black subordination wholly frustrate access to these norms. Given this understanding, perhaps we can begin to see why Black women have been dogged by the stereotype of the pathological matriarch,[40] or why there have been those in the Black liberation movement who aspire to create institutions and to build traditions that are intentionally patriarchal.[41]

Because ideological and descriptive definitions of patriarchy are usually premised upon white female experiences, feminists and others informed by feminist literature may make the mistake of assuming that since the role of Black women in the family and in other Black institutions does not always resemble the familiar manifestations of patriarchy in the white community, Black women are somehow exempt from patriarchal norms. For example, Black women have traditionally worked outside the home in numbers far exceeding the labour participation rate of white women.[42] An analysis of patriarchy that highlights the history of white women's exclusion from the workplace might permit the inference that Black women have not been burdened by this particular gender-based expectation .Yet the very fact that Black women must work conflicts with norms that women should not, often creating personal, emotional, and relationship problems in Black women's lives. Thus, Black women are burdened not only because they often have to take on responsibilities that are not traditionally feminine but, moreover, their assumption of these roles is sometimes interpreted within the Black community as either Black women's failure to live up to such norms or as another manifestation of racism's scourge upon the Black community.[43] This is one of the many aspects of intersectionality that cannot be understood through an analysis of patriarchy rooted in white experience.

Another example of how theory emanating from a white context obscures the multi-dimensionality of Black women's lives is found in feminist discourse on rape. A central political issue on the feminist agenda has been the pervasive problem of rape. Part of the intellectual and political effort to mobilize around this issue has involved the development of a historical critique of the role that law has played in establishing the bounds of normative sexuality and in regulating female sexual behaviour.[44] Early carnal knowledge statutes and rape laws are understood within this discourse to illustrate that the objective of rape statutes traditionally has not been to protect women from coercive intimacy but to protect and maintain a property-like interest in female chastity.[45] Although feminists quite rightly criticize these objectives, to characterize rape law as reflecting male control over female sexuality is for Black women an oversimplified account and an ultimately inadequate account.

Rape statutes generally do not reflect *male* control over *female* sexuality, but *white* male regulation of *white* female sexuality.[46] Historically, there has been absolutely no institutional effort to regulate Black female chastity.[47] Courts in some states had gone so far as to instruct juries that, unlike white women, Black women were not presumed to be chaste.[48] Also, while it was true that the attempt to regulate the sexuality of white women placed unchaste women outside the law's protection, racism restored a fallen white woman's chastity where the alleged assailant was a Black man.[49] No such restoration was available to Black women.

The singular focus on rape as a manifestation of male power over female sexuality tends to eclipse the use of rape as a weapon of racial terror.[50] When Black women were raped by white males, they were being raped not as women generally, but as Black women specifically: Their femaleness made them sexually vulnerable to racist domination, while their Blackness effectively denied them any protection.[51] This white male power was reinforced by a judicial system in which the successful conviction of a white man for raping a Black woman was virtually unthinkable.[52]

In sum, sexist expectations of chastity and racist assumptions of sexual promiscuity combined to create a distinct set of issues confronting Black women.[53] These issues have seldom been explored in feminist literature nor are they prominent in antiracist politics. The lynching of Black males, the institutional practice that was legitimized by the regulation of white women's sexuality, has historically and contemporaneously occupied the Black agenda on sexuality and violence. Consequently, Black women are caught between a Black community that, perhaps understandably, views with suspicion attempts to litigate questions of sexual violence, and a feminist community that reinforces those suspicions by focusing on white female sexuality.[54] The suspicion is compounded by the historical fact that the protection of white female sexuality was often the pretext for terrorizing the Black community. Even today some fear that antirape agendas may undermine anti-racist objectives. This is the paradigmatic political and theoretical dilemma created by the intersection of race and gender: Black women are caught between ideological and political currents that combine first to create and then to bury Black women's experiences.

III. WHEN AND WHERE I ENTER: INTEGRATING AN ANALYSIS OF SEXISM INTO BLACK LIBERATION POLITICS

Anna Julia Cooper, a 19th-century Black feminist, coined a phrase that has been useful in evaluating the need to incorporate an explicit analysis of patriarchy in any effort to address racial domination.[55] Cooper often criticized Black leaders and spokespersons for claiming to speak for the race, but failing to speak for Black women. Referring to one of Martin Delaney's public claims that where he was allowed to enter, the race entered with him, Cooper countered: 'Only the Black Woman can say, when and where I enter . . . then and there the whole Negro race enters with me.'[56]

Cooper's words bring to mind a personal experience involving two Black men with whom I had formed a study group during our first year of law school. One of our group members, a graduate from Harvard College, often told us stories about a prestigious and exclusive men's club that boasted memberships of several past United States presidents and other influential white males. He was one of its very few Black members. To celebrate completing our first-year exams, our friend invited us to join him at the club for drinks. Anxious to see this fabled place, we approached the large door and grasped the brass door ring to announce our arrival. But our grand entrance was cut short when our friend sheepishly slipped from behind the door and whispered that he had forgotten a very important detail. My companion and I bristled, our training as Black people having taught us to expect yet another barrier to our inclusion; even an informal one-Black-person quota at the establishment was not unimaginable. The tension broke, however, when we learned that *we* would not be excluded because of our race, but that *I* would have to go around to the back door because I was a female. I entertained the idea of making a scene to dramatize the fact that my humiliation as a female was no less painful and my exclusion no more excusable than had we all been sent to the back door because we were Black. But, sensing no general assent to this proposition, and also being of the mind that due to our race a scene would in some way jeopardize all of us, I failed to stand my ground. After all, the Club was about to entertain its first Black guests—even though one would have to enter through the back door.[57]

Perhaps this story is not the best example of the Black community's failure to address problems related to Black women's intersectionality seriously. The story would be more apt if Black women, and only Black women, had to go around to the back door of the club and if the restriction came from within, and not from the outside of the Black community. Still this story does reflect a markedly decreased political and emotional vigilance toward barriers to Black women's enjoyment of privileges that have been won on the basis of race but continue to be denied on the basis of sex.[58]

The story also illustrates the ambivalence among Black women about the degree of political and social capital that ought to be expended toward challenging gender barriers, particularly when the challenges might conflict with the antiracism agenda. While there are a number of reasons—including anti-feminist ones—why gender has not figured directly in analyses of the subordination of Black Americans, a central reason is that race is still seen by many as the primary oppositional force in Black lives.[59] If one accepts that the social experience of race creates both a primary group identity as well as a shared sense of being under collective assault, some of the reasons that Black feminist theory and politics have not figured prominently in the Black political agenda may be better understood.[60]

The point is not that African Americans are simply involved in a more important struggle. Although some efforts to oppose Black feminism are based on this assumption, a fuller appreciation of the problems of the Black community will reveal that gender subordination does contribute significantly to the destitute conditions of so many African Americans and that it must therefore be addressed. Moreover, the foregoing critique of the single-issue framework renders problematic the claim that the struggle against racism is distinguishable from, much less prioritized over, the struggle against sexism. Yet it is also true that the politics of racial otherness that Black women experience along with Black men prevent Black feminist consciousness from patterning the development of white feminism. For white women, the creation of a consciousness that was distinct from and in opposition to that of white men figured prominently in the development of white feminist politics. Black women, like Black men, live in a community that has been defined and subordinated by color and culture.[61] Although patriarchy clearly operates within the Black community, presenting yet another source of domination to which Black women are vulnerable, the racial context in which Black women find themselves makes the creation of a political consciousness that is oppositional to Black men difficult.

Yet while it is true that the distinct experience of racial otherness militates against the development of an oppositional feminist consciousness, the assertion of racial community sometimes supports defensive priorities that marginalize Black women. Black women's particular interests are thus relegated to the periphery in public-policy discussions about the presumed needs of the Black community. The controversy over the movie *The Color Purple* is illustrative. The animating fear behind much of the publicized protest was that by portraying domestic abuse in a Black family, the movie confirmed the negative stereotypes of Black men.[62] The debate over the propriety of presenting such an image on the screen overshadowed the issue of sexism and patriarchy in the Black community. Even though it was sometimes acknowledged that the Black community was not immune from domestic violence and other manifestations of gender subordination, some nevertheless felt that in the absence of positive Black male images in the media, portraying such images merely reinforced racial stereotypes.[63] The struggle against racism seemed to compel the subordination of certain aspects of the Black female experience in order to ensure the security of the larger Black community.

The nature of this debate should sound familiar to anyone who recalls Daniel Moynihan's diagnosis of the ills of Black America.[64] Moynihan's report depicted a deteriorating Black family, foretold the destruction of the Black male householder and lamented the creation of the Black matriarch. His conclusions prompted a massive critique from liberal sociologists[65] and from civil rights leaders.[66] Surprisingly, while many critics characterized the report as racist for its blind use of white cultural norms as the standard for evaluating Black families, few pointed out the sexism apparent in Moynihan's labelling Black women as pathological for their 'failure' to live up to a white female standard of motherhood.[67]

The latest versions of a Moynihanesque analysis can be found in the Moyers televised special, *The Vanishing Black Family*,[68] and, to a lesser extent, in William Julius Wilson's *The Truly Disadvantaged*.[69] In *The Vanishing Black Family*, Moyers presented the problem of female-headed households as a problem of irresponsible sexuality, induced in part by government policies that encouraged family breakdown.[70] The theme of the report was that the welfare state reinforced the deterioration of the Black family by rendering the Black male's role obsolete. As the argument goes, because Black men know that someone will take care of their families, they are free to make babies and leave them. A corollary to the Moyers view is that welfare is also dysfunctional because it allows poor women to leave men upon whom they would otherwise be dependent.

Most commentators criticizing the programme failed to pose challenges that might have revealed the patriarchal assumptions underlying much of the Moyers report. They instead focused on the dimension of the problem that was clearly recognizable as racist.[71] White feminists were equally culpable. There was little, if any, published response to the Moyers report from the white feminist community. Perhaps feminists were under the mistaken assumption that since the report focused on the Black community, the problems highlighted were racial, not gender-based. Whatever the reason, the result was that the ensuing debates over the future direction of welfare and family policy proceeded without significant feminist input. The absence of a strong feminist critique of the Moynihan/Moyers model not only impeded the interests of Black women, but it also compromised the interests of growing numbers of white women heads of household who find it difficult to make ends meet.[72]

William Julius Wilson's *The Truly Disadvantaged* modified much of the moralistic tone of this debate by reframing the issue in terms of a lack of marriageable Black men.[73] According to Wilson, the decline in Black marriages is not attributable to poor motivation, bad work habits, or irresponsibility but instead is caused by structural economics which have forced Black unskilled labour out of the workforce. Wilson's approach represents a significant move away from that of Moynihan/Moyers in that he rejects their attempt to centre the analysis on the morals of the Black community. Yet, he too considers the proliferation of female-headed households as dysfunctional *per se*, and fails to explain fully why such households are so much in peril. Because he incorporates no analysis of the way the structure of the economy and the workforce subordinates the interests of women, especially childbearing Black women, Wilson's suggested reform begins with finding ways to put Black men back in the family.[74] In Wilson's view, we must change the economic structure with an eye toward providing more Black jobs for Black men. Because he offers no critique of sexism, Wilson fails to consider economic or social reorganization that directly empowers and supports these single Black mothers.[75]

My criticism is not that providing Black men with jobs is undesirable; indeed, this is necessary not only for the Black men themselves, but for an entire community, depressed and subject to a host of sociological and economic ills that accompany massive rates of unemployment. But as long as we assume that the massive social reorganization Wilson calls for is possible, why not think about it in ways that maximize the choices of Black women?[76] A more complete theoretical and political agenda for the Black underclass must take into account the specific and particular concerns of Black women; their families occupy the bottom rung of the economic ladder, and it is only through placing them at the center of the analysis that their needs and the needs of their families will be directly addressed.[77]

IV. EXPANDING FEMINIST THEORY AND ANTIRACIST POLITICS BY EMBRACING THE INTERSECTION

If any real efforts are to be made to free Black people of the constraints and conditions that characterize racial subordination, then theories and strategies purporting to reflect the Black community's needs must include an analysis of sexism and patriarchy. Similarly, feminism must include an analysis of race if it hopes to express the aspirations of non-white women. Neither Black liberationist politics nor feminist theory can ignore the intersectional experiences of those whom the movements claim as their respective constituents. In order to include Black women, both movements must distance themselves from earlier approaches in which experiences are relevant only when they are related to certain clearly identifiable causes (for example, the oppression of Blacks is significant when based on race, of women when based on gender). The praxis of both should be centred on the life chances and life situations of people who should be cared about without regard to the source of their difficulties.

I have stated earlier that the failure to embrace the complexities of compoundedness is not simply a matter of political will, but is also due to the influence of a way of thinking about discrimination which structures politics so that struggles are categorized as singular issues. Moreover, this structure imports a descriptive and normative view of society that reinforces that status quo.

It is somewhat ironic that those concerned with alleviating the ills of racism and sexism should adopt such a top-down approach to discrimination. If their efforts instead began with addressing the needs and problems of those who are most disadvantaged and with restructuring and remaking the world where necessary, then others who are singularly disadvantaged would also benefit. In addition, it seems that placing those who currently are marginalized in the centre is the most effective way to resist efforts to compartmentalize experiences and undermine potential collective action.

It is not necessary to believe that a political consensus to focus on the lives of the most disadvantaged will happen tomorrow in order to recentre discrimination discourse at the intersection. It is enough, for now, that such an effort would encourage us to look beneath the prevailing conceptions of discrimination and to challenge the complacency that accompanies belief in the effectiveness of this framework. By so doing, we may develop language which is critical of the dominant view and which provides some basis for unifying activity. The goal of this activity should be to facilitate the inclusion of marginalized groups for whom it can be said: 'When they enter, we all enter.'

Notes

1. Gloria T. Hull *et al.* (eds.) (The Feminist Press, 1982).
2. For other work setting forth a Black feminist perspective on law, see Judy Scales-Trent, 'Black Women and the Constitution: Finding Our Place, Asserting Our Rights (Voices of Experience: New Responses to Gender Discourse)', *Harv CR-CL L Rev*, 24 (1989), 9; Regina Austin, 'Sapphire-Bound!', *Wise Women's L J* (1989).
3. The most common linguistic manifestation of this analytical dilemma is represented in the conventional usage of the term 'Blacks and women'. Although it may be true that some people mean to include Black women in either 'Blacks' or 'women', the context in which the term is used actually suggests that often Black women are not considered. See, for example, Elizabeth Spelman, *The Inessential Woman* (Beacon Press, 1988), discussing an article on Blacks and women in the military where 'the racial identity of those identified as "women" does not become explicit until reference is made to Black women, at which point it also becomes clear that the category of women excludes Black women', 114–15. It seems that if Black women were explicitly included, the preferred term would be either 'Blacks and white women' or 'Black men and all women'.
4. Civil Rights Act of 1964, 42 USC § 2000e, et seq. as amended (1982).
5. 413 F Supp 142 (E D Mo 1976).
6. 708 F2d 475 (9th Cir 1983).
7. 673 F2d 798 (5th Cir 1982).
8. *DeGraffenreid*, 413 F Supp at 143.
9. Id. at 144.
10. Id. at 145. In *Mosley* v. *General Motors*, 497 F Supp 583 (E D Mo 1980), plaintiffs, alleging broad-based racial discrimination at General Motors' St. Louis facility, prevailed in a portion of their Title VII claim. The seniority system challenged in *DeGraffenreid*, however, was not considered in *Mosley*.
11. Id. at 145.
12. Interestingly, no case has been discovered in which a court denied a white male's attempt to bring a reverse discrimination claim on similar grounds—that is, that sex and race claims cannot be combined because Congress did not intend to protect compound classes. White males in a typical reverse discrimination case are in no better position than the frustrated plaintiffs in *DeGraffenreid*: if they are required to make their claims separately, white males cannot prove race discrimination because white women are not discriminated against, and they cannot prove sex discrimination because Black males are not discriminated against. Yet it seems that courts do not acknowledge the compound nature of most reverse discrimination cases. That Black women's claims automatically raise the question of compound discrimination and white males' 'reverse discrimination' cases do not suggest that the notion of compoundedness is somehow contingent upon an implicit norm that is not neutral but is white male. Thus, Black women are perceived as a compound class because they are two steps removed from a white male norm, while white males are apparently not perceived to be a compound class because they somehow represent the norm.
13. I do not mean to imply that all courts that have grappled with this problem have adopted the *DeGraffenreid* approach. Indeed, other courts have concluded that Black women are protected by Title VII. See e.g. *Jefferies* v. *Harris*

Community Action Ass'n., 615 F2d 1025 (5th Cir 1980). I do mean to suggest that the very fact that the Black women's claims are seen as aberrant suggests that sex discrimination doctrine is centred in the experiences of white women. Even those courts that have held that Black women are protected seem to accept that Black women's claims raise issues that the 'standard' sex discrimination claims do not. See Elaine W. Shoben, *Compound Discrimination: The interaction of Race and Sex in Employment Discrimination*, 55 NYU L Rev 793, 803–4 (1980) (criticizing the *Jefferies* use of a sex-plus analysis to create a subclass of Black women).

14. 708 F2d 475.

15. See also *Moore* v. *National Association of Securities Dealers*, 27 EPD (CCH) ¶ 32,238 (D DC 1981); but see *Edmondson* v. *Simon*, 86 FRD 375 (N D Ill 1980), where the court was unwilling to hold as a matter of law that no Black female could represent without conflict the interests of both Blacks and females.

16. 708 F2d at 479. Between January 1976 and June 1979, the three years in which Moore claimed that she was passed over for promotion, the percentage of white males occupying first-level supervisory positions ranged from 70.3 to 76.8 per cent; Black males from 8.9 to 10.9 per cent; white women from 1.8 to 3.3 per cent; and Black females from 0 to 2.2 per cent. The overall male/female ratio in the top five labour grades ranged from 100/0 per cent in 1976 to 98/1.8 per cent in 1979. The white/Black ratio was 85/3.3 per cent in 1976 and 79.6/8 per cent in 1979. The overall ratio of men to women in supervisory positions was 98.2 to 1.8 per cent in 1976 to 93.4 to 6.6 per cent in 1979; the Black to white ratio during the same time period was 78.6 to 8.9 per cent and 73.6 to 13.1 per cent.

For promotions to the top five labour grades the percentages were worse. Between 1976 and 1979 the percentage of white males in these positions ranged from 85.3 to 77.9 per cent; Black males 3.3 to 8 per cent; white females from 1 to 1.4 per cent, and Black females from 0 to 0 per cent. Overall, in 1979, 98.2 per cent of the highest level employees were male; 1.8 per cent were female.

17. 708 F2d at 480 (emphasis added).

18. Id. at 484–6.

19. Under the disparate impact theory that prevailed at the time, the plaintiff had to introduce statistics suggesting that a policy or procedure disparately affects the members of a protected group. The employer could rebut that evidence by showing that there was a business necessity supporting the rule. The plaintiff then countered the rebuttal by showing that there was a less discriminatory alternative. See e.g. *Griggs* v. *Duke Power*, 401 US 424 (1971); *Connecticut* v. *Teal*, 457 US 440 (1982).

A central issue in a disparate impact case is whether the impact proved is statistically significant. A related issue is how the protected group is defined. In many cases a Black female plaintiff would prefer to use statistics which include white women and/or Black men to indicate that the policy in question does in fact disparately affect the protected class. If, as in *Moore*, the plaintiff may use only statistics involving Black women, there may not be enough Black women employees to create a statistically significant sample.

20. Id. at 484.

21. The court buttressed its finding with respect to the upper-level labour jobs with statistics for the Los Angeles Metropolitan Area which indicated that there were only 0.2 per cent Black women within comparable job categories. Id. at 485 n. 9.

22. Id. at 486.

23. Id.

24. See *Strong* v. *Arkansas Blue Cross & Blue Shield, Inc.*, 87 FRD 496 (E D Ark 1980); *Hammons* v. *Folger Coffee Co.*, 87 FRD 600 (W D Mo 1980); *Edmondson* v. *Simon*, 86 FRD 375 (N D Ill 1980); *Vuyanich* v. *Republic National Bank of Dallas*, 82 FRD 420 (N D Tex 1979); *Colston* v. *Maryland Cup Corp.*, 26 Fed Rules Serv 940 (D Md 1978).

25. 416 F Supp 248 (N D Miss 1976).

26. The suit commenced on 2 March 1972, with the filing of a complaint by three employees seeking to represent a class of persons allegedly subjected to racial discrimination at the hands of the defendants. Subsequently the plaintiffs amended the complaint to add an allegation of sex discrimination. Of the original named plaintiffs, one was a Black male and two were Black females. In the course of the three-year period between the filing of the complaint and the trial, the only named male plaintiff received permission of the court to withdraw for religious reasons. Id. at 250.

27. As the dissent in *Travenol* pointed out, there was no reason to exclude Black males from the scope of the remedy *after* counsel had presented sufficient evidence to support a finding of discrimination against Black men. If the rationale for excluding Black males was the potential conflict between Black males and Black females, then '[i]n this case, to paraphrase an old adage, the proof of plaintiffs' ability to represent the interests of Black males was in the representation thereof.' 673 F2d at 837–8.

28. 673 F2d 798 (5th Cir. 1982).

29. In much of anti-discrimination doctrine, the presence of intent to discriminate distinguishes unlawful from lawful discrimination. See *Washington* v. *Davis*, 426 US 229, 239–45 (1976) (proof of discriminatory purpose required to substantiate Equal Protection violation). Under Title VII, however, the Court has held that statistical data showing a disproportionate impact can suffice to support a finding of discrimination. See *Griggs*, 401 US at 432. Whether the distinction between the two analyses will survive is an open question. See *Wards Cove Packing Co., Inc.* v. *Atonio*, 109 S Ct 2115, 2122–23 (1989) (plaintiffs must show more than mere disparity to support a prima facie case of disparate impact). For a discussion of the competing normative visions that underlie the intent and effects analyses, see Alan David Freeman, 'Legitimizing Racial Discrimination Through Antidiscrimination Law: A Critical Review of Supreme Court Doctrine', *Minn. L. Rev.*, 62 (1978), 1049.

30. See e.g. *Moore*, 708 F2d at 479.

31. See Phyliss Palmer, 'The Racial Feminization of Poverty: Women of Color as Portents of the Future for All Women', *Women's Studies Quarterly*, 11/3–4 (Fall, 1983), posing the question of why 'white women in the women's movement had not created more effective and continuous alliances with Black women' when 'simultaneously . . . Black women [have] become heroines for the women's movement, a position symbolized by the consistent use of Sojourner Truth and her famous words, "Ain't I a Woman?" '.

32. See Paula Giddings, *When and Where I Enter: The Impact of Black Women on Race and Sex in America* (William Morrow, 1984).

33. Eleanor Flexner, *Century of Struggle: The Women's Rights Movement in the United States* (Belknap Press of Harvard University Press, 1975), 91. See also Bell Hooks, *Ain't I a Woman* (South End Press, 1981), 159–60.

34. ' "Objectivity" is itself an example of the reification of white male thought.' Hull *et al.* (eds.), *But Some of Us Are Brave*, p. xxv.
35. For example, many white females were able to gain entry into previously all-white male enclaves not through bringing about a fundamental reordering of male versus female work, but in large part by shifting their 'female' responsibilities to poor and minority women.
36. Feminists often discuss how gender-based stereotypes and norms reinforce the subordination of women by justifying their exclusion from public life and glorifying their roles within the private sphere. Law has historically played a role in maintaining this subordination by enforcing the exclusion of women from public life and by limiting its reach into the private sphere. See e.g. Deborah L. Rhode, 'Association and Assimilation', *Nw U L Rev.*, 81 (1986) 106; Frances Olsen, 'From False Paternalism to False Equality: Judicial Assaults on Feminist Community, Illinois 1869–95', *Mich. L. Rev.* 84 (1986) 1518; Martha Minow, 'Foreword: Justice Engendered', *Harv. L. Rev.* 101 (1987) 10; Nadine Taub and Elizabeth M. Schneider, 'Perspectives on Women's Subordination and the Role of Law', in David Kairys (ed.), *The Politics of Law* (Pantheon Books, 1982), 117–39.
37. Ibid.
38. This criticism is a discrete illustration of a more general claim that feminism has been premised on white middle-class women's experience. For example, early feminist texts such as Betty Friedan's *The Feminine Mystique* (W. W. Norton, 1963), placed white middle-class problems at the centre of feminism and thus contributed to its rejection within the Black community. See Hooks, *Ain't I a Woman*, 185–96, noting that feminism was eschewed by Black women because its white middle-class agenda ignored Black women's concerns.
39. Richard A. Wasserstrom, 'Racism, Sexism and Preferential Treatment: An Approach to the Topics', *UCLA L Rev*, 24 (1977), 581, 588. I chose this phrase not because it is typical of most feminist statements of separate spheres; indeed, most discussions are not as simplistic as the bold statement presented here. See e.g. Taub and Schneider, 'Perspectives on Women's Subordination and the Role of Law', 117–39.
40. For example, Black families have sometimes been cast as pathological largely because of Black women's divergence from the white middle-class female norm. The most infamous rendition of this view is found in the Moynihan report, which blamed many of the Black community's ills on a supposed pathological family structure. For a discussion of the report and its contemporary reincarnation, see above, pp. 332–3.
41. See Hooks, *Ain't I a Woman*, 94–9, discussing the elevation of sexist imagery in the Black liberation movement during the 1960s.
42. See generally Jacqueline Jones, *Labor of Love, Labor of Sorrow; Black Women, Work, and the Family from Slavery to the Present* (Basic Books, 1985), and Angela Davis, *Women, Race and Class* (Random House, 1981).
43. As Elizabeth Higginbotham noted, 'women, who often fail to conform to "appropriate" sex roles, have been pictured as, and made to feel, inadequate—even though as women, they possess traits recognized as positive when held by men in the wider society. Such women are stigmatized because their lack of adherence to expected gender roles is seen as a threat to the value system.' 'Two Representative Issues in Contemporary Sociological Work on Black Women', in Hull *et al.* (eds.), *But Some of Us Are Brave*, 95.

44. See generally Susan Brownmiller, *Against Our Will* (Simon and Schuster, 1975); Susan Estrich, *Real Rape* (Harvard University Press, 1987).
45. See Brownmiller, *Against Our Will*, 17; see generally Estrich, *Real Rape*.
46. One of the central theoretical dilemmas of feminism that is largely obscured by universalizing the white female experience is that experiences that are described as a manifestation of male control over females can be instead a manifestation of dominant group control over all subordinates. The significance is that other non-dominant men may not share in, participate in, or connect with the behaviour, beliefs, or actions at issue, and may be victimized themselves by 'male' power. In other contexts, however, 'male authority' might include non-white men, particularly in private sphere contexts. Efforts to think more clearly about when Black women are dominated as *women* and when they are dominated as *Black women* are directly related to the question of when power is *male* and when it is *white male*.
47. See Note, 'Rape, Racism and the Law', *Harv Women's L J*, 6 (1983), 103, 117–23, discussing the historical and contemporary evidence suggesting that Black women are generally not thought to be chaste. See also Hooks, *Ain't I a Woman*, 54, stating that stereotypical images of Black womanhood during slavery were based on the myth that 'all black women were immoral and sexually loose'; Beverly Smith, 'Black Women's Health: Notes for a Course', in Hull *et al.* (eds.), *But Some of Us Are Brave*, 110, noting that 'white men for centuries have justified their sexual abuse of Black women by claiming that we are licentious, always "ready" for any sexual encounter'.
48. The following statement is probably unusual only in its candour: 'What has been said by some of our courts about an unchaste female being a comparatively rare exception is no doubt true where the population is composed largely of the Caucasian race, but we would blind ourselves to actual conditions if we adopted this rule where another race that is largely immoral constitutes an appreciable part of the population.' *Dallas* v. *State*, 76 Fla 358, 79 So 690 (1918), quoted in Note, 'Rape, Racism and the Law', 121.

Espousing precisely this view, one commentator stated in 1902: 'I sometimes hear of a virtuous Negro woman but the idea is so absolutely inconceivable to me . . . I cannot imagine such a creature as a virtuous Negro woman' ibid. 82. Such images persist in popular culture. See Paul Grein, 'Taking Stock of the Latest Pop Record Surprises', LA Times § 6 (July 7, 1988), recalling the controversy in the late 70s over a Rolling Stones recording which included the line 'Black girls just wanna get fucked all night'.

Opposition to such negative stereotypes has sometimes taken the form of sexual conservatism. 'A desperate reaction to this slanderous myth is the attempt . . . to conform to the strictest versions of patriarchal morality', Smith, 'Black Women's Health', in Hull *et al.* (eds.), *But Some of Us Are Brave*, 111. Part of this reaction is reflected in the attitudes and policies of Black schools, which have been notoriously strict in regulating the behaviour of female students. See Gail Elizabeth Wyatt, 'The Sexual Experience of Afro-American Women', in Martha Kirkpatrick (ed.), *Women's Sexual Experience: Exploration of the Dark Continent* (Plenum, 1982), 24, noting 'the differences between the predominantly Afro-American universities, where there was far more supervision regarding sexual behaviour, and the majority of white colleges, where there were fewer curfews and restrictions placed on the resident'. Any attempt to understand and critique the emphasis on Black virtue without focusing on the racist ideology that places virtue beyond the reach of Black women would be incomplete and probably incorrect.

49. Because of the way the legal system viewed chastity, Black women could not be victims of forcible rape. One commentator has noted that '[a]ccording to governing stereotypes [*sic*], chastity could not be possessed by Black women. Thus, Black women's rape charges were automatically discounted, and the issue of chastity was contested only in cases where the rape complainant was a white women.' Note, 'Rape, Racism and the Law', 126. Black women's claims of rape were not taken seriously regardless of the offender's race. A judge in 1912 said: 'This court will never take the word of a nigger against the word of a white man [concerning rape]', ibid. 120. On the other hand, lynching was considered an effective remedy for a Black man's rape of a white woman. Since rape of a white woman by a Black man was 'a crime more horrible than death', the only way to assuage society's rage and to make the woman whole again was to brutally murder the Black man: ibid. 125.

50. See 'The Rape of Black Women as a Weapon of Terror', in Gerda Lerner (ed.), *Black Women in White America* (Pantheon Books, 1972), 172–93. See also Brownmiller, *Against Our Will*. Even where Brownmiller acknowledges the use of rape as racial terrorism, she resists making a 'special case' for Black women by offering evidence that white women were raped by the Klan as well: 139. Whether or not one considers the racist rape of Black women a 'special case', such experiences are probably different. In any case, Brownmiller's treatment of the Issue raises serious questions about the ability to sustain an analysis of patriarchy without understanding its multiple intersections with racism.

51. Lerner, *Black Women in White America*, 173.

52. See generally, Note, 'Rape, Racism and the Law', 103.

53. Paula Giddings notes the combined effect of sexual and racial stereotypes: 'Black women were seen having all of the inferior qualities of white women without any of their virtues.' Giddings, *When and Where I Enter*, 82.

54. Susan Brownmiller's treatment of the Emmett Till case illustrates why anti-rape politicization makes some African Americans uncomfortable. Despite Brownmiller's quite laudable efforts to discuss elsewhere the rape of Black women and the racism involved in much of the hysteria over the Black male threat, her analysis of the Till case places the sexuality of white women, rather than racial terrorism, at centre stage. Brownmiller states: 'Rarely has one single case exposed so clearly as Till's the underlying group-male antagonisms over access to women, for what began in Bryant's store should not be misconstrued as an innocent flirtation. . . . In concrete terms, the accessibility of all white women was on review.' Brownmiller, *Against Our Will*, 272. Later, Brownmiller argues:

And what of the wolf whistle, Till's 'gesture of adolescent bravado'? We are rightly aghast that a whistle could be cause for murder but we must also accept that Emmett Till and J. W. Millam shared something in common. They both understood that the whistle was no small tweet of hubba-hubba or melodious approval for a well-turned ankle. Given the deteriorated situation . . . it was a deliberate insult just short of physical assault, a last reminder to Carolyn Bryant that this black boy, Till, had a mind to possess her. (273)

While Brownmiller seems to categorize the case as one that evidences a conflict over possession, it is regarded in African American history as a tragic dramatization of the South's pathological hatred and fear of African Americans. Till's body, mutilated beyond recognition, was viewed by thousands so that, in the words of Till's mother, 'the world could see what they did to my boy'. Juan Williams, 'Standing for Justice', in *Eyes on the Prize* (Viking, 1987), 44. The Till tragedy is also regarded as one of the historical events that bore directly on the emergence of the Civil Rights movement. '[W]ithout question it moved black America in a way the Supreme Court ruling on school desegregation could not match' (ibid.). As Williams later observed, 'the murder of Emmett Till had a powerful impact on a generation of blacks. It was this generation, those who were adolescents when Till was killed, that would soon demand justice and freedom in a way unknown in America before' (57). Thus, while Brownmiller looks at the Till case and sees the vicious struggle over the possession of a white woman, African Americans see the case as a symbol of the insane degree to which whites were willing to suppress the Black race. While patriarchal attitudes toward women's sexuality played a supporting role, to place white women centre stage in this tragedy is to manifest such confusion over racism as to make it difficult to imagine that the white anti-rape movement could be sensitive to more subtle racial tensions regarding Black women's participation in it.

55. See Anna Julia Cooper, *A Voice from the South* (Negro Universities Press, 1969 reprint of the Aldine Printing House, Ohio, 1892).

56. Ibid. 31.

57. In all fairness, I must acknowledge that my companion accompanied me to the back door. I remain uncertain, however, as to whether the gesture was an expression of solidarity or an effort to quiet my anger.

58. To this one could easily add class.

59. An anecdote illustrates this point. A group of female law professors gathered to discuss 'Isms in the Classroom'. One exercise led by Pat Cain involved each participant listing the three primary factors that described herself. Almost without exception, white women in the room listed their gender either primarily or secondarily; none listed their race. All of the women of colour listed their race first, and then their gender. This seems to suggest that identity descriptions seem to begin with the primary source of opposition with whatever the dominant norm is. See Pat Cain, *Feminist Jurisprudence: Grounding the Theories* (unpublished manuscript on file with author), 19–20, explaining the exercise and noting that 'no white woman ever mentions race, whereas every woman of color does', and that, similarly, 'straight women do not include "heterosexual" . . . whereas lesbians who are open always include "lesbian" '.

60. For a comparative discussion of Third World feminism paralleling this observation, see Kumari Jayawardena, *Feminism and Nationalism in the Third World* (Zed Books, 1986), 1–24. Jayawardena states that feminism in the Third World has been 'accepted' only within the central struggle against international domination. Women's social and political status has improved most when advancement is necessary to the broader struggle against imperialism.

61. For a discussion of how racial ideology creates a polarizing dynamic which subordinates Blacks and privileges whites, see Kimberle Crenshaw, 'Race, Reform and Retrenchment: Transformation and Legitimation in Antidiscrimination Law', *Harv L Rev*, 101 (1988), 1331, 1371–76.

62. Jack Matthews, 'Three Color Purple Actresses Talk About Its Impact', *LA Times* § 6 (31 Jan. 1986), 1; Jack Matthews, 'Some Blacks Critical of Spielberg's Purple', *LA Times* § 6 (20 Dec. 1985), 1. But see Gene Siskel, 'Does Purple Hate

Men?', *Chicago Tribune* § 13 (5 Jan. 1986), 16; Clarence Page, 'Toward a New Black Cinema', *Chicago Tribune* § 5 (12 Jan. 1986), 3.

63. A consistent problem with any negative portrayal of African Americans is that they are seldom balanced by positive images. On the other hand, most critics overlooked the positive transformation of the primary male character in *The Color Purple*.

64. Daniel P. Moynihan, *The Negro Family: The Case for National Action* (Office of Policy Planning and Research, United States Department of Labour, 1965).

65. See Lee Rainwater and William L. Yancey, *The Moynihan Report and the Politics of Controversy* (MIT Press, 1967), 427–9, containing criticisms of the Moynihan Report by, among others, Charles E. Silberman, Christopher Jencks, William Ryan, Laura Carper, Frank Riessman and Herbert Gans.

66. Ibid. 395–7: critics included Martin Luther King, Jr., Benjamin Payton, James Farmer, Whitney Young, Jr., and Bayard Rustin.

67. One of the notable exceptions is Jacquelyne Johnson Jackson, 'Black Women in a Racist Society', in *Racism and Mental Health* (University of Pittsburgh Press, 1973), 185–6.

68. *The Vanishing Black Family* (PBS Television Broadcast, Jan. 1986).

69. William Julius Wilson, *The Truly Disadvantaged: The Inner City, The Underclass and Public Policy* (University of Chicago Press, 1987).

70. Columnist Mary McGrory, applauding the show, reported that Moyers found that sex was as common in the Black ghetto as a cup of coffee. McGrory, *Moynihan was Right 21 Years Ago*, *Washington Post*, B1 and B4 (26 Jan. 1986). George Will argued that over-sexed Black men were more of a menace than Bull Conner, the Birmingham Police Chief who in 1968 achieved international notoriety by turning fire hoses on protesting school children. George Will, 'Voting Rights Won't Fix It', *Washington Post*, A23 (23 Jan. 1986).

My guess is that the programme has influenced the debate about the so-called underclass by providing graphic support to pre-existing tendencies to attribute poverty to individual immorality. During a recent and memorable discussion on the public-policy implications of poverty in the Black community, one student remarked that nothing can be done about Black poverty until Black men stop acting like 'roving penises', Black women stop having babies 'at the drop of a hat', and they all learn middle-class morality. The student cited the Moyers report as her source.

71. Although the nearly exclusive focus on the racist aspects of the programme poses both theoretical and political problems, it was entirely understandable given the racial nature of the subsequent comments that were sympathetic to the Moyers view. As is typical in discussions involving race, the dialogue regarding the Moyers programme covered more than just the issue of Black families; some commentators took the opportunity to indict not only the Black underclass, but the Black civil-rights leadership, the war on poverty, affirmative action, and other race-based remedies. See e.g. Will, 'Voting Rights Won't Fix It', A23.

72. Their difficulties can also be linked to the prevalence of an economic system and family policy that treat the nuclear family as the norm and other family units are aberrant and unworthy of societal accommodation.

73. Wilson, *The Truly Disadvantaged*, 96.

74. Ibid. 154 (suggestions include macroeconomic policies which promote balanced economic growth, a nationally oriented labour-market strategy, a child

support assurance programme, a child-care strategy, and a family allowances programme which would be both means-tested and race-specific.

75. Nor does Wilson include an analysis of the impact of gender on changes in family patterns. Consequently, little attention is paid to the conflict that may result when gender-based expectations are frustrated by economic and demographic factors. This focus on demographic and structural explanations represents an effort to regain the high ground from the Moyers/Moynihan approach which is more psychosocial. Perhaps because psychosocial explanations have come dangerously close to victim-blaming, their prevalence is thought to threaten efforts to win policy directives that might effectively address deteriorating conditions within the working-class and poor Black communities.

76. For instance, Wilson only mentions in passing the need for daycare and job training for single mothers: *The Truly Disadvantaged*, 153. No mention at all is made of other practices and policies that are racist and sexist, and that contribute to the poor conditions under which nearly half of all Black women must live.

77. Pauli Murray observes that the operation of sexism is at least the partial cause of social problems affecting Black women. See Murray, 'The Liberation of Black Women', in Jo Freeman (ed.), *Women: A Feminist Perspective* (Mayfield, 1975), 351–62.

16   The Politics of Paradigms: Gender Difference and Gender Disadvantage

Deborah L. Rhode

Traditional approaches to gender difference have alternated between exaggeration and denial. On most issues of public policy, denial has been the preferred strategy; women's special interests have remained unacknowledged and unaddressed. By contrast, policy initiatives that have spoken to gender difference have often overstated its nature and amplified its adverse consequences. Feminist responses have frequently remained entrapped in similar patterns. Many theoretical approaches that have sought to celebrate women's distinctive attributes have homogenized and essentialized their content, while strategies of denial have ignored women's particular needs and circumstances.

The following analysis surveys the limitations of traditional frameworks from both a theoretical and a policy-oriented perspective. After first reviewing certain consistent inadequacies in legal and legislative approaches, it proposes an alternative strategy, one that focuses less on gender difference and more on gender disadvantage. Such an alternative would demand close attention to context and to the diversity of women's interests over time and across boundaries such as race, class, ethnicity, and sexual orientation.

Discussion then turns to related issues in feminist theory and to limitations in conventional strategies that celebrate or deny difference. Again, the alternative proposed here is a less dualistic, more contextual approach. Under this framework, the focus is less on difference *per se* than on the process by which sex-linked attributes acquire cultural meaning and significance. Such a perspective focuses not simply on women's differences from men, but also on their differences from each other, and on the ways that social context mediates gender relationships.

Before discussing the merits of these alternative approaches, one threshold observation is in order. How we talk about paradigms in

Chapter 8 in G. Bock and S. James (eds.), *Beyond Equality and Difference* (Routledge, 1992), 149–63. Reprinted by permission.

itself presupposes a choice of paradigms. My choice is to resist the temptations of theoretical purity. Rather than thinking in terms of either/or—sameness vs. difference, difference vs. disadvantage—we should focus on issues of when and why. If the subject is gender, we cannot entirely escape conventional questions of difference. We can, however, resist their limitations on fundamental issues of feminist theory and practice.[1]

I

Feminism in general, and the American women's movement in particular, emerged against a backdrop of social, economic, and political inequalities between the sexes. The prevailing assumption was that woman's nature was to nurture. Gender inequality appeared biologically grounded, spiritually ordained, and culturally essential.[2] Woman's brain was too small, her powers of reasoning too limited, and her 'tender susceptibility' too unsuited for demanding pursuits.[3]

According to scientific wisdom, women who diverted scarce physical resources from reproductive to productive pursuits risked permanent sterility.[4] Legal decision-makers similarly perceived a 'law of Nature and the Creator' that decreed domesticity as destiny and that justified females' exclusion from professional, political, and civic responsibilities.[5] Although the precise method of divine communication was never fully revealed, its message was widely acknowledged. Until the last century, women lacked the right to vote, to enter contracts, to hold property, or to stand for political office.[6]

Yet if the exaggeration of gender difference served to legitimate gender hierarchy, the denial of gender difference had similar consequences. Women's special vulnerability to sexual violence, harassment, and economic dependence was, for the most part, politely overlooked. Among married couples, rarely did the force of law intervene against the consequences of force. Spousal 'chastisement', or 'domestic disturbances', the law's euphemisms for wife-beating, almost never resulted in formal sanctions.[7] Harassment had no conceptual cubby-hole, and social welfare policies did little to address the causes or consequences of female poverty.[8] Although legal decision-makers often talked of 'we the people', they were not in fact using the term generically. Women were largely unacknowledged in official texts, uninvited in their formulation and, before the last quarter-century, largely uninvolved in their interpretation.

Early feminist responses to gender inequality challenged but also presupposed its underlying assumptions. One strategy was to deny the extent or essential nature of gender difference. Beginning in the late nineteenth century, many activists joined Elizabeth Cady Stanton in dismissing as 'mysterious Twaddle' the 'sentimental talk about the male and female element'.[9] By contrast, other feminists premised their arguments for women's equality on women's difference. Jane Addams, one of the early American proponents of this position, cast mothers as 'municipal housekeepers', and many European theorists sounded similar themes.[10] With her 'high code of morals, women would yet purify politics'.[11]

In some respects, the ambivalence about difference had its advantages. On issues of equal rights, feminists could embrace either perspective and arrive at similar conclusions. To the extent women were the same as men, both should enjoy the same status; to the extent women were different, their distinctive perspectives and concerns deserved a role in public life. Yet this dual strategy also carried a cost. The preoccupation with women's differences from men obscured women's differences from each other, and deflected attention from the class, racial, and ethnic bias of the early feminist agenda.[12] Claims about women's special moral sensibility oversimplified and over-claimed its importance, while ignoring its constraints. Moreover on some issues, such as protective statutes, competing views of difference could not happily coexist. As a consequence, feminists too often found themselves fighting with each other over the value of protection rather than uniting to challenge the conditions that made protection so valuable.

Such issues arose in the United States around the turn of this century as increasing numbers of state legislatures began passing regulations governing maximum hours, minimum wages, and working conditions. Controversies increased after a pair of Supreme Court decisions struck down such regulations for male workers as a violation of their freedom to contract, but upheld restrictions for female employees in light of their special vulnerabilities and reproductive responsibilities.[13] Even after the Supreme Court reversed its holding as to male workers, the disputes over gender-specific protections persisted. In part, the debate centred on concerns about the fate of such protections under a proposed Constitutional Equal Rights Amendment. Underlying that issue were deeper questions about mandates of formal equality in circumstances of social inequality.

Those same questions have resurfaced in the last decade, as the American women's movement divided over the merits of state legislation requiring employers to grant job-protected maternity leave but not paternity, parental, or temporary medical disability leaves.

Then, as now, feminists who supported gender-specific policies began from the premise that women are different and that their special needs justify special regulatory intervention. Earlier in the century, the focus was on female employees' unequal labour-force status and unequal domestic burdens. Most women workers were crowded into low-paying jobs with few advancement opportunities and little likelihood of improving their status through unionization. Female employees were also far more likely than their male counterparts to assume major family responsibilities, and the combination of those duties with prevailing twelve- to fourteen-hour work shifts imposed enormous hardships. For most of these women, statutory regulation of hours and wages meant a substantial improvement in their quality of life.[14]

Yet as feminists who opposed gender-specific statutes also noted, such protections made women more expensive, and often protected them out of any jobs desirable to male competitors. The ideology of gender difference served to rationalize gender exclusions in occupations ranging from bartending and shoeshining to military service. In some contexts, regulation also increased female unemployment and reinforced assumptions about the appropriateness of unequal family roles.[15]

Although both sides of the protection labour debate claimed to speak for women, women's interests were more divided than partisans acknowledged. Those who denied the significance of gender difference frequently understated the obstacles to securing sex-neutral mandates and the value of sex-specific regulation. For the majority of workers, clustered in female-dominated jobs, such regulation brought significant improvements. Yet those who stressed accommodation of gender difference often underestimated its price. Special protection for women restricted their employment opportunities, and thus reinforced the social inequalities that protection was meant to address. Moreover, the ideology of paternalism spilled over to other welfare, family, and criminal-law contexts in which paternalism was less advantageous.[16]

The contemporary debate about gender difference and public policy involves similar complexities. In the United States, major attention has focused on issues involving pregnancy and parental leaves, and on women's exclusion from occupational settings thought to present special demands or risks, such as military service or toxic work-sites. Here again, sex-linked differences have been both overlooked and overvalued. On some issues, courts have transformed biological distinctions into cultural imperatives. On other questions, women's special needs have remained unmet.

What makes the United States pregnancy cases particularly instructive as sex discrimination opinions is the Supreme Court's initial unwillingness to treat them as such. During the mid-1970s, a majority of Justices upheld policies providing employee benefits for virtually all medical treatment except that related to childbirth. Yet in the first of these cases, the court relegated the entire discussion of discrimination to a footnote. There the majority announced its somewhat novel conclusion that pregnancy policies did not even involve 'gender as such'. Rather, employers were simply drawing a distinction between—in the court's memorable phrase—'pregnant women' and 'non-pregnant persons'.[17] Preoccupied with issues of difference rather than disadvantage, the majority perceived no issue of discrimination; since pregnancy was a 'unique' and 'additional' disability for women, employers were entitled to exclude it from insurance coverage.[18]

Never did the majority explain why only pregnancy was 'unique', while men's disabilities, such as prostatectomies, were fully covered. Rather, the court's characterization assumed what should have been at issue and made the assumption from a male reference point. Men's physiology set the standard against which women's claims appeared only additional.

Following this line of cases, intense lobbying prompted passage of the federal Pregnancy Discrimination Act, which provided that pregnancy should be treated 'the same as' other medical risks for employment-related purposes.[19] This remains, however, one of the many contexts in which denials of difference serve only to reinforce the disadvantages that have accompanied it. The Act requires equality in form, not equality in fact. It demands only that employers treat pregnancy like other disabilities. It does not affirmatively require adequate disability policies. In the absence of statutory mandates, such policies have been slow to develop. Recent data have indicated that about three-fifths of female workers were not entitled to wage replacement, and a third could not count on returning to their same job after a normal period of leave. The United States has remained alone among major industrialized nations in failing to provide such benefits.[20]

In response to such inadequacies, many feminists have supported requirements that employers provide pregnancy leave whether or not leave is available for other disabilities or caretaking needs. Those who justify such policies generally begin from the premise that women are unequally situated with respect to reproduction. While no-leave policies pose hardships for both sexes concerning the disabilities they share, such policies present an additional burden for women. As a matter of principle, pregnancy should not have to seem just like other disabilities to obtain protection. As a practical matter, until legislatures are prepared to mandate adequate benefits for all workers, partial coverage seems like an appropriate goal.[21]

The danger, however, as other feminists have noted, is that settling for the proverbial half a loaf could erode efforts for more comprehensive approaches. Legislation that makes women more expensive also creates incentives for covert discrimination. Many feminists are unwilling to see women once again 'protected out' of jobs desirable to men.[22] To require maternity, but not paternity or parental leaves, is to reinforce a division of child-rearing responsibilities that has been more separate than equal. Difference-oriented approaches in various employment contexts have led to the establishment of special 'mummy tracks' that often turn into mummy traps.[23]

On these sorts of issues, a focus on differences is utterly unilluminating and misrepresents the controversy it seeks to resolve. Women are both the same and different. They are different in their needs at childbirth but the same in their needs for broader medical, child-rearing, and caretaking policies. To know which side of the sameness/difference dichotomy to emphasize in legal contexts requires some further analytic tool.

The advantage of talking in terms of disadvantage is that it emphasizes a different set of questions and encourages a more contextual analysis. The issue is not difference *per se*, but the consequences of addressing it in a particular way under particular social and historical circumstances. Such a framework demands acknowledgement of the variation in women's interests across race, class, and ethnicity, and recognizes that trade-offs may be necessary in terms of short- and long-term objectives.

From this perspective, the preferable strategy for resolving issues such as employee leave policy should be to press for the broadest possible coverage for all workers. While the importance of pregnancy benefits should not be overlooked, neither should they be over-emphasized. More employers provide job-protected childbirth leave than other forms of assistance that are equally critical to workers and their dependants. Pregnancy-related policies affect most women workers for relatively brief intervals. The absence of broader disability, health, child-rearing, and caretaking assistance remains a chronic problem for the vast majority of employees, male and female, throughout their working lives.[24] In such contexts, both men and women stand to gain if we press for more by refusing to settle for less. The stakes are not just equality for women but the quality of life for all individuals.[25]

Similar observations are applicable in a wide variety of other policy contexts. Many of the inadequacies in contemporary equal protection law stem from its preoccupation with difference. Traditional frameworks require only similar treatment for those similarly situated; sex discrimination is permissible if the sexes differ in ways relevant to a valid regulatory objective. Yet what differences matter and what objectives are legitimate remain open to dispute, and the responses have been less than satisfying. For example, women's continued exclusion from military leadership, combat, and draft registration systems reflects continued stereotypes about gender difference. Despite women's demonstrated competence in police, prison, and combat-related work, the assumption persists that they cannot or should not be trusted in the most demanding military positions.[26] So too, female workers have lost employment because of their different susceptibility to reproductive hazards and their different family obligations. Relatively little effort has been directed towards restructuring workplaces to minimize hazards or accommodate caretaking demands.[27]

To make significant progress will require an alternative form of analysis, one less fixated on difference and more attentive to the disadvantages that it has entailed. The most pressing problems now facing women do not generally find them 'similarly situated' to men: poverty, sexual violence, reproductive freedom, family responsibilities. The discourse of difference will sometimes have a place, but it should begin analysis, not end it. As deconstructionists remind us, women are always already the same and different: the same in their humanity, different in their anatomy. Whichever category we privilege in our legal discourse, the other will always be waiting to disrupt it.[28] By constantly presenting gender issues in difference-oriented frameworks, conventional legal discourse implicitly biases analysis. To pronounce women either the same or different from men allows men to remain the standard.

Under the disadvantage framework proposed here, a determination that the sexes are not 'similarly situated' only begins discussion. Analysis would then turn on whether legal recognition of sex-based differences is more likely to reduce or to reinforce sex-based disparities in political power, social status, and economic security. Such an approach would entail a more searching review than has generally been apparent in cases involving gender. Its focus would extend beyond the rationality of differential treatment and the legitimacy of governmental ends. Rather, this alternative would require that governmental objectives include a substantive commitment to gender equality—to a society in which women as a group are not disadvantaged in controlling their own destiny. So, for example, in employment settings, the issue becomes not whether gender is relevant to the job as currently structured, but how the workplace can be restructured to make gender less relevant. What sort of public and private sector initiatives are necessary to avoid penalizing parenthood? What changes in working schedules, hiring and promotion criteria, leave policies and childcare options are necessary to reconcile home and family responsibilities?

This alternative strategy will demand substantial changes in our legal paradigms and social priorities. It will also require a deeper understanding of the harms of sex-based classifications and the complexity of strategies designed to address them. Shifting focus from gender difference to gender disadvantage will not always supply definitive answers, but it can at least suggest the right questions. It can also point up the limitations of traditional strategies, which have to often offered only access to, not alteration of, existing social institutions.

This is not to discount the difficulties in applying a disadvantage framework. Such an approach confronts many of the same difficulties in assessing women's interests that plague other paradigms. The strategy proposed here at least minimizes these difficulties by limiting its aspirations and acknowledging its complexities. The point is not to advocate some grand theoretical structure, but rather to suggest an approach that will be useful in particular contexts under particular social conditions. We need not commit ourselves to some abstract assessment of the origins or extent of gender difference. Nor do we need to determine what women's 'authentic' interests may be; we know more than enough about what they will not be to provide a current legal agenda. Changes in law will not of themselves ensure our arrival at any predetermined destination, but they can change our pace and direction of travel, and our awareness of choices along the way. By challenging gender inequalities in political power, economic resources, and social status, a disadvantage framework imposes no fixed and final determinations of women's nature or women's interests. Rather, such an approach encourages us to confront that issue with greater sensitivity to social context and to the diversity of concerns at issue.

II

The limitations of difference as a policy framework have parallels in other more theoretical contexts. As previous discussion indicated, feminists have long differed over difference. During the last two decades, these controversies gained new dimensions. One branch of the feminist movement focused primary energy on challenging difference and exposing the cultural construction of ostensibly natural attributes.[29] By contrast, other theorists began emphasizing the centrality of sexual difference although disagreeing about its origins and consequences. Their discourse reflects a broad range of perspectives that do not easily fit under any single label. For present purposes, it is enough to summarize certain common themes which can be loosely grouped under the term 'relational feminism'.[30]

What unites these approaches is a focus on women's reproductive role and the nurturing relationships that it has encouraged. Some feminists, including those working within contemporary French traditions, attach overarching significance to biological difference.[31] Other theorists emphasize socialization and/or subordination; their frameworks underscore women's need to obtain status, control and approval through attachments to others.[32] A third approach draws most heavily on psychoanalytic theory. According to this last account, children develop closer attachments to a primary caretaker of the same sex. Individuals who form strong attachments in early life will be more likely later to define themselves in relation to others and to develop close nurturing bonds. Since more primary caretakers have been and continue to be female, girls grow up with a greater inclination towards, and capacity for, caretaking roles.[33]

One other relational feminist approach, which has been especially influential in the United States, focuses not on the origins of gender difference but on its normative significance. From this perspective, the problem for contemporary western women stems less from the exaggeration of difference than from its devaluation. This school of thought, popularized by Carol Gilligan, argues that conventional moral and legal theories have placed too great a priority on abstract rights, and too little to concrete relationships. Based on empirical and qualitative research, Gilligan claims that women tend to reason in 'a different voice', which is especially attentive to care, co-operation, and context in the resolution of human problems.[34]

Relational feminism has made important contributions, but they come at a cost. Its strengths lie in its demand that the values traditionally associated with women be valued, and that public policy focus on restructuring social institutions, rather than just assimilating women within them. By affirming characteristics traditionally associated with women, such approaches can encourage greater political cohesiveness and collective self-esteem. As other commentary in this collection suggests, making values such as empathy and nurturance more central to political discourse has significant transformative possibilities. Relational feminism can also provide theoretical underpinnings for legal policies that are responsive to women's distinctive concerns.

Yet as was true during earlier feminist campaigns, this validation of difference raises its own set of problems at both strategic and substantive levels. As a strategic matter, affirmation of women's voice can deflect attention from the structural circumstances that construct and constrain it.[35] Emphasizing males' association with abstract rationality and females' concern for interpersonal relationships reinforces long-standing stereotypes that have restricted opportunities for both sexes. However feminist in inspiration, any dualistic world view is likely to be appropriated for non-feminist objectives. As the previous discussion reflected, the perception that nurturance is women's responsibility has long served to justify women's under-representation in demanding positions and to reinforce roles that are more separate than equal.

Moreover, as a substantive matter, it is by no means clear how different women's 'different' voice is. Relational feminist work has generally failed to address variations across culture, class, race, ethnicity, age, and sexual orientation.[36] For example, Gilligan's data drew on small, unrepresentative samples, and most empirical studies of moral development do not disclose significant gender distinctions.[37] Nor does related research reveal the kind of strong sex-linked differences that relational feminism would suggest; there are few psychological attributes on which the sexes consistently vary.[38] For even these attributes, such as aggression, spatial ability, and helping behaviour, gender typically accounts for only about 5 per cent of the variance; the similarities between men and women are far greater than the disparities, and small statistical distinctions do not support sweeping sex-based dichotomies.[39]

Gender differences fall along a continuum, and context matters greatly in eliciting traits traditionally associated with women.[40] When pressures for sex-typed behaviour are strong, individuals generally will behave in expected ways, which helps transform sex-based stereotypes into self-fulfilling prophecies.[41] It is misleading to discuss gender-related attributes as if they can be abstracted from the distinctive social expectations, opportunities and hierarchies that are also linked to gender.[42]

Such findings suggest reasons to qualify relational claims but not to deny all of their potential implications. Although psychological variations between the sexes are relatively minor and socially contingent, the variation in their roles and experience continues to be substantial. As relational feminists have noted, the fact that men and women give similar answers in most surveys of moral reasoning does not mean that they would choose similar ways of framing the question.[43] Nor is it clear that most women would structure workplace policy and governmental priorities in the same way as men if given greater decision-making opportunities.[44] To make sense of gender dynamics, we need frameworks that neither overstate nor undervalue gender difference.

Reformulating the problem in these terms builds on more contextual, less dualistic strains of contemporary feminist theory, those concerned with differences within, as well as between, the sexes. Post-modern theoretical accounts have drawn increasing attention to the multiple forces that constitute women's identity across race, ethnicity, class, age, religion, sexual orientation, and so forth.[45] Yet this focus has also underscored a long-standing paradox in feminist theory and practice. What gives feminism its unique perspective is its claim to speak from women's experience. But that same experience counsels attention to the differences in women's backgrounds, perceptions, and priorities. There is no 'generic woman', nor any monolithic 'woman's point of view'.[46] Feminism has increasingly become 'feminisms', which complicates the search for theoretical coherence and political cohesion.[47]

Yet the factors that divide us could also be a basis for enriching our analysis and broadening our coalitions. As Audre Lorde has noted, it is not 'our differences which separate [us as] women but our reluctance to recognize those differences and deal effectively with the distances that have resulted'.[48] The same values that underpin feminism's struggle against gender inequality demand its opposition to other forms of group-based disadvantage. We cannot empower all women without challenging the multiple sources of disempowerment that many women face. The problem is how to make such challenges a basis for psychological affinity and political activism.

To realize its full potential, the feminist movement must both expand its practical agenda and qualify its theoretical claims. No single categorical framework can adequately address the dynamics of difference. We remain caught between the need to affirm our gender identity and the need to transcend its constraints, to claim solidarity and to acknowledge diversity. The sameness/difference dilemma cannot be resolved; it can only be reformulated. Our focus needs to shift from difference to disadvantage and to the social conditions that perpetuate it.[49]

To challenge those conditions, our strategies must rest on feminist principles, not feminine stereotypes. The issues of greatest concern to women are not simply 'women's issues'. Although the feminist agenda incorporates values traditionally associated with women, the stakes in its realization are ones that both sexes share.

Notes

1. For a fuller exploration of these themes see D. Rhode, *Justice and Gender* (Cambridge, Mass. and London; Harvard University Press, 1989); D. Rhode, 'Theoretical Perspectives on Sexual Difference', and 'Definitions of Difference', in D. Rhode (ed.), *Theoretical Perspectives on Sexual Difference* (New Haven and London: Yale University Press, 1990), 1, 197; D. Rhode, 'The No Problem Problem: Feminist Challenges and Cultural Change', *Yale Law Journal*, 100 (1991).

2. See, generally, S. Okin, *Women in Western Political Thought* (Princeton: Princeton University Press, 1979); E. Flexner, *A Century of Struggle: The Women's Rights Movement in the United States*, revised edn. (Cambridge, Mass.: Harvard University Press, 1975); L. Newman (ed.), *Men's Ideas/Women's Realities* (New York: Pergamon Press, 1985).

3. S. Gould, *The Mismeasure of Man* (New York and London: Norton, 1981), 103–22; H. Maudseley, 'Sex and Mind in Education', in J. Newman, *Men's Ideas/Women's Realities*, 197–219; J. Hyde, 'Meta Analysis and the Psychology of Gender Differences', *Signs*, 16 (1990), 54, 56–7; *In re Goodell*, 39 Wis. 232, 244–5 (1875).

4. B. Ehrenreich and D. English, *For Her Own Good: 150 Years of the Experts' Advice to Women* (Garden City, NY: Anchor, 1978), 113–17; C. Smith-Rosenberg, *Disorderly Conduct* (New York: Knopf, 1984), 259–60; E. Clarke, *Sex in Education* (New York: Houghton Mifflin 1873).

5. *Bradwell v. State*, 83 US 130, 137 (1872) (upholding exclusion of women from bar).

6. W. Blackstone, *Commentaries on the Laws of England* (Oxford: Oxfordshire

Professional Books, 15th edn., 1982); Rhode, *Justice and Gender*, 9–10, 20–9; M. Salmon, 'The Legal Status of Women in Early America: A Reappraisal', *Law and History Review*, 1 (1983), 129–51.

7. *State* v. *Hussey*, 44 NC 60, 61 (1824); *State* v. *Black*, 60 NC (Winn.) 266 (1864); E. Pleck, 'Wife Beating in Nineteenth Century America', *Victimology*, 4 (1979), 60; N. Oppenlander, 'The Evolution of Law and Wife Abuse', *Law and Policy Quarterly*, 3 (1981), 382–405.

8. For sexual harassment see C. MacKinnon, *Sexual Harassment of Working Women: A Case of Sex Discrimination* (New Haven and London: Yale University Press, 1979); M. Bularzik, 'Sexual Harassment at the Workplace: Historical Notes', *Radical America*, 12 (July–August 1978), 25–44. For welfare policies see M. Abramovitz, *Regulating the Lives of Women* (Boston, Mass.: South End Press, 1988); M. Katz, *Poverty and Policy in American History: Social Welfare Policy from Colonial Times to the Present* (New York: Academic Press, 1983), and *In the Shadow of the Poorhouse: A Social History of Welfare in America* (New York: Basic Books, 1986).

9. E. Stanton, quoted in W. Leach, *True Love and Perfect Union* (New York: Basic Books, 1980), 147.

10. J. Addams, 'Why Women Should Vote', in F. Bjorkman and A. Porritt, *Woman Suffrage: History, Arguments and Results* (New York: National Woman Suffrage Publishing Co., 1917), 110–29; J. Addams, 'The Modern City and the Municipal Franchise for Women', in S. Anthony and I. Harper (eds.), *History of Women Suffrage* (Indianapolis, Ind.: Hallenback Press, 1902), iv, 178. For related arguments by European feminists see K. Offen, 'Defining Feminism: A Comparative Historical Approach', *Signs*, 14 (1988), 119.

11. Anthony and Harper, *History*, 39, 308–9.

12. See P. Giddings, *When and Where I Enter: The Impact of Black Women on Race and Sex in America* (New York: Morrow, 1984), 127–9; B. Hooks, *Ain't I a Woman? Black Women and Feminism* (Boston: South End Press, 1981), 130–1; R. Terborg-Penn, 'Discrimination against Afro-American Women in the Women's Movement, 1830–1920', in S. Harley and R. Terborg-Penn (eds.), *The Afro-American Woman: Struggles and Images* (Port Washington, NY: Kennikut Press, 1978), 17–18.

13. *Lochner* v. *New York*, 198 US 45 (1905); *Mueller* v. *Oregon*, 208 US 412 (1908).

14. Women's Bureau, Bulletin 65, *The Effects of Labor Legislation on the Employment Opportunities of Women* (Washington, DC: US Government Printing Office, 1928; J. Baer, *The Chains of Protection* (Westport, Conn.: Greenwood Press, 1978; E. Baker, *Protective Labor Legislation* (New York: AMS Press, 1979; N. Cott, *The Grounding of Modern Feminism* (New Haven and London: Yale University Press, 1987).

15. J. Baer, *The Chains of Protection* (Westport, Conn.; Greenwood Press, 1978); A. Kessler Harris, *Out to Work* (New York: Oxford University Press, 1980); E. Landes, 'The Effect of State Maximum Hours Laws on the Employment of Women', *Journal of Political Economy*, 88 (1980), 476.

16. J. Johnston and C. Knapp, 'Sex Discrimination by Law: A Study in Judicial Perspective', *New York University Law Review*, 46 (1971), 675; W. Williams, 'Equality's Riddle: Pregnancy and the Equal Treatment–Special Treatment Debate', *New York University Review of Law and Social Change*, 13 (1985), 325; F. Olsen, 'From False Paternalism to False Equality: Assaults on Feminist

Community: Illinois', *University of Michigan Law Journal*, 58 (1986), 869–95; Rhode, 'Definitions of Difference', 200–11.

17. *Geduldig* v. *Aiello*, 417 US 484, n. 21 (1974); *General Electric Co.* v. *Gilbert*, 429 US 125 (1976).

18. *Geduldig* v. *Aiello*, 417 US 484, n. 21 (1974); *General Electric Co.* v. *Gilbert*, 429 US 125 (1976); K. Bartlett, 'Pregnancy and the Constitution: The Uniqueness Trap', *California Law Review*, 62 (1974), 1532.

19. 92 Stat. 2076 (Oct. 31, 1978).

20. S. Kammerman and A. Kahn, *The Responsive Workplace* (New York: Columbia University Press, 1987); Congressional Caucus for Women's Issues, fact sheet on parental leave legislation (Washington, DC, 1986); Rhode, 'The No-Problem Problem'.

21. L. Finley, 'Transcending Equality Theory: A Way Out of the Maternity and Workplace Debate', *Columbia University Law Review*, 86 (1986), 1118; H. Kay, 'Equality and Difference: The Case of Pregnancy', *Berkeley Women's Law Journal*, 1 (1985), 1.

22. Williams, 'Equality Riddle'; National Organization for Women, Brief in *California Federal Savings* v. *Guerra*, 479 US 272 (1987).

23. J. Kingston, 'Women in the Law Say Path is Limited by Mommy-Track', *New York Times* (8 Aug. 1988), A1. See T. Lewin, 'Women Say they Still Face Obstacles as Lawyers', *New York Times* (4 Dec. 1989), A15: 90 per cent of surveyed women lawyers believed their career would be slowed or blocked by accepting part-time or flexible-time schedules.

24. N. Taub, 'From Parental Leaves to Nurturing Leaves', *New York University Review of Law and Social Change*, 13 (1985), 381; Williams, 'Equality's Riddle', 325.

25. R. Spalter-Roth, *Unnecessary Losses: Costs to Americans for the Lack of Family and Medical Leave* (Washington, DC: Institute for Women's Policy Research, 1988).

26. For assumptions about women's unsuitability for combat see W. Webb, 'Women Can't Fight', in N. Davidson (ed.), *Gender Sanity* (New York: Lanham, 1989), 208; M. Levin, *Feminism and Freedom* (New Brunswick, NJ: Transaction, 1987), 239; and sources cited in Rhode, *Justice and Gender*, 98–100. See also *Rostker* v. *Goldberg*, 453 US 57 (1984), upholding male-only registration system for military service. For evidence concerning female performances see M. Binkin and S. Bach, *Women and the Military* (Washington, DC: Brookings Institution, 1977), 81–91; L. Laflin, *Women in Battles* (New York: Abelard Schuman, 1967), 10, 22, 62–79; H. Rogan, *Mixed Company: Women in the Modern Army* (New York: Putnam's, 1981), 258; J. Steihm, *Bring Me Men and Women: Mandated Change at the US Air Force Academy* (Berkeley, Calif.: University of California Press, 1981), 129–30, 167, 199, 250; E. Gemmette, 'Armed Combat: the Woman's Movement Mobilizes Troops in Readiness for the Inevitable Constitutional Attack on the Combat Exclusion for Women in the Military', *Woman's Rights Law Reporter*, 12 (1990), 89–102; L. Kornblum, 'Woman Warriors in a Men's World: The Combat Exclusion', *Law and Inequality*, 2 (1984), 351, 395–428.

27. For workplace safety see M. Becker, 'From *Muller* v. *Oregon* to fetal vulnerability policies', *University of Chicago Law Review*, 53 (1986), 1219–45; W. Chavkin (ed.), *Double Exposure: Women's Health Hazards on the Job and at Home* (New York: Monthly Review Press, 1984). For work–family conflicts see Rhode,

Justice and Gender, 172–5, and 'The No-Problem Problem'; S. Kamerman and A. Kahn, *The Responsive Workplace* (New York: Columbia University Press, 1987); N. Dowd, 'Work and Family: Restructuring the Workplace' *Arizona Law Review*, 32 (1990), 431–500.

28. J. Derrida, *Of Grammatology*, trans. G. Spivak (Baltimore: Johns Hopkins University Press, 1977); K. Silverman, *The Subject of Semiotics* (New York: Oxford University Press, 1983).

29. See e.g. A. Fausto-Sterling, *Myths of Gender* (New York: Basic Books, 1987); R. Lowe and R. Hubbard (eds.), *Women's Nature: Rationalizations of Inequality* (New York: Pergamon Press, 1983); A. Eagley, *Sex Differences in Social Behavior: A Social Role Interpretation* (Hillsdale, NJ: Erlbaum, 1987); R. Hubbard, 'The Political Nature of Human Nature', in Rhode, *Theoretical Perspectives*, 63.

30. See Offen, 'Defining Feminism', 134.

31. See C. Duchen, *Feminism in France* (London and Boston: Routledge and Kegan Paul, 1986); E. Marks and I. de Courtivron (eds.), *New French Feminisms: An Anthology* (Amherst, Mass.: University of Massachusetts Press, 1981); T. Moi, *Sexual Textual Politics: Feminist Literary Theory* (London and New York: Methuen, 1985); R. West, 'Jurisprudence and Gender', *University of Chicago Law Review*, 5 (1988), 1.

32. See C. MacKinnon, M. Dunlap, E. Dubois, C. Gilligan, and C. Menkel-Meadow, 'Feminist Discourse, Moral Values, and the Law: A Conversation', *Buffalo Law Review*, 34 (1985), 11, 71–4: comments of MacKinnon emphasizing subordination; E. Maccoby, 'Gender and Relationships', *American Psychology*, 45 (1990), 513, 516–19: emphasizing peer socialization.

33. N. Chodorow, *The Reproduction of Mothering: Psychoanalytic Feminism and the Sociology of Gender* (Berkeley: University of California Press, 1978); D. Dinnerstein, *The Mermaid and the Minotaur: Sexual Arrangements and the Human Malaise* (New York: Harper and Row, 1976); N. Chodorow, 'Psychoanalytic Feminism and the Psychoanalytic in the Psychology of Women', in Rhode, *Theoretical Perspectives*, 114.

34. C. Gilligan, *In a Different Voice: Psychological Theory and Women's Development* (Cambridge, Mass., and London: Harvard University Press, 1982).

35. R. Hare-Martin and J. Maracek, 'Gender and the Meaning of Difference: Postmodernism and Psychology', in R. Hare-Mustin and J. Maracek (eds.), *Making a Difference* (New Haven and London: Yale University Press, 1990), 22, 52. See also MacKinnon *et al.*, 'Feminist Discourse', 74: comments of MacKinnon, claiming that the voice Gilligan describes is the voice of the victim.

36. N. Fraser and L. Nicholson, 'Social Criticism without Philosophy: An Encounter Between Feminism and Postmodernism', in L. Nicholson (ed.), *Feminism/Postmodernism* (New York: Routledge, 1990), 19; J. Stacy and B. Thorne, 'The Missing Feminist Revolution in Sociology', *Social Problems*, 32 (1985), 301.

37. For critiques of Gilligan's methodology see C. Epstein, *Deceptive Distinctions: Sex, Gender, and the Social Order* (New Haven and London: Yale University Press, 1988), 76–94; S. Benhabib, 'The Generalized and the Concrete Other: The Kohlberg–Gilligan Controversy and Feminist Theory', in D. Cornell and S. Benhabib, *Feminism as Critique: Essays on the Politics of Gender in Late-Capitalist Societies* (Cambridge: Polity Press, 1987), 77–9; A. Colby and

W. Damon, 'Listening to a Different Voice: A Review of Gilligan's *In a Difference Voice*', in M. Walsh (ed.), *The Psychology of Women: Ongoing Debates* (New Haven and London: Yale University Press, 1987), 321; C. Greeno and E. Maccoby, 'How Different is the Different Voice?', *Signs*, 11 (1986), 310; see also Walsh, *Psychology*, 275–7, bibliography. For related criticisms of psychoanalytic theories such as those found in Chodorow and Dinnerstein's work see Fraser and Nicholson, 'Social Criticism'.

38. Eagley, *Sex Differences*; E. Maccoby and C. Jacklin, *The Psychology of Sex Differences* (Stanford, Calif.: Stanford University Press, 1974); Maccoby, 'Gender', 513–15; K. Deaux and M. Kite, 'Thinking about Gender', in B. Hess and M. Feree (eds.), *Analyzing Gender* (Beverly Hills, Calif.: Sage Publications, 1987), 93–4; Hyde, 'Meta Analysis', 64–8.

39. Epstein, *Deceptive Distinctions*; K. Deaux, 'From Individual Difference to Social Categories: Analysis of a Decade's Research on Gender', *American Psychology*, 39 (1984), 105; K. Deaux and B. Major, 'A Social-Psychological Model of Gender', in Rhode, *Theoretical Perspectives*, 89; and sources cited in notes 38 and 40.

40. Eagley, *Sex Differences*, 27–31, 125–32; Deaux and Kite, 'Thinking About Gender'; Epstein, *Deceptive Distinctions*; B. Thorne, 'Children and Gender: Constructions of Difference', in Rhode, *Theoretical Perspectives*, 100; R. Kanter, *Men and Women of the Corporation* (New York: Basic Books, 1977), 206–10.

41. R. Unger, 'Imperfect Reflections of Reality', in Hare-Mustin and Maracek, *Making a Difference*, 102–6.

42. B. Lott, 'Dual Natures or Learned Behavior', in Hare-Mustin and Maracek, *Making a Difference*, 70, noting that if average differences between women and men are attributed to gender rather than to different experiences correlated with gender, description is confused with explanation.

43. C. Gilligan, 'Reply', *Signs*, 11 (1986), 324, 328–31.

44. See e.g. J. Roesner, 'Ways Women Lead', *Harvard Business Review* (Nov.–Dec. 1990), 119, 120, finding that in certain medium-size organizational settings, women leaders are more likely than men to practise interactive leadership, i.e. to share knowledge and power, to encourage participation, and to enhance subordinates' self-worth.

45. C. Di Stefano, 'Dilemmas of Difference: Feminism, Modernity and Postmodernism', in Nicholson, *Feminism/Postmodernism*, 73; J. Flax, 'Postmodernism and Gender Relations in Feminist Theory', *Signs*, 12 (1987), 621, 634–9; R. Gagnier, 'Feminist Postmodernism: The End of Feminism or the Ends of Theory?', in Rhode, *Theoretical Perspectives*, 26.

46. E. Spellman, *Inessential Woman: The Problems of Exclusion in Feminist Thought* (Boston: Beacon Press, 1988), 114, 167; D. Rhode, 'The Woman's Point of View', *Journal of Legal Education*, 38 (1988), 39, 41, 44. For the failure of much feminist jurisprudence to take adequate account of diversity see A. Harris, 'Race and Essentialism in Feminist Legal Theory', *Stanford Law Review*, 42 (1990), 581, 585–608.

47. L. Alcoff, 'Cultural Feminism versus Post-Structuralism: The Identity Crisis in Feminist Theory', *Signs*, 13 (1988), 405; S. Bordo, 'Feminist Postmodernism and Gender Skepticism', in Nicholson, *Feminism/Postmodernism*, 133, 134–42; S. Harding, 'The Instability of the Analytic Categories of Feminist Theory', *Signs*, 11 (1986), 645, 647–64; E. Keller, 'Holding the Center of Feminist Theory', *Women's Studies International Forum*, 12 (1989), 313, 314; A. Rich,

'Disloyal to Civilization: Feminism, Racism, Cynephobia', in *On Lies, Secrets and Silence* (New York: Norton, 1975), 275, 299.

48. A. Lorde, *Sister Outsider* (Trumansberg, NY: Crossing Press, 1984), 116.

49. C. MacKinnon, *Towards a Feminist Theory of the State* (Cambridge, Mass., and London: Harvard University Press, 1989), 117–25, 180–8, 306–13; Rhode, *Justice and Gender* and *Theoretical Perspectives*. For an account of relational frameworks that focus on the construction and consequences of difference, see M. Minow, *Making All the Difference* (Ithaca, NY: Cornell University Press, 1990), 18, 19–23, 41–2, 56–60, 217–19, 375–7.

Part VI. Feminism and Citizenship

Antigone's Daughters

Jean Bethke Elshtain

This essay advances a note of caution. It argues that feminists should approach the modern bureaucratic state from a standpoint of scepticism that keeps alive a critical distance between feminism and statism, between female self-identity and a social identity tied to the public–political world revolving around the structures, institutions, values, and ends of the state. The basis for my caution and scepticism is a sober recognition that any political order in our time which culminates in a state is an edifice that monopolizes and centralizes power and eliminates older, less universal forms of authority; that structures its activities and implements its policies through unaccountable hierarchies; that erodes local and particular patterns of ethnic, religious, and regional identities; that standardizes culture, ideas, and ideals; that links portions of the population to it through a variety of dependency relationships; that may find it necessary or convenient to override civil liberties and standards of decency for *raison d'état* or executive privilege; and that, from time to time, commits its people to wars they have had neither the opportunity to debate fully nor the right to challenge openly.

For feminists to discover in the state the new 'Mr. Right', and to wed themselves thereby, for better or for worse, to a public identity inseparable from the exigencies of state power and policy would be a mistake. This is a serious charge. I shall defend and develop my argument by considering the ways in which certain important feminist thinkers, at times somewhat casually and carelessly, have presumed the superiority of a particular sort of public identity over a private one. I shall trace out the logic of these arguments, indicating what a fully public identity for women would require, including the final suppression of traditional female social worlds. Finally, I shall reclaim for women a social identity that locates them very much in and of the wider world but positions them against overweening state power and public identity defined in its terms. My aim is to define and to defend a female identity and a feminist perspective that

First published in Democracy in the World, 2/2 (1982), 46–59. Copyright © 1982 by Praeger Publishers. Reproduced by permission of Greenwood Publishing Group, Inc. Westport, CT, USA.

enables contemporary women to see themselves as the daughters of Antigone. To recognize that women as a group experience their social worlds differently from men as a group complicates feminist thinking, deepens female self-awareness, and calls attention to the complexity and richness of our social experiences and relations.

The feminist protest of the past several decades has largely concentrated on the ways—official and unofficial, ideological and practical—in which women have been excluded from equal participation in public life and equal share in official power in government and business. Responding to constraints that curbed their participation as citizens and limited expression of their individual autonomy, the end of feminist protest was conceived as the full incorporation of women into the power, privileges, and responsibilities of the public arena. The stated aim of the largest feminist political organization, the National Organization for Women (NOW), founded in October 1966, is to gain 'truly equal partnership with men'. To this end, NOW's Bill of Rights contains a list of proposals and demands required to attain such equal partnership. These demands include the establishment of government sponsored twenty-four-hours childcare centres, abortion on demand, equal pay for equal work, aggressive recruitment of women for top positions in all political and business hierarchies, and so on. Each demand requires action by the federal government to promote women's interests and to achieve NOW's version of sex equality. The presumption behind these demands, as stated by Betty Friedan's *The Feminine Mystique*, is that contemporary woman suffers a particular assault against her identity by being housebound; the man, however, with other 'able, ambitious' fellows, enters the success-driven ethos of the American public world and keeps 'on growing'.[1] Friedan contrasts, and devalues, the activities and identities of women in their 'comfortable concentration camps' with the exciting, fulfilling, and presumably worthwhile world of the successful professional male.[2] In her more recent *The Second Stage*, Friedan remains innocent of any intractable tensions between simultaneous commitments to full intimacy and mobile success on market terms. She evades any serious questioning of her rosy, upbeat feminist project by transcending (her favourite word) every conflict that poses an apparent clash of interests, values, or purposes, or that seems to present obstacles to her vision of feminism's 'second stage'.[3]

Liberal feminists have not been alone in urging that private woman join public man. Susan Brownmiller, a radical feminist, presumes that all the central features of the current male-dominated power structure will remain intact indefinitely; therefore, women must come to control these structures fifty-fifty. Armies, for instance,

must be fully integrated, as well as our national guard, our state troopers, our local sheriffs' offices, our district attorneys' offices, our state prosecuting attorneys' offices—in short the nation's entire lawful power structure (and I mean power in the physical sense) must be stripped of male dominance and control—if women are to cease being a colonized protectorate of men.[4]

Women should prepare themselves for combat and guard duty, for militarized citizenship with a feminist face.

Similarly, one fundamental presumption underlying more deterministic modes of Marxist feminism is the insistence that women will never be 'liberated' to join hands with those men whose identities bear the teleologic seed of the future revolutionary order—the proletariat—until they are sprung from the ghetto of the home and wholly absorbed in the labour force, there to acquire an overriding public identity as a member of the class of exploited workers. The realm of intimacy is recast, crudely, as the world of reproduction, an analogue of the productive process.

These moves to transform women into public persons, with a public identity that either primarily or exclusively defines them and takes precedence in cases of conflict with private lives, were embraced or implicitly adopted by the most widely disseminated statements of feminist politics. As a feminist project this ideology required 'the absorption of the private as completely as possible into the public'.[5] Women, formerly the private beings, would be 'uplifted' to the status of a pre-eminently public identity to be shared equally with men. Though this overstates the case for emphasis, it reflects accurately the main thrust of feminist thought and practice—particularly that of mainstream, liberal feminism—from the late 1960s through the 1970s. What was conspicuously missing from the discussion was any recognition of the potential dangers inherent in calling upon the state as an instrument for sexual emancipation. Concentrating only upon the good purposes to be served, feminists did not bring into focus the possibilities for enhanced powers of state surveillance and control of all aspects of intimate social relations.

In practice, the demand for a shift in the social identities of women involves their full assimilation into a combined identification with the state and the terms of competitive civil society, terms which have permeated all aspects of public life due to the close entanglements between government and corporations. The modern state, however, is the locus of structured, 'legitimate' public life. It is this state feminists look to to intervene, to legislate, to adjudicate, to police, and to punish on their behalf.

This process emerges in stark relief in an *amicus curiae* brief filed by NOW with the Supreme Court that argues that the all-male draft violates the constitutional rights of women. The brief asserts that 'compulsory universal military service is central to the concept of citizenship in a democracy' and that women suffer 'devastating long term psychological and political repercussions' because of their exclusion from such service.[6] Eleanor Smeal, president of NOW, insists that barring women from the military and from combat duty is based 'solely on archaic notions of women's role in society'.[7] Whatever one's position on women and the draft, NOW's stance and the stated defence for it embodies the conviction that women's traditional identities are so many handicaps to be overcome by women's incorporation into male public roles.

What all feminist protests that inveigh against women's contin- ued identification with the private sphere share is the conviction that women's traditional identities were wholly forced upon them— that all women have been the unwitting victims of deliberate exclu- sion from public life and forced imprisonment in private life. That is, women were not construed as agents and historic subjects who had, in their private identities as wives, mothers, and grandmothers, played vital and voluntary roles as neighbours, friends, social bene- factors, and responsible community members. Though these latter roles are not necessarily gender-related, historically they have been associated with women. Holding up the public world as the only sphere within which individuals made real choices, exercised authentic power or had efficacious control, the private world, in turn, automatically reflected a tradition of powerlessness, necessity, and irrationality. The darker realities of the public world, with the notable exception of its exclusion of women, went unexplored, just as the noble and dignified aspects of women's private sphere were ignored.[8]

Feminists who celebrated 'going public' could point to the long his- tory of the forced exclusion of women from political life and partic- ipation—whether the franchise, public office, or education and employment—as evidence that women's private identities were heavy-handed impositions by those with superior power. They could also recall a tradition of political thought in which great male theorists located women outside of, and frequently at odds with, the values and demands of politics and the sphere of public action. In contrast, another strain of feminist thought, best called 'difference feminism', questioned the move towards full assimilation of female identity with public male identity, and argued that to see women's traditional roles and activities as *wholly* oppressive was itself oppressive to women, denying them historic subjectivity and moral agency.[9] They could point to a first-person literature in which women defined and appropriated a particular female identity, rooted in private activities and relations, as a source of individual strength and social authority. They suggested that feminists should challenge rather than accept the present public world. And, rather than chastizing Western political thinkers for their failure to incorporate women into their scheme of things, why not question that very scheme with its devaluation of the traditional world and ways of women?

At this point it is important to take the measure of that public identity into which 'liberated' women are to be inducted. Contemporary American public identity is a far cry indeed from Jefferson's noble republican farmer or Lincoln's morally engaged citizen, the 'last best hope on earth'. Instead we find a public life, political and economic, marked by bureaucratic rationalization and culminating in the state's monopoly of authority in most vital fields of human activity. This process of rationalization and centralization, in the words of Brian Fay,

refers to the process by which growing areas of social life are subjected to decisions made in accordance with technical rules for the choice between alternative strategies given some set of goals or values. The characteristic features of these sorts of decisions are the quantification of the relevant data, the use of formal decision procedures, and the utilization of empirical laws; all of these are combined to form an attitude of abstraction from the traditional qualitative, and historically unique features of a situation in order to settle the question at hand 'objectively'. This sort of instrumental rationality is intimately connected with control over the various factors at hand, such that, by the manipulation of certain variables in accordance with some plan, some goal is best achieved.[10]

The aims are efficiency and control and powerful bureaucracies have been set up to implement these aims. Bureaucrats operate in conformity to certain impersonal, abstract, and rational standards: this is the price of entry into the predominant public identity available to anyone, male or female. It is the world Hegel called 'civil society', in which individuals treat others as means to some end and carry out actions to attain self-interest in public.

For women to identify fully with the present public order is for them to participate (and there is pathos if not tragedy in this) in the suppression of an alternative identity described by Dorothy Smith, a feminist sociologist, as 'the concrete, the particular, the bodily', an identity with which women have traditionally been defined and within which, for better *and* worse, they have located themselves as social and historic beings.[11] This world, once taken for granted and now problematic, exists in contrast to the abstracted 'mode of ruling', the ways of acting of the powerful. Women's historical social identity, at odds with extreme versions of abstract individualism, public-oriented behaviour aimed at good for others but not reducible to interest for self. The problem, as Jane Bennett points out in a recent study, is that women, as the 'exemplars/defenders of civic virtue', were pressed to sacrifice individual goals altogether in order to preserve 'a particular type of public good'.[12]

Feminist protest that seeks the elimination of this sphere of the concrete, particular, smaller social world—viewing only the sacrifices forced upon women, not the good attained by women—is one response to identities grown problematic under the pressures of social rationalization and modernization. A second response, where growth is a measure of the anger and despair of its adherents, is the militant reaffirmation of a rigid feminine identity, one that aims to leave all the political stuff to men who are better equipped for the task—ironically, of course, such feminine women are actively promoting this passive end. Somewhat lost in the cross-fire between these hostile camps is a third alternative, which I shall call 'social feminism', that opposes the rush toward a technocratic order and an overweening public identity and repudiates, as well, the standpoint of ardent feminine passivity.

The third way, a feminist *via media*, begins with a female subject located within a world that is particular, concrete, and social, and attempts to see it through her eyes. If one begins in this way, one cannot presume, with the feminists I discussed earlier, that this world is automatically one from which all women should seek, or need, to be wholly liberated. The French feminist writer, Julia Kristeva, observed in an interview: 'Feminism can be but one of capitalism's more advanced needs to rationalize.'[13] Those feminisms that embrace without serious qualification the governing consciousness and norms of social organization of the current public world serve in precisely this way.

To sketch my alternative requires that I begin from the standpoint of women within their everyday reality. Is it possible to embrace ideals and values from the social world of women, severed from male domination and female subordination? I am convinced this is possible only by not viewing women's traditional identities as devoid of vitality, as being tainted by relations of domination. What follows is my effort to reclaim for women, construed as social actors in the world, an identity that pits them against the imperious demands of public power and contractual relations, one that might serve as a locus for female thinking, acting, and being as transformed by social feminist imperatives. This locus is not some solid rock, not an ontological definition of female 'being'; rather, it is a series of overlapping intimations of a subject in the process of defining herself both with and against the available identities, public and private, of her epoch.

The female subject I have in mind is an identity-in-becoming, but she is located historically and grounded in tradition; she belongs to a heritage at least as old as Antigone's conflict with Creon. This powerful myth and human drama pits a woman against the arrogant insistencies of statecraft. Recall the story: the *dramatis personae* that matter for my purposes are Creon, King of Thebes, and his nieces, Antigone and her sister, Ismenê, daughters of the doomed Oedipus. Creon issues an order in the higher interests of state that violates the sacred familial duty to bury and honour the dead. Antigone, outraged, defies Creon. She defines their conflict with clarity and passion.

> Listen, Ismenê:
> Creon buried our brother Eteoclês
> With military honours, gave him a soldier's funeral,
> And it was right that he should; but Polyneicês,
> Who fought as bravely and died as miserably,—
> They say that Creon has sworn
> No one shall bury him, no one mourn for him
> But his body must lie in the fields, a sweet treasure
> For carrion birds to find as they search for food.
> That is what they say, and our good Creon is coming here
> To announce it publicly; and the penalty—
> Stoning to death in the public square
> There it is,
> And now you can prove what you are:
> A true sister, or a traitor to your family.[14]

369

Ismenê, uncomprehending, asks Antigone what she is going to do, and Antigone responds: 'Ismenê, I am going to bury him. Will you come?' Ismenê cries that the new law forbids it. Women, she cries, cannot fight with men nor against the law and she begs 'the Dead/To forgive me'. But Antigone, determined, replies: 'It is the dead, not the living, who make the longest demands.' Harshly, she orders Ismenê off with the words, 'I shall be hating you soon, and the dead will too,' for what is worse than death, or what is the worst of deaths, is 'death without honour'. Later, Antigone proclaims, 'There is no guilt in reverence for the dead' and 'there are honours due all the dead.' This primordial family morality precedes and overrides the laws of the state. Creon must be defied, for there are matters, Antigone insists, that are so basic they transcend *raison d'état*, one's own self-interest, even one's own life.

Creon's offence is his demand that political necessity justifies trampling upon a basic human duty, an imperative that lies at the heart of any recognizably human social life. In her loyalty to her slain brother and to family honour, Antigone asserts that there are matters of such deep significance that they begin and end where the state's right does not and must not run, where politics cannot presume to dictate to the human soul. In 'saving' the state, Creon not only runs roughshod over a centuries-old tradition, he presumed to override the familial order, the domain of women. In refusing to accept *raison d'état* as paramount, Antigone sets the course for her rebellion and pits the values of family and particular loyalties, ties, and traditions against the values of statecraft with its more abstract obligations. In her rebellion, Antigone is as courageous, honourable, and determined as Creon is insistent, demanding, and convinced of the necessity of his public decree.

Sophocles honors Antigone in her rebellion. He sees no need to portray a chastened Antigone, having confronted Creon but having failed to sway him, finally won over to the imperatives of *raison d'état*, yielding at last to Creon's fears of law-breakers and anarchy. Strangely, Antigone has not emerged as a feminist heroine. It is equally strange that a magisterial Greek thinker who would eliminate altogether the standpoint of Antigone is sometimes honoured by feminists for his 'radical' rearrangements without apparent regard to gender. I refer to Plato of *The Republic*, a Plato dedicated to eradicating and devaluing private homes and particular intimate attachments (principally for his Guardian class). Such private loyalties and passions conflicted with single-minded devotion to the city. Plato cries: 'Have we any greater evil for a city than what splits it and makes it many instead of one? Or a greater good than what binds it together and makes it one?'[15]

To see in Plato's abstract formulation for rationalized equality (for that minority of men and women who comprise his Guardian class) a move that is both radical and feminist is to accept public life and identity as, by definition, superior to private life and identity. Indeed, it is to concur in the wholesale elimination of the private social world to attain the higher good of a state without the points of potential friction and dissent private loyalties bring in their wake. This view accepts Plato's conviction that 'private wives' are a potentially subversive element within the city. Plato cannot allow women their own social location, for that would be at odds with his aim for a unified city. Instead, he provides for women's particulation under terms that deprivatize them and strip them of the single greatest source of female psychological and social power in fifth- and fourth-century Athens—their role in the household; their ties with their children. Effectively, he renders their sexual identities moot. In whose behalf is this dream of unity, and female public action, being dreamed?

The question of female identity and the state looks very different if one picks up the thread of woman's relationship to public power from the standpoint of an Antigone; if one adopts the sanctioned viewpoint of the handful of thinkers whose works comprise the canon of the Western political tradition; or if one tells the tale through the prism of unchecked *realpolitik*, from astride the horse of the warrior, or from the throne of the ruler. The female subject, excluded from legitimate statecraft unless she inherited a throne, is yet an active historic agent, a participant in social life who located the heart of her identity in a world bounded by the demands of necessity, sustaining the values of life-giving and preserving.

This sphere of the historic female subject generated its own imperatives, inspired its own songs, stories, and myths. It was and is, for many if not all, the crucible through which sustaining human relations and meaning are forged and remembered. It is easy to appreciate both the fears of traditionalists and the qualms of radicals at the suppression of this drama of the concrete and the particular in favour of some formal–legalistic, abstract 'personhood', or to make way for the further intrusion of an increasingly technocratic public order. To wholly reconstruct female social identity by substituting those identities available through the public order would be to lose the standpoint of Antigone, the woman who throws sand into the machinery of arrogant public power.

But how does one hold on to a social location for contemporary daughters of Antigone without simultaneously insisting that women accept traditional terms of political quiescence? The question answers itself: the standpoint of Antigone is of a woman who dares to challenge public power by giving voice to familial and social imperatives and duties. Hers is not the world of the *femme couverte*, the delicate lady, or the coy sex-kitten. Hers is a robust voice, a bold voice: woman as guardian of the prerogatives of the *oikos*, preserver of familiar duty and honour, protector of children, if need be their fierce avenger. To recapture that voice and to reclaim that standpoint, and not just for women alone, it is necessary to locate the daughters of Antigone where, shakily and problematically, they continue to locate themselves: in the arena of the social world where human life is nurtured and protected from day to day. This is a world women have not altogether abandoned, though it is one both male-dominant society and some feminist protest have devalued as the sphere of 'shit-work', 'diaper talk', and 'terminal social decay'. This is a world that women, aware that they have traditions and values, can bring forward to put pressure on contemporary public policies and identities.

Through a social feminist awareness, women can explore, articulate, and reclaim this world. To reaffirm the standpoint of Antigone for our own time is to portray women as being able to resist the imperious demands and overweening claims of state power when these run roughshod over deeply rooted values. Women must learn to defend without defensiveness and embrace without sentimentality the perspective that flows from their experiences in their everyday material world, 'an actual local and particular place in the world'.[16] To define this world simply as the 'private sphere' in contrast to 'the public sphere' is to mislead. For contemporary Americans, 'private' conjures up images of narrow exclusivity. The world of Antigone, however, is a *social* location that speaks of, and to, identities that are unique to a particular family, on the one hand; but, on another and perhaps even more basic level, it taps a deeply buried human identity, for we are first and foremost not political or economic men but family men and women. Family imagery goes deep and runs strong, and all of us, for better or worse, sporadically or consistently, have access to that imagery, for we all come from families even if we do not go on to create our own. The family is that arena that first humanizes us or, tragically, damages us. The family is our entry point into the wider social world. It is the basis of a concept of the social for, as Hegel recognized, 'the family is a sort of training ground that provides an understanding of another-oriented and public-oriented action.'[17]

What is striking about political theory in the Western tradition is the very thin notion of the social world so much of that theory describes. All aspects of social reality that go into making a person what he or she is fall outside the frame of formal, abstract analyses. In their rethinking of this tradition, many feminist thinkers, initially at least, locked their own formulations into an overly schematic public–private dichotomy, even if their intention was to challenge or to question it.[18] Those feminists who have moved in the direction of 'social feminism' have, in their rethinking of received categories, become both more historical and more interpretive in their approach to social life. One important female thinker whose life and work form a striking contrast to the classical vision and to overly rigid feminist renderings of the public and private, particularly those who disdain anything that smacks of the traditionally 'feminine', is Jane Addams. Addams embodies the standpoint of Antigone. A woman with a powerful public identity and following, who wielded enormous political power and influence, Addams's life work was neither grandly public nor narrowly private. Instead, she expressed the combined values of centuries of domestic tradition, and the dense and heady concoction of women's needs, and she brought these to bear on a political world that held human life very cheap indeed.

Addams recognized, in uncritical celebrations of heroic male action, a centuries-long trail of tears. What classical political theorists dismissed as ignoble—the sustenance of life itself—Addams claimed as truly heroic. Rather than repudiating human birth and the world surrounding it as a possible source of moral truth and political principle, Addams spoke from the standpoint of the 'suffering mothers of the disinherited', of 'women's haunting memories', which, she believed, 'instinctively challenge war as the implacable enemy of their age-long undertaking'.[19] At one point she wrote:

Certainly the women in every country who are under a profound imperative to preserve human life, have a right to regard this maternal impulse as important now as the compelling instinct evinced by primitive woman long ago, when they made the first crude beginnings of society by refusing to share the vagrant life of man because they insisted upon a fixed abode in which they might cherish their children. Undoubtedly women were then told that the interests of the tribe, the diminishing food supply, the honour of the chieftain, demanded that they leave their particular caves and go out in the wind and weather without regard to the survival of their children. But at the present moment the very names of the tribes and of the honors and the glories which they sought are forgotten, while the basic fact that the mothers held the lives of their children above all else, insisted upon staying where the children had a chance to live, and cultivate the earth for their food, laid the foundations of an ordered society.[20]

A feminist rethinking of Addams's category of the social, resituating it as an alternative to privatization and public self-interestedness, would allow us to break out of the rigidities into which current feminist discourse has fallen. Seeing human beings through the prism of a many-layered, complex social world suffused with diverse goods, meanings, and purposes opens up the possibility for posing a transformed vision of the human community against the arid plain of bureaucratic statism. This communitarian ideal involves a series of interrelated but autonomous social spheres. It incorporates a vision of human solidarity that does not require uniformity and of cooperation that permits dissent. The aim of all social activity would be to provide a frame within which members of a diverse social body could attain both individual and communal ends and purposes, without, however, presuming some final resolution of these ends and purposes; a social world featuring fully public activities at one end of a range of possibilities and intensely private activities at the other.

If this communal ideal is to be claimed as a worthy ideal for our time, a first requirement is a feminist framework that locates itself in the social world in such a way that our current public, political realities can be examined with a critical and reflective eye. One alternative feminist perspective, a variation on both 'difference' and 'social' feminism that helps us to do this is called 'maternal thinking' by its author, Sara Ruddick.[21] According to Ruddick, mothers have had a particular way of thinking that has largely gone unnoticed—save by mothers themselves. That is, women in mothering capacities have developed intellectual abilities that wouldn't otherwise have been developed; made judgements they wouldn't otherwise have been called upon to make; and affirmed values they might not otherwise have affirmed. In other words, mothers engage in a discipline that has its own characteristic virtues and errors and that involves, like other disciplines, a conception of achievement. Most important for the purposes of feminist theory, these concepts and ends are dramatically at odds with the prevailing norms of our bureaucratic, and increasingly technological, public order.

Ruddick claims that one can describe maternal practices by a mother's interest in the preservation, the growth, and the social acceptability of her child. These values and goods may conflict, for preservation and growth may clash with the requirements for social acceptability. Interestingly, what counts as a failure within the frame of maternal thinking, excessive control that fails to give each unique child room to grow and develop, is the *modus operandi* of both public and private bureaucracies. Were maternal thinking to be taken as the base for feminist consciousness, a wedge for examining an increasingly over-controlled public world would open up immediately. For this notion of maternal thought to have a chance to flourish as it is brought to bear upon the larger world, it must be transformed in and through social feminist awareness.

To repeat: the core concepts of maternal achievement put it at odds with bureaucratic manipulation. Maternal achievement requires paying a special sort of attention to the concrete specificity of each child; it turns on a special kind of knowledge of this child, this situation, without the notion of seizure, appropriation, control, or judgement by impersonal standards. What maternal thinking could lead to, though this will always be problematic as long as mothers are socially subordinated, is the wider diffusion of what attentive love to all children is about and how it might become a wider social imperative.

Maternal thinking opens up for reflective criticism the paradoxical juxtapositions of female powerlessness and subordination, in the overall social and political sense, with the extraordinary psycho-social authority of mothers. Maternal thinking refuses to see women principally or simply as victims, for it recognizes that much good has emerged from maternal practices and could not if the world of the mother were totally destructive. Maternal thinking transformed by feminist consciousness, hence aware of the binds and constraints imposed on mothers, including the presumption that women will first nurture their sons and then turn them over to sacrifice should the gods of war demand human blood, offers us a mode of reflection that links women to the past yet offers up hope of a future. It makes contact with the strengths of our mothers and grandmothers; it helps us to see ourselves as Antigone's daughters, determined, should it be necessary, to chasten arrogant public power and resist the claims of political necessity. For such power, and such claims, have, in the past, been weapons used to trample upon the deepest yearnings and most basic hopes of the human spirit.

Maternal thinking reminds us that public policy has an impact on real human beings. As public policy becomes increasingly impersonal, calculating, and technocratic, maternal thinking insists that the reality of a single human child be kept before the mind's eye. Maternal thinking, like Antigone's protest, is a rejection of amoral statecraft and an affirmation of the dignity of the human person.

Notes

1. Betty Friedan, *The Feminine Mystique* (New York: Dell Books, 1974), 201.
2. Ibid. 325.
3. Betty Friedan, *The Second Stage* (New York: Summit Books, 1981).
4. Susan Brownmiller, *Against Our Will: Men, Women and Rape* (New York: Simon and Schuster, 1975), 388.
5. Robert Paul Wolff, 'There's Nobody Here But Us Persons', in Carol Gould and Marx Wartofsky (eds.), *Women and Philosophy* (New York: Putnam, 1976), 140–1.
6. Linda Greenhouse, 'Women Join Battle on All-Male Draft', *New York Times* (22 March 1981), 19. We do have plenty of evidence on the devastating damage done to men and women who served in a variety of capacities in Vietnam.
7. Ibid.
8. My argument should not be taken as a denial that women, historically, *have* suffered in specific ways. It is, however, a denial that this suffering has been so total that women are reduced to the status of objects—whether in the name of feminism or in the name of defences of male supremacy.
9. Examples of 'difference feminism' include: Carol Gilligan, 'In a Different Voice: Women's Conception of Self and Morality', *Harvard Educational Review*, 47 (1977), 481–517; some of the essays in the volumes *Women, Culture and Society*, ed. Michelle Rosaldo and Louise Lamphere (Stanford, Calif.: Stanford University Press, 1974); and Sandra Harding and Merrill B. Hintikka (eds.), *Discovering Reality: Feminist Perspectives on Epistemology, Metaphysics, Methodology and the Philosophy of Science* (Amsterdam: Dordrecht-Reidel, 1983).
10. Brian Fay, *Social Theory and Political Practice* (London: George Allen and Unwin, 1975), 44.
11. Dorothy E. Smith, 'A Sociology for Women', in *The Prism of Sex: Essays in the Sociology of Knowledge*, ed. Julia A. Sterman and Evelyn Torton Beck (Madison, Wis.: University of Wisconsin Press, 1979), 135–88.
12. Jane Bennett, 'Feminism and Civic Virtue', unpublished paper (1981).
13. Julia Kristeva, 'Women Can Never Be Defined', in Elaine Marks and Isabelle de Courtivron (eds.), *New French Feminisms: An Anthology* (Amherst, Mass.: University of Massachusetts Press, 1980), 141.
14. Sophocles, *The Oedipus Cycle*, 'Antigone', trans. Dudley Fitts and Robert Fitzgerald (New York: Harvest Books, 1949), 186.
15. Plato, *The Republic*, trans. Allan Bloom (New York: Basic Books, 1968), Book V/460E–462D, 141.
16. Smith, 'A Sociology for Women', 168.
17. Bennett, 'Feminism and Civic Virtue'.

18. I consider myself guilty on this score. See one of my earlier formulations on the public–private dilemma, 'Moral Woman/Immoral Man: The Public/Private Distinction and its Political Ramifications', *Politics and Society*, 4 (1974), 453–73. I try to restore a richness this initial foray dropped out in *Public Man, Private Woman: Women in Social and Political Thought* (Princeton: Princeton University Press, 1981).

19. Jane Addams, *The Long Road of Woman's Memory* (New York: MacMillan, 1916), 40.

20. Ibid. 126–7.

21. Sara Ruddick, 'Maternal Thinking', typescript. A shortened version has appeared in *Feminist Studies* (Summer 1980), but I draw upon the original full-length draft.

18 Context Is All: Feminism and Theories of Citizenship

Mary G. Dietz

In Margaret Atwood's powerful novel *The Handmaid's Tale*,[1] the heroine Offred, a member of a new class of 'two-legged wombs' in a dystopian society, often thinks to herself, 'Context is all.' Offred reminds us of an important truth: at each moment of our lives our every thought, value, and act—from the most mundane to the most lofty—takes its meaning and purpose from the wider political and social reality that constitutes and conditions us. In her newly reduced circumstances, Offred comes to see that matters beyond one's immediate purview make a great deal of difference with respect to living a more or less free and fully human life. But her realization comes too late.

Unlike Offred, feminists have long recognized as imperative the task of seeking out, defining, and criticizing the complex reality that governs the ways we think, the values we hold and the relationships we share, especially with regard to gender. If context is all, then feminism in its various guises is committed to uncovering what is all around us and to revealing the power relations that constitute the creatures we become. 'The personal is the political' is the credo of this critical practice.

The political and ideological context that most deeply conditions the American experience is liberalism and its attendant set of values, beliefs, and practices. Without question, the liberal tradition can count many among its adherents but it has its critics as well. Over the past decade in the United States, few critics of liberalism have been as persistent or as wide-ranging as the feminists. Certainly no others have been as committed to articulating alternatives to the liberal vision of gender, the family, the sexual division of labour, and the relationship between the public and the private realm.[2]

Reprinted by permission of *Daedalus*, Journal of the American Academy of Arts and Sciences, from the issue entitled, 'Learning About Women: Gender, Politics, and Power', 116/4 (Fall 1987).

In this essay I shall focus on the aspect of the feminists' critique that concerns citizenship. First I will outline the dominant features of liberalism's conception of citizenship, and then I will introduce two current feminist challenges to that conception. What I ultimately want to argue, however, is that although both of these challenges offer important insights, neither of them leads to a suitable alternative to the liberal view or a sufficiently compelling feminist political vision. In the third section of the essay I will make a preliminary sketch of what such a feminist vision of citizenship might be. In part, I would have it reconfirm the idea that 'equal access is not enough'.

I

The terrain of liberalism is vast, and its historical basis has over the past century been extensively surveyed in social, political, and moral theory.[3] All I shall present here is the bare bones of the liberal conception of citizenship, but this skeletal construction may sufficiently set off the feminist critiques that follow. With this in mind and the caveat that all conceptions change through time, we can begin by considering the features that have more or less consistently distinguished the views of liberal political thinkers.

First, there is the notion that human beings are atomistic, rational agents whose existence and interests are ontologically prior to society.[4] In the liberal society one might say that context is not 'all'. It is nothing, for liberalism conceives of the needs and capacities of individuals as being independent of any immediate social or political condition.[5] What counts is that we understand human beings as rational individuals who have intrinsic worth.

A second tenet of liberal political thought is that society should ensure the freedom of all its members to realize their capabilities. This is the central ethical principle of the Western liberal tradition. Perhaps the classic formulation is John Stuart Mill's observation that 'the only freedom which deserves the name, is that of pursuing our own good in our own way, so long as we do not attempt to deprive others of theirs, or impede their efforts to obtain it'.[6]

Closely associated with the principle of individual liberty is a third feature—an emphasis on human equality. Liberal theorists may differ in their formulations of this principle but not on its centrality. Locke, for example, held that 'reason is the common rule and measure that God has given to mankind' and therefore that all men must be considered created equal and thereby worthy of the same dignity and respect. Bentham argued (not always consistently) that the case for equality rests on the fact that all individuals have the same capacity for pleasure and hence that the happiness of society is maximized when everyone has the same amount of wealth or income. In his 'Liberal Legislation and Freedom of Contract', T. H. Green proclaimed that 'every one has an interest in securing to every one else the free use and enjoyment and disposal of his possessions, so long as that freedom on the part of one does not interfere with a like freedom on the part of others, because such freedom contributes to that equal development of the faculties of all which is the highest good of all'.[7] Since liberal theories usually begin with some version of the presumption of perfect equality among individual men, it is a relatively small step from this to the related argument that societal justice entails equal suffrage, in which every single person should count, in Herbert Spencer's words, 'for as much as any other single individual in the community'.[8] As Alison Jagger writes, 'Liberalism's belief in the ultimate worth of the individual is expressed in political egalitarianism.'[9]

This egalitarianism takes the form of what theorists call 'negative liberty', which Sir Isaiah Berlin in his classic essay on freedom characterizes as 'the area within which a man can act unobstructed by others'.[10] It is the absence of obstacles to possible choices and activities. What is at stake in this liberal conception is neither the 'right' choice nor the 'good' action but simply the freedom of the individual to choose his own values or ends without interference from others and consistent with a similar liberty for others. At the core of negative liberty, then, is a fourth feature of liberalism that speaks to the individual in his political guise as citizen: the conception of the individual as the 'bearer of formal rights' designed to protect him from the infringement or interference of others and to guarantee him the same opportunities or 'equal access' as others.

The concept of rights is of fundamental importance to the liberal political vision. In *A Theory of Justice*, John Rawls offers this classic formulation of the liberal view: 'Each person possesses an inviolability founded on justice that even the welfare of society as a whole cannot override. . . . The rights secured by justice are not subject to political bargaining or the calculus of social interests.'[11]

Not only does the concept of rights reinforce the underlying liberal principles of individual freedom and formal equality; it also sets up the distinction between 'private' and 'public' that informs so much of the liberal perspective on family and social institutions. Individual rights correspond to the notion of a private realm of freedom, separate and distinct from that of the public. Although liberal theorists disagree about the nature and degree of state intervention in the public realm—and even about what counts as 'public'—they nevertheless accept the idea that certain rights are inviolable and exist in a private realm where the state cannot legitimately interfere. For much of liberalism's past this private realm has subsumed, in Agnes Heller's phrase, 'the household of the emotions'—marriage, family, housework, and childcare. In short, the liberal notion of 'the private' has included what has been called 'woman's sphere' as 'male property' and sought not only to preserve it from the interference of the public realm but also to keep those who 'belong' in that realm— women—from the life of the public.[12]

Another feature of liberalism tied to all of the above is the idea of the free individual as competitor. To understand it, we might recall liberalism's own context, its distinctive history and origin.[13] Liberalism emerged amid the final disintegration of, in Karl Marx's words, those 'motley feudal ties'—in the decline of aristocracy and the rise of a new order of merchants and entrepreneurs with a 'natural propensity', as Adam Smith wrote, 'to trade, truck, and barter.' The life of liberalism, in other words, began in capitalist market societies, and as Marx argued, it can only be fully comprehended in terms of the social and economic institutions that shaped it. For Max Weber, liberal political thought inherited the great transformation wrought by Protestantism and a new ethic of self and work soon to replace privilege, prescription, and primacy of rank. As both Marx and Weber recognized, liberalism was the practical consciousness, or the theoretical legitimation, of the values and practices emanating from the newly emergent market society. Accordingly, liberalism lent support to the active pursuit of things beneficial to an economic system based on production for the sake of profit.

Among these 'things beneficial' is the notion of the rational man as a competitive individual who tends naturally to pursue his own interest and maximize his own gain. Although it would be mistaken to suggest that all liberal theorists conceive of human nature as being egoistic, most do argue that people tend naturally in this direction and must work to develop moral capacities to counter their basic selfish, acquisitive inclinations.[14] Thus, we can at least generally conclude that, for liberals, the motive force of human action is not to be found in any noble desires to achieve 'the good life' or 'the morally virtuous society' but rather in the inclination toward individual advancement or (in capitalist terms) the pursuit of profit according to the rules of the market.[15] Taken in this light, then, the liberal individual might be understood as the competitive entrepreneur, his civil society as an economic marketplace, and his ideal as the equal opportunity to engage, as Adam Smith wrote, in 'the race for wealth, and honours, and preferments'.

Vital in this race is the issue of equality of access to the race itself, to the market society. What liberty comes to mean in this context is a set of formal guarantees to the individual that he (and later she) may enjoy a fair start in Smith's 'race'. What citizenship comes to mean in this liberal guise is something like equal membership in an economic and social sphere, more or less regulated by government and more or less dedicated to the assumption that the 'market maketh man'.[16] To put this another way, under liberalism, citizenship becomes less a collective, political activity than an individual, economic activity—the right to pursue one's interests, without hindrance, in the marketplace. Likewise, democracy is tied more to representative government and the right to vote than to the idea of the collective, participatory activity of citizens in the public realm.

This vision of the citizen as the bearer of rights, democracy as the capitalist market society, and politics as representative government is precisely what makes liberalism, despite its admirable and vital insistence on the values of individual freedom and equality, seem so politically barren to so many of its critics, past and present, conservative and radical. As far as feminism is concerned, perhaps Mary Shanley best sums up the problem liberalism poses when she writes:

While liberal ideals have been efficacious in overturning restrictions on women as individuals, liberal theory does not provide the language or concepts to help us understand the various kinds of human interdependence which are part of the life of both families and polities, nor to articulate a feminist vision of 'the good life.' Feminists are thus in the awkward position of having to use rhetoric in dealing with the state that does not adequately describe their goals and that may undercut their efforts at establishing new modes of life.[17]

II

For good and obvious reasons, one might expect that a feminist critique of liberalism would best begin by uncovering the reality behind the idea of equal access. Not only is equal access a central tenet of liberal thought; it is also a driving part of our contemporary political discourse that is used both to attack and to defend special pleas for women's rights. Just such a critique is what this volume undertakes.

But a complementary approach may be in order as well. There is merit, I think, to the argument that to begin with the question of equal access is already to grant too much, to deal too many high cards to the liberal hand. Quite literally, 'access is not enough', for once in the domain of 'equal access talk', we are tied into a whole network of liberal concepts—rights, interests, contracts, individuals, representative government, negative liberty. These open up some avenues of discourse but at the same time block off others. As Shanley implies, for feminists to sign on to these concepts may be to obscure rather than to illuminate a vision of politics, citizenship, and 'the good life' that is appropriate to feminine values and concerns.

By this I do not mean to suggest that feminists who proceed from the question of access are doing something unhelpful or unimportant. On the contrary, by using gender as a unit of analysis, feminist scholars have revealed the inegalitarianism behind the myth of equal opportunity and made us aware of how such presumptions deny the social reality of unequal treatment, sexual discrimination, cultural stereotypes, and women's subordination both at home and in the marketplace. To the extent that this sort of gender analysis leads to positive political programmes—the extension of pregnancy leaves, affirmative action plans, childcare facilities, comparable-worth wages, sexual harassment laws, healthcare benefits—feminists give indispensable assistance to liberal practice.

However, we should not overlook the fact that this sort of analysis has boundaries that are determined by the concepts of liberalism and the questions they entail. So, for example, when power is perceived in terms of access to social, economic, or political institutions, other possibilities (including the radical one that power has nothing to do with access to institutions at all) are left out. Or to take another example, if one establishes the enjoyment of rights or the pursuit of free trade as the criterion of citizenship, alternative conceptions like civic activity and participatory self-government are overlooked. Liberalism tends toward both an understanding of power as access and a conception of citizenship as civil liberty. What I want to emphasize is that neither of these formulations is adequate in and of itself or appropriate for a feminist political theory.

Of course, few feminist theorists would find these remarks startling or new. Indeed, much of recent feminist thought (liberal feminism notwithstanding) has been directed toward revealing the problems a liberal political theory poses for a vision of women's liberation and human emancipation. A variety of arguments and approaches has been articulated. Some have focused on the epistemological and ontological roots of liberalism, others on its implications for an ethical understanding of personhood, still others on the assumptions that underlie its methodology.[18]

On the political side and with regard to the liberal theory of freedom, the role of the state, the public and the private, and capitalism and democracy, feminist critics seem to fall into two camps—the Marxists and what I will call the maternalists.[19] These two camps are of primary concern in this essay because they address issues of 'the good life' and, more precisely, the nature of political community. A brief look at each should suffice to bring us up to date on the feminist alternatives to the liberal conception of the citizen—alternatives that are, as I shall go on to argue, not fully satisfactory counters to the liberal view, although they provide suggestive and thought-provoking contributions to the political debate.

First, the Marxists. Feminists working within the Marxist tradition seek to reveal the capitalist and patriarchal foundations of the liberal state as well as the oppression inherent in the sexual division of labour—or, as one thinker puts it, 'the consequences of women's dual contribution to subsistence in capitalism'.[20] At stake in this economic critique, as another theorist argues, is the notion of the 'state's involvement in protecting patriarchy as a system of power, much in the same way it protects capitalism and racism'.[21] In so far as they believe that the state participates in the oppression of women, Marxist feminists hold that the idea of the rights of citizenship granted by the state is a sham, a convenient ideological fiction that serves to obscure the underlying reality of a dominant male ruling class. Accordingly, so these theorists contend, the liberation of women will be possible only when the liberal state is overthrown and its capitalist and patriarchal structure dismantled. What will emerge is an end to the sexual division of labour and 'a feminist politics that moves beyond liberalism'.[22] What most Marxist feminists seem to mean by these politics is the egalitarian reordering of productive and reproductive labour and the achievement of truly liberating human relations, a society of 'propertyless producers of use values'.[23]

The strengths of this critique should be obvious. Marxist feminists would have us recognize that a system of economics and gender rooted in capitalist, male-dominant structures underlies much of liberal ideology, from the notion of independent, rational man to the conception of separate private and public realms, from the value of individualism to the equation of freedom with free trade. As such the Marxist-feminist analysis reveals numerous inadequacies in the liberal feminist position, particularly in its mainstream view of women's work and its reliance on the law, the state, interest groups, and state-instituted reforms as the source of social justice, individual equality, and 'access'. The advantage of the Marxist-feminist approach is not only its critique of capitalism, which reveals the exploitative and socially constructed nature of women's work, but also its political critique, which challenges the liberal assumption that representative government is the sole sanctuary for politics and the legitimate arbiter of social change.

Nevertheless, even though the Marxist-feminist critique has much to offer from the standpoint of historical materialism, it has little to say on the subject of citizenship. As Sheldon Wolin has noted, 'Most Marxists are interested in the "masses" or the workers, but they dismiss citizenship as a bourgeois conceit, formal and empty'.[24] Unfortunately, Marxist feminists are no exception to this generalization. *Citizenship* hardly appears in their vocabulary, much less any of the rest of its family of concepts: participation, action, democracy, community, and political freedom.

To the extent that Marxist feminists discuss citizenship at all, they usually conflate it with labour, class struggle, and socialist revolution, and with the advent of social change and certain economic conditions. In their view, true citizenship is realized with the collective ownership of the means of production and the end of oppression in the relations of reproduction. They associate both of these ideas with revolutionary action and the disappearance of the patriarchal state. In their approach to citizenship, Marxist feminists tend to reduce politics to revolutionary struggle, women to the category of 'reproducers', and freedom to the realization of economic and social equality and the overthrowing of natural necessity. Once freedom is achieved, they seem to say, politics ends or becomes little more than what Marx himself once termed 'the administration of things'.

Now no-one would deny that economic equality and social justice empower people. A society that values and strives for them with both men and women in mind deserves admiration and respect. What I am suggesting is that because Marxist feminism stops here, its liberatory vision of how things will be 'after the revolution' is incomplete, for what emerges is a picture of economic, not political, freedom and a society of autonomous and fulfilled social beings, not a polity of citizens. As a result, a whole complex of vital political questions is sidestepped or ignored: What is political freedom? What does it mean to be a citizen? What does an expressly feminist political consciousness require? Or, to put the matter more bluntly, is there more to feminist politics than revolutionary struggle against the state?

The second camp of feminist theorists, the maternalists, would answer this last question with a resounding yes. They would have us reconsider both the liberal and the Marxist views of citizenship[25] and become committed to a conception of female political consciousness that is grounded in the virtues of woman's private sphere, primarily in mothering. Unlike the Marxist feminists, the maternal feminists hold that, as important as social justice is, it is not a sufficient condition for a truly liberatory feminist politics. Women must be addressed as mothers, not as 'reproducers', and as participants in the public realm, not just as members of the social and economic orders.

Like the Marxist feminists, however, the maternal feminists eschew the liberal notion of the citizen as an individual holder of rights protected by the state. For the maternalist, such a notion is at best morally empty and at worst morally subversive since it rests on a distinctly masculine conception of the person as an independent, self-interested, economic being. When one translates this notion into a broader conception of politics, the maternal feminist argues, one is left with a vision of citizens as competitive marketeers and jobholders for whom civic activity is, at most, membership in interest groups. Thus, the maternal feminist would deny precisely what the liberal would defend—an individualist, rights-based, contractual conception of citizenship and a view of the public realm as one of competition. As one maternalist puts it:

The problem—or one of the problems—with a politics that begins and ends with mobilizing resources, achieving maximum impacts, calculating prudentially, articulating interest group claims . . . and so on, is not only its utter lack of imagination but its inability to engage in the reflective allegiance and committed loyalty of citizens. Oversimply, no substantive sense of civic virtue, no vision of political community that might serve as the groundwork of a life in common, is possible within a political life dominated by a self-interested, predatory, individualism.[26]

Maternal feminism is expressly designed to counter what it thinks are the arid and unimaginative qualities of the prevailing liberal view and, more emphatically, to present an alternative sense of civic virtue and citizenship. As a first step, it wants to establish the moral primacy of the family. Although this may seem to some a strange start for a feminist politics, the maternalists would have us rethink the rigid, liberal distinction of public and private realms and consider instead the 'private' as the locus for a possible public morality and as a model for the activity of citizenship itself. Or, to put this another way, maternal feminism criticizes 'statist' politics and individualist persons, and offers in their place the only other alternative it sees—a politics informed by the virtues of the private realm, and a personhood committed to relational capacities, love, and caring for others.

What makes this view expressly feminist (rather than, say, traditionally conservative) is its claim that women's experience as mothers in the private realm endows them with a special capacity and a 'moral imperative' for countering both the male liberal individualist world view and its masculinist notion of citizenship. Jean Bethke Elshtain describes mothering as a 'complicated, rich, ambivalent, vexing, joyous activity' that upholds the principle that 'the reality of a single human child [must] be kept before the mind's eye'.[27] For her, the implications mothering holds for citizenship are clear: 'Were maternal thinking to be taken as the base for feminist consciousness, a wedge for examining an increasingly overcontrolled public world would open immediately.'[28]

Not only would maternal thinking chasten the 'arrogant' (i.e. male) public; it would also provide the basis for a whole new conception of power, citizenship, and the public realm. The citizen that emerges is a loving being who, in Elshtain's words, is 'devoted to the protection of vulnerable human life' and seeks to make the virtues of mothering the 'template' for a new, more humane public world.

Much of the maternalist argument takes its inspiration from, or finds support in, the psychoanalytic object-relations theory of Nancy Chodorow and the moral development theory of Carol Gilligan.[29] These scholars argue that striking contrasts exist between men and women and can be understood in terms of certain experiential differences in the early stages of their development. At the crux of Chodorow and Gilligan's findings is the implication that women's morality is tied to a more mature and humane set of moral values than men's.[30] Gilligan identifies a female 'ethic of care' that differs from the male 'ethic of justice'. The ethic of care revolves more around responsibility and relationships than rights, and more around the needs of particular situations than the application of general rules of conduct. Maternal feminists seize upon this psycho-logical 'binary opposition' and, in effect, politicize it. In their work, 'the male voice' is that of the liberal individualist who stands in opposition to the female, whose voice is that of the compassionate citizen as loving mother. For maternal feminists, as for feminist psychologists, there is no doubt about which side of the opposition is normatively superior and deserving of elevation, both as a basis for political consciousness and as an ethical way of being. The maternalists might say that the female morality of responsibility 'must extend its imperative to men', but they nevertheless grant a pride of place to women and to 'women's sphere'—the family—as the wellspring of this new 'mode of public discourse'.[31] They also maintain that public discourse and citizenship should be informed by the virtues of mothering—love, attentiveness, compassion, care, and 'engrossment'—in short, by all the virtues, the liberal, statist, public realm disdains.

What are we to make of this vision of feminist citizenship? There is, I think, much to be gained from the maternalist approach, especially if we consider it within the context of the liberal and Marxist-feminist views. First, the maternalists are almost alone among other 'feminisms' in their concern with the meaning of citizenship and political consciousness. Although we may disagree with their formulations, they deserve appreciation for making citizenship a matter of concern in a movement that (at least on its academic side) is too often caught up in the psychological, the literary, and the social rather than in problems of political theory that feminists must face. Second, the maternalists remind us of the inadequacy and limitations of a rights-based conception of the individual and a view of social justice as equal access. They would have us understand the dimensions of political morality in other ways and politics itself as potentially virtuous. Third, in an era when politics has on all sides become something like a swear word, the maternal feminists would have us rehumanize the way we think about political participation and recognize how, as interrelated 'selves', we can strive for a more humane, relational, and shared community than our current political circumstances allow.

Despite these contributions, however, much is troubling about the maternalists' conception of citizenship. It has the same problems as do all theories that hold one side of an opposition to be superior to the other. For the maternalists, women are more moral than men because they are, or can be, or are raised by, mothers and because mothering itself is necessarily and universally an affective, caring, loving activity. Leaving aside what should be the obvious and problematic logical and sociological character of these claims, suffice it to say that the maternalists stand in danger of committing precisely the same mistake they find in the liberal view. They threaten to turn historically distinctive women into ahistorical, universalized entities.[32]

Even more serious is the conviction of the maternalists that feminists must choose between two worlds—the masculinist, competitive, statist public and the maternal, loving, virtuous private. To choose the public world, they argue, is to fall prey to both a politics and an ethic that recapitulates the dehumanizing features of the liberal-capitalist state. To choose the private world, however, is not only to reassert the value of a 'women's realm' but also to adopt a maternal ethic potentially appropriate for citizenship, a deeply moral alternative to the liberal, statist one.[33]

When we look to mothering for a vision of feminist citizenship, however, we look in the wrong place—or, in the language of the maternalists, to the wrong 'world'. At the centre of the mothering activity is not the distinctive political bond among equal citizens but the intimate bond between mother and child. But the maternalist would offer us no choice in the matter: we must turn to the 'intimate private' because the 'statist public' is corrupt. This choice is a specious one, however. Indeed, by equating the public with statist politics and the private with the virtue of intimacy, maternalist feminism reveals itself to be closer to the liberal view than we might at first suppose. Thus it is open to much the same charge as liberalism: its conception of citizenship is informed by a flawed conception of politics as impersonal, representative government. That liberalism is content to maintain such a conception and that maternalist feminism wants to replace it with a set of prescriptions drawn from the private is not the real issue. The problem for a feminist conception is that neither of the above will do, because both leave us with a one-sided view of politics and therefore of citizenship. What we need is an entirely different conception. For the remainder of this essay, I will sketch out an alternative basis for a feminist political vision, with a view to developing a more detailed feminist vision in the future. I offer the following recommendations more as a programmatic outline than as a comprehensive theory.

III

My basic point is a straightforward one: for a vision of citizenship, feminists should turn to the virtues, relations, and practices that are expressly political and, more exactly, participatory and democratic. What this requires, among other things, is a willingness to perceive politics in a way neither liberals nor maternalists do: as a human activity that is not necessarily or historically reducible to representative government or 'the arrogant, male, public realm'. By accepting such judgments, the feminist stands in danger of missing a valuable alternative conception of politics that is historically concrete and very much a part of women's lives. That conception is perhaps best called the democratic one, and it takes politics to be the collective and participatory engagement of citizens in the determination of the affairs of their community. The community may be the neighbourhood, the city, the state, the region, or the nation itself. What counts is that all matters relating to the community are undertaken as 'the people's affair'.[34]

From a slightly different angle, we might understand democracy as the form of politics that brings people together as citizens. Indeed, the power of democracy rests in its capacity to transform the individual as teacher, trader, corporate executive, child, sibling, worker, artist, friend, or mother into a special sort of political being, a citizen among other citizens. Thus, democracy offers us an identity that neither liberalism, with its propensity to view the citizen as an individual bearer of rights, nor maternalism, with its attentiveness to mothering, provides. Democracy gives us a conception of ourselves as 'speakers of words and doers of deeds' mutually participating in the public realm. To put this another way, the democratic vision does not legitimize the pursuit of every separate, individual interest or the transformation of private into public virtues. In so far as it derives its meaning from the collective and public engagement of peers, it sees citizens neither as wary strangers (as the liberal marketplace would have it) nor as 'loving intimates' (as the maternalist family imagines).

To return to my earlier point, democratic citizenship is a practice unlike any other; it has a distinctive set of relations, virtues, and principles all its own. Its relation is that of civic peers; its guiding virtue is mutual respect; its primary principle is the 'positive liberty' of democracy and self-government, not simply the 'negative liberty' of non-interference. To assume, then, that the relations that accompany the capitalist marketplace or the virtues that emerge from the intimate experience of mothering are the models for the practice of citizenship is to misperceive the distinctive characteristics of democratic political life and to misconstrue its special relations, virtues, and principles.

The maternalists would have us believe that this democratic political condition would, in fact, flow from the 'insertion' of women's virtues as mothers into the public world. There is no reason to think that mothering necessarily induces commitment to democratic practices. Nor are there good grounds for arguing that a principle like 'care for vulnerable human life' (as noble as that principle is) by definition encompasses a defense of participatory citizenship. An enlightened despotism, a welfare-state, a single-party bureaucracy, and a democratic republic may all respect mothers, protect children's lives, and show compassion for the vulnerable.

The political issue for feminists must not be just whether children are protected (or any other desirable end achieved) but how and by whom those ends are determined. My point is this: as long as feminists focus only on questions of social and economic concern— questions about children, family, schools, work, wages, pornography, abortion, abuse—they will not articulate a truly political vision, nor will they address the problem of citizenship. Only when they stress that the pursuit of those social and economic concerns must be undertaken through active engagement as citizens in the public world and when they declare the activity of citizenship itself a value will feminists be able to claim a truly liberatory politics as their own.

I hope it is clear that what I am arguing for is the democratization of the polity, not interest-group or single-issue politics-as-usual. A feminist commitment to democratic citizenship should not be confused with either the liberal politics of pressure groups and representative government or the idea that after victory or defeat on an issue, the game is over and we can 'go home'. As one democratic theorist writes:

> The radical democrat does not agree . . . that after solving [a] problem it will be safe to abandon the democratic struggle and disband the organizations. . . . The radical democrat does not believe that any institutional or social arrangement can give an automatic and permanent solution to the main question of political virtue, or can repeal what may be the only scientific law political science has ever produced: power corrupts.[35]

The key idea here is that citizenship must be conceived of as a continuous activity and a good in itself, not as a momentary engagement (or a socialist revolution) with an eye to a final goal or a societal arrangement. This does not mean, of course, that democratic citizens do not pursue specific social and economic ends. Politics is about such things, after all, and the debates and discussions of civic peers will necessarily centre on issues of social, political, and economic concern to the community. But at the same time the democratic vision is, and feminist citizenship must be, more than this. Perhaps it is best to say that this is a vision fixed not on an end but rather inspired by a principle—freedom—and by a political activity—positive liberty. That activity is a demanding process that never ends, for it means engaging in public debate and sharing responsibility for self-government. What I am pressing for, in both theory and practice, is a feminist revitalization of this activity.

The reader who has followed me this far is perhaps now wondering whether I have not simply reduced feminist political consciousness to democratic consciousness, leaving nothing in this vision of feminist citizenship for feminism itself. In concluding these reflections, let me suggest why I think the revitalization of democratic citizenship is an especially appropriate task for feminists to undertake. Although the argument can be made more generally, I will direct my remarks to feminism in the United States.

Like Offred in *The Handmaid's Tale*, we Americans live in reduced circumstances, politically speaking. How we understand ourselves as citizens has little to do with the democratic norms and values I have just defended, and it is probably fair to say that most Americans do not think of citizenship in this way at all. We seem hypnotized by a liberal conception of citizenship as rights, an unremitting consumerism that we confuse with freedom, and a capitalist ethic that we take as our collective identity.[36] Sheldon Wolin has noted that in the American political tradition there exist two 'bodies' within the historic 'body of the people'—a collectivity informed by democratic practices on the one hand and a collectivity informed by an anti-democratic political economy on the other.[37] The latter is a 'liberal-capitalist citizenship' that has emerged triumphant today. Truly democratic practices have nearly ceased to be a part of politics in the United States. They exist only on the margins. More disturbing still, I think, even the memory of these practices seems to elude our collective imagination. As Hannah Arendt puts it, citizenship is the 'lost treasure' of American political life.

What I want to argue is that we may yet recover the treasure. We may be able to breathe new life into the peoples' other 'body'—into our democratic 'selves'. This prospect brings us back to feminism, which I think is a potential source for our political resuscitation. Feminism has been more than a social cause; it has been a political movement with distinctive attributes. Throughout its second wave in America, the movement has been informed by democratic organization and practice—by spontaneous gatherings and marches, diverse and multitudinous action groups, face-to-face assemblies, consensus decision making, non-hierarchical power structures, open speech and debate.[38] That is, embodied within the immediate political past of feminism in this country are forms of freedom that are far more compatible with the 'democratic body' of the American experience than with the liberal-capitalist one.[39] These particular feminist forms are, potentially at least, compatible with the idea of collective, democratic citizenship on a wider scale.

I say 'potentially' because feminists must first transform their own democratic practices into a more comprehensive theory of citizenship before they can arrive at an alternative to the nondemocratic liberal theory. Feminist political practice will not in some automatic way become an inspiration for a new citizenship. Instead, feminists must become self-conscious political thinkers—defenders of democracy—in a land of liberalism. To be sure, this task is neither easy nor short-term, but it is possible for feminists to undertake it in earnest because the foundation is already set in the movement's own experiences, in its persistent attention to issues of power, structure, and democracy, and in the historical precedent of women acting as citizens in the United States.[40]

A warning is in order, however. What a feminist defence of democracy must at all costs avoid is the temptation of 'womanism'. To turn to 'women of the public' and to feminist organization for inspiration in articulating democratic values is one thing; it is quite another to conclude that therein lies evidence of women's 'superior democratic nature' or of their 'more mature' political voice. A truly democratic defence of citizenship cannot afford to launch its appeal from a position of gender opposition and women's superiority. Such a premise would posit as a starting-point precisely what a democratic attitude must deny—that one group of citizens' voices is generally better, more deserving of attention, more worthy of emulation, more moral, than another's. A feminist democrat cannot give way to this sort of temptation, lest democracy itself lose its meaning, and citizenship its special nature. With this in mind, feminists would be well advised to secure the political defence of their theory of democratic citizenship not only in their own territory but also in the diversity of other democratic territories historical and contemporary, male and female. We might include the townships and councils of revolutionary America, the populist National Farmers Alliance, the sit-down strikes of the 1930s, the civil rights movement, the soviets of the Russian Revolution, the French political clubs of 1789, the Spanish anarchist affinity groups, the KOR (Workers' Defense Committee) in Poland, the 'mothers of the disappeared ones' in Argentina, and so on. In short, the aim of this political feminism is to remember and bring to light the many examples of democratic practices already in existence and to use these examples as inspiration for a form of political life that would challenge the dominant liberal one.[41] What this aim requires is not only a feminist determination to avoid 'womanism' while remaining attentive to women, but also a commitment to the activity of citizenship, which includes and requires the participation of men.

I began these reflections by agreeing with Offred that 'context is all'. I end on what I hope is a complementary and not an overly optimistic note. We are indeed conditioned by the contexts in which we live, but we are also the creators of our political and social constructions, and we can change them if we are so determined. The recent history of democratic politics in this country has not been an altogether happy one, despite spontaneous movements and periodic successes. Rather than occasion despair, however, perhaps this realization can work to strengthen and renew our sense of urgency concerning our present condition and what is to be done.

First, however, the urgency must be felt, and the spirit necessary for revitalizing citizenship must be enlivened in the public realm. Democracy, in other words, awaits its 'prime movers'. My aim here has been to argue that one such mover might be feminism, and to suggest why I think feminism is well suited to this demanding and difficult task that would benefit us all.

Notes

1. Margaret Atwood, *The Handmaid's Tale* (New York: Simon and Schuster, 1986).
2. For some idea of the wide-ranging nature of the feminist critique of liberalism, see the following: Irene Diamond (ed.), *Families, Politics, and Public Policy: A Feminist Dialogue on Women and the State* (New York: Longman, 1983); Zillah Eisenstein, *The Radical Future of Liberal Feminism* (New York: Longman, 1981); Jean Bethke Elshtain, *Public Man, Private Woman* (Princeton: Princeton University Press, 1981); Sandra Harding and Merrill Hintikka, *Discovering Reality: Feminist Perspectives on Epistemology, Metaphysics, Methodology, and*

the Philosophy of Science (Dordrecht: Reidel, 1983); Allison Jagger, *Feminist Politics and Human Nature* (New York: Rowman and Allenheld, 1983); Juliet Mitchell and Ann Oakley, *The Rights and Wrongs of Women* (Harmondsworth: Penguin, 1976); Linda Nicholson, *Gender and History* (New York: Columbia University Press, 1986); and Susan Moller Okin, *Women in Western Political Thought* (Princeton: Princeton University Press, 1979). For a feminist critique of social contract theory, see Seyla Benhabib, 'The Generalized and Concrete Other: The Kohlberg-Gilligan Controversy and Feminist Theory', *Praxis International*, 5/4 (1986), 402–24; Christine Di Stephano, 'Masculinity as Ideology in Political Theory: Hobbesian Man Considered', *Women's Studies International Forum*, 6/6 (1983); Carole Pateman, 'Women and Consent', *Political Theory*, 8/2 (1980), 149–68; Carole Pateman and Teresa Brennan, 'Mere Auxiliaries to the Commonwealth: Women and the Origins of Liberalism', *Political Studies*, 27/2 (1979), 183–200; and Mary Lyndon Shanley, 'Marriage Contract and Social Contract in Seventeenth-Century English Political Thought', *Western Political Quarterly*, 32/1 (1979), 79–91. For a critique of the 'rational man', see Nancy Hartsock, *Money, Sex, and Power* (New York: Longman, 1983); Genevieve Lloyd, *Man of Reason* (Minneapolis: University of Minnesota Press, 1984); and Iris Marion Young, 'Impartiality and the Civic Public: Some Implications of Feminist Critiques of Moral and Political Theory', *Praxis International*, 5/4 (1986), 381–401. On Locke, see Melissa Butler, 'Early Liberal Roots of Feminism: John Locke and the Attack on Patriarchy', *American Political Science Review*, 72/1 (1978), 135–50; Lorenne M. G. Clark, 'Women and Locke: Who Owns the Apples in the Garden of Eden?' in Clark and Lynda Lange (eds.), *The Sexism of Social and Political Theory* (Toronto: University of Toronto Press, 1979); and Carole Pateman, 'Sublimation and Reification: Locke, Wolin, and the Liberal Democratic Conception of the Political', *Politics and Society*, 5 (1975), 441–67. On Mill, see Julia Annas, 'Mill and the Subjection of Women', *Philosophy*, 52 (1977), 179–94; Richard W. Krouse, 'Patriarchal Liberalism and Beyond: From John Stuart Mill to Harriet Taylor', in Jean Bethke Elshtain (ed.), *The Family in Political Thought* (Amherst, Mass.: University of Massachusetts Press, 1982); and Jennifer Ring, 'Mill's *Subjection of Women*: The Methodological Limits of Liberal Feminism', *Review of Politics* 47/1 (1985). On liberal moral theory, see Lawrence Blum, 'Kant and Hegel's Moral Paternalism: A Feminist Response', *Canadian Journal of Philosophy*, 12 (1982), 287–302.

3. For a sense of the historical and intellectual development of liberalism over the past three centuries, see the following (in chronological order): L. T. Hobhouse, *Liberalism* (London, 1911); Guido De Ruggiero, *The History of European Liberalism* (Oxford: Oxford University Press, 1927); Harold Laski, *The Rise of European Liberalism* (London: Allen and Unwin, 1936); George H. Sabine, *A History of Political Theory* (New York: Holt, 1937); Charles Howard McIlwain, *Constitutionalism and the Changing World* (New York: Macmillan, 1939); John H. Hallowell, *The Decline of Liberalism as an Ideology* (Berkeley: University of California Press, 1943); Thomas Maitland Marshall, *Citizenship and Social Class* (Cambridge: Cambridge University Press, 1950); Michael Polanyi, *The Logic of Liberty* (Chicago: University of Chicago Press, 1951); Louis Hartz, *The Liberal Tradition in America* (New York: Harcourt Brace, 1955); R. D. Cumming, *Human Nature and History, A Study of the Development of Liberal Democracy* (2 vols.; Chicago: University of Chicago

Press, 1969); C. B. MacPherson, *The Life and Times of Liberal Democracy* (Oxford: Oxford University Press, 1977); Alan Macfarlane, *Origins of English Individualism* (Oxford: Oxford University Press, 1978); Steven Seidman, *Liberalism and the Origins of European Social Theory* (Berkeley: University of California Press, 1983); and John Gray, *Liberalism* (Minneapolis: University of Minnesota Press, 1986).

4. Although Thomas Hobbes was not within the main (and broadly defined) tradition of liberal theory that includes but is not limited to Locke, Kant, Smith, Madison, Montesquieu, Bentham, Mill, T. H. Green, L. T. Hobhouse, Dewey, and, recently, Rawls, Dworkin, and Nozick, he set the stage for the view of man that came to distinguish much of liberal thought. In *De Cive*, Hobbes wrote, 'let us . . . consider men as if but even now sprung out of the earth, and suddenly, like mushrooms come to full maturity, without all kinds of engagement to each other'. 'Philosophical Rudiments Concerning Government and Society', in Sir W. Molesworth (ed.), *The English Works of Thomas Hobbes* (London: Longman, 1966), 102. This invocation to view man as an autonomous 'self' outside society is discernible, in varied forms, from Locke's state of nature to Rawls's 'veil of ignorance'. Contemporary critics of liberalism refer to this formulation as the 'unencumbered self'; see Michael Sandel, 'The Procedural Republic and the Unencumbered Self', *Political Theory*, 12/1 (1984), 81–96.

I will use the male referent in this discussion of liberalism for two reasons: first, it serves as a reminder of the exclusively male discourse used in traditional political theory, including that of the few theorists who are willing to concede that *he/him* means 'all'. Second, many feminist theorists have persuasively argued that the term *man* as used in liberal thought is not simply a linguistic device or a generic label but a symbol for a concept reflecting both masculine values and virtues and patriarchalist practices. See Brennan and Pateman, 'Mere Auxiliaries to the Commonwealth'.

5. As Brennan and Pateman point out in 'Mere Auxiliaries', the idea that the individual is by nature free—that is, outside the bonds of society, history, and tradition—was bequeathed to liberalism by social contract theorists. The emergence of this idea in the seventeenth century not only marked 'a decisive break with the traditional view that people were "naturally" bound together in a hierarchy of inequality and subordination' but also established a conception of 'natural' individual freedom as the condition of individual isolation from others prior to the (artificial) creation of 'civil society'.

6. John Stuart Mill, 'On Liberty', in Max Lerner (ed.), *The Essential Works of John Stuart Mill* (New York: Bantam, 1961), 266.

7. T. H. Green, 'Liberal Legislation and Freedom of Contract', in John R. Rodman (ed.), *The Political Theory of T. H. Green* (New York: Crofts, 1964).

8. Quoted in Sheldon Wolin, *Politics and Vision* (Boston: Little, Brown, 1963).

9. Jagger, *Feminist Politics*, 33.

10. Sir Isaiah Berlin, 'Two Concepts of Liberty', in *Four Essays on Liberty* (Oxford: Oxford University Press, 1969), 122. Berlin goes on to note something that will be important to the argument I make in Section III—that 'freedom [as negative liberty] is not, at any rate logically, connected with democracy or self-government. . . . The answer to the question "Who governs me?" is logically distinct from the question "How far does government interfere with me?" ' (129–30). The latter question, as we shall see, is the one that is of primary

concern for the liberal citizen; the former must be of concern to the democratic citizen, and accordingly to feminist political thought.

11. John Rawls, *A Theory of Justice* (Cambridge, Mass.: Harvard University Press, 1971).

12. The denial of citizenship to women is, of course, a historical but not a contemporary feature of liberalism. Nevertheless, it is worth noting that, at least in early liberal thought, the ethical principles that distinguish liberalism—individual freedom and social equality—were not in practice (and often not in theory) extended to women, but solely to 'rational men', whose 'rationality' was linked to the ownership of property.

13. Liberalism's context is actually a highly complex set of shifting social, political, and historical situations. We must not forget that in its earliest (seventeenth- and eighteenth-century) manifestations with the Levellers, the True Whigs, and Commonwealthmen, and revolutionary 'patriots', the proclamation of individual rights and social equality were acts of rebellion against king and court. The domain of capitalist 'possessive individualism' developed in a separate but related set of practices. Thus liberalism's legacy is a radical as well as a capitalist one.

14. See Jagger, *Feminist Politics*, 31.

15. As C. B. MacPherson rightly points out in *The Life and Times of Liberal Democracy*, 2, one of the prevailing difficulties of liberalism is that it has tried to combine the idea of individual freedom as 'self-development' with the entrepreneurial notion of liberalism as the 'right of the stronger to do down the weaker by following market rules'. Despite attempts by J. S. Mill, Robert Nozick, and others to reconcile market freedom with self-development freedom, a successful resolution has not yet been achieved. MacPherson argues that the two freedoms are profoundly inconsistent, but he also asserts that the liberal position 'need not be taken to depend forever on an acceptance of capitalist assumptions, although historically it has been so taken' (2). That historical reality is the one I focus on here, and is what I think predominates in the liberal American view of citizenship. However, like MacPherson, I do not think liberalism is necessarily bound (conceptually or practically) to what he calls the 'capitalist market envelope'.

16. Ibid. 1.

17. Mary Lyndon Shanley, 'Afterword: Feminism and Families in a Liberal Polity', in Diamond, *Families, Politics, and Public Policy*, 360.

18. For example, see Jagger, *Feminist Politics*; Naomi Scheman, 'Individualism and the Objects of Psychology', in Harding and Hintikka, *Discovering Reality*; Jean Grimshaw, *Philosophy and Feminist Thinking* (Minneapolis: University of Minnesota Press, 1986); Nicholson, *Gender and History*; and Young, 'Impartiality and the Civic Public'.

19. I intentionally leave radical feminism out of this discussion, not because it is insignificant or unimportant, but because it has not, to date, arrived at a consistent political position on the questions that concern us here. For a helpful critique of radical feminism's theoretical failings, see Jagger, *Feminist Politics*, 286–90, and Joan Cocks, 'Wordless Emotions: Some Critical Reflections on Radical Feminism', *Politics and Society*, 13/1 (1984), 27–57.

20. By delineating this category I do not mean to blur or erase the very real distinctions between various kinds of Marxist feminists or to obscure the importance of the 'patriarchy versus capitalism' debate. For a sense of the diversity of

Marxist (or socialist) feminism, see: Mariarose DallaCosta and Selma James, *Women and the Subversion of Community: A Woman's Place* (Bristol: Falling Wall Press, 1981); Hartsock, *Money, Sex, and Power*; Zillah Eisenstein, *Capitalist Patriarchy and the Case for Socialist Feminism* (New York: Monthly Review Press, 1978); Catherine A. MacKinnon, 'Feminism, Marxism, Method, and the State: An Agenda for Theory', in Nannerl O. Keohane, Michelle Rosaldo, and Barbara Gelpi (eds.), *Feminist Theory: A Critique of Ideology* (Chicago: University of Chicago Press, 1981); Sheila Rowbotham, *Women, Resistance, and Revolution* (New York: Vintage, 1974); and Lydia Sargent (ed.), *Women and Revolution* (Boston: South End Press, 1981). The quotations are from Hartsock, *Money, Sex, and Power*, 235.
21. Eisenstein, *The Radical Future of Liberal Politics*, 223.
22. Ibid. 222.
23. Hartsock, *Money, Sex, and Power*, 247.
24. Sheldon Wolin, 'Revolutionary Action Today', *Democracy*, 2/4 (1982), 17–28.
25. For various maternalist views see, among others, Jean Bethke Elshtain, 'Antigone's Daughters', *Democracy*, 2/2 (1982), 46–59; Elshtain, 'Feminism, Family and Community', *Dissent*, 29/4 (1982), 442–49; and Elshtain, 'Feminist Discourse and Its Discontents: Language, Power and Meaning', *Signs*, 3/7 (1982), 603–21; also Sara Ruddick, 'Maternal Thinking', *Feminist Studies*, 6/2 (1980), 342–67; Ruddick, 'Preservative Love and Military Destruction: Reflections on Mothering and Peace', in Joyce Treblicot (ed.), *Mothering: Essays on Feminist Theory* (Totowa, NJ: Littlefield Adams, 1983); and Hartsock, *Money, Sex, and Power* (Hartsock incorporates both Marxist and maternalist perspectives in her 'feminist standpoint' theory).
26. Elshtain, 'Feminist Discourse', 617.
27. Elshtain, *Public Man, Private Woman*, 243, and Elshtain, 'Antigone's Daughters', Chapter 17, 363–77.
28. Ibid. 375.
29. See Nancy Chodorow, *The Reproduction of Mothering: Psychoanalysis and the Sociology of Gender* (Berkeley: University of California Press, 1978), and Carol Gilligan, *In a Different Voice: Psychological Theory and Women's Development* (Cambridge, Mass.: Harvard University Press, 1982).
30. I qualify this with 'implication' because Gilligan is by no means consistent about whether the 'different voice' is exclusive to women or open to men. For an interesting critique, see Joan Tronto, 'Women's Morality: Beyond Gender Difference to a Theory of Care', in *Signs*, 12/4 (1987), 644–63.
31. Elshtain, 'Feminist Discourse', 621.
32. For a complementary and elegant critique of binary opposition arguments, see Joan Scott, 'Gender: A Useful Category of Historical Analysis', *American Historical Review*, 91/2 (1986), 1053–75.
33. For a more detailed critique, see Dietz, 'Citizenship with a Feminist Face: The Problem with Maternal Thinking', *Political Theory*, 13/1 (1985), 19–35.
34. The alternative conception introduced here—of politics as participatory and citizenship as the active engagement of peers in the public realm—has been of considerable interest to political theorists and historians over the past twenty years, and has developed in detail as an alternative to the liberal view. Feminists now need to consider the significance of this perspective in regard to their own political theories. Perhaps the leading contemporary exponent of politics as the active life of citizens is Hannah Arendt, *The Human Condition* (Chicago:

University of Chicago Press, 1958) and *On Revolution* (New York: Penguin, 1963). But alternatives to liberalism are also explored as 'civic republicanism' in the work of J. G. A. Pocock, *The Machiavellian Moment: Florentine Political Thought and the Atlantic Republican Tradition* (Princeton, NJ: Princeton University Press, 1975), and in the recent 'communitarian turn' articulated by Michael Sandel in his critique of the tradition of thinkers from Kant to Rawls, *Liberalism and the Limits of Justice* (Cambridge: Cambridge University Press, 1982). For other 'democratic' critiques of liberalism, see Benjamin Barber, *Strong Democracy: Participatory Politics for a New Age* (Berkeley: University of California Press, 1984); Joshua Cohen and Joel Rogers, *On Democracy: Toward a Transformation of American Society* (New York: Penguin, 1983); Russell Hanson, *The Democratic Imagination in America* (Princeton, NJ: Princeton University Press, 1985); Lawrence Goodwyn, *Democratic Promise: The Populist Movement in America* (New York: Oxford University Press, 1976); Carole Pateman, *Participation and Democratic Theory* (Cambridge: Cambridge University Press, 1970); Michael Walzer, *Radical Principles* (New York: Basic Books, 1980); and Sheldon Wolin, *Politics and Vision* (Boston: Little, Brown, 1963). Also see the short-lived but useful journal *Democracy* (1981–1983).

35. C. Douglas Lummis, 'The Radicalization of Democracy', *Democracy*, 2/4 (1982), 9–16.

36. I would reiterate, however, that despite its historical propensity to collapse democracy into a capitalist economic ethic, liberalism is not without its own vital ethical principles (namely, individual freedom and equality) that democrats ignore to their peril. The task for 'ethical liberals', as MacPherson puts it in *The Life and Times of Liberal Democracy*, is to detach these principles from the 'market assumptions' of capitalism and integrate them into a truly democratic vision of participatory citizenship. By the same token, the task for participatory democrats is to preserve the principles of freedom and equality that are the special legacy of liberalism.

37. Sheldon Wolin, 'The Peoples' Two Bodies', *Democracy* 1/1 (1981), 9–24.

38. I do not intend to imply that feminism is the only democratic movement that has emerged in the recent American past or that it is the only one from which we can draw examples. There are others—the civil rights movement, the populist resurgence, the collective political gatherings occasioned by the farm crises of the 1980s, gay liberation, and so on. But in its organization and decentralized practices, the feminist movement has been the most consistently democratic, its liberal, interest-group side (NOW) notwithstanding.

39. The phrase 'forms of freedom' comes from Jane Mansbridge, 'Feminism and the Forms of Freedom', in Frank Fischer and Carmen Siriani (eds.), *Critical Studies in Organization and Bureaucracy* (Philadelphia: Temple University Press, 1984), 472–86.

40. Some of the historical precedents I have in mind are developed in Linda Kerber's book, *Women of the Republic* (New York: Norton, 1980), especially in ch. 3, 'The Meaning of Female Patriotism', in which she reconsiders the political activism of women in revolutionary America. Other activist precedents that contemporary feminists might recall and preserve are discussed in Sara M. Evans and Harry C. Boyte, *Free Spaces: The Sources of Democratic Change in America* (New York: Harper and Row, 1986); these include the abolitionist movement, the suffrage movement, the Women's Christian Temperance Union, the settlement house movement, and the National Women's Trade

Union League, as well as contemporary forms of feminist organization and action.

41. My point here is not that the soviets of 1917 or the Polish KOR of 1978 can serve as models for participatory citizenship in late twentieth-century America, but rather that an alternative to liberal citizenship can take root only if it is distilled into a framework of conceptual notions. The historical moments I mention (and others) provide the experiential and practical reality for such a conceptual framework and thus merit incorporation into feminist democratic politics. Or, as Arendt writes in *On Revolution*, 'What saves the affairs of moral men from their inherent futility is nothing but the incessant talk about them, which in turn remains futile unless certain concepts, certain guideposts for future remembrance and even for sheer reference, arise out of it' (20). The diverse practices mentioned above should be perceived as guideposts and references that might inspire a democratic spirit rather than as literal examples to be emulated in keeping with such a spirit.

19 Polity and Group Difference: A Critique of the Ideal of Universal Citizenship

Iris Marion Young

An ideal of universal citizenship has driven the emancipatory momentum of modern political life. Ever since the bourgeoisie challenged aristocratic privileges by claiming equal political rights for citizens as such, women, workers, Jews, blacks, and others have pressed for inclusion in that citizenship status. Modern political theory asserted the equal moral worth of all persons, and social movements of the oppressed took this seriously as implying the inclusion of all persons in full citizenship status under the equal protection of the law.

Citizenship for everyone, and everyone the same *qua* citizen. Modern political thought generally assumed that the universality of citizenship in the sense of citizenship for all implies a universality of citizenship in the sense that citizenship status transcends particularity and difference. Whatever the social or group differences among citizens, whatever their inequalities of wealth, status, and power in the everyday activities of civil society, citizenship gives everyone the same status as peers in the political public. With equality conceived as sameness, the ideal of universal citizenship carries at least two meanings in addition to the extension of citizenship to everyone: (1) universality defined as general in opposition to particular; what citizens have in common as opposed to how they differ, and (2) universality in the sense of laws and rules that say the same for all and apply to all in the same way; laws and rules that are blind to individual and group differences.

During this angry, sometimes bloody, political struggle in the nineteenth and twentieth centuries, many among the excluded and disadvantaged thought that winning full citizenship status, that is, equal political and civil rights, would lead to their freedom and equality. Now, in the late twentieth century, however, when

Reprinted by permission from *Ethics*, 9 (1989), 250–74. Copyright © 1989 by the University of Chicago. All rights reserved.

citizenship rights have been formally extended to all groups in liberal capitalist societies, some groups still find themselves treated as second-class citizens. Social movements of oppressed and excluded groups have recently asked why extension of equal citizenship rights has not led to social justice and equality. Part of the answer is straightforwardly Marxist: those social activities that most determine the status of individuals and groups are anarchic and oligarchic; economic life is not sufficiently under the control of citizens to affect the unequal status and treatment of groups. I think this is an important and correct diagnosis of why equal citizenship has not eliminated oppression, but in this article I reflect on another reason more intrinsic to the meaning of politics and citizenship as expressed in much modern thought.

The assumed link between citizenship for everyone, on the one hand, and the two other senses of citizenship—having a common life with and being treated in the same way as the other citizens—on the other, is itself a problem. Contemporary social movements of the oppressed have weakened the link. They assert a positivity and pride in group specificity against ideals of assimilation. They have also questioned whether justice always means that law and policy should enforce equal treatment for all groups. Embryonic in these challenges lies a concept of *differentiated* citizenship as the best way to realize the inclusion and participation of everyone in full citizenship.

In this article I argue that far from implying one another, the universality of citizenship, in the sense of the inclusion and participation of everyone, stands in tension with the other two meanings of universality embedded in modern political ideas: universality as generality, and universality as equal treatment. First, the idea that the activities of citizenship express or create a general will that transcends the particular differences of group affiliation, situation, and interest has in practice excluded groups judged not capable of adopting that general point of view; the idea of citizenship as expressing a general will has tended to enforce a homogeneity of citizens. To the degree that contemporary proponents of revitalized citizenship retain that idea of a general will and common life, they implicitly support the same exclusions and homogeneity. Thus I argue that the inclusion and participation of everyone in public discussion and decision making requires mechanisms for group representation. Second, where differences in capacities, culture, values, and behavioural styles exist among groups, but some of these groups are privileged, strict adherence to a principle of equal treatment tends to perpetuate oppression or disadvantage. The inclusion and participation of everyone in social and political institutions therefore sometimes requires the articulation of special rights that attend to group differences in order to undermine oppression and disadvantage.

I. CITIZENSHIP AS GENERALITY

Many contemporary political theorists regard capitalist welfare society as depoliticized. Its interest group pluralism privatizes policy-making, consigning it to back-room deals and autonomous regulatory agencies and groups. Interest-group pluralism fragments both policy and the interests of the individual, making it difficult to assess issues in relation to one another and set priorities. The fragmented and privatized nature of the political process, moreover, facilitates the dominance of the more powerful interests.[1]

In response to this privatization of the political process, many writers call for a renewed public life and a renewed commitment to the virtues of citizenship. Democracy requires that citizens of welfare corporate society awake from their privatized consumerist slumbers, challenge the experts who claim the sole right to rule, and collectively take control of their lives and institutions through processes of active discussion that aim at reaching collective decisions.[2] In participatory democratic institutions citizens develop and exercise capacities of reasoning, discussion, and socializing that otherwise lie dormant, and they move out of their private existence to address others and face them with respect and concern for justice. Many who invoke the virtues of citizenship in opposition to the privatization of politics in welfare capitalist society assume as models for contemporary public life the civic humanism of thinkers such as Machiavelli or, more often, Rousseau.[3]

With these social critics I agree that interest group pluralism, because it is privatized and fragmented, facilitates the domination of corporate, military, and other powerful interests. With them I think democratic processes require the institutionalization of genuinely public discussion. There are serious problems, however, with uncritically assuming as a model the ideals of the civic public that come to us from the tradition of modern political thought.[4] The ideal of the public realm of citizenship as expressing a general will, a point of view and interest that citizens have in common which transcends their differences, has operated in fact as a demand for homogeneity among citizens. The exclusion of groups defined as different was explicitly acknowledged before this century. In our time, the excluding consequences of the universalist ideal of a public that embodies a common will are more subtle, but they still obtain.

The tradition of civic republicanism stands in critical tension with the individualist contract theory of Hobbes or Locke. Where liberal individualism regards the state as a necessary instrument to mediate conflict and regulate action so that individuals can have the freedom to pursue their private ends, the republican tradition locates freedom and autonomy in the actual public activities of citizenship. By participating in public discussion and collective decision making, citizens transcend their particular self-interested lives and the pursuit of private interests to adopt a general point of view from which they agree on the common good. Citizenship is an expression of the universality of human life; it is a realm of rationality and freedom as opposed to the heteronomous realm of particular need, interest, and desire.

Nothing in this understanding of citizenship as universal as opposed to particular, common as opposed to differentiated, implies extending full citizenship status to all groups. Indeed, at least some modern republicans thought just the contrary. While they extolled the virtues of citizenship as expressing the universality of humanity, they consciously excluded some people from citizenship on the grounds that they could not adopt the general point of view, or that their inclusion would disperse and divide the public. The ideal of a common good, a general will, a shared public life leads to pressures for a homogeneous citizenry.

Feminists in particular have analyzed how the discourse that links the civic public with fraternity is not merely metaphorical. Founded by men, the modern state and its public realm of citizenship paraded as universal values and norms which were derived from specifically masculine experience: militarist norms of honour and homoerotic camaraderie; respectful competition and bargaining among independent agents; discourse framed in unemotional tones of dispassionate reason.

Several commentators have argued that in extolling the virtues of citizenship as participation in a universal public realm, modern men expressed a flight from sexual difference, from having to recognize another kind of existence that they could not entirely understand, and from the embodiment, dependency on nature, and morality that women represent.[5] Thus the opposition between the universality of the public realm of citizenship and the particularity of private interest became conflated with oppositions between reason and passion, masculine and feminine.

The bourgeois world instituted a moral division of labour between reason and sentiment, identifying masculinity with reason and femininity with sentiment, desire, and the needs of the body. Extolling a public realm of manly virtue and citizenship as independence, generality, and dispassionate reason entailed creating the private sphere of the family as the place to which emotion, sentiment, and bodily needs must be confined.[6] The generality of the public thus depends on excluding women, who are responsible for tending to that private realm, and who lack the dispassionate rationality and independence required of good citizens.

In his social scheme, for example, Rousseau excluded women from the public realm of citizenship because they are the caretakers of affectivity, desire, and the body. If we allowed appeals to desires and bodily needs to move public debates, we would undermine public deliberation by fragmenting its unity. Even within the domestic realm, moreover, women must be dominated. Their dangerous, heterogeneous sexuality must be kept chaste and confined to marriage. Enforcing chastity on women will keep each family a separated unity, preventing the chaos and blood-mingling that would be produced by illegitimate children. Chaste, enclosed women in turn oversee men's desire by tempering its potentially disruptive impulses through moral education. Men's desire for women itself threatens to shatter and disperse the universal, rational realm of the public, as well as to disrupt the neet distinction between the public and private. As guardians of the private realm of need, desire, and affectivity, women must ensure that men's impulses do not subvert the universality of reason. The moral neatness of the female-tended hearth, moreover, will temper the possessively individualistic impulses of the particularistic realm of business and commerce, since competition, like sexuality, constantly threatens to explode the unity of the polity.[7]

It is important to recall that universality of citizenship conceived as generality operated to exclude not only women, but other groups as well. European and American republicans found little contradiction in promoting a universality of citizenship that excluded some groups, because the idea that citizenship is the same for all translated in practice to the requirement that all citizens be the same. The white male bourgeoisie conceived republican virtue as rational, restrained, and chaste, not yielding to passion or desire for luxury, and thus able to rise above desire and need to a concern for the common good. This implied excluding poor people and wage workers from citizenship on the grounds that they were too motivated by need to adopt a general perspective. The designers of the American constitution were no more egalitarian than their European brethren in this respect; they specifically intended to restrict the access of the labouring class to the public, because they feared disruption of commitment to the general interests.

These early American republicans were also quite explicit about the need for the homogeneity of citizens, fearing that group differences would tend to undermine commitment to the general interest. This meant that the presence of blacks and Indians, and later Mexicans and Chinese, in the territories of the republic posed a threat that only assimilation, extermination, or dehumanization could thwart. Various combinations of these three were used, of course, but recognition of these groups as peers in the public was never an option. Even such republican fathers as Jefferson identified the red and black people in their territories with wild nature and passion, just as they feared that women outside the domestic realm were wanton and avaricious. They defined moral, civilized republican life in opposition to this backward-looking, uncultivated desire that they identified with women and non-whites.[8] A similar logic of exclusion operated in Europe, where Jews were particular targets.[9]

These republican exclusions were not accidental, nor were they inconsistent with the ideal of universal citizenship as understood by these theorists. They were a direct consequence of a dichotomy between public and private that defined the public as a realm of generality in which all particularities are left behind, and defined the private as the particular, the realm of affectivity, affiliation, need, and the body. As long as that dichotomy is in place, the inclusion of the formerly excluded in the definition of citizenship—women, workers, Jews, blacks, Asians, Indians, Mexicans—imposes a homogeneity that suppresses group differences in the public and in practice forces the formerly excluded groups to be measured according to norms derived from and defined by privileged groups.

Contemporary critics of interest group liberalism who call for a renewed public life certainly do not intend to exclude any adult persons or groups from citizenship. They are democrats, convinced that only the inclusion and participation of all citizens in political life will make for wise and fair decisions and a polity that enhances rather than inhibits the capacities of its citizens and their relations with one another. The emphasis by such participatory democrats on generality and commonness, however, still threatens to suppress differences among citizens.

I shall focus on the text of Benjamin Barber, who, in his book, *Strong Democracy*, produces a compelling and concrete vision of participatory democratic processes. Barber recognizes the need to safeguard a democratic public from intended or inadvertent group exclusions, though he offers no proposals for safeguarding the inclusion and participation of everyone. He also argues fiercely against contemporary political theorists who construct a model of political discourse purified of affective dimensions. Thus Barber does not fear the disruption of the generality and rationality of the public by desire and the body in the way that nineteenth-century republican theorists did. He retains, however, a conception of the civic public as defined by generality, as opposed to group affinity and particular need and interest. He makes a clear distinction between the public realm of citizenship and civic activity on the one hand and a private realm of particular identities, roles, affiliations, and interests on the other. Citizenship by no means exhausts people's social identities, but it takes moral priority over all social activities in a strong democracy. The pursuit of particular interests, the pressing of the claims of particular groups, all must take place within a framework of community and common vision established by the public realm. Thus Barber's vision of participatory democracy continues to rely on an opposition between the public sphere of a general interest and a private sphere of particular interest and affiliation.[10]

While recognizing the need for majority rule procedures and means of safeguarding minority rights, Barber asserts that 'the strong democrat regrets every division and regards the existence of majorities as a sign that mutualism has failed' (207). A community of citizens, he says, 'owes the character of its existence to what its constituent members have in common' (232), and this entails transcending the order of individual needs and wants to recognize that 'we are a moral body whose existence depends on the common order of individual needs and wants into a single vision of the future in which all can share' (224). This common vision is not imposed on individuals from above, however, but is forged by them in talking and working together. Barber's models of such common projects, however, reveal his latent biases: 'Like players on a team or soldiers at war, those who practice a common politics may come to feel ties that they never felt before they commenced their common activity.

This sort of bonding, which emphasizes common procedures, common work, and a shared sense of what a community needs to succeed, rather than monolithic purposes and ends, serves strong democracy most successfully' (244).

The attempt to realize an ideal of universal citizenship that finds the public embodying generality as opposed to particularity, commonness versus difference, will tend to exclude or to put at a disadvantage some groups, even when they have formally equal citizenship status. The idea of the public as universal and the concomitant identification of particularity with privacy makes homogeneity a requirement of public participation. In exercising their citizenship, all citizens should assume the same impartial, general point of view transcending all particular interests, perspectives, and experiences.

But such an impartial general perspective is a myth.[1] People necessarily and properly consider public issues in terms influenced by their situated experience and perception of social relations. Different social groups have different needs, cultures, histories, experiences, and perceptions of social relations which influence their interpretation of the meaning and consequences of policy proposals and influence the form of their political reasoning. These differences in political interpretation are not merely or even primarily a result of differing or conflicting interests, for groups have differing interpretations even when they seek to promote justice and not merely their own self-regarding ends. In a society where some groups are privileged while others are oppressed, insisting that as citizens persons should leave behind their particular affiliations and experiences to adopt a general point of view serves only to reinforce the privilege; for the perspectives and interests of the privileged will tend to dominate this unified public, marginalizing or silencing those of other groups.

Barber asserts that responsible citizenship requires transcending particular affiliations, commitments, and needs, because a public cannot function if its members are concerned only with their private interests. Here he makes an important confusion between plurality and privatization. The interest group pluralism that he and others criticize indeed institutionalizes and encourages an egoistic, self-regarding view of the political process, one that sees parties entering the political competition for scarce goods and privileges only in order to maximize their own gain, and therefore they need not listen to or respond to the claims of others who have their own point of view. The processes and often the outcomes of interest group bargaining, moreover, take place largely in private; they are neither revealed nor discussed in a forum that genuinely involves all those potentially affected by decisions.

Privacy in this sense of private bargaining for the sake of private gain is quite different from plurality, in the sense of the differing group experiences, affiliations, and commitments that operate in any large society. It is possible for persons to maintain their group identity and to be influenced by their perceptions of social events derived from their group-specific experience, and at the same time to be public-spirited, in the sense of being open to listening to the claims of others and not being concerned for their own gain alone. It is possible and necessary for people to take a critical distance from their own immediate desires and gut reactions in order to discuss public proposals. Doing so, however, cannot require that citizens abandon their particular affiliations, experiences, and social location. As I will discuss in the next section, having the voices of particular group perspectives other than one's own explicitly represented in public discussion best fosters the maintenance of such critical distance without the pretence of impartiality.

A repoliticization of public life should not require the creation of a unified public realm in which citizens leave behind their particular group affiliations, histories, and needs to discuss a general interest or common good. Such a desire for unity suppresses but does not eliminate differences and tends to exclude some perspectives from the public.[12] Instead of a universal citizenship in the sense of this generality, we need a group differentiated citizenship and a heterogeneous public. In a heterogeneous public, differences are publicly recognized and acknowledged as irreducible, by which I mean that persons from one perspective or history can never completely understand and adopt the point of view of those with other group-based perspectives and histories. Yet commitment to the need and desire to decide together the society's policies fosters communication across those differences.

II. DIFFERENTIATED CITIZENSHIP AS GROUP REPRESENTATION

In her study of the functioning of a New England Town Meeting government, Jane Mansbridge discusses how women, blacks, working-class people, and poor people tend to participate less and have their interests represented less than whites, middle-class professionals, and men. Even though all citizens have the right to participate in the decision-making process, the experience and perspectives of some groups tend to be silenced for many reasons. White middle-class men assume authority more than others, and they are more practised at speaking persuasively; mothers and old people often find it more difficult than others to get to meetings.[13] Amy Gutmann also discusses how participatory democratic structures tend to silence disadvantaged groups. She offers the example of community control of schools, where increased democracy led to increased segregation in many cities because the more privileged and articulate whites were able to promote their perceived interests against blacks' just demand for equal treatment in an integrated system.[14] Such cases indicate that when participatory democratic structures define citizenship in universalistic and unified terms, they tend to reproduce existing group oppression.

Gutmann argues that such oppressive consequences of democratization imply that social and economic equality must be achieved before political equality can be instituted. I cannot quarrel with the value of social and economic equality, but I think its achievement depends on increasing political equality as much as the achievement of political equality depends on increasing social and economic equality. If we are not to be forced to trace a utopian circle, we need to solve now the 'paradox of democracy' by which social power makes some citizens more equal than others, and equality of citizenship makes some people more powerful citizens. That solution lies at least in part in providing institutionalized means for the explicit recognition and representation of oppressed groups. Before discussing principles and practices involved in such a solution, however, it is necessary to say something about what a group is and when a group is oppressed.

The concept of a social group has become politically important because recent emancipatory and leftist social movements have mobilized around group identity rather than exclusively class or economic interests. In many cases such mobilization has consisted in embracing and positively defining a despised or devalued ethnic or racial identity. In the women's movement, gay rights movement, or elders' movements, different social status based on age, sexuality, physical capacity, or the division of labour has been taken up as a positive group identity for political mobilization.

I shall not attempt to define a social group here, but I shall point to several marks which distinguish a social group from other collectivities of people. A social group involves first of all an affinity with other persons by which they identify with one another, and by which other people identify them. A person's particular sense of history, understanding of social relations, and personal possibilities, her or his mode of reasoning, values, and expressive styles are constituted at least partly by her or his group identity. Many group definitions come from the outside, from other groups that label and stereotype certain people. In such circumstances the despised group members often find their affinity in their oppression. The concept of social group must be distinguished from two concepts with which it might be confused: aggregate and association.

An aggregate is any classification of persons according to some attribute. Persons can be aggregated according to any number of attributes, all of them equally arbitrary—eye colour, the make of car we drive, the street we live on. At times the groups that have emotional and social salience in our society are interpreted as aggregates, as arbitrary classifications of persons according to attributes of skin colour, genitals, of years lived. A social group, however, is not defined primarily by a set of shared attributes, but by the sense of identity that people have. What defines black Americans as a social group is not primarily their skin colour; this is exemplified by the fact that some persons whose skin colour is fairly light, for example, identify as black. Though sometimes objective attributes are a necessary condition for classifying oneself or others as a member of a certain social group, it is the identification of certain persons with a social status, a common history that social status produces, and a self-identification that defines the group as a group.

Political and social theorists tend more often to elide social groups with associations rather than aggregates. By an association I mean a collectivity of persons who come together voluntarily—such as a club, corporation, political party, church, college, union, lobbying organization, or interest group. An individualist contract model of society applies to associations but not to groups. Individuals constitute associations; they come together as already formed persons and set them up, establishing rules, positions, and offices.

Since one joins an association, even if membership in it fundamentally affects one's life, one does not take that association membership to define one's very identity in the way, for example, being Navajo might. Group affinity, on the other hand, has the character of what Heidegger calls 'thrownness': one finds oneself as a member of a group, whose existence and relations one experiences as always already having been. For a person's identity is defined in relation to how others identify him or her, and others do so in terms of groups which always already have specific attributes, stereotypes, and norms associated with them, in reference to which a person's identity will be formed. From the thrownness of group affinity it does not follow that one cannot leave groups and enter new ones. Many women become lesbian after identifying as heterosexual, and anyone who lives long enough becomes old. These cases illustrate thrownness precisely in that such changes in group affinity are experienced as a transformation in one's identity.

A social group should not be understood as an essence or nature with a specific set of common attributes. Instead, group identity should be understood in relational terms. Social processes generate groups by creating relational differentiations, situations of clustering, and affective bonding in which people feel affinity for other people. Sometimes groups define themselves by despising or excluding others whom they define as other, and whom they dominate and oppress. Although social processes of affinity and separation define groups, they do not give groups a substantive identity. There is no common nature that members of a group have.

As products of social relations, groups are fluid; they come into being and may fade away. Homosexual practices have existed in many societies and historical periods, for example, but gay male group identification exists only in the West in the twentieth century. Group identity may become salient only under specific circumstances, when in interaction with other groups. Most people in modern societies have multiple group identifications, moreover, and therefore groups themselves are not discrete unities. Every group has group differences cutting across it.

I think that group differentiation is an inevitable and desirable process in modern societies. We need not settle that question, however. I merely assume that ours is now a group-differentiated society, and that it will continue to be so for some time to come. Our political problem is that some of our groups are privileged and others are oppressed.

But what is oppression? In another place I give a fuller account of the concept of oppression.[15] Briefly, a group is oppressed when one or more of the following conditions occurs to all or a large portion of its members: (1) the benefits of their work or energy go to others without those others reciprocally benefiting them (exploitation); (2) they are excluded from participation in major social activities, which in our society means primarily a workplace (marginalization); (3) they live and work under the authority of others, and have little work autonomy and authority over others themselves (power-lessness); (4) as a group they are stereotyped at the same time that their experience and situation is invisible in the society in general, and they have little opportunity and little audience for the expression of their experience and perspective on social events (cultural imperialism); (5) group members suffer random violence and harassment motivated by group hatred or fear. In the United States today at least the following groups are oppressed in one or more of these ways: women, blacks, Native Americans, Chicanos, Puerto Ricans and other Spanish-speaking Americans, Asian Americans, gay men, lesbians, working-class people, poor people, old people, and mentally and physically disabled people.

Perhaps in some utopian future there will be a society without group oppression and disadvantage. We cannot develop political principles by starting with the assumption of a completely just society, however, but must begin from within the general historical and social conditions in which we exist. This means that we must develop participatory democratic theory not on the assumption of an undifferentiated humanity, but rather on the assumption that there are group differences and that some groups are actually or potentially oppressed or disadvantaged.

I assert, then, the following principle: a democratic public, however that is constituted, should provide mechanisms for the effective representation and recognition of the distinct voices and perspectives of those of its constituent groups that are oppressed or disadvantaged within it. Such group representation implies institutional mechanisms and public resources supporting three activities: (1) self-organization of group members so that they gain a sense of collective empowerment and a reflective understanding of their collective experience and interests in the context of the society; (2) voicing a group's analysis of how social policy proposals affect them, and generating policy proposals themselves, in institutionalized contexts where decision-makers are obliged to show that they have taken these perspectives into consideration; (3) having veto power regarding specific policies that affect a group directly, for example, reproductive rights for women, or use of reservation lands for Native Americans.

The principles call for specific representation only for oppressed or disadvantaged groups, because privileged groups already are represented. Thus the principle would not apply in a society entirely without oppression. I do not regard the principle as merely provisional, or instrumental, however, because I believe that group difference in modern complex societies is both inevitable and desirable, and that wherever there is group difference, disadvantage or oppression always looms as a possibility. Thus a society should always be committed to representation for oppressed or disadvantaged groups and ready to implement such representation when it appears. These considerations are rather academic in our own context, however, since we live in a society with deep group oppressions the complete elimination of which is only a remote possibility.

Social and economic privilege means, among other things, that the groups which have it behave as though they have a right to speak and be heard, that others treat them as though they have that right, and that they have the material, personal, and organizational resources that enable them to speak and be heard in public. The privileged are usually not inclined to protect and further the interests of the oppressed partly because their social position prevents them from understanding those interests, and partly because to some degree their privilege depends on the continued oppression of others. So a major reason for explicit representation of oppressed groups in discussion and decision-making is to undermine oppression. Such group representation also exposes in public the specificity of the assumptions and experience of the privileged; for unless confronted with different perspectives on social relations and events, different values and language, most people tend to assert their own perspective as universal.

Theorists and politicians extol the virtues of citizenship because through public participation persons are called on to transcend merely self-centred motivation and acknowledge their dependence on and responsibility to others. The responsible citizen is concerned not merely with interests but with justice, with acknowledging that each other person's interest and point of view is as good as his or her own, and that the needs and interests of everyone must be voiced and be heard by the others, who must acknowledge, respect, and address those needs and interests. The problem of universality has occurred when this responsibility has been interpreted as transcendence into a general perspective.

I have argued that defining citizenship as generality avoids and obscures this requirement that all experiences, needs, and perspectives on social events have a voice and are respected. A general perspective does not exist which all persons can adopt and from which all experiences and perspectives can be understood and taken into account. The existence of social groups implies different, though not necessarily exclusive, histories, experiences, and perspectives on social life that people have, and it implies that they do not entirely understand the experience of other groups. No one can claim to speak in the general interest, because no one of the groups can speak for another, and certainly no-one can speak for them all. Thus the only way to have all group experience and social perspectives voiced, heard, and taken account of it is to have them specifically represented in the public.

Group representation is the best means to promote just outcomes to democratic decision-making processes. The argument for this claim relies on Habermas's conception of communicative ethics. In the absence of a Philosopher King who reads transcendent normative verities, the only ground for a claim that a policy or decision is just is that it has been arrived at by a public which has truly promoted free expression of all needs and points of view. In his formulation of a communicative ethic, Habermas retains inappropriately an appeal to a universal or impartial point of view from which claims in a public should be addressed. A communicative ethic that does not merely articulate a hypothetical public that would justify decisions, but proposes actual conditions tending to promote just outcomes of decision-making processes, should promote conditions for the expression of the concrete needs of all individuals in their particularity.[16] The concreteness of individual lives, their needs and interests, and their perception of the needs and interests of others, I have argued, are structured partly through group-based experience and identity. Thus full and free expression of concrete needs and interests under social circumstances where some groups are silenced or marginalized requires that they have a specific voice in deliberation and decision making.

The introduction of such differentiation and particularity into democratic procedures does not encourage the expression of narrow self-interest; indeed, group representation is the best antidote to self-deceiving self-interest masked as an impartial or general interest. In a democratically structured public where social inequality is mitigated through group representation, individuals or groups cannot simply assert that they want something; they must say that justice requires or allows that they have it. Group representation provides the opportunity for some to express their needs or interests who would not likely be heard without that representation. At the same time, the test of whether a claim on the public is just, or a mere expression of self-interest, is best made when persons making it must confront the opinion of others who have explicitly different, though not necessarily conflicting, experiences, priorities, and needs. As a person of social privilege, I am not likely to go outside of myself and have a regard for social justice unless I am forced to listen to the voice of those my privilege tends to silence.

Group representation best institutionalizes fairness under circumstances of social oppression and domination. But group representation also maximizes knowledge expressed in discussion, and thus promotes practical wisdom. Group differences not only involve different needs, interests, and goals, but probably more important different social locations and experiences from which social facts and policies are understood. Members of different social groups are likely to know different things about the structure of social relations and the potential and actual effects of social policies. Because of their history, their group-specific values or modes of expression, their relationship to other groups, the kind of work they do, and so on, different groups have different ways of understanding the meaning of social events, which can contribute to the others' understanding if expressed and heard.

Emancipatory social movements in recent years have developed some political practices committed to the idea of a heterogeneous public, and they have at least partly or temporarily instituted such publics. Some political organizations, unions, and feminist groups have formal caucuses for groups (such as blacks, Latinos, women, gay men and lesbians, and disabled or old people) whose perspectives might be silenced without them. Frequently these organizations have procedures for caucus voice in organization discussion and caucus representation in decision making, and some organizations also require representation of members of specific groups in leadership bodies. Under the influence of these social movements asserting group difference, during some years even the Democratic party, at both national and state levels, has instituted delegate rules that include provisions for group representation.

Though its realization is far from assured, the ideal of a 'rainbow coalition' expresses such a heterogeneous public with forms of group representation. The traditional form of coalition corresponds to the idea of a unified public that transcends particular differences of experience and concern. In traditional coalitions, diverse groups work together for ends which they agree interest or affect them all in a similar way, and they generally agree that the differences of perspective, interests, or opinion among them will not surface in the public statements and actions of the coalition. In a rainbow coalition, by contrast, each of the constituent groups affirms the presence of the others and affirms the specificity of its experience and perspective on social issues.[17] In the rainbow public, blacks do not simply tolerate the participation of gays, labour activists do not grudgingly work alongside peace movement veterans, and none of these paternalistically allow feminist participation. Ideally, a rainbow coalition affirms the presence and supports the claims of each of the oppressed groups or political movements constituting it, and it arrives at a political programme not by voicing some 'principles of unity' that hide differences, but rather by allowing each constituency to analyse economic and social issues from the perspective of its experience. This implies that each group maintains autonomy in relating to its constituency, and that decision-making bodies and procedures provide for group representation.

To the degree that there are heterogeneous publics operating according to the principles of group representation in contemporary politics, they exist only in organizations and movements resisting the majority politics. Nevertheless, in principle participatory democracy entails commitment to institutions of a heterogeneous public in all spheres of democratic decision making. Until and unless group oppression or disadvantages are eliminated, political publics, including democratized workplaces and government decision-making bodies, should include the specific representation of those oppressed groups, through which those groups express their specific understanding of the issues before the public and register a group-based vote. Such structures of group representation should not replace structures of regional or party representation, but should exist alongside them.

Implementing principles of group representation in national politics in the United States, or in restructured democratic publics within particular institutions such as factories, offices, universities, churches, and social-service agencies, would require creative thinking and flexibility. There are no models to follow. European models of consociational democratic institutions, for example, cannot be taken outside of the contexts in which they have evolved, and even within them they do not operate in a very democratic fashion. Reports of experiments with publicly institutionalized self-organization among women, indigenous peoples, workers, peasants, and students in contemporary Nicaragua offer an example closer to the conception I am advocating.[18]

The principle of group representation calls for such structures of representation for oppressed or disadvantaged groups. But what groups deserve representation? Clear candidates for group representation in policy making in the United States are women, blacks,

Native Americans, old people, poor people, disabled people, gay men and lesbians, Spanish-speaking Americans, young people, and non-professional workers. But it may not be necessary to ensure specific representation of all these groups in all public contexts and in all policy discussions. Representation should be designated whenever the group's history and social situation provide a particular perspective on the issues, when the interests of its members are specifically affected, and when its perceptions and interests are not likely to receive expression without that representation.

An origin problem emerges in proposing a principle such as this, which no philosophical argument can solve. To implement this principle a public must be constituted to decide which groups deserve specific representation in decision-making procedures. What are the principles guiding the composition of such a 'constitutional convention'? Who should decide what groups should receive representation, and by what procedures should this decision take place? No programme or set of principles can found a politics, because politics is always a process in which we are already engaged; principles can be appealed to in the course of political discussion, they can be accepted by a public as guiding their action. I propose a principle of group representation as a part of such potential discussion, but it cannot replace that discussion or determine its outcome.

What should be the mechanisms of group representation? Earlier I stated that the self-organization of the group is one of the aspects of a principle of group representation. Members of the group must meet together in democratic forums to discuss issues and formulate group positions and proposals. This principle of group representation should be understood as part of a larger programme for democratized decision-making processes. Public life and decision-making processes should be transformed, so that all citizens have significantly greater opportunities for participation in discussion and decision making. All citizens should have access to neighbourhood or district assemblies where they participate in discussion and decision-making. In such a more participatory democratic scheme, members of oppressed groups would also have group assemblies, which would delegate group representatives.

One might well ask how the idea of a heterogeneous public which encourages self-organization of groups and structures of group representation in decision-making is different from the interest-group pluralism criticism which I endorsed earlier in this article. First, in the heterogeneous public not any collectivity of persons that chooses to form an association counts as a candidate for group representation. Only those groups that describe the major identities and major status relationships constituting the society or particular institution, and which are oppressed or disadvantaged, deserve specific representation in a heterogeneous public. In the structures of interest group pluralism, Friends of the Whales, the National Association for the Advancement of Coloured People, the National Rifle Association, and the National Freeze Campaign all have the same status, and each influences decision making to the degree that their resources and ingenuity can win out in the competition for policy-makers' ears. While democratic politics must maximize freedom of the expression of opinion and interest, that is a different issue from ensuring that the perspective of all groups has a voice.

Second, in the heterogeneous public the groups represented are not defined by some particular interest or goal, or some particular political position. Social groups are comprehensive identities and ways of life. Because of their experiences their members may have some common interests that they seek to press in the public. Their social location, however, tends to give them distinctive understandings of all aspects of the society and unique perspectives on social issues. For example, many Native Americans argue that their traditional religion and relation to land gives them a unique and important understanding of environmental problems.

Finally, interest-group pluralism operates precisely to forestall the emergence of public discussion and decision making. Each interest group promotes only its specific interest as thoroughly and forcefully as it can, and it need not consider the other interests competing in the political marketplace except strategically, as potential allies or adversaries in the pursuit of its own. The rules of interest group pluralism do not require justifying one's interest as right or as compatible with social justice. A heterogeneous public, however, is a *public*, where participants discuss together the issues before them and are supposed to come to a decision that they determine as best or most just.

III. UNIVERSAL RIGHTS AND SPECIAL RIGHTS

A second aspect of the universality of citizenship is today in tension with the goal of full inclusion and participation of all groups in political and social institutions: universality in the formulation of law and policies. Modern and contemporary liberalism hold as basic the principle that the rules and policies of the state, and in contemporary liberalism also the rules of private institutions, ought to be blind to race, gender, and other group differences. The public realm of the state and law properly should express its rules in general terms that abstract from the particularities of individual and group histories, needs, and situations to recognize all persons equally and treat all citizens in the same way.

As long as political ideology and practice persisted in defining some groups as unworthy of equal citizenship status because of supposedly natural differences from white male citizens, it was important for emancipatory movements to insist that all people are the same in respect of their moral worth and deserve equal citizenship. In this context, demands for equal rights that are blind to group differences were the only sensible way to combat exclusion and degradation.

Today, however, the social consensus is that all persons are of equal moral worth and deserve equal citizenship. With the near-achievement of equal rights for all groups, with the important exception of gay men and lesbians, group inequalities nevertheless remain. Under these circumstances many feminists, black liberation activists, and others struggling for the full inclusion and participation of all groups in this society's institutions and positions of power, reward, and satisfaction, argue that rights and rules that are universally formulated and thus blind to differences of race, culture, gender, age, or disability, perpetuate rather than undermine oppression.

Contemporary social movements seeking full inclusion and participation of oppressed and disadvantaged groups now find themselves faced with a dilemma of difference.[19] On the one hand, they must continue to deny that there are any essential differences between men and women, whites and blacks, able-bodied and disabled people, which justify denying women, blacks, or disabled people the opportunity to do anything that others are free to do or to be included in any institution or position. On the other hand, they have found it necessary to affirm that there are often group-based differences between men and women, whites and blacks, able-bodied and disabled people that make application of a strict principle of equal treatment, especially in competition for positions, unfair because these differences put those groups at a disadvantage. For example, white middle-class men as a group are socialized into the behavioural styles of a particular kind of articulateness, coolness, and competent authoritativeness that are most rewarded in professional and managerial life. To the degree that there are group differences that disadvantage, fairness seems to call for acknowledging rather than being blind to them.

Though in many respects the law is now blind to group differences, the society is not, and some groups continue to be marked as deviant and as the other. In everyday interactions, images, and decision-making, assumptions continue to be made about women, blacks, Latinos, gay men, lesbians, old people, and other marked groups, which continue to justify exclusions, avoidances, paternalism, and authoritarian treatment. Continued racist, sexist, homophobic, ageist, and ableist behaviours and institutions create particular circumstances for these groups, usually disadvantaging them in their opportunity to develop their capacities and giving them particular experiences and knowledge. Finally, in part because they have been segregated and excluded from one another, and in part because they have particular histories and traditions, there are cultural differences among social groups—differences in language, style of living, body comportment and gesture, values, and perspectives on society.

Acknowledging group difference in capacities, needs, culture, and cognitive styles poses a problem for those seeking to eliminate oppression only if difference is understood as deviance or deficiency. Such understanding presumes that some capacities, needs, culture, or cognitive styles are normal. I suggested earlier that their privilege allows dominant groups to assert their experience of and perspective on social events as impartial and objective. In a similar fashion, their privilege allows some groups to project their group-based capacities, values, and cognitive and behavioural styles as the norm to which all persons should be expected to conform. Feminists in particular have argued that most contemporary workplaces, especially the most desirable, presume a life-rhythm and behavioural style typical of men, and that women are expected to accommodate to the workplace expectations that assume those norms.

Where group differences in capacities, values, and behavioural or cognitive styles exist, equal treatment in the allocation of reward according to rules of merit composition will reinforce and perpetuate disadvantage. Equal treatment requires everyone to be measured according to the same norms, but in fact there are no 'neutral' norms of behaviour and performance. Where some groups are privileged and others oppressed, the formulation of law, policy, and the rules of private institutions tend to be biased in favour of the

421

privileged groups, because their particular experience implicitly sets the norm. Thus where there are group differences in capacities, socialization, values, and cognitive and cultural styles, only attending to such differences can enable the inclusion and participation of all groups in political and economic institutions. This implies that instead of always formulating rights and rules in universal terms that are blind to difference, some groups sometimes deserve special rights.[20] In what follows, I shall review several contexts of contemporary policy debate where I argue such special rights for oppressed or disadvantaged groups are appropriate.

The issue of a right to pregnancy and maternity leave, and the right to special treatment for nursing mothers, is highly controversial among feminists today. I do not intend here to wind through the intricacies of what has become a conceptually challenging and interesting debate in legal theory. As Linda Krieger argues, the issue of rights for pregnant and birthing mothers in relation to the workplace has created a paradigm crisis for our understanding of sexual equality, because the application of a principle of equal treatment on this issue has yielded results whose effects on women are at best ambiguous and at worst detrimental.[21]

In my view an equal-treatment approach on this issue is inadequate, because it either implies that women do not receive any right to leave and job security when having babies, or it assimilates such guarantees under a supposedly gender-neutral category of 'disability'. Such assimilation is unacceptable, because pregnancy and childbirth are normal conditions of normal women, they themselves count as socially necessary work, and they have unique and variable characteristics and needs.[22] Assimilating pregnancy into disability gives a negative meaning to these processes as 'unhealthy'. It suggests, moreover, that the primary or only reason that a woman has a right to leave and job security is that she is physically unable to work at her job, or that doing so would be more difficult than when she is not pregnant and recovering from childbirth. While these are important reasons, depending on the individual woman, another reason is that she ought to have the time to establish breastfeeding and develop a relationship and routine with her child, if she chooses.

The pregnancy-leave debate has been heated and extensive because both feminists and non-feminists tend to think of biological sex difference as the most fundamental and ineradicable difference. When difference slides into deviance, stigma, and disadvantage, this impression can engender the fear that sexual equality is not attainable. I think it is important to emphasize that reproduction is by no means the only context in which issues of same versus different treatment arise. It is not even the only context where it arises for issues involving bodily difference. The last twenty years have seen significant success in winning special rights for persons with physical and mental disabilities. Here is a clear case where promoting equality in participation and inclusion requires attending to the particular needs of different groups.

Another bodily difference which has not been as widely discussed in law and policy literature, but should be, is age. With increasing numbers of willing and able old people marginalized in our society, the issue of mandatory retirement has been increasingly discussed. This discussion has been muted because serious consideration of working rights for all people able and willing to work implies major restructuring of the allocation of labour in an economy with already socially volatile levels of unemployment. Forcing people out of their workplaces solely on account of their age is arbitrary and unjust. Yet I think it is also unjust to require old people to work on the same terms as younger people. Old people should have different working rights. When they reach a certain age they should be allowed to retire and receive income benefits. If they wish to continue working, they should be allowed more flexible and part-time schedules than most workers currently have.

Each of these cases of special rights in the workplace—pregnancy and birthing, physical disability, and being old—has its own purposes and structures. They all challenge, however, the same paradigm of the 'normal, healthy' worker and 'typical work situation'. In each case the circumstance that calls for different treatment should not be understood as lodged in the differently treated workers *per se*, but in their interaction with the structure and norms of the workplace. Even in cases such as these, that is, difference does not have its source in natural, unalterable, biological attributes, but in the relationship of bodies to conventional rules and practices. In each case the political claim for special rights emerges not from a need to compensate for an inferiority, as some would interpret it, but from a positive assertion of specificity in different forms of life.[23]

Issues of difference arise for law and policy not only regarding bodily being, but just as importantly for cultural integrity and invisibility. By culture I mean group-specific phenomena of behaviour, temperament, or meaning. Cultural differences include phenomena of language, speaking style or dialectic, body comportment, gesture, social practices, values, group-specific socialization, and so on. To the degree that groups are culturally different, however, equal treatment in many issues of social policy is unjust because it denies these cultural differences or makes them a liability. There are a vast number of issues where fairness involves attention to cultural differences and their effects, but I shall briefly discuss three: affirmative action, comparable worth, and bilingual, bicultural education and service.

Whether they involve quotas or not, affirmative-action programmes violate a principle of equal treatment because they are race- or gender-conscious in setting criteria for school admissions, jobs, or promotions. These policies are usually defended in one of two ways. Giving preference to race or gender is understood either as just compensation for groups that have suffered discrimination in the past, or as compensation for the present disadvantage these groups suffer because of that history of discrimination and exclusion.[24] I do not wish to quarrel with either of these justifications for the differential treatment based on race or gender implied by affirmative-action policies. I want to suggest that, in addition, we can understand affirmative-action policies as compensating for the cultural biases of standards and evaluators used by the schools or employers. These standards and evaluators reflect at least to some degree the specific life and cultural experience of dominant groups—whites, Anglos, or men. In a group-differentiated society, moreover, the development of truly neutral standards and evaluations is difficult or impossible, because female, black, or Latino cultural experience and the dominant cultures are in many respects not reducible to a common measure. Thus affirmative-action policies compensate for the dominance of one set of cultural attributes. Such an interpretation of affirmative action locates the 'problem' that affirmative action solves partly in the understandable biases of evaluators and their standards, rather than only in specific differences of the disadvantaged group.

Although they are not a matter of different treatment as such, comparable-worth policies similarly claim to challenge cultural biases in traditional evaluation in the worth of female-dominated occupations, and in doing so require attending to differences. Schemes of equal pay for work of comparable worth require that predominantly male and predominantly female jobs have similar wage structures if they involve similar degrees of skill, difficulty, stress, and so on. The problem in implementing these policies, of course, lies in designing methods of comparing the jobs, which often are very different. Most schemes of comparison choose to minimize sex differences by using supposedly gender-neutral criteria, such as educational attainment, speed of work, whether it involves manipulation of symbols, decision-making, and so on. Some writers have suggested, however, that standard classifications of job traits may be systematically biased to keep specific kinds of tasks involved in many female-dominated occupations hidden.[25] Many female-dominated occupations involve gender-specific kinds of labour—such as nurturing, smoothing over social relations, or the exhibition of sexuality—which most task-observation ignores.[26] A fair assessment of the skills and complexity of many female-dominated jobs may therefore involve paying explicit attention to gender differences in kinds of jobs rather than applying gender-blind categories of comparison.

Finally, linguistic and cultural minorities ought to have the right to maintain their language and culture and at the same time be entitled to all the benefits of citizenship, as well as valuable education and career opportunities. This right implies a positive obligation on the part of governments and other public bodies to print documents and to provide services in the native language of recognized linguistic minorities, and to provide bilingual instruction in schools. Cultural assimilation should not be a condition of full social participation, because it requires a person to transform his or her sense of identity, and when it is realized on a group level it means altering or annihilating the group's identity. This principle does not apply to any persons who do not identify with majority language or culture within a society, but only to sizeable linguistic or cultural minorities living in distinct though not necessarily segregated communities. In the United States, then, special rights for cultural minorities applies at least to Spanish-speaking Americans and Native Americans.

The universalist finds a contradiction in asserting both that formerly segregated groups have a right to inclusion and that these groups have a right to different treatment. There is no contradiction here, however, if attending to difference is necessary in order to make participation and inclusion possible. Groups with different circumstances or forms of life should be able to participate together in public institutions without shedding their distinct identities or suffering disadvantage because of them. The goal is not to give special compensation to the deviant until they achieve normality, but rather to denormalize the way institutions formulate their rules by revealing the plural circumstances and needs that exist, or ought to exist, within them.

Many opponents of oppression and privilege are wary of claims for special rights because they fear a restoration of special classifications that can justify exclusion and stigmatization of the specially marked groups. Such fear has been particularly pronounced among feminists who oppose affirming sexual and gender difference in law and policy. It would be foolish for me to deny that this fear has some significant basis.

Such fear is founded, however, on accession to traditional identi-fication of group difference with deviance, stigma, and inequality. Contemporary movements of oppressed groups, however, assert a positive meaning to group difference, by which a group claims its identity as a group and rejects the stereotypes and labelling by which others mark it as inferior or inhuman. These social movements engage the meaning of difference itself as a terrain of political strug-gle, rather than leave difference to be used to justify exclusion and subordination. Supporting policies and rules that attend to group difference in order to undermine oppression and disadvantage is, in my opinion, a part of that struggle.

Fear of claims to special rights points to a connection of the prin-ciple of group representation with the principle of attending to dif-ference in policy. The primary means of defence from the use of special rights to oppress or exclude groups is the self-organization and representation of those groups. If oppressed and disadvantaged groups are able to discuss among themselves what procedures and policies they judge will best further their social and political equal-ity, and have access to mechanisms to make their judgements known to the larger public, then policies that attend to difference are less likely to be used against them than for them. If they have the insti-tutionalized right to veto policy proposals that directly affect them, and them primarily, moreover, such danger is further reduced.

In this article I have distinguished three meanings of universality that have usually been collapsed in discussions of the universality of citizenship and the public realm. Modern politics properly pro-motes the universality of citizenship in the sense of the inclusion and participation of everyone in public life and democratic processes. The realization of genuinely universal citizenship in this sense today is impeded rather than furthered by the commonly held conviction that when they exercise their citizenship, persons should adopt a universal point of view and leave behind the perceptions they derive from their particular experience and social position. The full inclusion and participation of all in law and public life is also sometimes impeded by formulating laws and rules in universal terms that apply to all citizens in the same way.

In response to these arguments, some people have suggested to

426

me that such challenges to the ideal of universal citizenship threaten to leave no basis for rational normative appeals. Normative reason, it is suggested, entails universality in a Kantian sense: when a person claims that something is good or right he or she is claiming that everyone in principle could consistently make that claim, and that everyone should accept it. This refers to a fourth meaning of universality, more epistemological than political. There may indeed be grounds for questioning a Kantian-based theory of the universality of normative reason, but this is a different issue from the substantive political issues I have addressed here, and the arguments in this paper neither imply nor exclude such a possibility. In any case, I do not believe that challenging the ideal of a unified public or the claim that rules should always be formally universal subverts the possibility of making rational normative claims.

Notes

1. Theodore Lowi's classical analysis of the privatized operations of interest group liberalism remains descriptive of American politics; see *The End of Liberalism* (New York: Norton, 1969). For more recent analyses, see Jürgen Habermas, *Legitimation Crisis* (Boston: Beacon, 1973); Claus Offe, *Contradictions of the Welfare State* (Cambridge, Mass.: MIT Press, 1984); John Keane, *Public Life in Late Capitalism* (Cambridge, Mass.: MIT Press,1984); and Benjamin Barber, *Strong Democracy* (Berkeley: University of California Press, 1984).
2. For an outstanding recent account of the virtues of and conditions for such democracy, see Philip Green, *Retrieving Democracy* (Totowa, NJ: Rowman and Allanheld, 1985).
3. Barber and Keane both appeal to Rousseau's understanding of civic activity as a model for contemporary participatory democracy, as does Carole Pateman in her classic work, *Participation and Democratic Theory* (Cambridge: Cambridge University Press, 1970). (Pateman's position has, of course, changed.) See also James Miller, *Rousseau: Dreamer of Democracy* (New Haven: Yale University Press, 1984).
4. Many who extol the virtues of the civic public, of course, appeal also to a model of the ancient polis. For a recent example, see Murray Bookchin, *The Rise of Urbanization and the Decline of Citizenship* (San Francisco: Sierra Club Books, 1987). In this article, however, I choose to restrict my claims to modern political thought. The idea of the ancient Greek polis often functions in both modern and contemporary discussion as a myth of lost origins, the paradise from which we have fallen and to which we desire to return; in this way, appeals to the ancient Greek polis are often contained within appeals to modern ideas of civic humanism.
5. Hannah Pitkin performs a most detailed and sophisticated analysis of the virtues of the civic public as a flight from sexual difference through a reading of the texts of Machiavelli; see *Fortune Is a Woman* (Berkeley: University of California Press, 1984). Carole Pateman's recent writing also focuses on such analysis. See e.g. Carole Pateman, *The Social Contract* (Stanford,

Calif.: Stanford University Press, 1988). See also Nancy Hartsock, *Money, Sex and Power* (New York: Longman, 1983), chs. 7 and 8.

6. See Susan Okin, 'Women and the Making of the Sentimental Family', *Philosophy and Public Affairs*, 11 (1982), 65–88, and Linda Nicholson, *Gender and History: The Limits of Social Theory in the Age of the Family* (New York: Columbia University Press, 1986).

7. For analyses of Rousseau's treatment of women, see Susan Okin, *Women in Western Political Thought* (Princeton: Princeton University Press, 1978); Lynda Lange, 'Rousseau: Women and the General Will', in *The Sexism of Social and Political Theory*, ed. Lorenne M. G. Clark and Lynda Lange (Toronto: University of Toronto Press, 1979); Jean Bethke Elshtain, *Public Man, Private Woman* (Princeton: Princeton University Press, 1981), ch. 4. Mary Dietz develops an astute critique of Elshtain's 'maternalist' perspective on political theory; in so doing, however, she also seems to appeal to a universalist ideal of the civil public in which women will transcend their particular concerns and become general; see 'Citizenship with a Feminist Face: The Problem with Maternal Thinking', *Political Theory*, 13 (1985), 19–37. On Rousseau on women, see also Joel Schwartz, *The Sexual Politics of Jean-Jacques Rousseau* (Chicago: University of Chicago Press, 1984).

8. See Ronald Takaki, *Iron Cages: Race and Culture in 19th Century America* (New York: Knopf, 1979). Don Herzog discusses the exclusionary prejudices of some other early American republicans; see 'Some Questions for Republicans', *Political Theory*, 14 (1986), 473–93.

9. George Mosse, *Nationalism and Sexuality* (New York: Fertig, 1985).

10. Barber, chs. 8 and 9. Future page references in parentheses are to this book.

11. I have developed this account more thoroughly in my paper, Iris Marion Young, 'Impartiality and the Civic Public: Some Implications of Feminist Critiques of Moral and Political Theory', in *Feminism as Critique*, ed. S. Benhabib and D. Cornell (Oxford: Polity Press, 1987), 56–76.

12. On feminism and participatory democracy, see Pateman.

13. Jane Mansbridge, *Beyond Adversary Democracy* (New York: Basic Books, 1980).

14. Amy Gutmann, *Liberal Equality* (Cambridge: Cambridge University Press, 1980), 191–202.

15. See Iris Marion Young, 'Five Faces of Oppression', *Philosophical Forum* (1988), in press.

16. Jürgen Habermas, *Reason and the Rationalization of Society* (Boston: Beacon, 1983), Pt. 3. For criticism of Habermas as retaining too universalist a conception of communicative action, see Seyla Benhabib, *Critique, Norm and Utopia* (New York: Columbia University Press, 1986); and Young, 'Impartiality and the Civic Public'.

17. The Mel King for mayor campaign organization exhibited the promise of such group representation in practice, which was only partially and haltingly realized: see special double issue of *Radical America* 17/6 and 18/1 (1984). Sheila Collins discusses how the idea of a rainbow coalition challenges traditional American political assumptions of a 'melting pot', and she shows how lack of coordination between the national level rainbow departments and the grass-roots campaign committees prevented the 1984 Jackson campaign from realizing the promise of group representation; see *The Rainbow Challenge: The Jackson Campaign and the Future of U.S. Politics* (New York: Monthly Review Press, 1986).

18. See Gary Ruchwarger, *People in Power: Forging a Grassroots Democracy in Nicaragua* (Hadley, Mass.: Bergin and Garvey, 1985).

19. Martha Minow, 'Learning to Live with the Dilemma of Difference: Bilingual and Special Education', *Law and Contemporary Problems*, 48 (1985), 157–211.

20. I use the term 'special rights' in much the same way as Elizabeth Wolgast, in *Equality and the Rights of Women* (Ithaca, NY: Cornell University Press, 1980). Like Wolgast, I wish to distinguish a class of rights that all persons should have, general rights, and a class of rights that categories of persons should have by virtue of particular circumstances. That is, the distinction should refer only to different levels of generality, where 'special' means only 'specific'. Unfortunately, 'special rights' tends to carry a connotation of *exceptional*, that is, specially marked and deviating from the norm. As I assert below, however, the goal is not to compensate for deficiencies in order to help people be 'normal', but to denormalize, so that in certain contexts and at certain levels of abstraction everyone has 'special' rights.

21. Linda J. Krieger, 'Through a Glass Darkly: Paradigms of Equality and the Search for a Women's Jurisprudence', *Hypatia: A Journal of Feminist Philosophy*, 2 (1987), 45–62. Deborah Rhode provides an excellent synopsis of the dilemmas involved in this pregnancy debate in feminist legal theory in 'Justice and Gender' (typescript), ch. 9.

22. See Ann Scales, 'Towards a Feminist Jurisprudence', *Indiana Law Journal*, 56 (1980), 375–444. Christine Littleton provides a very good analysis of the feminist debate about equal vs. different treatment regarding pregnancy and childbirth, among other legal issues for women, in 'Reconstructing Sexual Equality', *California Law Review*, 25 (1987), 1279–337. Littleton suggests, as I have stated above, that only the dominant male conception of work keeps pregnancy and birthing from being conceived of as work.

23. Littleton suggests that difference should be understood not as a characteristic of particular sorts of people, but of the interaction of particular sorts of people with specific institutional structures. Minow expresses a similar point by saying that difference should be understood as a function of the relationship among groups, rather than located in attributes of a particular group.

24. For one among many discussions of such 'backward looking' and 'forward looking' arguments, see Bernard Boxill, *Blacks and Social Justice* (Totowa, NJ: Rowman and Allanheld, 1984), ch. 7.

25. See R. W. Beatty and J. R. Beatty, 'Some Problems with Contemporary Job Evaluation Systems', and Ronnie Steinberg, 'A Want of Harmony: Perspectives on Wage Discrimination and Comparable Worth', both in *Comparable Worth and Wage Discrimination: Technical Possibilities and Political Realities*, ed. Helen Remick (Philadelphia; Temple University Press, 1981); D. J. Treiman and H. I. Hartmann (eds.), *Women, Work and Wages* (Washington, DC: National Academy Press, 1981), 81.

26. David Alexander, 'Gendered Job Traits and Women's Occupations' (Ph.D. diss., University of Massachusetts, Department of Economics, 1987).

From Redistribution to Recognition? Dilemmas of Justice in a 'Post-Socialist' Age

Nancy Fraser

The 'struggle for recognition' is fast becoming the paradigmatic form of political conflict in the late twentieth century. Demands for 'recognition of difference' fuel struggles of groups mobilized under the banners of nationality, ethnicity, 'race', gender, and sexuality. In these 'post-socialist' conflicts, group identity supplants class interest as the chief medium of political mobilization. Cultural domination supplants exploitation as the fundamental injustice. And cultural recognition displaces socioeconomic redistribution as the remedy for injustice and the goal of political struggle.

That, of course, is not the whole story. Struggles for recognition occur in a world of exacerbated material inequality—in income and property ownership; in access to paid work, education, health care and leisure time; but also more starkly in caloric intake and exposure to environmental toxicity, hence in life expectancy and rates of morbidity and mortality. Material inequality is on the rise in most of the world's countries—in the United States and in Haiti, in Sweden and in India, in Russia and in Brazil. It is also increasing globally, most dramatically across the line that divides North from South. How, then, should we view the eclipse of a socialist imaginary centred on terms such as 'interest', 'exploitation', and 'redistribution'? And what should we make of the rise of a new political imaginary centred on notions of 'identity', 'difference', 'cultural domination', and 'recognition'? Does this shift represent a lapse into 'false consciousness'? Or does it, rather, redress the culture-blindness of a materialist paradigm rightfully discredited by the collapse of Soviet Communism?

Neither of those two stances is adequate, in my view. Both are too wholesale and un-nuanced. Instead of simply endorsing or rejecting all of identity politics *simpliciter*, we should see ourselves

Reprinted by permission from *New Left Review*, 212 (July/August 1995), 68–93.

as presented with a new intellectual and practical task: that of developing a *critical* theory of recognition, one which identifies and defends only those versions of the cultural politics of difference that can be coherently combined with the social politics of equality.

In formulating this project, I assume that justice today requires *both* redistribution *and* recognition. And I propose to examine the relation between them. In part, this means figuring out how to conceptualize cultural recognition and social equality in forms that support rather than undermine one another. (For there are many competing conceptions of both!) It also means theorizing the ways in which economic disadvantage and cultural disrespect are currently entwined with and support one another. Then, too, it requires clarifying the political dilemmas that arise when we try to combat both those injustices simultaneously.

My larger aim is to connect two political problematics that are currently dissociated from one another, for only by articulating recognition and redistribution can we arrive at a critical-theoretical framework that is adequate to the demands of our age. That, however, is far too much to take on here. In what follows, I shall consider only one aspect of the problem. Under what circumstances can a politics of recognition help support a politics of redistribution? And when is it more likely to undermine it? Which of the many varieties of identity politics best synergize with struggles for social equality? And which tend to interfere with the latter?

In addressing these questions, I shall focus on axes of injustice that are simultaneously cultural and socioeconomic, paradigmatically gender and 'race'. (I shall not say much, in contrast, about ethnicity or nationality.[1]) And I must enter one crucial preliminary caveat: in proposing to assess recognition claims from the standpoint of social equality, I assume that varieties of recognition politics that fail to respect human rights are unacceptable even if they promote social equality.[2]

Finally, a word about method: in what follows, I shall propose a set of analytical distinctions, for example, cultural injustices versus economic injustices, recognition versus redistribution. In the real world, of course, culture and political economy are always imbricated with one another; and virtually every struggle against injustice, when properly understood, implies demands for both redistribution and recognition. Nevertheless, for heuristic purposes, analytical distinctions are indispensable. Only by abstracting from the complexities of the real world can we devise a conceptual schema that can illuminate it. Thus, by distinguishing redistribution and recognition analytically, and by exposing their distinctive logics, I aim to clarify—and begin to resolve—some of the central political dilemmas of our age.

My discussion proceeds in four parts. In Section 1, I conceptualize redistribution and recognition as two analytically distinct paradigms of justice, and I formulate 'the redistribution–recognition dilemma'. In Section 2, I distinguish three ideal-typical modes of social collectivity in order to identify those vulnerable to the dilemma. In Section 3, I distinguish between 'affirmative' and 'transformative' remedies for injustice, and I examine their respective logics of collectivity. Lastly, I use these distinctions, in Section 4, to propose a political strategy for integrating recognition claims with redistribution claims with a minimum of mutual interference.

I. THE REDISTRIBUTION–RECOGNITION DILEMMA

Let me begin by noting some complexities of contemporary 'post-socialist' political life. With the decentring of class, diverse social movements are mobilized around cross-cutting axes of difference. Contesting a range of injustices, their claims overlap and at times conflict. Demands for cultural change intermingle with demands for economic change, both within and among social movements. Increasingly, however, identity-based claims tend to predominate, as prospects for redistribution appear to recede. The result is a complex political field with little programmatic coherence.

To help clarify this situation and the political prospects it presents, I propose to distinguish two broadly conceived, analytically distinct understandings of injustice. The first is socioeconomic injustice, which is rooted in the political-economic structure of society. Examples include exploitation (having the fruits of one's labour appropriated for the benefit of others); economic marginalization (being confined to undesirable or poorly paid work, or being denied access to income-generating labour altogether); and deprivation (being denied an adequate material standard of living).

Egalitarian theorists have long sought to conceptualize the nature of these socioeconomic injustices. Their accounts include Marx's theory of capitalist exploitation, John Rawls's account of justice as fairness in the distribution of 'primary goods', Amartya Sen's view that justice requires ensuring that people have equal 'capabilities to function', and Ronald Dworkin's view that it requires 'equality of resources'.[3] For my purposes here, however, we need not commit ourselves to any one particular theoretical account. We need only subscribe to a rough and general understanding of socioeconomic injustice informed by a commitment to egalitarianism.

The second kind of injustice is cultural or symbolic. It is rooted in social patterns of representation, interpretation, and communication. Examples include cultural domination (being subjected to patterns of interpretation and communication that are associated with another culture and are alien and/or hostile to one's own); non-recognition (being rendered invisible via the authoritative representation, communicative, and interpretative practices of one's culture); and disrespect (being routinely maligned or disparaged in stereotypic public cultural representations and/or in everyday life interactions).

Some political theorists have recently sought to conceptualize the nature of these cultural or symbolic injustices. Charles Taylor, for example, has drawn on Hegelian notions to argue that:

Nonrecognition or misrecognition . . . can be a form of oppression, imprisoning someone in a false, distorted, reduced mode of being. Beyond simple lack of respect, it can inflict a grievous wound, saddling people with crippling self-hatred. Due recognition is not just a courtesy but a vital human need.[4]

Likewise, Axel Honneth has argued that:

we owe our integrity . . . to the receipt of approval or recognition from other persons. [Negative concepts such as 'insult' or 'degradation'] are related to forms of disrespect, to the denial of recognition. [They] are used to characterize a form of behaviour that does not represent an injustice solely because it constrains the subjects in their freedom for action or does them harm. Rather, such behaviour is injurious because it impairs these persons in their positive understanding of self—an understanding acquired by intersubjective means.[5]

Similar conception informs the work of many other critical theorists who do not use the term 'recognition.'[6] Once again, however, it is not necessary here to settle on a particular theoretical account. We need only subscribe to a general and rough understanding of cultural injustice, as distinct from socioeconomic injustice.

Despite the differences between them, both socioeconomic injustice and cultural injustice are pervasive in contemporary societies. Both are rooted in processes and practices that systematically disadvantage some groups of people *vis-à-vis* others. Both, consequently, should be remedied.[7]

Of course, this distinction between economic injustice and cultural injustice is analytical. In practice, the two are intertwined. Even the most material economic institutions have a constitutive, irreducible cultural dimension; they are shot through with significations and norms. Conversely, even the most discursive cultural practices have a constitutive, irreducible political-economic dimension; they are underpinned by material supports. Thus, far from occupying two airtight separate spheres, economic injustice and cultural injustice are usually interimbricated so as to reinforce one another dialectically. Cultural norms that are unfairly biased against some are institutionalized in the state and the economy; meanwhile, economic disadvantage impedes equal participation in the making of culture, in public spheres and in everyday life. The result is often a vicious circle of cultural and economic subordination.[8]

Despite these mutual entwinements, I shall continue to distinguish economic injustice and cultural injustice analytically. And I shall also distinguish two correspondingly distinct kinds of remedy. The remedy for economic injustice is political-economic restructuring of some sort. This might involve redistributing income, reorganizing the division of labour, subjecting investment to democratic decision-making, or transforming other basic economic structures. Although these various remedies differ importantly from one another, I shall henceforth refer to the whole group of them by the generic term 'redistribution'.[9] The remedy for cultural injustice, in contrast, is some sort of cultural or symbolic change. This could involve upwardly revaluing disrespected identities and the cultural products of maligned groups. It could also involve recognizing and positively valorizing cultural diversity. More radically still, it could involve the wholesale transformation of societal patterns of representation, interpretation and communication in ways that would change *everybody's* sense of self.[10] Although these remedies differ importantly from one another, I shall henceforth refer to the whole group of them by the generic term 'recognition'.

Once again, this distinction between redistributive remedies and recognition remedies is analytical. Redistributive remedies generally presuppose an underlying conception of recognition. For example, some proponents of egalitarian socioeconomic redistribution ground their claims on the 'equal moral worth of persons'; thus, they treat economic redistribution as an expression of recognition.[11] Conversely, recognition remedies sometimes presuppose an underlying conception of redistribution. For example, some proponents of multicultural recognition ground their claims on the imperative of a just distribution of the 'primary good' of an 'intact cultural structure'; they therefore treat cultural recognition as a species of redistribution.[12] Such conceptual entwinements notwith-standing, I shall leave to one side questions such as, do redistribu-tion and recognition constitute two distinct, irreducible, *sui generis* concepts of justice, or alternatively, can either one of them be reduced to the other?[13] Rather, I shall assume that however we account for it metatheoretically, it will be useful to maintain a work-ing, first-order distinction between socioeconomic injustices and their remedies, on the one hand, and cultural injustices and their remedies, on the other.[14]

With these distinctions in place, I can now pose the following questions: What is the relation between claims for recognition, aimed at remedying cultural injustice, and claims for redistribution, aimed are redressing economic injustice? And what sorts of mutual interferences can arise when both kinds of claims are made simulta-neously?

There are good reasons to worry about such mutual interferences. Recognition claims often take the form of calling attention to, if not performatively creating, the putative specificity of some group, and then of affirming the value of that specificity. Thus they tend to pro-mote group differentiation. Redistribution claims, in contrast, often call for abolishing economic arrangements that underpin group specificity. (An example would be feminist demands to abolish the gender division of labour.) Thus they tend to promote group de-differentiation. The upshot is that the politics of recognition and the politics of redistribution appear to have mutually contradictory aims. Whereas the first tends to promote group differentiation, the second tends to undermine it. The two kinds of claim thus stand in tension with each other; they can interfere with, or even work against, one another.

Here, then, is a difficult dilemma. I shall henceforth call it the redistribution–recognition dilemma. People who are subject to both cultural injustice and economic injustice need both recogni-tion and redistribution. They need both to claim and to deny their specificity. How, if at all, is this possible?

Before taking up this question, let us consider precisely who faces the recognition–redistribution dilemma.

II. EXPLOITED CLASSES, DESPISED SEXUALITIES, AND BIVALENT COLLECTIVITIES

Imagine a conceptual spectrum of different kinds of social collectivities. At one extreme are modes of collectivity that fit the redistribution model of justice. At the other extreme are modes of collectivity that fit the recognition model. In between are cases that prove difficult because they fit both models of justice simultaneously.

Consider, first, the redistribution end of the spectrum. At this end let us posit an ideal-typical mode of collectivity whose existence is rooted wholly in the political economy. It will be differentiated as a collectivity, in other words, by virtue of the economic structure, as opposed to the cultural order, of society. Thus any structural injustices its members suffer will be traceable ultimately to the political economy. The root of the injustice, as well as its core, will be socioeconomic maldistribution, while any attendant cultural injustices will derive ultimately from that economic root. At bottom, therefore, the remedy required to redress the injustice will be political-economic redistribution, as opposed to cultural recognition.

In the real world, to be sure, political economy and culture are mutually intertwined, as are injustices of distribution and recognition. Thus we may doubt whether there exist any pure collectivities of this sort. For heuristic purposes, however, it is useful to examine their properties. To do so, let us consider a familiar example that can be interpreted as approximating the ideal type: the Marxian conception of the exploited class, understood in an orthodox and theoretical way.[15] And let us bracket the question of whether this view of class fits the actual historical collectivities that have struggled for justice in the real world in the name of the working class.[16]

In the conception assumed here, class is a mode of social differentiation that is rooted in the political-economic structure of society. A class only exists as a collectivity by virtue of its position in that structure and of its relation to other classes. Thus, the Marxian working class is the body of persons in a capitalist society who must sell their labour-power under arrangements that authorize the capitalist class to appropriate surplus productivity for its private benefit. The injustice of these arrangements, moreover, is quintessentially a matter of distribution. In the capitalist scheme of social reproduction, the proletariat receives an unjustly large share of the burdens and an unjustly small share of the rewards. To be sure, its members also suffer serious cultural injustices, the 'hidden (and not so hidden) injuries of class'. But far from being rooted directly in an autonomously unjust cultural structure, these derive from the political economy, as ideologies of class inferiority proliferate to justify exploitation.[17] The remedy for the injustice, consequently, is redistribution, not recognition. Overcoming class exploitation requires restructuring the political economy so as to alter the class distribution of social burdens and social benefits. In the Marxian conception, such restructuring takes the radical form of abolishing the class structure as such. The task of the proletariat, therefore, is not simply to cut itself a better deal, but 'to abolish itself as a class'. The last thing it needs is recognition of its difference. On the contrary, the only way to remedy the injustice is to put the proletariat out of business as a group.

Now consider the other end of the conceptual spectrum. At this end we may posit an ideal-typical mode of collectivity that fits the recognition model of justice. A collectivity of this type is rooted wholly in culture, as opposed to in political economy. It only exists as a collectivity by virtue of the reigning social patterns of interpretation and evaluation, not by virtue of the division of labour. Thus, any structural injustices its members suffer will be traceable ultimately to the cultural-valuational structure. The root of the injustice, as well as its core, will be cultural misrecognition, while any attendant economic injustices will derive ultimately from that cultural root. At bottom, therefore, the remedy required to redress the injustice will be cultural recognition, as opposed to political-economic redistribution.

Once again, we may doubt whether there exist any pure collectivities of this sort, but it is useful to examine their properties for heuristic purposes. An example that can be interpreted as approximating the ideal type is the conception of despised sexuality, understood in a specific stylized and theoretical way.[18] Let us consider this conception, while leaving aside the question of whether this view of sexuality fits the actual historical homosexual collectivities that are struggling for justice in the real world.

Sexuality in this conception is a mode of social differentiation whose roots do not lie in the political economy, as homosexuals are distributed throughout the entire class structure of capitalist society, occupy no distinctive position in the division of labour, and do not constitute an exploited class. Rather, their mode of collectivity is that of a despised sexuality, rooted in the cultural-valuational structure of society. From this perspective, the injustice they suffer is quintessentially a matter of recognition. Gays and lesbians suffer from heterosexism: the authoritative construction of norms that privilege heterosexuality. Along with this goes homophobia: the cultural devaluation of homosexuality. Their sexuality thus disparaged, homosexuals are subject to shaming, harassment, discrimination, and violence, while being denied legal rights and equal protections—all fundamentally denials of recognition. To be sure, gays and lesbians also suffer serious economic injustices; they can be summarily dismissed from work and are denied family-based social-welfare benefits. But far from being rooted directly in the economic structure, these derive instead from an unjust cultural-valuational structure.[19] The remedy for the injustice, consequently, is recognition, not redistribution. Overcoming homophobia and heterosexism requires changing the cultural valuations (as well as their legal and practical expressions) that privilege heterosexuality, deny equal respect to gays and lesbians, and refuse to recognize homosexuality as a legitimate way of being sexual. It is to revalue a despised sexuality, to accord positive recognition to gay and lesbian sexual specificity.

Matters are thus fairly straightforward at the two extremes of our conceptual spectrum. When we deal with collectivities that approach the ideal type of the exploited working class, we face distributive injustices requiring redistributive remedies. When we deal with collectivities that approach the ideal type of the despised sexuality, in contrast, we face injustices of misrecognition requiring remedies of recognition. In the first case, the logic of the remedy is to put the group out of business as a group. In the second case, on the contrary, it is to valorize the group's 'groupness' by recognizing its specificity.

Matters become murkier, however, once we move away from these extremes. When we consider collectivities located in the middle of the conceptual spectrum, we encounter hybrid modes that combine features of the exploited class with features of the despised sexuality. These collectivities are 'bivalent'. They are differentiated as collectivities by virtue of *both* the political-economic structure *and* the cultural-valuational structure of society. When disadvantaged, therefore, they may suffer injustices that are traceable to both political economy and culture simultaneously. Bivalent collectivities, in sum, may suffer both socioeconomic maldistribution and cultural misrecognition in forms where neither of these injustices is an indirect effect of the other, but where both are primary and co-original. In that case, neither redistributive remedies alone nor recognition remedies alone will suffice. Bivalent collectivities need both.

Both gender and 'race' are paradigmatic bivalent collectivities. Although each has peculiarities not shared by the other, both encompass political-economic dimensions and cultural-valuational dimensions. Gender and 'race', therefore, implicate both redistribution and recognition.

Gender, for example, has political-economic dimensions. It is a basic structuring principle of the political economy. On the one hand, gender structures the fundamental division between paid 'productive' labour and unpaid 'reproductive' and domestic labour, assigning women primary responsibility for the latter. On the other hand, gender also structures the division within paid labour between higher-paid, male-dominated, manufacturing and professional occupations and lower-paid, female-dominated, 'pink-collar' and domestic-service occupations. The result is a political-economic structure that generates gender-specific modes of exploitation, marginalization, and deprivation. This structure constitutes gender as a political-economic differentiation endowed with certain class-like characteristics. When viewed under this aspect, gender injustice appears as a species of distributive injustice that cries out for redistributive redress. Much like class, gender justice requires transforming the political economy so as to eliminate its gender structuring. Eliminating gender-specific exploitation, marginalization, and deprivation requires abolishing the gender division of labour—both the gendered division between paid and unpaid labour and the gender division within paid labour. The logic of the remedy is akin to the logic with respect to class: it is to put gender out of business as such. If gender were nothing but a political-economic differentiation, in sum, justice would require its abolition.

That, however, is only half the story. In fact, gender is not only a political-economic differentiation, but a cultural-valuational differentiation as well. As such, it also encompasses elements that are more problematic of recognition. Certainly, a major feature of gender injustice is androcentrism: the authoritative construction of norms that privilege traits associated with masculinity. Along with this goes cultural sexism: the pervasive devaluation and disparagement of things coded as 'feminine', paradigmatically—but not only—women.[20] This devaluation is expressed in a range of harms suffered by women, including sexual assault, sexual exploitation, and pervasive domestic violence; trivializing, objectifying, and demeaning stereotypical depictions in the media; harassment and disparagement in all spheres of everyday life; subjection to androcentric norms in relation to which women appear lesser or deviant and which work to disadvantage them, even in the absence of any intention to discriminate; attitudinal discrimination; exclusion or marginalization in public spheres and deliberative bodies; and denial of full rights and equal protections. These harms are injustices of recognition. They are relatively independent of political economy and are not merely 'superstructural'. Thus they cannot be remedied by political-economic redistribution alone but require additional independent remedies of recognition. Overcoming androcentrism and sexism requires changing the cultural valuations (as well as their legal and practical expressions) that privilege masculinity and deny equal respect to women. It requires decentring androcentric norms and revaluing a despised gender. The logic of the remedy is akin to the logic with respect to sexuality: it is to accord positive recognition to a devalued group specificity.

Gender, in sum, is a bivalent mode of collectivity. It contains a political-economic face that brings it within the ambit of redistribution. Yet it also contains a cultural-valuational face that brings it simultaneously within the ambit of recognition. Of course, the two faces are not neatly separated from one another. Rather, they intertwine to reinforce one another dialectically, as sexist and androcentric cultural norms are institutionalized in the state and the economy, while women's economic disadvantage restricts women's 'voice', impeding equal participation in the making of culture, in public spheres, and in everyday life. The result is a vicious circle of cultural and economic subordination. Redressing gender injustice, therefore, requires changing both political economy and culture.

But the bivalent character of gender is the source of a dilemma. In so far as women suffer at least two analytically distinct kinds of injustice, they necessarily require at least two analytically distinct kinds of remedy—both redistribution and recognition. The two remedies pull in opposite directions, however. They are not easily pursued simultaneously. Whereas the logic of redistribution is to put gender out of business as such, the logic of recognition is to valorize gender specificity.[21] Here, then, is the feminist version of the redistribution–recognition dilemma: how can feminists fight simultaneously to abolish gender differentiation and to valorize gender specificity?

An analogous dilemma arises in the struggle against racism. 'Race', like gender, is a bivalent mode of collectivity. On the one hand, it resembles class in being a structural principle of political economy. In this aspect, 'race' structures the capitalist division of labour. It structures the division within paid work between low-paid, low-status, menial, dirty, and domestic occupations, held disproportionately by people of colour, and higher-paid, higher-status, white-collar, professional, technical, and managerial occupations, held disproportionately by 'whites'.[22] Today's racial division of paid labour is part of the historic legacy of colonialism and slavery, which elaborated racial categorization to justify brutal new forms of appropriation and exploitation, effectively constituting 'blacks' as a political-economic caste. Currently, moreover, 'race' also structures access to official labour markets, constituting large segments of the population of colour as a 'superfluous', degraded sub-proletariat or underclass, unworthy even of exploitation and excluded from the productive system altogether. The result is a political-economic structure that generates 'race'-specific modes of exploitation, marginalization, and deprivation. This structure constitutes 'race' as a political-economic differentiation endowed with certain class-like characteristics. When viewed under this aspect, racial injustice appears as a species of distributive injustice that cries out for redistributive redress. Much like class, racial justice requires transforming the political economy so as to eliminate its racialization. Eliminating 'race'-specific exploitation, marginalization, and deprivation requires abolishing the racial division of labour—both the racial division between exploitable and superfluous labour and the racial division within paid labour. The logic of the remedy is like the logic with respect to class: it is to put 'race' out of business as such. If 'race' were nothing but a political-economic differentiation, in sum, justice would require its abolition.

However, 'race', like gender, is not only political-economic. It also has cultural-valuational dimensions, which bring it into the universe of recognition. Thus, 'race' too encompasses elements that are more like sexuality than class. A major aspect of racism is eurocentrism: the authoritative construction of norms that privilege traits associated with 'whiteness'. Along with this goes cultural racism: the pervasive devaluation and disparagement[23] of things coded as 'black', 'brown', and 'yellow', paradigmatically—but not only—people of colour.[24] This depreciation is expressed in a range of harms suffered by people of colour, including demeaning stereotypical depictions in the media as criminal, bestial, primitive, stupid, and so on; violence, harassment, and dissing in all spheres of everyday life; subjection to Eurocentric norms in relation to which people of colour appear lesser or deviant and which work to disadvantage them, even in the absence of any intention to discriminate;

attitudinal discrimination; exclusion from and/or marginalization in public spheres and deliberative bodies; and denial of full legal rights and equal protections. As in the case of gender, these harms are injustices of recognition. Thus the logic of their remedy, too, is to accord positive recognition to devalued group specificity.

'Race', too, therefore, is a bivalent mode of collectivity with both a political-economic and a cultural-valuational, face. Its two faces intertwine to reinforce one another dialectically, as racist and Eurocentric cultural norms are institutionalized in the state and the economy, while the economic disadvantage suffered by people of colour restricts their 'voice'. Redressing racial injustice, therefore, requires changing both political economy and culture. And as with gender, the bivalent character of 'race' is the source of a dilemma. Insofar as people of colour suffer at least two analytically distinct kinds of injustice, they necessarily require at least two analytically distinct kinds of remedy, which are not easily pursued simultaneously. Whereas the logic of redistribution is to put 'race' out of business as such, the logic of recognition is to valorize group specificity.[25] Here, then, is the anti-racist version of the redistribution–recognition dilemma. How can anti-racists fight simultaneously to abolish 'race' and to valorize racialized group specificity?

Both gender and 'race', in sum, are dilemmatic modes of collectivity. Unlike class, which occupies one end of the conceptual spectrum, and unlike sexuality, which occupies the other, gender and 'race' are bivalent, implicated simultaneously in both the politics of redistribution and the politics of recognition. Both, consequently, face the redistribution–recognition dilemma. Feminists must pursue political-economic remedies that would undermine gender differentiation, while also pursuing cultural-valuational remedies that valorize the specificity of a despised collectivity. Anti-racists, likewise, must pursue political-economic remedies that would undermine 'racial' differentiation, while also pursuing cultural-valuational remedies that valorize the specificity of despised collectivities. How can they do both things at once?

III. AFFIRMATION OR TRANSFORMATION? REVISITING THE QUESTION OF REMEDY

So far I have posed the redistribution–recognition dilemma in a form that appears quite intractable. I have assumed that redistributive remedies for political-economic injustice always de-differentiate social groups. Likewise, I have assumed that recognition remedies for cultural-valuational injustice always enhance social group differentiation. Given these assumptions, it is difficult to see how feminists and anti-racists can pursue redistribution and recognition simultaneously.

Now, however, I want to complicate these assumptions. In this section, I shall examine alternative conceptions of redistribution, on the one hand, and alternative conceptions of recognition, on the other. My aim is to distinguish two broad approaches to remedy injustice that cut across the redistribution–recognition divide. I shall call them 'affirmation' and 'transformation' respectively. After sketching each of them generically, I shall show how each operates in regard to both redistribution and recognition. On this basis, finally, I shall reformulate the redistribution–recognition dilemma in a form that is more amenable to resolution.

Let me begin by briefly distinguishing affirmation and transformation. By affirmative remedies for injustice I mean remedies aimed at correcting inequitable outcomes of social arrangements without disturbing the underlying framework that generates them. By transformative remedies, in contrast, I mean remedies aimed at correcting inequitable outcomes precisely by restructuring the underlying generative framework. The nub of the contrast is end-state outcomes versus the processes that produce them. It is *not* gradual versus apocalyptic change.

This distinction can be applied, first of all, to remedies for cultural injustice. Affirmative remedies for such injustices are currently associated with mainstream multiculturalism.[26] This proposes to redress disrespect by revaluing unjustly devalued group identities, while leaving intact both the contents of those identities and the group differentiations that underlie them. Transformative remedies, by contrast, are currently associated with deconstruction. They would redress disrespect by transforming the underlying cultural-valuational structure. By destabilizing existing group identities and differentiations, these remedies would not only raise the self-esteem of members of currently disrespected groups. They would change *everyone's* sense of belonging, affiliation, and self.

To illustrate the distinction, let us consider, once again, the case of the despised sexuality.[27] Affirmative remedies for homophobia and heterosexism are currently associated with gay-identity politics, which aims to revalue gay and lesbian identity.[28] Transformative remedies, in contrast, include the approach of 'queer theory', which would deconstruct the homo–hetero dichotomy. Gay-identity poli-tics treats homosexuality as a substantive, cultural, identificatory positivity, much like an ethnicity.[29] This positivity is assumed to sub-sist in and of itself and to need only additional recognition. 'Queer theory', in contrast, treats homosexuality as the constructed and devalued correlate of heterosexuality; both are reifications of sexual ambiguity and are co-defined only in virtue of one another.[30] The transformative aim is not to solidify a gay identity, but to deconstruct the homo–hetero dichotomy so as to destabilize all fixed sexual iden-tities. The point is not to dissolve all sexual difference in a single, uni-versal human identity; it is rather to sustain a sexual field of multiple, debinarized, fluid, ever-shifting differences.

Both these approaches have considerable interest as remedies for misrecognition. But there is one crucial difference between them. Whereas gay-identity politics tends to enhance existing sexual group differentiation, queer-theory politics tends to destabilize it—at least ostensibly and in the long run.[31] The point holds for recog-nition remedies more generally. Whereas affirmative recognition remedies tend to promote existing group differentiations, transfor-mative recognition remedies tend, in the long run, to destabilize them so as to make room for future regroupments. I shall return to this point shortly.

Analogous distinctions hold for the remedies for economic injus-tice. Affirmative remedies for such injustices have been associated historically with the liberal welfare state.[32] They seek to redress end-state maldistribution, while leaving intact much of the underlying political-economic structure. Thus they would increase the con-sumption share of economically disadvantaged groups, without otherwise restructuring the system of production. Transformative remedies, in contrast, have been historically associated with social-ism. They would redress unjust distribution by transforming the underlying political-economic structure. By restructuring the rela-tions of production, these remedies would not only alter the end-state distribution of consumption shares; they would also change the social division of labour and thus the conditions of existence for everyone.[33]

Let us consider, once again, the case of the exploited class.[34] Affirmative redistributive remedies for class injustices typically include income transfers of two distinct kinds: social-insurance programmes share some of the costs of social reproduction for the stably employed, the so-called 'primary' sectors of the working class; public-assistance programmes provide means-tested, 'targeted' aid to the 'reserve army' of the unemployed and underemployed. Far from abolishing class differentiation *per se*, these affirmative remedies support it and shape it. Their general effect is to shift attention from the class division between workers and capitalists to the division between employed and nonemployed fractions of the working class. Public-assistance programmes 'target' the poor, not only for aid but for hostility. Such remedies, to be sure, provide needed material aid. But they also create strongly cathected, antagonistic group differentiations.

The logic here applies to affirmative redistribution in general. Although this approach aims to redress economic injustice, it leaves intact the deep structures that generate class disadvantage. Thus it must make surface reallocations time and again. The result is to mark the most disadvantaged class as inherently deficient and insatiable, as always needing more and more. In time such a class can even come to appear privileged, the recipient of special treatment and undeserved largesse. An approach aimed at redressing injustices of distribution can thus end up creating injustices of recognition.

In a sense, this approach is self-contradictory. Affirmative redistribution generally presupposes a universalist conception of recognition, the equal moral worth of persons. Let us call this its 'official recognition commitment'. Yet the practice of affirmation redistribution, as iterated over time, tends to set in motion a second—stigmatizing—recognition dynamic, which contradicts universalism. This second dynamic can be understood as the 'practical recognition-effect' of affirmative redistribution.[35] It conflicts with its official recognition commitment.[36]

Now contrast this logic with transformative remedies for distributive injustices of class. Transformative remedies typically combine universalist social-welfare programmes, steeply progressive taxation, macroeconomic policies aimed at creating full employment, a large non-market public sector, significant public and/or collective ownership, and democratic decision-making about basic socioeconomic priorities. They try to assure access to employment for all, while also tending to de-link basic consumption shares from employment. Hence their tendency is to undermine class differentiation. Transformative remedies reduce social inequality without, however, creating stigmatized classes of vulnerable people perceived as beneficiaries of special largesse.[37] They tend therefore to promote reciprocity and solidarity in the relations of recognition. Thus an approach aimed at redressing injustices of distribution can help redress (some) injustices of recognition as well.[38]

This approach is self-consistent. Like affirmative redistribution, transformative redistribution generally presupposes a universalist conception of recognition, the equal moral worth of persons. Unlike affirmative redistribution, however, its practice tends not to undermine this conception. Thus, the two approaches generate different logics of group differentiation. Whereas affirmative remedies can have the perverse effect of promoting class differentiation, transformative remedies tend to blur it. In addition, the two approaches generate different subliminal dynamics of recognition. Affirmative redistribution can stigmatize the disadvantaged, adding the insult of misrecognition to the injury of deprivation. Transformative redistribution, in contrast, can promote solidarity, helping to redress some forms of misrecognition.

What, then, should we conclude from this discussion? In this section, we have considered only the 'pure' ideal-typical cases at the two extremes of the conceptual spectrum. We have contrasted the divergent effects of affirmative and transformative remedies for the economically rooted distributive injustices of class, on the one hand, and for the culturally rooted recognition injustices of sexuality, on the other. We saw that affirmative remedies tend generally to promote group differentiation, while transformative remedies tend to destabilize or blur it. We also saw that affirmative redistribution remedies can generate a backlash of misrecognition, while transformative redistribution remedies can help redress some forms of misrecognition.

All this suggests a way of reformulating the redistribution–recognition dilemma. We might ask: for groups who are subject to injustices of both types, what combinations of remedies work best to minimize, if not altogether to eliminate, the mutual inferences that can arise when both redistribution and recognition are pursued simultaneously?

IV. FINESSING THE DILEMMA: REVISITING GENDER AND 'RACE'

Imagine a four-celled matrix. The horizontal axis comprises the two general kinds of remedy we have just examined, namely, affirmation and transformation. The vertical axis comprises the two aspects of justice we have been considering, namely, redistribution and recognition. On this matrix we can locate the four political orientations just discussed. In the first cell, where redistribution and affirmation intersect, is the project of the liberal welfare state; centered on surface reallocations of distributive shares among existing groups, it tends to support group differentiation; it can also generate backlash misrecognition. In the second cell, where redistribution and transformation intersect, is the project of socialism; aimed at deep restructuring of the relations of production, it tends to blur group differentiation; it can also help redress some forms of misrecognition. In the third cell, where recognition and affirmation intersect, is the project of mainstream multiculturalism; focused on surface reallocations of respect among existing groups, it tends to support group differentiation. In the fourth cell, where recognition and transformation intersect, is the project of deconstruction; aimed at deep restructuring of the relations of recognition, it tends to destabilize group differentiations.

	Affirmation	Transformation
Redistribution	*The liberal welfare state* surface reallocations of existing goods to existing groups; supports group differentiation; can generate misrecognition	*socialism* deep restructuring of relations of production; blurs group differentiation; can help remedy some forms of misrecognition
Recognition	*mainstream multiculturalism* surface reallocations of respect to existing identities of existing groups; supports group differentiations	*deconstruction* deep restructuring of relations of recognition; destabilizes group differentiation

This matrix casts mainstream multiculturalism as the cultural analogue of the liberal welfare state, while casting deconstruction as the cultural analogue of socialism. It thereby allows us to make some preliminary assessments of the mutual compatibility of various remedial strategies. We can gauge the extent to which pairs of remedies would work at cross-purposes with one another if they were pursued simultaneously. We can identify pairs that seem to land us squarely on the horns of the redistribution-recognition dilemma. We can also identify pairs that hold out the promise of enabling us to finesse it.

Prima facie at least, two pairs of remedies seem especially *un*promising. The affirmative redistribution politics of the liberal welfare state seems at odds with the transformative recognition politics of deconstruction; whereas the first tends to promote group differentiation, the second tends rather to destabilize it. Similarly, the transformative redistribution politics of socialism seems at odds with the affirmative recognition politics of mainstream multiculturalism; whereas the first tends to undermine group differentiation, the second tends rather to promote it.

Conversely, two pairs of remedies seem comparatively promising. The affirmative redistribution politics of the liberal welfare state seems compatible with the affirmative recognition politics of mainstream multiculturalism; both tend to promote group differentiation. Similarly, the transformative redistribution politics of socialism seems compatible with the transformative recognition politics of deconstruction; both tend to undermine existing group differentiations.

To test these hypotheses, let us revisit gender and 'race'. Recall that these are bivalent differentiations, axes of both economic and cultural injustice. Thus people subordinated by gender and/or 'race' need both redistribution and recognition. They are the paradigmatic subjects of the redistribution–recognition dilemma. What happens in their cases, then, when various pairs of injustice remedies are pursued simultaneously? Are there pairs of remedies that permit feminists and anti-racists to finesse, if not wholly to dispel, the redistribution–recognition dilemma?

Consider, first, the case of gender.[39] Recall that redressing gender injustice requires changing both political economy and culture, so as to undo the vicious circle of economic and cultural subordination. As we saw, the changes in question can take either of two forms, affirmation or transformation.[40] Let us consider, first, the *prima facie* promising case in which affirmative redistribution is combined with affirmative recognition. As the name suggests, affirmative redistribution to redress gender injustice in the economy includes affirmative action, the effort to assure women their fair share of existing jobs and educational places, while leaving unchanged the nature and number of those jobs and places. Affirmative recognition to redress gender injustice in the culture includes cultural feminism, the effort to assure women respect by revaluing femininity, while leaving unchanged the binary gender code that gives the latter its sense. Thus, the scenario in question combines the socioeconomic politics of liberal feminism with the cultural politics of cultural feminism. Does this combination really finesse the redistribution–recognition dilemma?

Despite its initial appearance of promise, this scenario is problematic. Affirmative redistribution fails to engage the deep level at which the political economy is gendered. Aimed primarily at combating attitudinal discrimination, it does not attack the gendered division of paid and unpaid labour, nor the gendered division of masculine and feminine occupations within paid labour. Leaving intact the deep structures that generate gender disadvantage, it must make surface reallocations again and again. The result is not only to underline gender differentiation. It is also to mark women as deficient and insatiable, as always needing more and more. In time women can even come to appear privileged, recipients of special treatment and undeserved largesse. Thus an approach aimed at redressing injustices of distribution can end up fuelling backlash injustices of recognition.

This problem is exacerbated when we add the affirmative recognition strategy of cultural feminism. That approach insistently calls attention to, if it does not performatively create, women's putative cultural specificity or difference. In some contexts, such an approach can make progress towards decentring androcentric norms. In this context, however, it is more likely to have the effect of pouring oil onto the flames of resentment against affirmative action. Read through that lens, the cultural politics of affirming women's difference appears as an affront to the liberal welfare state's official commitment to the equal moral worth of persons.

The other route with a *prima facie* promise is that which combines transformative redistribution with transformative recognition. Transformative redistribution to redress gender injustice in the economy consists in some form of socialist feminism or feminist social democracy. And transformative recognition to redress gender injustice in the culture consists in feminist deconstruction aimed at dismantling androcentrism by destabilizing gender dichotomies. Thus the scenario in question combines the socioeconomic politics of socialist feminism with the cultural politics of deconstructive feminism. Does this combination really finesse the redistribution–recognition dilemma?

This scenario is far less problematic. The long-term goal of deconstructive feminism is a culture in which hierarchical gender dichotomies are replaced by networks of multiple intersecting differences that are demassified and shifting. This goal is consistent with transformative socialist-feminist redistribution. Deconstruction opposes the sort of sedimentation or congealing of gender difference that occurs in an unjustly gendered political economy. Its utopian image of a culture in which ever new constructions of identity and difference are freely elaborated and then swiftly deconstructed is only possible, after all, on the basis of rough social equality.

As a transitional strategy, moreover, this combination avoids fanning the flames of resentment.[41] If it has a drawback, it is rather that both deconstructive-feminist cultural politics and socialist-feminist economic politics are far removed from the immediate interests and identities of most women, as these are currently culturally constructed.

Analogous results arise for 'race', where the changes can again take either of two forms, affirmation or transformation.[42] In the first *prima facie* promising case, affirmative action is paired with affirmative recognition. Affirmative redistribution to redress racial injustice in the economy includes affirmative action, the effort to assure people of colour their fair share of existing jobs and educational places, while leaving unchanged the nature and number of those jobs and places. And affirmative recognition to redress racial injustice in the culture includes cultural nationalism, the effort to assure people of colour respect by revaluing 'blackness', while leaving unchanged the binary black–white code that gives the latter its sense. The scenario in question thus combines the socioeconomic politics of liberal anti-racism with the cultural politics of black nationalism or black power. Does this combination really finesse the redistribution–recognition dilemma?

Such a scenario is again problematic. As in the case of gender, here affirmative redistribution fails to engage the deep level at which the political economy is radicalized. It does not attack the racialized division of exploitable and surplus labour, nor the racialized division of menial and non-menial occupations within paid labour. Leaving intact the deep structures that generate racial disadvantage, it must make surface reallocations gain and again. The result is not only to underline racial differentiation. It is also to mark people of colour as deficient and insatiable, as always needing more and more. Thus they too can be cast as privileged recipients of special treatment. The problem is exacerbated when we add the affirmative recognition strategy of cultural nationalism. In some contexts, such an approach can make progress toward decentring Eurocentric norms, but in this context the cultural politics of affirming black difference equally appears as an affront to the liberal welfare state. Fuelling the resentment against affirmative action, it can elicit intense backlash misrecognition.

In the alternative route, transformative redistribution is combined with transformative recognition. Transformative redistribution to redress racial injustice in the economy consists in some form of anti-racist democratic socialist or anti-racist democratic socialism or anti-racist social democracy. And transformative recognition to redress racial injustice in the culture consists in anti-racist deconstruction aimed at dismantling Eurocentrism by destabilizing racial dichotomies. Thus, the scenario in question combines the socioeconomic politics of socialist anti-racism with the cultural politics of deconstructive anti-racism or critical 'race' theory. As with the analogous approach to gender, this scenario is far less problematic. The long-term goal of deconstructive anti-racism is a culture in which hierarchical racial dichotomies are replaced by demassified and shifting networks of multiple intersecting differences. This goal, once again, is consistent with transformative socialist redistribution. Even as a transitional strategy, this combination avoids fanning the flames of resentment.[43] Its principal drawback, again, is that both deconstructive–anti-racist cultural politics and socialist–anti-racist economic politics are far removed from the immediate interests and identities of most people of colour, as these are currently culturally constructed.[44]

What, then, should we conclude from this discussion? For both gender and 'race', the scenario that best finesses the redistribution–recognition dilemma is socialism in the economy plus deconstruction in the culture.[45] But for this scenario to be psychologically and politically feasible requires that people be weaned from their attachment to current cultural constructions of their interests and identities.[46]

V. CONCLUSION

The redistribution–recognition dilemma is real. There is no neat theoretical move by which it can be wholly dissolved or resolved. The best we can do is try to soften the dilemma by finding approaches that minimize conflicts between redistribution and recognition in cases where both must be pursued simultaneously.

I have argued here that socialist economics combined with deconstructive cultural politics works best to finesse the dilemma for the bivalent collectivities of gender and 'race'—at least when they are considered separately. The next step would be to show that this combination also works for our larger sociocultural configuration. After all, gender and 'race' are not neatly cordoned off from one another. Nor are they neatly cordoned off from sexuality and class. Rather, all these axes of injustice intersect one another in ways that affect everyone's interests and identities. No one is a member of only one such collectivity. And people who are subordinated along one axis of social division may well be dominant along another.[47]

The task then is to figure out how to finesse the redistribution–recognition dilemma when we situate the problem in this larger field of multiple, intersecting struggles against multiple, intersecting injustices. Although I cannot make the full argument here, I will venture three reasons for expecting that the combination of socialism and deconstruction will again prove superior to the other alternatives.

First, the arguments pursued here for gender and 'race' hold for all bivalent collectivities. Thus, in so far as real-world collectivities mobilized under the banners of sexuality and class turn out to be more bivalent than the ideal-typical constructs posited above, they too should prefer socialism plus deconstruction. And that doubly transformative approach should become the orientation of choice for a broad range of disadvantaged groups.

Second, the redistribution–recognition dilemma does not only arise endogenously, as it were, within a single bivalent collectivity. It also arises exogenously, so to speak, across intersecting collectivities. Thus, anyone who is both gay and working-class will face a version of the dilemma, regardless of whether or not we interpret sexuality and class as bivalent. And anyone who is also female and black will encounter it in a multilayered and acute form. In general, then, as soon as we acknowledge that axes of injustice cut across one another, we must acknowledge cross-cutting forms of the redistribution–recognition dilemma. And these forms are, if anything, even more resistant to resolution by combinations of affirmative remedies than the forms we considered above. For affirmative remedies work additively and are often at cross purposes with one another. Thus, the intersection of class, 'race', gender, and sexuality intensifies the need for transformative solutions, making the combination of socialism and deconstruction more attractive still.

Third, that combination best promotes the task of coalition building. This task is especially pressing today, given the multiplication of social antagonisms, the fissuring of social movements, and the growing appeal of the Right in the United States. In this context, the project of transforming the deep structures of both political economy and culture appears to be the one over-arching programmatic orientation capable of doing justice to *all* current struggles against injustice. It alone does not assume a zero-sum game.

If that is right, then, we can begin to see how badly off track is the current US political scene. We are currently stuck in the vicious circles of mutually reinforcing cultural and economic subordination. Our best efforts to redress these injustices via the combination of the liberal welfare state plus mainstream multiculturalism are generating perverse effects. Only by looking to alternative conceptions of redistribution and recognition can we meet the requirements of justice for all.

Notes

1. This omission is dictated by reasons of space. I believe that the framework elaborated below can fruitfully address both ethnicity and nationality. In so far as groups mobilized on these lines do not define themselves as sharing a situation of socioeconomic disadvantage and do not make redistributive claims, they can be understood as struggling primarily for recognition. National struggles are peculiar, however, in that the form of recognition they seek is political autonomy, whether in the form of a sovereign state of their own (e.g. the Palestinians) or in the form of more limited provincial sovereignty within a multinational state (e.g. the majority of Québecois). Struggles for ethnic recognition, in contrast, often seek rights of cultural expression within polyethnic nation-states. These distinctions are insightfully discussed in Will Kymlicka, 'Three Forms of Group-Differentiated Citizenship in Canada', now in S. Benhabib (ed.), *Democracy and Difference: Contesting the Boundaries of the Political* (Princeton: Princeton University Press, 1996), 153–70.
2. My principal concern in this essay is the relation between the recognition of cultural difference and social equality. I am not directly concerned, therefore, with the relation between recognition of cultural difference and liberalism. However, I assume that no identity politics is acceptable that fails to respect fundamental human rights of the sort usually championed by left-wing liberals.
3. Karl Marx, *Capital*, John Rawls, *A Theory of Justice* (Cambridge, Mass.: Harvard University Press, 1971) and subsequent papers; Amartya Sen, *Commodities and Capabilities* (North-Holland, 1985); and Ronald Dworkin, 'What is Equality? Part 2: Equality of Resources', *Philosophy and Public Affairs*, 10/4 (Fall, 1981). Although I here classify all these writers as theorists of distributive economic justice, it is also true that most of them have some resources for dealing with issues of cultural justice as well. Rawls, for example, treats 'the social bases of self-respect' as a primary good to be fairly distributed, while Sen treats a 'sense of self' as relevant to the capability to function. (I am indebted to Mika Manty for his point.) Nevertheless, as Iris Marion Young has suggested, the primary thrust of their thought leads in the direction of distributive economic justice. See her *Justice and the Politics of Difference* (Princeton: Princeton University Press, 1990).
4. Charles Taylor, *Multiculturalism and 'The Politics of Recognition'* (Princeton: Princeton University Press, 1992), 25.

5. Axel Honneth, 'Integrity and Disrespect: Principles of a Conception of Morality Based on the Theory of Recognition', *Political Theory*, 20/2 (May 1992), 188–9. See also his *Kampf um Anerkennung* (Frankfurt, 1992; English translation, *Struggle for Recognition*, Oxford: Polity Press, 1995). It is no accident that both of the major contemporary theorists of recognition, Honneth and Taylor, are Hegelians.

6. See e.g. Patricia J. Williams, *The Alchemy of Race and Rights* (Cambridge, Mass.: Harvard University Press, 1991); and Young, *Justice and the Politics of Difference*.

7. Responding to an earlier draft of this paper, Mika Manty posed the question of whether a schema focused on classifying justice issues as either cultural or political-economic could accommodate 'primary political concerns' such as citizenship and political participation ('Comments on Fraser', unpublished typescript presented at the Michigan symposium on 'Political Liberalism'). My inclination is to follow Jürgen Habermas in viewing such issues bifocally. From one perspective, political institutions (in state-regulated capitalist societies) belong with the economy as part of the 'system' that produces distributive socioeconomic injustices; in Rawlsian terms, they are part of 'the basic structure' of society. From another perspective, however, such institutions belong with 'the lifeworld' as part of the cultural structure that produces injustices of recognition; for example, the array of citizenship entitlements and participation rights conveys powerful implicit and explicit messages about the relative moral worth of various persons. 'Primary political concerns' could thus be treated as matters either of economic justice or cultural justice, depending on the context and perspective in play.

8. For the interimbrication of culture and political economy, see my 'What's Critical About Critical Theory? The Case of Habermas and Gender', in Nancy Fraser, *Unruly Practices: Power, Discourse and Gender in Contemporary Social Theory* (Oxford: Polity Press, 1989); 'Rethinking the Public Sphere', in Fraser, *Justice Interruptus: Critical Reflections on the 'Postsocialist' Condition* (New York: Routledge, 1997); and Fraser, 'Pragmatism, Feminism, and the Linguistic Turn', in Benhabib, Butler, Cornell and Fraser, *Feminist Contentions: A Philosophical Exchange* (New York: Routledge, 1995). See also Pierre Bourdieu, *Outline of a Theory of Practice* (Cambridge: Cambridge University Press, 1977). For critiques of the cultural meanings implicit in the current US political economy of work and social welfare, see the last two chapters of *Unruly Practices* and the essays in Part 3 of *Justice Interruptus*.

9. In fact, these remedies stand in some tension with one another, a problem I shall explore in a subsequent section of this paper.

10. These various cultural remedies stand in some tension with one another. It is one thing to accord recognition to existing identities that are currently undervalued; it is another to transform symbolic structures and thereby alter people's identities. I shall explore the tensions among the various remedies in a subsequent section of the paper.

11. For a good example of this approach, see Ronald Dworkin, 'Liberalism', in his *A Matter of Principle* (Cambridge, Mass.: Harvard University Press, 1985).

12. For a good example of this approach, see Will Kymlicka, *Liberalism, Community and Culture* (Oxford: Clarendon Press, 1989). The case of Kymlicka suggests that the distinction between socioeconomic justice and cultural justice need not always map onto the distinction between distributive justice and relational or communicative justice.

13. Axel Honneth's *Kampf um Anerkennung* represents the most thorough and sophisticated attempt at such a reduction. Honneth argues that recognition is the fundamental concept of justice and can encompass distribution.

14. Absent such a distinction, we foreclose the possibility of examining conflicts between them. We miss the chance to spot mutual interferences that could arise when redistribution claims and recognition claims are pursued simultaneously.

15. In what follows I conceive class in a highly stylized, orthodox, and theoretical way in order to sharpen the contrast to the other ideal-typical kinds of collectivity discussed below. Of course, this is hardly the only interpretation of the Marxian conception of class. In other contexts and for other purposes, I myself would prefer a less economistic interpretation, one that gives more weight to the cultural, historical, and discursive dimensions of class emphasized by such writers as E. P. Thompson and Joan Wallach Scott. See Thompson, *The Making of the English Working Class* (London: Penguin, 1962); and Scott, *Gender and the Politics of History* (New York: Columbia University Press, 1988).

16. It is doubtful that any collectivities mobilized in the real world today correspond to the notion of class presented below. Certainly, the history of social movements mobilized under the banner of class is more complex than this conception would suggest. Those movements have elaborated class not only as a structural category of political economy, but also as a cultural-valuational category of identity—often in forms problematic for women and blacks. Thus, most varieties of socialism have asserted the dignity of labour and the worth of working people, mingling demands for redistribution with demands for recognition. Sometimes, moreover, having failed to abolish capitalism, class movements have adopted reformist strategies of seeking recognition of their 'difference' within the system in order to augment their power and support demands for what I below call 'affirmative redistribution'. In general, then, historical class-based movements may be closer to what I below call 'bivalent modes of collectivity' than to the interpretation of class sketched here.

17. This assumption does not require us to reject the view that distributive deficits are often (perhaps even always) accompanied by recognition deficits. But it does entail that the recognition deficits of class, in the sense elaborated here, derive from the political economy. Later, I shall consider other sorts of cases in which collectivities suffer from recognition deficits whose roots are not directly political-economic in this way.

18. In what follows, I conceive sexuality in a highly stylized theoretical way in order to sharpen the contrast to the other ideal-typical kinds of collectivity discussed here. I treat sexual differentiation as rooted wholly in the cultural structure, as opposed to in the political economy. Of course, this is not the only interpretation of sexuality. Judith Butler (personal communication) has suggested that one might hold that sexuality is inextricable from gender, which, as I argue below, is as much a matter of the division of labour as of the cultural-valuational structure. In that case, sexuality itself might be viewed as a 'bivalent' collectivity, rooted simultaneously in culture and political economy. Then the economic harms encountered by homosexuals might appear economically rooted rather than culturally rooted, as they are in the account I offer here. While this bivalent analysis is certainly possible, to my mind it has serious drawbacks. Yoking gender and sexuality together too tightly, it covers over the important distinction between a group that occupies a distinct position in the

division of labour (and that owes its existence in large part to this fact), on the one hand, and one that occupies no such distinct position, on the other hand. I discuss this distinction below.

19. An example of an economic injustice rooted directly in the economic structure would be a division of labour that relegates homosexuals to a designated disadvantaged position and exploits them as homosexuals. To deny that this is the situation of homosexuals today is not to deny that they face economic injustices. But it is to trace these to another root. In general, I assume that recognition deficits are often (perhaps even always) accompanied by distribution deficits. But I nevertheless hold that the distribution deficits of sexuality, in the sense elaborated here, derive ultimately from the cultural structure. Later, I shall consider other sorts of cases in which collectivities suffer from recognition deficits whose roots are not (only) directly cultural in this sense. I can perhaps further clarify the point by invoking Oliver Cromwell Cox's contrast between anti-Semitism and white supremacy. Cox suggested that for the anti-Semite, the very existence of the Jew is an abomination; hence the aim is not to exploit the Jew but to eliminate him/her as such, whether by expulsion, forced conversion, or extermination. For the white supremacist, in contrast, the 'Negro' is just fine—in his/her place: as an exploitable supply of cheap, menial labour power; here the preferred aim is exploitation, not elimination: see Cox's unjustly neglected masterwork, *Caste, Class, and Race* (New York: Monthly Review Press, 1970). Contemporary homophobia appears in this respect to be more like anti-Semitism than white supremacy: it seeks to eliminate, not exploit, homosexuals. Thus, the economic disadvantages of homosexuality are derived effects of the more fundamental denial of cultural recognition. This makes it the mirror image of class, as just discussed, where the 'hidden (and not so hidden) injuries' of misrecognition are derived effects of the more fundamental injustice of exploitation. White supremacy, in contrast, as I shall suggest shortly, is 'bivalent', rooted simultaneously in political economy and culture, inflicting co-original and equally fundamental injustices of distribution and recognition. (On this last point, incidentally, I differ from Cox, who treats white supremacy as effectively reducible to class.)

20. Gender disparagement can take many forms, of course, including conservative stereotypes that appear to celebrate, rather than demean, 'femininity'.

21. This helps explain why the history of women's movements records a pattern of oscillation between integrationist equal-rights feminisms and 'difference'-oriented 'social' and 'cultural' feminisms. It would be useful to specify the precise temporal logic that leads bivalent collectivities to shift their principal focus back and forth between redistribution and recognition. For a first attempt, see my 'Rethinking Difference' in *Justice Interruptus*.

22. In addition, 'race' is implicitly implicated in the gender division between paid and unpaid labour. That division relies on a normative contrast between a domestic sphere and a sphere of paid work, associated with women and men respectively. Yet the division in the United States (and elsewhere) has always also been racialized in that domesticity has been implicitly a 'white' prerogative. African-Americans especially were never permitted the privilege of domesticity either as a (male) private 'haven' or a (female) primary or exclusive focus on nurturing one's own kin. See Jacqueline Jones, *Labor of Love, Labor of Sorrow: Black Women, Work, and the Family from Slavery to the Present* (New York: Basic Books, 1985); and Evelyn Nakano Glenn, 'From Servitude to

Service Work: Historical Continuities in the Racial Division of Reproductive Labor', *Signs: Journal of Women in Culture and Society*, 18/1 (Autumn 1992).

23. In a previous draft of this paper I used the term 'denigration'. The ironic consequence was that I unintentionally perpetrated the exact sort of harm I aimed to criticize—in the very act of describing it. 'Denigration', from the Latin *nigrare* (to blacken), figures disparagement as blackening, a racist valuation. I am grateful to the Saint Louis University student who called my attention to this point.

24. Racial disparagement can take many forms, of course, ranging from the stereotypical depiction of African-Americans as intellectually inferior, but musically and athletically gifted, to the stereotypical depiction of Asian-Americans as a 'model minority'.

25. This helps explain why the history of black liberation struggle in the United States records a pattern of oscillation between integration and separatism (or black nationalism). As with gender, it would be useful to specify the dynamics of these alternations.

26. Not all versions of multiculturalism fit the model I describe here. The latter is an ideal-typical reconstruction of what I take to be the majority understanding of multiculturalism. It is also mainstream in the sense of being the version that is usually debated in mainstream public spheres. Other versions are discussed in Linda Nicholson, 'To Be or Not To Be: Charles Taylor on The Politics of Recognition', *Constellations*, 3/1 (1996), 1–16, and in Michael Warner *et al.*, 'Critical Multiculturalism', *Critical Inquiry*, 18/3 (Spring 1992).

27. Recall that sexuality is here assumed to be a collectivity rooted wholly in the cultural-valuational structure of society; thus, the issues here are unclouded by issues of political-economic structure, and the need is for recognition, not redistribution.

28. An alternative affirmative approach is gay-rights humanism, which would privatize existing sexualities. For reasons of space, I shall not discuss it here.

29. For a critical discussion of the tendency in gay-identity politics to tacitly cast sexuality in the mould of ethnicity, see Steven Epstein, 'Gay Politics, Ethnic Identity: The Limits of Social Constructionism', *Socialist Review*, 93/94 (May–Aug. 1987).

30. The technical term for this in Jacques Derrida's deconstructive philosophy is 'supplement'.

31. Despite its professed long-term deconstructive goal, queer theory's practical effects may be more ambiguous. Like gay-identity politics, it too seems likely to promote group solidarity in the here and now, even as it sets its sights on the promised land of deconstruction. Perhaps, then, we should distinguish what I below call its 'official recognition commitment' of group de-differentiation from its 'practical recognition effect' of (transitional) group solidarity and even group solidification. The queer-theory recognition strategy thus contains an internal tension: in order eventually to destabilize the homo–hetero dichotomy, it must first mobilize 'queers'. Whether this tension becomes fruitful or debilitating depends on factors too complex to discuss here. In either case, however, the recognition politics of queer theory remains distinct from that of gay identity. Whereas gay-identity politics simply and straightforwardly underlines group differentiation, queer theory does so only indirectly, in the undertow of its principal de-differentiating thrust. Accordingly, the two approaches construct qualitatively different kinds of groups. Whereas

gay-identity politics mobilizes self-identified homosexuals qua homosexuals to vindicate a putatively determinate sexuality, queer theory mobilizes 'queers' to demand liberation from determinate sexual identity. 'Queers', of course, are not an identity group in the same sense as gays; they are better understood as an anti-identity group, one that can encompass the entire spectrum of sexual behaviours, from gay to straight to bi. For a hilarious—and insightful—account of the difference, as well as for a sophisticated rendition of queer politics, see Lisa Duggan, 'Queering the State', *Social Text*, 39 (Summer 1994). Complications aside, then, we can and should distinguish the (directly) differentiating effects of affirmative gay recognition from the (more) de-differentiating (albeit complex) effects of transformative queer recognition.

32. By 'liberal welfare state', I mean the sort of regime established in the US in the aftermath of the New Deal. It has been usefully distinguished from the social-democratic welfare state and the conservative-corporatist welfare state by Gosta Esping-Andersen in *The Three Worlds of Welfare Capitalism* (Princeton: Princeton University Press, 1990).

33. Today, of course, many specific features of socialism of the 'really existing' variety appear problematic. Virtually no one continues to defend a pure 'command' economy in which there is little place for markets. Nor is there agreement concerning the place and extent of public ownership in a democratic socialist society. For my purposes here, however, it is not necessary to assign a precise content to the socialist idea. It is sufficient, rather, to invoke the general conception of redressing distributive injustice by deep political-economic restructuring, as opposed to surface reallocations. In this light, incidentally, social democracy appears as a hybrid case that combines affirmative and transformative remedies; it can also be seen as a 'middle position', which involves a moderate extent of economic restructuring, more than in the liberal welfare state but less than in socialism.

34. Recall that class, in the sense defined above, is a collectivity wholly rooted in the political-economic structure of society; the issues here are thus unclouded by issues of cultural-valuational structure; and the remedies required are those of redistribution, not recognition.

35. In some contexts, such as the United States today, the practical recognition-effect of affirmative redistribution can utterly swamp its official recognition commitment.

36. My terminology here is inspired by Pierre Bourdieu's distinction, in *Outline of a Theory of Practice*, between 'official kinship' and 'practical kinship'.

37. I have deliberately sketched a picture that is ambiguous between socialism and robust social democracy. The classic account of the latter remains T. H. Marshall's 'Citizenship and Social Class' in *Class, Citizenship, and Social Development: Essays by T. H. Marshall*, ed. Martin Lispet (Chicago, 1964). There Marshall argues that a universalist social-democratic regime of 'social citizenship' undermines class differentiation, even in the absence of full-scale socialism.

38. To be more precise: transformative redistribution can help redress those forms of misrecognition that derive from the political-economic structure. Redressing misrecognition rooted in the cultural structure, in contrast, requires additional independent recognition remedies.

39. Recall that gender, qua political-economic differentiation, structures the division of labour in ways that give rise to gender-specific forms of exploitation,

marginalization, and deprivation. Recall, moreover, that qua cultural-valuational differentiation, gender also structures the relations of recognition in ways that give rise to androcentrism and cultural sexism. Recall, too, that for gender, as for all bivalent group differentiations, economic injustices and cultural injustices are not neatly separated from one another; rather they intertwine to reinforce one another dialectically, as sexist and androcentric cultural norms are institutionalized in the economy, while economic disadvantage impedes equal participation in the making of culture, both in everyday life and in public spheres.

40. I shall leave aside the *prima facie* unpromising cases. Let me simply stipulate that a cultural-feminist recognition politics aimed at revaluing femininity is hard to combine with a socialist-feminist redistributive politics aimed at degendering the political economy. The incompatibility is overt when we treat the recognition of 'women's difference' as a long-term feminist goal. Of course, some feminists conceive the struggle for such recognition not as an end in itself but as a stage in a process they envision as leading eventually to degenderization. Here, perhaps, there is no formal contradiction with socialism. At the same time, however, there remains a practical contradiction, or at least a practical difficulty: can a stress on women's difference in the here and now really end up dissolving gender difference in the by and by? The converse argument holds for the case of the liberal-feminist-welfare state plus deconstructive feminism. Affirmative action for women is usually seen as a transitional remedy aimed at achieving the long-term goal of 'a sex-blind society'. Here, again, there is perhaps no formal contradiction with deconstruction. But there remains nevertheless a practical contradiction, or at least a practical difficulty: can liberal-feminist affirmative action in the here-and-now really help lead us to the deconstruction of gender in the by-and-by?

41. Here I am assuming that the internal complexities of transformative recognition remedies, as discussed in n. 31 above, do not generate perverse effects. If, however, the practical recognition effect of deconstructive feminist cultural politics is strongly gender-differentiating, despite the latter's official recognition commitment to gender de-differentiation, perverse effects could indeed arise. In that case, there could be interferences between socialist-feminist redistribution and deconstructive-feminist recognition. But these would probably be less debilitating than those associated with the other scenarios examined here.

42. The same can be said about 'race' here as about gender in n. 39 and 40.

43. See n. 31 above on the possible perverse effects of transformative recognition remedies.

44. Ted Koditschek (personal communication) has suggested to me that this scenario may have another serious drawback: 'The deconstructive option may be less available to African-Americans in the current situation. Where the structural exclusion of [many] black people from full economic citizenship pushes "race" more and more into the forefront as a cultural category through which one is attacked, self-respecting people cannot help but aggressively affirm and embrace it as a source of pride.' Koditschek goes on to suggest that Jews, in contrast, 'have much more elbow room for negotiating a healthier balance between ethnic affirmation, self-criticism, and cosmopolitan universalism—not because we are better deconstructionists (or more inherently disposed toward socialism) but because we have more space to make these moves'.

45. Whether this conclusion holds as well for nationality and ethnicity remains a question. Certainly bivalent collectivities of indigenous peoples do not seek to put themselves out of business as groups.
46. This has always been the problem with socialism. Although cognitively compelling, it is experientially remote. The addition of deconstruction seems to exacerbate the problem. It could turn out to be too negative and reactive, i.e. too *deconstructive*, to inspire struggles on behalf of subordinated collectivities attached to their existing identities.
47. Much recent work has been devoted to the 'intersection' of the various axes of subordination that I have treated separately in this essay for heuristic purposes. A lot of this work concerns the dimension of recognition; it aims to demonstrate that various collective identifications and identity categories have been mutually co-constituted or co-constructed. Joan Scott, for example, has argued (in *Gender and the Politics of History*) that French working-class identities have been discursively constructed through gender-coded symbolization; and David R. Roediger has argued, in *The Wages of Whiteness: Race and the Making of the American Working Class* (London: Verso, 1991) that US working-class identities have been racially coded. Meanwhile, many feminists of colour have argued both that gender identities have been racially coded and that racialized identities have been gender-coded. I myself have argued, with Linda Gordon, that gender, 'race', and class ideologies have intersected to construct current US understandings of 'welfare dependency' and 'the underclass'. See Fraser and Gordon, 'A Genealogy of "Dependency": Tracing a keyword of the U.S. Welfare State', *Signs: Journal of Women in Culture and Society*, 19/2 (Winter 1994).

Index

Notes: 1. Emboldened page numbers indicate main chapter references; 2. most references are to the United States, except where otherwise indicated; 3. feminism, politics, and gender are largely omitted as qualifiers; 4. names of authors in notes at end of chapters are only included when they are quoted.